Strategies and Tools for Managing Connected Consumers

Ree C. Ho
Taylor's University, Malaysia

A volume in the Advances in Marketing, Customer Relationship Management, and E-Services (AMCRMES) Book Series

IGI Global
DISSEMINATOR OF KNOWLEDGE

Published in the United States of America by
IGI Global
Business Science Reference (an imprint of IGI Global)
701 E. Chocolate Avenue
Hershey PA, USA 17033
Tel: 717-533-8845
Fax: 717-533-8661
E-mail: cust@igi-global.com
Web site: http://www.igi-global.com

Library of Congress Cataloging-in-Publication Data

Names: Ho, Ree C., 1986- editor.
Title: Strategies and tools for managing connected consumers / Ree C. Ho, editor.
Description: Hershey, PA : Business Science Reference, [2019]
Identifiers: LCCN 2019006557| ISBN 9781522596974 (hardcover) | ISBN 9781522596998 (ebook) | ISBN 9781522596981 (softcover)
Subjects: LCSH: Electronic commerce. | Social media--Economic aspects. | Customer relations.
Classification: LCC HF5548.32 .S7683 2019 | DDC 658.8/72--dc23 LC record available at https://lccn.loc.gov/2019006557

This book is published in the IGI Global book series Advances in Marketing, Customer Relationship Management, and E-Services (AMCRMES) (ISSN: 2327-5502; eISSN: 2327-5529)

British Cataloguing in Publication Data
A Cataloguing in Publication record for this book is available from the British Library.

Advances in Marketing, Customer Relationship Management, and E-Services (AMCRMES) Book Series

Eldon Y. Li
National Chengchi University, Taiwan & California Polytechnic State University, USA

ISSN:2327-5502
EISSN:2327-5529

Mission

Business processes, services, and communications are important factors in the management of good customer relationship, which is the foundation of any well organized business. Technology continues to play a vital role in the organization and automation of business processes for marketing, sales, and customer service. These features aid in the attraction of new clients and maintaining existing relationships.

The Advances in Marketing, Customer Relationship Management, and E-Services (AMCRMES) Book Series
addresses success factors for customer relationship management, marketing, and electronic services and its performance outcomes. This collection of reference source covers aspects of consumer behavior and marketing business strategies aiming towards researchers, scholars, and practitioners in the fields of marketing management.

Coverage

- Cases on CRM Implementation
- Telemarketing
- B2B marketing
- Mobile CRM
- Ethical Considerations in E-Marketing
- Customer Relationship Management
- Electronic Services
- Cases on Electronic Services
- Relationship Marketing
- Legal Considerations in E-Marketing

IGI Global is currently accepting manuscripts for publication within this series. To submit a proposal for a volume in this series, please contact our Acquisition Editors at Acquisitions@igi-global.com or visit: http://www.igi-global.com/publish/.

The Advances in Marketing, Customer Relationship Management, and E-Services (AMCRMES) Book Series (ISSN 2327-5502) is published by IGI Global, 701 E. Chocolate Avenue, Hershey, PA 17033-1240, USA, www.igi-global.com. This series is composed of titles available for purchase individually; each title is edited to be contextually exclusive from any other title within the series. For pricing and ordering information please visit http://www.igi-global.com/book-series/advances-marketing-customer-relationship-management/37150. Postmaster: Send all address changes to above address.

Titles in this Series

For a list of additional titles in this series, please visit: www.igi-global.com/book-series

Predicting Trends and Building Strategies for Consumer Engagement in Retail Environments
Giuseppe Granata (University of Cassino and Southern Lazio, Italy) Andrea Moretta Tartaglione (University of Cassino and Southern Lazio, Italy) and Theodosios Tsiakis (Alexander Technological Educational Institute of Thessaloniki, Greece)
Business Science Reference • ©2019 • 413pp • H/C (ISBN: 9781522578567) • US $245.00

Handbook of Research on Digital Marketing Innovations in Social Entrepreneurship and Solidarity Economics
Jose Manuel Saiz-Alvarez (Tecnologico de Monterrey, Mexico)
Business Science Reference • ©2019 • 438pp • H/C (ISBN: 9781522589396) • US $295.00

Structural Equation Modeling Approaches to E-Service Adoption
Yakup Akgül (Alanya Alaaddin Keykubat University, Turkey)
Business Science Reference • ©2019 • 350pp • H/C (ISBN: 9781522580157) • US $205.00

Leveraging Computer-Mediated Marketing Environments
Gordon Bowen (Regent's University London, UK) and Wilson Ozuem (University of Cumbria, UK)
Business Science Reference • ©2019 • 473pp • H/C (ISBN: 9781522573449) • US $205.00

Integrated Marketing Communications, Strategies, and Tactical Operations in Sports Organizations
Manuel Alonso Dos Santos (Universidad Católica de la Santísima Concepción, Chile)
Business Science Reference • ©2019 • 325pp • H/C (ISBN: 9781522576174) • US $215.00

Exploring the Dynamics of Consumerism in Developing Nations
Ayantunji Gbadamosi (University of East London, UK)
Business Science Reference • ©2019 • 428pp • H/C (ISBN: 9781522579069) • US $225.00

Evaluating the Gaps and Intersections Between Marketing Education and the Marketing Profession
Margarida M. Pinheiro (University of Aveiro, Portugal) Ana Estima (University of Aveiro, Portugal) and Susana Marques (University of Aveiro, Portugal)
Business Science Reference • ©2019 • 252pp • H/C (ISBN: 9781522562955) • US $190.00

Advanced Methodologies and Technologies in Digital Marketing and Entrepreneurship
Mehdi Khosrow-Pour, D.B.A. (Information Resources Management Association, USA)
Business Science Reference • ©2019 • 818pp • H/C (ISBN: 9781522577669) • US $315.00

IGI Global
DISSEMINATOR OF KNOWLEDGE

701 East Chocolate Avenue, Hershey, PA 17033, USA
Tel: 717-533-8845 x100 • Fax: 717-533-8661
E-Mail: cust@igi-global.com • www.igi-global.com

Editorial Advisory Board

Table of Contents

Detailed Table of Contents

Over the past two decades, social media has developed exponentially and significantly changed the customers' shopping behavior. Social media apps enable customers to interact with retailers and other customers closely, and influences their purchase decision. Hence, it is small wonder that businesses are investing time and resources to promote their products and brand image on social media applications. Instagram is best known for its enriched visual features in both image and footage and suitable for developing strong brand engagement. It is a viable platform for businesses to promote their products to customers. This chapter proposes a framework of product learning process with the use of Instagram. It contributes in effective management of social media marketing and provides marketers with the guidelines in using Instagram creatively to roll out customer engagement strategies.

In this chapter, the authors analyze the cultural, technological, and psychological factors that influence online young technology-literate consumer behavior in a densely populated urban area. This chapter starts with a literature review of factors that can explain the online behavior of people from various demographic and cultural backgrounds including education, occupation, income level, gender, ethnicity, and age (as a control). The authors also reviewed several empirical studies that examine online consumer behavior in India, where the population is the second highest in the world and a leader in global technology services. The purpose of the study is to develop a multi-cultural model that could predict the emerging shopping pattern of young and highly connected consumers in the high technology use metropolitan area, specifically in Northern India. The results can be used to generalize other online consumer behavior in other similar highly populated communities where internet technology use is high.

Consumers pay attention to other consumers' comments, advice, and interactions during the purchase decision process. Besides having a strong impact on consumers' brand decisions, these user-driven contents have an important effect on brand's online reputation, which is very important area for consumers to follow the information about the brand. Therefore, some of the public relations practices will be forced to change by this new communication eco-system. The increasing power of consumer-driven content could lead to the evolution of traditional public relations and marketing communication. Interaction and participation would be the main concepts in the coming future of public relations. Therefore, this chapter aims to explain the effect of consumers' interactions on brand's social media accounts that would lead to their brand selection decisions.

Governments across the world are looking at introducing the "digital tax," which will be imposed on technology companies and digital business players. Digital giants like Google, Amazon, Facebook, Apple, and Microsoft are benefiting from the strong growth of digital business. The Malaysian government has announced in the national 2019 budget that a digital tax will be implemented effective January 1, 2020. The rationale of the tax is that both the international and local businesses in the digital sector must pay their fair share of tax. Malaysia has been taxing income from e-commerce, but it has no guidelines on the taxation of income from digital business. Global digital businesses often avoid paying taxes in Malaysia because they have no physical presence in the country. This chapter looks at how Malaysia is reforming its laws and policies to ensure its tax base fully reflects the scale of transactions and profits generated by the digital economy.

Continuing to fulfill the requirements and needs of today's customer is a perplexing job for all the corporations. There have been a number of strategies developed to engage with customers, but few considerations have been paid to string them together in generating well-developed relationships. For of this reason companies are moving towards customer relationship management (CRM) to execute reliable strategies in engaging with customers. CRM emphasizes aiding companies thoroughly to manage the procedures involved in upholding good relationships with customers. This chapter discussed various strategies and examined case studies that adopted different techniques to engage with customers.

Foreword

Much has already been written about the technological revolution we are now experiencing with Industry 4.0 and its potential to transform manufacturing and communications, creating new occupations and making some irrelevant. Less attention has been given to the implications for e-commerce, which has already by stealth become the first choice of consumers over traditional 'high street' shopping. In the UK the demise of Thomas Cook, the world's first travel agency, is symptomatic of those changes and we can expect more restructuring in those sectors where consumers have already switched to the Internet. The new technologies will take e-commerce to a new phase of connectivity, empowering consumers who share information via social media, and leaving businesses with no option but to engage via the same channels, what Dr. Ho describes as 'socially connected businesses'.

This book is timely because we are at the start of the wave, where it is difficult to appreciate how much these new technologies will change consumer and business behaviour. What is predictable, is that digital connectivity and use of social media will continue to increase and that shopping will be transformed. That much is not a surprise, even if the scale of some of the implications are still to emerge. What is probably important is that companies will have less control over communication and marketing: the buyer-seller relationship will be less dyadic and its centre of gravity is in a community of users and commentators, not all of whom are necessarily even customers. The implications are many, and not all will be welcomed by businesses.

Companies will be called to account more easily and will need to ensure their corporate social responsibility policies are credible and not liable to exposure as 'greenwashing', for example. Employers will need to ensure their employees, and those working in their supply chains, are treated properly or risk a similar expose of inadequate terms and conditions, as has already happened to companies like Amazon and Ryanair. Those are positive effects, from the point of view of consumers, employees and society at large. However, the autonomy and absence of accountability that characterise social media, and which cannot be 'policed' by the creators of social media platforms nor by governments, except under totalitarian regimes, means that businesses could be more vulnerable to disinformation spread by competitors.

At the same time, companies are already using social media and mining big data to reap the enormous potential of the Internet to achieve 'richness and reach' that was previously impossible, tailoring pitches to consumers based on sophisticated analyses of purchasing behaviours of individuals or of specific groups in society. Those concerned with individual liberties see in this trend a risk of companies 'knowing too much' and using this to target them with products they do not need and possibly cannot afford. Indebtedness is a major consequence of societies obsessed with displaying wealth and over-consumption one of the major drivers of the environmental disaster we have created in the world.

We can only hope that these new rules of the game will help bring about more responsible capitalism but this book will certainly ensure those concerned are better informed of the limits and possibilities.

Jonathan Winterton
Taylor's University, Malaysia

Preface

OVERVIEW

Toward the next decade of the 21st century, businesses and consumers are facing one of the critical changes to the way business conducted in the networked world. Innovative communication technologies bring enormous changes in the new industrial 4.0 era. In the past decade, electronic commerce became the norm in which transactions take place over the network, predominantly via the Internet. The evolution of electronic commerce has shifted into another phase, i.e. online consumers are sharing and collaborating among themselves while shopping online.

This new wave is caused by the popularity and exponential increase use of social media users, cloud and mobile technologies. Besides, relevant information is readily accessible by both the consumers and businesses. This permit both parties to develop more engaging and interactive relationships between them. Furthermore, the advent of inexpensive computers and mobile devices close the digital divide and puts more people on riding the bandwagon of socially connected business. All this contributes to the development and growth of the field of digitally connected consumers, i.e. the subject of this book. These consumers are actively involved in transactions that take place over social media and digitally connected networks. Likewise, the businesses are electronically engaging the customers in the entire buying and selling process. However, it is not purely about buying and selling. It also involves the process of communication, collaboration and information sharing and co-creation.

THE RISE OF THE CONNECTED CONSUMER ERA

Customers are reaping the fruits of the closer engagement with the rise of social commerce and mobile commerce (Zhang, Guo, Hu, & Liu, 2017). The deployment of new technologies and business processes arise from social collaboration among the consumers. They learned about the shopping related information from media exposure and their collaboration with other consumers (Hong, 2015). This consideration is critical due to the ever-increasing social impact and influence of social media in current online business scenario. This new breed of customers socially and digitally linked in this new era.

The key objective of this book is to unravel and provide business managers and scholars with new theories, tools and strategies in managing the ever-increasing connected online consumers. The main contents include the critique of the current issues and concepts in online business environment. Consumers are connected with higher degree of social connectivity and collaboration in various channels in the Internet space. The growing penetration of new technologies and business processes reinvented through social collaboration among the consumers. This consideration is critical due to the ever-increasing social impact and influence of social media in current online business. This book draws from wide range of strategies and technologies used in current digital marketplace as well as recent development and empirical researches on the consumer behavior. As such, the book aims to contribute new dimensions in managing the new breed of consumers who are linked closely.

THE ISSUES AND CHALLENGES

Traditional e-commerce sites are under the threat from the increasing use of social commerce by online customers (Huang & Benyoucef, 2015). Purchases could be completed directly within the social media platforms and make it harder for traditional e-commerce practitioners to level the playing ground. Social commerce effectively delivered through apps, contents, and media in creative manner. More and more consumers are enjoying the shopping in this new platform because entertainment and hedonic values are attainable in social commerce over traditional e-commerce more easily (Sirakaya-Turk, Ekinci, & Martin, 2015). Adding to that, companies amass information from prospective visitors and create a sense of community. Hence, the consumers are gaining more attention from business companies directly as companies are able to develop individual customer profile with less effort (Saarijärvi, Joensuu, Rintamaki, & Yrjölä, 2018). The level of personalized services were intensified because of the closer engagement between the sellers and buyers. This is why social business begins to convert the actual purchases better and generate more sales.

Business firms are devoted efforts in managing their various social media channels due to its influential power on consumer buying behavior (Knoll, 2016). Facebook page, shopping tab and newsfeed are some of the popular tools. It is often just one click away for customers to purchase and complete the sales transactions. Clearly, companies started to add buy button in their companies' digital communication and social media platform. The challenge is the addition of these interactive buttons on more digitally engaged environment. Furthermore, social media page linked directly to third party payment gateways for faster processing (Zhong & Nieminen, 2015). On the other hand, trust is a precursor to brand building relationship with consumers (Calefato, Lanubile, & Novielli, 2015). The information learned, shared and even co-created is readily available and even more trustworthy. Hence, the pleasure and information elements are directly leading to more selling through the social conversion.

Companies would need to be aware of what they posted on the social media, or else ends up posting up the contents merely for the sake of posting. The importance in formulating the effective strategy cannot be underestimated. Strategic planning on clear goals, target population, and deliver what consumers want need to be carefully planned. Strategy around what the key selling points in term of relatedness and appealing to the target consumers. Undoubtedly, content is king and consumers are searching and learning via the connected networks (Hajli, Sims, Zadeh, & Richard, 2017). This relies on the effort of making shareable content that is engaging and available to right audience at the right time in the right place. It is about making the right contents that link and bond with the right customers.

The strategy in choosing the right platform is another critical decision. The need of the right business planning in selecting the right social media app to meet with the business objectives (Keegan & Rowley, 2017). Although the right platform may vary depending on the type of product, target consumers and many other considerations, at least it should reach the targeted consumers that match with their wants and interests. With that, the impact of the advertisement and promotion followed could be greater.

The argument is that current customers are socially connected, and technology savvy in utilizing the online technologies. They are experienced and readily sharing, co-create and consume the information from various social media means (Jones, Borgman, & Ulusoy, 2015). Therefore, this signals to the businesses the need to re-act to this paradigm shift. The ability and willingness of businesses to respond to serve this breed of customers is impending. While listening and serving the customers in online space, the companies should develop closer relationship with the customers by making full use of the social communication technologies.

ORGANIZATION OF THE BOOK

This book is organized into 17 chapters. A brief description of each of the chapters follows:

Chapter 1 discuss how companies are investing time and resources to promote their products and brand image with the use of social media platform, i.e. Instagram. It further explores the importance of the consumer socialization via frequent use of Instagram in enabling customers to interact with retailers and other customers, and subsequently learn about the product knowledge for making better purchase decision.

Chapter 2 analyzes the cultural, technological, and psychological factors that influence the behavior of young and technology-literate consumers who reside in densely populated urban areas. It explains the online behavior of digitally connected consumers from various demographic and cultural dimensions.

Chapter 3 addresses the impact of e-commerce on the urban landscape with reference to its multifaceted and diverse environments. It reviews the literature on the impact of e-commerce on the different aspects of urbanization to assists policy makers to understand the challenges and opportunities of the online economy.

Chapter 4 delves into the quality strategies for attaining customer loyalty in an e-service environment. By taking a case of mobile banking service, it discusses the major effects of relationship between e-service quality and customer loyalty.

Chapter 5 examines the nature and strength of the relationship between shopping mall attractiveness and customer loyalty. It offers detailed explanation on the quality dimensions of the malls in both offline and online environments, and further identifies factors needed for strategic management in enhancing the quality for modern shopping malls.

Chapter 6 concludes that organic foods consumers are driven by positive perceptions and preference towards green lifestyles. This is further supported by consumer possession of the knowledge on the benefits of organic farming production. These eco-friendly consumers have significant knowledge on conserving the environment and tend to consider the environmental impacts in their buying habits.

Chapter 7 focuses on the role of virtual communities in connecting the socially-linked customers. It provides the guidelines for managing various types of virtual communities and their impacts on different generations of online customers.

Chapter 8 examines how the act of live streaming could mold the viewers' impression towards the products' features and functionalities. It proposes that relative advantages of live stream footage are enhancing customer's learning on product knowledge, and subsequently useful for completing the product purchase process.

Chapter 9 investigated the current use of digital marketing, its impact and factors that influence the adoption of digital marketing in the context of South Africa. It highlights the increasing influential power of interactive digital marketing tools in building engaging customer relationships.

Chapter 10 addresses the current issues of online consumers' engagement among their virtual communities. Digital customers interact with each other while conducting online shopping activities such as discovering products, sharing product information and collaboratively making shopping decisions.

Chapter 11 establishes a comprehensive e-service framework by integrating both technology and functional aspects in the pursuit of improving the required services for online business. It addresses how new e-service refinements to replace the traditional customer service that are fast becoming obsolete.

Chapter 12 emphasizes on the role of social media communication in unravel the effect of collective communication for corporate accounts in social media platforms. This then translate into good management practice for improving the brand and corporate reputation.

Chapter 13 looks at how Malaysia is reforming its laws and policies to reflect the scale of transactions and profits generated by the digital economy. It examines current domestic tax incentives and analyze the need of compatibility in alignment with global standards and practices.

Chapter 14 reviews the different combinations of customer relationship solutions to serve the customer journey across marketing, sales and customer service. This prompts companies to develop relationships with individual customers through the experiences learned from their implemented customer relationship strategies.

Chapter 15 provides the knowhow and the development of the single platform E-payment systems devoted to the social media customers. The proposed functionalities of this new payment platform could promote and expedite the adoption of cardless, cashless and contactless payments for social commerce.

Chapter 16 offers a deeper understanding of impulse buying in the online purchase process and discuss different aspects of personal issues. This enables the online marketers to develop effective strategies to understand the consumer behavior in the networked business environment.

Chapter 17 deals with some of the most compelling problems and ethics relating to the use of social media in business. It highlights how these problems occur, their consequences, and what should be carry out to minimize the effects.

THE SOLUTIONS

This book intends to provide new insights and investigate the issues relating to this new trend of online business dominated by connected consumers. With the rise of the connected consumer, a myriad ways of conducting business in the Internet and social media are undergoing substantial changes. The key takeaway is clear. We need to understand the new digital shopping tools and processes influenced by the changing consumer behavior. Consumers are connected with higher degree of social connectivity within the digital networks.

The growing penetration of new technologies and a purchasing process reinvented through social collaboration. Consumers are empowered via connected networks by navigating the evolving new technologies to purchase through multiple, predominantly digital touch points. Consumers access the vast resources in the networked world before, during and after the shopping. Hence, both consumers and retailers are gearing into a more challenging and complex environment which disrupt the traditional retail business models. This book intends to provide new insights and investigate the issues relating to this new trend of online business dominated by connected consumers.

REFERENCES

Calefato, F., Lanubile, F., & Novielli, N. (2015). The role of social media in affective trust building in customer–supplier relationships. *Electronic Commerce Research, 15*(4), 453–482. doi:10.100710660-015-9194-3

Hajli, N., Sims, J., Zadeh, A. H., & Richard, M.-O. (2017). A social commerce investigation of the role of trust in a social networking site on purchase intentions. *Journal of Business Research, 71*, 133–141. doi:10.1016/j.jbusres.2016.10.004

Hong, I. B. (2015). Understanding the consumer's online merchant selection process: The roles of product involvement, perceived risk, and trust expectation. *International Journal of Information Management, 35*(3), 322–336. doi:10.1016/j.ijinfomgt.2015.01.003

Huang, Z., & Benyoucef, M. (2015). User preferences of social features on social commerce websites: An empirical study. *Technological Forecasting and Social Change, 95*, 57–72. doi:10.1016/j.techfore.2014.03.005

Jones, N., Borgman, R., & Ulusoy, E. (2015). Impact of social media on small businesses. *Journal of Small Business and Enterprise Development, 22*(4), 611–632. doi:10.1108/JSBED-09-2013-0133

Keegan, B. J., & Rowley, J. (2017). Evaluation and decision making in social media marketing. *Management Decision, 55*(1), 15–31. doi:10.1108/MD-10-2015-0450

Knoll, J. (2016). Advertising in social media: A review of empirical evidence. *International Journal of Advertising, 35*(2), 266–300. doi:10.1080/02650487.2015.1021898

Saarijärvi, H., Joensuu, J., Rintamaki, T., & Yrjölä, M. (2018). One person's trash is another person's treasure: Profiling consumer-to-consumer e-commerce in Facebook. *International Journal of Retail & Distribution Management, 46*(11/12), 1092–1107. doi:10.1108/IJRDM-04-2017-0091

Sirakaya-Turk, E., Ekinci, Y., & Martin, D. (2015). The efficacy of shopping value in predicting destination loyalty. *Journal of Business Research, 68*(9), 1878–1885. doi:10.1016/j.jbusres.2015.01.016

Zhang, M., Guo, L., Hu, M., & Liu, W. (2017). Influence of customer engagement with company social networks on stickiness: Mediating effect of customer value creation. *International Journal of Information Management, 37*(3), 229–240. doi:10.1016/j.ijinfomgt.2016.04.010

Zhong, J., & Nieminen, M. (2015). Resource-based co-innovation through platform ecosystem: Experiences of mobile payment innovation in China. *Journal of Strategy and Management, 8*(3), 283–298. doi:10.1108/JSMA-03-2015-0026

Chapter 1
Consumer Socialization Process for the Highly Connected Customers:
The Use of Instagram to Gain Product Knowledge

Ree C. Ho
Taylor's University, Malaysia

Teck Choon Teo
RVi Institute, Myanmar

ABSTRACT

Over the past two decades, social media has developed exponentially and significantly changed the customers' shopping behavior. Social media apps enable customers to interact with retailers and other customers closely, and influences their purchase decision. Hence, it is small wonder that businesses are investing time and resources to promote their products and brand image on social media applications. Instagram is best known for its enriched visual features in both image and footage and suitable for developing strong brand engagement. It is a viable platform for businesses to promote their products to customers. This chapter proposes a framework of product learning process with the use of Instagram. It contributes in effective management of social media marketing and provides marketers with the guidelines in using Instagram creatively to roll out customer engagement strategies.

DOI: 10.4018/978-1-5225-9697-4.ch001

INTRODUCTION

The emergence of the internet, particularly Web 2.0 has provided access to the views and opinions of a wide range of individuals opening up opportunities for new forms of communication and knowledge formation. Previous ways of navigating and filtering available information are likely to prove ineffective in today's context. Social media provides the connectivity needed for virtual environments (Kaplan & Haenlein, 2010). It has become a significant part of daily personal communication. In 2015 90% of young adults in the age group 18-29 often use of social media (Perrin, 2015). Additionally, social media enables users to share their product experiences through consumer reviews (Y. Chen, Fay, & Wang, 2011). Thus, it promotes communication among consumers (Abzari, Ghassemi, & Vosta, 2014). Social media referred as Social Networking Sites (SNS). Social networking sites is cyber-environment where individuals can create a personal profile, share photos, images and text with each other.

Arguably, Instagram may not be the most popular social media sites. However, known for its visual features in both image and footage with limited words. Does the lack of text by Instagram affect perceptions of popularity? This chapter explores the viability of Instagram in developing product attitude via consumer socialization process. Contents from Instagram are validated as antecedents in molding consumer socialization process. The two components of the consumer socialization process, namely peer communication and product involvement elucidates consumers learning about product knowledge.

Aims and Motivations

Social media generally refers to a collective of online communication channels built on community-based input, interaction, and collaboration. Typically, it is comprised of social networking sites, video sharing platforms, blogs and micro-blogging platforms, forums and messaging platforms. Social media channels are two-way communication platforms that enable people to respond and react to information. Primarily it is a medium for people to connect with each other; social media provides a unique opportunity for brands to leverage the power of peer-to-peer recommendation and word of mouth. The increasing marketing communication in the social media space has catapulted Instagram, translating into augmented popularity.

Instagram reaches the younger generation, and appeals to diverse societies more prevailingly than other social networking services (Abbott, Donaghey, Hare, & Hopkins, 2013; Salomon, 2013). As the reach and impact of social channels has grown and advertising models become established across key platforms, social media has evolved from being fan and community building platforms into highly powerful paid media channels capable of driving real business results at every stage of the customer touchpoints. As a result, social interaction gained in social media can assist consumer in making purchase decision. To tap into these opportunities, it is important to understand customer's purchase intent and delineate the moments in people's lives where social can play a role. For example, hospitality/tourism segment used social media for pre-trip planning as well as post-trip to share experiences with family and friends.

Understanding this initial start-point enable brands to define clearly their business objectives and strategies. Instagram is delivering clear business value beyond traditional likes, shares and comments in the form of images and videos. As such, the sharing of images rather than words alone has made communication with friends and broader groups of users who share similar interests more ideal, convenient and fascinating via the trend of aesthetic content in image and footage where consumers comment, post, and share consumer experience (Virtanen, Björk, & Sjöström, 2017). This chapter aims to uncover the consumer socialization process in the use of Instagram content, and the understanding of the product knowledge by consumers in facilitating the purchase decision. The elements such as the label and designs, color can sway the perception of consumers into actual purchase. Indeed, the consumer socialization process within Instagram can go beyond social purpose.

BACKGROUND

Growth of Social Commerce

Social commerce hawks merchandises directly through social media networks. It is unlike social media marketing i.e. you are not redirecting users to an online store, instead enabling them to checkout directly within the network they are using at that moment. It provides people the convenience to complete the transaction. One outstanding example is the Facebook Social Commerce; it is undoubtedly the biggest and most popular player. Facebook's major development such as Facebook Marketplace is hugely popular with people, giving Amazon and Google Shopping a "run" for their money. Another excellent example is the Instagram Social Commerce is the most promising platforms when it comes to creating a social selling strategy. Shoppable Posts, Instagram's latest development now allow brands the ability to tag items in organic posts which, when tapped, brings up a new page which leads to a checkout. It is small wonder that social commerce is making a huge impact on the world of e-commerce and marketing. Consequently, this led to the phenomenal growth of social commerce.

From marketing standpoint, social commerce has become part of our daily lives, particularly with the young people. Young people are ubiquitously known, have used social networking services, activities checking of their friends' updates, to catch up on the latest updates in their hobby, or simply to stalk the Instagram of their ex-girl/boyfriend. Consumers are exposed to brand and product via social network. Young people are more in tune with social media. They are also more prone to impulse purchases. Effectively, it capitalizes on young people's impulse urges by giving them a direct checkout within the updates they find most captivating.

Accordingly, social commerce giants are cashing in, changing their promotional tactics to align with customers' expectations vis-a-vis implementing highly engaging, eye-catching social promotions, etc. High level of interactions among consumers to learn about product and to share shopping experience with the use of consumer generated contents (Wang, Yu, & Wei, 2012). Consumers also use and distribute consumer related contents, such as product review, feedback and 'like' posts (Daugherty, Eastin, & Bright, 2008; Sparks & Bradley, 2017; Teixeira, Pereira, & Dionísio, 2018). The social media contents obtained via social media application is useful in the final purchase decision (Duverger, 2013; Fong & Burton, 2006).

Progressively, as more people are turning to social media in more areas of their lives, they are spending more time on their phone; expecting quick fix to every problem, and sharing everything they do on social media. It triggers companies and consumers alike to exploit full use of social media app, subsuming Instagram, for business purposes (Ashley & Tuten, 2015). The only logical action then is for marketers to take advantage of these behaviors and start selling through the channels that people engaged with the ease of checkout expectancy.

About Instagram

According to Salomon (2013), Instagram is the most popular image-based social media apps in both IOS and Android smart mobile device platform. In the initial years of the inception, it started as a photo sharing social network platform. However, gradually it evolved to include video, stories geo-tagged, live-stream video and linking to more social network accounts. The main feature is the distribution of short and interesting message mainly in the form of image and video footage that attracts many young people to use Instagram (H. Chen, 2018). Additionally, it has simple and straightforward short messages, which is easy to understand. As Ilich and Hardey (2018) puts it aptly, a picture tells thousand words. Instagram can reach followers instantaneously and the response is correspondingly efficient and effective. Resulting in businesses adopting Instagram's business account where it can specifically target their customers.

Instagram has excelled as an effective communication and marketing tool to display products with visual descriptions. Hence, it becomes a useful social networking platform instantly to individuals and companies. Interestingly, the acquisition of Instagram by Facebook has potentially made Instagram even more attractive and appealing to millions of users.

Use of Instagram in Business

Without a doubt, social media platforms today play a significant part in the growth of several businesses. Many marketers are quick to consider engaging various social media platforms to attract and reach their target customers. Aside from the hugely popular Facebook and Twitter, Instagram is the next best choice to market business on social media platforms. In social media marketing, it is essential to review the number of audiences that you can reach. It is astonishing that Instagram has that eminence, boasting of over one billion monthly active users.

Turning to visuals, it has always been an important element in marketing. For example, if a message released to the public but no one remembers it, then it has failed! Communicating does no good if it does not retained by the audience. Today, it is easy for information to be ignored if it is not in a digestible format. Thus, integrating visual content can enhance how much the audience absorbs and remembers.

In addition to helping marketers communicate a message that intrinsically remembered, Instagram proffer effective visuals content that is highly desirable when it comes to increasing customer engagement. Hautz, Füller, Hutter, and Thürridl (2014) posited that images and footage as determinant in influencing consumer to buy. By combining visual and text, Instagram is then able to maximize the marketing value. Given its usefulness and convenience, in the customer's memory recall process, other writers also cited that product information can be diffused faster with Instagram (De Veirman, Cauberghe, & Hudders, 2017). It increases higher publicity effectiveness with Instagram's image (Colliander & Marder, 2018) and the credibility of celebrities' Instagram profile in influencing female to purchase fashion (Djafarova & Rushworth, 2017).

CONCEPTUAL FRAMEWORK DEVELOPMENT

Instagram consists of two words, "instant' and "telegram". It captures and shares moments with a steady stream of images and footage. The principal application is connecting people and companies visually with its followers. Creators and publishers can tag business partners in branded content through feed and stories in Instagram. With countless followers tagging along, it translates into both social and business values. It is small wonder that the number of monthly active Instagram users increased exponentially. Due to the apps' visual nature and appeal, it enjoys a massive user engagement rate. In addition, Instagram is also a valuable marketing tool for fashion brands having an Instagram profile.

In present times, Instagram is more than attracting attention and admiration, arguably it is a moneymaking machine. Many companies acknowledged the tremendous influence of Instagrammers and companies are happy offering free products, hoping that Instagrammers will post pictures with their products and recommend them. Astutely some companies even willing to compensate Instagrammers to promote their products, without telling their followers that they are paid for doing so. It can be a product placement on social media, a combination of paid electronic Word-of-Mouth (eWOM) and paid user generated content (UGC). The product placement on social media is the contemporary form of celebrity endorsement and gravitate towards Influencer Marketing. Virtual word of mouth essentially focus was on specific individuals rather than a target market as a whole. According to Liu, Chou, and Liao (2015), product placement on social media was one of the most valuable marketing strategies.

Instagram Marketing

Social media are nowadays a central part of the personal social life. Besides communicating with friends, social media also allows users to connect to strangers all over the world with whom they share the same interest. Besides the continuous sales increment indicated that e-commerce has enormous market potential. The spectacular success of e-commerce conglomerates e.g. Alibaba, Amazon and Groupon, have set as an example for firms to change the brick-and-mortar model of their business to brick-and-click.

In the same vein, Instagram continues to grow and evolve as a marketing platform. Hence, it is imperative for businesses to build effective Instagram marketing strategies compared to having a thorough understanding of the Instagram marketing landscape and measurable outcomes. In light of this, Instagram created an algorithm that re-organized people's feeds so they would theoretically see more content that is relevant to them. This improves user-experience and the priorities of certain types of content. It can optimize one's posts to get the maximum engagement and reach possible. The principle of Instagram business viability is about its distribution of small chunk of contents, small size, short and fast enough for users to obtain and absorb it. It is efficient especially in the content creation as in the use of other social media case in making word of mouth spread faster and achieves its marketing value.

Studies shows that Instagram can increase the brand awareness leading to purchase decision (Colliander & Marder, 2018; Djafarova & Rushworth, 2017). High level of interactivity also facilitates good communication and collaboration within users in learning product information and experience (Tsekouropoulos et al., 2012). Invariably advertising on social media has become of big importance in the past years. Hence, what about the outcome of consumer socialization in product learning?

Consumer Socialization

Consumer socialization refers to collective processes by which young people acquire skills, knowledge, and attitudes relevant to their functioning as consumers in the marketplace (Basu & Sondhi, 2014). Quintal et al., 2016). It postulates that one obtains related skills in a social context that will subsequently affect the cognitive, effectiveness, and attitude while making decisions. Furthermore, socialization agents identified as the sources of influence that transfer norms, attitudes, motivations, and behaviors to children (Quintal, Phau, Sims, & Cheah, 2016). Children constitute a significant marketing segment. Today, they not only make purchases for themselves but also influence family purchase decisions. The purchase behavior determines the way they socialized with others to act as consumers.

According to Niu (2013), the purchasing power of teenagers has greatly increased and attributed to family communication patterns. In addition, the adolescent life cycle and family communication patterns, family socio-economic status and parental marital status also affect adolescent cyber purchasing behavior. Hence, the adolescent consumers do not gain these skills, knowledge and attitudes in solitary but through socialization. Other researchers such as Peters, Chen, Kaplan, Ognibeni, and Pauwels (2013) and Wang et al. (2012) shared the same view.

The impact of consumer socialization not just on the young people, but the entire population (De Gregorio & Sung, 2010; Taylor, Lewin, & Strutton, 2011). A significant relationship existed between social structural factors and socialization processes. Peers appear to be the most important agents of consumer socialization, contributing to a variety of desirable as well as undesirable consumer decision outcomes. Apart from this, the information can also be helpful in allowing marketers to be more effective in targeting various markets by formulating marketing strategies according to demographic factors, socialization process and decision-making styles. Hence, these consumer socialization dimensions are mediating the relationship between the contents obtained from Instagram and the intention to adopt purchase, as shown in Figure 1.

Figure 1. The conceptual framework

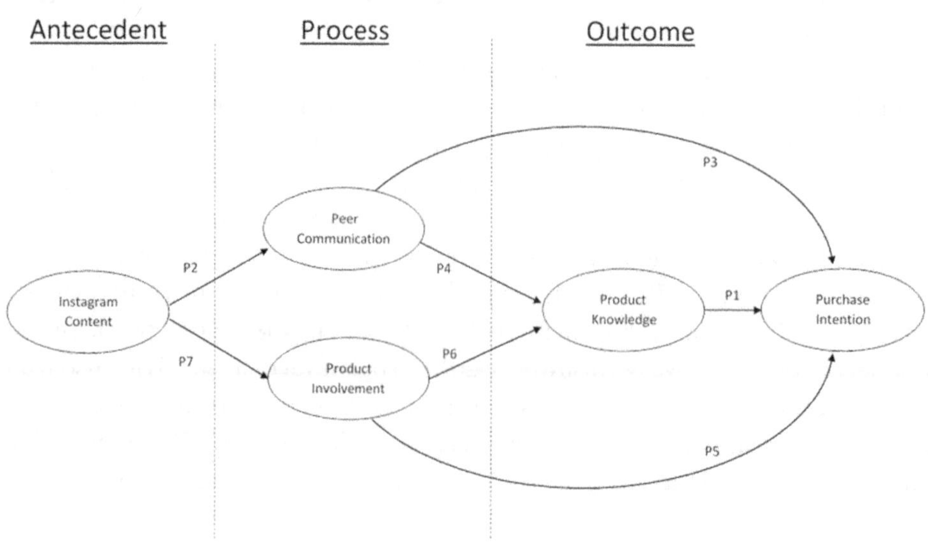

Product Knowledge

Product knowledge has gained attention in consumer behavior research. Product knowledge is an essential component in sales and marketing. Understanding products' features allows companies to present their benefits accurately and persuasively. Customers respond to enthusiastic sales staffs who are passionate about their products and eager to share the benefits with customers. By engaging customers, it is then possible to turn product features into benefits. Using one's knowledge to lead customer through the sales process, and make customer's experience an enjoyable one that they will want to revisit.

Customers have the tendency to know more of the product before purchase. The more customer know about the product, the more likely they will purchase the products and more competent in using it for full potential. Product learning is therefore important for all kinds of products and services. Wood and Lynch Jr (2002) accentuated that if customers are familiar with the product knowledge, they will invariably enjoy the product experience. Conversely, unfamiliarity may become disadvantageous for the customers.

Turning to self-service technologies with regard to technological interfaces, this allow customers to produce services independent of involvement of direct service employee. Increasingly Self-Service technologies are replacing many face-to-face service interactions with the intention to make service transactions more accurate, convenient and faster. With the widespread of contents by social media, people are becoming more comfortable and experience with technology, they are more willing to perform transactions over the Internet.

In other social media apps, the power of e-WoM (Electronic Word of Mouth) has been examined extensively (Hennig-Thurau, Gwinner, Walsh, & Gremler, 2004). People precisely like sharing information, social media, review websites and forums have become so successful. Therefore, e-WoM served as service chain, if one share information and then his/her friends shared the information with other friends and so on. This is the reason why e-WoM could become viral. Knowledge obtained from social media engagement is useful in helping consumer to make purchase decision. With refining image and video contents enriched with interactivity features, it is expecting that knowledge could be gained by following the Instagram posts. This then attributed to the high adoption and distribution speed of Instagram compared to other older social media apps. Therefore, we postulated the following proposition.

Proposition 1:

Product knowledge gained from consumer socialization can exert influence on purchase intention.

Instagram Content

Followers usually search for customized content from company that they are interested. In order to illustrate the application of the product, marketers must create engaging content on Instagram and show users how to use the products in their daily life. Consumers like to get ideas and see what products fit them personally. Hence, the trick is to keep content as actionable as possible.

In creating a thought-provoking story with the product, this can engage consumers and creates a compelling reason for them to click on the site and start shopping. This strategy can work for much of any product category. For example, agriculture revolution: agriculture technology uses storytelling to describe the communities benefiting from its sustainable food security initiatives around the world. The Instagram post can show a community that now has sustainable food security because of the nonprofit's project. Being open and telling brand story is a good way to build an online community.

With the high adoption of visual contents in social media, consumer socialization starts with the distribution of contents in the form of posts, image and footage. According to De Vries, Gensler, and Leeflang (2012), the most sought-after content has to be informative and entertaining. Interestingly, entertaining posts are the content normally do not directly relate to brand. The post published by the retailers should be customer-centric and this normally attracts the customers. If the content is relatable and can tell stories, then users will connect with the brand and will have a positive experience before they ever see the company's website. Consumer interaction with branded content becomes a matter of interest (Sabate, Berbegal-Mirabent, Cañabate, & Lebherz, 2014). Businesses should then recognize the benefits of getting closer to core customers in implementing customer centric strategies (Stefanou, Sarmaniotis, & Stafyla, 2003; Tian Xie & Johnston, 2004). Hashtags have become a uniform way to categorize content on many social media platforms. Hashtags allow Instagrammers to discover content and accounts to follow. It contributes to the increases of favorable posts, including the higher number of 'likes'. It also highlights the significance of high level of interactivity within social media users during the socialization process.

Peer Communication

By using social media marketing, companies virtually promote their brand image and MVC (Mission Vision and Culture) for minimum cost. This is an important advantage of word of mouth communication. Conversely, any errors or complaints on its services and/or products can adversely affect the companies' brand equity resulting in significant revenue loss. These errors affect the companies' images because young people communicate with their peers about everything at any time. Peer communication plays an important role in the socialization process fundamentally. As potential users develop greater independence from their parents and family, influence from peers and groups will have serious impact largely because of the large amount of time they spend together and the substantial behavioral and attitudinal similarities between them (Armağan & Çetin, 2013). These peers and groups become influential, important and valuable source of information on different brands and products.

Undoubtedly, Internet has the ability to link a piece of content to another. More specifically social media has transmuted how consumers and marketers communicate. Different social media platform (such as blogs, online discussion forums, and online communities) has an effect on marketing performance and especially social media has changed how consumers and marketers. For example, Instagram grabs attention of the younger generation, and is attractive to diverse societies, more appealing than other social networking services. Youngsters today spend more time on Instagram than Facebook (Salomon, 2013). This is because young mobile users who are extremely motivated to take photos or pictures using their mobile phones, and share them with others instantly. As such, the sharing of images rather than words alone has made communication with friends and broader groups of users who share similar interests conveniently. Social media provides firms with a more personal touch and communication channel with the consumers (Saji, Chauhan, & Pillai, 2013). It can enrich the two-way conversation in a shorter time possible as compared with traditional marketing communication channel. It is often wider coverage as it is much easier to find other users with similar interests together. From the business' perspective, friends with common interests invite and join the related retailer's social media, triggering the growth of social network groups. Hence, we developed the proposition as follow:

Proposition 2:

The contents gained from Instagram can exert influence on the peer communication during the consumer socialization.

Consumers often seek relevant information from various sources in their environment and attempt to make informed decisions. Hence, marketing through social media communication is new additional promotion mix strategy. In social networking, effective mode of communication between people and companies are crucial. Unlike traditional communication media, social networking site exploits its interactive images enabling the content to be more informative and representational. Users find social networking particularly useful because it can shared information and connected with their friends (Ho & Rezaei, 2018). From the decision-making stance, such online activities are crucial to companies as substantial amounts of users can make decision through social networking communication. It certainly has become an indispensable platform to get more customers and generate favorable attitude and intention in the marketplace in order to yield desired outcome (Brodie, Ilic, Juric, & Hollebeek, 2013; Mangold & Smith, 2012). Moreover, for the young online users, they tend to treat peer comments as important (Madell & Muncer, 2007). This led us to posit the proposition below:

Proposition 3:

Peer communication during consumer socialization can exert influence on purchase intention.

The elicitation of normative beliefs about Instagram provides knowledge about users' motivation to comply with relevant persons when it comes to using new application. Ting, Ming, de Run, and Choo (2015) accentuate that young people have no influence from their parents or the elderly. This indicates strong influence of people who are of similar age, such as their siblings, close friends and friends in the context of developing markets. Based on the consumer socialization process, peer communication at both individual and group levels are the antecedents for the product learning stage. Hence, it is critical for marketers to understand the social networking behavior as it is a contemporary phenomenon. Conversely, social networking is also a media for learning new things. The positive influence from siblings and friends, including Facebook friends, is important especially when it comes to new and innovative products.

With a variety of types of contents, Instagram can then be a platform for retailers to promote their products. Such understanding will assist companies in developing comprehensive strategies to not only target the users directly but also use referents to generate interest among potential users. During the consumer socialization process, followers and peers create information and shares experiences. The consumer learns more from peers rather than from retailer (Zhang & Daugherty, 2009). For instance, images posted in social media by local food and beverage industry can assist foreign travelers in understanding the local cuisines and impress them to patron the local restaurant.

Hence, consumers can expect to learn about efficacy of brand and product knowledge during their interactions with other users in Instagram. Indeed, social media is undergoing the socialization process which enables sharing and learning among the users by enjoying the outcomes of consumer socialization (Luczak & Younkin, 2012). Based on the discussion above, we developed the following proposition:

Proposition 4:

Peer communication during consumer socialization can exert influence on product knowledge.

Product Involvement

Product involvement is the degree of participation and actions conducted by consumers during the product consumption process. It is often associated with consumer's perceived enjoyment while consuming the product based on his own intrinsic values, needs and interests (Thong, Hong, & Tam, 2006). The user's predisposition to ponder over the outcome of a purchase and consumption experience will be contingent on their level of involvement and knowledge of the product itself. The possibility that any causal search occurs, users who are more knowledgeable were able to determine the correct underlying causes. This suggests that marketers need to be in a position to support less knowledgeable users in arriving at an accurate causal determination. Lee, Park, and Han (2008) further supports the notion that the level of involvement of Korean consumers tend to depend on the quality of information provided by the reviewers.

Instagram offers the hashtag (#) function in identifying relevant photos and videos. This way, users can browse specific hashtag to locate pictures/videos of their interest, such as "#travels" for travel destination or "#asianfood" for Asian food inspiration. Using suitable and relevant hashtags, the consumers can find the advertisement on their own. Thus, by identifying the key Instagrammers, the target audience faster and easily reached (Latiff & Safiee, 2015). Both through the Instagrammers' followers and hashtag posted by like-minded people.

Product Involvement During Consumer Socialization

Given the consumer socialization process, Lee et al. (2008) highlighted that the purchase intention is higher when there is higher level of customer's involvement in the negotiation stage with the retailer. Dellarocas (2003) reiterated that online word-of-mouth has imperative implications for managers in terms of brand building, product development, and quality assurance. Kim, Haley, and Koo (2009) provided further support to cues that the more effort and time spent by consumers in product evaluation, the higher possibility in product purchase.

Product involvement affects consumers in the decision-making process to purchase the products. The complexity of product search information, period in adopting, the level of the attitude and preferences about the product may lead to the customer perception on the various alternative in the same product category and brand loyalty (Bauer, Falk, & Hammerschmidt, 2006). Therefore, if a firm is seeking to win over consumer's loyalty of rival brand or enter into an established market may be better off targeting in its introductory efforts when consumers are already highly involved. The product involvement could be categorized into two major aspects with regard to enduring involvement and situational involvement (Bloch & Richins, 1983). In enduring involvement, it occurs when the consumer is actively involved in the process, and has more emotional attached during the purchase. While in situational involvement, it occurs when the consumer's perception on the product's importance is temporary as he/she is expecting to gain specific enjoyments or benefits from the product. The importance of product involvement in online shopping could understated during the consumer socialization process. Hence, we developed the following proposition:

Proposition 5:

Product involvement during consumer socialization can exert influence on purchase intention.

One significant factor that exerts influence on purchase intention is the influence of reference group. Reference group is people who act as a reference point for a consumer and with whom the consumer shares similar values, plays a major role in influencing the final purchase decision of the consumer. Rajput and Khanna (2014) concluded that reference groups are the external influencers such as favorite stars, celebrities, peers and relatives who considerably influence one's purchase decisions and behavior.

Product involvement in social commerce refers to as a situation where a particular consumer expresses constant interest with a particular product category (Peng, Zhang, Wang, & Liang, 2019). Herrington and Capella (1995) suggested that shoppers spend less time making a purchase when under time pressure. Significant factors are the influence of reference group and peer influence on purchase decisions (Akar & Nasir, 2015; Niu, 2013). According to Ting et al. (2015), communication is the foundation of social interaction, the essential means through which people initiate and maintain social relationships.

However, peers have increasing influence on their attitudes, beliefs, and behaviors. As young adults develop greater autonomy from their family, intrinsically peer influence becomes more important. They are particularly vulnerable to influence from their friends because of the considerable attitudinal and behavioral similarity between them and their friends (Armağan & Çetin, 2013). The main sources of information used by young adult concerning all kinds of products come mainly from peers. Consumers tend to interact with peers about consumption matters, which greatly influence their attitudes toward products and services (Wang et al., 2012). More importantly, they place greater level of trust in interpersonal information sources. Especially in their parents who are perceived as the most credible information source with respect to their learning about new products (Fan & Li, 2010). Hence, we posit the following proposition.

Proposition 6:

Product involvement during consumer socialization can exert influence on product knowledge.

An increasingly connected world has fast-forwarded the rate of information transfer across the globe. Social media has provided the platform for consumers to communicate simultaneously not only with their friends and acquaintances but also with relative strangers with unprecedented ease. Researchers who study consumer behavior attribute a great deal of importance to the product involvement variable (Charters & Pettigrew, 2006; Lin & Chen, 2006).

Product involvement can influence the decision-making process regarding a product. The extent to which consumers will search for information about the product, the timing in adoption of the product, the manner in which the consumer's attitudes and preferences regarding the product are influenced by the consumer's perceptions of alternatives in the same product category and brand loyalty (Hong, 2015).

It has facilitated the ability of people to share more about themselves, their families, and their friends through a variety of media. Thus, developing and sustaining social and business relationships. However, Fischer and Reuber (2011) observed that two factors that can moderate the social interaction, i.e. community orientation and community adherence. Conversely, findings of Lu, Zhao, and Wang (2010) revealed that the absence of physical contact between buyer and seller could reduce the likelihood for successful transaction.

It is common for Instagram to have a large number of 'likes' and 'follows" after more followers viewed images and watched the clip related to the product. With the increased adoption of visual contents, the customers' are more likely to distribute and co-create the contents. Hence, with these differences in research, it is imperative to ascertain the role of product involvement in Instagram with the following proposition.

Proposition 7:

The contents gained from Instagram can exert influence on the product involvement during the consumer socialization

CONCLUSION

Social networking has become an important communication tool enabling individuals and organizations to connect effectively. More specifically, Instagram utilizes its interactive images to make the content more representative and informative. This chapter focuses on consumer socialization process and the use of Instagram in providing practical implications for both consumers and marketers. Firstly, the peer communication and product involvement are important dimensions for better understanding the behavior of networked consumers. In addition, the effect of visual contents distributed by Instagram can stimulate the consumer shopping activities. It can expedite the marketing message diffusion with the simple liking or sharing the visual contents (Chang, Yu, & Lu, 2015).

Interestingly, the use of Instagram is less expensive and more effective as compared to conventional marketing tools. From the marketer's perspective, one of the biggest and the most obvious limitations of digital marketing is that there is no interaction between the customers and the medium used for marketing. Traditional marketing is a one-way street where a business is able to broadcast or provide information to their target audience about its product or service. This brand building exercise hopes to attract the attention of the right people and converting them into customers.

On the other hand, Instagram marketing conducted via the Internet or any electronic devices. Realistically any business, regardless of its size can leverage digital marketing to reach out to their target market, connect with prospects and convert more of them into customers/clients. By following the posts, image and video footage, prospect can learn about the new products and brand messaging. In addition to its role in brand awareness, there is also better engagement between customers and the retailers (Choudhury & Harrigan, 2014). Inversely, retailers can also learn, observe and gain new ideas from the followers. However, business need to ensure quality of its product and service is what they claimed to be.

In conclusion, social networks are mature and generated much business values. However, the most popular social media site contrasts greatly by level of usage in different online platforms. Understanding these differences in different types of social media is central when targeting specific audiences. Additionally, the popularity of one social media application in a specific context may not necessary be so in another context. The main finding of this chapter is to explore the consumer socialization process needed for online purchase via Instagram. Furthermore, this chapter confirmed that consumers' product knowledge acquired would ultimately lead to swift purchasing behavior. Instagram can be useful in providing a platform for customers to learn about product knowledge others. Therefore, consumer socialization process further enhanced with contents from Instagram that served as the antecedent. Hence, we learned that consumer socialization process could provide the necessary avenue to make Instagram the ideal shopping mode.

LIMITATIONS AND FUTURE RESEARCH DIRECTIONS

While this chapter emphasizes on the relationship of the contents distributed by Instagram and purchase intention, it is worthwhile to take note that consumer socialization process is ever changing in today's highly connected networked world. The importance of peer group factor and social media in building the knowledge, skills and attitudes required to function in the market place. It has an overwhelming impact on their brand choice and consumption behavior. Throughout the consumer socialization, consumers develop the knowledge, skills and values they will use in making and influencing purchases now and in future. Therefore, they not only are consumers, but also have a considerable influence in the purchase decisions depending on their purchase experience in different products. Invariably the amount of influence exerted by consumers differs from product group and during the decision-making process. As in some products, some consumers are merely purchasers while in other products they are influencers in their social networks for other consumers. Hence, the purchase behavior developed by the way they have been socialized to act as consumers. Hence, future researches could investigate the consumer socialization of Instagram based on the role of the consumer during product purchase process.

Instagram has a strongly visual-oriented focus as the photographs and short videos are the most common content (Murthy, Gross, & McGarry, 2016). Instagram users are mainly driven by social interaction (Blight, Ruppel, & Schoenbauer, 2017) which explains the higher level of engagement and brand community commitment found among its users (Phua, Jin, & Kim, 2017). High levels of interaction are important, because they can encourage a word-of-mouth effect and fan community building which are strong contributors to the success of social media campaigns (See-To & Ho, 2014). This raise an important question. Will the consumers engage in impulsive buying after they learned about the product knowledge from others? Further studies should investigate the relationship between Instagram contents and the likelihood of impulsive purchase behavior to examine how these two constructs correlate with each other.

REFERENCES

Abbott, W., Donaghey, J., Hare, J., & Hopkins, P. (2013). An Instagram is worth a thousand words: An industry panel and audience Q&A. *Library Hi Tech News*, *30*(7), 1–6. doi:10.1108/LHTN-08-2013-0047

Abzari, M., Ghassemi, R. A., & Vosta, L. N. (2014). Analysing the effect of social media on brand attitude and purchase intention: The case of Iran Khodro Company. *Procedia: Social and Behavioral Sciences*, *143*, 822–826. doi:10.1016/j.sbspro.2014.07.483

Akar, E., & Nasir, V. A. (2015). A review of literature on consumers' online purchase intentions. *Journal of Customer Behaviour*, *14*(3), 215–233. doi:10.1362/147539215X14441363630837

Armağan, E., & Çetin, A. (2013). Peer communication and impacts on purchasing decisions: An application on teenagers. *International Journal of Social Sciences and Humanity Studies*, *5*(2), 60–72.

Ashley, C., & Tuten, T. (2015). Creative strategies in social media marketing: An exploratory study of branded social content and consumer engagement. *Psychology and Marketing*, *32*(1), 15–27. doi:10.1002/mar.20761

Basu, R., & Sondhi, N. (2014). Child socialization practices: Implications for retailers in emerging markets. *Journal of Retailing and Consumer Services*, *21*(5), 797–803. doi:10.1016/j.jretconser.2014.06.008

Bauer, H. H., Falk, T., & Hammerschmidt, M. (2006). eTransQual: A transaction process-based approach for capturing service quality in online shopping. *Journal of Business Research*, *59*(7), 866–875. doi:10.1016/j.jbusres.2006.01.021

Blight, M. G., Ruppel, E. K., & Schoenbauer, K. V. (2017). Sense of community on Twitter and Instagram: Exploring the roles of motives and parasocial relationships. *Cyberpsychology, Behavior, and Social Networking*, *20*(5), 314–319. doi:10.1089/cyber.2016.0505

Bloch, P. H., & Richins, M. L. (1983). A theoretical model for the study of product importance perceptions. *Journal of Marketing*, *47*(3), 69–81. doi:10.1177/002224298304700308

Brodie, R. J., Ilic, A., Juric, B., & Hollebeek, L. (2013). Consumer engagement in a virtual brand community: An exploratory analysis. *Journal of Business Research*, *66*(1), 105–114. doi:10.1016/j.jbusres.2011.07.029

Chang, Y.-T., Yu, H., & Lu, H.-P. (2015). Persuasive messages, popularity cohesion, and message diffusion in social media marketing. *Journal of Business Research*, *68*(4), 777–782. doi:10.1016/j.jbusres.2014.11.027

Charters, S., & Pettigrew, S. (2006). Product involvement and the evaluation of wine quality. *Qualitative Market Research*, *9*(2), 181–193. doi:10.1108/13522750610658810

Chen, H. (2018). College-aged young consumers' perceptions of social media marketing: The story of Instagram. *Journal of Current Issues and Research in Advertising*, *39*(1), 22–36. doi:10.1080/10641734.2017.1372321

Chen, Y., Fay, S., & Wang, Q. (2011). The role of marketing in social media: How online consumer reviews evolve. *Journal of Interactive Marketing*, *25*(2), 85–94. doi:10.1016/j.intmar.2011.01.003

Choudhury, M. M., & Harrigan, P. (2014). CRM to social CRM: The integration of new technologies into customer relationship management. *Journal of Strategic Marketing*, *22*(2), 149–176. doi:10.1080/0965254X.2013.876069

Colliander, J., & Marder, B. (2018). 'Snap happy' brands: Increasing publicity effectiveness through a snapshot aesthetic when marketing a brand on Instagram. *Computers in Human Behavior*, *78*, 34–43. doi:10.1016/j.chb.2017.09.015

Daugherty, T., Eastin, M. S., & Bright, L. (2008). Exploring consumer motivations for creating user-generated content. *Journal of Interactive Advertising*, *8*(2), 16–25. doi:10.1080/15252019.2008.10722139

De Gregorio, F., & Sung, Y. (2010). Understanding attitudes toward and behaviors in response to product placement. *Journal of Advertising*, *39*(1), 83–96. doi:10.2753/JOA0091-3367390106

De Veirman, M., Cauberghe, V., & Hudders, L. (2017). Marketing through Instagram influencers: The impact of number of followers and product divergence on brand attitude. *International Journal of Advertising*, *36*(5), 798–828. doi:10.1080/02650487.2017.1348035

De Vries, L., Gensler, S., & Leeflang, P. S. H. (2012). Popularity of brand posts on brand fan pages: An investigation of the effects of social media marketing. *Journal of Interactive Marketing*, *26*(2), 83–91. doi:10.1016/j.intmar.2012.01.003

Dellarocas, C. (2003). The digitization of word of mouth: Promise and challenges of online feedback mechanisms. *Management Science*, *49*(10), 1407–1424. doi:10.1287/mnsc.49.10.1407.17308

Djafarova, E., & Rushworth, C. (2017). Exploring the credibility of online celebrities' Instagram profiles in influencing the purchase decisions of young female users. *Computers in Human Behavior*, *68*, 1–7. doi:10.1016/j.chb.2016.11.009

Duverger, P. (2013). Curvilinear effects of user-generated content on hotels' market share: A dynamic panel-data analysis. *Journal of Travel Research*, *52*(4), 465–478. doi:10.1177/0047287513478498

Fan, Y., & Li, Y. (2010). Children's buying behaviour in China: A study of their information sources. *Marketing Intelligence & Planning*, *28*(2), 170–187. doi:10.1108/02634501011029673

Fischer, E., & Reuber, A. R. (2011). Social interaction via new social media:(How) can interactions on Twitter affect effectual thinking and behavior? *Journal of Business Venturing*, *26*(1), 1–18. doi:10.1016/j.jbusvent.2010.09.002

Fong, J., & Burton, S. (2006). Electronic Word-of-Mouth: A Comparison of Stated and Revealed Behavior on Electronic Discussion Boards. *Journal of Interactive Advertising*, *6*(2), 7–62. doi:10.1080/15252019.2006.10722119

Hautz, J., Füller, J., Hutter, K., & Thürridl, C. (2014). Let users generate your video ads? The impact of video source and quality on consumers' perceptions and intended behaviors. *Journal of Interactive Marketing*, *28*(1), 1–15. doi:10.1016/j.intmar.2013.06.003

Hennig-Thurau, T., Gwinner, K. P., Walsh, G., & Gremler, D. D. (2004). Electronic word-of-mouth via consumer-opinion platforms: What motivates consumers to articulate themselves on the internet? *Journal of Interactive Marketing*, *18*(1), 38–52. doi:10.1002/dir.10073

Herrington, D. J., & Capella, L. M. (1995). Shopper reactions to perceived time pressure. *International Journal of Retail & Distribution Management*, *23*(12), 13–20. doi:10.1108/09590559510103963

Ho, R. C., & Rezaei, S. (2018). Social Media Communication and Consumers Decisions: Analysis of the Antecedents for Intended Apps Purchase. *Journal of Relationship Marketing*, *17*(3), 204–228. doi: 10.1080/15332667.2018.1492322

Hong, I. B. (2015). Understanding the consumer's online merchant selection process: The roles of product involvement, perceived risk, and trust expectation. *International Journal of Information Management*, *35*(3), 322–336. doi:10.1016/j.ijinfomgt.2015.01.003

Ilich, K. L., & Hardey, M. (2018). 'It's all about the packaging': Investigation of the motivations, intentions, and marketing implications of sharing photographs of secondary packaging on Instagram. *Information Communication and Society*. doi:10.1080/1369118X.2018.1478983

Kaplan, A. M., & Haenlein, M. (2010). Users of the world, unite! The challenges and opportunities of Social Media. *Business Horizons*, *53*(1), 59–68. doi:10.1016/j.bushor.2009.09.003

Kim, S., Haley, E., & Koo, G.-Y. (2009). Comparison of the paths from consumer involvement types to ad responses between corporate advertising and product advertising. *Journal of Advertising*, *38*(3), 67–80. doi:10.2753/JOA0091-3367380305

Latiff, Z. A., & Safiee, N. A. S. (2015). New business set up for branding strategies on social media–Instagram. *Procedia Computer Science*, *72*, 13–23. doi:10.1016/j.procs.2015.12.100

Lee, J., Park, D.-H., & Han, I. (2008). The effect of negative online consumer reviews on product attitude: An information processing view. *Electronic Commerce Research and Applications*, *7*(3), 341–352. doi:10.1016/j.elerap.2007.05.004

Lin, L.-Y., & Chen, C.-S. (2006). The influence of the country-of-origin image, product knowledge and product involvement on consumer purchase decisions: An empirical study of insurance and catering services in Taiwan. *Journal of Consumer Marketing*, *23*(5), 248–265. doi:10.1108/07363760610681655

Liu, S.-H., Chou, C.-H., & Liao, H.-L. (2015). An exploratory study of product placement in social media. *Internet Research*, *25*(2), 300–316. doi:10.1108/IntR-12-2013-0267

Lu, Y., Zhao, L., & Wang, B. (2010). From virtual community members to C2C e-commerce buyers: Trust in virtual communities and its effect on consumers' purchase intention. *Electronic Commerce Research and Applications*, *9*(4), 346–360. doi:10.1016/j.elerap.2009.07.003

Luczak, C., & Younkin, N. (2012). Net generation: A conceptual framework of the consumer socialization process. *Academy of Marketing Studies Journal*, *16*(2), 47.

Madell, D. E., & Muncer, S. J. (2007). Control over social interactions: An important reason for young people's use of the internet and mobile phones for communication? *Cyberpsychology & Behavior*, *10*(1), 137–140. doi:10.1089/cpb.2006.9980

Mangold, W., & Smith, K. T. (2012). Selling to Millennials with online reviews. *Business Horizons*, *55*(2), 141–153. doi:10.1016/j.bushor.2011.11.001

Murthy, D., Gross, A., & McGarry, M. (2016). Visual Social Media and Big Data. Interpreting Instagram Images Posted on Twitter. *Digital Culture & Society*, *2*(2), 113–134. doi:10.14361/dcs-2016-0208

Niu, H.-J. (2013). Cyber peers' influence for adolescent consumer in decision-making styles and online purchasing behavior. *Journal of Applied Social Psychology*, *43*(6), 1228–1237. doi:10.1111/jasp.12085

Peng, L., Zhang, W., Wang, X., & Liang, S. (2019). Moderating effects of time pressure on the relationship between perceived value and purchase intention in social E-commerce sales promotion: Considering the impact of product involvement. *Information & Management*, *56*(2), 317–328. doi:10.1016/j.im.2018.11.007

Perrin, Andrew. (2015). Social media usage. *Pew Research Center.*

Peters, K., Chen, Y., Kaplan, A. M., Ognibeni, B., & Pauwels, K. (2013). Social media metrics—A framework and guidelines for managing social media. *Journal of Interactive Marketing*, *27*(4), 281–298. doi:10.1016/j.intmar.2013.09.007

Phua, J., Jin, S. V., & Kim, J. J. (2017). Gratifications of using Facebook, Twitter, Instagram, or Snapchat to follow brands: The moderating effect of social comparison, trust, tie strength, and network homophily on brand identification, brand engagement, brand commitment, and membership intention. *Telematics and Informatics*, *34*(1), 412–424. doi:10.1016/j.tele.2016.06.004

Quintal, V., Phau, I., Sims, D., & Cheah, I. (2016). Factors influencing generation Y's purchase intentions of prototypical versus me-too brands. *Journal of Retailing and Consumer Services*, *30*, 175–183. doi:10.1016/j.jretconser.2016.01.019

Rajput, N., & Khanna, A. (2014). Dynamics of young indian consumers' buying behvior towards branded apparels: Gender perspective. *Archives of Business Research*, *2*(5), 84–106. doi:10.14738/abr.25.596

Sabate, F., Berbegal-Mirabent, J., Cañabate, A., & Lebherz, P. R. (2014). Factors influencing popularity of branded content in Facebook fan pages. *European Management Journal*, *32*(6), 1001–1011. doi:10.1016/j.emj.2014.05.001

Saji, K. B. (2013). Role of content strategy in social media brand communities: A case of higher education institutes in India. *Journal of Product and Brand Management*, *22*(1), 40–51. doi:10.1108/10610421311298687

Salomon, D. (2013). Moving on from Facebook: Using Instagram to connect with undergraduates and engage in teaching and learning. *College & Research Libraries News*, *74*(8), 408–412. doi:10.5860/crln.74.8.8991

See-To, E. W. K., & Ho, K. K. W. (2014). Value co-creation and purchase intention in social network sites: The role of electronic Word-of-Mouth and trust–A theoretical analysis. *Computers in Human Behavior*, *31*, 182–189. doi:10.1016/j.chb.2013.10.013

Sparks, B. A., & Bradley, G. L. (2017). A "Triple A" typology of responding to negative consumer-generated online reviews. *Journal of Hospitality & Tourism Research (Washington, D.C.)*, *41*(6), 719–745. doi:10.1177/1096348014538052

Stefanou, C. J., Sarmaniotis, C., & Stafyla, A. (2003). CRM and customer-centric knowledge management: An empirical research. *Business Process Management Journal*, *9*(5), 617–634. doi:10.1108/14637150310496721

Taylor, D. G., Lewin, J. E., & Strutton, D. (2011). Friends, fans, and followers: Do ads work on social networks? *Journal of Advertising Research*, *51*(1), 258–275. doi:10.2501/JAR-51-1-258-275

Teixeira, N., Pereira, H. G., & Dionísio, P. (2018). Online consumer generated content it's for real! the rise of social influence marketing. *The Business & Management Review*, *9*(3), 358–366.

Thong, J.YL, Hong, S.-J., & Tam, K.Y. (2006). The effects of post-adoption beliefs on the expectation-confirmation model for information technology continuance. *International Journal of Human-Computer Studies*, *64*(9), 799-810.

Ting, H., Ming, W. W. P., de Run, E. C., & Choo, S. L. Y. (2015). Beliefs about the use of Instagram: An exploratory study. *International Journal of business and innovation*, *2*(2), 15-31.

Tsekouropoulos, G., Andreopoulou, Z., Koliouska, C., Koutroumanidis, T., Batzios, C., & Lefakis, P. (2012). Marketing policies through the internet: The case of skiing centers in Greece. *Scientific Bulletin-Economic Sciences*, *11*(1), 66–78.

Virtanen, H., Björk, P., & Sjöström, E. (2017). Follow for follow: Marketing of a start-up company on Instagram. *Journal of Small Business and Enterprise Development*, *24*(3), 468–484. doi:10.1108/JSBED-12-2016-0202

Wang, X., Yu, C., & Wei, Y. (2012). Social media peer communication and impacts on purchase intentions: A consumer socialization framework. *Journal of Interactive Marketing*, *26*(4), 198–208. doi:10.1016/j.intmar.2011.11.004

Wood, S. L., & Jr, L. (2002). Prior knowledge and complacency in new product learning. *The Journal of Consumer Research*, *29*(3), 416–426. doi:10.1086/344425

Xie, T. (2004). Strategic alliances: Incorporating the impact of e-business technological innovations. *Journal of Business and Industrial Marketing*, *19*(3), 208–222. doi:10.1108/08858620410531342

Zhang, J., & Daugherty, T. (2009). Third-person effect and social networking: Implications for on-line marketing and word-of-mouth communication. *American Journal of Business*, *24*(2), 53–64. doi:10.1108/19355181200900011

KEY TERMS AND DEFINITIONS

Consumer Socialization: The process undergone by social media users in which they develop the skills, attitude and knowledge as consumers.

Instagram Marketing: The use of Instagram with the goal of developing a positive brand identity and building relationship with online customers.

Peer Communication: The exchange of information, product reviews and comments by peers in one's social virtual community.

Product Involvement: Defined as the perceived relevance of a product class based on the consumer's inherent needs, interest, and value during the purchase process.

Product Knowledge: The amount of accurate information about the products including the alternatives and product features that consumers believe they know.

Product Learning: It refers to learning about product consumption through interactions among the consumers, resellers and socialization agents in Instagram.

Purchase Attitude: Consumer's positive or negative feelings related to accomplishing product purchase in the Internet.

Purchase Intention: The possibility that the consumer would purchase the related products after the consumer socialization process.

Chapter 2
What Motivates Young Technology-Literate Consumers in Densely Populated Areas?

Narasimha Rao Vajjhala
https://orcid.org/0000-0002-8260-2392
American University of Nigeria, Nigeria

Kenneth D. Strang
https://orcid.org/0000-0002-4333-4399
Walden University, USA

ABSTRACT

In this chapter, the authors analyze the cultural, technological, and psychological factors that influence online young technology-literate consumer behavior in a densely populated urban area. This chapter starts with a literature review of factors that can explain the online behavior of people from various demographic and cultural backgrounds including education, occupation, income level, gender, ethnicity, and age (as a control). The authors also reviewed several empirical studies that examine online consumer behavior in India, where the population is the second highest in the world and a leader in global technology services. The purpose of the study is to develop a multi-cultural model that could predict the emerging shopping pattern of young and highly connected consumers in the high technology use metropolitan area, specifically in Northern India. The results can be used to generalize other online consumer behavior in other similar highly populated communities where internet technology use is high.

DOI: 10.4018/978-1-5225-9697-4.ch002

INTRODUCTION

There has been a dramatic increase in consumer shopping on the Internet in India (Nittala 2015). At 1.32 billion, India has the second largest population in the world after China although the Internet penetration is quite low and comprised mostly of young technology-literate people at or under the age of 30 (Khare 2016). Hence, the study of people in a densely populated urban area of India provides an ideal basis to study the online consumer behavior of the emerging technology-literate young generation while knowing or controlling for country level characteristics such as national culture, technological maturity, as well as examining the individual level psychological factors.

A review of the literature indicated that two broad approaches were being used to empirically examine consumer Internet behavior: psychological and technical. The consumer psychological approach for studying Internet behavior has focused on examining demographics, social factors, shopping motivation and personality orientation (Dennis et al. 2009; Zhou et al. 2007). The technology approach for examining consumer Internet behavior has focused on technical specifications of the website, payment, user intention, and ease of use (Dennis et al. 2009; Zhou et al. 2007). The authors have included an additional dimension, i.e. cultural factors to examine the influence of various cultural dimensions on online consumer behavior. According to Yoon (2009), e-commerce has an international scope so national culture can have an impact on the behavior of the consumers.

The authors have reviewed the various national cultural models and examined the various national cultural dimensions that are likely to influence online consumer behavior. Young technology-literate consumers, in particular, form a key demographic for online marketers as their Internet usage is significantly higher. As online shopping has already reached a saturation point in most of the European countries and in the USA, large online retailers, including Amazon and Walmart are focusing on countries with dense populations. The BRICS countries, namely, Brazil, Russia, India, China, and South Africa offer an opportunity for online companies because of dense population and low penetration rates in the context of online shopping. This chapter provides an understanding of the factors that motivate young technology literate consumers in dense population areas with focus on India. Therefore, the objective of this study was to develop a multi-cultural model that could predict emerging young consumer behavior in a high population high technology use metropolitan area, specifically India.

Problem and Background Marketing managers and other researchers do not have a current research model to use for studying the younger emerging generation of technology-literate consumers in densely populated BRICS regions with the national cultural dimensions unique to India. Since large retailers are expanding into BRICS regions, including India, new product developers and marketing professionals in these companies will need to understand the online behavior of the emerging generation of young technology-literate consumers, otherwise a lot of investment could be wasted and the national economy of India could suffer.

Online shopping provides several benefits to consumers as compared to the traditional offline shopping channels. These benefits include availability of information and lower information as well as search costs (Hwang & Jeong, 2016). There have been significant advances in technology over the last couple of decades because of which online shopping is gaining increasing popularity. However, there have not been any studies of the online behavior by young technology-literature consumers in a densely populated urban region of a BRICS country, specifically northern India.

The revenues from Business-to-Consumer (B2C) and Consumer-to-Consumer (C2C) forms of e-commerce have seen significant growth over the last decade. The online shopping and Internet penetration rates are quite high in the Western countries and online shopping has nearly reached a saturation point. Hence, large online retailers, including Walmart and Amazon are focusing on BRICS countries. BRICS countries are densely populated with the population in these countries constituting 40% of the global population (Bremmer, 2017). The problem is that there has been no research specifically directed at you technology-literate young consumers in densely populated urban regions of a BRICS country, with distinctive national level cultural characteristics such as India.

FACTORS INFLUENCING ONLINE CONSUMER BEHAVIOR

The online behavior of consumers is considerably different from the traditional consumer behavior because of the unique characteristics of technology coupled with culture (Bagga & Bhatt, 2013). Several studies have explored both the traditional offline as well as online consumer behavior. However, most of these studies have focused on the technical aspects of the website as well as the psychological factors influencing consumer purchasing decisions. This book chapter will focus on the third factor, in particular, the role of cultural factors in influencing online consumer purchasing decisions. National culture has been shown to impact technology avoidance in specific cultural dimensions (Strang & Vajjhala, 2017; Strang & Vajjhala, 2015). Malhotra and McCort (2001) state that behavioral intention models need not necessarily be universally applicable and must be operationalized with the distinctive thought processes of each culture.

National Level Cultural Factors

Examining global consumer behavior requires international consumer research to be done in a cross-cultural context (Park & Jun, 2003). Bagga and Bhatt (2013) state that different cultures exhibited different behaviors and attitudes to Internet and could lead to different impressions of the same websites. Researchers have been using theories, such as the Theory of Reasoned Action to explain the behavior of consumers but these theories may not be applicable across all cultures. Malhotra and McCort (2001) give the example of the criticism that the Fishbein and Ajzen theory contains Western cultural biases and might be suited and supported in US samples but not necessarily samples from other cultures.

According to Park and Jun (2003), cultural factors are likely to have a significant impact on the adoption and the use of the Internet. Examining cross-cultural behavior is a complex process and often researchers have sought the use of national cultural dimensions to characterize national culture at a country-level. Most of the studies have used the national cultural dimensions described by Hofstede (1984), Hofstede (2001), and Hofstede, Hofstede, and Minkov(2010). The national cultural dimensions listed by Trompenaar and Hampden-Turner (1997) are another set of cultural dimensions that are frequently used by researchers seeking to understand the national cultural behavior.

Hofstede's national culture model consisted of six dimensions, namely, power distance index (PDI), individualism versus collectivism (IDV), masculinity versus feminity (MAS), uncertainty avoidance index (UAI), long-term versus short-term normative orientation (LTO), and indulgence versus restraint

(IND). The PDI dimension is indicative of the degree to which the less powerful members of the society accept unequal distribution of power in the society (Hofstede, 1984). India ranks quite high in the PDI dimension with a score of 77 indicating an acceptance of unequal distribution of power (Insights, 2018).

PDI is used to measure the extent of power distribution in an organization and the level of equality between different members in a group. The choice of appropriate content and web features across cultures for web designers is more of an art than a science. Singh and Matsuo (2004) provide a content analysis of cultural website adaptation while Yun et al. (2008) describe the use of interactive features in countries with high versus low power differences. In high power distance societies, people are more task-oriented and less people-oriented. Hence, dominance and the feeling of control in completing the task is more critical for customers from high power distance cultures (Mazaheri et al., 2011).

The MAS dimension is indicative of the society's preference for achievement and material rewards in contrast to feminity indicated by a preference for cooperation and modesty (Hofstede, 1984). India is considered as a masculine society indicated by a marginally high score of 56 (Insights, 2018). Masculine societies place increased emphasis on wealth, success, ambition, achievement, etc., whereas feminine cultures place greater value on people, helping others, and preserving equality and environment (Hofstede, 1984). In the context of online consumer behavior, masculine societies are likely to choose products based on tangible features such as product quality and convenience.

The UAI dimension indicates the degree to which the members of the society feel uncomfortable with uncertainty and ambiguity (Hofstede, 1984). India is considered to have a medium to low preference for uncertainty with a score of 40 (Insights, 2018). Uncertainty avoidance includes the ability of a team of people to handle ambiguity and unplanned situations. In organizations high in levels of uncertainty avoidance, employees work efficiently with a clear set of guidelines and work descriptions, whereas, in societies with low uncertainty avoidance, employees can work efficiently without a clear set of instructions (Hofstede, 1984). In the context of uncertainty avoidance, the factors such as perceived risk of online shopping can influence the attitude of consumers to online purchasing. Park and Jun (2003) give an example of the importance of cultural factors through the early adoption of Internet marketing schemes which is relatively slower in countries characterized by high uncertainty avoidance. Customers from cultures with a lower level of uncertainty avoidance try to avoid uncertain situations and are more tolerant to risk. In countries with high uncertainty avoidance, the risk associated with online shopping is likely to influence the online shopping behavior. In such cultures, people usually trust and look forward to the government to provide regulation. Hence, the institutional and governmental policies are likely to help positively influence the online consumer behavior in such countries. One way of minimizing risk is through seeking and collecting additional information about online transactions before getting involved in online purchasing decisions (Mazaheri et al., 2011).

Although several demographic studies of online adoption and usage exist, researchers and research outlets will need to continue to focus on this area as increased global online adoption makes the existing research out-of-date and of little value to global e-marketers (Cummins et al., 2014). Several researchers have emphasized that the cultural background of the internet users influences the way the user perceives the importance of specific web design features (Mazaheri et al., 2014). For instance, people in high uncertainty avoidance cultures experience higher stress and have less emotional control contributing to the higher influence of pleasure (Mazaheri et al., 2014).

The IDV dimension is indicative of the preference for a loosely-knit social framework with emphasis on the individual and his immediate family (Hofstede, 1984). Collectivism in contrast is indicative of the preference for a tightly-knit social framework with emphasis on in-group loyalty and consideration (Hofstede, 1984). India has a mix of both individualistic and collectivist tendencies with an intermediate IDV score of 48 (Insights, 2018). Collectivist cultures are tightly integrated cultures in which members assume that individuals belong to one or more in-groups, through either birth or other events (Hofstede, 1984). In contrast, individualistic cultures exist in countries where a higher preference is given to the personal goals of individuals as compared to the larger societal benefits (Hofstede, 1984).

The comparison of collectivist and non-collectivist cultures offers valuable insights. For example, Lim et al. (2004) list out the differences in uncertainty avoidance in online shopping while Ko et al. (2006) describe the perceptions of interactivity in the context of culture. According to Moon et al. (2008), individuals from individualistic countries were more likely to purchase customized products online as compared to those of collectivistic cultures. Moon et al. (2008) also identified individualism as the most important of the cultural dimensions in explaining consumer purchasing intention for online personalized products. Based on this premise, we can argue that online personalization strategies would be ideal while targeting consumers in more individualistic countries like the USA, and European countries as compared to collectivistic societies, such as the Asian countries.

Customers from individualistic societies are likely to be high on self-reliance, competitiveness, aggressive creativity, and insecurity. Mazaheri et al. (2011) state that the effect of emotional experience is substantial in individualistic cultures as compared to collectivistic cultures. Collectivism is closely associated with high-context cultures, where there is an emphasis on causal reasoning and situational constraints. Hence, these cultures are more sensitive to site and service attitudes (Mazaheri et al., 2011). Customers in individualistic cultures are likely to make their decisions based on their interest as compared to collectivistic cultures where the decision-making behavior is likely to be influenced by the preferences of the society (Mazaheri et al., 2011). According to Khare (2012), individualist societies are likely to demonstrate positive online shopping behavior as compared to collectivistic cultures. As the decisions are based on individual interest, customers from individualistic cultures are likely to make online purchasing decisions quicker as compared to customers from collectivistic cultures.

Long-term orientation (LTO) is the "fostering of virtues oriented towards future rewards, in particular, perseverance and thrift" (Hofstede, 2001, p. 359). Customers from cultures with long-term orientation associate themselves with responsive and reliable service. India has an intermediate score of 51 indicating a mix of both long-term and short-term orientation (Insights, 2018). The level of expectation is also higher about the amount and quality of information provided on the website (Mazaheri et al., 2011).

Trompenaars and Hampden-Turner (1997) described seven dimensions of culture in their model: Universalism versus particularism, individualism versus collectivism, neutral versus emotional, specific versus diffused, sequential versus synchronic, inner versus outer direction, and achievement versus ascription. These cultural values can also be considered as variations of Hofstede's (1984) cultural factors (Strang, 2011, p. 9). Hall (1981) categorized cultures as low-context and high-context with cultures where most things are explicitly stated being categorized as low-context cultures. In contrast, a lot of information is in the context of low-context cultures. In the context of computer-mediated communication, low-context interactivity in a website is mostly represented in the form of human-message interaction as people from low-context culture rely mainly on the information they can find on the Internet (Ko et al., 2006). High-context interactivity in a website is related to human-human interaction because people from a high-context culture put in more emphasis on online bonds with other people (Ko et al., 2006).

Cultural dimensions also influence the tangibility dimension. Cultural context is quite useful in understanding some of the intangible differences between cultures (Ko et al., 2006). For instance, high-context cultures have indirect and ambiguous communication as compared to low-context cultures which depend on direct information and data. Examining the cultural differences in using and adopting technology is essential as the World Wide Web allows consumers to control the amount of data they choose to receive through their own navigational decisions on the website (Ko et al., 2006). For instance, individuals coming from a high context culture prefer to see and touch items (Mazaheri et al., 2014). Hence, service providers have a task at hand in trying to render tangible services to attract customers from high-context cultures. The emphasis is on building trust and relationships before undertaking any business in high-context cultures. Hence, communication is quite important as this is essential for creating and building relationships. Low-context cultures use communication only as a means for information interchange, and individual achievement is of utmost importance. Hence, physical and mental tangibility is of utmost importance for customers of low-context cultures.

Hence, understanding low-context cultures is harder and difficult to penetrate for marketers as compared to high-context cultures. Hofstede's cultural dimensions can also be explained by using the cultural context as there is a strong correlation between cultural context and the individualism/collectivism dimension (Hofstede, 1984). In marketing literature, culture is considered to be one of the most influential factors affecting the consumer motivation, attitudes, and purchasing behavior (Ko et al., 2006). Bagga and Bhatt (2013) emphasize that online consumer behavior is also influenced by external influences, including culture, sub-culture, locality, ethnicity, and social class. Mazaheri et al. (2011) emphasize on the need for more cross-cultural comparisons of accepted models and theories.

Individual Level Technological Factors Technology is the driver for internet marketing with changes in how consumers seek information and interact with prospective sellers in the marketplace determined by changes in technology (Banerjee and Dholakia, 2012). For instance, changes in technology from desktop computers to laptop computers to handheld devices, such as smartphones have influenced consumer use of technology (Banerjee and Dholakia, 2012). According to Khare et al. (2012), the acceptance of Internet is dependent on the quality of Internet connection, accessibility, technology-related laws, and power failures. Online shopping offers several benefits to consumers, including greater availability of information and lower search costs (Hwang & Jeong, 2016).

Several researchers have used the Technology Acceptance Model (TAM) to understand online consumer behavior (Khare et al., 2012; Tong, 2010). Davis (1989) proposed the initial Technology Acceptance Model (TAM) and then followed this up with the TAM 2 (Venkatesh & Davis, 2000) and TAM3 (Venkatesh & Bala, 2008) models. The TAM model remains the foundation for understanding technology acceptance with its iterations taking into considerations the advancements in technology and the way users adopted and used the technology (Tong, 2010). Another important set of theories that have been popular with researchers investigating the acceptance and continual use of technology in enterprises are the Unified Theory of Use and Acceptance of Technology (UTAUT)(Venkatesh et al., 2003) and UTAUT2 (Venkatesh et al., 2012).

Among the TAM factors, perceived usefulness and risk were identified to having an effect on the online consumer shopping behavior. According to Khare et al. (2012), perceived ease of use has a positive effect on the perceived usefulness and prior online shopping experience has a positive effect on the perceived ease of use and a negative effect on the perceived risks. Several factors influence the internet consumer behavior, including the perceived usefulness, perceived ease of use, length of time spent online and perceived enjoyment (Davis, 1989; Park & Jun, 2003). Bagga and Bhatt (2013) emphasize that the Internet shopping experience and perceived risk play an important role in the purchase likelihood of the consumer. Khare, Khare, and Singh (2012) suggest that the consumer attitude towards online shopping is influenced by the features of the website, such as convenience, navigability, information availability, and ease of use. Consumer demographics, social factors, risk factors, and Internet accessibility are other factors that could influence online consumer behavior (Khare et al., 2012).

Individual Level Psychological and Social FactorsCustomers' adoption of an innovation depends partially on the acceptance among social groups (Khare et al., 2012). Consumers are likely to adopt an innovation to maintain their standing in their respective social group. Hence, social factors play an important role in influencing the consumer's decision on acceptance of new retail channels. Barrutia and Gilsanz (2012) cite the Service-Dominant Logic (SDL) to illustrate the importance of viewing a customer as an operant resource and a collaborative partner contributing to value creation in a firm. Hence, understanding the social and psychological factors that influence the online shopping consumer behavior is imperative for online marketers.

Bagga and Bhatt (2013) identified seven intrinsic and extrinsic factors that are likely to influence the online consumer buying behavior. These factors include: need for recreation, convenience, website attributes, online advertising, social communication, information search, and security/privacy concerns (Bagga & Bhatt, 2013). These factors can offer an in-depth view into the online consumer buying behavior when considered together with demographic variables, such as age, income group of consumers, and gender. Amin and Amin (2013) stated that the individual attitudes to online shopping behavior were a direct predictor of the buying behavior. Hence, personal values, such as self-direction, enjoyment, and self-achievement could be considered as significantly related to positive attitudes to online shopping.

Amin and Amin (2013) claimed that the level of trust as a key factor influencing the online shopping behavior of the consumer. For instance, the reputation and size of the online store influences the consumer's trust of the retailer. Liao et al. (2011) look at online consumer behavior from the perspective of post-purchase evaluations by evaluating the impact of satisfaction or regret by the consumer. Liao et al. (2011) list out the antecedents of online consumer satisfaction, namely, information quality, system quality, and service quality. For instance, if consumers are not satisfied with the quality of the content in a website then they are likely to move on to other websites or return back to traditional channels of shopping (Lio et al., 2011). Similarly, service quality is equally important as consumers who cannot complete transactions, don't receive products in time or are having problems in contacting the customer support are likely to regret shopping online.

Koufaris (2002) looks at an online consumer from a dual perspective: both as a shopper as well as a computer user. Hence, online consumer behavior needs to take constructs from both technology acceptance as well as consumer behavior. Understanding the differences between online and traditional offline consumers is quite important. According to Koufaris (2002), online customers cannot depend on all the five senses and mostly rely on the visual descriptions provided through audio and video channels.

Hence, the design of the websites as well as the use of advanced technology to enhance the online shopping experience through means such as recommender systems is quite essential. The social conditions could also be different for online and the offline consumers. For instance, the intention to shop online could be motivated by the lack of leisure time or perhaps the preference for using technology for the online consumer (Koufaris, 2002).

Online consumers are also often concerned with the inherent risks of shopping online. For instance, risks such as credit card fraud or not receiving the right products could influence the overall shopping experience and also negative impact the online consumer behavior. One of the key challenges for online marketers is the low levels of loyalty among online shoppers. This is partially because of the low switching costs associated with online shopping (Koufaris, 2002). Online shoppers may also switch to other sites if they are not satisfied with the online shopping experience at a particular site. For instance, the lack of frequently asked questions (FAQ) or customer support could result in the customers moving to another site which offers these features. Khare et al. (2012) emphasize that consumer demographics, including education, national income levels, economic development, crime rate, and unemployment influence the Internet usage rates. Khare et al. (2012) state that the Indian consumer's online shopping behavior is influenced by the normative beliefs and gender. Consumers also tend to prefer online shopping if their social systems and groups have a positive opinion on online shopping.

Conclusions and Synthesis of Online Consumer Behavior Model for Urban India

In this book chapter, our focus was on proposing a research design for analyzing consumer behavior in a densely populated urban BRICS region based on the cultural, technological, and social as well as psychological factors influencing the online activity of young technology-literate people in India.

The scope of our study was to propose a model for studying the online acceptance behavior of technology-literate younger consumers in the northern urban region of India. India is a BRICS country and it is considered one of the most successful (as per literature review citations). We purposively selected the northern urban densely populated area of India as the sample frame. Thus, we intended to be able to generalize our findings to densely populated urban areas in India primarily, with a second possible assertion that the study could be replicated to other BRICS regions.

This study specifically focused on proposing a population sample frame to examine the densely populated urban area of Hyderabad in the newly formed Telangana state of India. The authors performed unstructured interviews of young consumers and developed a proposed theoretical factor model which could be used in future studies to predict consumer online behavior. We recommend this study be extended to test the model with a new formal sample.

India is the second largest populated country close behind China with a population of approximately 1.32 billion. However, the Internet penetration rate is quite low with only 503 million internet users in 2017 and most of these are the younger generation at or under the age of 30 (Khare, 2016). However, the annual growth rate of Internet users is quiet high at 41%. Online retailers and marketers have a huge untapped market that offers significant growth opportunities. Amazon has already invested significantly in the Indian online market with Walmart quickly following up with the acquisition of the largest Indian online retailer - Flipkart in 2018. Both these international online retailers have invested significantly in the Indian online shopping sector as they see huge potential growth opportunities. However, there is relatively limited research and literature to understand the online consumer shopping behavior of Indian consumers as compared to literature on Western European and American online consumers (Khare et al., 2012).

In the context of the geographical dispersion of cross-cultural e-commerce studies, most of the studies provide a comparison between or across cultures rather than analysis within a single non-US culture. Strang and Vajjhala (2015) indicate a literature gap in studies examining culture in the context of decision making. Some of the studies investigate as many as 12 countries (Lynch, 2001). Most of the studies compare the USA and Asian countries, most often China, Japan, and South Korea because of the high level of economic development and importance (Khare et al., 2012). Fewer comparison studies investigate the online environment, market or consumers in Europe, Canada, or Australia. National comparison studies also tend to have a narrow focus, examining on cultural differences within a particular group.

Very few studies investigate the markets that may be representational of a larger understudied group of countries (Khare et al., 2012). For instance, India with a multicultural population of more than 1.2 Billion is a potential market with significant economic clout as part of the BRIC countries. A Larger number of studies on these underrepresented countries will help e-marketers aid their company's strategic moves into these promising markets. This study focuses on young technology literate online shoppers from a densely populated area in India – Hyderabad in the newly formed state of Telangana in India. Telangana is one of the states with the highest Gross State Domestic Product (GSDP) which suggests that the availability and affordability of the use of technology and Internet was much higher in this state. Hyderabad is the capital city of Telangana and is one of the most populous cities in India with a population of over 8 million in 2018 (including the sub-urban areas).

SOLUTIONS AND RECOMMENDATIONS

The authors performed unstructured interviews with more than 60 young technology literature university students throughout densely populated urban areas in Northern India. We selected the two southern areas known to have a high concentration of Internet access: Andhra Pradesh and Telangana. These two states were chosen as they were among the top-5 states in the Gross State Domestic Product (GSDP) indicating that the affordability and availability of technology were much higher as compared to other Indian states. Andhra Pradesh and Telangana used to be one single state before the bifurcation in 2014. The state of Andhra Pradesh stood seventh regarding geographic area and 10th regarding population among the 29 Indian states. We used social media and email to identify participants who agreed to participate in an informal unstructured interview. The participants included a diverse demographic distribution with the main criteria being they had access to the online Internet shopping and they had shopped once online. We asked the participants which factors would likely influence their decision to purchase items online through the Internet, while specifically mentioning all the variables we had located through the literature review. This allowed the authors to confirm if and how the theoretical factors from the literature review were likely to be relevant to predict online consumer purchase behavior.

Based on the literature review and unstructured interviews, the authors can propose the following factors to be used for analyzing and predicting consumer behavior for technology-literate young consumers in a highly populated technology literature area in metropolitan India.

We found that the perceptions of participants differed based on their demographic characteristics namely gender and subcultural dialect (e.g., culture). Therefore gender would be the first important factor. Although we selected only young technology literate participants, we would recommend age and technology literacy is included in future models as a control.

We found satisfaction, positive feelings and pleasant feelings about the Internet tended to differ between participants so we would recommend these factors be included in a predictive model. Traditionally, socioeconomic factors such as income level have been included with predictive social models so this ought to be included in a future model. Also, as noted in the literature review, motivation to purchase or as it has been customarily termed; purchase intention behavior ought to be included in predictive model so as to capture this factor since it has been shown to be highly correlated with actual purchase behavior.

In summary, here are the factors we developed for this model, based on the literature review and data analysis:

- Gender.
- Socio-cultural background (local dialect).
- Trust of information from a friend (personal conversation or online).
- Trust of information from the social media (e.g., Facebook but not a friend)?
- Trust of information from the national news (e.g., Television, Google News or similar)?
- Trust of information from the local news (e.g., local radio station, local newspaper or flyer)?
- Trust of information from a public library provided by an employee or librarian?
- Trust of information from a Health Care Provider (e.g., Blue Cross, pharmaceutical, or insurance provider)?
- Trust of information from the government (e.g., Prime Minister Modi or other official announcement)?
- Trust of information from a bank or investment company?
- Willing to take risks to purchase online?
- Purchasing online helps to be more productive.
- Purchasing online saves time.
- Purchasing online requires fewer steps than other methods like catalog mail order or phone.
- Purchasing online makes the task easier than the other methods (easier than phone or catalog).
- Purchasing online is easy to learn (there is usually enough information to make it easy).
- Purchasing online provides satisfaction with the results.
- Purchasing online provides positive feelings about the effort.
- Purchasing online provides and pleasant feelings about the effort.
- Control variables (identified in literature review and recommended to be included in predictive model):
  - Age.
  - Socio-economic status through income level.
  - Technology literacy.
  - Motivation (behavioral intent to purchase online).

FUTURE RESEARCH DIRECTIONS

This study focused on developing a predictive consumer online purchase model based on young technology literate shoppers from one of major densely populated urban areas in India - Hyderabad city in the newly formed Telangana state. This study needs to be executed with a large sample size. This study also needs to be replicated in other major densely populated urban cities of India, including the metropolitan cities of New Delhi, Mumbai, Kolkata, and Chennai.

Researchers could also consider expanding this study to other major cities and states in India because of the diverse and heterogeneous mix of sub-cultures within India. In future, this study could also be expanded to other Asian and African countries which have a large young population and densely populated urban areas, such as Nigeria, Kenya, Indonesia, China, and Malaysia.

REFERENCES

Amin, B. J., & Amin, P. (2013). A conceptual framework to understanding online consumer buying behavior. *International Journal of Online Marketing*, *3*(1), 47–63. doi:10.4018/ijom.2013010104

Bagga, T., & Bhatt, M. (2013). A study of intrinsic factors influencing consumer buying behavior online. *Asia-Pacific Journal of Management Research and Innovation*, *9*(1), 77–90. doi:10.1177/2319510X13483515

Banerjee, S., & Dholakia, R. R. (2012). Location-based mobile advertisements and gender targeting. *Journal of Research in Interactive Marketing*, *6*(3), 198–214. doi:10.1108/17505931211274679

Barrutia, J. M., & Gilsanz, A. (2012). Electronic service quality and value: Do consumer knowledge-related resources matter? *Journal of Service Research*, *16*(2), 231–246. doi:10.1177/1094670512468294

Bremmer, I. (2017). The Mixed Fortunes of the BRICS Countries, in 5 Facts. Time.

Cummins, S., Peltier, J. W., Schibrowsky, J. A., & Nill, A. (2014). Consumer behavior in the online context. *Journal of Research in Interactive Marketing*, *8*(3), 169–202. doi:10.1108/JRIM-04-2013-0019

Davis, F. D. (1989). Perceived usefulness, perceived ease of use, and user acceptance of information technology. *Management Information Systems Quarterly*, *13*(3), 319–340. doi:10.2307/249008

Dennis, C., Merrilees, B., Jayawardhena, C., & Wright, L. T. (2009). E-Consumer behavior. *European Journal of Marketing*, *42*(9), 1121–1139. doi:10.1108/03090560910976393

Hall, E. T. (1983). *The Dance of Life*. Garden City, NY: Anchor Press.

Hofstede, G. (1984). The cultural relativity of the quality of life concept. *Academy of Management Review*, *9*(3), 389–398. doi:10.5465/amr.1984.4279653

Hofstede, G. (2001). *Culture's consequences: Comparing values, behaviors, institutions, and organizations across nations* (2nd ed.). Thousand Oaks, CA: Sage.

Hofstede, G., Hofstede, G. J., & Minkov, M. (2010). *Cultures and organizations: Software of the mind* (3rd ed.). New York, NY: McGraw-Hill.

Insights, H. (2018). *Country Comparison - India.* Retrieved December 1, 2018, from https://www.hofstede-insights.com/country-comparison/india/

Khare, A. (2016). Consumer shopping styles and online shopping: An empirical study of Indian consumers. *Journal of Global Marketing*, *29*(1), 40–53. doi:10.1080/08911762.2015.1122137

Khare, A., Khare, A., & Singh, S. (2012). Attracting shoppers to shop online - Challenges and opportunities for the Indian retail sector. *Journal of Internet Commerce*, *11*(1), 161–185. doi:10.1080/15332861.2012.689570

Ko, H., Roberts, M. S., & Cho, C.-H. (2006). Cross cultural differences in motivations and perceived interactivity: A comparative study of American and Korean internet users. *Journal of Current Issues and Research in Advertising*, *28*(2), 93–104. doi:10.1080/10641734.2006.10505201

Koufaris, M. (2002). Applying technology acceptance model and flow theory to online consumer behavior. *Information Systems Research*, *13*(2), 205–226. doi:10.1287/isre.13.2.205.83

Liao, C., Liu, C.-C., Liu, Y.-P., To, P.-L., & Lin, H.-N. (2011). Applying the expectancy disconfirmation and regret theories to online consumer behavior. *Cyberpsychology, Behavior, and Social Networking*, *14*(4), 241–246. doi:10.1089/cyber.2009.0236 PMID:21067306

Malhotra, N. K., & McCort, J. D. (2001). A cross-cultural comparison of behavior intention models: Theoretical consideration and an empirical investigation. *International Marketing Review*, *18*(3), 235–268. doi:10.1108/02651330110396505

Mazaheri, E., Richard, M. O., & Laroche, M. (2011). Online consumer behavior: Comparing Canadian and Chinese website visitors. *Journal of Business Research*, *64*(1), 958–965. doi:10.1016/j.jbusres.2010.11.018

Mazaheri, E., Richard, M. O., Laroche, M., & Ueltschy, L. C. (2014). The influence of culture, emotions, intangibility, and atmospheric cues on online behavior. *Journal of Business Research*, *67*(1), 253–259. doi:10.1016/j.jbusres.2013.05.011

Nittala, R. (2015). Factors influencing online shopping behavior of urban consumers in India. *International Journal of Online Marketing*, *5*(1), 38–50. doi:10.4018/IJOM.2015010103

Park, C., & Jun, J.-K. (2003). A cross-cultural comparison of Internet buying behavior: Effects of Internet usage, perceived risks, and innovativeness. *International Marketing Review*, *20*(5), 534–553. doi:10.1108/02651330310498771

Singh, N., & Matsuo, H. (2004). Measuring cultural adaptation on the web: A content analytic study of US and Japanese Web sites. *Journal of Business Research*, *57*(8), 864–872. doi:10.1016/S0148-2963(02)00482-4

Strang, K. D. (2011). Multicultural face of organizations. In M. A. Sarlak (Ed.), *The new faces of organizations in the 21st century* (Vol. 5, pp. 1–21). Duluth, MN: North American Institute of Science and Information Technology.

Strang, K. D., & Vajjhala, N. R. (2015). Impact of socialized uncertainty on group decision making: An experiment with emerging executives. *International Journal of Risk and Contingency Management*, *4*(2), 45–58. doi:10.4018/IJRCM.2015040104

Strang, K. D., & Vajjhala, N. R. (2017). Student resistance to a mandatory learning management system in online supply chain courses. *Journal of Organizational and End User Computing*, *29*(3), 49–67. doi:10.4018/JOEUC.2017070103

Trompenaars, F., & Hampden-Turner, C. (1997). *Riding the waves of culture: Understanding cultural diversity in business* (2nd ed.). Boston, MA: Nicholas Brealey.

Venaik, S., & Brewer, P. (2013). Critical issues in the Hofstede and GLOBE national culture models. *International Marketing Review*, *30*(5), 469–482. doi:10.1108/IMR-03-2013-0058

Venkatesh, V., & Bala, H. (2008). Technology acceptance model 3 and a research agenda on interventions. *Decision Sciences*, *39*(2), 273–315. doi:10.1111/j.1540-5915.2008.00192.x

Venkatesh, V., & Davis, F. D. (2000). A theoretical extension of the technology acceptance model: Four longitudinal field studies. *Management Science*, *46*(2), 186–204. doi:10.1287/mnsc.46.2.186.11926

Venkatesh, V., Morris, M. G., Davis, G. B., & Davis, F. D. (2003). User acceptance of information technology: Toward a unified view. *Management Information Systems Quarterly*, *27*(3), 425–478. doi:10.2307/30036540

Venkatesh, V., Thong, J. Y. L., & Xu, X. (2012). Consumer acceptance and use of information technology: Extending the unified theory of acceptance and use of technology. *Management Information Systems Quarterly*, *36*(1), 157–178. doi:10.2307/41410412

Yoon, C. (2009). The effects of national culture values on consumer acceptance of e-commerce: Online shoppers in China. *Information & Management*, *46*(1), 294–301. doi:10.1016/j.im.2009.06.001

Yun, G. W., Park, S.-Y., & Ha, L. (2008). Influence of cultural dimensions on online interactive review feature implementations: A comparison of Korean and US retail web sites. *Journal of Interactive Marketing*, *22*(3), 40–50. doi:10.1002/dir.20116

Zhou, L., Dai, L., & Zhang, D. (2007). Online shopping acceptance model - A critical survey of consumer factors in online shopping. *Journal of Electronic Commerce Research*, *8*(1), 41–62.

KEY TERMS AND DEFINITIONS

Collectivism: A cultural dimension characterized by preference and priority for a group as compared to individual self.

Consumer Behavior: Consumer behavior is the study of how individual or groups of customers make purchasing decisions and the underlying motivations for these purchasing decisions.

Individualism: A cultural dimension characterized by preference and priority for self over a group.

Indulgence: A cultural dimension encouraging societies to indulge and focus on individual happiness and wellbeing.

National Culture: National culture is inclusive of all the beliefs and values shared by the population of a particular nation.

Power Distance: A cultural dimension that is indicative of the extent to which the lower ranking individuals of the society accept the unequal distribution of power in the society.

Restraint: A cultural dimension in which societies control the desire to engage in individual happiness and leisure.

Uncertainty Avoidance: A cultural dimension dealing with the tolerance exhibited by the members of a society to ambiguous and uncertain circumstances.

Chapter 3
Impact of E-Commerce on the Urban Landscape

Sotheeswari Somasundram
Taylor's University, Malaysia

ABSTRACT

Consumers in large cities are projected to contribute 81% to global consumption in 2030 with B2C e-commerce sales growth projected to increase globally by 24% in 2020. The inquiry of the present study is to understand the impact of this growth on the urban landscape. Three key areas influenced by e-commerce which in turn impact the urban landscape, city logistics, warehousing, and retail experience. Rising home deliveries impact city logistics where delivery trucks contribute to traffic congestion and environmental hazards. E-commerce influences locational demand for warehouses differently, depending on the section of the logistic chain. The positive gains include reduced damage to road infrastructures and higher valuation of logistics real estate in urban areas. The final area, retail experience, influences the sustainability of malls in urban areas. Malls in urban centers could remain relevant by reconfiguring retail spaces to accommodate temporary guide stores and pop-up stores instead of anchor tenants.

DOI: 10.4018/978-1-5225-9697-4.ch003

INTRODUCTION

The migration, from brick and mortar to digital space, has impacted various facets of our interactional environment, including but not limited to, the business, social and economic aspects. To this list the present study appends, the impact e-commerce has on the urban landscape. According to a report by UNDESA (2014), urban population will account for 60% of the global population by 2030. While a report by United Nations Department of Economic and Social Affairs Population Division (2016) estimates that by 2030, 27% of the global population will be concentrated in cities. A rise likely to impact global consumption. A report by McKinsey Global Institute (2016) highlights, that 81% of global consumption in 2030 would be generated by consumers in large cities with a significant percentage coming from China and North America. In addition, the growing preference for e-commerce in developing markets, especially in China and India, sees both countries topping the list as the most frequent online purchasers (CIGI-IPSOS, 2018). Further, attractive features of e-commerce such as time saving, convenience, ease of use, flexible prices, a variety of choices, and availability of the products (CIGI-IPSOS, 2018) are pushing the penetration rates at the global level. The rising preference for e-commerce highlights the need for adjustment by the retail sectors, logistics and supply chains, and other connected industries which are predominately found in the urban setting.

The prelude above on the urban population and global consumption, specifically e-commerce, sets the context for the present study. The engagement, of the urban population with online commerce platforms, is likely to impact the various aspects of urbanization. A report by Federal Department of Town and Country Planning (2016) highlighted that urbanities in Kuala Lumpur (capital city of Malaysia) incurred an estimated cost of 1.1% to 2.2% of GDP in 2014 arising from transportation concerns such as wasted fuel, carbon (CO_2) emissions, delays and vehicle maintenance. The increased utilization and acceptance of e-commerce would be able to rectify these concerns and contribute towards improving the quality of life in the city. For instance, on-line shopping leads to less time on the road allowing for efficient time management and cost savings for the urban community. The proposition above is stated as an opportunity for the urban community. However, this might not always be the case. It is highly likely that e-commerce might adversely impact city logistics with increased presences of delivery trucks in residential areas. Thus, on whether the impact of e-commerce is positive or otherwise depends on how it is employed and deployed.

The present study is of the view that the impact of e-commerce on the urban landscape is multifaceted and diverse, with a range of opportunities and challenges. Thus, the aim of this study is to provide a synthesis of existing literature on the impact of e-commerce on the different aspects of urbanization to assists policy makers to understand the challenges and opportunities of e-commerce, which would be of use when devising policy strategies.

URBAN LANDSCAPE AND E-COMMERCE

The analysis on the interaction between e-commerce and the urban landscape is discussed from the perspective of city logistics, warehousing and retail experience.

City Logistics

A convenience that e-commerce provides is home delivery. A boon for consumers but a challenge for delivery companies and the man on the street. Carriers often face difficulties when delivering goods in urban areas due to road networks, especially in old European cities where the streets are narrow with limited parking spaces and one-way streets (Crainic, Ricciardi, & Storchi, 2004). Even in modern cities, the road networks force delivery trucks to cruise for parking space, or park illegally (Jaller, Holguín-Veras, & Hodge, 2013). Amer and Chow (2017) state that the problem is compounded as delivery trucks require more space with proximity to the destination and access routes with greater turning radii. The presences of these delivery trucks could lead to congestion and reduced accessibility to urban areas.

However, the severity of the problem depends on the volume transacted in an e-commerce delivery environment. According to Crainic, Ricciardi and Storchi (2009), number of freight vehicles moving in and within cities are increasing. Likely compounded by the B2C e-commerce sales growth projected to increase globally by 24% in 2020 (MITI, MDEC, & AT Kearney, 2016). In the case of the United States, parcel volume increased by 8.2% from 2015 to 2016, while global parcel growth was projected to increase from 17% to 28% from 2017 to 2021 (Pitney Bowes, 2017). Developed markets such as Japan and Singapore express higher preference for online transactions (Teo, Taniguchi, & Qureshi, 2012) pointing towards a possibility of higher freight traffic compared to emerging markets where the share of urban freight transport to total traffic is much lower (Kin, Verlinde, & Macharis, 2017).

Raising a question on whether the impact from e-commerce delivery is contained in cities within the developing and emerging markets. In response to this question, one has to be mindful that congestion and urban accessibility challenges can be exacerbated by high population density. Although concurring with Kin et al. (2017) that the share of urban freight transport is lower in developing countries but population density is much higher within cities in developing markets. Cities like Dhaka (44,500 people per square kilometer) and Mumbai (31,700 people per square kilometer) have far higher density compared to cities in developed countries (Paris, London, Barcelona, Yokohama) with density lower than 6,000 people per square kilometer (UN Habitat, 2013). It is inevitable that delivery trucks competing for space in densely populated city streets with passenger traffic would significantly contribute to traffic congestion and environmental hazards such as noise and air pollution. Studies highlight of the negative impact of urbanization on congestion and environmental degradation (Kang, Zhao and Yang, 2016 ; He *et al.*, 2017; Dong, Sun, Dong, *et al.*, 2018). However, a study by Wang *et al.*, (2015) states that carbon emission increases during the early stages of urbanization but declines as cities attain higher levels of urbanization. Cities at the early stages of urbanization, from the developing and emerging markets, are likely to contribute more towards environmental degradation. However, as cities mature and have a better grip on city logistics, the management of environmental challenges is likely to improve.

Challenges arising from e-commerce delivery have resulted in a number of innovative solutions aimed at reducing congestion and environmental hazards. United Parcel Service (UPS) in collaboration with the City of Seattle uses a cargo e-bike as a delivery vehicle (Seattle Traffic, 2019). The cargo e-bike addresses concerns of the conventional delivery trucks by ensuring direct access to drop-off points, preventing double parking and, reducing congestion, noise and air pollution. Another innovation is the use of autonomous vehicles (AVs) by retailers such as Walmart and Kroger. Kroger, a grocery chain in the US is piloting the use of AVs to deliver groceries (Howell, 2018). Groceries are loaded into a driverless vehicle and customers pick up from their curb by entering numeric code to open the vehicle to gain access to their online purchases. This solution reduces the delivery truck dwell time, as customers are onsite to immediately unload their purchases. In the case of Walmart, the retail chain in US is collaborating with Waymo, a self-driving vehicle company to ferry customers from their homes (Makena, 2018). Customers would make their purchases online and while their orders are prepared, Waymo will ferry the customers to Walmart to pick-up their purchases. A solution that is able to reduce congestion arising from double parking and hogging of parking spaces by delivery trucks.

Warehousing

The impact of e-commerce on the use of urban land space is investigated from the perspective of warehousing. In order to understand the impact on the urban landscape, the warehousing requirements are analyzed from the perspective of first mile and last mile deliveries. Before the 1970s, the supply chain in developed countries were decentralized with warehouses located closer to the manufacturers and consumers (Allen, Browne, & Cherrett, 2012) and warehousing space positively correlating with the population density of a metropolitan area (McKinnon, 1983). However this has changed in recent years. The location and size of warehouses are influenced by whether they are the first mile or last mile distribution centres. First mile is the first stage of the supply chain. Warehouses which are part of the first mile, accept parcels from suppliers. The last mile, the final stage of the supply chain, delivers products directly to customers.

The first mile distribution centres are relocating to suburban sites driven by structural shifts in the manufacturing industry, which includes among others, e-commerce (Hesse, 2004). The warehouses in urban areas were considered inefficient as these facilities were unable to accommodate the new operational requirements that is necessary to facilitate modern logistics (Leigh & Hoelzel, 2012). These newer facilities, serving the online market, require more inventory capacity as well as sophisticated technology systems such as automated picking and sortation systems (Carlson & Larco, 2017). The higher inventory capacity necessitates mega distribution centres. Warehouses with 500,000 to 1 million square feet and those over 1 million square feet is on the rise, when in 1998 it was less than 5% but has increased to 25% in 2006 (Andreoli, Goodchild, & Vitasek, 2010). These large storage spaces are cost inefficient if built in urban areas. Therefore, the preferred location for the first mile distribution is the suburban area due to lower land prices and more manageable traffic conditions (Allen et al., 2012).

The relocation of warehouses out of urban areas have impacted the urban landscape both favorably and adversely. On a positive note, the reduced presences of heavy trucks in urban areas (Crainic et al., 2004) minimizes infrastructure damages. On the down side, a study by Dablanc & Rakotonarivo (2010) highlighted that relocation to suburban areas resulted in 15,000 tonnes of CO_2 emission which was about 30 times higher compared to, if the warehouses were located within the urban area. The distance away from city centres requires increase use of smaller delivery vehicles to service these areas. In addition, the increase in delivery vehicles had also lead to higher noise pollution from these vehicles (S. Kang, 2018).

The last mile distribution is considered as the most inefficient and expensive section of the entire logistics chain (Gevaers, Van de Voorde, & Vanelslander, 2014). This is driven partly by consumers' expectation for same day or next-day delivery which has led to the need for more local and small-scale distribution centres in urban areas (Carlson & Larco, 2017). According to Prologis Research, (2016) online retailers need three times more distribution space compared to brick-and-mortar retailers for a given level of revenue. The increasing demand for logistics real estate in urban areas is double-edged as it increases rental returns to asset owners (Maidenberg, 2017) but forces other urban stakeholders to face higher real estate prices to own properties in these areas.

The growth of e-commerce and the resulting changes in warehousing has impacted the urban space. Warehouses moving to suburban sites have reduced damage to road infrastructures with the decrease in heavy vehicles plying urban roads. In addition, real estate owners have gained from higher rental returns due to higher demand for smaller distribution spaces by online retailers. According to Maidenberg (2017), struggling US retail properties are benefitting from increased demand for warehouses spaces citing an example of an empty mall been demolished to be replaced with warehouses. On the downside, freight transport operating from the smaller urban distribution centres contribute to congestion in urban roads, noise pollution and CO_2 emission.

Retail Experience

The competition to gain wider market share has led to the use of different channels, one of which is the showroom and home delivery mode (Chopra, 2016). This channel known as a guidestore or showroom model was pioneered by digitally-native brands transiting into brick and mortar such as Bonobos, Warby Parker, Frank & Oak (Carlson & Larco, 2017a) and Rent the Runway (Bergner, 2016). Guidestores are defined as physical stores that do not hold any inventory but ensures that customers are given the best service allowing for tactile experience. Customers would purchase via tablets, and the order would be shipped to a location of their choosing (Bell, Gallino, & Moreno, 2018). Guidestores place greater emphasis on retail experience rather than the actual act of shopping. This model allows consumers to browse through a limited number of products in the physical store, try the products, choose the specific size and color, which will then be delivered to their homes (Bergner, 2016).

Guidestores allow customers to experience the product first which increases the likelihood of a purchase (DeLoatch, 2018). The importance of retail experience has caught on even with traditional retailers. The traditional retailers are now incorporating retail experience into their retail channels. This has led to traditional retail stores in the US such as American Girl, selling dolls, books and accessories for girls; REI, the outdoor gear and clothing company; Sephora, beauty and cosmetic company; Walmart, retail chain; to incorporate retail experience in a relevant way (DeLoatch, 2018; Unglesbee, 2018).

If retail experience is the way forward, retailers might not need as much retail space. Guidestores do not carry inventories in the physical stores. The desired purchases are made online and shipped for free (Carlson & Larco, 2017a), thus reducing the need for large mall and departmental stores. It was highlighted that more than 6000 brick and mortar stores were closed in 2017 and an additional 3600 closures were expected in 2018 (Badrinarayanan & Becerra, 2018). A phenomena especially critical in the US where the ratio of retail space per person is much higher at 23.6 square feet compared to Australia (11.1) and U.K.(4.6) (Ritholtz, 2018). One recommendation is to convert the excess retail space to community spaces, apartments or offices (Ritholtz, 2018). However the viability of such a move will depend on whether there is sufficient demand for residential housing and office space given that high rental and asset prices might be of concern.

A study by McKinsey (2017) recommends moving away from anchor tenants in malls to experimenting with revolving storefronts and pop-up stores. Reconfigurable retail spaces are rented to pop-up stores for a short duration (Kim, Fiore, Niehm, & Jeong, 2010) for purposes of product launch, seasonal offerings or providing guidestores for online retailers. Customers seeking innovative experience are likely to appreciate the diverse offering of pop-up stores. The increase in popularity for pop-up stores can be measured by the increase in sales by these stores which accounts for £2.3 billion in 2015, up 12% compared to 2014 in United Kingdom (McKinsey, 2017) indicating a preference by the market for these types of stores. Another proposition by McKinsey (2017) is to convert retail spaces into co-working areas. Co-working space in malls are ideal as it is accessible during and after working hours. A further value add specially for start-up and entrepreneurs is the access to customers for validating business models, an attractive cost saving option for new ventures and start-ups (Resnick, 2015).

The changing urban landscape from the rise of e-commerce, retail experience and the sprouting of guidestores have resulted in a fair share of opportunities and challenges. The starkly different purchase approach of the millennials compared to the generations preceding them has been disruptive but not necessarily in a negative sense. Online and traditional retailers attuned to these changes and quick to adapt stand to gain from the millennials consumer spending. The malls and retail spaces, a common feature in cities, can withstand this disruptive change by re-innovating by accommodating pop-up stores, inviting guidestores to take up temporary tenancy instead of seeking anchor tenants. The change in approach by mall management would ensure more traffic and patronage translating to a sustainable presences of malls in the urban environment.

FUTURE RESEARCH DIRECTIONS

Digital technology is bringing about a change in the urban environment. Under the broad spectrum of technology and urbanism, studies have explored different aspects of this dynamic relationship. These include but not limited to the impact of technological infrastructure and networks on urbanism (Dupuy, van Schaick, & Klaasen, 2018); and planning of smart cites driven by urban applications, intelligent infrastructure and smart buildings (Luque-Ayala & Marvin, 2015) to name a few. However, literature specifically on the impact of e-commerce on urbanization is limited. Lin (2018) highlighted that the lack of studies include both theoretical and empirical evidence on the impact of e-commerce on urbanism.

A report by McKinsey (2017) highlighted key areas for consideration in the digital consumer era providing impetus for future research. One of the areas highlighted by the report is the need to reassess the challenges arising from e-commerce delivery. The current challenges highlighted by the present study may become redundant in the future due to technological changes taking place within the urban space. For instance, technology allowing for integration of parking space, parking applications, e-hailing pick-up and drop off zones and autonomous vehicles could change the urban real-estate environment. There is an opportunity for future studies to investigate the impact of the changing e-commerce delivery environment on the urban landscape.

McKinsey (2017) also highlighted that in 2017, online purchases were dominated by the millennial generation. A generation which the report states is guided by trust recommendations when making purchasing decisions. This points toward the presence of social commerce, a subset of e-commerce which is about the power of online social networking in shopping. Social commerce rides on the social networking capabilities encouraging customers to share personal experiences to boost sales (Li, 2017). Social commerce highlights the importance of validation from trusted recommendations in completing a purchase. McKinsey (2017) highlights how this might encourage the presences of communication channels such as digital screens in transport hubs and major junctions in cities providing information on products and reviews. This approach by businesses to reach out and connect with their customers and the impact on the urban landscape is a possible area for future research. The present study focused on the impact of e-commerce (product centered) commerce site on the urban landscape. However, future research can investigate the impact of social (social-centered) commerce sites on the urban environment.

CONCLUSION

The objective of this study was to explore the impact e-commerce has on the urban landscape. The analysis focused on three components – city logistics, warehousing and retail experience. The convenience of e-commerce is in its home deliveries. However, limited parking space, lack of proper loading/ unloading bays, and narrow streets within the urban space is a challenge for freight transport providers. In response to these challenges, delivery trucks flaunt the law by parking illegally or double parking to keep to their delivery promises. The presences of these delivery trucks in urban areas leads to traffic congestions and environmental hazards. However on a positive note, public-private sector initiatives such as UPS in collaboration with the City of Seattle in US; and private sector collaborations, such as Waymo and Walmart, are exploring other viable solutions.

On the warehousing front, higher capacity storage spaces are moving out of urban areas but smaller distribution centres are sprouting in cities to ensure faster deliveries to customers. There are fewer heavy vehicles on urban roads reducing damages to infrastructure but increased volume of smaller delivery trucks contribute to congestion and pollution. Literature highlights that growth in e-commerce has led to decline in demand for departmental stores and mall spaces. However, the increase in demand for smaller distribution centres provides opportunities for higher valuation of logistics real estate in urban areas.

The changing retail preference that is motivated more by multi-sensory experiences rather than product ownership is changing the retail front. The sprouting of more guidestores, allowing customers to try the products in-store, buy it online and have it delivered to their homes, translates to less requirement for inventory space. A decrease in demand for retail space requires a rethink on the part of urban planners on the future of malls and shopping centres in urban areas. Adapting to changes by moving away from current practices of depending on anchor tenants to drive traffic to malls might be a viable option to consider. Taking into consideration the preference for online patronage and multi-sensory retail experience, malls could attract more traffic by offering reconfigurable retail spaces to temporary guidestores and pop-up stores instead of anchor tenants.

In conclusion, the present study is of the opinion that development of e-commerce has disrupted the urban landscape. A disruption which is both a challenge and an opportunity. The urban community, freight companies, online and traditional businesses stand to gain from recognizing the opportunities and challenges, and incorporating these into the business and urban environment.

ACKNOWLEDGMENT

This research was supported by Taylor's University [TUFR/2017/001/03].

REFERENCES

Allen, J., Browne, M., & Cherrett, T. (2012). Investigating relationships between road freight transport, facility location, logistics management and urban form. *Journal of Transport Geography*, *24*, 45–57. doi:10.1016/j.jtrangeo.2012.06.010

Amer, A., & Chow, J. Y. J. (2017). A downtown on-street parking model with urban truck delivery behavior. *Transportation Research Part A, Policy and Practice*, *102*, 51–67. doi:10.1016/j.tra.2016.08.013

Andreoli, D., Goodchild, A., & Vitasek, K. (2010). The rise of mega distribution centers and the impact on logistical uncertainty. *Transportation Letters*, *2*(2), 75–88. doi:10.3328/TL.2010.02.02.75-88

Badrinarayanan, V., & Becerra, E. P. (2018). Shoppers' attachment with retail stores: Antecedents and impact on patronage intentions. *Journal of Retailing and Consumer Services*. doi:10.1016/j.jretconser.2018.07.012

Bell, D. R., Gallino, S., & Moreno, A. (2018). The Store Is Dead—Long Live the Store. *MIT Sloan Management Review*, *59*(3), 59–66. Retrieved from https://faculty.wharton.upenn.edu/wp-content/uploads/2018/03/Long-Live-the-Store.pdf

Bergner, M. (2016). *What Retailers Can Learn from the Showroom Model*. Retrieved January 22, 2019, from https://apparelmag.com/what-retailers-can-learn-showroom-model

Carlson, G., & Larco, N. (2017). *Warehousing*. Retrieved from https://cpb-us-e1.wpmucdn.com/blogs.uoregon.edu/dist/f/13615/files/2017/06/Warehousing-Urb-Next-SCI-Carlson-Larco-2017-19ymhh6.pdf

Chopra, S. (2016). How omni-channel can be the future of retailing. *Decision (Washington, D.C.)*, *43*(2), 135–144. doi:10.100740622-015-0118-9

CIGI-IPSOS. (2018). *Global Survey on Internet Security and Trust*. Retrieved from www.cigionline.org/internet-survey

Crainic, T. G., Ricciardi, N., & Storchi, G. (2004). Advanced freight transportation systems for congested urban areas. *Transportation Research Part C, Emerging Technologies*, *12*(2), 119–137. doi:10.1016/j.trc.2004.07.002

Crainic, T. G., Ricciardi, N., & Storchi, G. (2009). Models for Evaluating and Planning City Logistics Systems. *Transportation Science*, *43*(4), 432–454. doi:10.1287/trsc.1090.0279

Dablanc, L., & Rakotonarivo, D. (2010). The impacts of logistics sprawl: How does the location of parcel transport terminals affect the energy efficiency of goods' movements in Paris and what can we do about it? *Procedia: Social and Behavioral Sciences*, *2*(3), 6087–6096. doi:10.1016/j.sbspro.2010.04.021

DeLoatch, P. (2018). *Retailers lure shoppers with in-store holiday experiences*. Retrieved January 22, 2019, from https://www.retaildive.com/news/retailers-lure-shoppers-with-in-store-holiday-experiences/541471/

Dong, K., Sun, R., Dong, C., Li, H., Zeng, X., & Ni, G. (2018). Environmental Kuznets curve for PM 2.5 emissions in Beijing, China: What role can natural gas consumption play? *Ecological Indicators*, *93*, 591–601. doi:10.1016/j.ecolind.2018.05.045

Dupuy, G., van Schaick, J., & Klaasen, I. T. (2018). *Urban networks: Network urbanism*. Amsterdam: Techne press.

Federal Department of Town and Country Planning. (2016). *Malaysia National Report for the 3rd UNITED NATIONS Conference on Housing and Sustainable Urban Development (HABITAT III)*. Kuala Lumpur, Malaysia: Author.

Gevaers, R., Van de Voorde, E., & Vanelslander, T. (2014). Cost Modelling and Simulation of Last-mile Characteristics in an Innovative B2C Supply Chain Environment with Implications on Urban Areas and Cities. *Procedia: Social and Behavioral Sciences*, *125*, 398–411. doi:10.1016/j.sbspro.2014.01.1483

He, Z., Xu, S., Shen, W., Long, R., & Chen, H. (2017). Impact of urbanization on energy related CO2 emission at different development levels: Regional difference in China based on panel estimation. *Journal of Cleaner Production*, *140*, 1719–1730. doi:10.1016/j.jclepro.2016.08.155

Hesse, M. (2004). Land for Logistics: Locational Dynamics, Real Estate Markets and Political Regulation of Regional Distribution Complexes. *Tijdschrift voor Economische en Sociale Geografie*, *95*(2), 162–173. doi:10.1111/j.0040-747X.2004.t01-1-00298.x

Howell, A. (2018). *Why Kroger's Driverless Grocery Delivery Pilot Is a Harbinger of Disruption*. Retrieved January 10, 2019, from https://urbanismnext.uoregon.edu/2018/09/17/why-krogers-driverless-grocery-delivery-pilot-is-a-harbinger-of-disruption/

Jaller, M., Holguín-Veras, J., & Hodge, S. D. (2013). Parking in the City. *Transportation Research Record: Journal of the Transportation Research Board*, *2379*(1), 46–56. doi:10.3141/2379-06

Kang, S. (2018). Warehouse location choice: A case study in Los Angeles, CA. *Journal of Transport Geography*. doi:10.1016/j.jtrangeo.2018.08.007

Kang, Y.-Q., Zhao, T., & Yang, Y.-Y. (2016). Environmental Kuznets curve for CO 2 emissions in China: A spatial panel data approach. *Ecological Indicators*, *63*, 231–239. doi:10.1016/j.ecolind.2015.12.011

Kim, H., Fiore, A. M., Niehm, L. S., & Jeong, M. (2010). Psychographic characteristics affecting behavioral intentions towards pop-up retail. *International Journal of Retail & Distribution Management*, *38*(2), 133–154. doi:10.1108/09590551011020138

Kin, B., Verlinde, S., & Macharis, C. (2017). Sustainable urban freight transport in megacities in emerging markets. *Sustainable Cities and Society*, *32*, 31–41. doi:10.1016/j.scs.2017.03.011

Leigh, N. G., & Hoelzel, N. Z. (2012). Smart Growth's Blind Side. *Journal of the American Planning Association*, *78*(1), 87–103. doi:10.1080/01944363.2011.645274

Li, C.-Y. (2017). How social commerce constructs influence customers' social shopping intention? An empirical study of a social commerce website. *Technological Forecasting and Social Change*, *144*, 283–294. doi:10.1016/j.techfore.2017.11.026

Lin, Y. (2018). E-urbanism: E-commerce, migration, and the transformation of Taobao villages in urban China. *Cities (London, England)*. doi:10.1016/j.cities.2018.11.020

Luque-Ayala, A., & Marvin, S. (2015). Developing a critical understanding of smart urbanism? *Urban Studies (Edinburgh, Scotland)*, *52*(12), 2105–2116. doi:10.1177/0042098015577319

Maidenberg, M. (2017, October 24). As Amazon Moves In, Demand for Warehouse Space Climbs. *The New York Times*. Retrieved from www.nytimes.com/2017/10/24/business/amazon-ecommerce-warehouse-demand.html?smprod=nytcore-iphone&smid=nytcore-iphone-share&_r=0

Makena, K. (2018). *Waymo partners with Walmart to test grocery pickup service in Arizona*. Retrieved from www.theverge.com/2018/7/25/17611760/waymo-walmart-self-driving-vehicles-groceries-discounts

McKinnon, A. C. (1983). The development of warehousing in England. *Geoforum*, *14*(4), 389–399. doi:10.1016/0016-7185(83)90036-2

McKinsey. (2017). *Meeting millennials where they shop: Shaping the future of shopping malls*. Retrieved from www.mckinsey.com/industries/capital-projects-and-infrastructure/our-insights/meeting-millennials-where-they-shop-shaping-the-future-of-shopping-malls

McKinsey Global Institute. (2016). *Urban World: The Global Consumers to Watch*. Retrieved from https://www.mckinsey.com/global-themes/urbanization/urban-world-the-global-consumers-to-watch/~/media/57c6ad7f7f1b44a6bd2e24f0777b4cd6.ashx

MITI, MDEC, & AT Kearney. (2016). *National eCommerce Strategic Roadmap Overview*. Retrieved from http://www.miti.gov.my/miti/resources/Gallery_Walk.pdf

Peterson, E. R., Sillman, A., & McCaffrey, C. R. (2018). *Where Are the Global Millennials?* Retrieved January 24, 2019, from https://www.atkearney.com/web/global-business-policy-council/article?/a/where-are-the-global-millennials-

Pitney Bowes. (2017). *Pitney Bowes Parcel Shipping Index Reveals 48 Percent Growth in Parcel Volume since 2014*. Retrieved from http://news.pb.com/article_display.cfm?article_%0Aid=5784

Prologis Research. (2016). *Global E-Commerce Impact on Logistics Real Estate*. Retrieved January 21, 2019, from www.prologis.com/logistics-industry-research/global-e-commerce-impact-logistics-real-estate

Resnick, M. L. (2015). The Shopping Mall Of The Customer Experience Future. *Proceedings of the Human Factors and Ergonomics Society Annual Meeting*, *59*(1), 1127–1131. doi:10.1177/1541931215591164

Ritholtz, B. (2018). *Don't Blame Amazon for the Retail Apocalypse*. Retrieved from https://www.bloomberg.com/opinion/articles/2018-04-09/trump-is-wrong-that-amazon-caused-the-u-s-retail-apocalypse

Seattle Traffic. (2019). *UPS pilot kicks off with a public/private partnership of a new urban delivery system*. Retrieved January 10, 2019, from https://www.seattletraffic.org/a-special-delivery-ups-pilot-kicks-off-with-a-public-private-partnership-creating-a-new-urban-delivery-system/

Teo, J. S. E., Taniguchi, E., & Qureshi, A. G. (2012). Evaluating City Logistics Measure in E-Commerce with Multiagent Systems. *Procedia: Social and Behavioral Sciences*, *39*, 349–359. doi:10.1016/j.sbspro.2012.03.113

UN Habitat. (2013). *Explore data*. Retrieved January 10, 2019, from http://urbandata.unhabitat.org/explore-data/?indicators=urban_agglomeration_population_density

UNDESA. (2014). World Urbanization Prospects. *Undesa, 32*. doi:10.4054/DemRes.2005.12.9

Unglesbee, B. (2018). *Walmart has big plans to cash in on Toys R Us' demise*. Retrieved January 24, 2019, from https://www.retaildive.com/news/walmart-has-big-plans-to-cash-in-on-toys-r-us-demise/531413/

United Nations Department of Economic and Social Affairs Population Division. (2016). *The World's Cities in 2016 – Data Booklet* (ST/ESA/ SER.A/392). Retrieved from http://www.un.org/en/development/desa/population/publications/pdf/urbanization/the_worlds_cities_in_2016_data_booklet.pdf

Wang, Y., Zhang, X., Kubota, J., Zhu, X., & Lu, G. (2015). A semi-parametric panel data analysis on the urbanization-carbon emissions nexus for OECD countries. *Renewable & Sustainable Energy Reviews, 48*, 704–709. doi:10.1016/j.rser.2015.04.046

ADDITIONAL READING

Bell, D. R., Choi, J., & Lodish, L. (2012). What matters most in internet retailing? *Sloan Management Review, 54*(1), 27.

Dablanc, L., Ogilvie, S., & Goodchild, A. (2014). Logistics Sprawl: Differential Warehousing Development Patterns in Los Angeles, California, and Seattle, Washington. *Transportation Research Record: Journal of the Transportation Research Board, 2410*(1), 105–112. doi:10.3141/2410-12

Doha, A., Elnahla, N., & McShane, L. (2019). Social commerce as social networking. *Journal of Retailing and Consumer Services, 47*, 307–321. doi:10.1016/j.jretconser.2018.11.008

Jiang, M. (2005). UPS-k: A set partitioning problem with applications in UPS pickup-delivery system. *Information Processing Letters, 93*(4), 173–175. doi:10.1016/j.ipl.2004.10.010

Li, C.-Y., & Ku, Y.-C. (2018). The power of a thumbs-up: Will e-commerce switch to social commerce? *Information & Management, 55*(3), 340–357. doi:10.1016/j.im.2017.09.001

Ni, L., Wang, X., & Zhang, D. (2016). Impacts of information technology and urbanization on less-than-truckload freight flows in China: An analysis considering spatial effects. *Transportation Research Part A, Policy and Practice, 92*, 12–25. doi:10.1016/j.tra.2016.06.030

Saskia, S., Mareï, N., & Blanquart, C. (2016). Innovations in e-grocery and Logistics Solutions for Cities. *Transportation Research Procedia, 12*, 825–835. doi:10.1016/j.trpro.2016.02.035

Turkensteen, M., & Hasle, G. (2017). Combining pickups and deliveries in vehicle routing – An assessment of carbon emission effects. *Transportation Research Part C, Emerging Technologies, 80*, 117–132. doi:10.1016/j.trc.2017.04.006

van Duin, J. H. R., de Goffau, W., Wiegmans, B., Tavasszy, L. A., & Saes, M. (2016). Improving Home Delivery Efficiency by Using Principles of Address Intelligence for B2C Deliveries. *Transportation Research Procedia, 12*, 14–25. doi:10.1016/j.trpro.2016.02.006

KEY TERMS AND DEFINITIONS

Anchor Tenants: The leading or main tenant in a shopping mall, often a well-known departmental store or retail chain.

Autonomous Vehicles: A vehicle capable of self-directed navigation by sensing its environment with limited or no human input.

First Mile Delivery: Delivery of products from retailers' warehouses to distribution centers.

Guideshop: A physical store where customers can experience the products before purchasing it. The physical store only showcases the product for customer experience but do not sell any physical items. Customers place orders in the physical store and it will be delivered to their homes.

Last Mile Delivery: Delivery of a product from distribution centers to the doorstep of final consumers.

Millennials: Those born roughly between 1981 and 1997.

Pop-Up Store: A retail store is normally setup for a short duration in malls or shopping centers to promote and/or sell products that is currently trending the market or to sell seasonal products.

Social Commerce: A subset of e-commerce that employs social media as a tool for product reviews and recommendations. The social networks utilized in the context of e-commerce transactions.

Urbanization: A process where an increasing percentage of the population live in cities.

Chapter 4
Quality Strategies for Customer Loyalty in an E-Service Environment:
A Case of M-Banking Customers

Savdeep Vasudeva
DAV Institute of Engineering and Technology, India

ABSTRACT

This chapter focuses on the issue of quality strategies for attaining customer loyalty in an e-service environment. It takes into consideration the key relationship between e-service quality and customer loyalty. A case of mobile banking service acted as the basis for the formulation of quality strategies for customer retention. This study was conducted by a survey with a sample size of 524 mobile banking users in the state of Punjab in India. The survey instrument utilized the E-S-QUAL, E-RecS-QUAL, and loyalty scales proposed in the earlier research studies. Furthermore, the data generated was analyzed by using the statistical multiple regression. Findings of this chapter give important implications to the delivery of e-service for mobile banking. It could help service providers to gain proper insights into the issue of managing the customers in a virtual environment.

DOI: 10.4018/978-1-5225-9697-4.ch004

INTRODUCTION

In the last two decades, continuous changes in information and communication technology (ICT) have contributed towards the transformation of electronic commerce (e-commerce) into mobile commerce (m-commerce) and redefined the business operations. ICT involves the usage of technology in exchange of information and is generally considered as a starting point for both e-commerce and m-commerce. Increased implementation of ICT based applications in business has become an important trend (Rust, 2001). The transformation of e-commerce into m-commerce has been possible due to the fast growth in the field of wireless and mobile communication (Mohd & Osman, 2005). Greater popularity of mobile phones, personal digital assistants and other types of hand-held devices has contributed towards the m-commerce hype (Liang & Wei, 2004). M-commerce applications have gained popularity due to the unique feature of mobility offered by them. Different types of m-commerce applications include mobile banking, mobile shopping, mobile ticketing, mobile entertainment, mobile information services, mobile marketing and telematics services.

The present scenario depicts that due to the increased focus on electronic mode of business e-service quality has become a matter for concern as most of the businesses are going online. These businesses transformed from a traditional brick and mortar style to more refined and technology enabled e-business. Many of the service organizations have started distributing their services through electronic means (de Ruyter, Wetzels, & Kleijnen, 2001). Proper implementation of e-commerce based applications enables businesses to generate profits from technology-based exchange of goods and services (Magutu et al., 2011). In a similarity to the other sectors, the banking sector is not an exception to this e-commerce revolution. The electronic nature of loyalty in an e-banking system poses a great challenge to the banks in an online environment (Reichheld & Schefter, 2000). Loyal customers in an electronic environment are cost effective and help to lower the operating cost of organizations (van Riel, Liljander, & Jurriëns, 2001). There is an important role of electronic service (e-service) quality in building customer loyalty in case of financial institutions such as banks (Asgari, Ahmadi, Shamlou, Farokhi, & Farzin, 2014). Efficient delivery of service quality among e-services plays a crucial role in the success of banking system and helps the banks to sustain effectively in the competitive environment (Ariff, Leong, Norhayati, & Ahmad, 2012).

Nowadays, m-commerce is becoming more popular due to the greater focus on mobility. Maintaining customer loyalty in the m-commerce settings has been a matter of immense importance in case of more agile service business. The popularity of m-commerce applications has forced the banks to offer an alternative channel of banking using mobile phones. In the current chapter, the issue of customer loyalty in the m-commerce environment has been examined by taking the case of an e-service such as mobile banking. Mobile banking (popularly known as m-banking) is considered as a constituent of electronic banking service offered by banks (Chen, 2013; Jun & Palacios, 2016; Safeena, Hundewale, & Kammani, 2011). The implementation of mobile technology in financial services (Chung & Kwon, 2009). Paybox from Germany launched this service, in collaboration with Deutsche Bank in the later 1990s. Initially, the service was used in Sweden, Germany, Spain, Austria and United Kingdom in Europe and then, later on, this service was introduced among the developing countries starting from Kenya in the year 2007 (Shaikh & Karjaluoto, 2015). In India, this service first initiated by ICICI bank in the year 2008. M-banking being regarded as the first commercial application of m-commerce (Laukkanen & Lauronen, 2005) has been selected to represent an e-service due to its growing popularity among individual customers in personal banking. Mobility in banking provided by m-commerce makes m-banking most suitable for delivering personal banking or retail banking services to the customers. This latest channel of e-banking has redefined the personal banking operations among the banks. M-banking services could be accessed through various modes such as SMS (short message service) banking, WAP (wireless application protocol) based banking, USSD (unstructured supplementary service data) mode, mobile web banking and application on a mobile phone. It empowers the customers to access the services such as funds transfer, cheque book request, shopping from mobile, utility bills payment, balance enquiry, movie ticket, railway ticket and airline ticket booking form a remote location at their own discretion of time and place. It has now become a challenge for the banking organizations to keep the customers connected with them in a virtual environment. In addition, the transition in mobile technology has also increased the importance of maintaining service quality in the m-commerce settings. This calls for some strategies that can help to keep the service providers responsive to the needs of customers and help them to maintain better service quality. There has been a scarcity of studies concerning m-banking service quality in case of technology-based services (Malviya, 2015).

This chapter aims to formulate the quality strategies for increasing loyalty in an e-service environment by taking a case of m-banking customers. These strategies for promoting customer loyalty could be framed based on the different dimensions of e-service quality and further be formulated only after knowing the impact of each of these on the loyalty of customers. Previous studies depict that e-service quality comprises e-core service quality and e-recovery service quality (Parasuraman, Zeithaml, & Malhotra, 2005). Among these two, the former includes the quality of service given during the time of actual service delivery whereas the latter includes the quality of service provided after the delivery of service i.e. during any support or failure. Literature suggests that besides e-core service quality, the proper resolution of customer problems has a great impact on customer loyalty (Miller, Craighead, & Karwan, 2000; Robbins & Miller, 2004; Wu 2011). This increases the relevance of examining e-recovery service quality along with e-core service quality in an electronic environment. Customers become more satisfied when the firm follows adequate recovery service (Swanson & Kelley, 2001) in a combination to the core service strategies. Thus, the relationships between e-core service quality, e-recovery service quality and customer loyalty needs to be explored further.

BACKGROUND

A brief review of literature related to the constructs of this study needs some attention, and is presented further to gain a proper understanding of each of these.

E-Service Quality

Earlier studies show that an e-service focuses on providing continuous communication and flow of information to the customers (Rust & Lemon, 2001). Santos (2003) described e-service quality as the total assessment and evaluation of an e-service in the virtual environment. Rowley (2006) defines the delivery of e-service as a phenomenon whose effectiveness is mediated by the information technology based solutions. According to de Ruyte, Wetzel and Kleijnen (2001) "E-service is an interactive content-centered and Internet-based customer service, driven by customer and integrated with related organizational customer support processes and technologies with the goal of strengthening the customer-service provider relationship". Colier and Bienstock (2006, p. 260) defined e-service quality as "customer's perceptions of the outcome of the service along with recovery perceptions if a problem should occur".

Ease of customers in usage of technology-based services than the traditional services have increased the importance of examining service quality in the virtual environment (Santos, 2003). Amidst greater focus on electronic and mobile technologies, e-service quality has emerged as an important part of the modern days' business (Hussien & El Aziz, 2013; Yaya, Marimon, & Casadesus, 2011) and is considered as a key constituent for the successful e-commerce (Yang, 2001; Zeithaml, Parasuraman, & Malhotra, 2002). Oliveria, Roth and Gilland (2002) have also proposed that maintenance of e-service quality is important for attracting new customers as well as for retaining the earlier ones. It is considered distinct from the traditional service quality on the basis of communication between humans and technology (Rotchanakitumnuai, 2008). Even the measurement of e-service quality is different from the conventional service quality as the components of an e-commerce based business are apart from the traditional ones (Lin & Shih, 2013).

Customer Loyalty

Marketers believe that in the long run, success of any manufacturing or service organization depends upon the loyalty of customers. Customer loyalty has been defined as the strong willingness to make frequent purchases of a product or service in a stipulated time frame regardless of the marketing efforts which may induce switching behavior (Oliver, 1999). Most of the earlier studies have shown that loyalty is determined by making regular purchase of a product or service (Homburg & Giering, 2001). In marketing, every organization wants to keep a good number of loyal customers. Customer loyalty also has a strong relationship with customer satisfaction where the latter is considered as an antecedent of the former (Wu & Wang, 2005).

Loyal customers have a higher buying tendency and considered as the indirect promoters of business firms (Harris & Goode, 2004). They have a positive impact on the performance of the firm and a little increase in the number of loyal customers can increase the revenue to greater extent (Cyr, Hassanein, Head, & Ivanov, 2006; Reichheld & Schefter, 2000). Loyal customers also help the business organizations to gain a competitive edge and win over its rivals in the globalized world (Flavián, Guinalíu, & Gurrea, 2006; Keating, Rugimbana, & Quazi, 2003). Achieving greater levels of customer loyalty in an online business has become more challenging than a traditional business (Gommans, Krishnan, & Scheffold, 2001) and is generally considered an area of prime focus for the success of e-commerce (Vatanasombut, Stylianou, & Igbaria, 2004; Swaid, 2009). Further, the literature proposes that loyalty in the online settings has also been viewed as e-loyalty i.e. electronic loyalty and is regarded as an offshoot of loyalty concept adopted in e-commerce (Al-Agaga & Nor 2012). In a virtual environment, it is considered as the consumers' readiness to visit an electronic platform regularly or make a repeated purchase from an online portal (Cyr, Bonanni, Bowes, & Ilsever, 2005; Koernig, 2003).

E-Service Quality and Loyalty

Literature suggests that quality of service is considered as a driving force for achieving customer loyalty (Caruana, 2002; Izogo & Ogba, 2015; Parasuraman et al., 2005; Thaichon, Lobo, & Mitsis, 2014) and is also seen as one of its important determinant (Luarn & Lin, 2003). There is a direct relationship between service quality, customer satisfaction and loyalty (Kotler, Keller, Koshy, & Jha, 2009) and this relationship also holds true in case of online services (Chang & Wang, 2011; Jeong & Lee, 2010) where a higher level of e-service quality leads to greater loyalty (Romadhoni, Hadiwidjojo, Noermijati, & Aisjah, 2015). This association also holds true even in the field of banking (Chu, Lee, & Chao, 2012; Floh & Treiblmaier, 2006). Asgari et al. (2014) through their study have also supported these views and stated a positive and direct relationship between e-service quality and customer loyalty in e-banking services. Previous research shows that e-service quality is considered as an important prerequisite of customer loyalty in the electronic mode of banking (Alsamdyai, Yousif, & Al-khasawneh, 2012) and has also been viewed as a new field of research in m-banking (Ganguli & Roy, 2011). Romadhoni et al. (2015) have highlighted that e-service quality plays a crucial role in the formation of customer loyalty in case of m-banking service. Earlier studies reveal that the quality of service significantly affects loyalty towards m-banking (Puriwat & Tripopsakul, 2017; Widiatmika & Subawa, 2017). It has also been proposed that e-service quality could be effectively utilized in future m-banking research to provide greater insights into the issue of customer loyalty Malviya (2015).

THEORETICAL BASIS

Measurement and assessment of e-service quality dimensions seeks greater research attention due to the growing focus on the online means of business (Akinci, Inan, & Aksoy, 2008). In order to have an overall assessment of the e-service quality involving e-core and e-recovery service quality, the E-S-QUAL scale proposed by Parasuraman et al. (2005) has been used in the current chapter. Previous studies suggest that this scale could be effecttively utilized to assess the service quality of m-banking systems (Jo & Mo, 2018; Lin & Shih, 2013; Malviya, 2015; Puriwat & Tripopsakul, 2017). Parasuraman et al. (2005) in their original study leading to the development of E-S-QUAL scale used perceived value and loyalty as the indicators to measure the effectiveness of the e-service quality dimensions given in the scale. The current chapter intends to provide quality strategies for customer loyalty in an e-service environment. So, the E-S-QUAL, E-RecS-QUAL and loyalty scales have been used in a similarity to the original study to judge the overall impact of e-service quality dimensions on the loyalty by taking case of m-banking. These scales support in ascertaining these dimensions act as the theoretical foundation of the current study and are discussed further.

E-S-QUAL Scale

Parasuraman et al. (2005), had put forward two scales i.e. E-S-QUAL and E-RecS-QUAL for assessing e-service quality. E-S-QUAL has been termed as the extension of SERVQUAL scale by Parasuraman, Zeithaml, and Berry (1988). Previous studies on service quality show that SERVQUAL has been a famous scale widely used in the measurement of service quality of more physical or 'brick or mortar' type of business (Ladhari, 2009) and may not be suitable for measurement of online services. With a special focus on e-service quality, Zeithaml (2002) developed E-SERVQUAL scale with seven dimensions to support the assessment of an e-service. Parasuraman et al. (2005), further categorized these dimensions into four dimensions of E-S-QUAL i.e. efficiency, fulfillment, system availability and privacy, and the three dimensions of E-RecS-QUAL i.e. responsiveness, compensation and contact.

Among these, E-S-QUAL represents e-core service quality that deals with the quality of service provided during the real time of core service delivery, and E-RecS-QUAL represents e-recovery service quality related with quality of service provided after service delivery i.e. while handling any service problems or enquiries. Parasuraman et al. (2005) proposed these scales to assess the service quality of online web portals. Consumers use similar dimensions to figure e-service quality independent of the nature of a product or service (Zeithaml, Parasuraman, & Malhotra, 2000). Literature suggests that e-service quality scales have been quite popular to ascertain service quality in case of m-commerce based services (Negi, 2009; Ozer, Argan, & Argan, 2013). These scales have been equally used for research in the field of banking (Ganguli & Roy, 2011; Thuy & Hau, 2010) involving internet banking and m-banking. Thus, in the current chapter an effort has been made to apply the E-S-QUAL and E-RecS-QUAL scales to examine the issue of e-service quality in case of m-banking. These scales use 22 items in E-S-QUAL and 11 items in E-RecS-QUAL in a similarity with the original study conducted by Parasuraman et al. (2005). However, as a distinct feature, the description of the dimensions adjusted in the context of m-banking service and is given below:

E-S-QUAL

1. **Efficiency (EFF)**: Shown by the ease and convenience of using the m-banking service.
2. **Fulfillment (FUL)**: Refers to the extent to which m-banking service assures about completion of the customer's request.
3. **System Availability (SYS)**: Related with the proper reach and functioning of m-banking service.
4. **Privacy (PRI)**: Includes the security of m-banking transactions and safeguarding of customer records.

E-RecS-QUAL

1. **Responsiveness (RES)**: Reflected with proper handling of the customer issues and problems in case of a service failure.
2. **Compensation (COM)**: Specifies the benefit given to the customer for any problem related to m-banking service.
3. **Contact (CON)**: Refers to the ease with which telephone or online representatives contacted by customers in case of a service problem.

Loyalty Scale

Many researchers have used attitudinal measures to ascertain customer loyalty. In a step towards this direction, the five item loyalty scale has been given by Zeithaml, Berry and Parasuraman (1996). The current chapter uses this scale to ascertain the loyalty intentions of m-banking customers in a similarity to the study conducted by Parasuraman et al. (2005). However, the items of the loyalty scale were adjusted as per the nature of the current study and a brief description of these items is as follows:

1. **Loyalty to Service**: Shown by spreading positive word of mouth about m-banking service to other people.
2. **Propensity to Switch**: Reflected by recommending m-banking service to others looking for advice.
3. **Willingness to Pay More**: Displayed by inspiring family, friends and other people to make higher usage of m-banking.
4. **External Response to Problem**: Shown by considering m-banking service as the first preference for future transactions.
5. **Internal Response to Problem**: Refers to an internal readiness for service usage soon in the future.

E-Service Quality Dimensions and Loyalty

Different studies in the past used E-S-QUAL and E-RecS-QUAL scales proposed by Parasuraman et al. (2005) to explore the relationship between e-service quality dimensions and loyalty. Yang and Tsai (2007) conducted a study involving the application of general E-S-QUAL scales on the website satisfaction and loyalty model. The results of the study showed that dimension fulfillment had the highest impact on loyalty towards shopping websites followed by the dimension efficiency, responsiveness and contact. The dimensions system availability and compensation were found to be least important in determining loyalty but still had significant impacts on loyalty towards websites. Kortunay (2016) conducted a study using E-S-QUAL scales in Turkey to measure the internet service quality of e-commerce websites in which it reflected that all the quality dimensions significantly affect loyalty. Dimensions efficiency, fulfillment, privacy, system availability and responsiveness had a higher impact on loyalty than the dimensions compensation and contact.

In case of the banking sector, Alkhouli (2017) conducted a study on the effect of website service quality on the e-satisfaction and e-loyalty of customers by taking a case of Swedish banks using E-S-QUAL scale. The study revealed that the four dimensions of e-core service quality i.e. efficiency, fulfillment, privacy and system availability significantly affect the online loyalty of banking customers. Malviya (2015) conducted a study to analyze the issue of m-banking service quality dimensions in case of public and private sector banks in Indore district of Madhya Pradesh in India. The results revealed that dimensions security, efficiency, responsiveness and reliability have a key role to play in m-banking service quality. Jo and Mo (2018) conducted a study on the factors influencing customer satisfaction and loyalty towards internet banking services by taking the case of undergraduates of a Nigerian University. The findings revealed that out of the different E-S-QUAL dimensions, the only dimension significantly affecting customer loyalty towards internet banking was fulfillment. On the contrary, Dhurup, Surujlal and Redda (2014) in their study on the relationship between online banking service quality with satisfaction and loyalty have revealed an insignificant effect of dimension fulfillment on the customer loyalty in South Africa. Ariff, Yu, Zakuan and Ismail (2013) in their study focused on analyzing the impact of service quality and customer satisfaction on loyalty towards internet banking in Malaysia found that e-service quality dimensions fulfillment, efficiency and system availability have a crucial role to play in loyalty towards internet banking. Awan, Khan and Wenqing (2012) conducted a comparative study of online service quality perception of two regional economies. The study focused on analyzing the website service quality of banks from China and Kingdom of Saudi Arabia (KSA). The results revealed that in case of Chinese customers, the dimensions fulfillment and compensation had a significant effect on customer loyalty whereas the effect of dimensions system availability, privacy, contact and efficiency was comparatively weaker on banking websites. In a comparison to this, the customers from KSA exhibited somewhat different behavior, where the dimensions responsiveness and efficiency significantly affected loyalty intention and the effect of dimensions privacy, fulfillment and system availability on loyalty towards banking websites was not considerable among the customers.

MAIN FOCUS OF THE CHAPTER

Issues and Problems

The discussion during the review of the literature reveals that the dynamic nature of an e-service poses a great challenge for those who are engaged in its delivery. The main issues and concerns could be addressed with formulation of quality strategies for customer loyalty have been categorized as follows:

Issue of Customer Connection in an Online Environment

Wider adoption of technology among businesses has raised the issue of examining service quality in an electronic environment (Li, Liu, & Suomi, 2009). Customer retention in the virtual world has now become a new area for concern in modern day businesses as the loyalty behavior of customers in online settings may be different from the offline. Business organizations are making sincere efforts to stay closer to the customer and employ strategies and tools to keep the customers connected with them in a computer-mediated environment. The concern for customer connection has increased the importance of maintaining highest level of service quality in the delivery of an e-service. This could be possible by formulation of strategies based on the two determinants of service quality i.e. e-core and e-recovery service quality.

Issue of Operational Efficiency Among the Banks

Banking sector is going through a continuous transition with the implementation of technological solutions. These solutions have enabled the banks to increase their operational efficiency by the reduction in the cost of serving the customers. It further helps them to face the challenges of competition in the banking industry more effectively. The banks could only be able to leverage on the benefits of technology-based solutions if they are able to attain customer loyalty in case of e-services. Loyalty in an online environment is vital for the banks to generate revenue and attract more customers (Li, 2009). Banking sector has become more aware about reaping the benefits of information technology based applications which will further lead them towards customer loyalty (Bukhari & Kazi, 2016; Chen, 2015). This strategic change has revolutionized the field of relationship marketing and influenced the quality of operations in personal banking.

Issue of Mobility in Banking Services

E-banking has emerged as a new channel for the banks to increase their customer base (Mobarek, 2007). It is generally considered as a starting point for both internet banking and m-banking. The wider use of these two technology based channels for remotely accessing the banks' services has increased the relevance of observing the points of customer interaction in the virtual environment. This increases the need to deliver quality services with the highest level of accuracy as a small lapse in service delivery may induce the switching intention. The easy availability of close substitutes in an online environment may give more strength to this kind of behavior. These customer touch points are even more crucial in case of m-commerce services such as m-banking due to its ubiquitous nature. Mobile applications are rapidly becoming a popular medium for carrying out routine transactions by the customers (Del Giudice, Campanella, & Dezi, 2016). Different preferences of customers in the case of m-banking create more challenges for the service providers and need to be addressed with greatest care. Mobile phone has emerged as an important medium to depict the quality of banking services.

Thus, the issues discussed above call for certain strategies to be framed by the banks on the basis of quality dimensions which may reduce the switching behavior and promote customer loyalty. Formulation of strategies to maintain e-service quality considered as an important area for research (Sylvie & Ina, 2010) and regarded as a vital step towards this direction. The current chapter aims to address this issue and provides quality strategies for customer loyalty in a vibrant mobile environment. The discussion on the relationship between e-service quality dimensions and loyalty conducted earlier shows a shortage of studies focused on analyzing the impact of service quality dimensions on the loyalty of m-banking customers as most of the studies in this domain are concerned with website service quality or internet banking. An effort was made to throw light on the relationship between e-service quality and loyalty by taking the case of m-banking service. This may further help in generation of quality strategies and proper management of customers in an online environment.

Research Hypothesis and Model

Previous discussion reveals that different studies involving the impact of e-service quality dimensions on the customer loyalty have been conducted earlier. However, there has been a dearth of these studies in the field of m-commerce. So, the following hypotheses dealing with the relationship among the three constructs i.e. E-S-QUAL, E-RecS-QUAL and loyalty scales in an m-banking environment have been proposed and are tested subsequently:

H1: E-core service quality dimensions significantly affect customer loyalty in case of m-banking
H2: E-recovery service quality dimensions significantly affect customer loyalty in case of m-banking

This relationship between the constructs shown in the model of hypotheses presented in Figure 1. The model displays the association between service quality and customer loyalty in an e-service environment based on the literature review and earlier discussion. It further takes into account the two determinants of e-service quality i.e. e-core service and e-recovery service quality, and focuses on ascertaining their impact on the loyalty of customers in case of m-banking. Thus, it helps to determine the differences in the impact of quality dimensions on the customer loyalty.

Research Methodology

The data related to the constructs used in this study has been collected through a survey in the three most economically significant districts of the state of Punjab in India i.e. Ludhiana, Jalandhar and Amritsar. Apart from being economically significant, these districts had the highest number of banks' branches in the state. The sampling technique used during the survey has been convenience sampling and the data was collected through personal visits to the top ten public and private sector banks in the three districts. These banks were ranked based on the volume of m-banking transactions in India during the last one year. Initially, 600 questionnaires were distributed, with 200 each in the three districts. However, after the survey 524 usable questionnaires obtained thereby keeping the response rate to 87.3%. The missing values in the survey were handled using the best guess approach. Zikmund, Babin, Carr and Griffin (2013) have argued that this approach helps to fill the missing data based on the trend shown by earlier values. The sample data of 524 respondents collected from the survey consisted of 309 (58.96%) males

Figure 1. Model of hypotheses

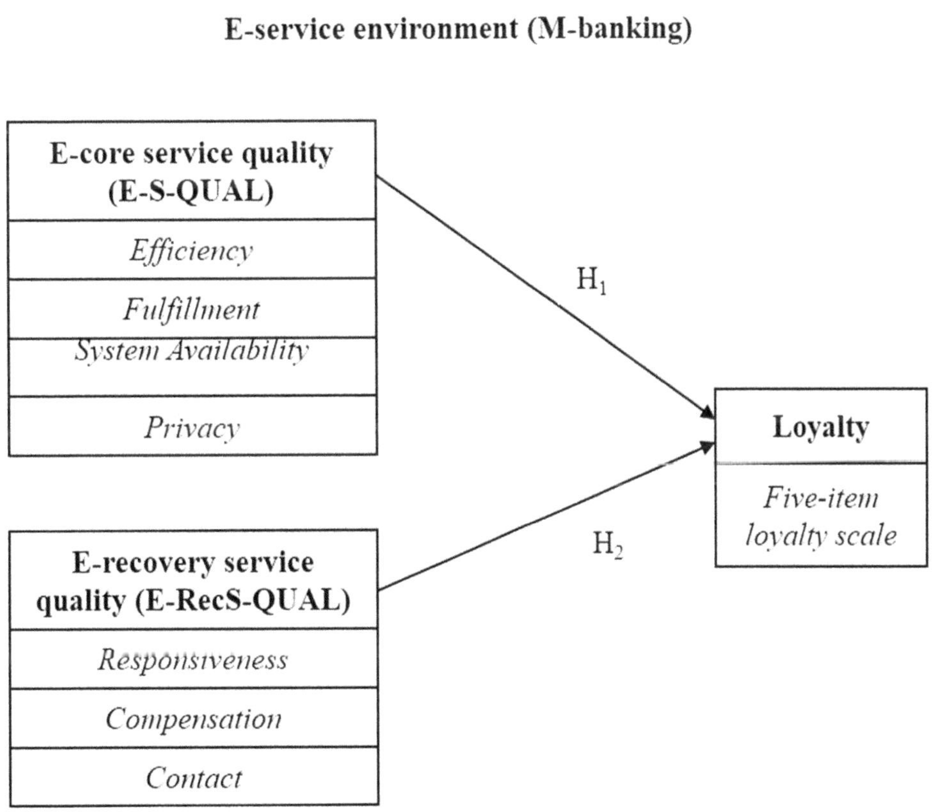

and 215 (41.04%) females. Whereas, 295 (56.29%) were between the age of 18 to 30 years, 194 (37.02%) between 31 to 45 years and 35 (6.67%) were of 46 years and above age. Further, the generated data was analyzed using Ms-Excel and SPSS.

Data Analysis

The current chapter uses 33 statements based on E-S-QUAL and E-RecS-QUAL scales to understand the relationship between service quality and loyalty in case of m-banking. These statements are presented in Table 1 and Table 2, respectively. Further, the statements related to the five item loyalty scale discussed earlier have been listed in Table 3. The survey instrument used during the study utilizes a seven point Likert scale with values ranging from 1 to 7 with 1 referring to the strong disagreement and 7 to strong agreement to the statements listed in Table 1, Table 2 and Table 3. It should be noted that each of these statements are concerned with a specific variable denoting quality dimension of e-core service quality (EFF, FUL, SYS, PRI), e-recovery service quality (RES, COM, CON), and loyalty (LOY).

Table 1. Statements representing e-core service quality dimensions

Variable	Statements
EFF	1. Mobile banking facility in my phone makes it easy to find what I need in personal banking.
	2. It is easy to get anywhere on the mobile banking menu in my phone.
	3. Mobile banking enables me to complete a personal banking transaction quickly.
	4. Information related to personal banking provided by mobile banking is well organized.
	5. Mobile banking menu loads fast on my phone.
	6. Personal banking services offered to me through mobile banking are simple to use.
	7. Mobile banking menu enables me to get on to the mobile banking service quickly.
	8. Mobile banking service provided by my bank is well organized.
SYS	1. Mobile banking service of my bank provides continuous connections to me.
	2. Mobile banking service is available on all mobile phone operating systems.
	3. Mobile banking service provided by my bank launches and runs right away.
	4. Mobile banking service offered by my bank does not crash.
FUL	1. Mobile banking interface does not freeze after I enter my information.
	2. Mobile banking completes my personal banking transactions when promised.
	3. My banking transactions are fulfilled using mobile banking within suitable timeframe.
	4. Mobile banking completes my personal banking request as per the order.
	5. Mobile banking offers me those personal banking services that the bank claims to have.
	6. Mobile banking service provided to me is truthful about its offerings.
	7. Mobile banking service provided by my bank makes accurate promises about completion of request.
PRI	1. Mobile banking does not share my personal information to others.
	2. Mobile banking protects information about my bank account.
	3. Mobile banking is safe to use.

Table 2. Statements representing e-recovery service quality dimensions

Variable	Statements
RES	1. Mobile banking provides me with convenient options to solve my banking problems.
	2. Mobile banking service appropriately handles my banking related problems.
	3. Mobile banking offers a meaningful solution to my banking problems.
	4. Mobile banking service tells me what to do if my transaction is not processed.
	5. Mobile banking takes care of my banking problems promptly.
COM	1. Mobile banking service compensates me in case I suffer some problem which is created by the bank.
	2. Mobile banking compensates me when my transactions are not fulfilled in time.
	3. Mobile banking service provides me with a telephone number to dial in case of any problem related to banking.
CON	1. The customer service representatives of mobile banking are always available online.
	2. Mobile banking offers me the ability to speak to a live person in case there is a problem.
	3. Customer service representatives of mobile banking provide best solution to my problem.

Table 3. Statements representing loyalty items

Variable	Statements
LOY	1. I always say positive things about mobile banking to other people
	2. I recommend mobile banking to someone who seeks my advice on personal banking.
	3. I always encourage friends and others to use mobile banking service.
	4. I consider mobile banking as the first choice while deciding the mode of Banking
	5. I will do more transactions using mobile banking in the coming months

Reliability of the Measures

D In order to find out whether the three scales qualify to be the reliable measure of e-core service quality, e-recovery service quality and loyalty intentions in case of m-banking, the values of coefficient Cronbach's alpha have been computed and are listed in Table 4.

It has been observed that the alpha values related to the dimensions of E-S-QUAL are ranging from .748 to .868 and those of E-RecS-QUAL are ranging from .733 to .861 whereas the alpha value in case of loyalty scale is .882. This tells about the internal consistency with in the data and thus, the three constructs prove to be the reliable measure of e-core service quality, e-recovery service quality and customer loyalty in case of m-banking.

Table 4. Reliability statistics – E-S-QUAL, E-RecS-QUAL and loyalty scale

	E-S-QUAL Scale				E-RecS-QUAL Scale			Loyalty Scale
Cronbach's Alpha	EFF	SYS	FUL	PRI	RES	COM	CON	LOY
	.868	.850	.848	.748	.816	.861	.733	.882

Appropriateness of the Statistical Model

Further, multiple regression analysis has been applied to test the relationships given in Figure 1 and is used as a statistical technique for this study. It has been depicted in the past that multiple regression is considered as a useful technique when the motive of a task is to test the impact of different independent variables on the dependent variable with the goal of generalizing the results to a larger community (Osborne, 2000). However, before the application of multiple regression, its suitability for judging the relationships was checked by testing its assumptions and the values obtained thereafter have been listed in Table 5.

Independence of Residuals: Table 5 presents the model summary and displays the overall regression values in case of e-core service quality and e-recovery service quality represented by model-1 and model-2, respectively. The Durban-Watson values of 1.994 and 1.861 suggest that there is no autocorrelation in the sample, and the residuals are found to be independent.

Multicollinearity: It is considered as a situation in which the variables in the regression model may show a high correlation may affect the appropriateness of the regression model. Table 5 depicts that the VIF (variance inflation factor) values in case of all the dimensions of E-S-QUAL and E-RecS-QUAL scales are less than 10 that reflects that there is no correlation between the independent variables in the sample and this confirms the non-existence of multicollinearity.

Residual Mean and Outliers: Table 5 presents that residual in case of model-1 and model-2 has a mean value equal to .000 indicates about the accuracy of the regression fit. Further, the Cook's Distance values of .075 and .089 in these models show that there are no possible outliers or extreme values in the sample data. Cook and Stanford (1982) quoted that the presence of outliers has an unfavorable effect on the prediction of the regression model and the distance value of less than 1 confirms about their non-existence.

Table 5. Values showing appropriateness of regression model

Model	Durbin-Watson	Collinearity Statistics			Residual Means	Outliers
		Tolerance		VIF		Cook's Distance
1	1.994	EFF SYS FUL PRI	387 .475 .459 .571	2.585 2.106 2.178 1.751	.000	.002
2	1.861	RES COM CON	.435 .563 .602	2.300 1.775 1.662	.000	.003

a. Predictors: (constant), Model-1: PRI, SYS, FUL, EFF; Model-2: RES, COM, CON
b. Dependent variable: LOY

Effect of Quality Dimensions on the Loyalty

Legitimacy of the regression model and reliability of measures were used to ascertain e-core service quality, e-recovery service quality and customer loyalty. After that, the summated score of the items of each of the dimensions of E-S-QUAL and E-RecS-QUAL scales have been fitted as independent variables in the least squares regression equation whereas the summated score of the five item loyalty scale has been fitted as the dependent variable.

The equation related to the impact of E-S-QUAL dimensions on customer loyalty has been included in model-1 and that of E-RecS-QUAL dimensions on customer loyalty in model-2. These equations are listed below for further analysis:

Model-1: E-S-QUAL

$$LOY = a + b1\ (EFF) + b2\ (SYS) + b3\ (FUL) + b4\ (PRI) \quad (1)$$

Model-2: E-RecS-QUAL

$$LOY = a + b1\ (RES) + b2\ (COM) + b3\ (CON) \quad (2)$$

Where, a = intercept

b1, b2, b3, b4 = regression coefficients

EFF, SYS, FUL, PRI, RES, COM, CON= independent variables

LOY = dependent variable

Further, multiple regression analysis has been applied on the equations (1) and (2), and the results obtained have been presented in Table 6.

The values of adjusted R2 in Table 6 that the regression is positive and significant among both E-S-QUAL and E-RecS-QUAL scales represented by model-1 and model-2. The values of F-Cal and F-Crit show that the hypothesis H1 and H2 are accepted and there is a significant effect of e-core service quality (E-S-QUAL) and e-recovery service quality (E-RecS-QUAL) on the loyalty of respondents towards m-banking. However, the effect of e-core service quality on the loyalty is more in comparison to e-recovery service quality.

In case of the different dimensions of e-core service quality, p-value in efficiency, system availability and privacy is less than 0.05, and is statistically significant. However, this relationship is not true in case of the other dimension fulfillment with a p-value greater than 0.05. Further, the regression coefficients show that dimension privacy has the highest value of .717 followed by efficiency with a value of .319

Table 6. Multiple regression results showing the effect of quality dimensions

Hypothesis	Relationship	Adjusted R^2	F-Cal	F-Crit
H_1	E-S-QUAL → LOY	.590	189.268	.000
	Dimensions	*Coefficients*	*P-Value*	
	EFF	.319	.000	
	SYS	.222	.000	
	FUL	.065	.221	
	PRI	.717	.000	
H_2	E-RecS-QUAL → LOY	.442	139.220	.000
	Dimensions	*Coefficients*	*P-Value*	
	RES	.431	.000	
	COM	.210	.013	
	CON	.581	.000	

and system availability with a value of .222. In the context of e-recovery service quality, p-value of the dimensions responsiveness and contact is less than 0.05 and is statistically significant whereas the p-value in case of the dimension compensation is greater than 0.05, and is insignificant. Further, the regression coefficients reveal that dimension contact has the highest value of .581 followed by responsiveness with a value of .431.

SOLUTIONS AND RECOMMENDATIONS

Data analysis conducted earlier reflects that both e-core service quality and e-recovery service quality have a positive association with customer loyalty in case of m-banking, and these two indicators may be effectively utilized for formulating quality strategies in an e-service environment. But, among the two, e-core service quality has the higher impact on loyalty towards m-banking and should be given prime importance by the service providers.

In case of different dimensions of each of these indicators, it has been found that dimensions privacy, efficiency and system availability significantly affect loyalty towards m-banking whereas the effect of dimension fulfillment is found to be insignificant. In addition, it has also been revealed that dimension privacy has the highest effect on loyalty towards m-banking followed by efficiency and system availability whereas the effect of fulfillment is found to be least. Further in case of e-recovery service quality, the dimensions responsiveness and contact have a significant impact on the loyalty towards m-banking. However, this impact is found to be insignificant in case of the dimension compensation. It has also been found that responsiveness has the highest impact on loyalty towards m-banking followed by contact and compensation.

These findings generate important implications for quality strategies involving e-core service quality and e-recovery service quality. These strategies could be followed for managing the loyalty of connected customers in an e-service environment and have been discussed further.

Quality Strategies

E-Core Service Quality: It has been revealed that dimension privacy has a significant impact on the loyalty of customers towards m-banking. Consequently, the banks should focus on making the m-banking applications more secure and should take due care in protection of the customer record. There should be a greater concern for maintaining the privacy of customers. This includes providing them with up to date and state-of-the-art applications to ensure safety of their record and transactions. Apart from the implementation of latest security provisions, the customers should also be educated through different print and electronic means about the safe conduct of transactions in an electronic environment. Banks should educate their customers about safer ways of conducting m-banking transactions and try to clarify any myths in their minds. In addition, dimension of privacy has the highest impact on customer loyalty in comparison to the other dimensions. Hence, ensuring customer privacy should be of prime importance for the banking sector in case of e-services. Next, it has been found that the dimension efficiency also significantly affects the loyalty of customers towards m-banking. The banks should work on making the service more simple and convenient to use. Clark (2001) has also considered convenience as one of the important driver of the usage of m-commerce applications. In order to increase the efficiency of customers, the banks should work on making the user interface of the different m-banking applications simple and easy to use. A customer friendly interface should have the ability to adapt to the language preference of m-banking customers. This will help the customers to locate the desired option of service with ease and in lesser timeframe. The dimension efficiency also has the second highest impact on the loyalty towards service after privacy in case of e-core service quality so it should be given due attention for the retention of the customers. Further, e-core service quality dimension system availability also has a significant impact on the loyalty of m-banking customers. Earlier studies reveal that ubiquity is usually considered as an important driving force for the usage of m-commerce applications (Clarke, 2001; Hameed, Ahsan, & Yang, 2010; Nysveen, Pedersen, & Skard, 2015). This anywhere anytime usage of m-banking service could only be possible through continuous availability and reach of m-banking network on different types of phones and hand-held devices with varying operating systems. Efforts should also be made to ensure the functioning of service in the urban as well as rural areas. The banks should work on making the service available through different mediums that could be used round the clock at the discretion of the customer. Furthermore, it has been revealed that the impact of dimension fulfillment on the loyalty towards m-banking is found to be insignificant. It might be due to the reason that m-banking being an electronic service automatically completes the request after its execution so this may reduce the relevance of this dimension in the formation of customer loyalty.

E-Recovery Service Quality: It has been found that the dimension contact significantly affects the loyalty of customers towards m-banking. Hence, the banks should maintain proper service support for the customers by providing them with telephone numbers to dial in case of a service failure. These helpline numbers could be made toll-free and be further complimented with online support provided by banks' representatives. This will equip the m-banking customers with the ease of contact in case of a service support or a problem. In addition, this dimension also has the highest impact on the loyalty of customers towards m-banking so it should be considered as the top priority by the banks in case of e-recovery service quality. Further, it has been revealed that other e-recovery service quality dimension responsiveness also has a significant effect on the loyalty of customers towards m-banking. Hence, the banks should give prompt support to the service-related issues of the customers. The problems in case of any service failure should be handled diligently and due consideration should be given to the customers for providing adequate recovery service quality. This dimension has the second highest impact on the loyalty of customers towards m-banking so its role in delivery of the desired level of e-recovery service quality should never be overlooked by the banks. Furthermore, it has been found that the dimension compensation does not significantly affect the loyalty of customers towards m-banking. It reflects that in case of e-recovery service quality instead of looking for compensation, the m-banking customers give more value to the other dimensions i.e. contact and responsiveness, which have a considerable impact on their loyalty towards the service.

FUTURE RESEARCH DIRECTIONS

This chapter focuses on the issue of quality strategies for customer loyalty in case of m-banking and includes a survey conducted in the state of Punjab in India. However, future research may be conducted by expanding the scope of data collection to the other geographical domain, which may depict the quality preferences of people from a distinct background. In addition, different studies can be conducted to explore the role of consumer demographics in the formation of quality strategies for customer loyalty. Separate research work may be carried out involving e-core service and e-recovery service quality to find out the differences in the impact of dimensions on the loyalty based on the customers' demographics. Apart from this, future studies could formulate the quality strategies for customer loyalty by taking the case of the other applications of m-commerce such as mobile entertainment, mobile marketing, mobile shopping, mobile ticketing and mobile information services. This will help the researchers to explore the field of service quality and customer loyalty in case of other m-commerce services apart from m-banking.

CONCLUSION

The issue of e-service quality poses great challenges for banking Industry in future and should be given utmost focus. The banks need to implement sophisticated technological solutions, which may help the customers to gain more confidence in terms of security of their record and transactions. In future, these service providers may work on making the m-banking applications more robust by enabling their functioning on varied operating systems and types of devices with different browsers and screen sizes. There is a greater possibility that the customers may demand more personalized m-banking experience based on their individual preferences. There may be a concern for newer ways of operating the service and the banks need to respond appropriately to this challenge. It may also require assisting the customers in the real-time service environment i.e. while performing a service transaction or making an enquiry request.

The greater focus on the implementation of technology-based solutions across different business organizations has increased the relevance of strategies and tools for managing the customers in a virtual environment. This chapter was intended to focus on this issue and throws light on the linkage between e-service quality and customer loyalty in the m-banking scenario based on a survey based approach. The results obtained have shown the differences in the importance of the dimensions of both e-core service quality and e-recovery service quality in determining customer loyalty. The dimensions efficiency, privacy and system availability proved to be significant in case of the core service, and the dimensions contact and responsiveness were crucial in case of the recovery service. Further, these findings were utilized to formulate the quality strategies for customer loyalty in case of m-banking. Thus, the current chapter provides key inferences for those doing research or involved in the delivery of m-banking service. It also helps to gain valuable insights into the issue of e-service quality and customer loyalty, which further enables the service providers to maintain better customer connectivity in an e-service environment.

REFERENCES

Akinci, S., Inan, E. A., & Aksoy, Ş. (2008). Re-assessment of E-S-Qual and E-RecS-Qual in a pure service setting. *Journal of Business Research*, *63*(3), 232–240. doi:10.1016/j.jbusres.2009.02.018

Al-Agaga, A. M., & Nor, K. H. M. (2012). Factors that influence e-loyalty of internet banking users. *International Journal of Electronic Commerce Studies*, *3*(2), 297–304. doi:10.7903/ijecs.1097

Alkhouli, S. (2017). The effect of banks website service quality and e-satisfaction on e-loyalty: An empirical study on Swedish banks. *International Journal of Business and Management*, *13*(1), 1–12. doi:10.5539/ijbm.v13n1p1

Alsamdyai, M. J., Yousif, R. O., & Al-khasawneh, M. H. (2012). The factors influencing consumer satisfaction and continuity to deal with e-banking services in Jordan. *Global Journal of Management and Business Research*, *12*(14), 129–142.

Ariff, M. S. M., Leong, O. Y., Norhayati, Z., & Ahmad, J. (2012). Examining dimensions of electronic service quality for internet banking services. *Proceedings of International Congress on Interdisciplinary Business and Social Science 2012*, *65*, 854-859. 10.1016/j.sbspro.2012.11.210

Ariff, M. S. M., Yun, L. O., Zakuan, N., & Ismail, K. (2013). The impacts of service quality and customer satisfaction on customer loyalty in internet banking. *Procedia: Social and Behavioral Sciences*, *81*, 469–473. doi:10.1016/j.sbspro.2013.06.462

Asgari, N., Ahmadi, M. H., Shamlou, M., Farokhi, A. R., & Farzin, M. (2014). Studying the impact of e-service quality on e-loyalty of customers in the area of e-banking services. *Journal of Management and Sustainability*, *4*(2), 126–133. doi:10.5539/jms.v4n2p126

Awan, M. A., Khan, H. U., & Wenqing, Z. (2012). A comparative study on online service quality perception of two major regional economies. *International Journal of e-Education, e-Business, e-Management and e-Learning, 2*(6), 529-533.

Bukhari, A. N., & Kazi, R. (2016). CRM triggers effectiveness through customer selection orientation, business cycle orientation, cross-functional integration and dual value creation: Myth or reality. *Journal of Marketing Management*, *4*(1), 163–171.

Caruana, A. (2002). Service loyalty: The effects of service quality and the mediating role of customer satisfaction. *European Journal of Marketing*, *36*(7/8), 811–828. doi:10.1108/03090560210430818

Chang, H. H., & Wang, H.-W. (2011). The moderating effect of customer perceived value on online shopping behaviour. *Online Information Review*, *35*(3), 333–359. doi:10.1108/14684521111151414

Chen, C. (2013). Perceived risk, usage frequency of mobile banking services. *Managing Service Quality: An International Journal, 23*(5), 410–436. doi:10.1108/MSQ-10-2012-0137

Chen, S.-C. (2015). Customer value and customer loyalty: Is competition a missing link? *Journal of Retailing and Consumer Services, 22*, 107–116. doi:10.1016/j.jretconser.2014.10.007

Chu, P.-Y., Lee, G.-Y., & Chao, Y. (2012). Service quality, customer satisfaction, customer trust, and loyalty in an e-banking context. *Social Behavior and Personality, 40*(8), 1271–1283. doi:10.2224bp.2012.40.8.1271

Chung, N., & Kwon, S. J. (2009). The effect of customers' mobile experience and technical support on the intention to use mobile banking. *Cyberpsychology & Behavior, 12*(5), 539–543. doi:10.1089/cpb.2009.0014 PMID:19772441

Clarke, I. (2001). Emerging value propositions for m-commerce. *The Journal of Business Strategy, 18*(2), 133–149.

Colier, J. E., & Bienstock, C. C. (2006). Measuring service quality in e-retailing. *Journal of Service Research, 8*(3), 260–275. doi:10.1177/1094670505278867

Cook, R. D., & Sanford, W. (1982). *Residuals and influence in regression*. New York: Chapman and Hall.

Cyr, D., Bonanni, C., Bowes, J., & Ilsever, J. (2005). Beyond trust: Web site design preferences across cultures. *Journal of Global Information Management, 13*(4), 25–54. doi:10.4018/jgim.2005100102

Cyr, D., Hassanein, K., Head, M., & Ivanov, A. (2006). The role of social presence in establishing loyalty in e-service environments. *Interacting with Computers, 19*(1), 43–56. doi:10.1016/j.intcom.2006.07.010

de Ruyter, K., Wetzels, M., & Kleijnen, M. (2001). Customer adoption of e-service: An experimental study. *International Journal of Service Industry Management, 12*(2), 184–207. doi:10.1108/09564230110387542

Del Giudice, M., Campanella, F., & Dezi, L. (2016). The bank of things: An empirical investigation on the profitability of the financial services of the future. *Business Process Management Journal, 22*(2), 324–340. doi:10.1108/BPMJ-10-2015-0139

Dhurup, M., Surujlal, J., & Redda, E. (2014). Customer perceptions of online banking service quality and its relationship with customer satisfaction and loyalty. *Mediterranean Journal of Social Sciences, 5*, 72–80.

Flavián, C., Guinalíu, M., & Gurrea, R. (2006). The role played by perceived usability, satisfaction and consumer trust on website loyalty. *Information & Management, 43*(1), 1–14. doi:10.1016/j.im.2005.01.002

Floh, A., & Treiblmaier, H. (2006). What keeps the e-banking customer loyal? A multigroup analysis of the moderating role of consumer characteristics on e-loyalty in the financial service industry. *Journal of Electronic Commerce Research, 7*(2), 97–110.

Ganguli, S., & Roy, S. K. (2011). Generic technology-based service quality dimensions in banking impact on customer satisfaction and loyalty. *International Journal of Bank Marketing, 29*(2), 168–189. doi:10.1108/02652321111107648

Gommans, M., Krishnan, K. S., & Scheffold, K. B. (2001). From brand loyalty to e-loyalty: A conceptual framework. *Journal of Economic and Social Research*, *3*(1), 43–58.

Hameed, K., Ahsan, K., & Yang, W. (2010). Mobile commerce and applications: An exploratory study and review. *Journal of Computers*, *2*(4), 110–114.

Harris, L. C., & Goode, M. M. (2004). The four levels of loyalty and the pivotal role of trust: A study of online service dynamics. *Journal of Retailing*, *80*(2), 139–158. doi:10.1016/j.jretai.2004.04.002

Homburg, C., & Giering, A. C. (2001). Personal characteristics as moderators of the relationship between customer satisfaction and loyalty - An empirical analysis. *Psychology and Marketing*, *18*(1), 43–66. doi:10.1002/1520-6793(200101)18:1<43::AID-MAR3>3.0.CO;2-I

Hussien, M. I., & El Aziz, R. A. (2013). Investigating e-banking service quality in one of Egypt's banks: A stakeholder analysis. *The TQM Journal*, *25*(5), 557–576. doi:10.1108/TQM-11-2012-0086

Izogo, E. E., & Ogba, I.-I. (2015). Service quality, customer satisfaction and loyalty in automobile repair services sector. *International Journal of Quality & Reliability Management*, *32*(3), 250–269. doi:10.1108/IJQRM-05-2013-0075

Jeong, Y., & Lee, Y. (2010). A study on the customer satisfaction and customer loyalty of furniture purchaser in on-line shop. *Asian Journal on Quality*, *11*(2), 146–156. doi:10.1108/15982681011075952

Jo, A., & Mo, A. (2018). Factors influencing customer satisfaction and loyalty to internet banking services among undergraduates of a Nigerian University. *Journal of Internet Banking and Commerce*, *23*(1), 1–20.

Jun, M., & Palacios, S. (2016). Examining the key dimensions of mobile banking service quality: An exploratory study. *International Journal of Bank Marketing*, *34*(3), 307–326. doi:10.1108/IJBM-01-2015-0015

Keating, B., Rugimbana, R., & Quazi, A. (2003). Differentiating between service quality and relationship quality in cyberspace. *Managing Service Quality: An International Journal*, *13*(3), 217–232. doi:10.1108/09604520310476481

Koernig, S. K. (2003). E-scapes: The electronic physical environment and service tangibility. *Psychology and Marketing*, *20*(2), 151–167. doi:10.1002/mar.10065

Kortunay, N. (2016). *Measuring internet service quality of e-commerce web sites by using E-S-QUAL in Turkey*. European Scientific Journal.

Kotler, P., Keller, K. L., Koshy, A., & Jha, M. (2009). *Marketing management - A South Asian perspective* (13th ed.). New Delhi, India: Pearson Education.

Ladhari, R. (2009). A review of twenty years of SERVQUAL research. *International Journal of Quality and Service Sciences*, *1*(2), 172–198. doi:10.1108/17566690910971445

Laukkanen, T., & Lauronen, J. (2005). Consumer value creation in mobile banking services. *International Journal of Mobile Communications*, *3*(4), 325–338. doi:10.1504/IJMC.2005.007021

Li, H., Liu, Y., & Suomi, R. (2009). Measurement of e-service quality: An empirical study in online travel service. *Proceedings of 17th European Conference on Information Systems*, 1127-1139.

Li, Y. (2009). Measuring e-commerce dimensions. *Journal of Computer Information Systems*, 2–12.

Liang, T., & Wei, C. P. (2004). Introduction to the special issue: Mobile commerce applications. *International Journal of Electronic Commerce*, *8*(3), 7–17. doi:10.1080/10864415.2004.11044303

Lin, C.-Y., & Shih, K.-H. (2013). Service quality of mobile banking systems. In *Proceedings of Confernence on Active Citizenship by Management Knowledge Management and Innovation* (pp. 515–521). Zadar, Croatia: Knowledge and Learning.

Luarn, P., & Lin, H. (2003). A customer loyalty model for e-serve context. *Journal of Electronic Commerce Research*, *4*(4), 156–167.

Magutu, P. O., Mwangi, M., Nyaoga, R. B., Ondimu, G. M., Kagu, M., Mutai, K., ... Nthenya, P. (2011). E-commerce products and services in the banking industry: The adoption and usage in commercial banks in Kenya. *Journal of Electronic Banking Systems*, *2011*, 1–19.

Malviya, S. (2015). Exploring mobile banking service quality dimensions for public and private sector banks in Indore district of Madhya Pradesh. *International Journal of Advance Research in Computer Science and Management Studies*, *3*(1), 243–252.

Miller, J. L., Craighead, C. W., & Karwan, K. R. (2000). Service recovery: A framework and empirical investigation. *Journal of Operations Management*, *18*(4), 387–400. doi:10.1016/S0272-6963(00)00032-2

Mobarek, A. (2007). E-banking practices and customer satisfaction - a case study in Botswana. *Proceedings of 20th Australasian Finance & Banking Conference 2007 Paper*. Retrieved from http://ssrn.com/abstract=1011112

Mohd, F., & Osman, S. (2005). Towards the future of mobile commerce (m-commerce) in Malaysia. *Proceedings of IADIS International Conference Web Based Communities 2005*, 276-280.

Negi, R. (2009). User perceived service quality of mobile communications: Experience from Ethiopia. *International Journal of Quality & Reliability Management*, *26*(7), 699–711. doi:10.1108/02656710910975769

Nysveen, H., Pedersen, P. E., & Skard, S. E. R. (2015). *A review of mobile services research: Research gaps and suggestions for future research on mobile apps.* SNF Working Paper No 01/15.

Oliver, R. L. (1999). Whence customer loyalty. *Journal of Marketing*, *63*(4), 33–44. doi:10.1177/00222429990634s105

Oliveria, P., Roth, A. V., & Gilland, W. (2002). Achieving competitive capabilities in e-services. *Technological Forecasting and Social Change*, *69*(7), 721–739. doi:10.1016/S0040-1625(01)00188-3

Osborne, J., & Waters, E. (2002). Four assumptions of multiple regression that researchers should always test. *Practical Assessment, Research & Evaluation*, *8*(2). Retrieved from http://PAREonline.net/getvn.asp?v=8&n=2

Ozer, A., Argan, M. T., & Argan, M. (2013). The effect of mobile service quality dimensions on customer satisfaction. *Social and Behavioral Sciences, 11*(99), 428–438.

Parasuraman, A., Zeithaml, V. A., & Berry, L. L. (1988). Servqual. *Journal of Retailing, 64*(1), 12–37.

Parasuraman, A., Zeithaml, V. A., & Malhotra, A. (2005). E-S-QUAL a multiple-item scale for assessing electronic service quality. *Journal of Service Research, 7*(3), 1–21. doi:10.1177/1094670504271156

Puriwat, W., & Tripopsakul, S. (2017). The impact of e-service quality on customer satisfaction and loyalty in mobile banking usage: Case study of Thailand. *Polish Journal of Management Studies, 15*(2), 183–193. doi:10.17512/pjms.2017.15.2.17

Reichheld, F. F., & Schefter, P. (2000). E-loyalty: Your secret weapon on the web. *Harvard Business Review, 78*, 105–113.

Robbins, T. L., & Miller, J. L. (2004). Considering customer loyalty in developing service recovery strategies. *The Journal of Business Strategy, 21*(2), 95–109.

Romadhoni, B., & Hadiwidjojo, D., Noermijati, & Aisjah, S. (2015). Relationship between e-service quality, e-satisfaction, e-trust, e-commitment in building customer e-loyalty: A literature review. *International Journal of Business and Management Invention, 4*(2), 1–9.

Rotchanakitumnuai, S. (2008). Measuring e-government service value with the EGOVSQUAL-RISK model. *Business Process Management Journal, 14*(5), 724–737. doi:10.1108/14637150810903075

Rowley, J. (2006). An analysis of the e-service literature: Towards a research agenda. *Internet Research, 16*(3), 339–359. doi:10.1108/10662240610673736

Rust, R. T. (2001). The rise of e-service. *Journal of Service Research, 3*(4), 283–284. doi:10.1177/109467050134001

Rust, R. T., & Lemon, K. N. (2001). E-service and the consumer. *International Journal of Electronic Commerce, 5*(3), 85–101. doi:10.1080/10864415.2001.11044216

Safeena, R., Hundewale, N., & Kamani, A. (2011). Customer's adoption of mobile-commerce a study on emerging economy. *International Journal of e-Education, e-Business, e-. Management Learning, 1*(3), 228–233.

Santos, J. (2003). E-service quality: A model of virtual service quality dimensions. *Managing Service Quality, 13*(3), 233–246. doi:10.1108/09604520310476490

Shaikh, A. A., & Karjaluoto, H. (2015). Mobile banking adoption: A literature review. *Telematics and Informatics, 32*(1), 129–142. doi:10.1016/j.tele.2014.05.003

Swaid, S. I. (2009). Measuring the quality of e-service: Scale development and initial validation. *Journal of Electronic Commerce Research, 10*(1), 13–28.

Swanson, S. R., & Kelley, S. W. (2001). Attributions and outcomes of the service recovery process. *Journal of Marketing Theory and Practice, 9*(4), 50–65. doi:10.1080/10696679.2001.11501903

Sylvie, R., & Ina, F. (2010). A new measure of e-service quality in France. *International Journal of Retail & Distribution Management*, *38*(7), 497–517. doi:10.1108/09590551011052106

Thaichon, P., Lobo, A., & Mitsis, A. (2014). An empirical model of home internet services quality in Thailand. *Asia Pacific Journal of Marketing and Logistics*, *26*(2), 190–210. doi:10.1108/APJML-05-2013-0059

Thuy, P. N., & Hau, L. N. (2010). Service personal values and customer loyalty: A study of banking services in a transitional economy. *International Journal of Bank Marketing*, *28*(6), 465–478. doi:10.1108/02652321011077706

van Riel, A. C. R., Liljander, V., & Jurriens, P. (2001). Exploring consumer evaluations of e-services: A portal site. *International Journal of Service Industry Management*, *12*(4), 359–377. doi:10.1108/09564230110405280

Vatanasombut, B., Stylianou, A., & Igbaria, M. (2004). How to retain online customers. *Communications of the ACM*, *47*(6), 65–69. doi:10.1145/990680.990682

Widiatmika, G. N., & Subawa, N. S. (2017). Effect of e-service quality and recovery service quality mobile banking services to e-trust, e-satisfaction and e-loyalty mobile banking users of local bank customer in Bali, Indonesia. *Imperial Journal of Interdisciplinary Research*, *3*(3), 1252–1260.

Wu, J., & Wang, S. (2005). What drives mobile commerce? An empirical evaluation of the revised technology acceptance model. *Information & Management*, *42*(5), 719–729. doi:10.1016/j.im.2004.07.001

Wu, K. W. (2011). Customer loyalty explained by electronic recovery service quality: Implications of the customer relationship re-establishment for consumer electronics e-tailers. *Contemporary Management Research*, *7*(1), 21–44. doi:10.7903/cmr.1101

Yang, H., & Tsai, F.-S. (2007). General E-S-QUAL scales applied to websites satisfaction and loyalty model. *Communications of the IIMA*, *7*(2), 115–126.

Yang, Z. (2001). Consumer perceptions of service quality in internet-based electronic commerce. *Proceedings of EMAC Conference.*

Yaya, L. H. P., Marimon, F., & Casadesus, M. (2011). Customer's loyalty and perception of ISO 9001 in online banking. *Industrial Management and Data Systems, 111*(8), 1194-1213. doi:10.1108/02635571111170767

Zeithaml, V. A. (2002). Service excellence in electronic channels. *Managing Service Quality*, *12*(3), 135–138. doi:10.1108/09604520210429187

Zeithaml, V. A., Berry, L. L., & Parasuraman, A. (1996). The behavioral consequences of service quality. *Journal of Marketing*, *60*(2), 31–46. doi:10.2307/1251929

Zeithaml, V. A., Parasuraman, A., & Malhotra, A. (2000). *Conceptual framework for understanding e-service quality: Implications for future research and managerial practice.* Retrieved from http://www.msi.org/reports/a-conceptual-framework-for-understanding-e-service-quality-implications-for/

Zeithaml, V. A., Parasuraman, A., & Malhotra, A. (2002). Service quality delivery through web sites: A critical review of extant knowledge. *Journal of the Academy of Marketing Science*, *30*(4), 362–375. doi:10.1177/009207002236911

Zikmund, W. G., Babin, B. J., Carr, J. C., & Griffin, M. (2013). *Business research methods*. Mason, OH: Cengage Learning.

KEY TERMS AND DEFINITIONS

Application on Mobile Phone: An advanced mode of accessing m-banking service using an application (popularly known as app) installed on the mobile device.

E-Commerce: A business model involving exchange of goods and services using internet and computer-mediated equipment.

M-Commerce: An extension of e-commerce which supports in buying and selling of products using mobile devices.

Mobile Entertainment: Provides entertainment to the users based on services like video, audio, mobile gaming, downloading of ringtones.

Mobile Information Services: Helps to provide information to the users related to certain fields such as current affairs, travel, sports, news.

Mobile Web Banking: A special type of m-banking which works in a similarity with internet banking based on advanced web browsers on a mobile phone.

Personal Banking: An individualistic type of banking which helps to deliver customer specific services (also known as retail banking).

SMS Banking: A basic m-banking service offered to customers through SMS (Short Message Service) communication.

USSD-Based Banking: A USSD (unstructured supplementary service data) based on a menu-driven interface, and helps to use m-banking service without internet.

WAP-Based Banking: A WAP (wireless application protocol)-based communication, works on a mobile phone and helps to access m-banking service in a more secure way than SMS banking.

Chapter 5
Offline vs. Online Quality Dimension:
The Relationship Between Shopping Mall Quality Dimensions and Customer Loyalty

Cecilia Silvestri
https://orcid.org/0000-0003-2528-601X
University of Tuscia, Italy

Eleonora Rapiti
University of Tuscia, Italy

Michela Piccarozzi
https://orcid.org/0000-0001-9717-9462
University of Tuscia, Italy

ABSTRACT

The study examines the nature and the strength of the relationship between shopping mall attractiveness, in the form of offline and online quality dimensions and customer loyalty. A survey was conducted on consumers of a shopping mall in Viterbo, Italy. In particular, this study aims to meet two objectives: (1) to identify, through factor analysis, offline and online shopping mall quality dimensions and (2) to analyze, through multiple regression models, the relationship between offline and online quality dimensions and customer loyalty. The regression models showed that both offline and online the quality dimensions have positive effect on customer loyalty. More precisely, all quality factors have a positive effect on loyalty, excluding internet browsing. This result contributed to the existing literature in understanding the importance of shopping mall attractiveness to develop customer loyalty.

DOI: 10.4018/978-1-5225-9697-4.ch005

INTRODUCTION

Narahari and Kuvad (2017) defined a shopping mall as "a huge building or group of buildings that contain various stores and other business establishments (or) solely sells various products / brands in retailing mode. If it is a collection of multiple stores, they are connected by walkways so that consumers can easily walk and shop between the stores" (p. 3978). However, in recent years, shopping malls are gaining importance as a place of leisure, becoming an "onestop solution for various needs of the customers—from entertainment to buying daily groceries" (Ammani, 2013, p. 7). In today's consumer culture, the shopping mall can be defined as "center of the Universe" (Feinberg and Meoli, 1991, p. 426) as demonstrated by numbers. In fact, the total shopping center floor space in Europe increased by 2.9% over twelve months to June 2017, reaching 160.8 million square meters. Western Europe currently accounts for 68% of the total built shopping centre space (Cushman & Wakefiled, 2017). According to the International Council of Shopping Centers (ICSC), the shopping malls in the United States grew more than 300% over the last 45 years (Max, 2018).

Shopping Mall and the New Internet Oriented Strategies

Aliagha et al., (2015) suggested that "the implication of competition and increasing number of shopping malls is that customers find it easier with least cost to defect or switch to other malls particularly now most of the shopping centers are offering identical goods and services" (p. 16). In this domain, the implementation of strategies aimed at improving customer loyalty and retaining customers plays a crucial role for the managers of shopping malls. According to Wallace et al., (2004) customer loyalty generates a stable pool of customers for a product or a service of a firm; loyal customers tend to buy more, are willing to pay higher prices and have good opinion about the firm. For this reason, it is more convenient to retain customers than acquire them (Aliagha et al., 2015). Moreover, Keating et al., 2003 argued that loyalty is a key factor to achieve organization success and sustainability over time. According to Hallowell (1996), loyalty also favors positive word-of-mouth (WOM), relevant to generate profits. Since it is important to understand what are the attractiveness quality dimensions for a shopping mall that impact on customer loyalty, several studies have focused on this topic. Moreover, some authors (i.e. Yu et al., 2017) introduced a new dimension that should be analyzed in relation to customer loyalty: the Internet. In particular, Yu et al., 2017 proposed a model to investigate the interrelationship between the constituent factors of Chinese internet shopping mall, purchase satisfaction, customer loyalty and repurchase intention, focusing on the role of the shopping mall website.

However, the relationship between website factors in the internet shopping mall and customer loyalty has not been widely studied, and this research aimed to fill this gap. The study examines the nature and the strength of the relationship between shopping mall attractiveness (the latter classified for dimensions of quality in offline and online services) and customer loyalty, based on a survey conducted on consumers of a shopping mall in Viterbo, Italy. In particular, this study aims to reach two objectives: (1) to identify, through factor analysis, the offline and online shopping malls dimensions of quality (2) to analyze, through multiple regression models, the relationships between offline and online dimensions of quality and customer loyalty. Then, the methodology used will be outlined and the results will follow.

BACKGROUND

Quality Dimensions *Offline* of the Mall

In the last twenty years (1998-2018), several authors tried to explore the quality dimensions in order to understand how these can affect: (1) Customer/Shopping Behaviour; (2) Shopping Experience; (3) Customer Loyalty; (4) Shopping Mall Attractiveness; (5) Customer Satisfaction (6) Mall Image. In fact, the study of literature highlighted six main topics of analysis by the authors.

Customer/Shopping Behaviour

Customer/Shopping Behaviour topic is the most studied and the first authors who analyzed the relationship between quality dimensions and Shopping Behaviour was Severin et al. (2001). These authors, in their study conducted in Canada, used random utility theory in order to compare models of shopping center choice based on nine perceived quality attributes: (1) Convenience; (2) Atmosphere; (3) Functionality; (4) Product/Service Quality; (5) Structure/ Layout; (6) Parking Facility/Security; (7) Price & Promotion; (8) Product and store variety; (9) Updation. Laroche et al., (2005), instead, compared English and French-Canadian consumers' shopping mall decision process. They proved that: (1) consumers' evaluations of service quality in a shopping environment mediate their pleasure and purchase intention and (2) consumer mall shopping decision is invariant across English and French-Canadian consumers. Parsons (2003), studied how sales drivers and visit drivers can be combined together in order to obtain combinations that would be effective in generating the optimum customer behaviour. In particular, the authors identified three quality dimensions: (1) Aesthetics; (2) Recreation; (3) Merchandise Variety that can affect customer behaviour. Michon et al., (2005), instead, focused only on the mall atmosphere and environment, highlighting how these macro quality dimensions interact with the customer behaviour. Also, Massicotte et al., (2011) and Chebat et al., (2014) studied the role of mall atmosphere dimension on customer behavior. In particular, Massicotte et al., (2011) found that the mall atmosphere positively affects functional congruity for both adults and teenage shoppers; a few years later Chebat et al., (2014) investigated the consumers psychological processes that trigger changes in the spending behaviour in the renovated mall, exploring the effects of mall renovation (or mall atmosphere) on the shoppers spending.

Mall atmosphere represents a crucial macro quality dimensions and Cai and Shannon (2012) tested a theory developed in the West in a non-Western country (i.e. China). It showed how "consumers who have a favorable attitude towards malls are more likely to visit the mall frequently and spent more money during their Mall visit" (p.305). Also Ahmed et al., (2007) studied the international consumer behavior in shopping malls in a non-Western country, as Malaysia, and the macro quality dimensions analyzed are: (1) Aesthetics (2) Recreation (3) Convenience (4) Social interaction. Aesthetics dimension is also studied by Rajagopal (2011) and Khare (2011, 2012). In his study, Rajagopal (2011) explored the influence of a quality dimension of malls, as aesthetics, on customer behavior, analyzing retailing patterns and establishing customer-centric strategies. Khare (2011, 2012), instead, developed his study in India and suggested that Mall attributes such as "décor, layout, services, variety of stores, and entertainment facilities, must be considered while planning malls in smaller cities as they have an effect on consumer buying behaviour" (Khare, 2011, p. 110). Ammani (2013) as well conducted his study in Hyderabad (India), analyzing the preferences of the young, and the factors that drove them to visit shopping malls. In particular, the author found out that (1) Quality Environment, (2) Convenience, (3) Place for celebrations, are the factors the young considered as important.

According to Narahari and Kuvad (2017) shopping Malls are the best locations to socialize, to hang out, especially for younger generations, to spend quality time with their family, to dine out, even more than actually shopping. Through their study conducted in Bhavnagar, Gujarat (India), the authors proved how shopping in malls has become a major leisure activity. According to Rousseau and Venter (2014), mature shoppers, compared to young consumers, are wiser, more experienced and have plenty of time to observe the products as well as to gather information before making decisions. Also mature shoppers look for social and leisure experiences. The study of shopping Malls as recreational and socializing place had already been analyzed by Rajagopal (2008) who demonstrated that "shopping malls attract buyers and sellers, and induce customers providing enough time to make choices as well as a recreational means of shopping" (p. 1). According to Yiu and Yau (2006) and Yiu and Xu (2012), the quality dimension that affects costumer behaviour on shopping mall is the tenant's space allocation. Reimers and Clulow (2009) suggested that time convenience has a salient influence on consumers' patronage behaviour, while Farrag et al (2010) developed a model of shopper experiences at the Mall in Egypt. They identified seven main shopping motives: three functional motives—safety, bargain hunting, and convenience—and four hedonic motives—entertainment, freedom, appreciation of modernity, and self-identity. Finally, Dilek and Top (2013) conducted their study in Turkey focusing on mall parking management and Katrodia et al., (2018) developed the research in the seven shopping malls of Durban, South Africa. They focused on the determinants which influence the shopping behaviour, showing how factors such as services, accessibility, and sales dynamics have a significant influence on the consumer buying behaviour.

Shopping Experience

The shopping experience theme is the second more studied topic over the last twenty years. According to Castaldo and Botti (1999), the shopping experience derives from the combined effect of several factors. Among them, there are primarily the psychological and socio-demographic elements, which determine the individual's inclination towards recreational shopping. This is not enough, however, to outline the person involved in the experiential shopping, strongly influenced also by the benefits sought. The same person, in fact, can find in shopping different replies to his emotional and/or functional needs, at different times and towards different product categories. Secondly, the stimuli factors must be considered; they come from the environment where the buyer acts. For this reason, he is particularly sensitive and receptive towards them. The shopping experience, that is buying commercial services and goods, is determined by the joint effect, inside the shop, of sensory stimuli - aimed to give an emotional response - on the individual showing a hedonistic attitude towards shopping, for his characteristics and the advantages he is searching (Castaldo & Botti, 1999). Kim et al., (2005) focused on mature consumers (55 years old or over). He developed a structural model proving that "mall can be a place to reduce older consumers' loneliness and that retailers in the mall can attract and make older consumers spend more by emphasizing value consumption and service consumption" (p. 995). Whereas Jackson et al., (2011) suggested that "shopping value is a two-dimensional concept that captures the hedonic and utilitarian benefits derived from a consumer visit to a retail store" (p.1); extending this concept to the context of a shopping mall, the authors analyzed the perception of the mall attributes and the shopping value distinguishing by gender and generational cohort.

According to Anuradha and Manohar (2011), consumers visit the Malls for social and entertainment purposes, while Singh and Sahay (2012) and Singh and Prashar (2014) suggested that shoppers visualize the shopping experience as a combination of more quality dimensions: ambience, physical infrastructure, marketing focus, convenience, safety and security. According to El Hedhli et al. (2013), shopping in a mall may contribute to life satisfaction through four key life domains: (1) Consumer Life, (2) Social Life, (3) Leisure Life, and (4) Community Life. A shopping mall can contribute significantly to consumer well-being by providing shoppers with an assortment of stores that carry many needed goods and services, or allow them to gather with other people, such as friends and relatives, to interact and socialize. At the same time, a shopping mall can contribute significantly to leisure well-being by providing shoppers with an entertainment venue.

Many shopping malls host implicit and explicit entertainment programs. Implicit entertainment may occur in the form of browsing through the mall and stores within. Explicit entertainment occurs, for example, when shoppers go to a movie theatre inside the mall or go to a video arcade. Finally, a shopping mall can contribute significantly to community well-being by providing a meeting place for community residents to assemble, socialize, and experience a sense of community. Enhancing well-being in the consumer, social, leisure, and community life domains helps to increase overall life satisfaction (El Hedhli et al. 2013). Tsai (2010) proposed the 'Holistic Entertainment Experience for Wooing Shoppers' model, empirically testing his hypotheses with a cross-regional survey; Chang (2013) developed a new technique using a combination of SEM and MEC proving that the atmosphere, the environment and the facilities, influences the shopping experience. Keng (2007) and Lloyd et al., (2014) as well, in order to analyze the shopping experience, used the SEM model. Keng (2007) used this model in order to explore how the counter service impacts the customer experiential value and subsequently customer behavioral intentions in a shopping mall context, in Taiwan. Lloyd et al., (2014), demonstrated that "for shoppers who place high economic value on time, the effects of service convenience are greater on hedonic value. Conversely, those who place low economic value on time, effects of service convenience are greater on utilitarian value" (p.36). Tandon et al. (2016) conducted the study in four metro cities of India: New Delhi, Kolkata, Chennai and Mumbai, and analyzed how the dimension of Mall attractiveness can affect shoppers' mall experience.

Customer Loyalty, Shopping Mall Attractiveness and Customer Satisfaction

Customer loyalty in shopping mall is in-depth analyzed in the literature of the twenty years from 1998 to -2018. Hedhli and Chebat (2009) proposed the concept of the shopper-based mall equity (SBME); Chebat et al., (2009), based on this new retailing concept, tested a conceptual model designed to explain the psychological processes related to mall loyalty. Rabbanee et al., (2012) focused on the relationship between store loyalty and shopping mall loyalty showing "that store loyalty influences shopping mall loyalty under certain conditions and that such an influence is moderated by the geographic distance between the consumer and the shopping mall" (p. 271). Ahmad (2012) and Aliagha et al., (2015) investigated the nature and the strength of the relationship between shopping mall attractiveness and customer loyalty, the first author developing the study in Saudi shopping mall centers while Aliagha et al., (2015) examining this relationship in Sungai Petani, Kedah, Malaysia. Both of them, basing on the attributes of shopping mall attractiveness, tried to identify those models that best explain customer loyalty. Haj-Salem et al. (2016), testing the literature-based model in two North American shopping malls, studied which factors drive Mall loyalty of male and female shoppers, proving how the atmosphere affects Mall loyalty and the shoppers' identification with the Mall. According to Prashar et al., (2017), "convenience" is the most influencing factor in selecting Malls and customer loyalty for Indian mall shoppers. Jenifer (2016) studied the customer orientation as a drive able to create superior customer value that results in an enhanced customer satisfaction and strong brand loyalty. He developed his research in the shopping malls of South Chennai (India).

Finally, Kursunluoglu (2011) conducted his study in shopping centers in Izmir City (Turkey) and examined the customer service effects on customer satisfaction and customer loyalty. Khare and Rakesh (2010) focused on customer satisfaction and found that three attributes of Malls (mall management, entertainment facilities and quality service) have relevant effects on the shopper's preferences and their satisfaction. In particular, according to the authors, the shopping malls should convey the image of providing parking facilities, easy accessibility, elevators, clean spaces with wide space for walking, spacious dining areas and recreational facilities, since these quality dimensions can generate more consumer bustling. Also Hui et al. (2013) analyzed customer satisfaction and carried out a five-year longitudinal survey in five selected shopping malls in Hong Kong. The authors assert "that management and maintenance of communal facilities is the most crucial dimension, with regard to the overall customer satisfaction; the condition of a washroom is another important dimension for customer satisfaction; communication efficiency and efficacious promotion events are also important for maintaining customer satisfaction" (p. 194).

Mall Image

Dubihlela & Dubihlela (2014), instead, conducted their research in Gauteng South in South African. The study revealed interesting findings regarding the creation of the mall image and the interrelationship between its diverse dimensions. In particular, (1) Merchandising, (2) Atmosphere, (3) Accessibility, (4) Entertainment, and (5) In-mall Convenience are the five major features that affect customers satisfaction of South African market. The creation of the mall image topic is thoroughly examined by Chebat et al. (2010) and Gudonaviciene and Alijosiene, (2013). In particular, Chebat et al. (2010) suggested that "one way to generate more traffic in a mall is to build a strong mall image perceived by shoppers as delivering a unique bundle of benefits"(p.735). He identified five major dimensions that contribute to building up a strong mall image: (1) Access, (2) Store Atmosphere, (3) Price and Promotion, (4) Cross-category Assortment, and (5) Within-category Assortment. Gudonaviciene & Alijosiene, (2013) studied the attributes of the main image which determine shopping mall selection in Lithuania and developed suggestions of which attributes of the shopping mall image should be emphasized in promotional campaigns and how to improve the perceptions of the overall mall image in shopping mall patrons.

Other authors from Turkey (i.e. Wakefield & Baker, 1998; Erkip, 2005; Ismail El-Adly, 2007; Debek, 2015; Mittal & Jhamb, 2016; Said et al., 2016) studied the shopping mall attractiveness. In particular, Wakefield and Baker (1998) examined the relationship between three factors - tenant variety, Mall environment and shopping involvement - on shoppers' excitement and desire to stay in the Mall. Out-

Table 1. Offline Quality Dimensions of Shopping Mall (1998-2018)

Authors	Topic	Offline Quality Dimensions of Shopping Mall
Katrodia *et al.* (2018)	Customer/Shopping Behaviour	(1) Social Factor, (2) Cultural Factor, (3) Psychological Factor
Narahari and Kuvad (2017)	Customer/Shopping Behaviour	(1) Ambience (2) Air Conditioning (3) Safety and Security (4) Parking Facility/Security (5) Cleanliness/ Hygiene (6) Toilet Facilities (7) Personal / Friendly staff
Prashar *et al.* (2017)	Customer Loyalty	(1) Convenience to Shoppers (2) Safety & Security (3) Ambience (4) Physical Infrastructure (5) Marketing Focus
Jenifer (2016)	Customer Loyalty	(1) Convenience (2) Product/Service Quality (4) Price & Promotion (5) Product and Store Variety
Haj-Salem *et al.* (2016)	Customer Loyalty	(1) Employees (2) Service Quality (3) Physical Layout (4) Atmosphere (5) Product Quality (6) Price
Mittal & Jhamb (2016)	Shopping Mall Attractiveness	(1) Merchandising (2) Variety & Selection (3) Milieu & Facilities, (4) Convenience
Said *et al.* (2016)	Shopping Mall Attractiveness	(1) Location of Mall (2) Facilities and Services (3) Aesthetics and Design (4) Quality of Structures
Tandon *et al.* (2016)	Shopping experience	(1) Atmospherics (2) Entertainment (3) Tenant Management (4) Facilities Management
Aliagha *et al.* (2015)	Customer Loyalty	(1) Physical Elements, (2) Quality Service, (3) Quality Building Facilities, (4) Entertainment, (5) Price and Variety, (6) Accessibility
Debek (2015)	Shopping Mall Attractiveness	(1) Aesthetics (2) Atmosphere (3) Commerce (4) Convenience (5) Layout (6) Leisure (7) Safety (8) Social Positioning
Chebat *et al.* (2014)	Customer/Shopping Behaviour	(1) Mall Atmosphere (2) Utilitarian Value (3) Hedonic Value
Dubihlela & Dubihlela (2014)	Customer Satisfaction	(1) Merchandising (2) Atmosphere (3) Accessibility (4) Entertainment (5) In-mall Convenience
Lloyd *et al.* (2014)	Shopping experience	(1) Service Convenience (2) Hedonic Value (3) Utilitarian Value (4) Desire to Stay (5) Economic Value of Time
Rousseau & Venter (2014)	Customer/Shopping Behaviour	(1) Personal Factors (2) Emotional Factors (3) Mall Environment (4) Situational Factors
Singh & Prashar (2014)	Shopping experience	(1) Ambience (2) Convenience to Shoppers (3) Marketing Focus (3) Safety&Security (4) Physical Infrastructure
Ammani (2013)	Customer/Shopping Behaviour	(1) Convenience, (2) Quality Environment (3) Ambience (4) Value for Money (5) Celebrations (6) Parking Facility
Chang (2013)	Shopping experience	(1) Required Services (2) Subsidiary Services (3) Facilitates (4) Attractiveness of Merchandise (5) Price & Promotion (6) Convenience (7) Display & Arrangement (8) Location
Dilek & Top, (2013)	Customer/Shopping Behaviour	(1) Parking
El Hedhli *et al.* (2013)	Shopping experience	(1) Functionality, (2) Convenience, (3) Safety, (4) Leisure, (5) Atmospherics
Gudonaviciene & Alijosiene (2013)	Mall image	(1) Merchandising (2) Accessibility (3) Entertainment (4) Atmosphere
Hui *et al.* (2013)	Customer satisfaction	(1) Safety and Security (2) Price & Promotion (3) Cleanliness/Hygiene
Ahmad (2012)	Customer Loyalty	(1) Aesthetic (2) Convenience and Sccessibility (3) Product variety (4) Entertainment (5) Service quality
Cai & Shannon (2012)	Customer/Shopping Behaviour	(1) Price (2) Merchandise Quality (3) Return Policy (4) Fast Checking (5) Atmosphere (6) Security (7) Cleanness
Khare (2012)	Customer/Shopping Behaviour	(1) Store Relationship Commitment (2) Perceived Value of Store (3) Distance
Rabbanee *et al.* (2012)	Customer Loyalty	(1) Ambience (2) Design (3) Interiors (4) Service (5) Assortment (6) Socializing
Singh & Sahay (2012)	Shopping experience	(1) Ambience (2) Physical infrastructure (3) Marketing focus (4) Convenience (5) Safety & Security
Yiu & Xu (2012)	Customer/Shopping Behaviour	(1) Tenant Space Allocation
Anuradha & Manohar (2011)	Shopping experience	(1) Shopping Ambience (2) Layout of Store (3) Variety of Shops (4) Service Offered at Mall (5) Design

continued on following page

Table 1. Continued

Authors	Topic	Offline Quality Dimensions of Shopping Mall
Massicotte *et al.* (2011)	Customer/Shopping Behaviour	(1) Mall Atmosphere (2) Functional Congruity (3) Self-congruity
Jackson *et al.* (2011)	Shopping experience	(1) Convenience (2) Safety and Security (3)Physical Infrastructure/Facilities (4)Atmosphere (5) Structure/ Layout (6) Event/Entertainment (7) Parking Facility/Security (8) Cleanliness/ Hygiene (9) Personal / Friendly Staff (10) Distance to Home/to Work (11) Accessibility (12) Mall Hours (13) Design & Architecture
Khare (2011)	Customer/Shopping Behaviour	(1) Aesthetics (2) Escape (3) Flow (4) Exploration (5) Role enactment (6) Social (7) Convenience
Kursunluoglu (2011)	Customer Loyalty	(1) Product/Service Quality
Rajagopal, (2011)	Customer/Shopping Behaviour	(1) Aesthetics (2) Recreation (3) Marketing Communications (4) Hedonic Pleasure (5) Convenient Location
Chebat *et al.* (2010)	Mall image	(1) Access (2) Store Atmosphere (3) Price/Promotion (4) Cross-Category Assortment (5) Within Category Assortment
Farrag *et al.* (2010)	Customer/Shopping Behaviour	(1) Appreciation of Modernity (2) Freedom (3) Self-Identity (4) Entertainment (5) Bargain Hunting (6) Convenience (7) Safety
Khare & Rekesh, (2010)	Customer satisfaction	(1) Entertainment Facilities/Services (2) Ambience (3) Mall Management
Tsai (2010)	Shopping experience	(1) Variety and Prestige of Retailers (2) Aesthetics (3) Physical Infrastructure and Layout (4) Recreation/ Entertainment (5) Displays and Signage (6) Mall Image (7) Special Events
Chebat *et al.* (2009)	Customer Loyalty	(1) Convenience (2) Environment (3) Product Quality (4) Services Quality
Reimers and Clulow (2009)	Customer/Shopping Behaviour	(1) Spatial Convenience (2) Temporal Convenience (3) Car Convenience (4) Hedonic Attributes (5) Shopping Services
Rajagopal, (2008)	Customer/Shopping Behaviour	(1) Sales Promotion (2) Market Ambiance (3) Leisure Shopping (4) Recreational Services
Ahmed *et al.* (2007)	Customer/Shopping Behaviour	(1) Aesthetics (2) Recreation (3) Convenience (4) Social interaction
Ismail El-Adly (2007)	Shopping Mall Attractiveness	(1) Comfort, (2) Entertainment, (3) Diversity (4) Mall Essence, (5) Convenience (6) Luxury
Keng *et al.* (2007)	Shopping experience	(1) Aesthetics (2) Physical Infrastructure and layout (3) Convenience (4) Safety & security (5) Merchandise variety (6) Employee (7) Parking (8) Social interaction (9) Hedonic pleasure (10) Traffic management (11) Billing (12) Convenient Location
Yiu & Yau. (2006)	Customer/Shopping Behaviour	(1) Tenant Space Allocation
Erkip (2005)	Shopping Mall Attractiveness	(1) Leisure (2) New Experience (3) Retail Environment (4) Security (5) Accessibility (6) Socializing (7) Social environment
Laroche *et al.* (2005)	Customer/Shopping Behaviour	(1) Mall Perception (2) Product Perception (3) Arousal (4) Pleasure (5) Service Quality
Kim *et al.* (2005)	Shopping experience	Mall-shopping motivation: (1) Service Consumption, (2) Value Consumption (3) Eating Experiential mall-shopping motivation: (1) Diversion (2) Aesthetic
Michon *et al.* (2005)	Customer/Shopping Behaviour	(1) Mall Atmospherics/Mall Environment
Parsons (2003)	Customer/Shopping Behaviour	(1) Aesthetics (2) Recreation (3) Merchandise Variety
Severin *et al.* (2001)	Customer/Shopping Behaviour	(1) Convenience (2) Atmosphere (3) Functionality (4) Product/Service Quality (5) Structure/ Layout (6) Parking Facility/Security (7) Price & Promotion (8) Product and Store Variety (9) Updating
Castaldo & Botti, (1999)	Shopping experience	(1) Layout (2) Variety of Store (3) Services (4) Interactions with Product and People
Wakefield & Baker (1998)	Shopping Mall Attractiveness	(1) Ambient Factors (2) Design Factors (3) Layout (4) Variety

Source: Our elaborations

lining the results, the authors also discussed the contribution of individual environmental factors to the excitement and desire to stay in the Mall. In his study the Ambient Factors, appear the most important factors. Erkip (2005) conducted the study in the shopping mall in Ankara (Turkey) and identified in (1) Leisure (2) New experience (3) Retail environment (4) Security (5) Accessibility (6) Socializing (7) Social environment, the most important attractiveness factors for the shopping mall.

El-Adly (2007) examined the attractiveness factors of UAE shopping malls from the shoppers' perspective, segmenting shoppers according to these factors. The results revealed six Mall attractiveness factors from the shoppers' perspective (Table 1). Debek (2015) as well investigated the drivers of shopping mall attractiveness. After surveying 384 Polish adult, he found out that shopping mall attractiveness was mainly driven by its atmosphere and social positioning. Said et al., (2016), examined instead the architectural factors attracting customers to shop in the Malaysian shopping malls. The results showed differences in the customers' ranking of different factors. Moreover, the authors suggested the best positions to locate shopping malls, the facilities to provide thehigh quality materials and nice aesthetics beautification to use for a mall. Finally, Mittal & Jhamb (2016) identified the main attributes that lead to shoppers' patronage in an Indian shopping mall, literature review on this topic. The authors identified dimensions that can be considered as determinants for shopping mall attractiveness: (1) merchandising (2) variety & selection (3) milieu & facilities, and (4) convenience. The results showed a fair degree of convergence between the preferences of shoppers in India and shoppers in other parts of the world, when referring to shopping mall evaluation criteria.

Table 1 shows the quality dimensions offline of shopping mall identified by authors in the last twenty years (1998-2018).

Online Website Quality Dimensions

In the last twenty years (1998-2018), several authors tried to explore the quality dimensions of websites in different contexts such as e-commerce, cellular phone service, tourism and shopping mall. In particular, the effect of quality dimension of web sites on (1) Purchase Intention, (2) Customer Satisfaction and (3) Customer Loyalty have been studied. Spiteri (2000) focused on electronic commerce (e-commerce) sites, stating that their success depends on a number of factors, such as the quality, variety and price of their products, their guarantees, return policies, etc. In particular, he took into consideration the following quality dimensions (1) Information quality (2) Security/Privacy. Lin and Lu (2000) have also focused on e-commerce and have investigated why users accept or reject a web site and how the user's acceptance is affected by: (1) Information quality (2) Access Speed (3) Functionality of the web Site. The results highlighted that the response time is an important quality dimension that affects the user's opinions of the web site.

Liu and Arnett (2000), in order to assess the factors associated with the web site success, in the e-commerce context, have identified four crucial factors: (1) Information and Service Quality, (2) System Use, (3) Playfulness, and (4) System Design quality. Ivory et al. (2001) focused their attention only on layout quality dimension. The results provide an empirical foundation for web site design guidelines. Instead, Cox and Dale (2002) focused to identify the key quality factors in web site design and use. They have developed a conceptual model to assess how a web site can deliver what its users expect. The model is based on: (1) Ease of Use, (2) Customer Confidence, (3) On-line Resources, and (4) Relationship Services.

Van Iwaarden et al. (2003) identified the most important quality factors perceived, when using web sites, through a questionnaire based on the SERVQUAL instrument (Parasuraman et al., 1985, 1988) that evaluated five quality dimensions. The results indicate that the quality dimensions identified are (1) Security/Privacy (2) Internet Browsing (3) Layout (4) Responsiveness (5) Reliability. Song and Zinkhan (2003) also employed the SERVQUAL model to develop their conceptual framework. They examined three issues: antecedents of web site quality, dimensions of this quality judgment, and consequence of web site quality. Moreover, they employed the Technology Acceptance Model (TAM) (Davis 1989, Davis et al. 1989). Both models are popular in the marketing and MIS literatures. They created an overall conceptual model in order to summarize the key relationships. Instead, Cao et al. (2005) proposed to identify what determines the web site quality or what makes a web site effective. They used an IS success model - based on the following quality dimensions: system quality, information quality, service quality, and attractiveness) together with SERVQUAL and TAM. A set of reliable instruments for web site quality has then been developed and empirically validated. Aquilani et al. (2015) compared the traditional service quality dimensions (SERVQUAL scale) with e-service Quality Dimension (e-SQ dimension) and described a framework of overall customer satisfaction developed from B2C markets. The authors adopted the IS Success Model (DeLone & McLean, 1992), which distinguishes between informational and system features. They discussed the offline literature separating the relationship between customer satisfaction (CS), customer relationship management (CRM), the concept of CS, its measurement tools and methodologies. They examined the literature on the relationship between e-CS and e-CRM, the concept of e-CS, its drivers and effects and the tools used over the years to measure it. The website quality dimensions are divided into three level: information level, system level and service level. The information level includes: (1) Accuracy, (2) Usefulness, (3) Completeness, (4) Relevance, (5) Timeliness, (6) Security of transaction. The system level includes: (1) Accessibility, (2) Usability, (3) Navigation, (4) Interactivity, (5) Design. The service level includes: (1) Delivery processes, (2) Perceived control, (3) Responsiveness, (4) Reliability/Trust.

Santouridis et al. (2012) examined the applicability of the electronic service quality measurement instrument (E-S-QUAL) and its factor structure in the context of e-commerce in Greece. Moreover, they investigated the effects of E-S-QUAL factors on customer perceived overall quality, value and loyalty. E-S-QUAL includes four dimensions: (1) Efficiency, (2) Fulfillment, (3) System availability, (4) Privacy (Parasuraman et al., 2005). They replicated the work of the E-S-QUAL model developers. The results confirmed the four factor structure of E-S-QUAL in the context of e-commerce in Greece. Efficiency is the principal quality dimension and it has a significantly positive effect on all three dependent variables, namely perceived overall quality, value and loyalty. Instead, privacy has a positive significant effect on both perceived overall quality and value, but not on loyalty.

Kim et al. (2003) proposed web site evaluation criteria for firms engaged in e-commerce and applied these criteria to different industry groups within Korea. They have evaluated web sites in 12 industries to determine any differences in the design. The results showed significant differences in the design of web sites across these different industry groups. Signore (2005) wanted to define a quality model and a set of characteristics relating to internal and external quality factors, to identify potential problems. He mainly described external requirements, specifying how they can be related to the internal characteristics: (1) Correctness, (2) Presentation (Layout, Text, Multimedia, Links, Forms), (3) Content, (4) Navigation, (5) Interaction, (6) Additional Consideration. He proposed a quality model which can be used as a framework of reference to evaluate existing sites and fix errors. Instead, Kamesh et al. (2018)

identified five quality dimensions: (1) Aesthetics (2) Ease of use (3) Multimedia (4) Rich Content (5) Reputation. The results have offered the framework that can be used for calculating the quality of any web sites. Finally, Faraoni et al. (2018) investigated the micro-linkages fostering consumer e-loyalty in the context of grocery retailers B2C e-commerce. Specifically, they focused on the role of (1) security, (2) privacy and (3) website design. The main results were related to the importance of website characteristics as antecedents of e-loyalty in online grocery retailing.

Moustakis et al. (2004) presented a hierarchical framework, which supports website quality assessment. Website quality was explained by five main criteria: (1) Content, (2) Navigation, (3) Structure and design, (4) Appearance and multimedia, (5) Uniqueness. Each criterion contained some sub-criteria. They conducted an experiment in order to validate the framework. The websites of three cellular phone service providers in Greece were assessed of the. The results confirmed the framework validity. The statistical factor analysis supported the reduction of the original model to a website quality scoring framework, which involves nine composite criteria.

Park and Gretzel (2007) studied and presented a qualitative meta-analysis methodology in the context of "destination marketing organizations" (p.4). Specifically, a unified framework of commonly used web site success factors emerged from the analysis and included nine factors: 1) Information Quality; 2) Ease of Use; 3) Responsiveness; 4) Security/Privacy; 5) Visual Appearance; 6) Trust; 7) Interactivity; 8) Personalization; 9) Fulfillment. Similarly, Singh et al. (2016) focused their study on the context of market tourism in India. They developed a research model to understand the relationship between e-service quality dimensions and overall service quality perceptions related to these sites. This model identified six quality dimensions: (1) Convenience, (2) Understanding the customer, (3) Security, (4) Reliability, (5) Credibility, (6) Responsiveness. They suggested that, in order to enhance the overall service quality, the online reservation sites should point up on responsiveness and reliability to attract and retain customers.

Instead, Razak et al. (2016) examined the relationship between web site quality and repurchase intention. They believed that the website quality has an impact on repurchase intention in the context of travel agencies in Malaysia. The analyzed dimensions of web site quality are divided as follows: (1) System quality, (2) Information quality, (3) Service quality, (4) Security quality. This study supported the contentions forwarded by the Technology Acceptance Model (TAM) and the Social Capital Theory (SCT) as well as S-D Logic Theory. A conclusion was that the socio economics variables, traditionally considered as important, were not discriminating. Laureti et al. (2017) studied the real role of historical satisfaction (HSat), i.e., satisfaction only deriving from past experiences, excluding the most recent ones in B2C service contexts. They focused on a particular travel industry firm which provides travel services and manages the web site where these services are purchased. The results showed that HSat directly affects encounter overall satisfaction with a higher impact (EOS) than its indirect effect through offline service dimensions and web site dimensions. They also observed that offline service dimensions have a direct impact on EOS. Therefore, e-customer satisfaction could be indirectly linked to web site quality dimensions.

Kim and Song (2010) examined the relationships among the quality of WOM, online trust, perceived usefulness, perceived ease of use, and online shopping intention in the online shopping mall. They found that the quality of WOM has positive effects on online trust, and the latter has positive effects on perceived usefulness, shopping intention and perceived ease of use. Moreover, the results demonstrated that perceived ease of use and perceived usefulness have positive effects on shopping intention. Ha and

Table 2. Online Quality Dimensions of Web site (1998-2018)

Authors	Online Quality Dimension	Context
Faraoni *et al.* (2018)	(1) Security/Privacy	E-commerce (Grocery retailers)
Kamesh *et al.* (2018)	(1) Information Quality (2) Easiness (3) Layout (4) Reputation	E-commerce
Laureti *et al.* (2017)	(1) Information Quality (2) System quality (3) Service quality	Tourism (Travel industry)
Yu *et al.* (2017)	(1) Information Quality (2) Security/Privacy (3) Easiness (4) Layout (5) Service Quality (6) Convenience	Shopping mall
Razak *et al.* (2016)	(1) Information Quality (2) Security/Privacy (3) System quality (4) Service quality	Tourism (Travel agency)
Singh *et al.* (2016)	(1) Updating (2) Information Quality (3) Easiness (4) Internet Browsing (5) Layout (6) Level of Interactivity (7) Usefulness	Tourism
Aquilani *et al.* (2015)	(1) Information Quality (2) System Quality (3) Service Quality	E-commerce
Kwon *et al.* (2013)	(1) Updating (2) Easiness (3) Level of Interactivity (4) Accuracy	Shopping mall
Ha & Im (2012)	(1) Information Quality (2) Layout	E-commerce
Santouridis *et al.* (2012)	(1) Security/Privacy (2) System Quality (3) Service Quality (4) Functionality	E-commerce
Kim & Song (2010)	(1) Easiness (2) Usefulness	Shopping mall
Park & Greztel (2007)	(1) Information Quality (2) Security/Privacy (3) Easiness (4) Internet Browsing (5) Layout (6) Level of Interactivity (7) Service Quality (8) Access Speed (9) Reputation (10) Responsiveness (11) Reliability	Tourism (Destination marketing organization)
Cao *et al.* (2005)	(1) Information Quality (2) Easiness (3) Layout (4) Usefulness (5) System Quality (6) Service Quality	E-commerce
Signore (2005)	(1) Information Quality (2) Internet Browsing (3) Layout (4) Accuracy	E-commerce
Moustakis *et al.* (2004)	(1) Information Quality (2) Easiness (3) Internet Browsing (4) Layout (5) Convenience (6) Access Speed (7) Uniqueness	Cellular phone service
Kim *et al.* (2003)	(1) Internet Browsing (2) Layout (3) System Quality (4) Reliability	E-commerce
Song & Zinkhan (2003)	(1) Information Quality (2) Security/Privacy (3) Layout (4) Level of Interactivity (5) Usefulness (6) System Quality (7) Service Quality (8) Reliability	E-commerce
Van Iwaarden *et al.* (2003)	(1) Security/Privacy (2) Internet Browsing (3) Layout (4) Responsiveness (5) Reliability	E-commerce
Cox & Dale (2002)	(1) Easiness	E-commerce
Ivory *et al.* (2001)	(1) Layout	E-commerce
Liu & Arnett (2000)	(1) Information Quality (2) Security/Privacy (3) Easiness (4) Internet Browsing (5) Level of Interactivity (6) Usefulness (7) System Quality (8) Service Quality (9) Accuracy	E-commerce
Lin & Lu (2000)	(1) Information Quality (2) Access Speed (3) Functionality	E-commerce
Spiteri, L. F. (2000)	(1) Information Quality (2) Security/Privacy	E-commerce

Source: Our elaboration

Im (2012) studied WOM communication. They examined a comprehensive model explaining how web site design influences the consumer's emotional and cognitive responses and contributes to satisfaction and WOM communication in an online shopping context. The following measures were used: (1) Quality of web site design, (2) Pleasure and arousal, (3) Perceived quality of information, (4) Satisfaction, (5) WOM intention, (6) Demographic information. They focused their research on a total of 804 female college students. The results showed that web site design quality had positive direct effects on pleasure, arousal, and perceived information quality and indirect effects on satisfaction and WOM intention. Moreover, satisfaction mediated the relationship between emotional and cognitive responses and positive WOM intention. Instead, Kwon et al. (2013) mainly focused on the system quality factors of the targeted shopping mall web site in China and Korea, surveying undergraduate students. They classified six system quality dimensions: (1) Quick Transition of the Image and Page, (2) Accuracy, (3) Ease of Use, (4) Reliability, (5) Access Speed, (6) Short Cut Function. Subsequently, they formulated hypotheses about how those six factors are different, developing an empirical study to verify those hypotheses. The results showed that the shopping mall web sites of two countries are different in terms of quick transition of the web pages or images, ease of use, reliability, and accessibility, while there was no difference in terms of accuracy and short cut function. Finally, they analyzed the causes of the research results and suggested a strategy implementing the effective shopping mall web sites.

Yu et al. (2017) focused on the context of internet shopping mall in order to investigate the relationship between the constituent factors of Chinese internet shopping mall, purchase satisfaction, customer loyalty and repurchase intention. The subjects of their study were Chinese female college students. The results revealed five evaluation dimensions that include (1) general service factor, (2) information providing factor, (3) system factor, and (4) visual factor of design. Regarding the information provider factor: convenience, information providing ability, ease of product search and service quality were the most significant. Moreover, the ease of retrieving products was found to be the most influential factor in purchase satisfaction of internet shopping mall. Regarding the visual factor of design, the type, the graphic, the color, the multimedia, the layout and the product assortment affected the purchase satisfaction. Another important result is that purchase satisfaction has a strong relationship with customer loyalty and repurchases intention. In addition, customer loyalty is strongly related to repurchase intention. In practice, these results showed that the consumer purchase satisfaction is an important factor for the development of firms and that purchase satisfaction has a strong influence on brand loyalty and repurchase intention. Table 2 shows the Quality Dimensions Online of web site from 1998 to 2018.

Customer Loyalty

According to Oliver (1997, p. 392), customer loyalty can be defined as a "deeply held commitment to rebuy or re-patronize a preferred product or service consistently in the future, thereby causing repetitive same-brand or same brand-set purchasing, despite situational influences and marketing efforts having the potential to cause switching behavior". George and Stavros (2013) suggested that customer loyalty can be considered as a key determinant of customer retention and according to Reichheld and Sasser (1990) firms that want to achieve superior performance and gain long-term profitability should focus on customer loyalty. Nyadzayo and Khajehzadeh (2016) confirmed that customer loyalty "helps firms to lower marketing costs, solicit more customers, effectively increase market share and are willing to pay premium prices (p. 263)".

Pearson (1996) and Lee et al. (2001) defined customer loyalty as the mindset of the customers who hold favorable attitudes toward a firm, commit to repurchase the company's product/service and spread word-of-mouth recommendation to others. Therefore, several scholars, as i.e. Rasheed and Abadi (2014), have identified customer loyalty as a primary driver to organizational success. Lam and Burton (2006), Wills (2009), and Yap et al. (2012), in their study, claimed that loyal customers significantly contribute to market share growth. Bennet and Rundle-Thiele (2002) suggested that loyalty can be define as a psychological process and composed by two dimensions: behavioral and attitudinal. Dick and Basu, (1994) defined "behavioral dimension" as a propensity of customers to repurchase and it can actually drive customers to repurchase products and services. The "Attitudinal dimension", according to Parasuraman, et al., (1991) refers to parameters such as repurchasing, resistance to buy from other firms, WOM recommendation to others to use a specific product or service of a company. According to e.g. Day (1969) and Jacoby (1971) the "composite loyalty" is the third component of loyalty. Loyalty produces many benefits. Reichheld and Sasser (1990) demonstrated that the improvement of customer loyalty has increased profits; it reduced the costs to acquire new customers and decreased the costs to serve current customers.

However, according to Moliner et al. (2007) and Abdul-Rahman and Kamarulzaman (2012) "relationship quality is an emerging mega-construct in marketing literature and has become a strategic imperative since good relationship is associated with loyalty creation, close collaboration, improved operational planning, security and business flow continuity" (p.608). Several scholars (i.e. Hennig-Thurau et al., 2002, Athanasopoulou, 2009) suggested that loyalty, commitment, and satisfaction are the core dimensions of relationship quality. Szwarc (2005) and Jiang and Zhang (2016) claimed that improved factors quality in the service industry generated improvement of customer satisfaction and loyalty, and in turn leads to increased corporate profits.

Several studies have been developed on the relationship between quality and loyalty. McCain et al. (2005) conducted a gap analysis between loyalty and potential switchers in evaluating casinos service quality attributes. Rauyruen and Miller (2006) analyzed how the relationship quality can influence customer loyalty in the business-to-business context by developing an empirical study. Čater and Čater, (2010) studied how product quality and relationship quality influence the customer commitment along with their combined effect on customer loyalty, so demonstrating how the product quality positively and negatively influences calculative commitment. Rasheed and Abadi (2014) studied the effect of quality dimensions, trust and customer perceived value, on customer loyalty demonstrating how the quality can be considered the antecedent of loyalty. Quach et al. (2016), in their research, investigated the quality dimensions and their effects on customer loyalty, thus contributing to explain the impact of quality on loyalty in high-tech service settings. Jiang and Zhang (2016) investigated the service quality of four major airlines in Chinese domestic market and explored the links between their service quality and customer satisfaction. Furthermore, they explored the relationship between customer satisfaction and customer loyalty as well as the roles of service quality and demographic variables in explaining customer loyalty. Rahman and Ramli, (2016) claimed that "relationship quality has been known as one of the most influential predictors of customer loyalty" (p. 606) and they studied this link in business-to-consumer context. Finally, Nyadzayo and Khajehzadeh (2016) examined the antecedents of customer loyalty in the automotive industry; the results showed that loyalty is influenced by quality factors, customer satisfaction and customer value.

The study of shopping mall attractiveness factors and customer loyalty in shopping mall has been widely illustrated in the previous sections. According to what has been observed it is possible to assume that:

H1: Offline Quality Dimension (OfQD) has a positive effect on Customer Loyalty (CL);
H2: Online Quality Dimension (OnQD) has a positive effect on Customer Loyalty (CL);
H3: Quality Dimensions (OfQD and OnQD) have a positive effect on Costumer Loyalty (CL).

Methodology

The research, developed in December 2018 (one week-end, from Friday, 30 November to Sunday, 2 December 2018), was carried out in the service sector and, more precisely, in a Shopping Centre in Viterbo (central Italy).

Since it was difficult to clearly identify the exact population of the hypermarket, as widely occurs in market research, a sampling scheme of non-probabilistic kind and in particular a sampling of accidental type, was adopted (Bracalente et al., 2009). The sample of respondents is composed of approximately 250 individuals.

To validate the formulated hypotheses (H1, H2, H3) the analyses was divided into two different steps. The first step includes two models: one for the OfQD effect on customer loyalty and one for the OnQD effect on customer loyalty. The two models were structured so as to understand how different quality dimensions, offline and online, separately impact on customer loyalty; afterwards, these results have been compared with the model which includes the effects of both quality dimensions on customer loyalty. The second step is only dedicated to validate H3, concerning the impact of all quality dimensions effect on customer loyalty.

First of all, the empirical analysis was implemented in the factor analysis. To summarize, all the variables, were considered homogeneous, and then multivariate regression models were used. The data collection was carried out inside the Mall, through a questionnaire which was either self-compiled or with direct interview. The whole data collection phase was carried out over the weekend, at different time slots within the days. On one hand this methodology ensures,, a uniform condition degree of the data collection (which instead could not be respected if data were collected over a long period of time) and, on the other hand, different type of customer of the Mall are best represented.

As mentioned above, a questionnaire was the surveying instrument, and was structured in the following three main areas of analysis:

1. Customer profile, containing information on socio-demographic and customer behavior, necessary to identify personal characteristics.
2. Quality dimension, containing questions concerning the size (1) Functionality, (2) Convenience, (3) Safety, (4) Leisure, (5) Atmosphere (6) Online.
3. Customer loyalty to the mall.

The answers to the questions on the customer perception of quality have been structured on the basis of the Likert-type measurement scale, with a score, assigned by the respondents, between 1 and 7, where 7 expresses the maximum positive evaluation (fully satisfied) and 1 the negative evaluation (very little satisfied) (Likert, 1932).

The data were processed through multivariate tool analysis and the different elaborations were performed using the statistical program "STATA Statistics/Data Analysis" (www.stata.com).

The aim of the analysis was to verify the existence of a relationship between quality dimensions (QDOf and QDOn) of the Mall and customer loyalty (CL).

Through the analysis by main components, the dimensionality of the information from variables has been reduced. In market research, especially based on consumer surveys, as in this case, information regarding various characteristics of a product or service, are often collected with ten variables; they

Table 3. Classifications of items and reliability analysis

Dimensions	Items	Items tot	Number of cases	Cronbach's alpha	KMO
OfQD	Structure: variety stores	27	250	0.9556	0.9042
	Structure: assortment of product				
	Structure: quality of product				
	Staff: costumer services				
	Structure: relationship quality/price				
	Distance of the mall from home				
	Adequacy opening time				
	Parking: access				
	Parking: security				
	Parking: capacity				
	Parking: illumination				
	Parking: signage				
	Cleanness shops				
	Cleanness: toilette				
	Cleanness: atrium and corridor of the mall				
	Cleanness: parking				
	Toilet: adequacy spaces				
	Toilet: basic services				
	Toilet: accessories (e.g. changing table)				
	Security: availability				
	Pleasant atmosphere				
	Area restaurants: assortment				
	Events: interesting				
	Events: funny				
	Events: involving				
	Socialization				
	Additional services				
OnQD	Updating	8	250	0.9587	0.9182
	Information quality				
	Easiness				
	Internet browsing				
	Layout				
	Level of interactivity				
	Usefulness				
CL	Overall satisfaction	3	250	0.9036	0.7337
	Intention to WOM				
	Intention to repurchase				

Source: Our elaboration

concern different topics but are conceptually related and overlapping. Some variables sometimes provide information already included in other variables and only partially, provide an original explanatory contribution. That is why the factor analysis is of great help in these cases.

Once the explicative quality variable has been synthesized in macro elements, the regression model has been structured. In structuring the multiple linear regression model, the new six variables (OfQD and OnQD) obtained from the factor analysis are the explanatory variables, while customer loyalty is the dependent variable.

RESULTS

Factor Analysis

To verify whether or not the observed variables contain misleading redundancies or make the results insignificant, the correlation study has been used. The values contained in the correlation matrices in the attached tables (Tables 8-10) show a strong link between the variables under analysis. The factor analysis is generally useful to provide a brief explanation of all the relationships identified through the market investigation. When it is necessary to "condense" and "reduce" the data, in order to lose the least amount of relevant information.

The six items of measurement (1. Functionality; 2. Convenience; 3. Safety; 4. Leisure and Atmosphere; 5. Online; 6. Customer Loyalty). They were classified according to three quality dimensions: (1) Offline Quality Dimensions, (2) Online Quality Dimensions (3) Customer Loyalty.

Once classified, Cronbach α was used to test the internal consistency for all items under respective variables (Namukasa, 2013). Hair at al. (2006) suggested that Cronbach α coefficient over 0.6 was adequate for basic research; therefore, the reliability of each construct was tested by this indicator and the results prove good internal consistency.

Furthermore, the Kaiser-Meyer-Olkin value (KMO) was used to verify the appropriateness of the sample for performing factor analysis, as it exceeds the 0.5 limit (Kaiser, 1974; Hair et al., 2006; Santouridis and Trivellas, 2010). A varimax orthogonal rotation method of Kaiser (1958) was used to rotate the factors. This method works by trying to maximize the high saturations, minimizing the low ones,

Table 4. New variables

Measures	New Variables Code	New Variables
OfflineQuality Dimension	P&S	Parking and Security
	C&H	Cleanliness/Hygiene
	E	Entertainment
	S	Socialization
	C	Convenience
Online Quality Dimension	IQ	Information Quality
	IB	Internet Browsing
Customer Loyalty	CL1	Customer Loyalty

Source: Our elaboration

Table 5. Regression Model1 – Hypothesis H1 – Costumer loyalty (dependent variable), new variables of Offline Quality Dimensions (independent variable)

Variable dependent Customer Loyalty (CL)					
New Variables of Offline Quality Dimensions	**New Variables Code**	**Coef.**	**Std. Err**	**Sig.**	**P>t**
Parking and Security	P&S	0.329	0.054	***	**0.000**
Cleanliness/ Hygiene	C&H	0.294	0.054	***	**0.000**
Entertainment	E	0.387	0.054	***	**0.000**
Socialization	S	0.286	0.054	***	**0.000**
Convenience	C	0.409	0.054	***	**0.000**
	_cons	0.004	0.054	*	0.943
Adj R-squared = 0.5790				Number of Obs = 250	

Source: Our elaboration
Notes: Significant at *90%; **95%; ***99%

Table 6. Regression Model2 – Hypothesis H2 – Costumer loyalty (dependent variable), new variables of Online Quality Dimensions (independent variable)

Variable dependent Customer Loyalty (CL)					
New Variables of Online Quality Dimensions	**New Variables Code**	**Coef.**	**Std. Err**	**Sig.**	**P>t**
Information Quality	**IQ**	**0.416**	**0.082**	***	**0.000**
Internet Browsing	**IB**	**0.440**	**0.084**	***	**0.000**
	_cons	0.003	0.066	*	0.967
Adj R-squared = 0.3456				Number of Obs = 250	

Source: our elaboration
Notes: Significant at *90%; **95%; ***99%

Table 7. Regression Model3 – Hypothesis H3 – Costumer loyalty (dependent variable), new variables of Quality Dimensions (independent variable)

Variable dependent Customer Loyalty (CL)					
New Variables of Quality Dimensions Online	**New Variables Code**	**Coef.**	**Std. Err**	**Sig.**	**P>t**
Parking and security	**P&S**	**0.203**	**0.057**	***	**0.000**
Cleanliness/Hygiene	**C&H**	**0.282**	**0.051**	***	**0.000**
Entertainment	**E**	**0.324**	**0.056**	***	**0.000**
Socialization	**S**	**0.186**	**0.061**	***	**0.003**
Convenience	**C**	**0.377**	**0.053**	***	**0.000**
Information quality	**IQ**	**0.290**	**0.067**	***	**0.000**
Internet Browsing	IB	0.039	0.081	*	0.631
	_cons	0.000	0.051	*	0.992
Adj R-squared = 0.6254				Number of Obs = 250	

Source: our elaboration
Notes: Significant at *90%; **95%; ***99%

within single factors. Further, reliability tests were used for items referring to Customer Loyalty. Table 3 shows the classification of the items and the value of indicators of reliability.

Table 8 to 10 in the appendix show the correlation matrix concerning the three analyzed variables, namely Offline Quality Dimensions (OnQD), Online Quality Dimensions (OnQD), Customer Loyalty (CL). Table 11 to 16 in the appendix show the results of factor analysis [1] concerning the three analyzed variables. Table 4 shows the new variables.

Through factor analyses, eight factors have been identified. They represented the variables used in the research to run the regression models. These variables are the most relevant to the phenomenon observed, since they are able to explain most of the variance of the original data set. *Table 4* shows the new variables.

Regression Model

To assess the regression model, the variables obtained from the results of factor analysis were used in order to eliminate redundancies in the variables observed. The new six variables of Offline Quality Dimensions and Online Quality Dimensions (OfQD and OnQD) obtained from the factor analysis are the explanatory variables, while the new variable of customer loyalty (CL) is the dependent variable.

The Adj R-squared index provides information on the goodness of the model as a whole and shows how the dependent variable can be totally and proportionally variable. This attributed to the linear relationship with the independent variables considered. Having a considerable interpretative effectiveness, it can also be used to summarize the results of a regression model (Bracalente et al., 2009).

Tables 5 to 7 show the three regression models, implemented in order to find a relationship between quality dimensions and customer loyalty. Table 5 shows the first regression model. It was implemented to validate the hypothesis H1. The value of "Adj R-Squared" shows that 57.90% of the variability of customer loyalty is explained by offline quality dimension variables. A more in-depth analysis of the p-values shows a sound evidence against the null hypothesis when an alternative exists for the P&S, C&H, E, S and C variables. These variables are significantly related to Customer Loyalty.

Model 1 – H1: Offline Quality Dimension (OfQD) has a positive effect on Customer Loyalty (CL).

Table 6 shows the second regression model. It was implemented to validate the hypothesis H2. The value of "Adj R-Squared" shows that 34.56% of the variability of customer loyalty is explained by online quality dimension variables. A more in-depth analysis of the p-values shows a sound evidence against the null hypothesis when an alternative exists for the IQ and IB variables. These variables are significantly related to Customer Loyalty.

Model 2 – H2: Online Quality Dimension (OnQD) has a positive effect on Customer Loyalty (CL).

In *Table 7*, the value of "Adj RSquared" shows that 62.54% of the variability of customer loyalty is explained by Quality Dimensions Offline and Online variables. A more in-depth analysis of the p-values shows a sound evidence against the null hypothesis when an alternative exists for the P&S, C&H, E, S, C and IQ variables. These variables are significantly related to Customer Loyalty.

Model 3 – H3: Quality Dimensions (OfQD and OnQD) have a positive effect on Costumer Loyalty (CL).

SOLUTIONS AND RECOMMENDATIONS

The first objective of this study has been to identify the offline and online quality dimensions of the shopping mall through factor analysis. Seven factors have been identified. They summarize the variables related to offline and online quality dimensions. In particular, for OfQD, the factor analysis identified five factors: (1) Parking and Security, (2) Cleaning and Hygiene, (3) Entertainment, (4) Socialization and (5) Convenience. These results are in line with those highlighted in literature.

The topic of safety and parking is in fact widely developed by authors such as Severin et al. (2001), Jackson et al. (2011), and Narahari and Kuvad (2017). According to Gentry and Burns (1977) parking, together with traffic and hours of operation, are the fundamental criteria on which older consumers evaluated shopping malls. Narahari and Kuvad (2017) and Jackson et al. (2011) analyzed also the cleanliness and hygiene factor and Hui et al. (2013) defined it as one of the crucial facility management (FM) service dimensions. Entertainment and Socialization are other shopping mall attractiveness factors analyzed by several authors (i.e. Ismail El-Adly 2007 and Katrodia et al. 2018). Their studies highlight how these dimensions are becoming increasingly important for those consumers when evaluating shopping centers.

Finally, convenience is the most important factor for consumers. Prashar et al., (2017) in their study, established mall shoppers value 'convenience' as the most influencing factor when selecting a mall and Singh and Prashar (2014) argued that convenience, together with ambience, marketing focus, safety & security and physical infrastructure, can be defined as vital factors when defining the shopping experience. Instead, for OnQD, the factor analysis identified two factors: (1) Information Quality and (2) Internet Browsing. These results are in line with those of the literature. The topic of information quality, which includes updating and easiness is largely developed by authors. Such as Spiteri (2000), Lin and Lu (2000), Liu and Arnett (2000), Cox and Dale (2002), Song & Zinkhan (2003), Signore (2005), Cao et al. (2005), Ha & Im (2012), Aquilani et al. (2015) and Kamesh et al. (2018) in the context of e-commerce; Moustakis et al. (2004) in the context of cellular phone service; Park and Gretzel (2007) and Razak et al. (2016) in the context of tourism. While, in the context of shopping mall, the topic is widely developed by Yu et al. (2017). Information quality appears to be the most important factor for consumers. The topic of internet browsing, which includes layout, level of interactivity and usefulness, is analyzed by several authors (i.e. Kim et al. 2003 and Signore 2005), in the context of e-commerce. In the same context, the layout is studied by Ivory et al. (2001). While, in the context of shopping mall, this topic is developed by authors such as Kim and Song (2010), who focused on usefulness and Know et al. (2013), who focused on the level of interactivity.

The second objective of this study, however, was to analyze, through multiple regression models, the relationships between Offline and Online Quality Dimensions and Customer Loyalty in order to examine the nature and the strength of their relationship. Results of the first regression model confirm the H1 hypothesis, namely that Offline Quality Dimensions (OfQD) have a positive effect on Customer Loyalty, and they are aligned with those of the literature. In particular, Aliagha et al. (2015) in their study, demonstrated that the shopping mall attractiveness, expressed in terms of physical elements such as cleanliness, quality of building facilities, restrooms and car park, contributed significantly in explaining customer loyalty. According to Haj-Salem et al., (2016), instead, the atmosphere affects mall loyalty, in particular for female shoppers. This variable contributes to build the Socialization factor that positively affects customer loyalty.

However, socialization is strongly linked to Entertainment, because it is through the latter that the shopping mall attracts people who can establish connections among them. In our study, it appears that the Entertainment factor has a positive effect on Customer Loyalty. Findings of the research confirms with what claimed by Aliagha et al. (2015). They argued that in our modern-day life, entertainment is an increasingly integral part of the shopping mall experience. Bloch et al. (1994) claimed that malls were viewed by consumers as a place not only for shopping but also for other activities, such as Entertainment. Similarly, Sit et al. (2003) found that Entertainment is pivotal to shopping malls because it induces an exciting and fun shopping experience, which in turn could entice consumer patronage. In particular, White (2008) argued that consumers are no longer looking only for shopping malls that offer shopping, but also for places that entertain. Therefore, shopping mall is perceived by consumers as place for meeting and socializing.

Moreover, Srivastava and Kaul (2014) noted a positive influence of social interaction and convenience on both customer experience as well as customer satisfaction. Indeed, findings of this research show that Italian loyal shoppers not only look for hedonic benefits but also for utilitarian benefits, during their visit to the shopping mall. In fact, results show that Convenience is an important dimension that may affect customer loyalty and increase the value of shopping malls. These findings are also consistent with other research findings (i.e. Ahmad. 2012; Jenifer. 2016; Prashar et al. 2017). In particular, Prashar et al. (2017), in their study conducted in India, established that Mall shoppers predominantly look for convenience.

Results of the second regression model confirm hypothesis H2, namely that Online Quality Dimensions (OnQD) have a positive effect on Customer Loyalty. This result is aligned with those of the literature. In our model, the items of Customer Loyalty are overall satisfaction, intention to WOM and intention to repurchase. According to Kim and Song (2010), the quality of WOM has positive effects on online trust, which in turn has positive effects on perceived usefulness, shopping intention and perceived ease of use. The result of Ha and Him (2012) showed that web site design quality had positive indirect effects on satisfaction and WOM intention, confirming Kim and Song (2010). Yu et al. (2017) revealed five evaluation dimensions: (1) General Service Factor, (2) Information Providing Factor, (3) System Factor and (4) Visual Factor of Design. Their results emphasize that Customer loyalty is strongly related to repurchase intention. In practice, they showed that the consumer purchase satisfaction is an important factor for the development of a company and purchase satisfaction has a strong influence on brand loyalty and repurchase intention. Instead, Santouridis et al. (2012) confirmed the four-factor structure of E-S-QUAL. The most important dimension is Efficiency because it has a significant positive effect on all three dependent variables, namely perceived overall quality, value and loyalty.

Finally, the results of the third regression model suggest that Italian loyal shoppers of the mall where the study has been developed are influenced by mixed factors (physical elements, hedonistic benefits and information quality of website) except by Internet Browsing factor.

This result is justified and related to the scarce use of the online available communication tools. In fact, the web site is just one of the possible online tools that the shopping mall uses to communicate with its customers. The research was developed at a shopping mall, located in a medium-sized city (Viterbo had a population of about 67.488 in 2017, ISTAT data) that not only uses the web site as an online communication tool but also Instagram and Facebook. However, these tools are not used by regular customers of the Mall, whose decision to go to the shopping mall based on other factors identified by the study. The most used online tool is the web site. In fact, the sample was composed by 370 people and only 250 (67%) affirmed to surf and use the web site of the shopping mall. 69 respondents (19% of the sample) consult Facebook page and 48 (13% of sample) visit the Instagram page. This result explains why loyalty does not depend on the Internet Browsing factor.

CONCLUSION

As a final remark, factor analysis and multiple regression models have allowed us to analyze in detail the consumer behavior and his loyalty in relation to some strategic factors for the management and enhancement of a mall. First, through factor analysis, it was possible to identify the offline and online quality dimensions of the shopping center. In particular, for OfQD the factor analysis identified five factors: (1) Parking and Security, (2) Cleaning and Hygiene, (3) Entertainment, (4) Socialization and (5) Convenience. These factors make it possible to understand how the consumer looks at the Mall not only in search of concrete aspects (parking, hygiene and entertainment), but he also gives it a social role. As noted by the literature, the environment of the mall therefore contributes to create the optimal condition for social and convivial moments.

Looking at OnQD, the factor analysis identified two factors: (1) Information Quality and (2) Internet Browsing. The online factors identified and underlined by the literature (updating and easiness, layout, level of interactivity and usefulness) are an expression of the increasing awareness of customers and their attention to purchase choices. But, these factors must be analyzed separately to understand which of theme is actually correlated with customer loyalty (as seen with the third regression model).

After identifying the online and offline factors, the second objective of this study was to analyze, through multiple regression models, the relationships between Offline and Online Quality Dimensions and Customer Loyalty in order to examine the nature and the strength of relationship. Through the regression models, all the hypotheses have been verified and it was possible to state how the entire dimensions (Offline and Online) have a positive effect on Customer Loyalty. However, it should be underlined that in the third regression model it emerges that customer loyalty does not related to the Internet Browsing factor. Although widely used in everyday life and for many buying choices and more, web sites and social networks do not seem to influence consumers in their choice of purchasing and repurchasing. This result can be explained by the limited size of the sample city, Viterbo, which also represents a limit to this work (see below).

The knowledge of the territory and the frequency with which consumers go to the shopping center can make the consultation of these information channels meaningless. This aspect is certainly more relevant in a large city, where a longer journey may be required to reach a mall. This could motivate a prior consultation of the Mall site and/or social pages.

Beyond these considerations, the research has also some implications. From the theoretical point of view, this work contributes to further enhanced the literature on Offline Quality Dimension, Online Quality Dimension and Customer Loyalty, and confirms, through further empirical analysis, what was underlined by other authors. At the same time, the results focus on the Internet Browsing factor on its lack of relationship with Customer Loyalty.

From a managerial point of view, this research provides crucial implications for entrepreneurs and Mall managers who want to formulate strategies to increase customer loyalty. Indeed, today retail market is highly competitive. For mall, he challenges on the horizon are many and they involve strategies to attract new customers and retain customers already acquired. In this domain, therefore, it is essential that the actions to attract and retain customers are directly been assessed by their preferences and on the factors that they consider relevant.

Some future avenues of research are possible. It will be interesting to apply the proposed analysis model in a large Mall, in the future, in order to analyze the impact of social networks on loyalty, compared to the online dimensions. At the same time, it will be interesting to match the results of small and large cities to identify any differences/similarities related to the territorial dimension. Furthermore, it would be interesting to study the same phenomenon using the qualitative technique of the "Focus group".

This study also presents some limitations. In conclusion, the limited number of the sample (only 250 people) should be emphasized. It is also important to underline how Viterbo is a medium-sized city (as already highlighted, having about 67.488 people in 2017). This can lead to a distortion in the perception consumers have about the qualitative characteristics of the Mall.

REFERENCES

Abdul-Rahman, M., & Kamarulzaman, Y. (2012). The influence of relationship quality and switching costs on customer Loyalty in the Malaysian Hotel Industry. *Procedia: Social and Behavioral Sciences*, *62*, 1023–1027. doi:10.1016/j.sbspro.2012.09.174

Ahmad, A. E. M. K. (2012). Attractiveness factors influencing shoppers' satisfaction, loyalty, and word of mouth: An empirical investigation of Saudi Arabia shopping malls. *International Journal of Business Administration*, *3*(6), 101–112.

Ahmed, Z. U., Ghingold, M., & Dahari, Z. (2007). Malaysian shopping mall behavior: An exploratory study. *Asia Pacific Journal of Marketing and Logistics*, *19*(4), 331–348. doi:10.1108/13555850710827841

Aliagha, G. U., Qin, Y. G., Ali, K. N., & Abdullah, M. N. (2015). Analysis of shopping mall attractiveness and customer loyalty. *Journal Teknologi*, *74*(2), 15–21.

Ammani, P. (2013). A study of the factors that influence customer preference for shopping malls over local markets. *IUP Journal of Management Research*, *12*(1), 7–21.

Anuradha, D., & Manohar, H. (2011). Customer shopping experience in malls with entertainment centres in Chennai. *African Journal of Business Management*, *5*(31), 12319–12324. doi:10.5897/AJBM11.902

Aquilani, B., Serpico, E., Silvestri, C., & Ruggieri, A. (2015). Offline and online customer satisfaction in B2C markets: Towards an overall customer satisfaction framework. In *Handbook of Research on Managing and Influencing Consumer Behavior* (pp. 311–364). IGI Global. doi:10.4018/978-1-4666-6547-7.ch014

Athanasopoulou, P. (2009). Relationship quality: A critical literature review and research agenda. *European Journal of Marketing*, *43*(5/6), 583–610. doi:10.1108/03090560910946945

Bennett, R., & Rundle-Thiele, S. (2002). A comparison of attitudinal loyalty measurement approaches. *Journal of Brand Management*, *9*(3), 193–209. doi:10.1057/palgrave.bm.2540069

Bloch, P. H., Ridgway, N. M., & Dawson, S. A. (1994). The shopping mall as consumer habitat. *Journal of Retailing*, *70*(1), 23–42. doi:10.1016/0022-4359(94)90026-4

Bracalente, B., Cossignani, M., & Mulas, A. (2009). *Statistica aziendale*. Milan: McGraw-Hill.

Cai, Y., & Shannon, R. (2012). Personal values and mall shopping behaviour: The mediating role of intention among Chinese consumers. *International Journal of Retail & Distribution Management*, *40*(4), 290–318. doi:10.1108/09590551211211783

Cao, M., Zhang, Q., & Seydel, J. (2005). B2C e-commerce web site quality: An empirical examination. *Industrial Management & Data Systems*, *105*(5), 645–661. doi:10.1108/02635570510600000

Castaldo, S., & Botti, S. (1999). La dimensione emozionale dello shopping. *Economia & Management*, *1*, 17–37.

Čater, T., & Čater, B. (2010). Product and relationship quality influence on customer commitment and loyalty in B2B manufacturing relationships. *Industrial Marketing Management*, *39*(8), 1321–1333. doi:10.1016/j.indmarman.2010.02.006

Chang, Y. F. (2013). Exploration of shopping mall customer value propositions in the experience economy. *Актуальні проблеми економіки*, (5), 566-576.

Chebat, J. C., El Hedhli, K., & Sirgy, M. J. (2009). How does shopper-based mall equity generate mall loyalty? A conceptual model and empirical evidence. *Journal of Retailing and Consumer Services*, *16*(1), 50–60. doi:10.1016/j.jretconser.2008.08.003

Chebat, J. C., Michon, R., Haj-Salem, N., & Oliveira, S. (2014). The effects of mall renovation on shopping values, satisfaction and spending behaviour. *Journal of Retailing and Consumer Services*, *21*(4), 610–618. doi:10.1016/j.jretconser.2014.04.010

Chebat, J. C., Sirgy, M. J., & Grzeskowiak, S. (2010). How can shopping mall management best capture mall image? *Journal of Business Research*, *63*(7), 735–740. doi:10.1016/j.jbusres.2009.05.009

Cox, J., & Dale, B. G. (2002). Key quality factors in Web site design and use: An examination. *International Journal of Quality & Reliability Management*, *19*(7), 862–888. doi:10.1108/02656710210434784

Cushman & Wakefiled. (2017) *European Shopping Centres The Development Story*. A Cushman & Wakefield Research Publication. Retrieved from http://www.cushmanwakefield.com/en/research-and-insight/2017/european-shopping-centres-the-development-story-nov-17

Davis, F. D. (1989). Perceived usefulness. perceived ease of use. and user acceptance of information technology. *Management Information Systems Quarterly*, *13*(3), 319–340. doi:10.2307/249008

Davis, F. D., Bagozzi, R. P., & Warshaw, P. R. (1989). User acceptance of computer technology: A comparison of two theoretical models. *Management Science*, *35*(8), 982–1003. doi:10.1287/mnsc.35.8.982

Day, G. S. (1969). A two-dimensional concept of brand loyalty. *Journal of Advertising Research, 9*(3), 29–35.

Debek, M. (2015). What Drives Shopping Mall Attractiveness? *Polish Journal of Applied Psychology, 13*(1), 67–118. doi:10.1515/pjap-2015-0026

DeLone, W. H., & McLean, E. R. (1992). Information systems success: The quest for the dependent variable. *Information Systems Research, 3*(1), 60–95. doi:10.1287/isre.3.1.60

Dick, A. S., & Basu, K. (1994). Customer loyalty: Toward an integrated conceptual framework. *Journal of the Academy of Marketing Science, 22*(2), 99–113. doi:10.1177/0092070394222001

Dilek, S., & Top, S. (2013). Charges on parking in shopping malls: Evidence from Turkey. *Procedia: Social and Behavioral Sciences, 99*, 382–390. doi:10.1016/j.sbspro.2013.10.506

Dubihlela, D., & Dubihlela, J. (2014). Attributes of shopping mall image. customer satisfaction and mall patronage for selected shopping malls in Southern Gauteng. South Africa. *Journal of Economics and Behavioral Studies, 6*(8), 682.

El Hedhli, K., & Chebat, J. C. (2009). Developing and validating a psychometric shopper-based mall equity measure. *Journal of Business Research, 62*(6), 581–587. doi:10.1016/j.jbusres.2008.05.016

Erkip, F. (2005). The rise of the shopping mall in Turkey: The use and appeal of a mall in Ankara. *Cities (London, England), 22*(2), 89–108. doi:10.1016/j.cities.2004.10.001

Faraoni, M., Rialti, R., Zollo, L., & Pellicelli, A. C. (2018). Exploring e-Loyalty Antecedents in B2C e-Commerce: Empirical results from Italian grocery retailers. *British Food Journal, 121*(2), 574–589. doi:10.1108/BFJ-04-2018-0216

Farrag, D. A., El Sayed, I. M., & Belk, R. W. (2010). Mall shopping motives and activities: A multimethod approach. *Journal of International Consumer Marketing, 22*(2), 95–115. doi:10.1080/08961530903476113

Feinberg, R. A., & Meoli, J. (1991). A brief history of the mall. *ACR North American Advances, 18*, 426–427.

Gentry, J. W., & Burns, A. C. (1978). How important are evaluative criteria in shopping center patronage. *Journal of Retailing, 53*(4), 73.

George, T., & Stavros, T. (2013). *The role of psychological commitment and attitudinal loyalty on the relationship between involvement and behavioral loyalty of sports fans*. Available from: http://www.thesportjournal.org

Gudonaviciene, R., & Alijosiene. S. (2013). Influence of shopping centre image attributes on customer choices. *Economics and Management, 18*(3), 545-552.

Ha, Y., & Im, H. (2012). Role of web site design quality in satisfaction and word of mouth generation. *Journal of Service Management, 23*(1), 79–96. doi:10.1108/09564231211208989

Hair, J., Black, W. C., Babin, B. J., Anderson, R. E., & Tatham, R. (2006). *Multivariate Data Analysis*. New York, NY: Pearson Education.

Haj-Salem, N., Chebat, J. C., Michon, R., & Oliveira, S. (2016). Why male and female shoppers do not see mall loyalty through the same lens? The mediating role of self-congruity. *Journal of Business Research*, *69*(3), 1219–1227. doi:10.1016/j.jbusres.2015.09.011

Hallowell, R. (1996). The relationships of customer satisfaction, customer loyalty, and profitability: An empirical study. *International Journal of Service Industry Management*, *7*(4), 27–42. doi:10.1108/09564239610129931

Hennig-Thurau, T., Gwinner, K. P., & Gremler, D. D. (2002). Understanding relationship marketing outcomes. *Journal of Service Research*, *4*(3), 230–247. doi:10.1177/1094670502004003006

Hui, E. C., Zhang, P. H., & Zheng, X. (2013). Facilities management service and customer satisfaction in shopping mall sector. *Facilities*, *31*(5/6), 194–207. doi:10.1108/02632771311307070

Ismail El-Adly, M. (2007). Shopping malls attractiveness: A segmentation approach. *International Journal of Retail & Distribution Management*, *35*(11), 936–950. doi:10.1108/09590550710828245

Istat. (2017). *Data*. Retrieved from https://www.istat.it/

Ivory, M. Y., & Hearst, M. A. (2001). The state of the art in automating usability evaluation of user interfaces. *ACM Computing Surveys*, *33*(4), 470–516. doi:10.1145/503112.503114

Jackson, V., Stoel, L., & Brantley, A. (2011). Mall attributes and shopping value: Differences by gender and generational cohort. *Journal of Retailing and Consumer Services*, *18*(1), 1–9. doi:10.1016/j.jretconser.2010.08.002

Jacoby, J. (1971). A model of multi-brand loyalty. *Journal of Advertising Research*, *11*(3), 25–31.

Jenifer, L. (2016). Customer orientation in shopping malls of South Chennai - An exploratory study. *International Journal of Applied Research*, *2*(3), 124–128.

Jiang, H., & Zhang, Y. (2016). An investigation of service quality, customer satisfaction and loyalty in China's airline market. *Journal of Air Transport Management*, *57*, 80–88. doi:10.1016/j.jairtraman.2016.07.008

Kaiser, H. F. (1958). The Varimax criterion for analytic rotation in factor analysis. *Psychometrika*, *23*(3), 187–200. doi:10.1007/BF02289233

Kaiser, H. F. (1974). An index of factor simplicity. *Psychometrika*, *39*(1), 31–36. doi:10.1007/BF02291575

Kamesh, D. B. K., Sasi Bhanu, J., & Sastry, J. K. R. (2018). An architectural approach for assessing quality of web sites. *Journal of Engineering and Applied Sciences (Asian Research Publishing Network)*, *13*(15), 4503–4513.

Katrodia, A., Naude, M. J., & Soni, S. (2018). Determinants of shopping and buying behaviour: A case at Durban shopping malls. *African Journal of Business and Economic Research*, *13*(1), 219–241. doi:10.31920/1750-4562/2018/v13n1a8

Keng, C. J., Huang, T. L., Zheng, L. J., & Hsu, M. K. (2007). Modeling service encounters and customer experiential value in retailing: An empirical investigation of shopping mall customers in Taiwan. *International Journal of Service Industry Management*, *18*(4), 349–367. doi:10.1108/09564230710778137

Khare, A. (2011). Mall shopping behaviour of Indian small town consumers. *Journal of Retailing and Consumer Services*, *18*(1), 110–118. doi:10.1016/j.jretconser.2010.10.005

Khare, A. (2012). Influence of mall attributes and demographics on Indian consumers' mall involvement behavior: An exploratory study. *Journal of Targeting. Measurement and Analysis for Marketing*, *20*(3-4), 192–202. doi:10.1057/jt.2012.15

Khare, A., & Rakesh, S. (2010). Retailers in malls: Retailers' preferences for store space in Indian malls. *Journal of Retail & Leisure Property*, *9*(2), 125–135. doi:10.1057/rlp.2010.1

Kim, H., & Song, J. (2010). The quality of word-of-mouth in the online shopping mall. *Journal of Research in Interactive Marketing*, *4*(4), 376–390. doi:10.1108/17505931011092844

Kim, S. E., Shaw, T., & Schneider, H. (2003). Web site design benchmarking within industry groups. *Internet Research*, *13*(1), 17–26. doi:10.1108/10662240310458341

Kim, Y., Kang, J., & Kim, M. (2005). Family and Social Interaction, Loneliness, Mall Shopping Motivation, and Mall Spending of Older Consumers. *Psychology and Marketing*, *22*(12), 995–1015. doi:10.1002/mar.20095

Kursunluoglu, E. (2011). Customer service effects on customer satisfaction and customer loyalty: A field research in shopping centers in Izmir City-Turkey. *International Journal of Business and Social Science*, *2*(17).

Kwon, Y. J., Cui, J., & Kwon, D. (2013). A Study on Comparison Analysis of the System Quality Factors between Korea and China Shopping mall Websites. *Journal of Korea Multimedia Society*, *16*(11), 1315–1324. doi:10.9717/kmms.2013.16.11.1315

Lam, R., & Burton, S. (2006). SME banking loyalty (and disloyalty): A qualitative study in Hong Kong. *International Journal of Bank Marketing*, *24*(1), 37–52. doi:10.1108/02652320610642335

Laroche, M., Teng, L., Michon, R., & Chebat, J. C. (2005). Incorporating service quality into consumer mall shopping decision making: A comparison between English and French Canadian consumers. *Journal of Services Marketing*, *19*(3), 157–163. doi:10.1108/08876040510596830

Laureti, T., Piccarozzi, M., & Aquilani, B. (2018). The effects of historical satisfaction, provided services characteristics and website dimensions on encounter overall satisfaction: A travel industry case study. *The TQM Journal*, *30*(3), 197–216. doi:10.1108/TQM-07-2017-0080

Lee, J., Lee, J., & Feick, L. (2001). The impact of switching costs on the customer satisfaction-loyalty link: Mobile phone service in France. *Journal of Services Marketing*, *15*(1), 35–48. doi:10.1108/08876040110381463

Likert, R. (1932). A technique for the measurement of attitudes. *Archives de Psychologie*, *22*, 5–55.

Lin, J. C. C., & Lu, H. (2000). Towards an understanding of the behavioural intention to use a web site. *International Journal of Information Management*, *20*(3), 197–208. doi:10.1016/S0268-4012(00)00005-0

Liu, C., & Arnett, K. P. (2000). Exploring the factors associated with Web site success in the context of electronic commerce. *Information & Management*, *38*(1), 23–33. doi:10.1016/S0378-7206(00)00049-5

Lloyd, A. Y. K., Chan, R. S. C., Yip, L., & Chan, A. (2014). Time buying and time saving: Effects on service convenience and the shopping experience at the mall. *Journal of Services Marketing*, *28*(1), 36–49. doi:10.1108/JSM-03-2012-0065

Massicotte, M. C., Michon, R., Chebat, J. C., Sirgy, M. J., & Borges, A. (2011). Effects of mall atmosphere on mall evaluation: Teenage versus adult shoppers. *Journal of Retailing and Consumer Services*, *18*(1), 74–80. doi:10.1016/j.jretconser.2010.10.001

Max, R. (2018). *Mall Analytics*. Retrieved from https://behavioranalyticsretail.com/mall-analytics/

McCain, S. L. C., Jang, S., & Hu, C. (2005). Service quality gap analysis toward customer loyalty: Practical guidelines for casino hotels. *International Journal of Hospitality Management*, *24*(3), 465–472. doi:10.1016/j.ijhm.2004.09.005

Michon, R., Chebat, J. C., & Turley, L. W. (2005). Mall atmospherics: The interaction effects of the mall environment on shopping behavior. *Journal of Business Research*, *58*(5), 576–583. doi:10.1016/j.jbusres.2003.07.004

Mittal, A., & Jhamb, D. (2016). Determinants of shopping mall attractiveness: The Indian context. *Procedia Economics and Finance*, *37*, 386–390. doi:10.1016/S2212-5671(16)30141-1

Moliner, M. A., Sánchez, J., Rodríguez, R. M., & Callarisa, L. (2007). Relationship quality with a travel agency: The influence of the postpurchase perceived value of a tourism package. *Tourism and Hospitality Research*, *7*(3-4), 194–211. doi:10.1057/palgrave.thr.6050052

Moustakis, V., Litos, C., Dalivigas, A., & Tsironis, L. (2004). *Website Quality Assessment Criteria. IQ*, *5*, 59–73.

Namukasa, J. (2013). The influence of airline service quality on passenger satisfaction and loyalty: The case of Uganda airline industry. *The TQM Journal*, *25*(5), 520–532. doi:10.1108/TQM-11-2012-0092

Narahari, A. C., & Kuvad, D. (2017). Customer Behaviour towards Shopping Malls – A Study in Bhavnagar (Gujarat State, India). *IJARIIE*, *3*(2), 211–224.

Nyadzayo, M. W., & Khajehzadeh, S. (2016). The antecedents of customer loyalty: A moderated mediation model of customer relationship management quality and brand image. *Journal of Retailing and Consumer Services*, *30*, 262–270. doi:10.1016/j.jretconser.2016.02.002

Oliver Richard, L. (1997). *Satisfaction: A behavioral perspective on the consumer*. New York, NY: Irwin-McGraw-Hill.

Parasuraman, A., Berry, L. L., & Zeithaml, V. A. (1991). Understanding customer expectations of service. *Sloan Management Review*, *32*(3), 39–48.

Parasuraman, A., Zeithaml, V. A., & Berry, L. L. (1985). A conceptual model of service quality and its implications for future research. *Journal of Marketing*, *49*(4), 41–50. doi:10.1177/002224298504900403

Parasuraman, A., Zeithaml, V. A., & Berry, L. L. (1988). Servqual: A multiple-item scale for measuring consumer perc. *Journal of Retailing*, *64*(1), 12.

Parasuraman, A., Zeithaml, V. A., & Malhotra, A. (2005). ES-QUAL: A multiple-item scale for assessing electronic service quality. *Journal of Service Research*, *7*(3), 213–233. doi:10.1177/1094670504271156

Park, Y. A., & Gretzel, U. (2007). Success factors for destination marketing web sites: A qualitative meta-analysis. *Journal of Travel Research*, *46*(1), 46–63. doi:10.1177/0047287507302381

Parsons, A. G. (2003). Assessing the effectiveness of shopping mall promotions: Customer analysis. *International Journal of Retail & Distribution Management*, *31*(2), 74–79. doi:10.1108/09590550310461976

Pearson, S. (1996). Building brands directly: Creating business value from customer relationships. *Macmillan Business*, *20*(6), 68–82.

Prashar, S., Singh, H., Parsad, C., & Vijay, T. S. (2017). Predicting Indian Shoppers' Malls Loyalty Behaviour. *Vikalpa*, *42*(4), 234–250.

Quach, T. N., Thaichon, P., & Jebarajakirthy, C. (2016). Internet service providers' service quality and its effect on customer loyalty of different usage patterns. *Journal of Retailing and Consumer Services*, *29*, 104–113. doi:10.1016/j.jretconser.2015.11.012

Rabbanee, F. K., Ramaseshan, B., Wu, C., & Vinden, A. (2012). Effects of store loyalty on shopping mall loyalty. *Journal of Retailing and Consumer Services*, *19*(3), 271–278. doi:10.1016/j.jretconser.2012.02.001

Rahman, M. A., & Ramli, M. F. (2016). The influence of relationship quality on customer loyalty in the dual-banking system in the northern states of peninsular Malaysia. *Procedia: Social and Behavioral Sciences*, *219*, 606–613. doi:10.1016/j.sbspro.2016.05.040

Rajagopal, D. (2008). *Growing Shopping Malls and Behavior of Urban Shoppers.* EGADE Working Paper No. 2008-05-MKT. Available at SSRN: https://ssrn.com/abstract=1299024

Rajapopal, P. (2011). Determinants of shopping behavior of urban consumers. *Journal of International Consumer Marketing*, *23*(2), 83–104. doi:10.1080/08961530.2011.543051

Rasheed, F., & Abadi, M. F. (2014). Impact of Service Quality. Trust and Perceived Value on Customer Loyalty in Malaysia Services Industries. *Procedia: Social and Behavioral Sciences*, *164*(August), 298–304. doi:10.1016/j.sbspro.2014.11.080

Rauyruen, P., & Miller, K. E. (2006). Relationship quality as a predictor of B2B customer loyalty. *Journal of Business Research*, *60*(1), 21–31. doi:10.1016/j.jbusres.2005.11.006

Razak, N. S. A., Ahmad, A. H., & Marimuthu, M. (2016). The Effect of Website Quality on Repurchase Intention in Travel Agency's Website in Malaysia. *First International Conference on Advance Business and Social Sciences*, 21-29.

Rechinhheld, F., & Sasser, W. (1990). Zero defections: Quality comes to service. *Harvard Business Review*, *68*(5), 105–111.

Reimers, V., & Clulow, V. (2009). Retail centres: It's time to make them convenient. *International Journal of Retail & Distribution Management*, *37*(7), 541–562. doi:10.1108/09590550910964594

Rousseau, G. G., & Venter, D. J. (2014). Mall shopping preferences and patronage of mature shoppers. *SA Journal of Industrial Psychology, 40*(1), 1-12.

Said, I., Gambo, N., & Ismail, R. (2016). An evaluation into the architectural factors attracting customers to Malaysian shopping malls. *Journal of Business and Retail Management Research*, *11*(1), 138–153.

Santouridis, I., & Trivellas, P. (2010). Investigating the impact of service quality and customer satisfaction on customer loyalty in mobile telephony in Greece. *The TQM Journal*, *22*(3), 330–343. doi:10.1108/17542731011035550

Santouridis, I., Trivellas, P., & Tsimonis, G. (2012). Using ES-QUAL to measure internet service quality of e-commerce web sites in Greece. *International Journal of Quality and Service Sciences*, *4*(1), 86–98. doi:10.1108/17566691211219751

Severin, V., Louviere, J. J., & Finn, A. (2001). The stability of retail shopping choices over time and across countries. *Journal of Retailing*, *77*(2), 185–202. doi:10.1016/S0022-4359(01)00043-4

Signore, O. (2005, September). A comprehensive model for web sites quality. In *Web Site Evolution, 2005, (WSE 2005). Seventh IEEE International Symposium on* (pp. 30-36). IEEE. 10.1109/WSE.2005.1

Singh, H., & Prashar, S. (2014). Anatomy of shopping experience for malls in Mumbai: A confirmatory factor analysis approach. *Journal of Retailing and Consumer Services*, *21*(2), 220–228. doi:10.1016/j.jretconser.2013.08.002

Singh, H., & Sahay, V. (2012). Determinants of shopping experience: Exploring the mall shoppers of national capital region (NCR) of India. *International Journal of Retail & Distribution Management*, *40*(3), 235–248. doi:10.1108/09590551211207184

Singh, J., Srivastava, S., Sharma, S., Nath, S., & Karmakar, A. (2016). Customer perception of e-service quality in online travel companies in India. *International Journal of Applied Business and Economic Research.*, *14*(7), 5245–5254.

Sit, J., Merrilees, B., & Birch, D. (2003). Entertainment-seeking shopping centre patrons: The missing segments. *International Journal of Retail & Distribution Management*, *31*(2), 80–94. doi:10.1108/09590550310461985

Song, J. H., & Zinkhan, G. M. (2003, March). Features of web site design, perceptions of web site quality, and patronage behavior. In ACME 2003 proceedings (pp. 106-114). ACME.

Spiteri, L. F. (2000). Access to electronic commerce sites on the World Wide Web: An analysis of the effectiveness of six Internet search engines. *Journal of Information Science*, *26*(3), 173–183. doi:10.1177/016555150002600307

Srivastava, M., & Kaul, D. (2014). Social interaction, convenience and customer satisfaction: The mediating effect of customer experience. *Journal of Retailing and Consumer Services*, *21*(6), 1028–1037. doi:10.1016/j.jretconser.2014.04.007

Szwarc, P. (2005). *Researching customer satisfaction and loyalty: how to find out what people really think*. London, UK: Kogan Page.

Tandon, A., Gupta, A., & Tripathi, V. (2016). Managing shopping experience through mall attractiveness dimensions: An experience of Indian metro cities. *Asia Pacific Journal of Marketing and Logistics*, *28*(4), 634–649. doi:10.1108/APJML-08-2015-0127

Tsai, S. P. (2010). Shopping mall management and entertainment experience: A cross-regional investigation. *Service Industries Journal*, *30*(3), 321–337. doi:10.1080/02642060802123376

Van Iwaarden, J., Van der Wiele, T., Ball, L., & Millen, R. (2003). Applying SERVQUAL to web sites: An exploratory study. *International Journal of Quality & Reliability Management*, *20*(8), 919–935. doi:10.1108/02656710310493634

Wakefield, K. L., & Baker, J. (1998). Excitement at the mall: Determinants and effects on shopping response. *Journal of Retailing*, *74*(4), 515–539. doi:10.1016/S0022-4359(99)80106-7

Wallace, D. W., Giese, J. L., & Johnson, J. L. (2004). Customer retailer loyalty in the context of multiple channel strategies. *Journal of Retailing*, *80*(4), 249–263. doi:10.1016/j.jretai.2004.10.002

White, R. (2008). The Role of Entertainment in Shopping Centers & Malls. *Leisure eNewsletter, 8*(5), 1-15.

Wills, B. (2009). The business case for environmental sustainability (Green): Achieving rapid returns from the practical integration of lean & green. *Business Case for Environmental Sustainability*, 1-15.

Yap, B. W., Ramayah, T., & Shahidan, W. N. W. (2012). Satisfaction and trust on customer loyalty: A PLS approach. *Business Strategy Series*, *13*(4), 154–167. doi:10.1108/17515631211246221

Yim Yiu, C., & Xu, S. Y. (2012). A tenant-mix model for shopping malls. *European Journal of Marketing*, *46*(3/4), 524–541. doi:10.1108/03090561211202594

Yiu, C. Y., & Yau, Y. (2006). An ecological framework for the strategic positioning of a shopping mall. *Journal of Retail & Leisure Property*, *5*(4), 270–280. doi:10.1057/palgrave.rlp.5100037

Yu, M., Lee, Y.-S., & Lee, J.-E. (2017). A study on the constituent factors and customer characteristics of Chinese internet shopping malls (centering around purchase satisfaction, customer loyalty and repurchase intention of Chinese female college students). *Journal of Engineering and Applied Sciences (Asian Research Publishing Network)*, *12*(2), 6344–6349.

KEY TERMS AND DEFINITIONS

Customer Loyalty: The set of all those activities aimed at creating a commercial and personal link.

Factor Analysis: A statistical method used to describe variability between the observed correlated variables in terms of a potentially lower number of unobserved variables called factors.

Offline Quality Dimension: A measure of the hedonistic and physical aspects of the shopping mall.

Online Quality Dimension: A measure of the qualitative aspects of online communication tools.

Regression Model: A model of several variables with the focus is on the relationship between a dependent variable and one or more independent variables (or "predictors").

Shopping Mall: A specially built covered area containing shops, restaurants, and based service that people can walk between and where cars are not allowed.

Web Site: A collection of interlinked and publicly accessible web pages that share a domain name.

ENDNOTE

1 Factor analysis was used in order to eliminate problems of multicollinearity, and the criterion adopted for the identification of new factors was Eigenvalues <1. For an easier interpretation, the so-called "rotation" of the initial factor solution was applied. Because the following step of the research involves the use of regression analysis, an orthogonal rotation of factors (the rotated factors remain uncorrelated) was applied using the Varimax method (Kaiser, 1958).

APPENDIX

See Tables 8-16.

Table 8. Correlation Matrix of Offline Quality Dimension

	f1	f2	f3	f4	c1	c2	c3	c4	c5	c6	c7	s1	s2	s3	s4	s5	s6	s7	s8	la1	la2	la3	la4	la5	la6	la7	la8
f1	1.00																										
f2	0.43	1.00																									
f3	0.42	0.68	1.00																								
f4	0.37	0.36	0.36	1.00																							
c1	0.54	0.39	0.44	0.48	1.00																						
c2	0.48	0.38	0.30	0.53	0.51	1.00																					
c3	0.46	0.42	0.32	0.28	0.39	0.39	1.00																				
c4	0.29	0.29	0.24	0.40	0.47	0.37	0.57	1.00																			
c5	0.52	0.42	0.37	0.43	0.57	0.38	0.70	0.57	1.00																		
c6	0.35	0.27	0.27	0.47	0.53	0.43	0.50	0.70	0.63	1.00																	
c7	0.52	0.32	0.34	0.32	0.47	0.39	0.67	0.60	0.70	0.49	1.00																
s1	0.41	0.40	0.39	0.38	0.39	0.37	0.46	0.39	0.48	0.41	0.39	1.00															
s2	0.27	0.41	0.27	0.36	0.36	0.42	0.40	0.43	0.44	0.42	0.46	0.51	1.00														
s3	0.50	0.47	0.38	0.41	0.53	0.43	0.54	0.53	0.60	0.46	0.49	0.76	0.60	1.00													
s4	0.37	0.36	0.30	0.34	0.49	0.35	0.51	0.61	0.59	0.57	0.51	0.64	0.63	0.68	1.00												
s5	0.32	0.44	0.41	0.45	0.44	0.34	0.39	0.37	0.54	0.39	0.44	0.46	0.64	0.54	0.45	1.00											
s6	0.42	0.46	0.42	0.46	0.49	0.40	0.43	0.33	0.53	0.37	0.49	0.54	0.72	0.63	0.50	0.85	1.00										
s7	0.30	0.43	0.39	0.43	0.43	0.36	0.37	0.36	0.45	0.41	0.37	0.60	0.71	0.55	0.52	0.68	0.83	1.00									
s8	0.59	0.36	0.31	0.43	0.61	0.50	0.51	0.47	0.63	0.48	0.51	0.45	0.36	0.52	0.50	0.39	0.43	0.36	1.00								
la1	0.55	0.48	0.38	0.58	0.63	0.54	0.37	0.48	0.50	0.52	0.40	0.39	0.30	0.51	0.48	0.35	0.36	0.31	0.47	1.00							
la2	0.45	0.36	0.24	0.54	0.56	0.37	0.33	0.40	0.47	0.41	0.36	0.22	0.21	0.33	0.39	0.21	0.28	0.29	0.35	0.70	1.00						
la3	0.43	0.39	0.34	0.54	0.55	0.46	0.38	0.36	0.45	0.36	0.31	0.39	0.41	0.49	0.41	0.45	0.49	0.45	0.41	0.51	0.51	1.00					
la4	0.42	0.34	0.29	0.56	0.50	0.48	0.37	0.37	0.42	0.37	0.31	0.28	0.32	0.41	0.35	0.38	0.42	0.33	0.45	0.54	0.49	0.80	1.00				
la5	0.38	0.39	0.39	0.50	0.51	0.40	0.30	0.30	0.38	0.34	0.29	0.37	0.35	0.44	0.39	0.48	0.45	0.40	0.36	0.49	0.44	0.79	0.76	1.00			
la6	0.20	0.31	0.17	0.20	0.18	0.18	0.22	0.34	0.27	0.16	0.29	0.23	0.29	0.24	0.41	0.26	0.23	0.27	0.30	0.22	0.17	0.15	0.25	0.29	1.00		
la7	0.36	0.38	0.31	0.72	0.50	0.43	0.29	0.45	0.54	0.53	0.43	0.23	0.37	0.35	0.37	0.42	0.40	0.40	0.47	0.59	0.66	0.49	0.52	0.47	0.23	1.00	
la8	0.40	0.32	0.27	0.58	0.44	0.43	0.28	0.42	0.40	0.43	0.36	0.28	0.34	0.37	0.35	0.37	0.31	0.25	0.41	0.51	0.55	0.56	0.53	0.53	0.19	0.58	1.00
Number of Obs = 250																											

Source: Our elaboration

Table 9. Correlation Matrix of Online Quality Dimension

	online1	online2	online3	online4	online5	online6	online7
online1	1.000						
online2	0.844	1.000					
online3	0.783	0.838	1.000				
online4	0.712	0.777	0.769	1.000			
online5	0.758	0.769	0.760	0.790	1.000		
online6	0.745	0.807	0.744	0.810	0.890	1.000	
online7	0.732	0.747	0.699	0.671	0.756	0.777	1.000
Number of Obs = 250							

Source: Our elaboration

Table 10. Correlation Matrix of Customer Loyalty

	cl1	cl2	cl3
cl1	1.000		
cl2	0.759	1.000	
cl3	0.701	0.819	1.000
Number of Obs = 250			

Source: Our elaboration

Table 11. Main Factors Matrix (eigenvalues) – Offline Quality Dimension

Factors	Eigenvalue	Difference	Proportion	Cumulative
Factor1	4.84581	0.40978	0.1795	0.1795
Factor2	4.43603	0.46215	0.1643	0.3438
Factor3	3.97387	0.6257	0.1472	0.4910
Factor4	3.34817	1.04394	0.124	0.6150
Factor5	2.30423	.	0.0853	0.7003

Source: Our elaboration

Notes: *The Factor represent the 70.03% of the variability of the whole sample. The factors of Offline Quality Dimensions (OfQD) have an eigenvalue greater than 1 and contain 70.03% of the information included in the original data set. The use of the above criterion, in order to identify the new variables, is adequate because the factor extracted include a sufficient number of original variables.*

Table 12. Rotated factor loadings (pattern matrix) and unique variances – Offline Quality Dimesion

Dimension	Items	Factor1	Factor2	Factor3	Factor4	Factor5	Uniqueness
Quality Dimensions Offline	Distance of the mall from home	**0.4319**	0.1799	0.4213	0.3410	0.3114	0.3903
	Parking: access	**0.7426**	0.2162	0.1382	0.0529	0.2025	0.3390
	Parking: security	**0.6852**	0.2443	0.0519	0.4289	-0.0886	0.2763
	Parking: capacity	**0.6981**	0.2897	0.1751	0.2879	0.2099	0.2712
	Parking: illumination	**0.6028**	0.2589	0.0842	0.5090	-0.0462	0.3012
	Parking: signage	**0.7107**	0.2436	0.0546	0.2193	0.1862	0.3499
	Cleanness: atrium and corridor of the mall	**0.5469**	0.5188	0.3111	0.0209	0.2080	0.2914
	Cleanness: parking	**0.6246**	0.4724	0.2040	0.1423	0.0100	0.3248
	Security: availability	**0.6247**	0.1344	0.3636	0.1520	0.2364	0.3805
	Cleanness shops	0.4698	**0.5373**	0.2421	-0.0896	0.2102	0.3798
	Cleanness: toilette	0.2880	**0.7948**	0.1282	0.1391	0.0156	0.2494
	Toilet: adequacy spaces	0.1548	**0.7772**	0.1999	0.1882	0.1962	0.2581
	Toilet: basic services	0.1981	**0.8236**	0.2458	0.1105	0.2429	0.1508
	Toilet: accessories (e.g. changing table)	0.1609	**0.8376**	0.1533	0.1583	0.1637	0.1971
	Structure: relationship quality/price	0.3337	0.3271	**0.5218**	0.1793	0.2221	0.4279
	Adequacy opening time	0.3275	0.1767	**0.4271**	0.2781	0.2437	0.5424
	Events: interesting	0.1436	0.2886	**0.7999**	0.2400	0.0986	0.1889
	Events: funny	0.1597	0.1562	**0.8105**	0.2897	0.0688	0.2046
	Events: involving	0.0704	0.2848	**0.7841**	0.2163	0.1365	0.2336
	Staff: costumer services	0.0921	0.2993	0.3811	**0.6587**	0.1647	0.2956
	Pleasant atmosphere	0.3575	0.0640	0.3762	**0.5522**	0.3427	0.3042
	Area restaurants: assortment	0.2472	-0.0198	0.3430	**0.6813**	0.2066	0.314
	Socialization	0.1764	0.2219	0.2557	**0.7997**	0.1388	0.1954
	Additional services	0.1928	0.1323	0.4847	**0.5487**	0.0597	0.4057
	Structure: variety stores	0.4932	0.0180	0.4065	0.0784	**0.5166**	0.3181
	Structure: assortment of product	0.1431	0.3273	0.1245	0.2103	**0.7481**	0.2530
	Structure: quality of product	0.1062	0.2774	0.1122	0.1395	**0.7944**	0.2486

Source: Our elaboration

Notes: The table shows the correlation of each variable observed with the new variables obtained through the factor analysis and derived from the factors through the Factor loadings. Each extracted factor was named accordingly. The table presents the rotated factor loadings matrix for Offline Quality Dimensions. It can be observed that Factor1 contains information related to Parking and Security (P&S), Factor2 related to Cleanliness and Hygiene (C&H), Factor3 related to Entertainment (E), Factor4 related to Socialization (S), Factor5 related to Convenience (C). The new five variables have been considerate to also validate Hypothesis 1 and Hypothesis 3 of the regression model.

Table 13. Main Factors Matrix (eigenvalues) – Online

Factors	Eigenvalue	Difference	Proportion	Cumulative
Factor1	2.86653	0.15007	0.5289	0.5289
Factor2	2.71646	.	0.5012	1.0301

Source: Our elaboration

Notes: The first factor of Online has an eigenvalue greater than 1 and contains 52.89% of the information included in the original data set. In this case the use of the above criterion, in order to identify the new variables, is adequate because the factor extracted include a sufficient number of original variables.

Table 14. Rotated factor loadings (pattern matrix) and unique variances – Online Quality Dimensions

Dimension	Items	Factor1	Factor2	Uniqueness
Online Quality Dimensions	Updating	0.5007	**0.7288**	0.2181
	Information quality	0.5277	**0.7658**	0.1352
	Easiness	0.5125	**0.7213**	0.2170
	Internet Browsing	**0.6531**	0.5565	0.2638
	Layout	**0.7864**	0.4866	0.1448
	Level of Interactivity	**0.8084**	0.4807	0.1154
	Usefulness	**0.6134**	0.5487	0.3227

Notes: The table presents the rotated factor loadings matrix for Online Quality Dimensions. It can be observed that Factor 1 contains information related to variables Updating, Information Quality and Easiness while Factor 2 related to variables Internet Browsing, Layout, Level of Interactivity and Usefulness. The new two variables, named, respectively, Information Quality (IQ) and Internet Browsing (IB), have been considerate to also validate Hypothesis 2 and Hypothesis 3 of the regression model.

Table 15. Main Factors Matrix (eigenvalues) – Customer Loyalty

Factors	Eigenvalue	Difference	Proportion	Cumulative
Factor1	**2.52058**	.	**0.8402**	**0.8402**

Source: Our elaboration

Notes: The first Factor represent the 84.02% of the variability of the whole sample. For Customer Loyalty. On the basis of the eigenvalues. only component 1 has eigenvalue greater than 1; for this reason it has been chosen for detecting the new factor named Customer Loyalty (CL).

Table 16. Rotated factor loadings (pattern matrix) and unique variances – Customer Loyalty

Dimension	Items	Factor1	Uniqueness
Customer Loyalty	Overall satisfaction	0.8922	0.2040
	Intention to WOM	0.9396	0.1171
	Intention to repurchase	0.9174	0.1583

Notes: The table shows the relationships of each variable observed with the new variables introduced for customer loyalty. Each extracted factor was named accordingly.

Chapter 6
Consumer Perception of Purchasing Organic Foods: A Case Study of Online Consumer Behavior

Ernest K. S. Lim
Taylor's University, Malaysia

ABSTRACT

The aim of this study is to identify the consumer perception of buying the organic foods online in Malaysia. Consumer perception is typically affected by the variables such as purchase intention, price, health consciousness, organic certification and labeling, consumer knowledge, availability, and environmental concern. This study attempts to identify the relationship and linearity between the dependent and independent variables. Survey questionnaire was targeted to 200 online consumers aged between 18 to 65 years old who buy organic foods. The results indicate a significant positive relationship between price, health consciousness, organic certification and labeling, consumer knowledge, availability, and environmental concern and the purchase of organic food. It shows that purchase intention is linearly related to price, health consciousness, availability, and environmental concern.

ORGANIC FOOD MARKET

Organic food refers to food that meets the strict standards of the National Health Security in supervision, production, storage and distribution (Cheng, 2014). Organic food comprises a wide range of products such as fruits and vegetables, nuts, grains, liquors and beverages, poultry, eggs and dairy products (Lu, et al., 2012). Organic farming system does not uses chemical fertilisers, pesticides, herbicides and growth hormones. Organic meat, eggs-and-dairy-products are obtained from animals-that-are raised by organic crops without antibiotics and growth hormones (Dickieson & Arkus, 2009). The food is not permitted to go through irradiation process and is excluded from solvents, stabilisers and additional ingredients (Albala & Allen, 2007).

DOI: 10.4018/978-1-5225-9697-4.ch006

The global consumption of organic food has increased intensely over the years. According to International Federation of Organic Agriculture Movements (IFOAM) annual report 2017, global organic food sales was approximately 89.7 billion in 2016. This is due to consumers becoming more concern about their health, environment and harmful chemicals present in conventional food. More consumers are getting attracted to the health effects or benefits that organic food offers to human beings and its positive effects on the environment (Yin, et al., 2010). Likewise, global consumption of organic food grows substantially owning to the rise in income and improvements in living standards (Dettmann & Dimitri, 2009). Consumers purchase organic food more to upgrade their standards of living when their purchasing power increases. Besides, there is an increase in the awareness of organic food among consumers in Malaysia recently where consumers are exposed to the health effects of organic fruits and vegetables and environmental benefits by consuming organic food (Vazifehdoust, et al., 2013). However, the demand of organic food is relatively low in Malaysia (Hassan, et al., 2015).

ONLINE PURCHASE OF ORGANIC FOOD

The technology advancement particularly after the launch of various internet services and the widespread of using smart phones, it is easier for internet users to perform their online shopping. According to Internet World Stats (2015), internet users marked up to 3,366,261,156 which is 46.4% of the world population. Statistics shows that 40% of these internet users had bought products online via desktop, mobile, tablet or other online devices (Peyper, Liesl, 2015). Euromonitor International survey indicated that Malaysian online shoppers were sophisticated and spent an average of RM 2,461 per person. On top of that, the online shopping market in Malaysia was expected to grow at an accelerated pace from RM842 million in 2011 and to exceed RM1.9 billion by 2016. Today, 70% of Malaysians do online shopping at least once a month (Ahmad, Sharina & Rosli, Jamny, 2015). Marketing Magazine (2014) indicated that Malaysians ranked among the nation of world top online shoppers. Malaysian were more open to online shopping and ecommerce compared to other nations. eCommerceMILO (2014) surveyed 626 Malaysia online users, 91% of them had experienced online shopping with 49% of these online shoppers spent on food and beverages. This has created a business opportunity for marketers where interaction can be performed online, thus eliminating the traditional brick and mortar and effectively reducing the cost of business setup.

Organic food industry is very competitive throughout the world nowadays. To sharpen the marketing advantages, marketers have begun to provide extra services to customers beyond physical distances. Shopping malls provide delivery services for homes and offices. Online shopping is slowly becoming a trend of purchasing worldwide. It possesses great advantages and benefits to the consumers and the retailers. With online shopping, customers merely order organic food online via internet device, and waiting for the organic food to be delivered at their doorsteps.

CONSUMER PERCEPTION OF ORGANIC FOOD

Consumer intention to purchase a good is defined as consumer willingness to purchase certain goods or services (Mirabi, et al., 2015). Consumers more likely to perform a particular behaviour when they have strong intention towards the behaviour. This also applies in the case of purchasing organic food.

A consumer's willingness to purchase an organic food increases if he or she perceives organic food is beneficial for his or her health (Chen, 2007). Thus, there is a high probability that consumers will make the actual purchase of organic food if they have strong purchase intention towards the food. Besides behavioural reasons, there are several key attributes for a consumer to purchase an organic food which include price, health consciousness, organic certification and labelling, consumer knowledge, availability and environmental concern.

Price

Price is known as the value needed to purchase a product in monetary terms (Britannica, 2016). Price has an impact on the buying behaviour of consumer. When the price of a product increases, consumers are less likely to purchase the product (Al-Salamin & Al-Hassan, 2016). Price of organic food is affected by consumers' demand towards organic food. Hossain and Lim (2016) stressed that increasing demands for organic food cause its price to rise in most markets. This concept also applies in developing countries (Tshuma, et al., 2010). When the demand for organic food is higher than the supply of the food, shortage of organic food occurs (Somasundram, et al., 2016). Since the marketers and suppliers of organic food are unable to fulfil every consumer's demand, they will raise the price of organic food so that only the consumers that have willingness to offer more price for organic food-will make the purchase.

Likewise, the intention to purchase organic meat was influenced by price (Anders and Moeser, 2008). The purchase intention of organic meat among consumers decreased when there was a price premium for the product. Organic food such as fruits and vegetables are known to be more expensive because of the time required to produce them and also the natural agricultural practices that covers higher costs. (Achilleas & Anastasios, 2008). Consumers will more likely purchase organic food if they think that it is worth for the price. Consumers perceive that organic food is very beneficial to their health and has good quality (Chen, 2007). Therefore, consumers have positive perception towards purchasing organic food and think that the food is worth the price even if there is a price premium. However, some consumers are unwilling to pay the premium prices even if they have positive perceptions on organic food (Dardak, et al., 2009).

Conversely, price does not always influence consumers' purchase behaviours. Consumers might be willing to purchase organic food at premium prices due to the rise in their income levels. This was supported by the fact that middle income consumers' willingness to pay premium prices for organically farmed meat in Buenos Aires, Argentina (Rodriguez, et al., 2009). Thus, price of organic food does not impact the purchases of organic food negatively when the consumers think that the price is still reasonable.

Health Consciousness

Health consciousness is a state of readiness to take on healthy actions (Michaelidou & Hassan, 2008). Consumers are known to be health conscious when they are aware and concern about their state of healthiness (Dickieson & Arkus, 2009). These consumers being motivated by improving their health by adopting healthy lifestyles such as exercise regularly, eat a balanced-diet and chose the food they are eating. (Gracia & Magistris, 2007). Health conscious consumers are particularly care about their food intake and tend to consume organic food only. The perception that organic food is safe to consume and contains health benefits caused consumers to have positive attitude on organic consumption (Suh, et al., 2012). These consumers perceive organic food contains more nutrition value than conventional or processed food. Likewise, Lester and Saftner (2011) stressed that organic food has higher nutritional value and is less harmful than conventional food. Therefore, positive attitude on organic consumption motivates consumers to purchase organic food.

Consumers become more concern and conscious about their own health particularly when their family members have health issues such as obesity, diabetes or cancer, which indirectly increase their intention to consume more organic food (Ahmad and Juhdi, 2010). Consumers aware of their own health if people around them have health issues after consuming conventional food. These consumers will switch to consume organic food in prevention of getting illnesses. This situation indicates that surrounding situations can influence consumers to purchase organic food. Some consumers purchase organic food for the well-being of others. For instance, consumers purchase organic vegetables for their children's consumption as they are aware of the amount of pesticides used in conventional farming (Yin, et al., 2010).

Organic Certification and Labelling

Organic certification and labelling plays a vital role in helping consumers to differentiate between organic food and conventional food. Consumers do not view organic food as being different from conventional food when they do not trust the labels (Smed et al., 2013). Aryal et al. (2009) reported that 60% of the respondents did not trust a food to be organic without organic label despite having organic certification. Hence, informative organic labels are important to gain consumers' trust and also in aiding them to identify organic food by disclosing how the food is produced according to the required standards and in environmental friendly ways. By gaining access to this information, consumers are more likely to trust the food is organic and make the purchase (Sønderskov and Daugbjerg, 2011).

Bellows et al. (2008) claimed that consumers were actually placing their trust blindly when buying organic food from supermarkets, retailers and marketers. Padel and Foster (2008) survey showed that 52% of the consumers in United Kingdom only search for ''organic'' word on product packaging in order to identify organic food. This implies that 'organic' word acts as a symbol of trust and may possess greater impact than organic certificates and labels on consumers' behaviour. Moreover, there are cases of companies using fake organic certificates. This affects consumers that have intention to purchase organic product by deceiving them into thinking that a food is organic and organically certified. Consumers tend to distrust all organic products when there are incidents of falsely certified and labelled organic products (Voon, et al., 2011). Thus, creates a purchase barrier and causes consumers to have negative attitudes towards organic food even if it is genuinely certified and labelled.

Consumer Knowledge

According to Hossain and Lim (2016), consumer knowledge reflects a consumer's understanding of a product and this information could be used by consumers in the decision making process. Saleki et al. (2012) suggested that consumers with significant knowledge on organic food were more likely to purchase the food. Conversely, Yiridoe et al. (2005) argued that consumers did not purchase organic food when they were unable to distinguish organic food from conventional food due to lack of knowledge which included ingredients content, nutritional values and production methods of the food. Generally, organic food is more nutritious than conventional food because organic fruits and vegetables are grown without chemical fertilisers and artificial pesticide while organic meat, eggs and dairy products are produced by animals that are fed with organic crops and not injected with growth hormones (Lu, et al., 2012).

Hence, consumers' organic food purchase intention increase if they know the unique food contents or attributes that help them to identify the organic food. Yin et al. (2010) stated that consumers would not purchase organic meat if they were lacking of organic knowledge or would not buy organic meat as they were unfamiliar with the benefits from the product.

Organic food knowledge can be obtained from variety sources such as interaction with others, social media, advertisements and government resources (Gracia & Magistris, 2007). Consumers have to depend on the experiences and views from others if they have low knowledge on organic food (Zagata, 2012). Some consumers may be new to the product or have limited access on organic food. Hence, past experiences and information from others can influence consumers' organic food purchase intention. It is difficult to predict the amount of consumer knowledge needed for a consumer to make actual purchase of organic food. Furthermore, everyone has different past experiences and views on organic food. This will lead to inaccurate information on organic food and likely to affect their perception on purchasing organic food. For instance, some consumers believe that farmers use raw sewage sludge or human waste as fertilisers. In fact, raw sludge or waste must be treated before being used as fertilisers as those substances may be contaminated with other harmful materials (Lu, et al., 2012).

Availability

The availability of organic food increases over the years and organic food can be found in organic retail stores, supermarkets and hypermarkets. Therefore, marketers start to offer more organic food stores in the market in order to meet the demand (Hossain & Lim, 2016). A study by Ahmad and Juhdi (2010) indicated that less availability of organic food in shops and supermarkets was a barrier for consumers to purchase organic food. Similarly, Chakrabarti (2010) identified that product range of organic food affects consumer's purchase intention. For instance, consumers intended to buy organic dairy products in an organic store but the store only sells organic vegetables and fruits. This will indirectly limit their food options. Moreover, some consumers felt difficult to locate organic food stores due to less of information (Brown, 2003).

Convenience can influence consumers to purchase an organic food. The distance between organic food stores and households or workplaces would affect consumer's organic food purchase intention (Pomsanam, et al., 2014). Consumers who live or work near an organic food store tend to visit the shop more frequently. Dimitri and Dettmann (2012) observed that consumers purchased organic food if it was available in the shops as it would save their time for buying at another stores. Thus, high availability increases the convenience for consumers to purchase organic food.

Environmental Concern

Environmental concern can be defined as the worriedness about the quality of air, water and soil in the natural environment. The harmful effects of the methods used in conventional farming have caused consumers to be more concerned about the environment and focused on the benefits of organic farming (Gomiero, et al., 2011). Chemical fertiliser and pesticides are used in the growth of fruits and vegetables in conventional farming. By comparison, conventional farming contaminates the quality of the soil and sea; while organic farming helps to reduce contamination and preserve quality (Yin, et al., 2010). Consumers buy organic food as they perceived that organic farming has less impact on the environment (Gomiero et al., 2011). Likewise, Saleki et al. (2012) identified that consumers purchased organic food because they understood that organic farming causes less harm to environment. Therefore, consumers' intention to buy organic food is motivated by positive perceptions and actual knowledge on the benefits of organic farming.

Research shows that consumers practising green lifestyles have stronger intentions to purchase organic food. (Voon, et al., 2011). These eco-friendly consumers have significant knowledge on conserving the environment and tend to consider the environmental impacts in their actions. They have positive attitudes towards organic food because they know that consuming more organic food will stimulate the growth of organic farming which reduces environmental pollutions. Hence, stronger purchase intention occurs among this group of consumer as they understand their actions will bring positive impact to the environment.

DISCUSSION AND RECOMMENDATIONS

Malaysia female consumers are more health concern as compared to their male counterparts. Likewise, female consumers more likely to purchase organic food as they are more concerned on their own health as well as members of their families (Zhen and Mansori, 2012). Malaysia young adults are more likely to purchase organic food as they are more exposed to organic food. In Malaysia, different ethnic groups portray different organic purchase behaviour (Tan and Huey's, 2009). Survey also shows that married consumers tend to purchase organic food because they are concerned about well-being of their children (Yin, et al., 2010). High income group has more buying power to purchase organic food. Survey shows that 70% of the Malaysians purchase organic food at least once a week and they mostly purchased fruits and vegetables, followed by meat, fish and poultry.

Previous studies (Chen, 2007; Gracia & Magistris, 2007; Dettmann & Dimitri, 2009; Aryal, et al., 2009; Saleki, et al., 2012; Ahmad & Juhdi, 2010) suggested that consumers paid premium prices for organic food when they perceived the benefits of the food were worth than its price (Chen, 2007; Hughner, et al., 2007). Health conscious consumers tend to purchase more organic food than conventional food (Gracia & Magistris, 2007; Ahmad & Juhdi, 2012). The information of organic certifications and labels help consumers to identify the organic food and gain confidence to purchase the food (Aryal, et al., 2009). Consumers' purchase intention on organic food increase if adequate information on organic food. Similarly, consumers are more likely to purchase organic food if they can locate the organic food stores easily (Dimitri and Dettmann, 2012). Besides, available choices of organic food will increase consumers' purchase intention. Green consumers tend to purchase organic food because they are concerned about the environment and understand that organic farming conserves the environment by reducing environmental pollution (Saleki, et al., 2012).

REFERENCES

Achilleas, K., & Anastasios, S. (2008). Marketing aspects of quality assurance systems: The organic food sector case. *British Food Journal*, *110*(8), 829–839. doi:10.1108/00070700810893359

Ahmad, S., & Rosli, J. (2015). The Rise of Online Shopping. *Malaysian Business.*, *1*, 20–27.

Ahmad, S. N., & Juhdi, N. (2010). Organic Food: A Study on Demographic Characteristics and Factors Influencing Purchase Intentions among Consumers in Klang Valley, Malaysia. *International Journal of Business and Management*, *5*(2), 105–118. doi:10.5539/ijbm.v5n2p105

Al-Salamin, H., & Al-Hassan, E. (2016). The Impact of Pricing on Consumer Buying Behavior in Saudi. *European Journal of Business and Management*, *8*(12), 62–73.

Albala, K., & Allen, G. (2007). The Business of Food: Encyclopedia of the Food and Drink Industries. Greenwood.

Anders, S., & Moeser, A. (2008). Assessing the demand for value-based organic meats in Canada: A combined retail and household scanner-data approach. *International Journal of Consumer Studies*, *32*(5), 457–469. doi:10.1111/j.1470-6431.2008.00707.x

Aryal, K., Chaudhary, P., Pandit, S., & Sharma, G. (2009). Consumers' Willingness To Pay For Organic Products: A Case From Kathamandu Valley. *The Journal of Agriculture and Environment*, *10*, 12–22. doi:10.3126/aej.v10i0.2126

Bellows, A. C., Onyango, B., Diamond, A., & Hallman, W. K. (2008). Understanding Consumer Interest in Organics: Production Values vs. Purchasing Behaviour. *Journal of Agricultural & Food Industrial Organization*, *6*(2), 12–28.

Britannica. (2016). *Price*. Encyclopedia Britannica.

Brown, C. (2003). Consumers' preferences for locally produced food: A study in southeast MIssouri. *American Journal of Alternative Agriculture*, *18*(4), 213–224. doi:10.1079/AJAA200353

Chakrabarti, S. (2010). Factors influencing organic food purchase in India – expert survey insights. *British Food Journal*, *112*(8), 902–915. doi:10.1108/00070701011067497

Chen, M. F. (2007). Consumer Attitude towards organic meats and purchase intentions in relation to organic foods in Taiwan: Moderating effects of food-related personality traits. *Food Quality and Preference*, *18*, 1008–1021. doi:10.1016/j.foodqual.2007.04.004

Cheng, R. (2014). Strategy Research on Development of Green Food and Security Control in Heilongjiang Province. *International Conference on Agricultural and Biosystem Engineering*, *8*, 24-29. 10.1016/j.ieri.2014.09.005

Dardak, R. A., Zainol, A. Z., & Kasim, A. (2009). Consumer's perception, consumption and preference on organic product: Malaysian perspective. *Economic and Technology Management Review*, *4*, 95–107.

Dettmann, R. L., & Dimitri, C. (2009). Who's Buying Organic Vegetables? Demographic Characteristics of U.S. Consumers. *Journal of Food Products Marketing*, *16*(1), 79–91. doi:10.1080/10454440903415709

Dickieson, J., & Arkus, V. (2009). *Factors that influence the purchase of organic food: A study of consumer behaviour in the UK*. Cass Business School.

Dimitri, C., & Dettmann, R. L. (2012). Organic Food Consumers: What Do We Really Know About Them? *British Food Journal*, *114*(8), 1157–1183. doi:10.1108/00070701211252101 eCommerceMILO. (2014). Retrieved from https://www.ecinsider.my/2014/12/top-malaysia-ecommerce-stories-2014.html

Gomiero, T., Pimentel, D., & Paoletti, M. (2011). Environmental Impact of Different Agricultural Management Practices: Conventional vs. Organic Agriculture. *Critical Reviews in Plant Sciences*, *30*(1), 95–124. doi:10.1080/07352689.2011.554355

Gracia, A., & Magistris, T. (2007). Organic Food Product Purchase Behaviour: A Pilot Study. *Spanish Journal of Agricultural Research*, *5*(4), 439–451. doi:10.5424jar/2007054-5356

Hassan, S. H., Loi, W. Y., & Kok, J. R. (2015). Purchasing Intention Towards Organic Food Among Gen Y In Malaysia. *Journal of Agribusiness Marketing*, *7*(2), 16–32.

Hossain, M. T., & Lim, P. X. (2016). Consumers' Buying Behavior towards Organic Foods. *Journal of Malaysian Insititute of Management*, *51*(2), 7–25.

Hughner, R. S., McDonagh, P., Prothero, A., Shultz, C. J., & Stanton, J. (2007). Who are organic food consumers? A compilation and review of why people purchase orgnic food. *Journal of Consumer Behaviour*, *6*(2-3), 94–110. doi:10.1002/cb.210

International Federation of Organic Agriculture Movements. (2018). *2017 Annual Report of the Organics International*. Retrieved from https://www.ifoam.bio/en/our-library/annual-reports

Internetworldstats.com. (2015). *World Population Stats*. Available at: http://www.internetworldstats.com/stats.htm

Lester, G., & Saftner, R. A. (2011). Organically versus Conventionally Grown Produce: Common Production Inputs, Nutritional Quality, and Nitrogen Delivery between the Two Systems. *Journal of Agricultural and Food Chemistry*, *59*(19), 10401–10406. doi:10.1021/jf202385x PMID:21910454

Lu, Q., He, Z. L., & Stoffella, P. J. (2012). Land Application of Biosolids in the USA: A Review. *Applied and Environmental Soil Science*, *11*, 1–3. doi:10.1155/2012/201462

MagazineM. (2014). Retrieved from https://marketingmagazine.com.my/magazines/

Michaelidou, N., & Hassan, L. M. (2008). The role of health consciousness, food safety concern and ethical identity on attitudes and intentions towards organic food. *International Journal of Consumer Studies*, *32*(2), 163–170. doi:10.1111/j.1470-6431.2007.00619.x

Mirabi, V., Akbariyeh, H., & Tahmasebifard, H. (2015). A Study of Factors Affecting on Customers Purchase Intention. *Journal of Multidisciplinary Engineering Science and Technology*, *2*(1), 267–273.

Padel, S., & Foster, C. (2005). Exploring the gap between attitudes and behaviour: Understanding why consumers buy or do not buy organic food. *British Food Journal*, *107*(8), 606–625. doi:10.1108/00070700510611002

Peyper, L. (2015). *Trends and tastes in e-commerce*. Finweek.

Pomsanam, P., Napompech, K., & Suwanmaneepong, S. (2014). Factors Driving Thai Consumers' Intention to Purchase Organic Foods. *Asian Journal of Scientific Research*, *7*(4), 434–446. doi:10.3923/ajsr.2014.434.446

Saleki, Z. S., Seyedsaleki, S. M., & Rahimi, M. R. (2012). Organic Food Purchasing Behaviour in Iran. *International Journal of Business and Social Science*, *3*(13), 278–285.

Smed, A. S., Kærgård, L. M., & Daugbjerg, C. (2013). A Matter of Trust: How Trust Influence Organic Consumption. *The Journal of Agricultural Science*, *5*(7), 91–106.

Somasundram, C., Razali, Z., & Santhirasegaram, V. (2016). A Review on Organic Food Production in Malaysia. *Horticulturae*, *2*(3), 4–12. doi:10.3390/horticulturae2030012

Sønderskov, K. M., & Daugbjerg, C. (2011). The state and consumer confidence in eco-labeling: Organic labeling in Denmark, Sweden, The United Kingdom and The United States. *Agriculture and Human Values*, *28*(4), 507–517. doi:10.100710460-010-9295-5

Suh, B. W., Eves, A., & Lumbers, M. (2012). Consumers' Attitude and Understanding of Organic Food: The Case of South Korea. *Journal of Foodservice Business Research*, *12*(1), 49–63. doi:10.1080/15378020.2012.650524

Tan, A., & Huey, Q. S. (2009). Consumer Purchase Decisions of Organic Food Products: An Ethnic Analysis. *Journal of International Consumer Marketing*, *22*(1), 47–58. doi:10.1080/08961530902844949

Tshuma, P., Makhathini, S., Siketile, P. N., & Taruvinga, A. (2010). Consumer perceptions on organic products in the Eastern Cape; the case of East London: South Africa. *Journal of Environmental. Agricultural and Food Chemistry*, *9*(3), 458–467.

Vazifehdoust, H., Taleghani, M., Esmaeilpour, F., Nazari, K., & Khadang, M. (2013). Factors influence consumers' green purchasing behavior. *Management Science Letters*, *2*(9), 2489–2500. doi:10.5267/j.msl.2013.08.013

Voon, J. P., Ngui, K. S., & Agrawal, A. (2011). Determinants of Willingness to Purchase Organic Food: An Exploratory Study Using Structural Equation Modeling. *The International Food and Agribusiness Management Review*, *14*(2), 103–120.

Yin, S., Wu, L., Du, L., & Chen, M. (2010). Consumers' Purchase Intention of Organic Food in China. *Journal of the Science of Food and Agriculture*, *90*(8), 1361–1367. doi:10.1002/jsfa.3936 PMID:20474056

Yiridoe, E. K., Bonti-Ankomah, S., & Martin, R. C. (2005). Comparison of consumer perceptions and preference toward organic versus conventionally produced foods: A review and update of the literature. *Renewable Agriculture and Food Systems*, *20*(4), 193–205. doi:10.1079/RAF2005113

Zagata, L. (2012). Consumers' beliefs and behavioural intentions towards organic food. Evidence from the Czech Republic. *Appetite*, *59*(1), 81–89. doi:10.1016/j.appet.2012.03.023 PMID:22504401

Zhen, J., & Mansori, S. (2012). Young Female Motivations for Purchase of Organic Food in Malaysia. *International Journal of Contemporary Business Studies*, *3*(5), 61–72.

KEY TERMS AND DEFINITIONS

Availability: The possibility that one can buy, get, or obtain organic foods.

Consumer Behavior: Customers buy organic foods to satisfy their needs and wants. It refers to the actions that consumers taken and the underlying motives for those actions.

Consumer Knowledge: A consumer's understanding of a product and this information could be used by consumers in the decision-making process.

Consumer Perception: Consumer's awareness or consciousness about organic foods. It is typically affected by environmental and health concerns, pricing, availability, knowledge, and certification.

Environmental Concern: The worriedness about the quality of air, water and soil in the natural environment and the harmful effects of conventional farming being compared to organic farming.

Health Consciousness: Concerned about how healthy one's diet and lifestyle by consuming organic foods.

Online Purchase: A form of electronic commerce which allows consumers to directly buy goods or services from a seller over the Internet using a web browser.

Organic Certification and Labelling: A certification process for producers of organic food and other organic agricultural products.

Organic Food: Organic food is food produced by methods that comply with the standards of organic farming.

Price: The amount of money that has to be paid to acquire an organic product.

Chapter 7
Understanding Generational Impact on Online Business:
The Virtual Communities and Social Collaborations Scenario

Karthikeyan Shanmugam
https://orcid.org/0000-0003-4276-2663
SASTRA University (Deemed), India

Vijayabanu C
SASTRA University (Deemed), India

ABSTRACT

In today's age of technology and exploding internet penetration, customers are rapidly moving toward continuous connectivity across every facet of their lives. Similarly, business is also changing in response to this digital boom. This chapter analyzes digital tools such as virtual communities, social collaboration, and its impact on the multiple generations in managing connected customers for organizations. The technological tools make it simple for customers to be connected at all times, which has become the major challenge for organizations to formulate strategies and be competent in the market. The major types of virtual communities that can be associated with businesses were discussed in detail. This chapter proposes a model for organization to manage their customers effectively. The above-mentioned digital tools are playing vital role in retaining customers and strategies can be formulated to manage the connected customers successfully. Thus, the chapter analyzed the major areas that are important to the organizations in order to succeed in formulating competitive strategy.

INTRODUCTION

Evolution of information sharing is worldwide and it is to the extent of around 10 percent of the total population. They are sharing information through informal networks frequently, for various purposes. When information sharing is intelligently accessed, it acts as an efficient method for any organization

DOI: 10.4018/978-1-5225-9697-4.ch007

either it is public or private. Information sharing is essential to most of the businesses, aiding quickly to meet customer desires through CRM systems.

In today's age of technology and exploding Internet penetration, Indian retail customers are rapidly moving toward continuous connectivity across every facet of their lives. Today's customers are more tech-savvy and more open than ever before to try out new experiences enabled by unfettered digital access. Virtual communities are virtual in some extent. However, they are not something beyond our conventional societies. Virtual communities are genuine parts of our public and in that capacity additionally part of the progressing change and advancement of society. Regardless of whether we trust that a virtual community is just a gathering of individuals utilizing the equivalent "news" gathering, or meeting around an accumulation of homepages, or imparting through a "mailing list", it is considered as a "basic" specialized frameworks will impact the manner in which society is organized and how that structure will change (Schuler, 1996).

This digital transformation is bringing about a profound shift in how customers interact with retailers as they make their purchase decisions. Indian retailers that take note of, and act on, these changes would best placed to win customers in this connected retail environment. A number of researches have discounted that how an exchange of information and societal support are the two major facts behind why people join and then chose a virtual community.

Virtual Communities

Virtual community is web-based gathering of individuals who share similar interests, fears, and sincere beliefs. (Dennis, Pootheri, & Natarajan, 1998), a subject important to all individuals have been discussed by the groups of individuals who meet frequently (Figallo, 1998), and the shared interests or a geographic bond which brings groups of individuals together (Kilsheimer, 1997). Virtual communities are defined as "social aggregations that emerge from the Internet when enough people carry on those public discussions long enough, with sufficient human feeling, to form webs of personal relationships in cyberspace" (Rheingold, 1993).

Virtual communities and collaborations facilitate various value additions like active participation and promotion. (Pentina et al., 2008). Virtual communities are online spaces where individuals serach for peples and talk with them electronically about the similar interested topics. Being competent for enhancing attachment to online and the websites, virtual communities can possibly develop future plans of action, particularly in business to consumers. Hagel and Armstrong (1997) discussed the business viewpoint and characterize virtual communities as a gathering of individuals drawn together by a chance to impart a feeling of the network to similarly invested outsiders having normal premium. Virtual communities are fundamentally characterized as the gatherings of similarly invested outsiders who interface prevalently on the internet to frame connections, share learning, have a great time or take part in economic transactions.

Among the rapidly growing different types of websites (Peterson, 1999; Wingfield and Hanrahan, 1999), community sites places the major role. Assessments of virtual community membership have surpassed twenty-five million (Gross, 1999) and the Pew Internet and American Life Project reports that ninety million Americans have taken part in an online gathering (Horrigan, Rainie, and Fox, 2001). Along these lines, important reasons why users join specific communities and build up a web presence and for scholastics attempting to comprehend user behavior. Hence, it becomes essential for organizations to understand the virtual communities that facilitate them to take advantage of using vast information for enhancing income expanding potential. The introduction of virtual communities related to the recent trends of e-commerce (Othmani and Bouslama, 2015). Acquiring high technology security along with sociability is easy to use which helps virtual communities to collect the needs of customers and their interest.

BACKGROUND OF THE STUDY

Almost twenty-five years from now officially, digital has been transforming our society by changing the everyday life of markets and general peoples. One important dimension of this digital advancement is the expanded probability for customers to make a move in all directions.

In the mid-90s, because of sites and the advancement of web-based business (e-commerce), consumers used the capacity to influence demand and "churn". This impact keeps on developing and, towards the end of the 90s, customers started the attack by delivering information, positioning the products and brands on an expanding number through blogs and forums. The customer's impact escalated significantly due to social networks as "Facebook, Twitter and YouTube" in the 21st century: for huge sharing of information. Towards the end of the 2000s, consumer's empowerment achieved peak, in light of groups: the group and communities even helped consumers to mold up themselves as service providers.

Today the period is, described by the rise of connected devices and the expansion of the social networks of individuals through networks by both individuals and devices. This period of the Social Internet of Things addresses a huge change for market borders, focused universes and economic stakeholders. In this new universe, consumer behavior is always an unexplored field of research. The "Connected Consumers in a Digital World" inquire and disclose to the organizations how to adjust their marketing strategies and techniques to stay aggressive in markets where rivalry is expected.

In recent years, efforts to create innovations and new values accelerated by utilizing networked machines and information in the industry. We expected that not only the manufacturing industry but also the service industry are going to change with the use of Internet of Things (IoT). An effective platform creates an interdependent ecosystem in which companies collaborate independently seeking their own goals. The system that has contributed to the development of the hyper-connected society is especially depends on information and communication. Including the emergence of information exchange, the typical changes in through various equipment and systems such as smartphones, ICT convergence, media convergence, the emergence of big data, and cloud computing. In the pre-connectivity era, the customer buying behavior typically followed the 4A's framework that consists of awareness, attitude, and actions. In this straightforward process of the network era, the company's touch points have a major influence on customer decision making.

In the high connectivity era, customers tend to connect with their peers and ask their opinions. They are influenced by the netizens who are considered as one of the most active players in the consumer's forums and communities. Besides that, customers who need more information would go online and read the reviews to see what other consumers have told about the product or service. The amount of positive or negative opinions, reviews and recommendations will either strengthen or weaken the brand's initial appeal through the connectivity among the customers.

Social media platforms and live chat put organizations directly before customer; organizations could not forfeit their customer to keep up the brand position. In fact, when organizations do not react to an inquiry, it harms the brand reputation since that information is open to a huge number of individuals. The upside of these new devices is that it has a more extensive information accumulation pool; organizations can quickly track their innovative work by using this huge information. The studies show that behaviors of consumers in virtual community were influenced by the recommendations and online reviews plays a vital role (Menon et al, 2005; Bickart and Schindler, 2001).

Consumers and Digital Marketing (E-Commerce and Mobile App)

Digital marketing is a form of marketing that can be accessed either through online or offline utilization of electronic gadget, it brings completely every form of advertising via electronic gadget and inclines to view it on screen through television sets or electronic billboards, also it can be viewed through the internet via social media and through radio termed as offline.

Some of the benefits of social media are

Reduced Cost: The cost for creating a digital marketing strategy through online is comparatively lower than telecasted on televisions, radios and paper media.

Flexibility: The digital form has more flexibility with the advantage of easily moving from one channel to another with very little or no cost incurred compared to other forms.

Viral: Social media plug-ins is helpful in making viral the products and services of top app development companies on websites.

Measurable Result: Digital marketing makes it easy to know, evaluate the number of views or click of the content at the back end but it is hard to get the same evaluation on either TV, radio or billboard commercials.

Saves Time: With the use of digital marketing, the consumer can purchase the products of their need at ease with a simple click from where they reside. This saves more time for the customers.

The magnitude of digital marketing and its impact on the current business world is undoubtedly huge despite its contributing factors. Thus, E-commerce has emerged as a lifestyle for millions of people over the globe. As much as e-commerce has turned out to be instilled in everyday existence, so has the utilization of apps, those help to link our short-lived interests, benefits and specific needs in a given activity cycle.

With social media outlets being so predominant, apps that encourage the communication process between users are fundamental to everybody's shared digital encounters, by means of Facebook, Instagram, or Twitter. As everything changing into digital, that states every company getting themselves into online for marketing. Brands have to stay alive with recent trends that help them to face the challenges of digital marketing. The leading digital marketing trends that are paving the way in 2018 are Interactive Chatbots, Voice Search, Integrating AI and Blockchain Technologies, Influencer marketing.

OBJECTIVES OF THE STUDY

- To know and understand the role of virtual communities of connecting consumers.
- To identify the various types of virtual communities and their relationship to various generations.
- To identify the need of virtual communities to face future challenges for various generation of consumers.

Table 1. Types of virtual communities (e-commerce, Web 2.0)

Type	Details	Websites
Commercial communities	"To encourage business transactions and other businesses". They are related to e-commerce and centered on a commercial area.	Amazon, e-Bay
Communities of practice	Impart ideas, experiences, and opinions.	Twitter
Virtual reality communities	Imaginary environments experiences.	Second Life (Site 24)
Social communities	To set up or keep up social or expert or professional associations.	Facebook, Linkedin, MySpace

Source: (Turban et al. 2008)

Types of Virtual Communities

Typology of virtual communities is not conformed to the single, widely accepted classification and definitions of "virtual community". According to Preece(2000) Stanoevska – Slabeve (2002) most of the researchers, likely to classify virtual communities with a single variable which they feel the prime source of their discipline. For instance, researchers based on information system often classify by the supporting communication technology design like chat, blogs or other functional requirements. On the other side, there are researcher's looks through sociological perspective, who uses the structure of interaction network or the location of interaction like physical or virtual space as a classifying variable, Virnoche & Marx (1997).

Another major categorization by business researchers based on the purpose of communities such as revenue generation or consumer needs satisfaction based on the attributes like fantasy and interaction.

Classification Based on Information System Researchers

Virtual community is where people joining and meeting together with related interests, and connected over the Internet. Virtual communities based on usage of information systems can be distinguished, as shown in Table 1. Even though the reasons behind these virtual communities are amazing, creation and support of social networks became general among these communities.

Commercial Communities

The commercial communities are the type of virtual communities that are strongly associated with businesses, and e-commerce sites are the options how they directly associated with businesses. Some of them are developing normally towards such ideas, especially to encourage greater associations with their users or to give them information needed for making a better purchase. Nowadays e-commerce sites permit buyers to review the purchases they made using the e-commerce sites, which enables prospective customers to think and decide about future purchases based on these reviews (Easley and Kleinberg, 2010). Thus, e-commerce sites are advancing into virtual communities, and virtual communities supported by online social networks incorporated with the features of e-commerce.

Figure 1. Typology of virtual communities
Source: Porter, 2004

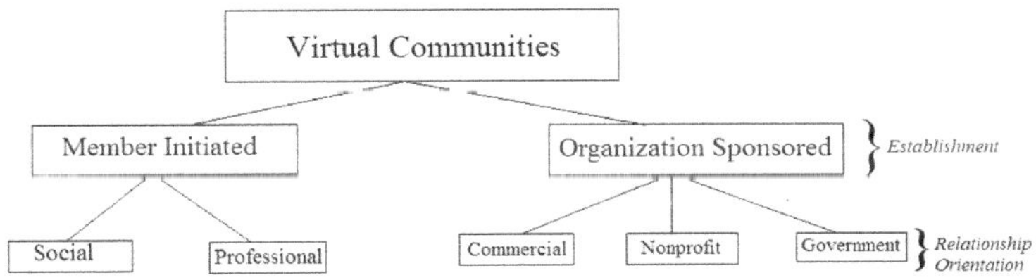

Communities of Practice

Communities of practice also termed as a virtual community of practice and is developed and maintained by using the internet. Professionals are grouped together by shared objectives and common concerns about participation, exchange of inferred and clear knowledge to improve their professional experience and the performance of their organizations. Communities of practice are mainly characterized by self-regulations. These communities depend majorly on internet virtual space like social networks. Professionals use communities of practice as a critical resource to provide them the need of suggestions, best practices, tips and tricks, insights. Along with these facts, which makes a community of practice strong is the collection of relationships, i.e., people and information are associated to a rational set of the area which people will find helpful, interesting and potentially profitable.

CLASSIFICATIONS BASED ON BUSINESS RESEARCHERS

Content-Based Classifications

The virtual communities include two first-level categories, and they are Member-initiated and Organization-sponsored. The second level category of virtual communities' states is the kind of association or affiliation prevails between the participants of society. "Member-initiated communities promoting either social or professional relationships among members have been done by the member-initiated communities". "Organization-sponsored communities promote develop relationships both among members and between individual members and the sponsoring organization".

Member-initiated communities and member-generated content focused majorly by the maximum researchers moderate than on organizations of virtual communities sponsored. Virtual communities of these types are becoming popular with organizations (Bughin & Zeisser, 2001; Balasubramanian & Mahajan, 2001). Member-generated content communities are widely accessed by both the members and organizations, which also contributes to the content as well as participation in building relationships (Mcwilliam, 2002). Thus, the proposed classifications are helpful across many disciplines for both the researchers and organizations as well.

Individuals create and set up virtual communities online to offer a forum by which people can share information paying little mind to the topic. Some virtual communities developed for individuals and occupied with business-related activities. In this kind of community, individuals normally share trade secrets. Moreover, a customer based virtual community shaped by business organizations builds up a situation where customers can transparently share and spread information to different customers and company agents.

From the past researches to characterize virtual communities, we suggested the following attributes: "Purpose, Place, Platform, Population Interaction Structure, and Profit Model". It will be thoughtful to have essential attributes in conceptualizing virtual communities as it is consistent and easy to describe them while organizations and researchers planning. The distinctive mixtures of features comprises precarious success factors and relative results that help both members and organizations. The differentiating variables, establishment, and relationships differentiate each kind of virtual community from others. Hence, the attributes explained below helps in label any virtual community despite its type.

The key attributes of virtual communities can be termed as the Five Ps of virtual community. The summarized attributes as follows:

Purpose: This attribute describes the specific focus of discourse, or focal content of the communication, among community members.

Place: This attribute defines the location of the interaction, where interaction occurs either completely virtually or only partially virtually.

Platform: This attribute refers to the technical design of interaction in the virtual community where designs enable synchronous communication, asynchronous communication or both.

Population: This attribute refers to the pattern of interaction among community members as described by group structure (e.g. small group or network) and type of social ties (e.g. strong, weak, stressful).

Profit Model: This attribute refers to whether a community creates tangible economic value where value is the revenue-generation.

Revenue-Based Classifications

The revenue-based classification of virtual community focuses not only on the content but also on the profitability that relates more to the business model perspective. The revenue-based virtual communities can be classified into two main groups namely standalone or add-on according to revenue generation model (Franz and Wolkinger, 2003). The organizations concentrate more towards indirect effects of the virtual communities rather than generating revenues through the standalone basis includes revenues from e-commerce trading, subscriptions, advertising, and other relevant sources. However, an add-on basis community includes revenues from integrating various customer, analyzing research about markets, and product development.

There are some additional elements frequently mentioned that provide indirect revenue for the company:

- Customer Loyalty
- Customer Feedbacks / Suggestions
- Improve products
- Consumer Stickiness
- discover new streams of revenue
- Innovation process
- Customer Information

The virtual community based on revenue by Cothrel (2000) has similar objectives of Franz and Wolkinger (2003) model. The Cothrel (2000) model aims to build a stronger relationship, innovations,

Table 2. Key attributes of virtual communities

Attribute	Explanation
Purpose - content of interaction	The content of information which is used for interaction, (Example., Sports or general discussions on the environment, politics, etc.,)
Place - extent of technology mediation of interaction	• Virtual "exists only in virtual space" • Hybrid "exists in both physical and virtual space"
Platform - design of interaction	• Synchronous for example chat. • Asynchronous for example email • Hybrid
Population interaction structure - pattern of interaction	• computer oriented social networks • small groups or networks • virtual public
Profit model - return on interaction	This attributes concentrates in identifying the creation of tangible economic value by virtual communities. • Income -generating (host, facilitator, owner) - host communities by the enablers of certain community's (e.g.Yahoo) • Non-revenue generating

Source: (Porter, 2004)

increase efficiency, acquiring new customers and direct revenues. The first three elements of the model envelop add-on part and the direct earnings are comparable to standalone elements of previous model.

IMPACT OF VIRTUAL COMMUNITIES ON MULTI-GENERATIONS

Generations are a group of people who born during a particular timeframe. They have more similar life circumstances, same perspectives, and dispositions, and separated from different ages. Currently, five generations namely Maturists, Baby Boomers, Gen X, Gen Y or Millennials ad Gen Z are prevailing. Multi-Generations has a greater impact on the virtual world. Understanding these issues is indispensable for organizations: they can influence everything at various stages to connect with customers and other stakeholders. The organizations should handle the issues of the virtual world across generations. Generally, millennials spend much time on the web, and live in internet-based life for various individual reasons. More youthful millennial tend to balance life, work, daily activities, network, etc., through tech-

Figure 2. Types of virtual communities (revenue based)Source: (Franz and Wolkinger 2003)

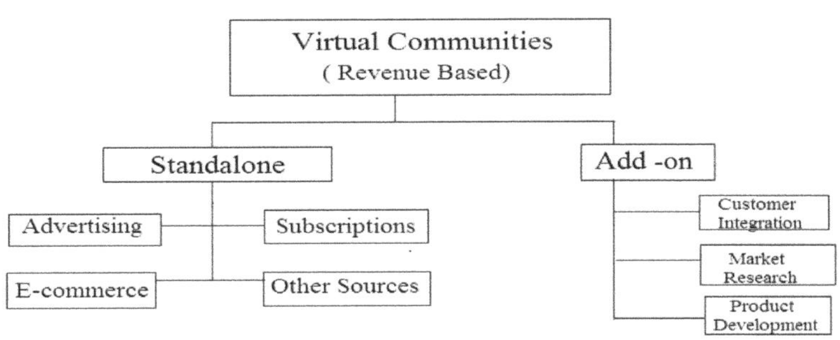

nology. Internet users of the Middle Ages are more inclined towards information technology than older ages to understand other people's perspectives through blogs compared to older generations. The middle ages also utilize social networking sites to make profiles on that locale. In contrast, teenagers and Gen Y utilize virtual communities to mingle and develop a relationship, business databases, and grouping. Hence, the challenge for the organization lies with the product, quality, competition and price wars that managed through effective social collaboration and with different generations.

Raymond Morin, Canada-based social media expert, speaker, author in his new book "Generation C - The Confluence Marketing at the Era of Connected Consumers" in which he examines the challenges and opportunities presented by content and influencer marketing in relation to successive generations that are increasingly less receptive to traditional communication. He explores the evolution of individuals' behavior as consumers but also workers and members of society. Raymond provides invaluable insights and advice for anyone interested in marketing in our digital age.

The new connected generation, also known as Generation C, encompasses successive generations of active users and consumers on the internet. From elders and baby boomers to digital natives, they are now all involved in the social and digital transformation of organizations. Today, as technological innovations transform society at an accelerated pace, we see micro-generations emerging, each with specific characteristics and motivations. In reality, the concept of Generation C is not new and goes back to 2004 with the appearance of social networks, and when Dutch magazine TrendWatching.com observed behavioral traits linking the different generations of connected consumers. Each of these new generations of "connected consumers" wants to be heard, and demands that companies and brands respond to their requests. Fourteen years later, they each uniquely influenced several aspects of society: from home to the workplace, to education, communication, social relations, and entertainment.

The connected consumer is empowered by the endless choices resulting from accessibility to the web and social media, which profound changes the business/customer relationship. Today, connected consumers rely more on their peers' recommendations to seek information and prioritize the quality of their experience and the brand. This forces companies and brands to adapt their message and communicate differently with their clients. In this context and thanks to new technological innovations (augmented reality, artificial intelligence, 3D printing) and the analysis of personal data accessible online, it is believed that marketing campaigns will be more personalized, more targeted towards the connected consumers, and will have the priority to satisfy the customer's experience.

SOCIAL COLLABORATION: IMPORTANCE AND BENEFITS

Sharing and interacting information with more people in a public forum to achieve a common goal, support, acceptance are about social collaboration. Social collaboration plays a vital role in improving the enhanced perception of the quality of products and services. This complex problem, by far more assorted and least consistent of all business software categories, is social collaboration. Among other business software category in social collaboration is fair and diverse in solving various diverse problems. When the collaboration tool is properly utilized it creates more positive eWOM, ends in satisfied customers. The organization can use these satisfied customers as their brand ambassadors whose perception results in sharing positive experiences via reviews, feedbacks, and conversations with their friends, family, and colleagues. Most of the time this will be based on the what are the products and services, overall objectives, and only the tip of the iceberg. Social collaboration tools simply help to do existing business activities in a faster and easier way.

Generally, social collaboration software classified into three different types, relevant to businesses, namely people oriented, task-oriented and file oriented. Social collaboration tools aims to promote impulsive, non-mandated knowledge between customers in the form of comments, status updates, microblogs etc.

Below are some neglected advantages:

- **Time-Saving:** One of the major crux of any industry is its effective usage of its time and the way they spent it with their customers. This also include how employees of the organization spent their time in accomplishing their tasks to attain the objectives of the organization.
- **Strong Relationship Among Team Members:** Building effective working relationships among employees is vital in any organization. Collaboration tools are path development for employees of a team to work conveniently for achieving a common goal.
- **Goal-Based Performance:** The Better organization is something that each organization ought to make progress toward, regardless of whether things are as of now going great. Collaboration tools are the best medication when you are endeavoring to enhance the organization.
- **Increased Productivity:** Employees spend almost 50 percent of their time searching for information and managing communications. Social collaboration tools dramatically streamline that process, enabling people to find what and whom they need more efficiently and effectively - which means they have more time to get real work done.
- **Clear, Consistent Communication:** Social collaboration tools allow organizations to communicate meaningfully at every level. Corporate-wide and executive announcements shared and interacted. Therefore, everyone aligned with the company vision, mission, and news. Departments gain a digital meeting space to work on projects and build relationships.
- **Stronger Corporate Memory:** Corporate culture – and its longer-term counterpart, corporate memory – stem from a communal understanding of an organization's values and knowledge. Social collaboration provides the framework to connect people to each other and to the historical and real-time information that is critical to organizational success.

Online collaboration tools help in enhancing efficiency, productivity, and innovation, online collaboration aspects of social media, traditional business, and crowdsourcing to create an experience, not at all like whatever else. Collaboration tools also include a broad range of functions, from instant messaging to company intranets to document collaboration to knowledge bases, forums, and user groups. At the highest level, social collaboration tools break down silos to improve access to the people and information that help work done more quickly and accurately. Those silos may be technological, geographical, organizational, personal, or all of the above.

The advantages of social collaboration enhance profitability, knowledge management, group commitment, and competitiveness. It is useful for a group of people to work together, and ideally dealt with each sort of information - records, projects, plans, and discussions. Social collaboration enables committed workspaces for customers and partners to share information, and arrange exertion or construct customer communities. In addition to the fact that it bring customers and partners into collaboration work process, to inspire and build more strong relationships.

Future of Social Collaboration Tools

Emerging technologies like artificial intelligence (AI) and machine learning will transform social collaboration tools into smart, predictive hubs when and where you need it. Foreseeing the future of work has become a most loved pastime for most of the people. More important, it is accomplished a lot of progress – with constant revolution. Creation of a perfect flawless collaboration tool experience to all stakeholders will be the future of business collaboration. Such tools experience and their collaborative processes would save money on travel and other material costs. Important conclusions about consumer behavior attained by decision-makers with the aid of integrated systems and data collaboration. Social collaboration aids the organizations to take advantage over their businesses in everything from innovation, design, invention, marketing plans and a million other tasks easily. According to Holly Simmons, senior director of marketing for SAP's cloud collaboration and analysis products, "Social collaboration is not just about replacing email or sharing a document, it is about moving the business ahead, solving problems and making strategic decisions".

In comparing with traditional marketing method, virtual communities are promising and increase efficiency element. The new combinations of information, products and services and innovative integrations of resources and relationships between consumers and companies seemed to provide more market potential with the addition of virtual communities. It is in the preliminary stages, the studies on understanding the impact of virtual communities on marketing strategies. As a result, there are other studies in the future. Above all the literature indicates that the degree of consumer commitment towards virtual community is the major factor in deciding the success of virtual communities (Cothrel 2000). Hence, it is important to plan a reliable measuring scale for the degree of individual involvement in the community. While measuring these following aspects are need to be taken into considerations like the trust or increasing degree of commitment one have on the brand as a limitation in representing a particular community (Morgan and Hunt, 1994). Until now, online auctions and the retail markets are some of the sectors. A full assessment of the consequences of virtual communities in different sectors will also be required. However, the use of virtual communities could also address broader types of relationships.

CONNECTING CONSUMERS OF VARIOUS GENERATIONS

Organizations that will succeed in retaining new recruits and in collaborating with the Generations Y and Z are those who know how to integrate them into their change-management process and appeal to their curiosity and natural creativity, notably for content creation and duration. Some of the measures to regain trust among customers are:

- Never walk away from the commitments you make
- Make sure of quicker response to all situations
- Show integrity in approach
- Adopt an open and transparent set of guidelines
- Establish a history of positive actions with the customers

The type of influencers and the role they play in online and social media marketing strategies will always depend on the objectives and target audiences. Celebrity or social media celebrity endorsement will never generate the same impact as a corporate ambassador program or a long-term business relationship. Companies and organizations must clearly define their objectives first, and identify the type of influencers that will best fit the context of the new era. The four generations have shared the same working environments. This is a new paradigm of today's digital society, which will accelerate the social and digital transformation of organizations. At this level, Generation X, which has just taken over decision-making positions, also has a new responsibility to undertake, and handle connected generations. The digital era has led to the emergence of micro-generations with specific expectations and needs, and it is time for marketing to adapt to this new reality.

CONCLUSION

The chapter reviewed and analyzed the impact of virtual communities and social collaboration for the effective performance of an organization. It states the realistic situations in breaking down generation and age barriers to access the information shared through virtual communities. It also confirms that the primary reasons why virtual communities and social collaboration are essential in managing the global business through connected customers, e-commerce, e-tailing of new emerging economies. Businesses can gain by enriching their websites to present highly interactive sessions. This can restrained through experts and motivates sharing opinions, exchanging various thoughts and news that effects in the discussions product related decisions. Valuable information can be created with the help of these events to increase loyalty among customers and able to develop potential customers concurrently. Additionally, by creating an online space in the trading website will attract customers in socializing and in turn helps the organizations to build loyal customers.

REFERENCES

Bagozzi, R. P., & Dholakia, U. M. (2002). Intentional social action in virtual communities. *Journal of Interactive Marketing*, *16*(2), 2–21. doi:10.1002/dir.10006

Balasubramanian, S., & Mahajan, V. (2001). The Economic Leverage of the Virtual Community. *International Journal of Electronic Commerce*, *5*(3), 103–138. doi:10.1080/10864415.2001.11044212

Bughin, J., & Zeisser, M. (2001). The marketing scale effectiveness of virtual communities. *Electronic Markets*, *11*(4), 258–262. doi:10.1080/101967801753405544

Cothrel, J. P. (2000). Measuring the success of an online community. *Strategy and Leadership*, *28*(2), 7–21. doi:10.1108/10878570010341609

Dennis, A. R., Pootheri, S. K., & Natarajan, V. L. (1998). Lessons from the early adopters of Web groupware. *Journal of Management Information Systems*, *14*(4), 65–86. doi:10.1080/07421222.1998.11518186

Easley & Kleinberg. (2010). Networks, Crowds, and Markets: Reasoning about a Highly Connected World. Cambridge University Press.

Figallo, C. (1998). *Hosting Web communities: Building relationships, increasing customer loyalty and maintaining a competitive edge*. New York: John Wiley & Sons, Inc.

Franz, R., & Wolkinger, T. (2003). Customer Integration with Virtual Communities. Case study: The online community of the largest regional newspaper in Austria. *Proceedings of the Hawaii International Conference on System Sciences.*

Gross. (1999, March 22). Building global communities: How business is partnering with sites that draw together like-minded consumers. *BusinessWeek Online*. Retrieved October 17, 2004, from http://businessweek.com/datedtoc/1999/9912.htm

Hagel, J., & Armstrong, A. G. (1997). *Net Gain: Expanding Markets through Virtual Communities.* Harvard Business School Press.

Horrigan, J. B., Rainie, L., & Fox, S. (2001). *Online communities: networks that nurture long-distance relationships and local ties.* Washington, DC: Pew Internet & American Life Project. Available at: http://www.pewinternet.org

Kilsheimer, J. (1997, April 7). Virtual communities; Cyberpals keep in touch online. *The Arizona Republic*, p. E3.

McWilliam, G. (2002). Building stronger brands through online communities. *Sloan Management Review, 41*(3), 43–54.

Morgan, R. M., & Hunt, S. D. (1994). The commitment-trust theory of relationship marketing. *Journal of Marketing, 58*, 20–38. doi:10.1177/002224299405800302

Othmani, L., & Bouslama, P. N. (2015). Highlighting the Influence of Virtual Communities on the online shoppers trust. *Journal of Internet Social Networking & Virtual Communities, 6*, 1–8.

Pentina, I., Prybutok, V. R., & Zhang, X. (2008). The Role of Virtual Communities as Shopping Reference Groups. *Journal of Electronic Commerce Research, 9*(2), 114–136.

Petersen, A. (1999, January 6). Some places to go when you want to feel right at home: Communities focus on people who need people. *The Wall Street Journal*, p. B6.

Porter, C. E. (2004). A Typology of Virtual Communities: A Multi-Disciplinary Foundation for Future Research. *Journal of Computer-Mediated Communication, 10*(1), 101–121. Retrieved from https://academic.oup.com/jcmc/article/10/1/JCMC1011/4614445

Preece, J. (2001). Sociability and usability in online communities: Determining and measuring success. *Behaviour & Information Technology, 20*(5), 347–356. doi:10.1080/01449290110084683

Schindler, R. M. (2001). Internet Forums as Influential Sources of Consumer Information. *Journal of Interactive Marketing, 15*(3), 31–40. doi:10.1002/dir.1014

Schuler, D. (1996). *New Community Networks – Wired for Change*. New York: Addison-Wesley.

Smith, D., Menon, K. S., & Sivakumar, K. (2005). Online Peer and Editorial Recommendations, Trust, and Choice in Virtual Markets. *Journal of Interactive Marketing, 19*(3), 15–37. doi:10.1002/dir.20041

Stanoevska-Slabeva, K. (2002). Toward a community-oriented design of Internet platforms. *International Journal of Electronic Commerce, 6*(3), 71–95. doi:10.1080/10864415.2002.11044244

Turban, E., King, D., McKay, J., Marshall, P., Lee, J., & Viehland, D. (2008). *Electronic Commerce 2008: A Managerial Perspective*. Pearson.

Virnoche, M. E., & Marx, G. T. (1997). Only connect-E. M. Forster in an age of electronic communication: Computer-mediated association and community networks. *Sociological Inquiry*, 67(1), 85–100. doi:10.1111/j.1475-682X.1997.tb00431.x

Wingfield, N., & Hanrahan, T. (1999). Web firm salon buys 'the Well,' an online pioneer. *The Wall Street Journal*, p. B9.

KEY TERMS AND DEFINITIONS

Digital Marketing: Marketing products and services with the use of internet, mobile phones, and social media are termed as digital marketing.

E-Commerce: Buying and selling of goods and services using internet, also referred as E-commerce or Electronic Commerce.

Gen X: Gen X is referred to as Baby Boomers, who are the group of people born during 1960s to 1980.

Gen Y: Gen Y is referred to as Millennials, who are the group of people born during 1980s to 2000.

Gen Z: Gen Z is the group of people born after 2000.

Online Business: Any business activity such as advertising, selling, and buying handled through internet.

Social Collaboration: The process that aids various people or group to interact and share information to achieve common goals.

Virtual Communities: A group of people with similar interests, ideas, and feelings share their views through online networks or society.

Chapter 8
Live Streaming Meets Online Shopping in the Connected World:
Interactive Social Video in Online Marketplace

Ree C. Ho
Taylor's University, Malaysia

Kanesh Gopal Rajadurai
Taylor's University, Malaysia

ABSTRACT

With the increased usage of live stream video, this chapter examined consumer product learning process in using it as a platform to shop online. Live stream video has been utilized to show and demonstrate product specifications and information. By depending on it, the prospective consumer uses the interactive videos to help them make purchase decision. However, the extent of the social live video in promoting the product knowledge is not examined yet. Hence, there is a need to examine the power of social live video in enhancing customer learning during the shopping. The main objective is to understand how the act of live streaming may change the viewer impression towards a brand or product. Secondly, the authors also investigate the subsequent knowledge gained by watching the live stream footage and how could it exert influence on product purchase. This study developed an integrative framework by combining the theories of relative advantage and absorptive capacity to examine the underlying factors in the use of social live stream video.

DOI: 10.4018/978-1-5225-9697-4.ch008

INTRODUCTION

There has been an exponential growth of video applications (apps) as seen on social media and altered the way businesses conducted online (Todd & Melancon, 2018). This provides a new opportunities as well as challenges to businesses and consumers. Companies are getting aware of the benefits of social media marketing as a tool in communicating with target customers (Ashley & Tuten, 2015; Felix, Rauschnabel, & Hinsch, 2017; A. J. Kim & Ko, 2012). Furthermore, social media also engages people much more intimately, while interactive videos aid in a much better communication in social commerce. The contents shared and even co-created by its followers via social media networks.

Traditional online business models are slowing losing its edge as consumers advance to social media spaces, while more and more people prefer to learn about products from social media (L. F. Lee, Hutton, & Shu, 2015; Xia Wang, Yu, & Wei, 2012). This is because social commerce has high trustworthiness as data gained from reliable sources. This has prompted online retailers to revise marketing efforts and plan to make full use of social media for promotional purposes. Having said that, the technological tools and applications are often in revolutionary basis. Evidently, video marketing as combined with social media, spawning a new technology to attract the consumers. Social media players such as "Vloggers" seem to influence the brand perception for luxury brands (J. E. Lee & Watkins, 2016). Consumer attitudes and intentions towards user-generated product content on Youtube is prolific (Harris, Kelly, & Wyatt, 2014). Live streaming became the digital social video platform, eroding the shares used to belong to blogs and social posts while video's can obtain more exposure as compared to texts, images or the combination of both. This prompts more innovative retailers to jump on this new idea and set up their own live stream channels. Hence, this is an indication on the importance of live streaming in marketing strategies for today's connected marketplace.

Livestream is source of credibility because consumers engage in real time basis with the streamers, and motivated consumers to pay more attention to the promoted product (Todd & Melancon, 2018). Apparently, live stream is used by small retailers in having a closer relationship with customers of the social commerce diaspora. Furthermore, the knowledge obtained from the closer engagement was useful in helping consumers make a purchase decision (Xia Wang et al., 2012). Thus, we identify the importance of livestreaming in assisting the shopping process by providing the information and knowledge about the product. This subsequently increases the absorptive capability of the consumers during product learning process. This study is aimed to fill in the research gap exist in the current literature on the emerging online retailing phenomenon in the use of social livestreaming. The research questions of this study are as follows. First, do the relative advantage of livestream influence the intended purchase behavior of consumers? Second, what are the knowledge dimensions gained by the viewers for shopping purposes?

The use of social live streaming in improving consumer knowledge is not examined yet. Majority of The studies related to the use of live stream lie in attracting customer to buy and its use in fostering customer engagement (Todd & Melancon, 2018; Yu, Jung, Kim, & Jung, 2018). Therefore, this study would investigate the usefulness of livestream in enhancing the ability of consumers to absorb knowledge needed in determining the purchase decision. The major contributions of this paper is to propose a new integrative model in combining theories of relative advantage and absorptive capacity in the acquisition for product learning with the use of livestreaming. Another contribution of this paper is to show the importance of live stream usage in increasing absorptive capacity of consumer's product knowledge. With its enriching interactivity and higher quality of visualization, it is interesting to know how much knowledge from livestreaming is attainable. These contributions are vital to explain the ever-growing use of social video for online shopping.

THEORETICAL BACKGROUND AND CONCEPTUAL FRAMEWORK DEVELOPMENT

The act of live streaming refers to the distribution of video contents via Internet on a real-time basis. While it includes both audio and video broadcast, it also consist of creative interaction, i.e. live conversation and response. It is a real-time interactive experience between the creator and consumer of the contents shared (Yu et al., 2018). Live streaming became popular with the growth of mobile devices such as smart phone and devices. Popular live streaming platforms are YouTube, Live.ly, YouNow, and Twitch. There have been new development in the live streaming process such as immersive and spherical videos in the recent development. This further enhanced the interactivity of the social video streaming (Rupp et al., 2019). Due to its high acceptance rate, other social media platforms also venturing into live streaming. New live stream applications such as Facebook Live, Twitter Periscope and Instagram Live were integrated into the mainstream social media applications. The inclusion of this innovative technology is obvious as it has the capability to grow a business quickly due to its wide acceptance by young people.

Theory Development

Two underpinning theories were used in this study. The theory of absorptive capacity developed by Cohen and Levinthal (1990) and Rogers (1962)'s diffusion of innovation theory. The perceived relative advantage of social live streaming was based on Choudhury and Karahanna (2008)'s work and we integrated it with the concept of potential absorptive capacity by Zahra and George (2002). The relative advantages, i.e. convenience, interactivity trust and information efficacy are posited to influence the potential absorptive capacity in attaining the product knowledge. The conceptual framework is shown in Figure 1.

Figure 1. The conceptual framework

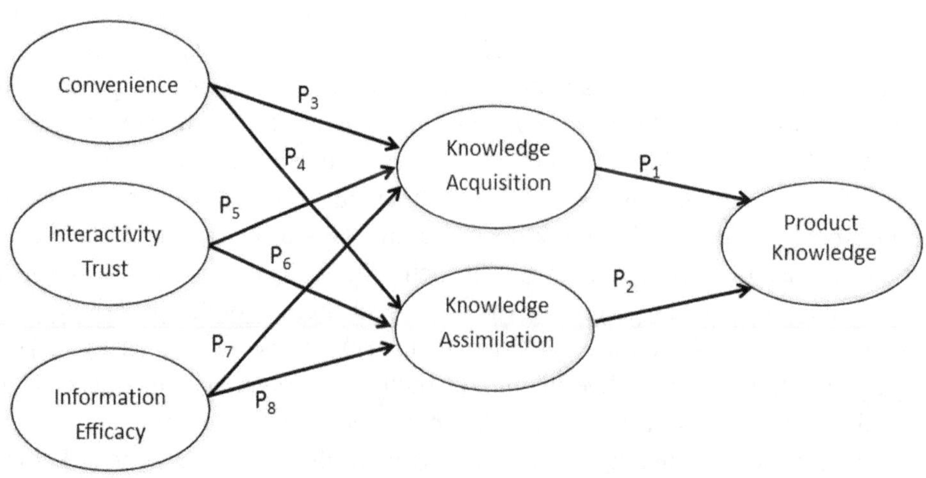

Table 1. Potential absorptive capacity of live stream users

Construct	Definition	References
Knowledge Acquisition	The ability to identify and acquire information and knowledge generated from social live stream video.	Zahra and George (2002)
Knowledge Assimilation	The ability to analyze, process, interpret and understand the information and knowledge from social live stream video.	Zahra and George (2002)

Absorptive Capacity

The theory of absorptive capacity developed by Cohen and Levinthal (1990) clearly describes one's ability to use past experiences to learn and apply new knowledge. People develop the ability to further understand and assimilate external knowledge with the use of relevant activities. There are four dimensions of this theory, which are acquisition, assimilation, transformation and exploitation while Zahra and George (2002) categorized it into two major sub-groups, potential absorptive capacity and realized absorptive capacity. Potential absorptive capacity consists of acquisition and assimilation, while realized absorptive capacity made up of transformation and exploitation. Table 1 shows the definition of the potential absorptive capacity of live stream users.

In the social video sharing platform, the act of learning is more personal during the transfer of product knowledge process. With social media, the relationship among the users are closer and more engaging, and as the intensity increases, a collaborative learning environment exists to manage knowledge learning better (Zhang et al., 2015). It is common for a business to roll out the use of social media strategies to engage with the customers and these collaborations enhance absorptive capacity (Culnan, McHugh, & Zubillaga, 2010; Siamagka, Christodoulides, Michaelidou, & Valvi, 2015; Tsitsi Chikandiwa, Contogiannis, & Jembere, 2013). According to absorptive capacity theory, the surroundings of the learning environment would influence the knowledge transfer, while a more vivid and live demonstration of the product in social media would allow consumers to improve the ability to learn and assimilate the external knowledge.

Acquisition and Assimilation of Product Knowledge

It is normal for customers to search for more information about the products they intend to purchase. Customers are more likely to purchase the products when they are familiar with the product features and believe they can enjoy the benefits of consuming the product. Latour and Latour (2010) supported the need of both formal and informal learning platforms to guide the consumers on the product features. If there is no such provision, the likeliness of customers to search for external knowledge on their own (Kirmani & Rao, 2000).

The livestream process is an external stimulus provided by the streamers. Absorptive capacity permits customers to be receptive in obtaining and integrating information demonstrated by the streamers. These external information and knowledge are being transfer to the viewers who might be interested to buy the products. As stated above, the two main processes in potential absorptive capacity, i.e. knowledge acquisition and knowledge assimilation are more likely to be involved in the process. Knowledge acquisition is the ability to identify and acquire external generated information and knowledge. While knowledge assimilation is the ability to analyze, process, interpret and understand the information and

Table 2. Relative advantage of social live streaming

Construct	Definition	References
Convenience	The benefits of easy to use, less effort and shorter time in using live stream as shopping channel.	Schaupp and Bélanger (2005)
Interactivity Trust	Trustworthiness over the ability of social live stream community's in providing high level of interactivity and closer engagement.	Sjöblom, Törhönen, Hamari, and Macey (2019)
Information Efficacy	Social live steaming provision of sufficient useful information to support customers' shopping experience.	Choudhury and Karahanna (2008)

knowledge from external source. Therefore, we would focus on the potential absorptive capacity since consumers are largely dependent on the exposure provided by streaming video in this study. We developed the propositions as follow:

Proposition 1:

Acquisition dimension of absorptive capacity gained from live stream leads to product knowledge

Proposition 2:

Assimilation dimension absorptive capacity gained from live stream leads to product knowledge

Relative Advantage

The diffusion of innovation theory stated that people accept new innovative technology after they appreciate the relative advantage gained from it. This theory served as theoretical lens in many studies relating to electronic commerce (Liu & Forsythe, 2010; Molesworth & Suortti, 2002; Xueqin Wang, Yuen, Wong, & Teo, 2018). In the realm of online shopping channel, Choudhury and Karahanna (2008) concluded that the relative advantages of the online channels are the major determinant in molding the purchase intention. Similar findings in confirming the importance of the relative advantage for social commerce also existed (Ahmad, Abu Bakar, & Ahmad, 2019; C.-Y. Li & Ku, 2018). In this proposed study, we would focus on the conceptual understanding of relative advantage and further explore the viability of livestream for social media shopping. The customer's salient beliefs in the relative advantage obtained by following livestream videos would influence the intention to buy the product promoted by it. Table 2 illustrates the main elements of relative advantage for social live streaming.

Convenience

Convenience is the key determinant in the adoption of electronic (Palmer, 2000; Sundström & Radon, 2015). Many functions and features are included on the retailers' web interface to enhance the relative advantages, i.e. product recommendation, price comparison and adjustment functionalities (Daoud, Naqvi, & Ahmad, 2014; KoçAs, 2005). This increased the accessibility of the retailers' channels and led to higher degree of convenience. The exponential growth of social media has changed the way consumers are taking part in online shopping due it higher level of its perceived usefulness and social interaction (Agnihotri, Dingus, Hu, & Krush, 2016). Customers are listening to their peers on their own social network for more product knowledge and shopping experience in social commerce (N. Kim & Kim, 2018; Lu, Fan, & Zhou, 2016).

Both product reviews and e-word of mouth contributed and shared on social media are more influential than the information provided by the sellers (Liang & Turban, 2011; Q. Ye, Law, Gu, & Chen, 2011; Yusuf, Che Hussin, & Busalim, 2018). The relationship and trust cultivated were often sought from social media apps, such as Twitter and Facebook. In this study, the readily available product demonstration and video footage provided the visual assistance in molding the customer product knowledge, as seen with the rapid use of Livestream among social media users, while online customers think that convenience of this new channel will make them learn about the product much more intensely. The following propositions were developed based on the discussion above:

Proposition 3

Convenience derived from live Stream of online resellers exerts influences on the acquisition dimension of absorptive capacity in learning product knowledge

Proposition 4

Convenience derived from live stream of online resellers exerts influences on the assimilation dimension of absorptive capacity in learning product knowledge

Interactivity Trust

Interactivity refers to the degree of interactive communication perceived by one as controllable, dual-directions and responsive to one's actions (Mollen & Wilson, 2010). This includes the feedback, real-time interaction and self-control in facilitating the process. One major distinctive feature contributed to the high adoption of social livestreaming is the high level of interactivity (Sjöblom et al., 2019). The customer experience is the result from the engagement and interaction with the e-retailers (Rose, Clark, Samouel, & Hair, 2012). The richness in interactivity of the social commerce mold positive attitudes toward branded websites, especially with more emphasis on product-related information (Y.-W. Li, Yang, & Liang, 2015; B. H. Ye, Barreda, Okumus, & Nusair, 2019). In the case of conducting business livestream, not only the channel itself, but also the involvement of streamers' emotion and personal attitude. This enhances the engagement with the customer. For example, in the use of para-social emotion like emoji further increase the interactivity of the live streaming channel (Yu et al., 2018).

Consumers often look for and are willing to buy from reliable and trustworthy retailers of traditional electronic commerce (Y. Kim & Peterson, 2017; Qu, Pinsonneault, Tomiuk, Wang, & Liu, 2015). Obviously, both sellers and customers need the trust to facilitate the purchase process (Ba & Pavlou, 2002). The emergence of social commerce provided the remedy for solving the lack of the social exchange process in the traditional electronic commerce process. Social media vitalizes the mechanism and provides the high interactivity found in social livestreaming can unlock this gap with clearer visual and footage. This can be further developed into long lasting relationship because more emotional connection between the streamers and viewers. De Vries, Gensler, and Leeflang (2012) found that brand related social media contents were highly sought by the interested consumers. This notion supported by Sashi (2012)'s study that confirmed customer relationship management is better improved with effective usage of social media among highly connected customers. Hence, we developed the following propositions:

Proposition 5:

Interactivity trust derived from live stream of online resellers exerts an influence on the acquisition dimension of absorptive capacity in learning product knowledge.

Proposition 6:

Interactivity trust derived from live stream of online resellers exerts an influence on the assimilation dimension of absorptive capacity in learning product knowledge.

Information Efficacy

Information efficacy refers to online channel's provision of clear and easily understood information to assist customers' online shopping experience (Choudhury & Karahanna, 2008). In tandem with current trends, one of the major shopping activities is the search for brand and product information prior to the purchase. There has been two major considerations, namely the quality and, the credibility of the information gained. Nusair and Kandampully (2008) examined that volume, form, and correctness of information about the brand, products and services are critical in assisting customer's purchase decision. Third-party shopping-related functionalities such as price, product comparison and product rating apps, were useful in promoting the products. More collaborative effort among consumers as well as the retailers exists during the operations of social commerce (Lu et al., 2016).

Consumer generated contents that are co-created by friends are useful in learning the product better because of its higher trustworthiness (Ho & Vogel, 2014). Adding to this, these contents are also widely available in the social media space. The availability of product-related information is one of the key drivers to influence the consumers purchase, especially in the early stages of purchase activities. However, the trustworthiness of such product information was needed prior to the purchase. Furthermore, consumers referred to high number of "likes" and positive comments by the followers in the social media (Zheng, Cheung, Lee, & Liang, 2015).

It is noted that the issue of credibility in the comments given by the followers found in the social commerce (Chai, Das, & Rao, 2011). Social media users often search for information and feedback from peers whom they trust to learn about products and services (Flanagin, Metzger, Pure, Markov, & Hartsell, 2014). With more enriched features in video footage provided by live stream video, information is easy to understand compare to other social media platforms but it has to be sufficient for use. However, such related research was not examined yet. Because the focus was information quality supplied by the online retailers (Kang & Namkung, 2019; Wixom & Todd, 2005). Hence, this study would seek to find out the how much useful information can gained from live stream. There has to be sufficient information from live stream obtainable by the customers to learn about the product and purchase process. Hence, we posit the following propositions.

Proposition 7:

Information efficacy derived from live stream of online resellers exerts influences on the acquisition dimension of absorptive capacity in learning product knowledge.

Proposition 8:

Information efficacy derived from live stream of online resellers exerts influences on the assimilation dimension absorptive capacity of learning product knowledge.

CONCLUSION

This chapter focuses on the impact of social live streaming data in influencing and helping consumers to understand product better. It is obvious that the usage of live streaming is a vital tool for consumers to apprehend product knowledge more efficiently. It exhibits the exponential use of social live video in promoting brands and products due to its popularity among the highly connected consumers. Live stream, a popular app in sharing live stream videos is slowly become one of the major channels in demonstrating the product and collaborating with customers in real-time basis. Data gained from social media is useful source of information for shopping purpose, but not manageable due to its lack of persuasive power if not obtain from right people (Leonardi, 2017). The contents provided in live stream are more easily captured and absorb by the followers. Three main relative advantages of live stream for shopping were developed in this study, i.e. convenience, interactivity trust and information efficacy. Hence, live stream with its higher interactivity in connecting both the sellers and customers in real-time basis can be the key in unlocking the diffusion of product knowledge. The relative advantage of social live video rooted in its interactive nature and making product knowledge learning to be much easier and faster (Todd & Melancon, 2018).

This chapter aimed to connect the missing link between social live stream data and absorptive capacity in attaining the product knowledge. With this proposed framework, social media with enhanced video footage can enhance consumer learning by creating the content that is useful for purchase purpose. Secondly, the study also developed an integrative framework in amalgamating the theories of relative advantages and absorptive capacity to investigate the use of social live stream for promoting products. It explores the relative advantage of live streaming needed to improve the product knowledge. This in turn assists consumers to make better buying decisions.

LIMITATIONS AND FUTURE RESEARCH DIRECTIONS

With its main feature in enriched interactivity in real time basis, the contents are more convincing and readily accepted for the followers. This theoretical framework concluded that consumers comprehend product knowledge in a more efficient manner. In this study, we examined potential absorptive capacity of the consumers in acquiring and assimilating the product knowledge via social live streaming. However, we suggest that perhaps future scholars may investigate how the consumers can become more proficient in using the product. Subsequently, consumers themselves elevated to become "expert" in the use of the product. Hence, we suggest future researchers to apply the other dimension of absorptive capacity, i.e. realized absorptive capacity in this area of study.

Social media users tended to follow their peers by accepting the feedbacks frequently (VanMeter, Syrdal, Powell-Mantel, Grisaffe, & Nesson, 2018). This presumably apply to the users of the live streaming as well. We expect the live stream followers would trust the friends and follow the trends of these friends. Will they buy something they do not need and develop impulsive purchase behavior? We aware that impulsive buying exists in traditional online shopping and social commerce (Chung, Song, & Lee, 2017; Yoon & Lim, 2018). Hence, future scholars can explore the likelihood of impulsive buying behavior in social live stream video.

REFERENCES

Agnihotri, R., Dingus, R., Hu, M. Y., & Krush, M. T. (2016). Social media: Influencing customer satisfaction in B2B sales. *Industrial Marketing Management*, *53*, 172–180. doi:10.1016/j.indmarman.2015.09.003

Ahmad, S. Z., Abu Bakar, A. R., & Ahmad, N. (2019). Social media adoption and its impact on firm performance: The case of the UAE. *International Journal of Entrepreneurial Behaviour & Research*, *25*(1), 84–111. doi:10.1108/IJEBR-08-2017-0299

Ashley, C., & Tuten, T. (2015). Creative strategies in social media marketing: An exploratory study of branded social content and consumer engagement. *Psychology and Marketing*, *32*(1), 15–27. doi:10.1002/mar.20761

Ba, S., & Pavlou, P. A. (2002). Evidence of the effect of trust building technology in electronic markets: Price premiums and buyer behavior. *Management Information Systems Quarterly*, *26*(3), 243–268. doi:10.2307/4132332

Chai, S., Das, S., & Rao, H. R. (2011). Factors affecting bloggers' knowledge sharing: An investigation across gender. *Journal of Management Information Systems*, *28*(3), 309–342. doi:10.2753/MIS0742-1222280309

Chikandiwa, T., & Sarah, C. (2013). The adoption of social media marketing in South African banks. *European Business Review*, *25*(4), 365–381. doi:10.1108/EBR-02-2013-0013

Choudhury, V., & Karahanna, E. (2008). The relative advantage of electronic channels: A multidimensional view. *Management Information Systems Quarterly*, *32*(1), 179–200. doi:10.2307/25148833

Chung, N., Song, H. G., & Lee, H. (2017). Consumers' impulsive buying behavior of restaurant products in social commerce. *International Journal of Contemporary Hospitality Management*, *29*(2), 709–731. doi:10.1108/IJCHM-10-2015-0608

Cohen, W. M., & Levinthal, D. A. (1990). Absorptive capacity: A new perspective on learning and innovation. *Administrative Science Quarterly*, *35*(1), 128–152. doi:10.2307/2393553

Culnan, M. J., McHugh, P. J., & Zubillaga, J. I. (2010). How large US companies can use Twitter and other social media to gain business value. *MIS Quarterly Executive*, *9*(4), 243–259.

Daoud, M., Naqvi, S.K., & Ahmad, A. (2014). Opinion Observer: Recommendation System on ECommerce Website. *International Journal of Computers and Applications*, *105*(14), 37–42.

De Vries, L., Gensler, S., & Leeflang, P. S. H. (2012). Popularity of brand posts on brand fan pages: An investigation of the effects of social media marketing. *Journal of Interactive Marketing*, *26*(2), 83–91. doi:10.1016/j.intmar.2012.01.003

Felix, R., Rauschnabel, P. A., & Hinsch, C. (2017). Elements of strategic social media marketing: A holistic framework. *Journal of Business Research*, *70*, 118–126. doi:10.1016/j.jbusres.2016.05.001

Flanagin, A. J., Metzger, M. J., Pure, R., Markov, A., & Hartsell, E. (2014). Mitigating risk in ecommerce transactions: Perceptions of information credibility and the role of user-generated ratings in product quality and purchase intention. *Electronic Commerce Research*, *14*(1), 1–23. doi:10.100710660-014-9139-2

Harris, A., Kelly, S. E., & Wyatt, S. (2014). Autobiologies on YouTube: Narratives of direct-to-consumer genetic testing. *New Genetics & Society*, *33*(1), 60–78. doi:10.1080/14636778.2014.884456 PMID:24772003

Ho, R., & Vogel, D. (2014). The impact of social networking functionalities on online shopping: An examination of the web's relative advantage. *International Journal of Business Information Systems*, *16*(1), 25–41. doi:10.1504/IJBIS.2014.060834

Kang, J.-W., & Namkung, Y. (2019). The information quality and source credibility matter in customers' evaluation toward food O2O commerce. *International Journal of Hospitality Management*, *78*, 189–198. doi:10.1016/j.ijhm.2018.10.011

Kim, A. J., & Ko, E. (2012). Do social media marketing activities enhance customer equity? An empirical study of luxury fashion brand. *Journal of Business Research*, *65*(10), 1480–1486. doi:10.1016/j.jbusres.2011.10.014

Kim, N., & Kim, W. (2018). Do your social media lead you to make social deal purchases? Consumer-generated social referrals for sales via social commerce. *International Journal of Information Management*, *39*, 38–48. doi:10.1016/j.ijinfomgt.2017.10.006

Kim, Y., & Peterson, R. A. (2017). A Meta-analysis of Online Trust Relationships in E-commerce. *Journal of Interactive Marketing*, *38*, 44–54. doi:10.1016/j.intmar.2017.01.001

Kirmani, A., & Rao, A. R. (2000). No pain, no gain: A critical review of the literature on signaling unobservable product quality. *Journal of Marketing*, *64*(2), 66–79. doi:10.1509/jmkg.64.2.66.18000

Koças, C. (2005). A model of Internet pricing under price-comparison shopping. *International Journal of Electronic Commerce*, *10*(1), 111–134. doi:10.1080/10864415.2005.11043959

Latour, K. A., & Latour, M. S. (2010). Bridging aficionados' perceptual and conceptual knowledge to enhance how they learn from experience. *The Journal of Consumer Research*, *37*(4), 688–697. doi:10.1086/655014

Lee, J. E., & Watkins, B. (2016). YouTube vloggers' influence on consumer luxury brand perceptions and intentions. *Journal of Business Research*, *69*(12), 5753–5760. doi:10.1016/j.jbusres.2016.04.171

Lee, L. F., Hutton, A. P., & Shu, S. (2015). The role of social media in the capital market: Evidence from consumer product recalls. *Journal of Accounting Research*, *53*(2), 367–404. doi:10.1111/1475-679X.12074

Leonardi, P. M. (2017). The social media revolution: Sharing and learning in the age of leaky knowledge. *Information and Organization*, *27*(1), 47–59. doi:10.1016/j.infoandorg.2017.01.004

Li, C.-Y., & Ku, Y.-C. (2018). The power of a thumbs-up: Will e-commerce switch to social commerce? *Information & Management*, *55*(3), 340–357. doi:10.1016/j.im.2017.09.001

Li, Y.-W., Yang, S.-M., & Liang, T.-P. (2015). Website interactivity and promotional framing on consumer attitudes toward online advertising: Functional versus symbolic brands. *Pacific Asia Journal of the Association for Information Systems*, *7*(2), 41–58. doi:10.17705/1pais.07203

Liang, T.-P., & Turban, E. (2011). Introduction to the special issue social commerce: A research framework for social commerce. *International Journal of Electronic Commerce*, *16*(2), 5–14. doi:10.2753/JEC1086-4415160201

Liu, C., & Forsythe, S. (2010). Post-adoption online shopping continuance. *International Journal of Retail & Distribution Management*, *38*(2), 97–114. doi:10.1108/09590551011020110

Lu, B., Fan, W., & Zhou, M. (2016). Social presence, trust, and social commerce purchase intention: An empirical research. *Computers in Human Behavior*, *56*, 225–237. doi:10.1016/j.chb.2015.11.057

Molesworth, M., & Suortti, J.-P. (2002). Buying cars online: The adoption of the web for high-involvement, high-cost purchases. *Journal of Consumer Behaviour: An International Research Review*, *2*(2), 155–168. doi:10.1002/cb.97

Mollen, A., & Wilson, H. (2010). Engagement, telepresence and interactivity in online consumer experience: Reconciling scholastic and managerial perspectives. *Journal of Business Research*, *63*(9-10), 919–925. doi:10.1016/j.jbusres.2009.05.014

Nusair, K., & Kandampully, J. (2008). The antecedents of customer satisfaction with online travel services: A conceptual model. *European Business Review*, *20*(1), 4–19. doi:10.1108/09555340810843663

Palmer, J. W. (2000). Electronic commerce in retailing: Convenience, search costs, delivery and price across retail formats. *Information Technology Management*, *1*(1-2), 25–43. doi:10.1023/A:1019152403937

Qu, W. G., Pinsonneault, A., Tomiuk, D., Wang, S., & Liu, Y. (2015). The impacts of social trust on open and closed B2B e-commerce: A Europe-based study. *Information & Management*, *52*(2), 151–159. doi:10.1016/j.im.2014.07.002

Rogers, E. M. (1962). *Diffusions of Innovations. The Free Press.*

Rose, S., Clark, M., Samouel, P., & Hair, N. (2012). Online customer experience in e-retailing: An empirical model of antecedents and outcomes. *Journal of Retailing*, *88*(2), 308–322. doi:10.1016/j.jretai.2012.03.001

Rupp, M. A., Odette, K. L., Kozachuk, J., Michaelis, J. R., Smither, J. A., & McConnell, D. S. (2019). Investigating learning outcomes and subjective experiences in 360-degree videos. *Computers & Education*, *128*, 256–268. doi:10.1016/j.compedu.2018.09.015

Sashi, C. M. (2012). Customer engagement, buyer-seller relationships, and social media. *Management Decision, 50*(2), 253–272. doi:10.1108/00251741211203551

Schaupp, L. C., & Bélanger, F. (2005). A Conjoint Analysis of Online Consumer Satisfaction. *Journal of Electronic Commerce Research, 6*(2), 95–111.

Siamagka, N.-T., Christodoulides, G., Michaelidou, N., & Valvi, A. (2015). Determinants of social media adoption by B2B organizations. *Industrial Marketing Management, 51*, 89–99. doi:10.1016/j.indmarman.2015.05.005

Sjöblom, M., Törhönen, M., Hamari, J., & Macey, J. (2019). The ingredients of Twitch streaming: Affordances of game streams. *Computers in Human Behavior, 92*, 20–28. doi:10.1016/j.chb.2018.10.012

Sundström, M., & Radon, A. (2015). Utilizing the concept of convenience as a business opportunity in emerging markets. *Organizations and Markets in Emerging Economies, 6*(2), 7–21.

Todd, P. R., & Melancon, J. (2018). Gender and live-streaming: Source credibility and motivation. *Journal of Research in Interactive Marketing, 12*(1), 79–93. doi:10.1108/JRIM-05-2017-0035

VanMeter, R., Syrdal, H. A., Powell-Mantel, S., Grisaffe, D. B., & Nesson, E. T. (2018). Don't Just "Like" Me, Promote Me: How Attachment and Attitude Influence Brand Related Behaviors on Social Media. *Journal of Interactive Marketing, 43*, 83–97. doi:10.1016/j.intmar.2018.03.003

Wang, X., Yu, C., & Wei, Y. (2012). Social media peer communication and impacts on purchase intentions: A consumer socialization framework. *Journal of Interactive Marketing, 26*(4), 198–208. doi:10.1016/j.intmar.2011.11.004

Wang, X., Yuen, K. F., Wong, Y. D., & Teo, C. C. (2018). An innovation diffusion perspective of e-consumers' initial adoption of self-collection service via automated parcel station. *International Journal of Logistics Management, 29*(1), 237–260. doi:10.1108/IJLM-12-2016-0302

Wixom, B. H., & Todd, P. A. (2005). A theoretical integration of user satisfaction and technology acceptance. *Information Systems Research, 16*(1), 85–102. doi:10.1287/isre.1050.0042

Ye, B. H., Barreda, A. A., Okumus, F., & Nusair, K. (2019). Website interactivity and brand development of online travel agencies in China: The moderating role of age. *Journal of Business Research, 99*, 382–389. doi:10.1016/j.jbusres.2017.09.046

Ye, Q., Law, R., Gu, B., & Chen, W. (2011). The influence of user-generated content on traveler behavior: An empirical investigation on the effects of e-word-of-mouth to hotel online bookings. *Computers in Human Behavior, 27*(2), 634–639. doi:10.1016/j.chb.2010.04.014

Yoon, C.-H., & Lim, D.-S. (2018). The Effect of the Big Five and the MBTI on Impulsive and Compulsive Buying Behaviors: An Integrated Analysis in Online Shopping. *Journal of International Trade & Commerce, 14*(3), 101–117.

Yu, E., Jung, C., Kim, H., & Jung, J. (2018). Impact of viewer engagement on gift-giving in live video streaming. *Telematics and Informatics, 35*(5), 1450–1460. doi:10.1016/j.tele.2018.03.014

Yusuf, A. S., Hussin, C., Razak, A., & Busalim, A. H. (2018). Influence of e-WOM engagement on consumer purchase intention in social commerce. *Journal of Services Marketing, 32*(4), 493–504. doi:10.1108/JSM-01-2017-0031

Zahra, S. A., & George, G. (2002). Absorptive capacity: A review, reconceptualization, and extension. *Academy of Management Review, 27*(2), 185–203. doi:10.5465/amr.2002.6587995

Zhang, X., Gao, Y., Yan, X., de Pablos, P. O., Sun, Y., & Cao, X. (2015). From e-learning to social-learning: Mapping development of studies on social media-supported knowledge management. *Computers in Human Behavior, 51*, 803–811. doi:10.1016/j.chb.2014.11.084

Zheng, X., Cheung, C. M. K., Lee, M. K. O., & Liang, L. (2015). Building brand loyalty through user engagement in online brand communities in social networking sites. *Information Technology & People, 28*(1), 90–106. doi:10.1108/ITP-08-2013-0144

KEY TERMS AND DEFINITIONS

Absorptive Capacity: The ability of one to use past experiences to learn and apply new knowledge.

Convenience: The benefits of easy to use, less effort, and shorter time in using live stream as shopping channel.

Information Efficacy: Provision of sufficient useful information to support customers' shopping experience by social live streaming.

Interactivity Trust: Trustworthiness over the ability of social live stream community's in providing high level of interactivity and closer engagement.

Knowledge Acquisition: The ability to identify and acquire information and knowledge generated from social live stream video.

Knowledge Assimilation: The ability to analyze, process, interpret and understand the information and knowledge from social live stream video.

Product Knowledge: The amount of accurate information about the products including the alternatives and product features that consumers believe they know.

Relative Advantage: The perceived efficiencies gained by the innovation relative to social live streaming.

Chapter 9
A Systematic Review of Digital Marketing in South Africa

Vera Nsahlai
University of KwaZulu-Natal, South Africa

Refiloe Khoase
University of KwaZulu-Natal, South Africa

Patrick Ndayizigamiye
https://orcid.org/0000-0001-5721-6070
University of Johannesburg, South Africa

Shopee M. Dube
https://orcid.org/0000-0003-0033-7992
University of Johannesburg, South Africa

ABSTRACT

This chapter investigates the extent of digital marketing usage in South Africa, its perceived impact, and factors that influence its adoption in the South African context. The methodology adopted is the systematic review using the preferred reporting items for systematic reviews and meta-analyses (PRISMA) framework. The results show that digital platforms currently used include mobile marketing (SMS) and social media platforms. The findings suggest that SMS-based marketing may be appealing to other market segments but not to young adults. The findings further suggest that social media marketing has had a significant influence on the purchase intentions among South African millennials (Generation Y). Moreover, the findings suggest that marketers, in their quest to influence customer purchasing decisions, should consider the knowledge that social media followers have regarding a subject matter (such as a product), and make an effort to educate those followers on the subject (or product) before suggesting a purchase.

DOI: 10.4018/978-1-5225-9697-4.ch009

INTRODUCTION AND BACKGROUND

The Evolution of Digital Marketing

Over the years, the Internet has evolved into one of the most significant marketplaces for businesses to sell their services and products worldwide. For instance, in the United States, online consumers spent over $100 billion in 2007. Goods such as software, magazines, and books have an average online demand growth rate of 25% to 50% (Leeflang, Verhoef, Dahlström, & Freundt, 2014). In November 2012, Amazon had over 26.5 million items ordered by customers all around the globe, that is, 306 items bought every second. Digital platforms have undoubtedly enabled the success of Business-to-Business (B2B), Business-to-Customer (B2C) and Customer-to-Customer (C2C) markets such as YouTube, eBay and Lulu. There has also been an increase in the use of online source of information over the years, thus resulting in the decline of shares of hard copies of magazines and newspapers (Leeflang et al., 2014). More people are relying on digital platforms to seek information.

Digital technologies, as we know them today, were developed over numerous years and are still being enhanced. In 1991, the first search engine called Gopher emerged and allowed users to search and use queries to search for information. Businesses started to optimise their websites' ranking after Yahoo's launch in 1994. Yahoo and Google took over the search optimisation market after the dot. com crash in 2001. In 2006, search traffic on the Internet grew and as a result companies like Google increased their investments in Search Engine Optimisation (SEO). The Internet usage increased drastically in 2007 due to the increase in the adoption and use of mobile devices. Consistently, digital platforms like social media has enabled people to conveniently connect with each other globally (Malik, 2017).

The online world has become more and more populated over the years, due to people's need to connect with each other. In January 2018, there were over 4 billion Internet users worldwide of which over 3 billion were social media users. There were 50 million Facebook users just 2 years after it was created. Recently, there were 2.167 billion active monthly users on Facebook worldwide (Chaffey, 2018). In addition, 42% of the global population is active on at least one social media network (Chaffey, 2018). Interestingly, social media has become an attractive medium for advertisements. In 2011, $4.3 billion was spent globally on advertising on social media. According to Leeflang et al. (2014:1), companies aim to make "brand fans" by investing in social media advertising to recruit brand loyal customers who will then advertise the brand through word of mouth. There are many online marketing creators that produce content regularly. These include not only brand managers who seek to attract customers by creating messages about the brand but also customers now have the platform (social media) to also create and disseminate messages about brands (Leeflang et al., 2014; Chaffey, 2018). This could be the reason why advertising through social media has become very attractive to marketers.

The Concept of Digital Marketing

Digital marketing is defined by Malik (2017) and Kumar and Verma (2017) as the marketing of services and products through digital channels. Digital marketing is a strategic process that marketers use to build relationships with their target audience across digital platforms. Organisations can create loyal customers by improving their relationships with them, thus increasing the lifetime value of their customers. Digital marketing can positively affect an organisation's revenue if properly executed (Rishika, Kumar, Janakiraman, & Bezawada, 2013). The term digital "refers to a number of different channels, all used to uniquely engage audiences and tackle various goals of the conversion funnel" (Malik, 2017, pp.1). Mobile devices, Internet, displays, video messages, social media and search engines can be regarded as digital channels. These channels not only allow marketers to reach out their audience in "real time" but also enable the audience to respond back immediately, providing the marketer with valuable information. This is also known as "Inbound Marketing". The development of these digital platforms for communication was steered by the globalised world. The vast amount of personal data that is continuously captured by digital technologies enables marketers to develop target markets profiles accurately, allowing them to reach the smallest segment as well as large target audiences (Malik, 2017). Companies can now target their audience based on the audience's attributes such as behavioural, psychographic, geographic or demographic information. Marketers can also target specific devices and even individual users irrespective of the digital devices they are using (Fierro, Cardona Arbelaez, & Gavilanez, 2017; Malik, 2017).

In addition, remarketing helps marketers to target interested customers directly by placing adverts in front of them with the intention to redirect them to the company's website (Kumar & Verma, 2017; Malik, 2017). In this case, a customer would have expressed his/her interest through keyword (s) search or by visiting particular web pages and based on such Internet search behaviour a specific advert will appear on the customer's screen while surfing on the internet. This has greatly reduced the time and financial resources required to conduct a marketing campaign and or run an advert. By using digital media tools, organisations no longer pay for accessing a specific media platform like in the traditional media, but are charged according to the scope of audience they intend to reach (Fierro et al., 2017; Kumar & Verma, 2017). Traditional media refer to "mediums that are part of our culture for over half a century" (Shah, 2017, pp.1).

Digital marketers are also required to keep track of the success of their marketing campaigns. To do this, many digital channels track information about the target audience such as their interests and preferences and use such information to provide customised adverts. This information is derived from clicks, impression, leads, website hits, and conversations. Additionally, marketers analyse this information to predict future behaviour and then devise adequate strategies that will assist in meeting customers' needs. Marketers can now use digital media to monitor their Return on Investment (ROI) effectively (compared to traditional media), which enables them to make strategic decisions for the short or long term.

Multiple digital marketing channels can be used by B2C and B2B businesses. Social media marketing (SEO), automation marketing, e-Commerce SEO, content marketing, search engine marketing (SEM), paid advertising to name a few, are important digital marketing tools and practices that are regularly used by B2C and B2B organisations. Marketers from both types of businesses should always keep up with the current trends in digital marketing that suits their line of business (Kumar & Verma, 2017; Malik, 2017).

In digital marketing, the results of a marketing campaign are easily monitored and tracked which could be a source of competitive advantage. Speed, navigation and accessibility are a few important characteristics for marketers to keep in mind when trying to produce good results in digital marketing. Word of mouth (WOM) is a proven strategy to succeed in digital marketing by using social media to drive traffics to the site. Blogs is one of the strategies that exemplify the use of WOM in digital marketing. Customers can write products reviews and their personal experience with certain products. Businesses can then incorporate online reviews in their marketing strategies.

Contemporarily, the development of e-commerce and social commerce has made WOM even more powerful. Turban (2010) defined e-commerce as the exchange of products or services and money via the Internet by individuals and entities. This transaction is supported by electronic monetary systems and Internet-mediated systems. Social commerce stems from e-commerce, by taking advantage of popular social networks that inherently have interaction data and social capital. The purpose of social commerce is to offer personalised products and services based on the users' interest and interaction on the Internet. Whereas social commerce allows customers to review and purchase products without leaving the social platforms, e-commerce on the other hand requires customers to leave their social platform to the website of the vendor to make purchases. Social commerce is comprised of two types. The first type can be seen on website like Amazon and Takealot, which enable customers and potential customers to read and write comments and reviews. The second type can be seen on social media sites like Twitter, Facebook and Instagram. These social platforms give users access to companies' social media business pages in order to view information regarding their products and services. The social platforms, however, had certain limitations, for instance, the inability to provide information about prices and not being able to facilitate online monetary transactions. However, these limitations have been mitigated by the introduction of action buttons in the social networks. Examples of action buttons are ''Shop now" on Facebook, ''Buy" on Twitter, ''Buy it" on Pinterest and ''Shop now" on Instagram (Huang & Benyoucef, 2013; Gibreel, AlOtaibi, & Altmann, 2018).

All the above described capabilities of digital marketing are designed to be mobile phones' friendly to enhance customers' convenience. Mobile commerce, involves the exchange of products and services online with the use of mobile phones (Chong, 2013). With the proliferation of smartphones, tablets and notebooks, this concept provides businesses with great opportunities to market their goods and services in both developed and developing countries (Zhang, Zhu, & Liu, 2012; Cullen, & Kabanda, 2018).

According to Agarwal and Wu (2018), an online survey conducted in Norway indicated that social media plays an important role in promoting e-commerce. Hence, there is a need for businesses and organisations to ensure a presence on such platforms as customers are increasingly accessing and using social networking sites. It is perceived that the presence on these platforms enhances corporate visibility (brand awareness, value equity, product knowledge).

Digital Media Elements

There are many digital media elements available to marketers. Search Engine Optimisation (SEO) Pay Per Click (PPC), web banner, pop up advert, Search Engine Marketing (SEM), social media marketing, mobile Advertising, affiliate marketing, online classified advertisements, and email advertising, are a few digital media elements.

One of the best forms of digital marketing is Search Engine Optimisation (SEO). Unlike paid adverts, (for example, Pay Per Click (PPC)), organic listings on Google get up to 94% of all clicks. The SEO helps businesses to rank higher on the list of resorts for customers to see. Studies show that only 3% of users (excluding researchers) click to the next pages for more results. As a result, businesses that have websites that rank low on the 3rd or 4th page have lower chances of getting returns on their investment. Many companies are investing time and money in SEO to increase their visibility in web searches (Malik, 2017; Fierro et al., 2017).

Pay Per Click (PPC) are sponsored links or adverts that are often found on Google. However, they can also be found on other search engines such as Bing and Yahoo. Pay Per Click is the only digital marketing method that is entirely short term, that is, the adverts stop when the company stops paying. In addition, the key difference between PPC and SEO is that PPC is a marketing model in which a company only pays the cost of advertisement when users click on the company's link or its adverts (Dodson, 2016; Chaffey & Ellis-Chadwick, 2019). However, SEO's model requires marketers to pay the cost of advertising regardless of the user's response to the advert (Malik, 2017). Companies pay for links to their website in order to be ranked amongst or above the organic listings that appear in a search. Companies normally use PPC and SEOs to rank as high as possible in a web search.

Another digital marketing element is web banner adverts. This form of advertisement is graphical, and it is displayed within a web site. A central ad server delivers many banner adverts. Programs like Adobe, and Java display adverts and incorporate interactive elements like forms, buttons, animations, audio, and video (Chaffey, 2010). A pop-up advert opens in a new web browser window that displays above the initial browser window, and a pop under advert is displayed under the initial browser in a new browser window (Malik, 2017).

Search Engine Marketing (SEM) is another tool that digital marketers use. This tool is used to increase the visibility of websites in Search Engine Results Pages (SERPs). Based on a query search on the web, organic and sponsored results are provided by search engines. Visual cues are often used by the search engine to differentiate between organic and sponsored results (Malik, 2017).

Social media is another widely used digital media element. Social media marketing is essentially using social media platforms (Facebook, Instagram, Twitter, Pinterest, YouTube and so on) for promotional purposes. Social media advertising has become very popular because companies can promote their products and services at a low cost. Numerous businesses use their social media platforms to reach their target audience by providing valuable content when promoting their products and/or services (Chaffey, 2018; Chaffey & Ellis-Chadwick, 2019).

As depicted in Figure 1, Facebook is the world's most used digital media platform, followed by YouTube and WhatsApp. A study by Negoita, Purcarea, Popescu, Niculescu, & Coman (2018) found that Facebook is the most used digital marketing tool by SMEs in Romania. In addition, research conducted by Jawaid & Ahmed (2018) showed that physicians in Pakistan prefer using Facebook as a digital marketing tool. These platforms also allow customers to share their opinions about products and their experience (Malik, 2017; Baltes, 2015; Kumar & Verma, 2017).

Due to social media's global coverage, adverts on social media are sent to a large network of people at a low cost. According to Duggan & Brenner (2012) most (83%) of individuals between the ages of 18 and 29 use various social media platforms, hence the media platform provides the opportunity for targeting this age group. In the United States of America (USA), the young generation prefers digital platforms for advertisement (Pate & Adams, 2013).

Marketers can also use Mobile Adverts. Mobile Advertising is essentially the delivery of ad copies through wireless mobile devices like tablet computers, feature phones and smartphones. Advertisement copy refers to the text of a clickable advert. These adverts can either be rich media display adverts, static adverts, short message service (SMS), multimedia messaging service (MMS), mobile application/game adverts, mobile website adverts, and mobile search adverts. The mobile ad unit specifications are regulated by an industry group known as Mobile Marketing Association (Malik, 2017).

Affiliate marketing is an effective digital marketing element. Affiliate marketing is the leveraging of third parties to generate leads for the organisation. Payment for the third-party affiliates is based on the number of sales generated through online promotion (Malik, 2017).

Online classified adverts are another tool that marketers can use. Online classified advertisements are adverts placed in an online categorical listing of particular services or product. For instance, websites like property24 that show real estate listings, and online "Yellow pages" that has a database of contact details (Malik, 2017).

Figure 1. Global usage of digital media platforms
Source: (Chaffey, 2018)

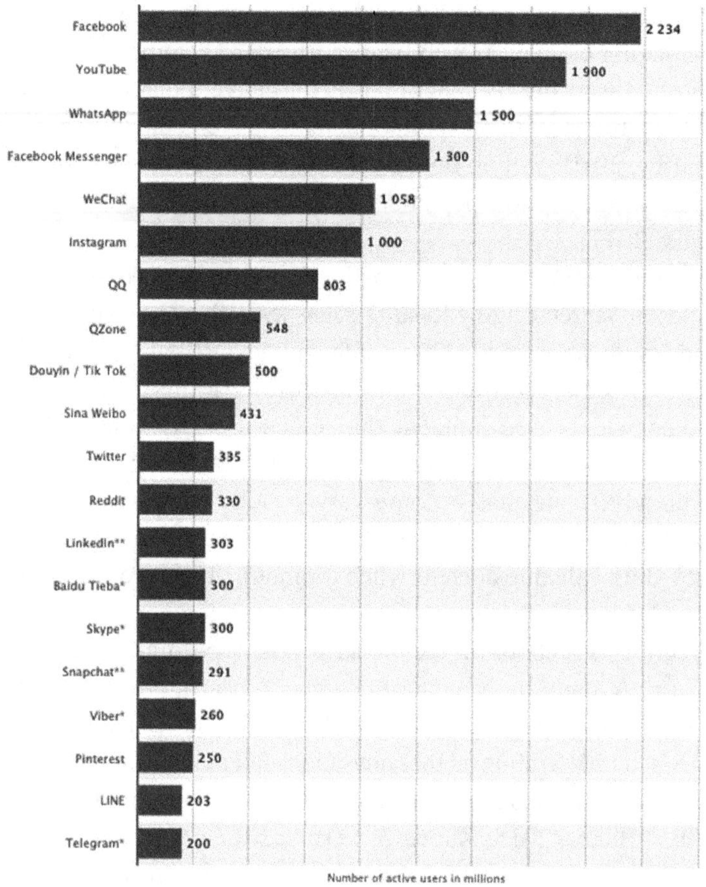

Figure 2. Use of digital platforms for marketing in the USA
Source: (Hanna et al. 2015)

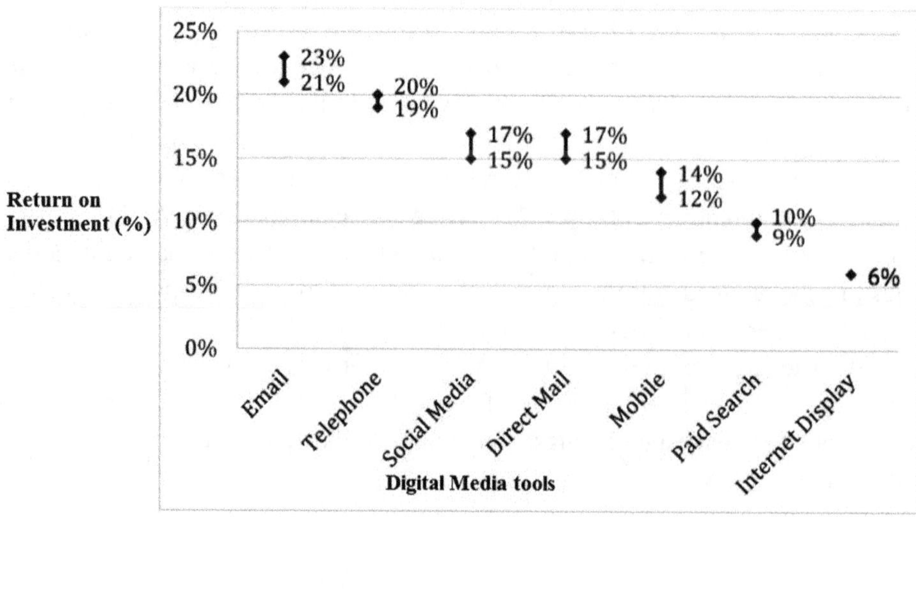

Email marketing is one of the oldest digital marketing elements. Email advertising is an email message that contains an ad copy. Sometimes email marketing is unrequested, in this case the marketer may give an opt-out option to the recipient for future emails, or they may request the recipients consent by availing an opt-in option for the recipient to receive emails in the future (Malik, 2017). In 2015, a survey of about 300 digital marketers found that email marketing was the most effective digital marketing tool to retain customer and generate revenues. This is due to the fact that over 50% of USA's general consumers check their emails multiple times in a day (Hanna, Swain, & Smith, 2015). This phenomenon is shown in Figure 2, as Email marketing produces the highest (23%) Return on Investment (ROI) (Hanna et al., 2015).

All digital marketers are faced with the challenge of managing changes and innovations in marketing strategies and technology. Branded mobile utilities, in-game adverts, and augmented reality are examples of recent approaches in marketing endeavours (Hanna et al., 2015; Malik, 2017).

Digital Marketing Communication

According to Leeflang et al. (2014), 90% of customers seek out online reviews prior to purchasing a product, and 67% of all consumers' goods purchases are a result of user-generated content. Reviews have a significant influence on consumer purchase decisions, because, an average of four reviews are read by consumers before they make a purchase (Leeflang et al., 2014). Thus, digital content reviewers have a greater influence on customers than adverts. This has resulted in the emergence of another marketing orientation called customer engagement. This is the degree to which the potential customer engages with the digital content. Insights on customer interactions with one another and the services and products they consume can be captured through the use of social media. "Blogs, product reviews, discussion groups, product ratings, just to mention a few, are new important sources of information describing how customers collect information, use that information, and how that information is used in their decision-making, shopping behavior, and post-purchase behavior," (Leeflang et al., 2014, pp.2). Organisation can collect and use this information to their advantage by improving their products and or service offerings to meet their customers' expectations, or to get ideas for new product or service development (Leeflang et al., 2014, pp.2).

Content Marketing

Content marketing has no universally accepted definition, however, the content marketing institute defines content marketing as "the marketing and business process for creating and distributing relevant and valuable content to attract, acquire, and engage a clearly defined and understood target audience with the objective of driving profitable customer action" (Baltes, 2015, pp.116). Content marketing, if executed correctly, has the potential to cement a company as an expert in their industry, thus giving them a competitive advantage (Anyanwu, Nelson, & Salawu, 2018). In order for companies to become and or remain competitive in the digital market, they must create content that is tailored to their target audience and disseminate it on the social networks that are used by the target audience. If done correctly, content marketing can help companies create an audience, test product ideas, build loyalty with customers, attracting new leads, build a relationship with customers and brand awareness. In the B2B markets, 70% of businesses are creating more content than they created in the previous years. This is because brand generated content helps 60% of decision makers in companies to make better purchase decisions in the aforementioned market. In addition, 61% of consumers are more inclined to purchase from business that provides custom content.

Content marketing is basically the art of communication, which organisations use to form relationships with existing and potential customers without necessarily selling. Marketers would provide information that adds value to their customers instead of pitching products and services to them. Due to the over-saturation of online advertisement, consumers are becoming less influenced by them. Thus, consumers ultimately patronise and stay loyal to businesses that consistently deliver information that is valuable to them. Content marketing retains the reader's attention, thus, improving brand loyalty. Email, events, custom magazines, print or online newsletters, digital content, websites or microsites, white papers, webcasts/webinars, podcasts, video portals or series, in-person roadshows, roundtables and interactive online are examples of content marketing products. The aim of content marketing is to educate existing and prospective customers on the important issues sometimes involving the marketers' products. "The motivation behind content marketing is the belief that educating the customer results in the brand's recognition as a thought leader and industry expert" (Baltes, 2015, pp.116). Content marketing also helps marketers provide content or campaigns around buying patterns and personalities. In order to win the trust of their target market, businesses, need to create a strong brand by being relevant to their target audiences. The consumer's perception about the quality of information provided is very important as 51% of consumers, in a study conducted in the USA, concluded that they will unfollow a brand that posts irritating information while 27% will block them (Chaffey, 2018). By creating content that is valuable to the target audience, interest is built and is transformed into long lasting relationships. This then translates into lifetime value of customers (Dickey & Lewis, 2010; Pate & Adams, 2013; Rishika et al., 2013; Dodson, 2016; Chaffey, & Ellis-Chadwick, 2019).

Digital marketing provides marketers with feedback, in real time on their marketing efforts. For instance, marketers can determine the success of an advert, a campaign or determine the number of customers interested in a product by counting the total number of clicks on the advert. Online behaviour and data can be easily analysed with the aid of modern software.

Digital marketing tools increase customer patronage and potentially increase revenue as noted by Kawira, Mukulu, & Odhiambo's (2019) study in Kenya. These tools are cheaper than traditional marketing, hence leveling the playing field for both large and small businesses. Therefore, if the advantages of these platforms are harnessed, it can lead to significant returns. This study aims to identify the extent of digital marketing usage in South Africa, its perceived impact and ways to maximise its impact.

METHODOLOGY

Research Design

This study uses the systematic review approach, using the Preferred Reporting Items for Systematic Reviews and Meta-Analyses (PRISMA) Framework. A systematic review is a collection of empirical evidence that fits pre-specified eligibility criteria to answer a specific research question. It uses clearly defined, procedural methods that in order to minimise biasness. This leads to reliable findings from which conclusions are made. Systematic reviews have key characteristics which are: a set of clearly defined objectives that have a methodology that is explicit and replicable; a systematic search method that helps to find all studies that meet the eligibility criteria; an evaluation of validity of the findings in the studies that were included; the synthesis and systematic presentation of findings and characteristics of the qualified studies (Liberati et al., 2009).

The PRISMA Guideline for Conducting Systematic Reviews

Preferred Reporting Items for Systematic Reviews and Meta-Analyses is based on evidence from a minimum set of items to be reported in a meta-analyses and systematic review. The PRISMA framework is used in research as a foundation for systematic reviews (PRISMA, 2015). This framework focuses on helping authors to ensure that the systematic review is reported with transparency and clarity (Liberati et al., 2009). It can also be used to critically assess systematic reviews that are published. However, it is not considered a quality assessment tool (PRISMA, 2015).

A literature review of published articles was conducted in four databases; Google Scholar, ScienceDirect, EBSCOHost, and Scopus using the PRISMA guideline. The PRISMA guideline has four stages that need to be followed. The first stage entails the identification of search engines and articles that fit the key phrases/words chosen for the study. Secondly, there is the screening of the articles to ensure that the abstracts are in line with the subject matter and duplicates are removed. After screening, the next step is determining which of the articles are eligible to be used in the study. This is done by reviewing the articles entirely to ensure that they are aligned with the study's objectives. The objectives of the study are: 1. to investigate the extent of digital marketing usage in South Africa; 2. to determine the perceived impact of digital marketing and; 3. to identify factors that influence its adoption. The Inclusion phase is the final stage, which involves the analysis of the eligible articles (PRISMA, 2015).

In the current study, the search was limited to articles published within 10 years span (2007-2018). Firstly, a combination of mesh terms "digital marketing + South Africa", were used as keywords for the search in all the databases. Secondly, a combination of free-text words such mobile marketing, social media marketing and South Africa were used as search terms. A total of 40 studies were retrieved from the search. A manual screening was done to ensure that duplicate articles were removed (12 articles were duplicated and hence removed). The abstract of the remaining 28 articles were screened to ensure that the articles are in line with the research objectives. A total of 16 articles met the pre-specified eligibility criteria and were used for the textual analysis. For articles to qualify to be included in the final analysis, they had to:

Figure 3. PRISMA flow chart
Source: Author's own

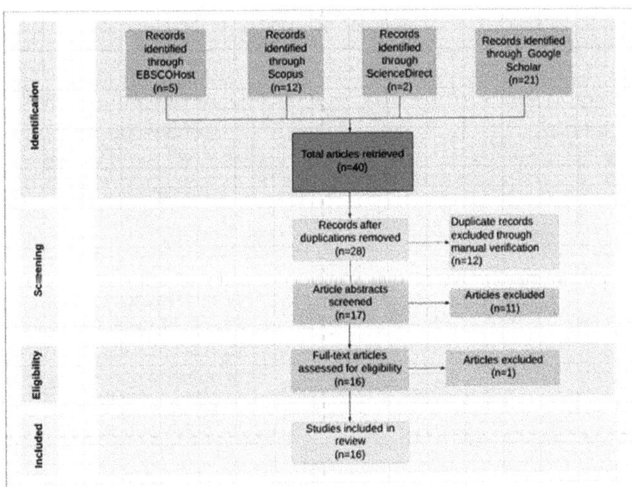

1. Discuss a form of digital marketing in South Africa.
2. Contribute to answering at least one of the research objectives.

Figure 3 shows the systematic review process.

PRESENTATION, ANALYSIS AND DISCUSSION OF RESEARCH FINDINGS

This section presents the research findings, analysis and discussion as well as recommendations in relation to the objectives of the study. Firstly, a table consisting of the selected articles for review is presented. The table shows details of authors, the setting, participants, objectives and a summary of results of each study. Secondly, the results from the selected articles are analysed and discussed in relation the research objectives. Then, recommendations and suggestions for further studies are provided.

Presentation of Data

The sixteen articles that qualified to be included in the study, are presented in Table 1.

Table 1. Selected articles for review

No	Author and year	Setting	Participants	Objectives	Results
1	Radder, Pietersen, Wang,& Han (2010)	High Schools in Port Elizabeth, South Africa	Pre-final year high school pupils	To explore the experiences of pre-final year high school pupils' approval of South African universities' SMS advertising.	Social norms, which is the perceived social pressure to engage or not to engage in an activity, is the most important determinant in school pupils' acceptance of SMS advertising.
2	Van der Waldt, Rebello,& Brown (2009)	Gauteng Province, South Africa.	Full-time registered undergraduate university students.	To determine the perceptions of younger consumers' segment towards SMS advertisements.	Generally, consumers have negative overall attitudes towards SMS advertisements, hence, it may not be effective in creating favourable attitudes towards the advertised product or service especially in the younger segment of consumers.
3	Sotiriadis, & Van Zyl (2013)	European countries (mainly Greece) and South Africa	Twitter users	To explore the factors influencing Twitter users' decision about the purchase of tourism services.	Follower's perception of the reliability of other followers, degree of involvement in terms of posting and the knowledge and expertise of other Twitter followers (based on their written reviews) influences the purchase of tourism services.
4	Dlodlo & Dhurup (2013)	South Africa	General consumers	To determine the factors that determine the use of social media tools such as social networking sites and Web 2.0 sharing applications.	The usage of social media is highly determined by factors such as the pleasure, enjoyment and value derived, user-friendliness as well as availability of communities on the online systems.

continued on following page

Table 1. Continued

No	Author and year	Setting	Participants	Objectives	Results
5	Duffett (2015)	Western Cape Province, South Africa	South African millennials students.	To investigate the effect of behavioural attitudes of millennials in South Africa towards Facebook.	Advertising on Facebook positively influences the behavioural attitudes of Millennials in South Africa in terms of their intention to purchase and actually purchasing the product.
6	Duffett (2017)	South Africa	College and high school students	To explore the effect of interactive social media marketing communications on students' cognitive, affective and behavioural attitude components.	Interactive social media marketing communications positively influences each attitude component (cognitive, affective and behavioral attitude components) among teenagers as they are no longer influenced by traditional marketing methods. Black and coloured teenagers are more susceptible to be influenced by social media marketing communications.
7	Akpojivi & Bevan-Dye (2014)	North West University and Vaal University of Technology, South Africa	Generation Y students	To determine the trend of mobile advertising in South Africa.	Generation Y students are not influenced by the usefulness of mobile advertising message. They are also uneasy about the privacy of personal information relating to mobile advertising.
8	Makgopa (2016)	Gauteng province, South Africa	Car dealerships	To determine the social media platforms used in marketing in the car dealership industry.	Facebook, Twitter, WhatsApp and YouTube are the platforms used by the car dealers, however, due to Facebook's popularity amongst the target audience, it emerged as the most used platform, followed by Twitter and WhatsApp.
9	Duffett & Wakeham (2016).	Western Cape province, South Africa	Millennials (18 to 30 years old) exposed to marketing communication on social media	To investigate the influence social media marketing communications has on the purchase process (attention, interest, desire, and action) among millennials in South Africa.	Social media marketing is found to have a significant influence on the purchase process. However, the magnitude of influence reduces at the later stages of the purchasing process.
10	Rambe (2017)	Free State province, South Africa	Tourism SMMEs owners/managers	To ascertain the extent to which tourism SMMEs utilize social media platforms in expanding their market share. Additionally, to assess the impact of social media use by the firms on their competitiveness.	Social media marketing is used predominantly for online marketing and promoting of products/services, to retain existing customers, attract new ones, and promote new offerings. Social media marketing positively influenced the competitiveness of tourism SMMEs.

continued on following page

Table 1. Continued

No	Author and year	Setting	Participants	Objectives	Results
11	Snyman & Visser (2014)	South Africa	Dentists who are members of the South African Dental Association	To find out the social media usage behaviour of South African dentists who are members of the South African Dental Association.	Most (50.2%) dentists use social media (especially GooglePlus and Facebook), however, only 13.2% use it as a marketing tool while the rest use the platform to connect with friends.
12	Chikandiwa, Contogiannis & Jembere, (2013)	South Africa	South African banks	To analyse how social media is being adopted by South African banks.	Facebook and Twitter are the main platforms being used by banks for customer service and advertising purposes. On the other hand, obstacles such as legal and regulatory issues are limitations to the adoption of social media. Since the SA bank customers are consumers both the new and traditional media, there is the need to integrate social media with traditional media.
13	Chinomona & Sandada, (2013)	Gauteng Province, South Africa	Mobile service customers or clients who partake in marketing activities	To find out if mobile marketing activities impact customer purchase intentions.	Mobile marketing activities highly influences consumer purchasing intentions, however, there is a stronger influence if marketers trigger the customer's acceptance of mobile marketing.
14	Sikundla, Mushunje & Akinyemi, (2018)	Eastern Cape province, South Africa.	Smallholder farmers	To investigate the adoption of mobile phone marketing by the farmers	Majority of farmers use local market contacts, family and acquaintances, social groups and state marketing agencies to market their goods. Although in the minority, some farmers use voice calls and SMS as forms of mobile marketing. Males were also found to easily adopt mobile phone marketing as compared to their female counterparts.
15	Oni, Shumba & Matiza, (2014)	Limpopo province, South Africa.	Retailers	To discover whether social media marketing has an impact on the turnover of retailers	Marketing through social media platforms such as Facebook, Twitter LinkedIn, BBM and Mxit were found to positively impact turnovers of retailers. Retailers employ social media to strengthen their brands, increase their reach to customers as well as boost their overall turnover.
16	Maduku, Mpinganjira & Duh, (2016).	Gauteng	SME owners/decision makers (Manufacturing, tourism, wholesale and retail sectors)	To ascertain the major drivers that influence the intention to adopt mobile marketing by South African SMEs	Most critical driver of the intention to adopt mobile marketing is perceived management support in the SME. In addition to this, anticipated competitive advantage, cost and perceived IT employee capacity are factors aiding the adoption intentions of SME owners

Source: Authors' own compilation

Analysis of Findings Based on the Research Objectives

The Current Use of Digital Marketing in South Africa

The final articles that were reviewed ranging between 2009 and 2018 show that digital marketing is being employed in the manufacturing, agricultural and service sectors of South Africa. The digital platforms currently used include mobile marketing (SMS) and social media, Facebook, Twitter, LinkedIn, YouTube, WhatsApp, Instagram, Tumblr, Pinterest, Blackberry Messenger, Google Plus, Mxit and WeChat (Van der Waldt et al., 2009; Sotiriadis & Van Zyl, 2013; Duffett, 2015; Makgopa, 2016; Duffett, 2017).

Studies in the banking, tourism and retail industries in South Africa suggest that, businesses use social media marketing to attract new customers, promote products and services, serve existing customers, boost business turnover and have a "customer first approach" (Chikandiwa et al., 2013; Oni et al., 2014; Rambe, 2017).

Although social media marketing has been widely adopted in various industries in South Africa, a study by Snyman & Visser, (2014) found that, social media marketing has not been widely adopted amongst registered dentists. However, in the same study most of the respondents (84%) indicated that social media marketing usage would increase in the future.

The Perceived Impact of Digital Marketing in South Africa

Van der Waldt et al.'s (2009) study that aimed at assessing the perceptions of undergraduate university students towards SMS advertisements in South Africa, found that consumers generally maintain a negative overall attitude towards SMS advertisements. This means that, SMS advertisement may not be effective in influencing purchasing intentions of the students. Hence, it may not be effective in creating favourable attitudes towards the advertised product or service especially in the younger segment of consumers.

The above finding is supported by Akpojivi and Bevan-Dye (2014) and Duffett, (2017) who explored mobile advertising in Generation Y (born in the period of 1981-1994) and Generation Z (born in the period of 1995-2012) age groups. These studies purported that the influence of mobile marketing on customers is dropping as consumers in these age groups are more influenced by interactive social media.

On the other hand, a study by Chinomona and Sandada (2013) investigated the impact of mobile marketing activities on purchasing intentions and found that, mobile marketing activities highly influence purchasing intentions. These findings, therefore, suggest that some digital platforms are peculiar to certain demographics as mobile marketing activities may still be relevant to the general customer (older generation) but not for young adults (Generations Y and Z).

In terms of social media marketing, Duffett and Wakeham's (2016) investigated the extent to which social media marketing impacts the purchase process (attention, interest, desire, and action) among South African millennials (Generation Y). The findings suggest that, social media marketing had a significant influence on the purchase process in the age group. However, its impact reduces at the later stages of the purchasing process (desire, and action). This implies that, this marketing strategy may work well in capturing the customer's attention but may not convince one to make the purchase. However, Duffett (2015) and Duffett (2017) on the other hand emphasize that, social media marketing, especially using Facebook, positively influences millennials in terms of their intention to purchase and actual buying behaviour.

The impact of social media marketing cannot be overstated as previous studies amongst Small, Medium and Micro Enterprises (SMMEs) in the tourism industry, car dealers and retailers in South Africa show that the marketing tool greatly influences business activities. In these business sectors, social media marketing assists businesses to expand their market share and increase their competitiveness (Oni et al., 2014; Makgopa, 2016; Rambe, 2017). The aforementioned studies suggest that Facebook is the most employed marketing tool due to its popularity within the target market and its comprehensiveness.

Factors That Affect the Adoption of Digital Marketing in South Africa

Although social media marketing has positively affected many industries as discussed in the section above, some industries are yet to benefit from its positive impact. A study conducted by Snyman and Visser (2014); Sikundla et al. (2018) amongst registered dentists and smallholder farmers in South Africa indicated that farmers faced issues such as their inability to afford airtime and unreliable network, and hence could not adopt social media marketing. The dentists on the other hand, stated challenges such as time constraints, lack of social media marketing know-how, security concerns, and not believing in the marketing and promotion of dental practice (i.e. their work speaks for itself). These dentists however, indicated that they are willing to adopt social media marketing in the future.

According to Maduku, Mpinganjira and Duh's (2016) study on Small and Medium Enterprises (SMEs), factors such as management support of digital marketing, anticipated competitive advantage and the perceived digital marketing know-how of the IT employees influence the SMEs intention to adopt digital marketing. Other studies conducted amongst twitter users, mobile service subscribers and millennial students suggest that marketers, in their quest to influence customer purchasing decisions, should consider the knowledge level of social media followers regarding a subject matter, and make an effort to educate followers (Chinomona & Sandada, 2013; Sotiriadis & Van Zyl, 2013; Duffett, 2015). Hence, providing a platform for customers to discuss their product experience through a forum as well as providing feedback and suggestions, is key to helping marketers to adapt their advertising to suit the target audience.

Furthermore, studies conducted on teenagers and young adults in high school and the university posit that marketers need to appeal to their social norms, which entails considering the influence of perceived external social pressure to engage or not to engage in a specific medium of advertising. Marketers should, therefore, ensure that, the language and content provided should match the profile of the target audience. Privacy of users of online medium of marketing should be provided through opt-in and opt-out options regarding a specific advertisement (Van der Waldt et al., 2009; Radder et al., 2010; Akpojivi & Bevan-Dye, 2014).

In choosing digital marketing platforms, marketers must ensure that the chosen platform is enjoyable for the target audience, user friendly as well as one that has an available online community (Dlodlo & Dhurup, 2013). A study by Chikandiwa et al. (2013) in South Africa's banking sector, and Afolabi, Ojelabi and Oyeyipo, (2018) in Nigeria's construction sector concluded that typical business customers consist of both users of the traditional and new media, therefore, marketers should combine both to ensure optimum results.

Summary of Main Findings

Table 2 depicts the main findings from the systematic review.

Table 2. Summary of main findings

Current usage	Perceived impact	Factors that affect the adoption of digital marketing
Used in manufacturing, agriculture and services sectors in South Africa (Van der Waldt et al., 2009; Sotiriadis & Van Zyl, 2013; Duffett, 2015; Makgopa, 2016; Duffett, 2017).	SMS advertisement may not effectively influence purchasing intentions of university undergraduate students ((Van der Waldt et al., 2009).	Inability by registered dentists and smallholder farmers to afford airtime. Unreliable network, lack of social media marketing know-how, and security concerns amongst others (Snyman & Visser, 2014; Sikundla et al., 2018).
Not widely adopted amongst registered dentists in South Africa (Snyman & Visser, 2014).	Influence of mobile marketing on Generation Y and Z customers is dropping as these consumers are more influenced by interactive social media (Akpojivi & Bevan-Dye, 2014; Duffett, 2017).	Management support of digital marketing, anticipated competitive advantage, and the perceived digital marketing know-how of the IT employees (Maduku et al., 2016).
	Mobile marketing highly influences purchasing intentions of older generation, but not for young adults (Chinomona & Sandada, 2013).	Knowledge level of social media followers and educating of such followers by the marketers. Providing a platform for customers to discuss their product experience, and providing feedback and suggestions (Chinomona & Sandada, 2013; Sotiriadis & Van Zyl, 2013; Duffett, 2015).
	Social media marketing has a significant influence on the purchase process, especially on capturing customer's attention but may not convince one to make a purchase (Duffett & Wakeham, 2016).	Language and content provided by marketers should match the profile of the target audience. Privacy of users of online medium should be provided through opt-in and opt-out options (Van der Waldt et al., 2009; Radder et al., 2010; Akpojivi & Bevan-Dye, 2014).
	Social media marketing especially using Facebook, positively influences millennials in terms of intention to purchase and actually buying behaviour (Duffett, 2015, 2017).	Enjoyable, user friendly digital marketing platform for the target audience (Dlodlo & Dhurup, 2013).
	Social media marketing assists tourism SMMEs, car dealers and retailers to expand their market share and increase their competitiveness (Oni et al., 2014; Makgopa, 2016; Rambe, 2017).	Taking into consideration both traditional and new media customers in South Africa's banking sector (Chikandiwa et al., 2013).

DISCUSSION AND RECOMMENDATIONS

The study investigated the current use of digital marketing, its impact and factors that influence the adoption of digital marketing in the context of South Africa. Digital marketing was found to be used by South African marketers. However, they are not taking advantage of all the digital media offerings. Based on the reviewed articles, some key tools were not used by South African marketers, such as email marketing, SEO, pay per click, web banner advertising and pop up adverts. A study by Hanna et al., (2015) in the USA concluded that adopting email marketing leads to customer retention and revenue generation. Other tools such as SEO and pay per click were reported in various literature to increase online visibility while web banner advertising and pop up adverts helps marketers target a specific audience. It is recommended that marketers in South Africa explore the aforementioned tools by incorporating them into their marketing strategy.

Furthermore, in order to fully benefit from digital marketing, a marketer has to effectively engage with the target audience. This can be done through content marketing, which was found to improve customer decision making regarding a product by 61% in the USA (Baltes, 2015). In study that involved Kenyan SMEs, Wilson, and Makau (2018) recommend marketers to plan their online content before implementing their digital marketing strategies. South African marketers are therefore recommended, to provide adequate and relevant information about their products and services in order to be considered as "experts" in that industry. As previously mentioned, products and services offered by perceived "experts", improves profitability and competitiveness.

FUTURE RESEARCH DIRECTIONS

One major limitation of the study was the paucity of peer reviewed articles regarding digital marketing in South Africa. Furthermore, most platforms required payment to access data, and this reduced the number of articles available to the researcher. Additionally, the reviewed studies did not indicate any use of certain tools such as email marketing, SEO, pay per click, web banner advertising and pop up adverts. Hence, more studies need to be conducted to ascertain whether these tools are being used and if not, why marketers do not use them.

CONCLUSION

Sixteen articles were selected for the analysis. All these articles confirmed that digital marketing has been adopted by South African marketers. It was also discovered that, mobile marketing is losing its influence in digital marketing, especially in the generation Y and Z age groups, as they are more influenced by interactive digital media. Generally, in South Africa, both mobile and digital marketing, were found to positively impact customer buying decisions as well as increase total revenue. This implies that businesses that adopt digital marketing platforms such as mobile and social media, have a high possibility of increasing revenue. However, the study found that a number of tools are yet to be fully explored by marketers.

Just merely adopting digital media for marketing purposes does not guarantee increased revenue. Marketers have to put some measures in place to reap the benefits of digital marketing. This entails understanding their target audience, educating them, providing avenues for customers to discuss and provide feedback on the company's products as well as designing adverts to suit the profile of their target audience.

REFERENCES

Afolabi, A. O., Ojelabi, R. A., & Oyeyipo, O. (2018). An analysis of social media marketing of indigenous construction firms in Nigeria: A tool for sustainable growth. *International Journal of Construction Supply Chain Management*, *8*, 60–72.

Agarwal, J., & Wu, T. (Eds.). (2018). *Emerging Issues in Global Marketing: A Shifting Paradigm*. New York: Springer. doi:10.1007/978-3-319-74129-1

Akpojivi, U., & Bevan-Dye, A. (2014). Mobile advertisements and information privacy perception amongst South African Generation Y students. *Telematics and Informatics*, *32*(1), 1–10. doi:10.1016/j.tele.2014.08.001

Anyanwu, G., Nelson, O., & Salawu, A. (2018). Online Advertising Influence for Promoting Preference for E-Shopping in Nigeria: A Study of Jumia. *Academy of Strategic Management Journal*, *17*, 1–9.

Baltes, L. P. (2015). Content marketing-the fundamental tool of digital marketing. *Bulletin of the Transilvania University of Brasov. Economic Sciences. Series V*, *8*, 111.

Chaffey, D. (2010). Applying organisational capability models to assess the maturity of digital-marketing governance. *Journal of Marketing Management*, *26*(3-4), 187–196. doi:10.1080/02672571003612192

Chaffey, D. (2018). *Global social media research summary 2018*. Retrieved from https://www.smartinsights.com/social-media-marketing/social-media-strategy/new-global-social-media-research/

Chaffey, D., & Ellis-Chadwick, F. (2019). *Digital Marketing*. London: Pearson.

Chikandiwa, T. S., Contogiannis, E., & Jembere, E. (2013). The adoption of social media marketing in South African banks. *European Business Review*, *25*(4), 365–381. doi:10.1108/EBR-02-2013-0013

Chinomona, R., & Sandada, M. (2013). The influence of market related mobile activities on the acceptance of mobile marketing and consumer intention to purchase products promoted by SMS in South Africa. *Journal of Applied Business Research*, *29*(6), 1897–1908. doi:10.19030/jabr.v29i6.8225

Chong, A. Y. L. (2013). Understanding mobile commerce continuance intentions: An empirical analysis of Chinese consumers. *Journal of Computer Information Systems*, *53*(4), 22–30. doi:10.1080/08874417.2013.11645647

Cullen, M., & Kabanda, S. K. (2018). The role of demographic and motivational factors on mobile commerce usage activities in South Africa. *South African Journal of Information Management*, *20*(1), 1–8. doi:10.4102ajim.v20i1.817

Dickey, I. J., & Lewis, W. F. (2010). Social Media Perceptions and Usage by Generation Y and Relevant Marketing Implications. In *2010 Conference Proceedings of the Society for Marketing Advances*. University of Dayton.

Dlodlo, N., & Dhurup, M. (2013). Examining social media dimensions among a cohort of Generation Y consumers in South Africa. *Mediterranean Journal of Social Sciences*, *4*, 329.

Dodson, I. (2016). *The Art of Digital Marketing*. John Wiley & Sons.

Duffett, R. G. (2015). Facebook advertising's influence on intention-to-purchase and purchase amongst Millennials. *Internet Research*, *25*(4), 498–526. doi:10.1108/IntR-01-2014-0020

Duffett, R. G. (2017). Influence of social media marketing communications on young consumers' attitudes. *Young Consumers*, *18*(1), 19–39. doi:10.1108/YC-07-2016-00622

Duffett, R. G., & Wakeham, M. (2016). Social media marketing communications effect on attitudes among Millennials in South Africa. *The African Journal of Information Systems*, *8*, 2.

Duggan, M., & Brenner, J. (2012). The demographics of social media users. *Pew Research Center's Internet & American Life Project*. Retrieved from https://www.pewinternet.org/2013/02/14/the-demographics-of-social-media-users-2012/

Fierro, I., Cardona Arbelaez, D. A., & Gavilanez, J. (2017). Digital marketing: A new tool for international education. *Pensamiento & Gestión*, *43*, 220–240.

Gibreel, O., AlOtaibi, D. A., & Altmann, J. (2018). Social commerce development in emerging markets. *Electronic Commerce Research and Applications*, *27*, 152–162. doi:10.1016/j.elerap.2017.12.008

Hanna, R. C., Swain, S. D., & Smith, J. (2015). *Email Marketing in a Digital World: The Basics and Beyond*. New York, NY: Business Expert Press.

Huang, Z., & Benyoucef, M. (2013). From e-commerce to social commerce: A close look at design features. *Electronic Commerce Research and Applications*, *12*(4), 246–259. doi:10.1016/j.elerap.2012.12.003

Jawaid, M., & Ahmed, S. J. (2018). Pharmaceutical Digital Marketing and Its Impact on Healthcare Physicians of Pakistan: A National Survey. *Cureus*, *10*(6), e2789. doi:10.7759/cureus.2789 PMID:30112265

Kawira, D. K., Mukulu, E., & Odhiambo, R. (2019). Effect of Digital Marketing on the Performance of MSMES in Kenya. *Journal of Marketing Communications*, *2*, 1–23.

Kumar, P., & Verma, A. (2017). Impact of Digital Marketing on Rural Marketing. *Imperial Journal of Interdisciplinary Research*, *3*, 705–708.

Leeflang, P. S., Verhoef, P. C., Dahlström, P., & Freundt, T. (2014). Challenges and solutions for marketing in a digital era. *European Management Journal*, *32*(1), 1–12. doi:10.1016/j.emj.2013.12.001

Liberati, A., Altman, D. G., Tetzlaff, J., Mulrow, C., Gøtzsche, P. C., Loannidis, J. P., ... Moher, D. (2009). The PRISMA statement for reporting systematic reviews and meta-analyses of studies that evaluate health care interventions: Explanation and elaboration. *Italian Journal of Public Health*, *6*, 354–391. PMID:19621070

Maduku, D. K., Mpinganjira, M., & Duh, H. (2016). Understanding mobile marketing adoption intention by South African SMEs: A multi-perspective framework. *International Journal of Information Management*, *36*(5), 711–723. doi:10.1016/j.ijinfomgt.2016.04.018

Makgopa, S. S. (2016). Online social media usage of car dealerships in Gauteng Province, South Africa. *Problems and Perspectives in Management*, *14*, 601–607. doi:10.21511/ppm.14(3-3).2016.02

Malik, R. (2017). An Empirical Study of Digital Marketing and its Elements. *IJSRST*, *3*, 715–718.

Negoita, O. D., Purcarea, A. A., Popescu, M., Niculescu, A., & Coman, C. N. (2018). Digital Marketing Tools Used by Companies. *FAIMA Business & Management Journal*, *6*, 66–76.

Oni, O. A., Shumba, P. M., & Matiza, T. (2014). The Impact of Social Media-Based Marketing on the Turnover of Retailers Based in Polokwane, South Africa. *Mediterranean Journal of Social Sciences*, *5*, 307–316.

Pate, S. S., & Adams, M. (2013). The influence of social networking sites on buying behaviors of millennials. *Atlantic Marketing Journal*, *2*, 92–109.

PRISMA. (2015). *Welcome to the Preferred Reporting Items for Systematic Reviews and Meta-Analyses (PRISMA) website!* Retrieved from http://www.prisma-statement.org/

Radder, L., Pietersen, J., Wang, H., & Han, X. (2010). Antecedents of South African high school pupils' acceptance of universities' SMS advertising. *International Business & Economics Research Journal*, *9*, 29–39.

Rambe, P. (2017). Social media marketing and business competitiveness: Evidence from South African tourism SMMEs. *Problems and Perspectives in Management*, *15*(2), 411–423. doi:10.21511/ppm.15(2-2).2017.10

Rishika, R., Kumar, A., Janakiraman, R., & Bezawada, R. (2013). The effect of customers' social media participation on customer visit frequency and profitability: An empirical investigation. *Information Systems Research*, *24*(1), 108–127. doi:10.1287/isre.1120.0460

Shah, M. (2017). *Traditional Media vs New Media: Which is Beneficial?* Retrieved from https://www.techfunnel.com/martech/traditional-media-vs-new-media-beneficial/

Sikundla, T., Mushunje, A., & Akinyemi, B. E. (2018). Socioeconomic drivers of mobile phone adoption for marketing among smallholder irrigation farmers in South Africa. *Cogent Social Sciences*, *4*(1), 1–12. doi:10.1080/23311886.2018.1505415 PMID:30310826

Snyman, L., & Visser, J. H. (2014). The adoption of social media and social media marketing by dentists in South Africa. *South African Dental Journal*, *69*, 258–264. PMID:26548200

Sotiriadis, M. D., & Van Zyl, C. (2013). Electronic word-of-mouth and online reviews in tourism services: The use of twitter by tourists. *Electronic Commerce Research*, *13*(1), 103–124. doi:10.100710660-013-9108-1

Turban, E., Lee, J. K., King, D., Liang, T. P., & Turban, D. (2010). *Electronic Commerce 2010: A Managerial Perspective*. Prentice Hall.

Van der Waldt, D. R., Rebello, T. M., & Brown, W. J. (2009). Attitudes of young consumers towards SMS advertising. *African Journal of Business Management*, *3*, 444–452.

Wilson, V., & Makau, C. (2018). Online marketing use: Small and medium enterprises (SMEs) experience from Kenya. *ORSEA Journal*, *7*, 63–77.

Zhang, L., Zhu, J., & Liu, Q. (2012). A meta-analysis of mobile commerce adoption and the moderating effect of culture. *Computers in Human Behavior*, *28*(5), 1902–1911. doi:10.1016/j.chb.2012.05.008

KEY TERMS AND DEFINITIONS

Affiliate Marketing: A type of performance-based marketing in which a business rewards one or more affiliates for each visitor or customer brought by the affiliate's own marketing efforts.

Augmented Reality: An interactive experience of a real-world environment where the objects that reside in the real world are "augmented" by computer-generated perceptual information.

Business-to-Business (B2B): Business-to-business is a situation where one business makes a commercial transaction with another.

Business-to-Customer (B2C): Refers to the process of selling products and services directly between consumers.

Content Marketing: A form of marketing focused on creating, publishing, and distributing content for a targeted audience online.

Customer-to-Customer (C2C): Customer to customer markets provide an innovative way to allow customers to interact with each other.

Generation Y: Also known as millennials, include people who were born between the early 1980s and early 2000s.

Generation Z: Refers to people who were born after Generation Y.

In-Game Adverts: Refers to advertising in computer and video games.

Pay per Click: Also known as cost per click, is an internet advertising model used to drive traffic to websites, in which an advertiser pays a publisher when the advert is clicked.

Chapter 10
Customer Engagement:
From Social Shoppers to Social Learners and Collaborators

Robin Cheng
Taylor's University, Malaysia

ABSTRACT

This chapter focused on exploring the engagement in which consumers interact with each other while conducting online shopping activities, such as discovering products, sharing product information, and/or collaboratively making shopping decisions. At the core of the product/service offering, successful shopping models will be able to meet the needs of highly engaged shoppers. In order to develop sustainable shopping model for this group of shoppers, social support theory could explain the current phenomenon of the use of social media for shopping. The social media technologies facilitated collaborative learning and collaborative improvement on the sale of unconventional and innovative products. The chapter contributes in social commerce innovations and provides managerial implications for understanding the overall interactions of social commerce.

INTRODUCTION

In the fierce competition, technological advancement, product choices and well-informed customers on the social commerce, the ability to engage customers is considered a strategic tool to build a sustainable competitive advantage (Van Doorn et al., 2010; Brodie et al., 2013; Islam & Rahman, 2016) and has emerged. Customer engagement is portrayed as an approach to create, build and enhance customer relationships (Brodie et al., 2013).

Information is the most important aspect of any decision-making process, whether it is engaging the customers in browsing or force them to buy the product or service (Kumar & Kashyap, 2018). Since the availability of adequate information on a website (Close and Kinney, 2010; Shim et al., 2001) may convert the browsing into buying, the information related to company and product is important to customers (Kaur and Quareshi, 2015) and for customer support services. Moreover, it enables the shoppers to gather information about products without the necessity of placing the items of interest (Close and Kinney, 2010).

DOI: 10.4018/978-1-5225-9697-4.ch010

In the United States, the survey from the Pew Research Centre shows that the top seven social media sites are YouTube, Facebook, Instagram, Pinterest, Snapchat, LinkedIn and Twitter (Spisak, 2019). Social media in Malaysia has grown due to the ease of Internet connection in the city around Malaysia. The top 8 social media in Malaysia is Facebook, Whatsapp, Youtube, Twitter, Linkin, Pinterest, Instagram and Weibo (Social Media Marketing, 2019)

The objective of the chapter is to understand the use of social networking site to gain information and social support with learning being thrust at the central role at the preliminary phrase of a pre-shopping journey. The chapter also examine the quality contents in the social media that compels users to engage with the social networking sites.

BACKGROUND

Social support and Web site quality plays a critical role by positively influencing the user's intention to use social commerce and to continue using a social networking site. The two effects are found to be mediated by the quality of the relationship between the user and the social networking Web site. Digital shoppers are increasingly hitting the "buy" button on social media sites (Amato-Mccoy, 2018), and possess the ability to influence purchase decisions. Social media is also considered a large part of the product discovery and research phase of the shopping journey (Pandolph, 2018), shoppable content is becoming more popular, it's likely that social media will play an even larger role in e-commerce, with Facebook, the clear winner in social commerce, with its huge user base and wide-ranging demographics.

Three case studies in Malaysia have been selected. The hosts are actively providing shoppable contents for the users, who are shopping for information or their services.

USER ENGAGEMENT

A user engagement is 'a quality of user experience with technology' (O'Brien's, 2011). A broader definition of social media engagement is 'a quality of user experience with web-based technologies that enable users to interact with, create, and share content with individuals and organizations in their social networks' (McCay-Peet and Quan-Haase, 2016). Users are actively engaged in decisions about what information to share and with whom, rather than being simply passive consumers of content after a great shopping experience (Young and Quan-Haase, 2013).

ENGAGED HOST-USERS / FOLLOWERS: HARNESSING POSITIVE EXPERIENCES

Individuals are using digital platform to disseminate knowledge for survival over the long term. During the social learning process, the highly engaged followers/users will be contributing to the conversation post threads and the core group of highly engaged fans is more valuable than millions of disengaged followers/users, and they can have a huge impact on the marketing efforts (Ackroyd, 2018). In the experiential journey, the followers/users may discover a small, real, relevant and quality of audience contributing to the content of the engaged champion.

If there are a few followers/users who are very influential, this type of indirect influence is very important on social media and can lead to significant amplification of your content. Things move fast on social media. New content can have a big impact on how it received. However, where highly engaged host and followers using average weekly working hours as the primary measure does not measure quality of work or actual productivity (Fuller and Shikaloff, 2017)

TECHNOLOGY ACCEPTANCE MODEL (TAM)

Technology Acceptance Model, developed by Davis(1989) to predict use and acceptance of information systems and technology by individuals, examines the individual technology acceptance behavior in different information systems constructs. In TAM model, there are two factors perceived usefulness and perceived ease of use is relevant in computer use behaviors. The perceived usefulness as the prospective user's subjective probability that using a specific application system will enhance his or her job or life performance. Perceive ease of use (EOU) can be defined as the degree to which the prospective user expects the target system to be free of effort.

Lim(2000) proposed to modify TAM by adding variables like experience, self efficacy, perceived risk and social influence. Agarwal and Karahanna added cognitive absorption, playfulness and self-efficacy to the TAM model. Van der Heijden(2000) after analyzing the individual acceptance and usage of the website added two new constructs to TAM:perceived entertainment value and perceived presentation attractiveness

Chau and Hu (2001) compared three models Technology Acceptance Model (TAM), the Theory of Planned Behavior (TPB), and a decomposed TPB model that is potentially adequate in the targeted healthcare professional setting in Hong Kong. The results indicated that TAM was superior to TPB in explaining the physicians' intention to use telemedicine technology. Voluntariness can be factor in determining the behavioral intention to use (Sun and Zhang, 2003). Hun-Pin Shih (2004) combined the TAM and the information behavioral model of Choo (1991) that takes notice of the relevance of the information. Lee (2009) combined the Technology Acceptance Model with Theory of Planned Behavior, perceived risk and perceived benefit to understand the adoption of internet banking

SOCIAL SUPPORT IN ONLINE COMMUNITIES

Social support is a multidimensional construct whose components could differ from context to context (Huang, Nambisan, Uzuner, 2010; Madjar, 2005). House (1981) argued that there are four types of social support that could reduce work stress, including emotional, instrumental, informational, and appraisal support.

People need emotional and informational support (which are intangible) as well as tangible support under health stress (Schaefer et al, 1981). Since interactions on the Internet are virtual in nature and are often relied-on messages, online social support that may help social media users usually is intangible in nature, including informational support and emotional support (Huang, Nambisan, Uzuner, 2010; Madjar, 2005). Informational support refers to providing messages, in the form of recommendations, advice, or knowledge, that could be helpful for solving problems. Emotional support refers to providing messages that involve emotional concerns such as caring, understanding, or empathy (House, 1981). Both types of messages are the major support mechanisms for social interactions in online communities.

In the virtual environment, informational support could provide solutions, plans, or interpretation. Emotional support focuses on expressing one's concerns and hence can help to solve problems indirectly. These two types of support are the main target for investigating social support in virtual communities.

When social support exists in a social network or social commerce, it would be natural for community members to share commercial information and recommendations as an extension of their sharing of other supportive information. When a user perceives that other members have been caring and helpful in providing useful information, then acquiring or sharing valuable shopping information with others would be obligatory (Crocker and Canevello, 2008). The frequent sharing of supportive information can also enhance friendship and trust among members, which may further increase the intention to conduct commercial activities in the social media.

SOCIAL MEDIA ENGAGEMENT MODEL

The model of social media engagement by McCay-Peet and Quan-Haase (2016) comprises of six elements: (1) presentation of self; (2) action and participation; (3) uses and gratifications; (4) positive experiences; (5) usage and activity counts; and (6) social context.

In this model, the quality and degree of social media engagement helps explain why people choose to adopt and continue to engage with the social media. Engagement can promote feelings of belonging to a community and occur at a deep level without much awareness on the part of users and demonstrates the relationship between positive experiences and different elements of the model of social media engagement through presentation of self and action and participation. This element enables people to keep up with the news. The emotional valence of content—positive or negative—has the potential to influence action and participation and thus usage and activity counts at the Action and Participation level. While there is often a wealth of user reviews or indicators (e.g. 'likes'), which help consumers make informed decisions, buyers would need to beware that some companies exist to create false reviews and inflate reputations (Griffith-Greene, 2014). The false user engagement has not been determined despite numerous network experiences that motivates users to engage with content created, shared, or endorsed by people in their social networks and encourage them to linger and return.

SOCIAL EXCHANGE THEORY

The social exchange theory postulates that consumers are socially interdependent (Emerson, 1976; Homans, 1958). Consumers may develop a sense of online community through mutually sharing product information and exchanging shopping experiences (Rese et al., 2014). They may also obtain product and service information that is useful for participating in online group-buying. However, online group-buying transactions involve risks that are intrinsically embedded in virtual environments, because of information asymmetry and potential opportunistic behavior of counterparts (Shiau and Luo, 2012). Information sharing and trust of community are relational bonds between exchange parties to cope with risks and opportunistic behaviors, hence may therefore foster consumers' trust in online intermediary

SOCIAL MEDIA LEARNERS

One reason social media is so popular is that it allows individuals to personalize the way they experience and interact with the Web. Tools such as Facebook, Twitter, and Instagram are increasingly being leveraged as a study tool for today's tech-savvy students (Ackroyd, 2018). There exists a synergy between knowledge management and e-learning through these social networking tools (Kane, Robinson-Combre and Berge, 2010). Social support and Web site quality positively influence the user's intention to use social commerce and to continue using a social networking site and these effects are found to be mediated by the quality of the relationship between the user and the social networking Web site (Liang, Ho, Li, Turbun, 2012)

In the case studies presented below: Dr Othman Talib, who has the largest number of engagement and actively promoted learning among his followers in his social media network; Dr Heshmael from Heshmael's Clinic for Pets and Cotton Mermaids.

CASE STUDY 1: DR OTHMAN TALIB (DR OT)

In the education industry, postgraduate research doctorates often experience independent information seeking. Learning may become a complex and arduous task with a lot of wasted time, money personal heartache and psychological distress as the feeling of inadequacy, lack of fundamental and higher order research skill. When the postgraduates are applying the social and emotional learning, they are participating in order to graduate on time.

In the last decade, there has been an increase in skills training, support and guidelines of good practice to support postgraduate students through their research. The training was provided by private organizations, research fellows and faculty members all over the world. With 46, 364 followers in his facebook and 2,610,147 visitors in his blog[1]. Dr. Othman Talib's videos, personal logs and research related logs and family related logs champion the cause of learning and research among his followers who are shadowing him. He brings together local and international postgraduate who wishes to learn research skills.

During the last ten years, Dr. Othman build his personal brand as Dr OT[2]. As one of the distinguished mainstream postgraduate writing champions and sought after speaker nationwide, he forms partnership with Malaysian Postgraduate Academy (MPA)[3] With more than 20 writing title listing in the postgraduate process from getting ready for postgraduate writing to viva voce that costs 1500 Ringgit, MPA certificate is endorsed by a local university. MPA also organizes independent research writing workshop titles at the request of participants and prominent research speakers, who are invited to facilitate the workshops at an affordable fee ranging from 150 Ringgit for participants and 50 Ringgit for MPA members.

Participants who are keen in the workshop titles will be invited to the whatsapp group. Dr OT has conducted numerous times in Malay Language medium such as 'Seminar Penulisan Tesis Pantas & Pengurusan Artikel Mendely'; 'Nipis Tapi Kritis'; translating to English 'Writing the First Three Chapter Thesis and Mendely'; 'Thin but Critical Writeup'. MPA manages the potential leads and actual sale leads. With permission of Dr OT, occasionally MPA will put up tips and guide on the research writing; promote the workshop on the whatsapp group. Despite seldom use his personal facebook page and blog page to promote his expertise, Dr OT followers have turned his fans nationwide to sales leads at MPA.

Primarily, Dr OT uses his personal facebook page and blog page to engage with his followers who face problems in postgraduate research writing. He also includes his insights and personal views on wide range of holistic education related discipline from early years of education as he has a young child, international trips to universities and various engagements with stakeholders from the education government officers, fellow researchers to his students. He even shares the success stories of his students and sometimes uploads his class of students, his wife, his children, and his personal well-being workout at the gymnasium on his personal facebook. His daily journey can be followed or shadowed by anyone interested in upskilling research writing, as well as in a typical Malaysian 'family life' of an academia.

CASE STUDY 2: HESHMAEL'S CLINIC FOR PETS

There are a total of 2,512 veterinarians nationwide registered with the Malaysian Veterinary Council. The ratio of vets to one for every 12,000 citizens in 2017 – an improvement from one to 15,000 in 2015. However, Malaysia will need to more than double the existing number of vets to 6,200 in order to achieve the ideal ratio of one doctor per 5,000 population, as seen in developed nations such as the United States (Yuen, 2018). About 150 new doctors are registered with the council every year, but Malaysia still need more veterinarians, especially in the clinical practice such as treating pets.

Incorporated in 2002, Heshmael's Clinic for Pets provides hospitalization, boarding services and treatment to pets. In 2015, the clinic adopted facebook[4] as its mainstream social media tool to create public awareness on the role of veterinarians in the society in Malaysia.

Several types of posts uploaded as newsfeed by Dr Heshmael daily. The sick animals, depending on the level of critical illness, will be treated and hospitalised at the clinic. Pedigreed and non-pedigreed cats, poodles, terrier breeds and such, guinea pigs, hamsters and rabbits. These animals with various types of illness from failing kidneys, enlarged bladder, ulcers, ear mites. It can be benign, malignant or aggressive growth (could be tumors or cancerous in nature) at various parts of the body from the eyes, mouth, tongue, gums, teeth, nose, shoulder, mammary glands, spleen, lungs, testes, stomach, hips, legs and tail will be required to undergo minor or major surgery. The images of X-ray results, castrated testes and microscopic images of parasites, together with a brief diagnosis, will be loaded to its news feed for the ardent fans, who are following the veterinary work up close. The clinic will emotionally connect the public with its decision-making on biopsies and pre-surgery videos of a few minutes; and emotionally excites the public with its post-surgery efforts on the health conditions of the sick animals during the recovery period.

There are also quick tips and tricks on handling grumpy animals during daily 5 – 10 minutes grooming sessions. On the occasions where a professional trainer is required, the clinic cautioned owners not to conduct the grooming sessions on their own despite appearing 'easy to handle' on the videos and encourage the pets to be brought to their veterinarians or regular groomers for the usual nail clips, fur brushing and combing, plus eye checking routines.

During the months where animals are prone to infection, the avid reader Dr Heshmael will alert the public on the zoonotic diseases that can be transmitted from animals to people like fleas, rabies and avian flu, from the local and international bodies, to increase awareness of its followers towards prevention. He also helps to reduce anxieties of the pets by providing consultation on the handling and bonding techniques.

Stray animals are rescued by independent rescuers or individuals, the clinic promotes in adoption initiatives where the animals are vaccinated, dewormed, spay/castrated. The clinic will assist in the rehoming initiatives by regularly posting on its feed.

The clinic has assisted some pet rescuers with their crowd fund-raising by posting their campaigns on its feed. The newsfeeds also include animals that are not found in Malaysia. Dr Heshmael aims to provide educational contents on wild life such as hedgehogs; by using hilarious posts and videos.

CASE STUDY 3: COTTON MERMAID SHARE AND CHAT

Having to endure unbearable rashes using disposable pads for decades, Chong Yeelin a 30 year old mother begin to help women by improving menstruating experiences by innovating and selling her menstrual cups brand and cloth pad brands[5] and at a closed group in the facebook in 2017. In the closed group, women are encouraged to be share their menstruation experiences and to be volunteers for a series of limited edition of test cups sets before actual production takes off.

As women are born with different cervix height, the founder will share her testing experiences of her new products and her newsfeed will be receiving comments, suggestions, with personal questions posted quite regularly. Volunteers will be sought at every product development stage. Following feedback from the volunteers trial testing, the cup innovation will be improved further.

Yeelin also takes the opportunity to update the members each testing phrase from her design, product development, mold development, raw material and colouring procurement, website development and marketing development stages. It also enables Yeelin to highlight the changes of the features on the existing cups and new cups with revised images, made announcements on discontinuing the least popular cups and its colors. Occasionally, Yeelin will give surprises to the group members by offering free give away for members from Malaysia, Singapore and international members. Recently, members were cautioned to select their products with care as all liquids, cream, wax products are no allowed to be shipped internationally, and discourage members to cart these items if members are from outside Malaysia and Singapore

The members asked the founder various questions on the difference of glossy and non-glossy cups, how to use the cups, will it be comfortable, will there be leaking, how to manage leaking. The founder also process the orders through the group page. It has enabled members to discuss about their problems and opportunities using the current range cup products and cloth products, exchange brand new mermaid pads, members' review[6]

In 2018, Ella Sarkadi, a Hungarian shared Mermaid brand within her community and organized group buy for the brand. The response was too overwhelming that Mermaid needed to stop taking orders after exceeding the amount for production.

DISCUSSIONS

Dr Othman Talib (Dr OT), Dr Hasnul Ismail Founder of the Heshmael's Clinic for Pets, Yeelin, Founder of Cotton Mermaid Share and Chat had been genuine advocators for their own niche on a problem or/ and pain that continues to be part of the life. The three advocating champions aims to minimize the pain by engaging with the group members with a few posts, daily.

Table 1. Summary of the selected three case studies in the social media

Solution Provider	Dr Othman Talib (Dr OT)	Heshmael's Clinic for Pets	Cotton Mermaid Share and Chat
Type of Group	Support	Support	Support
The Pain	Lack of Research Writing Skills in the postgraduate thesis	Lack of Hospitalisation, and Treatment Services for terminally ill and very sick (pedigree) pets	Sharing experiences on healthy and sustainable menstruation
The Niche	Postgraduate students & researchers	Pet Owners	Women
No. of Newsfeed	>10 posts	>4 posts	>2 posts
Web Links	http://drotspss.blogspot.com/	https://www.facebook.com/HeshmaelsClinic/	http://cottonmermaid.com/

The advocating champions put up engaging discussion posts that enabled its social learners with the same frustrations emotionally connected with the personal life and personal journey and stayed on with the champions. Social learners undertaking postgraduate studies may feel lonely and helpless whenever experience research roadblocks. Hence, the conversations on the postgraduate topic may become motivation and emotional supports, hence supporting the social support and social exchange theories.

At Dr Othman (Dr OT) facebook page, social learners know they are still 'in relevant and their cause matter' despite the adversities. For animal lovers who are single or married, home pets are the center of their life. The pain that their pets faced are not simply understood and the process of recovery could be long. The pet owners and animal lovers, however, found solace at Heshmael's Clinic for Pets. Pets can return to home safely after getting the correct diagnose, medical treatment and hospitalization for a few days. Women who are looking out for healthy and sustainable menstruation may find their concerns being addressed at Cotton Mermaid Share and Chat. By sharing positive and negative experiences on personal menstruation with others, women can feel more confident and look out for potential challenges when using similar products when engaged in the threads of conversation, hence supporting the social media engagement model.

Within the core pain, members were not only able to feel connected and engaged, they were able to emotionally feel that the champion/host possess high level of empathy and personally curated messages. Concepts that are difficult to handle, the champions will made efforts to develop short videos at anytime of the day. When the engaged host takes personal interests to invest time on the members and customer engagement as a process at the beginning of the painful journey: it will be known as a psychological process leads to the formation of loyalty (Bowden, 2009).

Members are increasingly drawn to products that are being shared and validated on the social media platforms. These platforms help provide "word-of-mouth" justification for a purchase. As an academician Dr Othman (Dr OT) and as a veterinarian Dr Hasnul Ismail, both did not pursue online group buying or individual buying as the main objective of their social media. They are more interested to bring together individuals, to socialize and share their experiences; updating and instilling love towards the academic and animals discipline. In the case of Dr OT, an external training provider handled the group purchase. He has never promoted his workshops on his social media problem; while animal lovers are aware of Heshmael's Clinic and may/may not assume the role of client in its customer database. Cotton

Mermaid Share and Chat uses its group to conduct testing as its first objective and announce the availability date and order processing of its new product as its second objective in the era where customers expect efficiency and fast shopping experiences (Kanwar, 2018).

FUTURE RESEARCH DIRECTIONS

Social media has become an important aspect in marketing mix and revolutionizing the way companies interact with customers. There is still limited research of small business owners using the emergence of social media as a marketing tool. Empirical data using small business owners to create influence by asserting relevant information pertaining could be explored. Further research could include explore whether users are primarily shopping or seeking information as part of their learning process before making decision to purchase the products; the duration of seeking information which could or not eventually lead to a purchase or group purchase.

CONCLUSION

The three case studies allow us to appreciate how the social networking sites are being used to gain information and social support with learning being thrust at the central role at the preliminary phrase of a pre-shopping journey. The quality contents in the social networking media sites have been examined from 2016-2018 to enable the researcher to appreciate the what compels users to staying on and engaging with the social networking sites, rather than leaving the social sites with or without purchase intentions.

Social media or social networking sites (SNS) is now part of the routine of the society. In this new era, creating engaging experiences and personalization will be more important than ever before. As shown in the case studies, product information is considered as a major reason for shopping online (Kaur and Quareshi, 2015) and would be directly relevant to the shopper's task of finding (Walther, 1992). As shown from the case studies, the social networks can be implemented and achieve greater results as a learning tool (Bartlett-Bragg, 2009).

Consumers may be directed online to purchase a product they have or have not experienced before. In the case studies, the motivation to gain information and knowledge from the social media learning is more prevalent. When the consumers are engaged in the contents of the social media, social members will be more likely to make decisions to purchase the products online, over time when strong credibility and trusts are reinforced by the host or the brand champion or the users from the group.

In the social learning process, members in the group learn that the content will differentiate one brand champion to another. Learners are strongly drawn to the quality of social media content, known as the instrument that stimulates interaction with the brand champion (Rapp, Beitelspacher, Grewal, and Hughes, 2013) which appeared to empower members to be closely connected with their service/product brand as they have developed belongingness and experienced incremental 'value' by staying in the group. Staying on or leaving the group will be determined by the shoppable contents, sense of belongingness, perceived benefits-risks, perceived usefulness, acceptance the value of information, acceptance of behaviours of the group and hosts, consideration of opportunity loss of staying out of the group, likelihood of purchase consideration later, while using the social technology.

REFERENCES

Ackroyd, A. (2018). *How to Turn Fans Into Brand Champions.* Retrieved from https://www.socialmediaexaminer.com/brand-champions-social-media/

Agarwal, R., & Prasad, J. (1998). A conceptual and operational definition of personal innovativeness in the domain of Information technology. *Information Systems Research, 9*(2), 204–215. doi:10.1287/isre.9.2.204

Amato-Mccoy, D. M. (2018, May 30). Study: Social commerce sales are on the rise. *Chain Store age: The business of retail.*

Bartlett-Bragg, A. (2009). Reframing practice: Creating social learning networks. *Development and Learning in Organizations: An International Journal, 23*(4), 16–20.

Bowden, J. L.-H. (2009). The Process of Customer Engagement: A Conceptual Framework. *Journal of Marketing Theory and Practice, 17*(1), 63–74. doi:10.2753/MTP1069-6679170105

Brodie, R. J., Ilic, A., Juric, B., & Hollebeek, L. (2013). Consumer engagement in a virtual brand community: An exploratory analysis. *Journal of Business Research, 66*(1), 105–114. doi:10.1016/j.jbusres.2011.07.029

Chau, P. Y. K., & Hu, P. J.-H. (2001). Information Technology Acceptance by Individual Professionals: A Model of Comparison Approach. *Decision Sciences, 32*(4), 699–719. doi:10.1111/j.1540-5915.2001.tb00978.x

Chretien, K. C., & Kind, T. (2013). Social media and clinical care: Ethical, professional, and social implications. *Circulation, 127*(13), 1413–1421. doi:10.1161/CIRCULATIONAHA.112.128017 PMID:23547180

Close, A. G., & Kinney, M. K. (2010). Beyond buying: Motivations behind consumer's online shopping cart use. *Journal of Business Research, 63*(9/10), 986–992. doi:10.1016/j.jbusres.2009.01.022

Crocker, J., & Canevello, A. (2008). Creating and undermining social support in communal relationships: The role of compassionate and self-image goals. *Journal of Personality and Social Psychology, 95*(3), 555–575. doi:10.1037/0022-3514.95.3.555 PMID:18729694

Davis. (1989). Perceived Usefulness, Perceived Ease of Use, and User Acceptance of Information Technology. *MIS Quarterly, 13*(3), 319-339.

De Vries, N. J., & Carlson, J. (2014). Examining the drivers and brand performance implications of customer engagement with brands in the social media environment. *Journal of Brand Management, 21*(6), 495–515. doi:10.1057/bm.2014.18

Edelman, B., Jaffe, S., & Kominers, S. D. (in press). To Groupon or not to Groupon: The profitability of deep discounts. *Marketing Letters.*

Ellison, N. B., Steinfield, C., & Lampe, C. (2007). The benefits of Facebook "friends:" Social capital and college students' use of online social network sites. *Journal of Computer-Mediated Communication, 12*(4), 1143–1168. doi:10.1111/j.1083-6101.2007.00367.x

Fei, B. (2011). *Study of China's online catering market under the booming of online group purchasing*. UNLV Theses/Dissertations/Professional Papers/Capstones, Paper 648. Retrieved 14 March, from: http://digitalcommons.library.unlv.edu/cgi/viewcontent.cgi?article=1649&context=thesesdissertations

Fuller, R., & Shikaloff, N. (2017). Being Engaged at Work Is Not the Same as Being Productive. *Harvard Business Review, 16*. Retrieved from https://hbr.org/2017/02/being-engaged-at-work-is-not-the-same-as-being-productive

Gottlieb, B. H. (1985). Social Networks and Social Support: An Overview of Research, Practice, and Policy Implications. *Health Education Quarterly*, *12*(1), 5–22. doi:10.1177/109019818501200102 PMID:3980240

Griffith-Greene, M. (2014). Fake online reviews: 4 ways companies can deceive you. *CBC News*. Retrieved from http://www.cbc.ca/

House, J. S. (1981). *Work Stress and Social Support*. Reading, MA: Addison- Wesley.

Hu, M., Shi, M., & Wu, J. (2013). Simultaneous vs. sequential group-buying mechanisms. *Management Science*, *59*(12), 2805–2822. doi:10.1287/mnsc.2013.1740

Huang, K.-Y., Nambisan, P., & Uzuner, Ö. (2010). *Informational support or emotional support: Preliminary study of an automated approach to analyze online support community contents*. Paper presented at the International Conference on Information Systems (ICIS 2010), St. Louis, MO.

Islam, J. U., & Rahman, Z. (2016). The transpiring journey of customer engagement research in marketing. *Management Decision*, *54*(8), 2008–2034. doi:10.1108/MD-01-2016-0028

Jiang, L., Yang, Z., & Jun, M. (2013). Measuring consumer perceptions of online shopping convenience. *Journal of Service Management*, *24*(2), 191–214. doi:10.1108/09564231311323962

Jing, X., & Xie, J. (2011). Group buying: A new mechanism for selling through social interactions. *Management Science*, *57*(8), 1354–1372. doi:10.1287/mnsc.1110.1366

Kane, K., Robinson-Combre, J., & Berge, J. L. (2010). Tapping into social networking: Collaborating enhances both knowledge management and e-learning. *Vine*, *40*(1), 62–70. doi:10.1108/03055721011024928

Kanwar, S. (2018). *Here is why retailers need to invest in social commerce, 21 Feb 2018, Shopping habits are changing*. Retrieved from https://www.digitalcommerce360.com/2018/02/21/retailers-need-invest-social-commerce/

Kaur, G., & Quareshi, T. K. (2015). Factors obstructing intentions to trust and purchase products online. *Asia Pacific Journal of Marketing and Logistics*, *27*(5), 758–783. doi:10.1108/APJML-10-2014-0146

Kumar, A., & Kashyap, A. K. (2018). Leveraging utilitarian perspective of online shopping to motivate online shoppers. *International Journal of Retail & Distribution Management*, *46*(3), 247–263. doi:10.1108/IJRDM-08-2017-0161

Liang, T. P., Ho, Y. T., Li, Y. W., & Turban, E. (2012). What Drives Social Commerce: The Role of Social Support and Relationship Quality. *International Journal of Electronic Commerce*, *16*(2), 69–90. doi:10.2753/JEC1086-4415160204

Madjar, N. (2008). Emotional and informational support from different sources and employee creativity. *Journal of Occupational and Organizational Psychology*, *81*(1), 83–100. doi:10.1348/096317907X202464

McCay-Peet, L., & Quan-Haase, A. (2016). A model of social media engagement: User profiles, gratifications, and experiences. In H. O'Brien & M. Lalmas (Eds.), *Why engagement matters: Cross-disciplinary perspectives and innovations on user engagement with digital media*. Heidelberg, Germany: Springer Verlag. doi:10.1007/978-3-319-27446-1_9

O'Brien, H. (2011). Exploring user engagement in online news interactions. *Proc. Am. Soc. Information Science Technology*, *48*(1), 1–10.

Pandolph, S. (2018). *The Social Commerce Report: How Facebook, YouTube, Pinterest, and other popular apps are upending the e-commerce space*. Business Insider. Retrieved from https://www.businessinsider.my/social-commerce-report-2018-1/?r=US&IR=T

Pepitone, J. (2011). Groupon anxiety: The online-coupon firm will have to move fast to retain its impressive lead. *Economist*, *17*, 70–71.

Rapp, A., Beitelspacher, L., Grewal, D., & Hughes, D. (2013). Understanding social media effects across seller, retailer, and consumer interactions. *Journal of the Academy of Marketing Science*, *41*(5), 547–566. doi:10.100711747-013-0326-9

Rose, S., Hair, N., & Clark, M. (2011). Online customer experience: A review of the business to consumer online purchase context. *International Journal of Management Reviews*, *13*(1), 24–39. doi:10.1111/j.1468-2370.2010.00280.x

Schaefer, C., Coyne, J. C., & Lazarus, R. S. (1981). The health-related functions of social support. *Journal of Behavioral Medicine*, *4*(4), 381–406. doi:10.1007/BF00846149 PMID:7338894

Shim, S., Eastlick, M., Lotz, S. L., & Warrington, P. (2001). An online pre-purchase intentions model: The role of intention to search. *Journal of Retailing*, *77*(3), 397–416. doi:10.1016/S0022-4359(01)00051-3

Social Media Marketing. (2019). *The No 1 Social Media Agency in Malaysia Discusses the Trends*. Retrieved from https://www.dmhubtraining.com

Social Media. (n.d.). *Merriam-Webster online*. Retrieved from http://www.merriam-webster.com/dictionary/socialmedia

Spisak, K. (2019). *2019 Social Media Trends & Statistics*. Retrieved from http://Business2community.com

Sun, H., & Zhang, P. (2003). *A new perspective to analyze user technology acceptance*. Working Paper, Syracuse University.

Tee, M. T. (2017). *She Bet RM60k On Women Wanting A Better Way To Deal With "That" Monthly Flow*. Retrieved from https://vulcanpost.com/621319/malaysia-cotton-mermaid-reusable-cloth-pad/

Van der Heijden. (2000). *Using the technology acceptance model to predict website usage: Extensions and Empirical Test*. Serie Research Memoranda.

Van Doorn, J., Lemon, K. N., Mittal, V., Nass, S., Pick, D., Pirner, P., & Verhoef, P. C. (2010). Customer engagement behavior: Theoretical foundations and research directions. *Journal of Service Research*, *13*(3), 253–266. doi:10.1177/1094670510375599

Verhoef, P. C., & Langerak, F. (2001). Possible determinants of consumers' adoption of electronic grocery shopping in the Netherland. *Journal of Retailing and Consumer Services*, *8*(5), 275–285. doi:10.1016/S0969-6989(00)00033-3

Wang, J. (2009). *Study of online group purchasing*. Retrieved from from: http://d.g.wanfangdata.com.cn/Periodical_scxdh200928025.aspx

Whiting, A., & Williams, D. (2013). Why people use social media: A uses and gratifications approach. *Qualitative Market Research*, *16*(4), 362–369. doi:10.1108/QMR-06-2013-0041

Wu, Shi, & Hu. (2015). Threshold Effects in Online Group Buying. *Management Science*, *61*(9), 2025–2040.

Xiong, L., & Hu, C. (2010). Harness the power of viral marketing in hotel industry: A network discount strategy. *Journal of Hospitality and Tourism Technology*, *1*(3), 234–244. doi:10.1108/17579881011078368

Xiong, L., & Hu, C. (2011). *Hotel Viral Marketing via Social Networks: A Strategic Pricing Lesson from Group Buying*. Retrieved from http://scholarworks.umass.edu/cgi/viewcontent.cgi?article=1312&context=gradconf_hospitality

Young, A. L., & Quan-Haase, A. (2013). Privacy Protection Strategies on Facebook. *Information Communication and Society*, *16*(4), 479–500. doi:10.1080/1369118X.2013.777757

Yuen, M. K. (2018). *Animal doctors needed*, 6 May 2018. Retrieved from https://www.thestar.com.my/news/nation/2018/05/06/animal-doctors-needed/

Yusta, A. I., & Newell, S. J. (2011). Consumer beliefs and motivations that influence repeat online purchases. *International Journal of Electronic Marketing and Retailing*, *4*(4), 270–292. doi:10.1504/IJEMR.2011.045611

KEY TERMS AND DEFINITIONS

Engaged Users/Followers: The core group of fans who will be contributing to the conversation post or contents of the post threads.

Model of Social Media Engagement: It comprises of these elements: presentation of self, action and participation, uses and gratifications, positive experiences, usage and activity counts, and social context.

Social Exchange Theory: It postulates that consumers are socially interdependent.

Social Media Engagement: A quality of user experience with web-based technologies that enable users to interact with, create, and share content with individuals and organizations in their social networks.

Social Media Learners: Individuals personalize the way they experience and interact with the web and web tools.

User Engagement: A quality of user experience with technology.

ENDNOTES

1 http://drotspss.blogspot.com/
2 https://www.facebook.com/DrOthmanTalib/
3 https://www/.postgraduateworkshop.com/mpa; https://www.facebook.com/mpws.training
4 https://www.facebook.com/HeshmaelsClinic/
5 http://cottonmermaid.com/why-cloth-pads/
6 http://thegreenvagina.com/mermaidcup-review/

Chapter 11
Development of an E-Service Quality Model (eSQM) to Assess the Quality of E-Service

Hamed Taherdoost
Hamta Group, Malaysia

Ali Hassan
Hamta Academy, Malaysia

ABSTRACT

E-service quality is known as a critical factor for successful implementation and decent performance of any business in electronic environment. Although many researches have been carried out in the field of service quality, there is a clear need for a theoretical model that integrates all aspects of e-service quality. This chapter responded to this need by developing a theoretical model to assess the quality of e-service. In the first phase, e-service quality dimensions were extracted from the literature. Exploratory factor analysis was applied to cluster the factors effectively in developing the conceptual model. Confirmatory approach was conducted with structural equation modeling to test and validate the proposed model. The contribution of this research is the integration of various relevant dimensions affecting e-service quality into a unified e-service quality model (eSQM).

INTRODUCTION

Today, the Internet is using with a wide range of industries to deliver or receive the required services. In fact, the term "service" has a variety of meaning depending on the angel that is viewed (Kardaras & Karakostas, 2006). Yang, Peterson, and Cai (2003) defined services as "a benefit providing object of transaction that is a more or less abstract activity or process of activities essentially produced, marketed and consumed in a simultaneous interaction". Besides, Hoffman and Bateson (1997) defined service as efforts, deeds or performance and also Lovelock (2001) defined it as "an act or performance offered by one party to another". The main distinction between electronic services and traditional services are the channels they use to deliver their services and they interact with their users (Taherdoost, Sahibuddin,

DOI: 10.4018/978-1-5225-9697-4.ch011

& Jalaliyoon, 2013). According to Taherdoost et al. (2012), e-service is defined as "the provision of interactional, content centered and electronic-based service over electronic networks".

Service is an endeavor of an enterprise, and it is achieved by satisfying the needs of customers by increasing the quality of the provided service (Chang, Pang, Tarn, Liu, & Yen, 2015). Consumers commonly use service quality as the comprehensive superiority of an enterprise. Raising the quality of services provided electronically will help organizations to achieve their goal which is making their customers satisfied (Chang et al., 2015). In a recent competitive business environment, the delivery of high-quality service to customers is very crucial for business survival, sustainability, growth and profitability (Suki, 2014). Thus, managers, developers and researchers need to understand what the quality determinants are to address them in order to increase user satisfaction.

Furthermore, lack of physical and direct human interaction in an electronic environment raised up the concern of organizations about the quality of their services (Grigoroudis, Litos, Moustakis, Politis, & Tsironis, 2008; Manasra, Zaid, & TaherQutaishat, 2013). Although measuring the quality of e-services is more complex than good/product (Manasra et al., 2013), there is no integrated method to evaluate the e-service quality (Loiacono, Watson, & Goodhue, 2007; Manasra et al., 2013). The notion of e-service has increasingly recognized as one of the key determinants in successful e-service by both researchers and practitioners. In brief, there is no particular technique to evaluate the interactional, content centered and electronic-based services.

In this research, the theoretical foundation of e-service quality is reviewed and we examined through in-depth exploratory and confirmatory analysis. In the first phase, the e-service quality dimensions are extracted from the literature and then survey is distributed among e-service users to categorize the quality dimensions using exploratory factor analysis. After introducing the e-service quality factors, an instrument is developed by extracting the related measurement items from previous studies. Afterward, validity (discriminate and convergent) and reliability tests are examined to validate the measurement tool. Finally, structural equation modeling is applied to validate the proposed model and instrument. The contribution of this chapter relates to the fact that the proposed theoretical framework integrates in a holistic way various relevant factors affecting e-service quality into a single template.

E-SERVICE QUALITY

Service quality is a key determinant in differentiating service offered and building competitive advantage (Bauer, Hammerschmidt, & Falk, 2005; Gronroos, Heinonen, Isoniemi, & Lindholm, 2000; Santos, 2003), the importance of measuring and monitoring e-service quality has been recognized by managers and academics (Johnson & Whang, 2002). Service quality determines the willingness of customers to purchase a service again in the future or to accept additional add-on services (Chang et al., 2015).

Service quality can potentially increase attractiveness, hit rate, customer retention, stickiness, and positive word-of-mouth. It can maximize the online competitive advantages of e-service. The concern about e-service quality becomes greater important because of the absence of direct human interaction in offered services (Grigoroudis et al., 2008).

As stated by Einasto (2014), quality development requires a well-defined quality concept, for which it is necessary to understand how users estimate the quality. To do so and thereby deliver superior service quality, decision makers of companies providing e-services need to first understand what is the perception of customers' towards e-service quality. This involves defining what e-service quality is, identifying its underlying dimensions, and determining how it can be conceptualized and measured.

There are many different definitions for terms related to service quality. Asubonteng, McCleary, and Swan (1996) defined service quality as customers' expectations for service performed prior to the service encounter and their perceptions of the service received. Whilst, Parasuraman, Zeithaml, and Berry (1988) defined it as the consumer's judgment about an entity's overall excellence or superiority. Likewise, service quality is defined as the extent to which a Website facilitates efficient and effective shopping, purchasing and delivery of products and services (Zeithaml, Parasuraman, & Malhotra, 2002). In this chapter, e-service quality is defined as a global judgment, or attitude, relating to the superiority of the service that a consumer obtained or is obtaining from the current service provider.

BACKGROUND

Service quality is vital for firms because it forms the behavioral intention of customers (Gilmore, 1997), for example in the high-level service quality lead to customer loyalty and repeat patronage loyalty (Van Riel, Semeijn, & Janssen, 2003; Zeithaml, Berry, & Parasuraman, 1996). On the other point of view, in an electronic environment, perceived a high-level of service quality is crucial for enterprises and service providers since in such an environment customers are able to easily compare the service enterprises and the switching cost is low (Van Riel, Liljander, & Jurriëns, 2001). Increased e-service quality on the Web can make online companies more effective and appealing, and can help them to achieve higher levels of customer satisfaction and retention (Gronroos et al., 2000).

The success and prevalence of the Internet have made web-based systems become an important medium in connecting service/product providers with their customers. It also created a new arena for firms in various industries (Chang et al., 2015). Service is an endeavor of an enterprise, and it is achieved by satisfying the needs of customers, and improved by increasing the quality of the service provided (Chang et al., 2015). Consumers commonly use service quality as the comprehensive superiority of an enterprise. It is an attitude, not a satisfaction measure, and a cognitive difference comparison between the consumers' acceptance of service level and their service expectation. Also, service quality determines the willingness of customers to purchase a service again in the future or to accept additional add-on services (Chang et al., 2015). Organizations are increasingly having a growing concern with respect to the quality of their websites. This concern becomes of greater importance because of the absence of the human interaction offered (Grigoroudis et al., 2008). The website quality is a very important part of companies' image that can influence shopping behavior in a similar way to those aspects of traditional establishments (Manasra et al., 2013).

Service quality is an important differentiator in a competitive business environment, and a driver of service-based businesses (Thaichon, Lobo, Prentice, & Quach, 2014). In a highly competitive environment, the delivery of high-quality service to the client is vital for the businesses' survival, competitiveness, profitability and sustained growth (Suki, 2014).

The relevant literature on e-service quality indicates that many instruments have been developed to measure the quality of service and e-service. Such as SERVQUAL (Parasuraman et al., 1988), SERVPER (Cronin & Taylor, 1992), SITEQUAL (Yoo & Donthu, 2001), e-SERVQUAL (V.A. Zeithaml et al., 2002), WebQual (Loiacono, Watson, & Hoodhue, 2002), E-Qual (Barnes & Vidgen, 2007), eTailQ (Wolfinbarger & Gilly, 2003), E-S-Qual (Parasuraman, Zeithaml, & Malhotra, 2005), eTransQual

(Bauer, Falk, & Hammerschmidt 2006), and PeSQ (Cristobal, Flavian, & Guinalıu, 2007). The studies reviewed have some limitations. First, the samples used in most of the studies consist of student populations, which may limit the general is the ability of the scales and reduce their applicability to the broader population of online users (Ladhari, 2010). Students are not sufficiently experienced in online shopping, they are neither familiar with particular businesses behind particular Web sites and nor with products offered on these Web sites (Hudek & Vrcek, 2006). Second, several studies use mostly US respondents. The reasons for internet use and the behavior of these participants may differ from those in other countries. Therefore, future studies should use more diversified samples (Ladhari, 2010). The literature on traditional service quality shows that dimensions of service quality differ from one country to another. Third, many respondents in these studies use the internet as an information source and not for commercial transactions (Ladhari, 2010). Most systems focus solely on the customer's interaction

Figure 1. E-service Quality Instruments and Their Criticisms

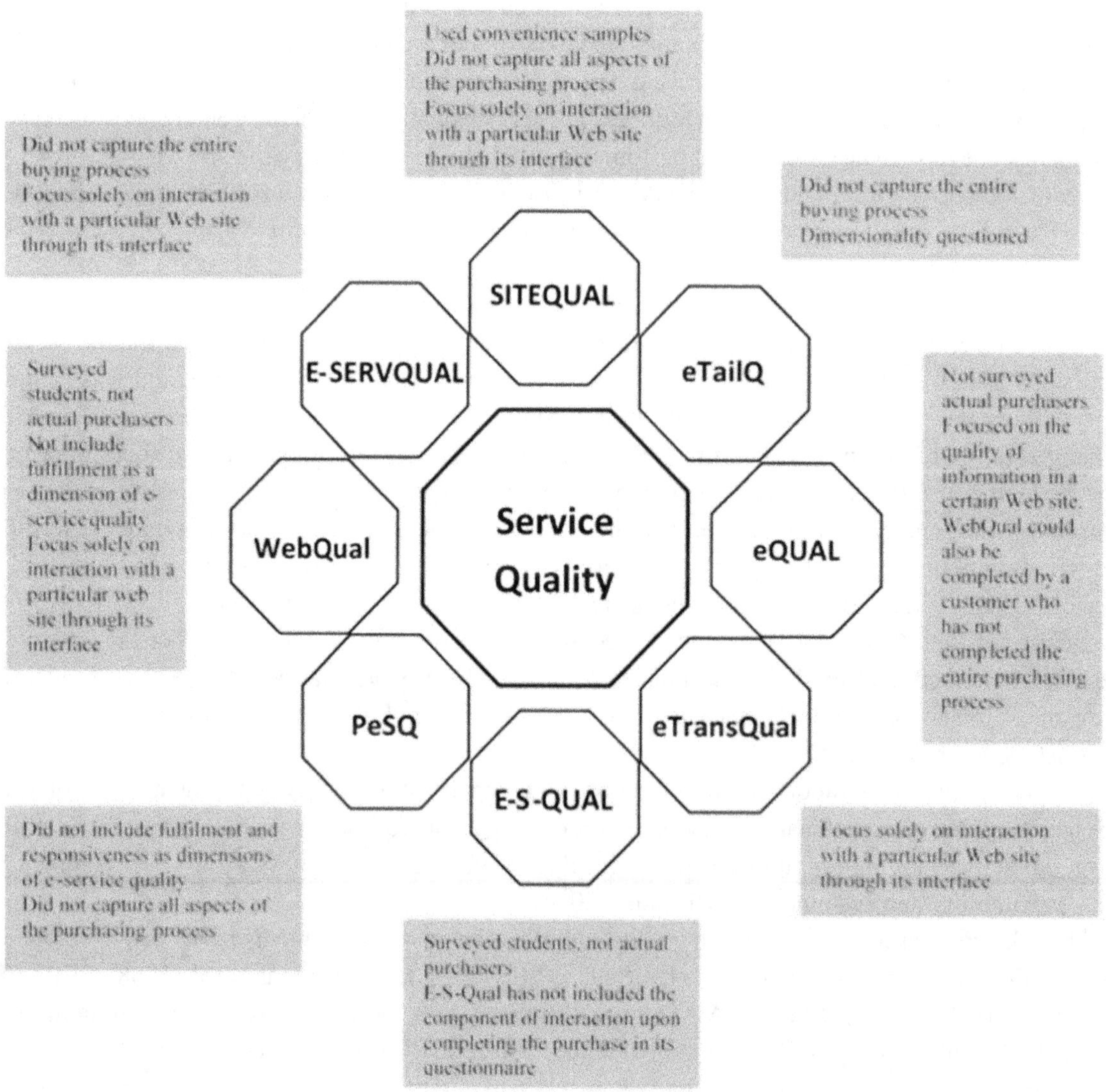

with the Web site, whilst ignoring the importance of interaction with the Web site upon completing the purchase (Hudek & Vrcek, 2006). Thus, they only focused on the transactional part or interface part of service quality, therefore, these scales might not be relevant to assess the complete service offering and capture electronic services in a broader sense (Gummerus, Liljander, Pura, & Riel, 2004). Respondents who have not engaged in commercial transactions on the internet may have concerns about security compared to experienced internet buyers. Finally, several studies used limited sample sizes, for instance, Cai and Jun (2003) use a sample of only 171 respondents, Ibrahim, Joseph, and Ibeh (2006) use a sample of 131 customers, Aladwani and Palvia (2002) use a sample of 101 students in their first study and 127 students in their second study. These sample sizes are relatively small for developing new scales and larger and diversified samples are required for survey instrument development (Ladhari, 2010).

The absence of a valid and reliable instrument to measure e-service quality in online environment has however, bedeviled the endeavors of both scholars and practitioners. Ladhari (2010) articulated that future research should develop a more specific theoretical framework that defines the e-service quality construct and its dimensions more consistently and identifies pertinent scale-items. Therefore, there is a need to address the gaps by developing a new instrument to be deployed in information systems research (Stamenkov & Dika, 2016). Figure 1 summarizes the previously developed instruments and criticisms.

DEVELOPMENT PROCESS

This research uses a questionnaire method to collect the required data. Collected data are either numerical (a measurement) or represent numerically (ranked in order of preference for example). In order to develop the eSQM (e-Service Quality Model) and the survey instrument, four surveys are conducted.

Step 1 – Extraction of E-service Quality Dimensions: Since this study is going to develop a new model and survey instrument so the dimensions affecting e-service quality are extracted from the literature.

Step 2 – Factor Identification: Exploratory Survey is conducted to categorize the extracted dimensions and reduce the number of factors.

Step 3 – Survey Development: Related items for each dimension and factor are extracted from the literature and new questions are designed for the final survey.

Step 4 – Content Validity Survey: Since a new instrument is developed and also existing scales have to be applied to examine new object so Content Validity Survey is conducted to confirm the content validity to propose the Final Survey.

Step 5 – Pilot Survey: In order to assist in improving the questionnaire in terms of detecting errors and limitation of the questionnaire, a pilot survey is conducted.

Step 6 – Data Collection: Final Survey is conducted to collect the data.

Step 7 – Validity and Reliability: After data collection, discriminate and convergent validity are examined utilizing principal component analysis (PCA) with varimax rotation method. Furthermore, the Cronbach Alpha is applied to confirm the internal consistency of measures.

Step 8 – Model Test: To evaluate the plausibility of a hypothesized model, Structural Equation Modeling is applied.

QUALITY DIMENSIONS

Unlike goods quality, which can be measured objectively by such indicators as durability and number of defects (Garvin, 1983), service quality is an abstract and elusive construct because of three features unique to services: intangibility, heterogeneity, and inseparability of production and consumption (Parasuraman & Berry, 1985). According to previous researches all service quality dimensions have not the same influence on consumers' quality perceptions, therefore, it is significant to identify which dimensions are more important than others to enhance the level of overall service quality as perceived by customers (Minjoon Jun, Yang, & Kim, 2004).

In this section, dimensions of service quality which identified by researchers are presented in Table 1. According to the literature review, thirty-five dimensions have been extracted from previous studies in the field of information system. Namely; Accessibility, Aesthetic Design, Appearance of Website, Assurance, Credibility, Currency, Communication, Content Quality, Customer Service, Customer Support, Customization, Delivery, Empathy, Ease of Use, Efficiency, Enjoyment, Flexibility, Fulfillment, Functionality, Information Accuracy, Information Quality, Navigation, Processing Speed, Recovery, Relevancy, Responsiveness, Reliability, Security, Site Attraction, Site Presentation, Structure and Layout, Tangibility, Timeliness, User Control, and Web Usability.

Table 1. Dimensions of E-service quality

Dimension	Source
Accessibility	(Cox & Dale, 2001; Finn, 2011; Janda, Trocchia, & Gwinner, 2002; M. Jun & Cai, 2001; Kaynama & Black, 2000)
Aesthetic Design	(Cheung & Lee, 2005; Collier & Bienstock, 2006; Cristobal et al., 2007; Dabholkar, 1996; Fassnacht & Koese, 2006; Finn, 2011; Fogg et al., 2003)
Appearance of Website	(Cox & Dale, 2001; Dabholkar, 1996; Fassnacht & Koese, 2006; Finn, 2011; Fogg et al., 2003)
Assurance	(Cristobal et al., 2007; Einasto, 2014; Lin, Huarng, Y.-M. Chen, & Lin, 2004; Finn, 2011; Kardaras & Karakostas, 2006; Li, Tan, & Xie, 2002)
Credibility	(Cox & Dale, 2001; Li et al., 2002; Madu & Madu, 2002; Wang & Strong, 1996)
Currency	(Alexander & Tate, 1999; Hussain, Nasser, & Hussain, 2014; Wixom & Todd, 2005)
Communication	(Cox & Dale, 2001; Hussain et al., 2014; Kardaras & Karakostas, 2006; Loiacono et al., 2002; Sohn & Tadisina, 2008; Yang et al., 2003)
Content Quality	(Fassnacht & Koese, 2006; Fogg et al., 2003; Janda et al., 2002; Kaynama & Black, 2000; Palmer, 2002; Santos, 2003; Sohn & Tadisina, 2008)
Customer Service	(Cheung & Lee, 2005; Cristobal et al., 2007; Fogg et al., 2003; Ho & Lee, 2007; Van Riel et al., 2001; Wolfinbarger & Gilly, 2003)
Customer Support	(DeLone & McLean, 2003; Finn, 2011; J Santos, 2003; Van Riel et al., 2001)
Customization / Personalization	(Finn, 2011; Joseph, McClure, & Joseph, 1999; Kardaras & Karakostas, 2006; Kaynama & Black, 2000; Lee & Lin, 2005; Loonam & O'Loughlin, 2008; Tan, Xie, & Li, 2003; Yang & Jun, 2002)
Delivery	(Dabholkar, 1996; Surjadaja, Ghosh, & Antony, 2003; Wolfinbarger & Gilly, 2003)
Empathy	(Gefen, 2002; Y. Li et al., 2002; Madu & Madu, 2002; A Parasuraman & Berry, 1985; Stiglingh, 2014; Yang & Jun, 2002)
Ease of Use	(Bressolles, Durrieu, & Senecal, 2014; Collier & Bienstock, 2006; Dabholkar, 1996; Einasto, 2014; Fassnacht & Koese, 2006; Finn, 2011; Sheng & Liu, 2010; Stiglingh, 2014; Udo, Bagchi, & Kirs, 2010; Z Yang et al., 2003)

continued on following page

Table 1. Continued

Dimension	Source
Efficiency	(Joseph et al., 1999; Kim, Kim, & Lennon, 2006; Parasuraman et al., 2005; Santos, 2003; Stiglingh, 2014; Zeist & Hendriks, 1996)
Enjoyment	(H. H. Bauer et al., 2006; Dabholkar, 1996)
Flexibility	(Loonam & O'Loughlin, 2008; Tan et al., 2003; Wixom & Todd, 2005; Zeithaml, Parasuraman, & Malhotra, 2000)
Fulfillment	(Cheung & Lee, 2005; Fogg et al., 2003; Kim et al., 2006; Sheng & Liu, 2010; Stiglingh, 2014; Wolfinbarger & Gilly, 2003; Zeithaml et al., 2000)
Functionality	(Bauer et al., 2006; Collier & Bienstock, 2006; Fassnacht & Koese, 2006; Fogg et al., 2003; Ho & Lee, 2007; Sohn & Tadisina, 2008; Zeist & Hendriks, 1996)
Information Accuracy	(Alexander & Tate, 1999; Collier & Bienstock, 2006; Fogg et al., 2003; Janda et al., 2002; Joseph et al., 1999; Jun & Cai, 2001; Wixom & Todd, 2005; Zeithaml et al., 2000)
Information Quality	(Bressolles et al., 2014; Ho & Lee, 2007; Jun & Cai, 2001; Ladhari, 2010; Li et al., 2002; Loonam & O'Loughlin, 2008; Udo et al., 2010; Zeithaml et al., 2000)
Navigation	(Alexander & Tate, 1999; Dabholkar, 1996; Finn, 2011; Kaynama & Black, 2000; Palmer, 2002; Tan et al., 2003; Van Riel, Semeijn, & Pauwels, 2004)
Processing Speed	(DeLone & McLean, 2003; Einasto, 2014; Palmer, 2002; Sohn & Tadisina, 2008; Sweeney & Lapp, 2004; Wolfinbarger & Gilly, 2003; Yoo & Donthu, 2001)
Recovery	(Collier & Bienstock, 2006; Kim et al., 2006; Loonam & O'Loughlin, 2008)
Relevancy	(Wang & Strong, 1996; Zeithaml et al., 2000)
Responsiveness	(Bauer et al., 2006; Lin et al., 2004; Finn, 2011; Gefen, 2002; Hussain et al., 2014; Jun & Cai, 2001; Minjoon Jun et al., 2004; Lee & Lin, 2005; Palmer, 2002)
Reliability	(Bauer et al., 2006; Bressolles et al., 2014; Dabholkar, 1996; Einasto, 2014; Lin et al., 2004; Fassnacht & Koese, 2006; Finn, 2011; Ladhari, 2010; Santos, 2003; Stiglingh, 2014)
Security	(Bressolles et al., 2014; DeLone & McLean, 2003; Einasto, 2014; Finn, 2011; Ho & Lee, 2007; Hussain et al., 2014; Ladhari, 2010; Loonam & O'Loughlin, 2008; Stiglingh, 2014; Taherdoost, 2017b)
Site Attraction	(Minjoon Jun et al., 2004; Kardaras & Karakostas, 2006; Van Riel et al., 2001; Yang, Peterson, & Huang, 2001)
Site Presentation	(Fogg et al., 2003; Kaynama & Black, 2000; Udo et al., 2010; Van Riel et al., 2001)
Structure & Layout	(Fassnacht & Koese, 2006; Santos, 2003; Udo et al., 2010)
Tangibility	(Lin et al., 2004; Gefen, 2002; Hussain et al., 2014; Parasuraman & Berry, 1985; Parasuraman et al., 2005)
Timeliness	(Collier & Bienstock, 2006; Wang & Strong, 1996; Wixom & Todd, 2005; Zeithaml et al., 2000)
User Control on Process	(Bauer et al., 2006; Cheung & Lee, 2005; Dabholkar, 1996; Loiacono et al., 2002; Sweeney & Lapp, 2004)
Web Usability	(Loiacono et al., 2002; Loonam & O'Loughlin, 2008; Zhilin Yang, Cai, Zhou, & Zhou, 2005; Zeist & Hendriks, 1996)

EXPLORATORY FACTOR ANALYSIS TO IDENTIFY THE QUALITY FACTORS

The main aim of this research is to develop a theoretical model and survey instrument to assess the e-service quality. In this step, quality dimensions are classified, however, terminologies are varying. Therefore, to achieve this goal, Exploratory Factor Analysis is used as a theory generating procedure (Stevens, 2001). The reason for applying exploratory analysis to this study is to determine factors that are affecting the quality of e-service. Thus, it is used to identify a number of key factors (principal factors) that explains the majority of the variance (Kline, 1997) among defined quality dimensions.

A structured questionnaire was used as a data collection instrument, because the questionnaire is very flexible to use (Moore, 2006; Taherdoost, 2016a). The subject of the chapter was a group of e-service users in the e-banking and e-commerce sectors who conduct transactions. As Taherdoost (2017) stated that e-commerce and e-banking are two applications of e-service. Hair, Anderson, Tatham, and Black (1995a) suggested that the sample size for exploratory analysis should be 100 or greater. For the current study, the researcher obtained 193 questionnaires after data filtering to eliminate invalid responses. Almost the same sample size has been chosen by other researchers, (Brensinger & Lambert, 1990; Churchill, 1979; Lai & Lai, 2013; Lean, Zailani, Ramayah, & Fernando, 2009; Lederer, Maupin, Sena, & Zhuang, 2000; A. Parasuraman et al., 1988; Saxe & Weitx, 1982; Semeijn, Riel, Birgelen, & Streukens, 2005; Vijayasarathy, 2004).

The Cronbach's Alphas range is spanned from 0.924 to 0.929, thereby, the given constructs are deemed to have adequate reliability (Hair, Anderson, Tatham, & Black, 1998; Robinson, 2009). Furthermore, the KMO (Kaiser-Meyer-Olkin) index which is a measure of sampling adequacy (Taherdoost, 2017b) is measured. The statistical analysis indicates that the KMO = 0.883 which confirms that the sampling adequacy as the suggested score is 0.70 (Leech, Barrett, & Morgan, 2005).

In the next step, it should be decided how many factors must be retained for rotation. In order to make this decision, the Kaiser criterion (Kraiser, 1958) was applied and factors with Eigenvalues greater than 1.0 are selected. the Kaiser criterion is the most used approach since it is easy to use (Fabrigar, Wegener, MacCallum, & Strahan, 1999; Gorsuch, 1983). According to the results, eight constructs should be retained. Table 2 summarizes the initial Eigenvalues and proportions of variance explained by the first eight factors.

Varimax rotation which was developed by Thompson (2004) and is the most common form of rotational methods for exploratory factor analysis is utilized in this study. The items with loading factor less than 0.4 are the minimum value suggested for Information System studies (Straub, Boudreau, & Gefen, 2004) and cross-loading greater than 0.4 are eliminated (Dwivedi, Choudrie, & Brinkman, 2006; Straub et al., 2004; Taherdoost, 2016b). Therefore, only one item, i.e. Empathy was deleted. In the next step, the interpretation process is carried out for allocating a name for each of eight remained constructs. The labeling of constructs is a theoretical, subjective and inductive process (Pett, Lackey, & Sullivan, 2003). It is significant that labels of constructs reflect the theoretical and conceptual intent. Table 3 presents the quality factor classifications and their loadings. Figure 2 shows the proposed model of eSQM (e-Service Quality Model).

Table 2. Total Variance Explained

	Initial Eigenvalues			Extraction Sums of Squared Loadings			Rotation Sums of Squared Loadings		
Component	**Total**	**% of Var**	**Cum %**	**Total**	**% of Var**	**Cum %**	**Total**	**% of Var**	**Cum %**
1	10.420	29.770	29.770	10.420	29.770	29.770	5.796	16.560	16.560
2	3.439	9.827	39.597	3.439	9.827	39.597	3.750	10.715	27.275
3	2.180	6.230	45.827	2.180	6.230	45.827	2.656	7.589	34.864
4	1.721	4.917	50.744	1.721	4.917	50.744	2.493	7.121	41.985
5	1.377	3.935	54.679	1.377	3.935	54.679	2.288	6.538	48.523
6	1.302	3.720	58.399	1.302	3.720	58.399	1.971	5.630	54.153
7	1.218	3.479	61.878	1.218	3.479	61.878	1.937	5.536	59.689
8	1.032	2.948	64.826	1.032	2.948	64.826	1.798	5.137	64.826

Table 3. E-Service Quality Dimensions Classifications and Their Loadings

NO	Factor	Dimension	Loading							
1	Performance	*Accessibility*	.417							
		Delivery	.560							
		Ease of Use	.703							
		Flexibility	.754							
		Fulfillment	.772							
		Functionality	.617							
		Processing Speed	.832							
		Recovery	.759							
		Timeliness	.742							
2	Dependability	*Assurance*		.672						
		Credibility		.759						
		Reliability		.596						
		Security		.472						
3	Design	*Aesthetic Design*			.790					
		Appearance of Website			.718					
		Customization			.421					
		Navigation			.702					
		Site Presentation			.657					
		Site Attraction			.581					
		Structure and Layout			.497					
4	Content	*Content Quality*				.706				
		Currency				.452				
		Enjoyment				.751				
		Information Quality				.400				
		Information Accuracy				.455				
		Relevancy				.543				
5	Usability	*Efficiency*					.711			
		Web Usability					.691			
6	Interaction	*Communication*						.698		
		Responsiveness						.726		
7	Support	*Customer Service*							.683	
		Customer Support							.682	
8	Expectation	*Tangibility*								.715
		User Control on Process								.663

SURVEY DEVELOPMENT

In order to develop the survey, in-depth literature review has been done to extract the existing items for each of the e-service quality constructs. Although some of the items were specifically composed for the purpose of this research since measures suitable for this study were not available. Table 4 presents the number of survey items with their references.

CONTENT VALIDITY OF THE FINAL SURVEY

Engaging review of the literature review helps to identify a sample of items for each construct. A total of 312 items for eight constructs related to the e-service quality were identified. Then, a content validity questionnaire which is highly recommended to apply while the new instrument is developed (Taherdoost,

Figure 2. E-Service Quality Model (eSQM)

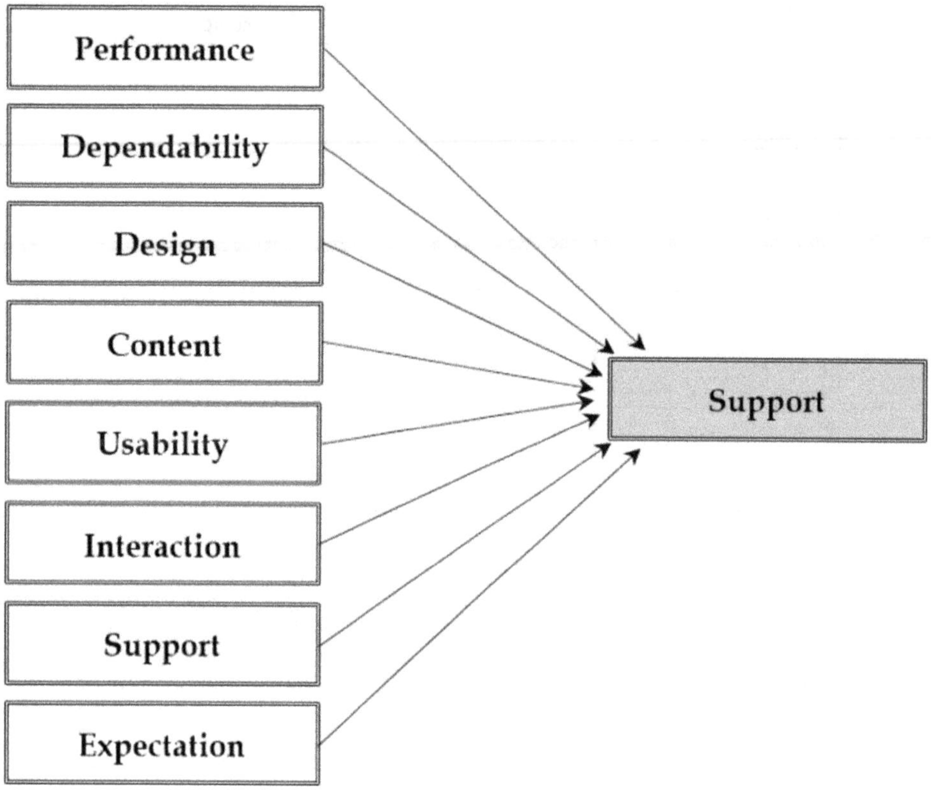

2016b) in information system research, was generated that comprised definitions of the constructs and associated items on a three-point scale (not necessary, useful but not essential and essential). A total of twelve experts (Dwivedi et al., 2006; Taherdoost, 2016b, 2018) were identified on the basis of their experience in the field of e-services quality. Then, a survey was sent to them and responses have been collected. In the next step, the content validity ratio (CVR) for each of the items was calculated and estimated. Items that were not significant at the 0.05 level were eliminated (Lawshe 1975). The finding illustrates that among the 332 items, 36 items remained for the final questionnaire. Table 5 shows the items included in the survey with their abbreviations used for further analysis. The experts also suggested using 7-point scale because its values are widely spread in comparison to 5 points scale and respondents would have more choices to select.

PILOT STUDY

A pilot study was conducted before the distribution of the final questionnaire to determine the response rate and any disharmony within the questions such as questionnaire format and questions' understandability. The survey was sent to thirty (Luo, Remus, & Chea, 2006) e-service users in Malaysia by email. The majority of the respondents reported that the questionnaire was easily understandable and required 15-20 minutes for completion.

Table 4. Number of initial items for final survey with their related sources

Construct	Research	Number of Items
Usability	(Anandarajan, Igbaria, & Anakwe, 2000; Carter & Bélanger, 2005; Davis, 1989; Davis, Bagozzi, & Warshaw, 1989; Gwebu & Wang, 2011; Jiang, Klein, & Crampton, 2000a; Loonam & O'Loughlin, 2008; M. M. Luo, Chea, & Chen, 2011; Mahinda & Whitworth, 2006; Mao & Palvia, 2006; Ok & Shon, 2006; Parasuraman, Berry, & Zeithaml, 1991a; Pavlou, 2003; Taherdoost (2018b); Riel, Semeijn, & Pauwels, 2003; Sheikhshoaei & Oloumi, 2011; Tan et al., 2003; Taylor & Todd, 1995a; Venkatesh, Morris, Davis, & Davis, 2003; Vijayasarathy, 2004; Wixom & Todd, 2005; Wu, Tao, & Yang, 2008; Yu, Ha, Choi, & Rho, 2005)	47
Design	(X. Li, Hess, & Valacich, 2006; Loonam & O'Loughlin, 2008; Mahinda & Whitworth, 2006; Mittal & Tsiros, 2007; Riel et al., 2003; Semeijn et al., 2005; Tan et al., 2003; Tsai, Huang, Jaw, & Chen, 2006; Wixom & Todd, 2005)	45
Dependability	(Anthopoulos, Siozos, & Tsoukalas, 2007; Bélanger & Carter, 2008; Carter & Bélanger, 2005; Collier & Bienstock, 2006; Janda et al., 2002; Jiang et al., 2000a; X. Li et al., 2006; Lu, Yu, Liu, & Yao, 2003; Mahinda & Whitworth, 2006; McKnight, Choudhury, & Kacmar, 2002b; Parasuraman et al., 1991a; Parasuraman et al., 1988; Riel et al., 2003; Ruyter, Wetzels, & Kleijnen, 2001; Salisbury, Pearson, Pearson, & Miller, 2001; Semeijn et al., 2005; Shachaf & Oltmann, 2007; Shareef, Kumar, Kumar, & Dwivedi, 2009; Shin, 2010; Taherdoost, 2017b, 2018; Tan et al., 2003; Torkzadeh & Dhillon, 2002; Vijayasarathy, 2004; Wolfinbarger & Gilly, 2003; Yenisey, Ozok, & Salvendy, 2005; Yoo & Donthu, 2001; Zhang & Prybutok, 2005)	57
Performance	(Al-Gahtani & King, 1999; Davis, 1989; Davis et al., 1989; Dickerson & Gentry, 1983; Dwivedi et al., 2006; Janda et al., 2002; Ko, 1990; Leong, 1997; X. Li et al., 2006; Loonam & O'Loughlin, 2008; Lu, 2001; Lu et al., 2003; Luo et al., 2011; Mahinda & Whitworth, 2006; Mosbeh & Soliman, 2008; Pavlou, 2003; Pedersen, 2005; Premkumar & Bhattacherjee, 2008; Riel et al., 2003; Ruyter et al., 2001; Semeijn et al., 2005; Stephanie, Abdul Nasir, & Nur Fadziana, 2008; Tan et al., 2003; Taylor & Todd, 1995a; Torkzadeh & Dhillon, 2002; Venkatesh et al., 2003; Wixom & Todd, 2005)	73
Content	(Luo et al., 2011; Riel et al., 2003; Smith, 2001; Wixom & Todd, 2005)	31
Interaction	(Carter & Bélanger, 2005; Janda et al., 2002; Jiang et al., 2000a; Li et al., 2006; Loonam & O'Loughlin, 2008; Lu et al., 2003; Parasuraman et al., 1991a; Riel et al., 2003; Semeijn et al., 2005; Smith, 2001; Tan et al., 2003; Torkzadeh & Dhillon, 2002; Tsai et al., 2006; Zhang & Prybutok, 2005)	34
Support	(Al-Gahtani & King, 1999; Li et al., 2006; Mosbeh & Soliman, 2008; Venkatesh et al., 2003)	9
Expectation	(Jiang et al., 2000a; M. M. Luo et al., 2011; Parasuraman et al., 1991a; Parasuraman et al., 1988; Premkumar & Bhattacherjee, 2008; Riel et al., 2003; Seneler, Basoglu, & Daim, 2010; Shachaf & Oltmann, 2007; Venkatesh et al., 2003; V.A. Zeithaml et al., 2002)	16

DATA COLLECTION OF FINAL SURVEY

An online survey was conducted to collect the data from e-service users in Malaysia in the e-banking and e-commerce sectors. The collected data was filtered and improper responses were removed. The remaining data was 403 valid responses which were taken as the sample of the study followed the sample size guideline of (Krejcie & Morgan, 1970).

RELIABILITY

In the case, Likert Scales were utilized for this study; Cronbach Alphas are considered the most appropriate measures of reliability (Robinson, 2009; Taherdoost, 2016b). As it is shown in Table 6, the Cronbach's Alphas range from 0.930 to 0.935, thus, the constructs are deemed to have adequate reliability

Table 5. Survey Items after Content Validity

Factor	Abb	Items
Content	CON1	The information provided by e-service is accurate.
	CON2	In general, e-service provides me with high-quality information.
	CON3	E-service provides me what I want or require.
	CON4	E-service provides me with the most recent information.
	CON5	I use e-service because it is enjoyable.
	CON6	E-service provides the information content which meets my needs.
Design	DSN1	I am satisfied with design of e-service.
	DSN2	Websites are organized logically and by anticipated user need.
	DSN3	I believe that e-service would be employed in my best interest.
	DSN4	E-service attractively displays Information.
Performance	PER1	E-service delivers product/ service in a way that I like.
	PER2	It is fast to use e-service.
	PER3	I successfully use e-service to perform my job.
	PER4	It is not too costly to use e-services.
	PER5	E-service provides service in a timely fashion.
	PER6	E-service makes information very accessible.
	PER7	E-service can be adapted to meet a variety of needs.
Usability	USB1	I accomplish my tasks easier and quicker with e-service.
	USB2	Using e-service improves the quality of the work I do.
	USB3	Using e-service is helpful and influential.
	USB4	E-service makes information very accessible.
Expectation	EXP1	E-service will provide me flexibility to work on my own time.
	EXP2	E-service will give the ability to work at my own place.
	EXP3	Using e-service is very compatible with the way I like to work.
	EXP4	Excellent e-service providers will have modern-looking equipment.
Dependability	DEP1	I feel assured that legal and technological structures adequately protect me from problems on the e-service.
	DEP2	E-service has the ability to perform the promised service dependably and accurately.
	DEP3	In general, e-services are robust and safe.
Interaction	INT1	E-service providers provide prompt responses to my questions.
	INT2	Using e-service would make it easier to interact.
Support	SUP1	A specific person (or group) is available for assistance with system difficulties.
	SUP2	There is extensive support to help with problems related to e-service.

Table 6. Cronbach's Alpha Statistics for Final Survey

	Scale Mean if Item Deleted	Corrected Item-Total Correlation	Cronbach's Alpha if Item Deleted
INT1	128.9231	0.429	0.933
INT2	128.9355	0.497	0.932
PER1	128.9653	0.574	0.931
PER2	128.8536	0.693	0.930
PER3	128.8139	0.605	0.931
PER4	128.8660	0.703	0.930
PER5	128.8387	0.681	0.930
PER6	128.7692	0.680	0.930
PER7	128.7146	0.605	0.931
DEP1	129.0546	0.494	0.932
DEP2	129.1340	0.447	0.932
DEP3	129.1166	0.412	0.933
EXP1	129.0422	0.501	0.932
EXP2	129.1489	0.483	0.932
EXP3	129.1588	0.506	0.932
EXP4	129.0720	0.450	0.932
SUP1	128.8015	0.245	0.935
SUP2	128.8561	0.243	0.935
CON1	128.3201	0.486	0.932
CON2	128.2978	0.480	0.932
CON3	128.3821	0.482	0.932
CON4	128.7841	0.596	0.931
CON5	128.2854	0.466	0.932
CON6	128.5633	0.450	0.933
USB1	128.9950	0.515	0.932
USB2	128.9454	0.522	0.932
USB3	129.0124	0.547	0.931
USB4	128.9975	0.475	0.932
DSN1	128.7221	0.545	0.931
DSN2	128.7122	0.531	0.932
DSN3	128.6675	0.598	0.931
DSN4	128.8189	0.475	0.932
QUL1	129.0968	0.575	0.931
QUL2	129.1017	0.649	0.931
QUL3	129.0695	0.624	0.931

(Taherdoost, 2017a). On the other hand, to measure the sampling adequacy, a KMO and Bartlett test were conducted. The KMO overall (0.887) is higher than the conventional cut-off point and the Bartlett has a significant value (p = .000). This indicates that the correlations observed in the variables are likely to contain common variance and the data are likely to factor well (Taherdoost, 2017b).

INSTRUMENT VALIDATION

Factor analysis using Principal Component Analysis (PCA) was applied using SPSS software to verify the construct validity (discriminant and convergent validity). Table 7 presents the Eigenvalues and explained total variance for the extracted factors. According to Straub, et al. (2004), only factors with Eigenvalues greater than one are considered for further analysis. Results indicate that all eight factors possess Eigenvalues greater than one. Results from the analysis also suggest that no extracted new factor consisted of an Eigenvalue greater than 1.

Extraction Method: Principal Component Analysis

Table 8 presents the factor loadings for all eight factors. Results clearly suggest that all eight components loaded on their corresponding factor. Items loaded above 0.40 are considered for further analysis. Therefore, both convergent and discriminant validity met the baseline criteria in IS research (Taherdoost, 2016b).

MODEL VALIDATION

Figure 3 shows the results of Structural Equation Modelling analysis. SEM is considered as an integration of path analysis and confirmatory factor analysis that studies measured variables. The advantage of path analysis is that it concurrently performs multiple regression analyses while it produces an overall assessment of the model's fit, usually based on a chi-square statistic (Singh & Wilkes, 1996). In addition, several goodness-of-fit indexes are available to better judge the model's fit. In order to test and evaluate the model proposed, a path analysis was performed using SPSS AMOS version 24 was employed, to fit a structural equation model to the values of a sample, the dataset used was extracted from analysis results after the CFA performed.

The estimated path coefficients support the argument that all the dimensions positively affect e-service quality, the dimensions managed to explain 39 percent (R2= 0.386) of the variance of overall as the dependent variable (e-service quality).

The coefficients of Content, Design and Performance were all significant (standardized value = . .11*, .16*, .17* respectively). Other factors also have significant and direct influence on e-service quality (see Figure 3).

All the constructs presented higher values to the level proposed by Chin (1998) for the evaluation of the measurement model, which is 0.7 for composite reliability (Table 9). Besides, they presented convergent validity, with AVE (average extracted variance) above 0.5 (Fornell & Larcker, 1981) and discriminant validity, with validation through the criterion of cross-loads, where each item showed a greater factorial load for the construct to which it belongs.

Table 7. Total Variance Explained for Final Survey

Component	Initial Eigenvalues			Extraction Sums of Squared Loadings			Rotation Sums of Squared Loadings		
	Total	% of Variance	Cumulative %	Total	% of Variance	Cumulative %	Total	% of Variance	Cumulative %
1	11.491	31.919	31.919	11.491	31.919	31.919	5.234	14.538	14.538
2	4.581	12.724	44.643	4.581	12.724	44.643	5.103	14.174	28.712
3	2.768	7.689	52.333	2.768	7.689	52.333	3.282	9.118	37.830
4	2.328	6.467	58.800	2.328	6.467	58.800	2.967	8.241	46.071
5	1.806	5.015	63.816	1.806	5.015	63.816	2.948	8.189	54.260
6	1.548	4.301	68.117	1.548	4.301	68.117	2.509	6.970	61.229
7	1.486	4.127	72.244	1.486	4.127	72.244	2.299	6.385	67.615
8	1.269	3.524	75.768	1.269	3.524	75.768	2.231	6.197	73.811
9	1.209	3.358	79.126	1.209	3.358	79.126	1.913	5.314	79.126
10	.709	1.969	81.094						
11	.550	1.527	82.621						
12	.535	1.485	84.107						
13	.497	1.381	85.487						
14	.481	1.336	86.823						
15	.395	1.096	87.919						
16	.388	1.077	88.996						
17	.344	.955	89.951						
18	.335	.930	90.881						
19	.320	.890	91.771						
20	.298	.828	92.600						
21	.282	.784	93.384						
22	.250	.695	94.079						
23	.241	.669	94.748						
24	.223	.620	95.368						
25	.196	.546	95.913						
26	.194	.539	96.453						
27	.181	.504	96.957						
28	.172	.477	97.434						
29	.162	.450	97.884						
30	.159	.442	98.326						
31	.152	.421	98.747						
32	.134	.371	99.118						
33	.118	.329	99.447						
34	.102	.283	99.730						
35	.072	.199	99.928						
36	.026	.072	100.000						

Table 8. Factor Loading for Final Survey Items

	Component								
	1	2	3	4	5	6	7	8	9
INT1	.091	.086	.092	.095	.158	.870	.088	.090	-.024
INT2	.184	.085	.054	.158	.157	.773	.154	.114	.052
PER1	.754	.147	.075	.111	.105	-.049	.144	.081	.069
PER2	.804	.237	.044	.128	.195	.090	.099	.104	.041
PER3	.811	.096	.052	.143	.134	.236	-.025	.005	.078
PER4	.790	.214	.139	.103	.187	.000	.188	.111	.046
PER5	.797	.239	.100	.098	.143	-.036	.226	.100	.023
PER6	.768	.195	.114	.057	.138	.239	.092	.103	.073
PER7	.825	.173	.051	.112	.109	.103	.045	.007	.023
DEP1	.162	-.085	.177	.127	.235	.138	.199	.752	.150
DEP2	.085	-.019	.113	.286	.086	.078	.243	.773	.059
DEP3	.130	-.016	.213	.151	.046	.177	-.025	.833	.051
EXP1	.114	.137	.217	.749	.077	.099	.058	.168	.016
EXP2	.200	.004	.104	.831	.098	.124	.086	.024	.122
EXP3	.196	-.047	.042	.771	.163	.119	.155	.146	.213
EXP4	.097	.040	.144	.783	.080	-.026	.201	.211	-.024
SUP1	.114	.003	.011	.139	-.005	-.030	.075	.110	.916
SUP2	.104	-.016	.066	.094	.009	-.014	.081	.076	.927
CON1	.200	.921	.059	.029	.025	-.025	.066	.002	-.018
CON2	.184	.930	.040	.010	.016	.033	.057	.009	-.024
CON3	.203	.867	.071	-.001	.090	.057	.032	-.049	-.016
CON4	.222	.833	.185	.080	.154	.067	.133	-.028	-.080
CON5	.182	.941	.033	.016	-.013	-.017	.072	.012	-.010
CON6	.113	.795	.114	.039	.036	.156	.010	-.027	.121
USB1	.089	.157	.806	.072	.148	.039	.158	.105	.094
USB2	.111	.062	.790	.077	.162	.095	.232	.128	.050
USB3	.095	.098	.871	.193	.106	.123	.140	.125	-.002
USB4	.116	.121	.856	.157	.056	.081	.003	.121	-.037
DSN1	.196	.029	.167	.104	.838	.087	.091	.146	.041
DSN2	.310	.051	.031	.125	.703	.205	.046	.072	.090
DSN3	.240	.141	.134	.145	.787	.165	.081	.074	.044
DSN4	.134	.052	.164	.057	.785	.103	.247	.052	-.162
QUL1	.229	.147	.216	.180	.129	.125	.717	.052	.057
QUL2	.214	.097	.218	.179	.180	.181	.781	.207	.118
QUL3	.212	.122	.168	.205	.183	.152	.780	.169	.067

Extraction Method: Principal Component Analysis.
Rotation Method: Varimax with Kaiser Normalization.
a. Rotation converged in 6 iterations.

Figure 3. The results of Structural Equation Modelling analysis

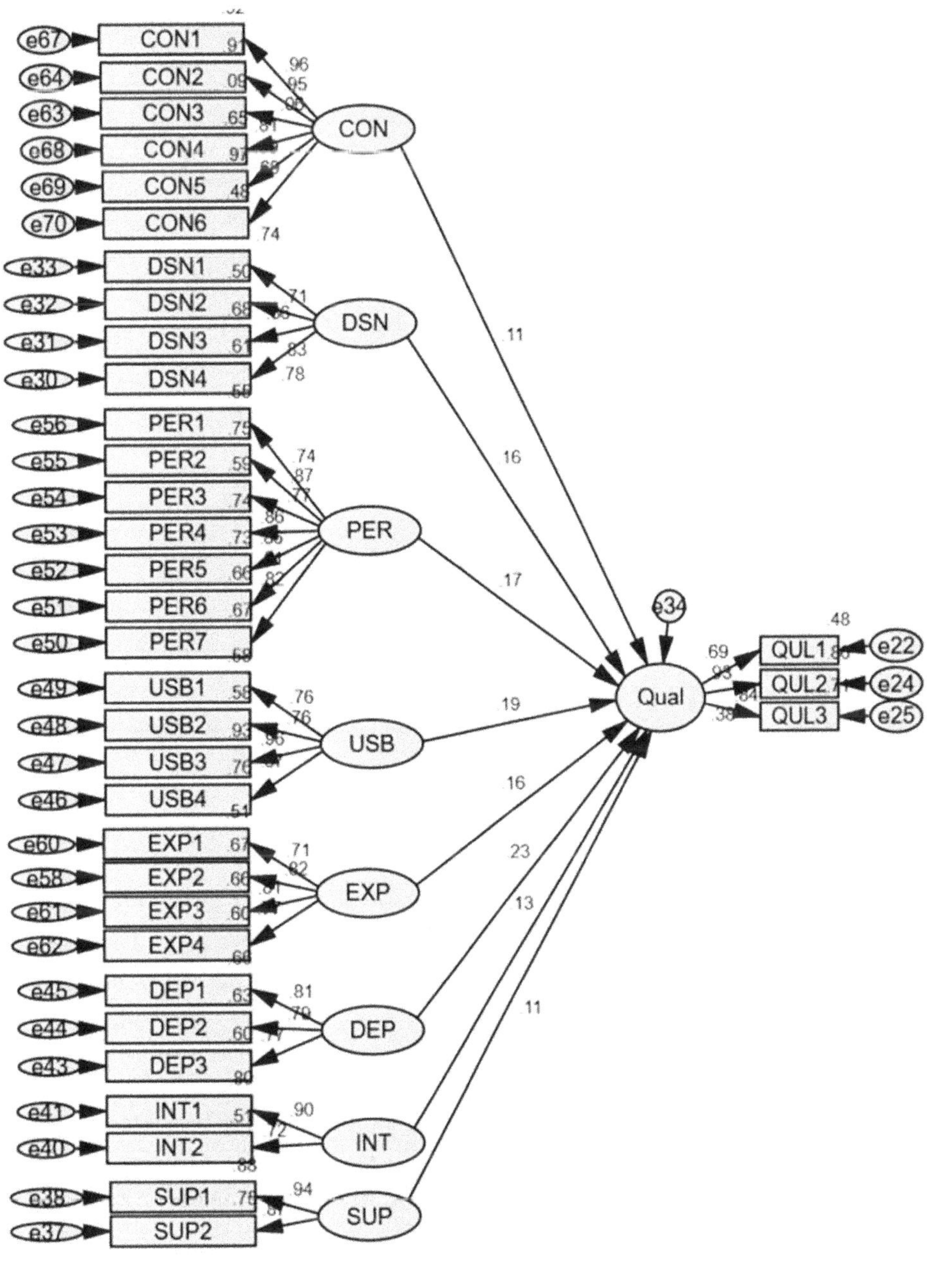

The Goodness-of-Fit Index (GFI) indicates the overall degree of model fit. The GFI should be greater than .90 (Bagozzi & Yi, 1988) and the Adjusted Goodness of Fit Index (AGFI) preferably greater than .80 (Etezadi-Amoli & Farhoomand, 1996; Saha, Nath, & Salehi-Sangari, 2010). In this case, GFI is 0.91 and AGFI 0.87 and indicating that the model fits the sample data reasonably well. The Normed Fit Index (NFI) measures the fit of the proposed model against the null model (Bentler & Bonett, 1980). The NFI for this study is 0.93, exceeding the acceptable value of 0.9 (Fornell & Larcker, 1981), once again indicating that the model fits the sample data well. Moreover, the Comparative Fit Index (CFI) is

Table 9. Summary of the Composite Reliability

	Cronbach's Alpha	Composite Reliability	Average Variance Extracted (AVE)
INT	0.794	0.677	0.807
PER	0.937	0.629	0.922
DEP	0.844	0.619	0.847
EXP	0.864	0.615	0.864
SUP	0.897	0.85	0.919
CON	0.948	0.779	0.955
USB	0.908	0.691	0.899
DSN	0.874	0.608	0.861
QUL	0.879	0.577	0.803

Table 10. The Values of Fit Indexes

Fit Index	Acceptable Value	e-SQM Value
Goodness-of-Fit Index (GFI)	0.90	0.91
Adjusted Goodness of Fit Index (AGFI)	0.80	0.87
Normed Fit Index (NFI)	0.90	0.93
Comparative Fit Index (CFI)	0.90	0.97

another index of overall fit (Gerbing, Anderson, & Carlo, 1993). The recommended threshold for CFI is 0.90 (Bentler, 1990; Doll, Xia, & Torkzadeh, 1994) and for this study, the CFI is 0.971. Therefore, it can be concluded that the measurement model has a good fit with the collected data. Table 10 summarizes the values of fit indexes.

DISCUSSION AND CONCLUSION

In order to deliver superior service quality, managers of companies with Web presences must first understand how customers perceive and evaluate electronic service quality. This involves defining what e-service quality is, identifying its underlying dimensions, and determining how it can be conceptualized and measured.

Minjoon Jun et al. (2004) mentioned that it is vital to recognize the priority of the e-service quality dimensions. By addressing these important questions, an organization can understand what service areas should be concentrated on to improve its service quality and customer satisfaction effectively. The contribution of this chapter relates to the fact that the proposed theoretical framework integrates in a holistic way various relevant factors affecting e-service quality into a single template.

In this chapter, concepts and special characteristics of e-service based on the existing literature have been discussed. The concept of e-service quality considering its features and dimensions. Then, it examined various research findings on e-service quality dimensions in which they categorized through exploratory factor analysis.

According to Manasra et al. (2013), evaluation of the service quality is more complex than good/product, nonetheless an integrated method for e-service quality assessment has not been developed (Eleanor T. Loiacono et al., 2007; Manasra et al., 2013). Although some instruments have been developed to assess the quality of e-service but there are still some limitations. Some of the developed tools focused on the customer's interaction with the web site (Hudek & N. Vrcek, 2006), some only focused on the transactional part, some solely focused on interface part of service quality (Gummerus et al., 2004), hence they might not be applicable to evaluate the complete e-service offering. While the eSQM assesses the quality of e-service is based on the evaluation of the experience the customer acquires during the process of e-service usage which is ranging from the search for information, product evaluation, decision making, order, delivery and a possible return of goods.

Furthermore, some other developed service quality instruments (such as E-S-Qual and WebQual) surveyed only the students and not the actual purchasers. Students are not sufficiently experienced in online shopping, they are neither familiar with particular businesses behind particular Web sites and nor with products offered on these Web sites (Hudek & Vrcek, 2006). Besides, in eTailQ, the surveyed respondents were those who purchased goods, not services and received packages rather than downloading products. Although, eSQM used e-service users (e-banking and e-commerce users) for validation of the instrument.

The findings indicate that performance (including; accessibility, delivery, ease of use, flexibility, fulfillment, functionality, and processing), dependability (including; assurance, credibility, reliability, and security), design (including; aesthetic design, appearance of Website, customization, navigation, site presentation, site attraction, and structure and layout), content (including; content quality, currency, enjoyment, information quality, information accuracy, and relevancy), usability (including; efficiency and Web usability), support (including; customer service, and customer support), interaction (responsiveness and communication) and expectation (including; tangibility and user control on process) are most important characteristics of e-service quality in which should be taken into consideration in order to have high quality e-service.

Measuring the quality of e-service is the concern of both researchers and practitioners, thus, many tools have been developed to assess service quality but there is no specific theoretical framework that defines the e-service quality construct and its dimensions consistently. Service-centered firms may give more attention to their e-service quality especially in eight e-service canon of performance, dependability, design, content, usability, support, interaction and expectation. The perceived quality of a service has two dimensions; the technological dimension, which refers to what is delivered, and the functional dimension, which refers to how the service is delivered. However, for more specific gauging of service maturity, users, IT experts, and other audiences can refer to sub-clusters of each canon. Therefore, it will be valuable to find out the solutions as well as perceptions of service quality and fill gaps between what is perceived by customers view through in-depth investigation. The findings will help e-service policy makers in which they can increase their customers' perceived quality.

On the other hand, the knowledge generated from this research can be used as a platform for e-service providers on how to increase the quality of their e-service. With careful strategy implementation by policy makers, agencies, and system developers, high-quality e-services could be successfully implemented. However, additional steps need to be taken to encourage users to use e-service more frequently.

ACKNOWLEDGMENT

This research was supported by Research Club & Hamta Academy at Hamta Group I Hamta Business Solution Sdn Bhd; and Tablokar Co I Switchgear Manufacturer.

REFERENCES

Al-Gahtani, S., & King, M. (1999). Attitudes. Satisfaction and usage: Factors contributing to each in the acceptance of information technology. *Behaviour and Information Technology Studies: Special Issue on Research Methodology*, *18*(4), 277–297. doi:10.1080/014492999119020

Aladwani, A. M., & Palvia, P. C. (2002). Developing and validating an instrument for measuring user-perceived web quality. *Information & Management*, *39*(6), 467–476. doi:10.1016/S0378-7206(01)00113-6

Alexander, J. E., & Tate, M. A. (1999). *Web wisdom: How to evaluate and create information quality on the web*. Mahwah, NJ: Erlbaum.

Anandarajan, M., Igbaria, M., & Anakwe, U. P. (2000). Technology Acceptance in the Banking Industry: A prospective from a less developed country. *Information Technology & People*, *13*(4), 298–312. doi:10.1108/09593840010359491

Anthopoulos, L. G., Siozos, P., & Tsoukalas, L. A. (2007). pplying Participatory Design and Collaboration in Digital Public Services for Discovering and Re-designing E-government Services. *Government Information Quarterly*, *24*(2), 353–376. doi:10.1016/j.giq.2006.07.018

Asubonteng, P., McCleary, K. J., & Swan, J. (1996). Servqual revisited: A critical review of service quality. *Journal of Services Marketing*, *10*(6), 62–81. doi:10.1108/08876049610148602

Bagozzi, R., & Yi, Y. (1988). On the evaluation of structural equation models. *Journal of the Academy of Marketing Science*, *16*(1), 74–94. doi:10.1007/BF02723327

Barnes, S., & Vidgen, R. (2007). Interactive e-government: Evaluating the web site of the UK Inland Revenue. *Journal of Electronic Government Research*, *3*(1), 19–37. doi:10.4018/jegr.2007010102

Bauer, H. H., Falk, T., & Hammerschmidt, M. (2006). Etransqual: A Transaction Process-Based Approach for Capturing Service Quality in Online Shopping. *Journal of Business Research*, *59*(7), 866–875. doi:10.1016/j.jbusres.2006.01.021

Bauer, H. H., Hammerschmidt, M., & Falk, T. (2005). Measuring the quality of e-banking portals. *International Journal of Bank Marketing*, *23*(2), 153–175. doi:10.1108/02652320510584395

Bélanger, F., & Carter, L. (2008). Trust and risk in e-government adoption. *The Journal of Strategic Information Systems*, *17*(2), 165–176. doi:10.1016/j.jsis.2007.12.002

Bentler, P., & Bonett, D. (1980). Significance tests and goodness of fit in the analysis of covariance structures. *Psychological Bulletin*, *88*(3), 588–606. doi:10.1037/0033-2909.88.3.588

Bentler, P. M. (1990). Comparative fit indexes in structural models. *Psychological Bulletin*, *107*(2), 238–246. doi:10.1037/0033-2909.107.2.238 PMID:2320703

Brensinger, R. P., & Lambert, D. M. (1990). *Can the SERVQUAL Scale be Generalized to Business-to-Business Services?* Paper presented at the Knowledge Development in Marketing1990 AMA's Summer Educators' Conference.

Bressolles, G., Durrieu, F., & Senecal, S. (2014). A consumer typology based on e-service quality and e-satisfaction. *Journal of Retailing and Consumer Services*, *21*(6), 889–896. doi:10.1016/j.jretconser.2014.07.004

Cai, S., & Jun, M. (2003). Internet Users Perceptions of On-line Service Quality: A Comparison of On-line Buyers and Information Searchers. *Managing Service Quality*, *13*(6), 504–519. doi:10.1108/09604520310506568

Carter, L., & Bélanger, F. (2005). The utilization of e-government services: Citizen trust, innovation and acceptance factors. *Information Systems Journal*, *15*(1), 5–26. doi:10.1111/j.1365-2575.2005.00183.x

Chang, M.-Y., Pang, C., Tarn, J. M., Liu, T.-S., & Yen, D. C. (2015). Exploring user acceptance of an e-hospital service: An empirical study in Taiwan. *Computer Standards & Interfaces*, *38*, 35–43. doi:10.1016/j.csi.2014.08.004

Cheung, C. M. K., & Lee, M. K. O. (2005). The Asymmetric Effect of Website Attribute Performance on Web Satisfaction: An Empirical Study. *e-Service Journal*, *3*(3), 65–90. doi:10.2979/esj.2004.3.3.65

Chin, W. W. (1998). Issues and opinions on structural equation modeling. *Management Information Systems Quarterly*, *22*(1), 7–16.

Churchill, G. A. Jr. (1979). A paradigm for developing better measures of marketing constructs. *JMR, Journal of Marketing Research*, *16*(1), 64–73. doi:10.1177/002224377901600110

Collier, J. E., & Bienstock, C. C. (2006). Measuring Service Quality in E-Retailing. *Journal of Service Research*, *8*(3), 260–275. doi:10.1177/1094670505278867

Cox, J., & Dale, B. G. (2001). Service quality and e-commerce: An exploratory analysis. *Managing Service Quality*, *11*(2), 121–131. doi:10.1108/09604520110387257

Cristobal, E., Flavian, C., & Guinalıu, M. (2007). Perceived E-Service Quality: Measurement Validation and Effects on Consumer Satisfaction and Website Loyalty. *Managing Service Quality*, *17*(3), 317–340. doi:10.1108/09604520710744326

Cronin, J. J. Jr, & Taylor, S. A. (1992). Measuring Service Quality: A Reexamination and Extension. *Journal of Marketing*, *56*(3), 55–68. doi:10.1177/002224299205600304

Dabholkar, P. (1996). Consumer evaluations of new technology-based self-service options: An investigation of alternative modes of service quality. *International Journal of Research in Marketing*, *13*(1), 29–51. doi:10.1016/0167-8116(95)00027-5

Davis, F. D. (1989). Perceived usefulness, perceived ease of use and user acceptance of information technology. *Management Information Systems Quarterly*, *13*(3), 319–340. doi:10.2307/249008

Davis, F. D., Bagozzi, R. P., & Warshaw, P. R. (1989). User Acceptance of Computer Technology: A Comparison of two Theoretical models. *Management Science*, *35*(8), 982–1003. doi:10.1287/mnsc.35.8.982

DeLone, W. H., & McLean, E. R. (2003). The DeLone and McLean model of information systems success: A ten-year update. *Journal of Management Information Systems, 19*(4), 9–30. doi:10.1080/07421222.2003.11045748

Dickerson, M. D., & Gentry, J. W. (1983). Characteristics of adopters and non-adopters of home computers. *The Journal of Consumer Research, 10*(2), 225–235. doi:10.1086/208961

Doll, W. J., Xia, W., & Torkzadeh, G. (1994). A confirmatory factor analysis of the end-user computing satisfaction instrument. *Management Information Systems Quarterly, 18*(4), 453–461. doi:10.2307/249524

Dwivedi, Y. K., Choudrie, J., & Brinkman, W.-P. (2006). Development of a survey instrument to examine consumer adoption of broadband. *Industrial Management & Data Systems, 106*(5), 700–718. doi:10.1108/02635570610666458

Einasto, O. (2014). E-service Quality Criteria in University Library: A Focus Group Study. *Procedia: Social and Behavioral Sciences, 147*, 561–566. doi:10.1016/j.sbspro.2014.07.163

Etezadi-Amoli, J., & Farhoomand, A. (1996). A structural model of end user computing satisfaction and user performance. *Information & Management, 30*(2), 65–73. doi:10.1016/0378-7206(95)00052-6

Fabrigar, L. R., Wegener, D. T., MacCallum, R. C., & Strahan, E. J. (1999). Evaluating the use of exploratory factor analysis in psychological research. *Psychological Methods, 4*(3), 272–299. doi:10.1037/1082-989X.4.3.272

Fassnacht, M., & Koese, I. (2006). Quality of electronic services: Conceptualizing and testing a hierarchical model. *Journal of Service Research, 9*(1), 19–31. doi:10.1177/1094670506289531

Finn, A. (2011). Investigating the non-linear effects of e-service quality dimensions on customer satisfaction. *Journal of Retailing and Consumer Services, 18*, 27-37.

Fogg, B. J., Soohoo, C., Danielson, D. R., Marable, L., Stanford, J., & Tauber, E. R. (2003). *How do Users Evaluate the Credibility of Web Sites? A Study with over 2500 Participants.* Paper presented at the Conference on Designing for User Experiences, San Francisco, CA.

Fornell, C., & Larcker, D. (1981). Structural equation models with unobservable variables and measurement error: Algebra and statistics. *JMR, Journal of Marketing Research, 14*(3), 382–388. doi:10.1177/002224378101800313

Garvin, D. A. (1983). Quality on the Line. *Harvard Business Review, 61*, 65–73.

Gefen, D. (2002). Customer loyalty in e-commerce. *Journal of the Association for Information Systems, 3*(1), 27–51. doi:10.17705/1jais.00022

Gerbing, D. W., Anderson, J. C., & Carlo, M. (1993). Evaluation of goodness-of-fit indeces for Stractural Equations Models. *Sociological Methods & Research, 21*(2), 132–160. doi:10.1177/0049124192021002002

Gilmore, A. (1997). Implementing quality in a services marketing context. *Marketing Intelligence & Planning, 15*(4), 185–189. doi:10.1108/02634509710185306

Gorsuch, R. (1983). *Factor Analysis*. Hillsdale, NJ: Erlbaum.

Grigoroudis, E., Litos, C., Moustakis, V. A., Politis, Y., & Tsironis, L. (2008). The assessment of user-perceived web quality: Application of a satisfaction benchmarking approach. *European Journal of Operational Research, 187*(3), 1346–1357. doi:10.1016/j.ejor.2006.09.017

Gronroos, C., Heinonen, F., Isoniemi, K., & Lindholm, M. (2000). The NetOffer model: A case example from the virtual marketplace. *management. Decision (Washington, D.C.), 38*(4), 243–252.

Gummerus, J., Liljander, V., Pura, M., & Riel, A. V. (2004). Customer loyalty to content-basedWeb sites: The case of an online healthcare service. *Journal of Services Marketing, 18*(3), 175–186. doi:10.1108/08876040410536486

Gwebu, K. L., & Wang, J. (2011). Adoption of Open Source Software: The role of social identification. *Decision Support Systems, 51*(1), 220–229. doi:10.1016/j.dss.2010.12.010

Hair, J., Anderson, R., Tatham, R., & Black, W. (1995a). Multivariate data analysis. (4th ed.). Prentice-Hall Inc.

Hair, J. F., Anderson, R. E., Tatham, R. L., & Black, W. C. (1998). Multivariate Data Analysis (5th ed.). Englewood Cliffs, NJ: Prentice Hall.

Ho, C.-I., & Lee, Y.-L. (2007). The development of an e-travel service quality scale. *Tourism Management, 26*(6), 1434–1449. doi:10.1016/j.tourman.2006.12.002

Hoffman, K. D., & Bateson, J. E. G. (1997). *Essentials of service marketing.* Fort Worth, TX: The Dryden Press.

Hudek, R., & Vrcek, N. (2006). *E-service quality evaluation instruments.* Paper presented at the 29th International Convention Proceedings: Microelectronics, Electronics and Electronic Technologies, MEET, Hypermedia and Grid Systems HGS (MIPRO), Croatia.

Hussain, R., Nasser, A. A., & Hussain, Y. K. (2014). Service quality and customer satisfaction of a UAE-based airline: An empirical investigation. *Journal of Air Transport Management,* 1–9.

Ibrahim, E. E., Joseph, M., & Ibeh, K. I. N. (2006). Customers'perception of electronic service delivery in the UK retail banking sector. *International Journal of Bank Marketing, 24*(7), 475–493. doi:10.1108/02652320610712094

Janda, S., Trocchia, P. J., & Gwinner, K. P. (2002). Consumer perceptions of Internet retail service quality. *International Journal of Service Industry Management, 13*(5), 412–431. doi:10.1108/09564230210447913

Jiang, J. J., Klein, G., & Crampton, S. M. (2000a). A Note on SERVQUAL Reliability and Validity in Information System Service Quality Measurement. *Decision Sciences, 31*(3), 725–744. doi:10.1111/j.1540-5915.2000.tb00940.x

Johnson, M. E., & Whang, S. (2002). E-business supply chain management: An overview and framework. *Production and Operations Management, 11*(4), 413–423. doi:10.1111/j.1937-5956.2002.tb00469.x

Joseph, M., McClure, C., & Joseph, B. (1999). Service quality in the banking sector: The impact of technology in service delivery. *International Journal of Bank Marketing, 17*(4), 182–191. doi:10.1108/02652329910278879

Jun, M., & Cai, S. (2001). The key determinants of Internet banking service quality: A content analysis. *International Journal of Bank Marketing*, *19*(7), 276–291. doi:10.1108/02652320110409825

Jun, M., Yang, Z., & Kim, D. (2004). Customers' perceptions of online retailing service quality and their satisfaction. *International Journal of Quality & Reliability Management*, *21*(8), 817–840. doi:10.1108/02656710410551728

Kardaras, D., & Karakostas, B. (2006). *E-service adaptation using fuzzy cognitive maps*. Paper presented at the 3rd International IEEE Conference Intelligent Systems.

Kaynama, S. A., & Black, C. I. (2000). A proposal to assess the service quality of online travel agencies: An exploratory study. *Journal of Professional Services Marketing*, *21*(1), 63–88. doi:10.1300/J090v21n01_05

Kim, M., Kim, J.-H., & Lennon, S. J. (2006). Online service attributes available on apparel retail web sites: An E-S-QUAL approach. *Managing Service Quality*, *16*(1), 51–77. doi:10.1108/09604520610639964

Kline, P. (1997). *An Easy Guide to Factor Analysis*. London: Routledge.

Ko, K. H. (1990). Promotion of IT Applications in Singapore: Policy Issues and Strategic Thrusts. In C. M. L. C. Y. Kuo & K. S. Raman (Eds.), *Information Technology and Singapore Society: Trends, Policies and Applications*. Singapore: Singapore University Press.

Kraiser, H. (1958). The varimax criterion for analytic rotation in factor analysis. *Psychometrika*, *23*(3), 187–200. doi:10.1007/BF02289233

Krejcie, R. V., & Morgan, D. W. (1970). Determining sample size for research activities. *Educational and Psychological Measurement*, *30*(3), 607–610. doi:10.1177/001316447003000308

Ladhari, R. (2010). Developing e-service quality scales: A literature review. *Journal of Retailing and Consumer Services*, *17*(6), 464–477. doi:10.1016/j.jretconser.2010.06.003

Lai, I. K. W., & Lai, D. C. F. (2013). User acceptance of mobile commerce: An empirical study in Macau. *International Journal of Systems Science*, *45*(6), 1321–1331. doi:10.1080/00207721.2012.761471

Lean, O. K., Zailani, S., Ramayah, T., & Fernando, Y. (2009). Factors influencing intention to use e-government services among citizens in Malaysia. *International Journal of Information Management*, *29*(6), 458–475. doi:10.1016/j.ijinfomgt.2009.03.012

Lederer, A. L., Maupin, D. J., Sena, M. P., & Zhuang, Y. (2000). The technology acceptance model and the World Wide Web. *Decision Support Systems*, *29*(3), 269–282. doi:10.1016/S0167-9236(00)00076-2

Lee, G.-G., & Lin, H.-F. (2005). Customer perceptions of e-service quality in online shopping. *International Journal of Retail & Distribution Management*, *33*(2), 161–176. doi:10.1108/09590550510581485

Leech, N., Barrett, K., & Morgan, G. A. (2005). *SPSS for intermediate statistics: Use and interpretation* (2nd ed.). London: Lawrence Erlbaum Associates.

Leong, Y. L. (1997). ECH Programme Hits Its Stride. *Computerworld*, *3*(13).

Li, X., Hess, T. J., & Valacich, J. S. (2006). Using Attitude and Social Influence to Develop an Extended Trust Model for Information Systems. *The Data Base for Advances in Information Systems*, *37*(2 & 3), 108–124. doi:10.1145/1161345.1161359

Li, Y., Tan, K., & Xie, M. (2002). Measuring web-based service quality. *Total Quality Management*, *13*(5), 685–700. doi:10.1080/0954412022000002072

Lin, F.-J., Huarng, K., Chen, Y.-M., & Lin, S.-M. (2004). *Quality Evaluation of Web Services*. Paper presented at the IEEE International Conference on E-Commerce Technology for Dynamic E-Business, Beijing, China.

Loiacono, E. T., Watson, R. T., & Goodhue, D. L. (2007). WebQual: An Instrument for Consumer Evaluation of Web Sites. *International Journal of Electronic Commerce*, *11*(3), 51–87. doi:10.2753/JEC1086-4415110302

Loiacono, E. T., Watson, R. T., & Hoodhue, D. L. (2002). WEBQUAL: measure of web site quality. *Marketing Educators Conference: Marketing Theory and Applications*, *13*, 432-437.

Loonam, M., & O'Loughlin, D. (2008). Exploring e-service quality: A study of Irish online banking. *Marketing Intelligence & Planning*, *26*(7), 759–780. doi:10.1108/02634500810916708

Lovelock, C. (2001). *Services Marketing: People, Technology and Strategy*. Upper Saddle River, NJ: Prentice Hall.

Lu, J. (2001). Measuring cost/benefits of e-business applications and customer satisfaction. *Proceedings of the 2nd International Web Conference*.

Lu, J., Yu, C. S., Liu, C., & Yao, J. E. (2003). Technology acceptance model for wireless Internet. *Internet Research*, *13*(3), 206–222. doi:10.1108/10662240310478222

Luo, M. M., Chea, S., & Chen, J.-S. (2011). Web-based information service adoption: A comparison of the motivational model and the uses and gratifications theory. *Decision Support Systems*, *51*(1), 21–30. doi:10.1016/j.dss.2010.11.015

Luo, M. M.-l., Remus, W., & Chea, S. (2006). Technology Acceptance of Internet-based Information Services: An Integrated Model of TAM and U&G Theory. *Proceedings of the Twelfth Americas Conference on Information Systems*.

Madu, C. N., & Madu, A. A. (2002). Dimensions of e-quality. *International Journal of Quality & Reliability Management*, *19*(3), 246–259. doi:10.1108/02656710210415668

Mahinda, E., & Whitworth, B. (2006). *Using The WOSP Model To Improve End-User Productivity Of Information Systems*. Paper presented at the International Conference on Business IT (BIZIT 2006): Collaborating with ICT Innovations for Business Survival, Kuala Lumpur, Malaysia.

Manasra, E. A. A., Zaid, M. K. S. A., & TaherQutaishat, F. (2013). Investigating the Impact of Website Quality on Consumers' Satisfaction in Jordanian Telecommunication Sector. *Arab Economic and Business Journal, 8*, 31-37.

Mao, E., & Palvia, P. (2006). Testing an Extended Model of IT Acceptance in the Chinese Cultural Context. *The Data Base for Advances in Information Systems, 37*(2 & 3), 20–32. doi:10.1145/1161345.1161351

McKnight, D. H., Choudhury, V., & Kacmar, C. (2002b). Developing and Validating Trust Measures for e-Commerce: An Integrative Typology. *Information Systems Research, 13*(3), 334–359. doi:10.1287/isre.13.3.334.81

Mittal, V., & Tsiros, M. (2007). Customer Loyalty in Electronically Mediated Environments. *Journal of Value Chain Management, 1*(1/2), 80–109.

Moore, N. (2006). *How to do research: a practical guide to designing and managing research projects* (3rd ed.). London: Facet Publishing.

Mosbeh, R., & Soliman, K. S. (2008). An exploratory analysis of factors affecting users' adoption of corporate intranet; A Tunisian study. *Management Research News, 31*(5), 375–385. doi:10.1108/01409170810865172

Ok, S.-J., & Shon, J.-H. (2006, December). *The Determinant of Internet Banking Usage Behavior in Korea: A Comparison of Two Theoretical Models.* Paper presented at the CollECTeR '06, Adelaide, Australia.

Palmer, J. W. (2002). Web Site Usability, Design and Performance Metrics. *Information Systems Research, 13*(2), 151–167. doi:10.1287/isre.13.2.151.88

Parasuraman, A., & Berry, L. L. (1985). A conceptual model of service quality and its implications for future research. *Journal of Marketing Science, 49*, 41–50.

Parasuraman, A., Berry, L. L., & Zeithaml, V. A. (1991a). Refinement and Reassessment of the SERVQUAL Scale. *Journal of Retailing, 67*(4), 420–450.

Parasuraman, A., Zeithaml, V. A., & Berry, L. L. (1988). SERVQUAL: A multi-item scale for measuring consumer perceptions of service quality. *Journal of Retailing, 64*, 2–40.

Parasuraman, A., Zeithaml, V. A., & Malhotra, A. (2005). E-S-QUAL: A multiple-item scale for assessing electronic service quality. *Journal of Service Research, 7*(3), 213–234. doi:10.1177/1094670504271156

Pavlou, P. (2003). Consumer acceptance of electronic commerce: Integrating trust and risk with the technology acceptance model. *International Journal of Electronic Commerce, 7*, 69–103.

Pedersen, P. E. (2005). Adoption of mobile Internet services: An exploratory study of mobile commerce early adopters. *Journal of Organizational Computing and Electronic Commerce, 15*(2), 203–222. doi:10.120715327744joce1503_2

Pett, M. A., Lackey, N. R., & Sullivan, J. J. (2003). *Making Sense of Factor Analysis: The use of factor analysis for instrument development in health care research.* Sage Publications Inc. doi:10.4135/9781412984898

Premkumar, G., & Bhattacherjee, A. (2008). Explaining information technology usage: A test of competing models. *Omega, 36*(1), 64–75. doi:10.1016/j.omega.2005.12.002

Riel, A. C. R. v., Semeijn, J., & Pauwels, P. (2003). Online Travel Service Quality: The Importance of Pre-transaction Services. METEOR, Maastricht research school of Economics of Technology and Organizations.

Robinson, J. (2009). *Triandis theory of interpersonal behaviour in understanding software privace behaviour in the South African context (Masters degree)*. Johannesburg: University of the Witwatersrand.

Ruyter, K., Wetzels, M., & Kleijnen, M. (2001). Customer adoption of e-service: An experimental study. *International Journal of Service Industry Management*, *12*(2), 184–207. doi:10.1108/09564230110387542

Saha, P., Nath, A., & Salehi-Sangari, E. (2010). Success of Government E-Service Delivery. Does Satisfaction Matter? In EGOV 2010 LNCS (Vol. 6228, pp. 204-215). IFIP International Federation for Information Processing.

Salisbury, W. D., Pearson, R. A., Pearson, A. W., & Miller, D. W. (2001). Perceived security and World Wide Web purchase intention. *Industrial Management & Data Systems*, *101*(4), 165–176. doi:10.1108/02635570110390071

Santos, J. (2003). E-service quality – a model of virtual service dimensions. *Managing Service Quality*, *13*(3), 233–247. doi:10.1108/09604520310476490

Santos, J. (2003). E-service quality: A model of virtual service quality dimensions. *Managing Service Quality*, *13*(3), 233–246. doi:10.1108/09604520310476490

Saxe, R., & Weitx, B. A. (1982). The SOCO Scale: A Measure of the Customer Orientation of Sales people. *Journal of Marketing*, *19*, 343–351. doi:10.1177/002224378201900307

Semeijn, J., Riel, A. C. R., Birgelen, M. J. H., & Streukens, S. (2005). E-services and offline fulfilment: How e-loyalty is created. *Managing Service Quality*, *15*(2), 182–194. doi:10.1108/09604520510585361

Seneler, C. O., Basoglu, N., & Daim, T. U. (2010). An empirical analysis of the antecedents of adoption of online services; A prototype-based framework. *Journal of Enterprise Information Management*, *23*(4), 417–438. doi:10.1108/17410391011061753

Shachaf, P., & Oltmann, S. M. (2007). E-quality and e-service equality. *Proceedings of the 40th Hawaii International Conference on System Sciences*.

Shareef, M. A., Kumar, U., Kumar, V., & Dwivedi, Y. K. (2009). Identifying critical factors for adoption of e-government. *Electronic Government: An International Journal*, *6*(1), 70–96. doi:10.1504/EG.2009.022594

Sheikhshoaei, F., & Oloumi, T. (2011). Applying the technology acceptance model to Iranian engineering faculty libraries. *The Electronic Library*, *29*(3), 367–378. doi:10.1108/02640471111141106

Sheng, T., & Liu, C. (2010). An empirical study on the effect of e-service quality on online customer satisfaction and loyalty. *Nankai Business Review International*, *1*(3), 273–283. doi:10.1108/20408741011069205

Shin, D.-H. (2010). The effects of trust, security and privacy in social networking: A security-based approach to understand the pattern of adoption. *Interacting with Computers*, *22*(5), 428–438. doi:10.1016/j.intcom.2010.05.001

Singh, J., & Wilkes, R. (1996). When consumers complain: A path analysis of the key antecedents of consumer complaint response estimates. *Journal of the Academy of Marketing Science*, *24*(4), 350–365. doi:10.1177/0092070396244006

Smith, A. G. (2001). Applying evaluation criteria to New Zealand government Web sites. *International Journal of Information Management*, *21*(2), 137–149. doi:10.1016/S0268-4012(01)00006-8

Sohn, C., & Tadisina, S. K. (2008). Development of e-service quality measure for internet-based financial institutions. *Total Quality Management & Business Excellence*, *19*(9), 903–918. doi:10.1080/14783360802224412

Stamenkov, G., & Dika, Z. (2016). Bank employees' internal and external perspectives on e-service quality, satisfaction and loyalty. *Electronic Markets*, *26*(3), 291–309. doi:10.100712525-016-0221-6

Stephanie, A. J., Abdul Nasir, Z., & Nur Fadziana, F. M. (2008). *A Study on the Acceptance of E-Ticketing in Universiti Utara Malaysia Bus Service*. Paper presented at the Knowledge Management International Conference, Langkawi, Malaysia.

Stevens, J. (2001). Applied multivariate statistics for the social sciences (3rd ed.). Mahwah, NJ: Lawrence Erlbaum.

Stiglingh, M. (2014). A measuring instrument to evaluate e-service quality in arevenue authority setting. *Public Relations Review*, *40*(2), 216–225. doi:10.1016/j.pubrev.2013.12.001

Straub, D., Boudreau, M.-C., & Gefen, D. (2004). Validation guidelines for IS positivist research. *Communications of the Association for Information Systems*, *13*, 380–427. doi:10.17705/1CAIS.01324

Suki, N. M. (2014). Passenger satisfaction with airline service quality in Malaysia: A structural equation modeling approach. *Research in Transportation Business & Management*, *10*, 26–32. doi:10.1016/j.rtbm.2014.04.001

Surjadaja, H., Ghosh, S., & Antony, F. (2003). Determining and assessing the determinants of e-service operations. *Managing Service Quality*, *13*(1), 39–44. doi:10.1108/09604520310456708

Sweeney, J. C., & Lapp, W. (2004). Critical Service Quality Encounters on the Web: An Exploratory Study. *Journal of Services Marketing*, *18*(4), 276–289. doi:10.1108/08876040410542272

Taherdoost, H. (2016a). How to Design and Create an Effective Survey/Questionnaire; A Step by Step Guide. *International Journal of Academic Research in Management*, *5*(4), 37–41.

Taherdoost, H. (2016b). Validity and Reliability of the Research Instrument; How to Test the Validation of a Questionnaire/Survey in a Research. *International Journal of Academic Research in Management*, *5*(3), 28–36.

Taherdoost, H. (2017a). Determining Sample Size; How to Calculate Survey Sample Size. *International Journal of Economics and Management Systems*, *2*, 237–239.

Taherdoost, H. (2017b). Understanding of E-service Security Dimensions and its effect on Quality and Intention to Use. *Information and Computer Security*, *25*(5), 535–559. doi:10.1108/ICS-09-2016-0074

Taherdoost, H. (2018). Development of an adoption model to assess user acceptance of e-service technology: E-Service Technology Acceptance Model. *Behaviour & Information Technology*, *37*(2), 173–197. doi:10.1080/0144929X.2018.1427793

Taherdoost, H. (2018b). A review of technology acceptance and adoption models and theories. *Journal of Procedia Manufacturing*, *22*, 960–967. doi:10.1016/j.promfg.2018.03.137

Taherdoost, H., Sahibuddin, S., Ibrahim, S., Kalantari, A., Jalaliyoon, N., & Ameri, S. (2012). *Examination of Electronic Service Definitions* Paper presented at the International Conference on Advanced Computer Science Applications and Technologies (ACSAT), Kuala Lumpur, Malaysia. 10.1109/ACSAT.2012.51

Taherdoost, H., Sahibuddin, S., & Jalaliyoon, N. (2013). E-Services Usage Evaluation; Applications' level of Co-Creation and Digitalization. *International Journal of Academic Research in Management*, *2*(1), 10–18.

Tan, K. C., Xie, M., & Li, Y. N. (2003). A service quality framework for Web-based information systems. *The TQM Magazine*, *15*(3), 164–172. doi:10.1108/09544780310469262

Taylor, S., & Todd, P. (1995a). Understanding information technology usage: A Test of Competing Models. *Information Systems Research*, *6*(2), 144–176. doi:10.1287/isre.6.2.144

Thaichon, P., Lobo, A., Prentice, C., & Quach, T. N. (2014). The development of service quality dimensions for internet service providers: Retaining customers of different usage patterns. *Journal of Retailing and Consumer Services*, *21*(6), 1047–1058. doi:10.1016/j.jretconser.2014.06.006

Thompson, B. (2004). *Exploratory and confirmatory factor analysis: understanding concepts and applications*. Washington, DC: American Psychological Association. doi:10.1037/10694-000

Torkzadeh, G., & Dhillon, G. (2002). Measuring factors that influence the success of Internet commerce. *Information Systems Research*, *13*(2), 187–204. doi:10.1287/isre.13.2.187.87

Tsai, H.-T., Huang, H.-C., Jaw, Y.-L., & Chen, W.-K. (2006). Why on-line customers remain with a particular e-retailer: An integrative model and empirical evidence. *Psychology and Marketing*, *23*(5), 447–464. doi:10.1002/mar.20121

Udo, G. J., Bagchi, K. K., & Kirs, P. J. (2010). An assessment of customers' e-service quality perception, satisfaction and intention. *International Journal of Information Management*, *30*(6), 481–492. doi:10.1016/j.ijinfomgt.2010.03.005

Van Riel, A. C. R., Liljander, V., & Jurriëns, P. (2001). Exploring consumer evaluations of e-services: A portal site. *International Journal of Service Industry Management*, *12*(4), 359–377. doi:10.1108/09564230110405280

Van Riel, A. C. R., Semeijn, C., & Janssen, W. (2003). E-service quality expectations: A case study. *Total Quality Management*, *14*(4), 437–450. doi:10.1080/1478336032000047255

Van Riel, C. R. A., Semeijn, J., & Pauwels, P. (2004). Online travel service quality: The importance of pre-transaction services. *Total Quality Management & Business Excellence*, *15*(4), 475–493. doi:10.1080/1478336042000183578

Venkatesh, V., Morris, M. G., Davis, G. B., & Davis, E. D. (2003). User acceptance of information technology: Towards a unified view. *Management Information Systems Quarterly*, *27*(3), 425–478. doi:10.2307/30036540

Vijayasarathy, L. R. (2004). Predicting consumer intentions to use on-line shopping: The case for an augmented technology acceptance model. *Information & Management*, *41*(6), 747–762. doi:10.1016/j.im.2003.08.011

Wang, R. Y., & Strong, D. M. (1996). Beyond accuracy: What data quality means to data consumers. *Journal of Management Information Systems, 12*(4), 5-33.

Wixom, B. H., & Todd, P. A. (2005). A theoretical integration of user satisfaction and technology acceptance. *Information Systems Research*, *16*(1), 85–102. doi:10.1287/isre.1050.0042

Wolfinbarger, M., & Gilly, M. C. (2003). Etailq: Dimensionalizing, Measuring and Predicting Etail Quality. *Journal of Retailing*, *79*(3), 183–198. doi:10.1016/S0022-4359(03)00034-4

Wu, Y.-L., Tao, Y.-H., & Yang, P.-C. (2008). The use of unified theory of acceptance and use of technology to confer the behavioral model of 3G mobile telecommunication users. *Journal of Statistics & Management Systems*, *11*(5), 919–949. doi:10.1080/09720510.2008.10701351

Yang, Z., Cai, S., Zhou, Z., & Zhou, N. (2005). Development and validation of an instrument to measure user perceived service quality of information presenting Web portals. *Information & Management*, *42*(4), 575–589. doi:10.1016/S0378-7206(04)00073-4

Yang, Z., & Jun, M. (2002). Consumer perception of e-service quality: From Internet purchaser and non-purchaser perspectives. *Journal of Business Strategies Huntsville*, *19*(1), 19–41.

Yang, Z., Peterson, R. T., & Cai, S. (2003). Services quality dimension of Internet retailing: An exploratory analysis. *Journal of Services Marketing Science*, *17*(7), 685–690. doi:10.1108/08876040310501241

Yang, Z., Peterson, R. T., & Huang, L. (2001). Taking the pulse of internet pharmacies. *Marketing Health Services*, *21*(2), 5–10. PMID:11406905

Yenisey, M. M., Ozok, A. A., & Salvendy, G. (2005). Perceived security determinants in ecommerce among Turkish University students. *Behaviour & Information Technology*, *24*(4), 259–274. doi:10.1080/0144929042000320992

Yoo, B., & Donthu, N. (2001). Developing a scale to measure perceived quality of an Internet shopping site (SITEQUAL). *Quarterly Journal of Electronic Commerce*, *2*(1), 31–46.

Yu, J., Ha, I., Choi, M., & Rho, J. (2005). Extending the TAM for a t-commerce. *Information & Management*, *42*(7), 965–976. doi:10.1016/j.im.2004.11.001

Zeist, R. H. J., & Hendriks, P. R. H. (1996). Specifying software quality with the extended ISO model. *Software Quality Journal*, *5*(4), 273–284. doi:10.1007/BF00209185

Zeithaml, V. A., Berry, L., & Parasuraman, A. (1996). The behavioral consequences of service quality. *JMR, Journal of Marketing Research*, *60*(2), 31–46.

Zeithaml, V. A., Parasuraman, A., & Malhotra, A. (2000). *A conceptual framework for understanding e-service quality: Implications for future research and managerial practice*. MSI Working Paper Series, Report No. 00-115, Cambridge.

Zeithaml, V. A., Parasuraman, A., & Malhotra, A. (2002). Service quality delivery through web sites: A critical review of extant knowledge. *Journal of the Academy of Marketing Science*, *30*(4), 362–375. doi:10.1177/009207002236911

Zhang, X., & Prybutok, V. (2005). A consumer perspective of e-service quality. *IEEE Transactions on Engineering Management*, *52*(4), 461–477. doi:10.1109/TEM.2005.856568

KEY TERMS AND DEFINITIONS

E-Service: The provision of interactional, content-centered, and electronic-based service over electronic networks.

E-Service Quality: A global judgment, or attitude, relating to the superiority of the service that a consumer obtained or is obtaining from the current service provider.

eSQM: The e-service quality model and instrument to assess the quality of electronic services.

Exploratory Factor Analysis (EFA): Used as a theory generating procedure. It is used to uncover the underlying structure of a relatively large set of variables and identifies representative variables from a much larger set of variables for use in subsequent multivariate analysis.

Service: An act or performance offered by one party to another.

Service Quality: Customers' expectations for service performed prior to the service encounter and their perceptions of the service received.

Structural Equation Modeling (SEM): Considered as an integration of path analysis and confirmatory factor analysis. It is a statistical technique that evaluates the plausibility of a hypothesized model.

Chapter 12
The New Horizon of Public Relations:
Community Management

Zeynep Genel
Okan University, Turkey

ABSTRACT

Consumers pay attention to other consumers' comments, advice, and interactions during the purchase decision process. Besides having a strong impact on consumers' brand decisions, these user-driven contents have an important effect on brand's online reputation, which is very important area for consumers to follow the information about the brand. Therefore, some of the public relations practices will be forced to change by this new communication eco-system. The increasing power of consumer-driven content could lead to the evolution of traditional public relations and marketing communication. Interaction and participation would be the main concepts in the coming future of public relations. Therefore, this chapter aims to explain the effect of consumers' interactions on brand's social media accounts that would lead to their brand selection decisions.

INTRODUCTION

The reputation is described as the management of communications between an organization and its target public groups (Hunt and Grunig 1984) represents the quality of an organization' communication skills with each member in its communication environment. The reputation indicates how effective or ineffective the communication approach of organization is on its publics' perception. In the early stage of the discussion about the reputation, the corporate managements adopted the strategic communication approaches based on achieving the main business objectives of an organization. The public's expectations were taken into consideration in the second step. As Grunig (2009) stated in his study titled Excellence Theory in Public Relations, these approaches started the discussion of one-way symmetrical communication management, which might be disadvantageous from in terms of the reputation (pp.92). In parallel with these discussions, the change in communication technology and its impact on the social

DOI: 10.4018/978-1-5225-9697-4.ch012

behavior and collective perception made the perceived reputation a fundamental effort in the practical communication area (Grunig and Hunt, 2002).

The constantly developing communication technologies brought new aspects in discussions on the survival in newborn communication fields accepted by the publics as a determinant factor in creating the beliefs and thoughts by reconsidering the sum of a corporates images on cyberspace. Within this scope, this chapter fundamentally discusses the issues that are crucial for establishing an efficient and sustainable reputation in the digital communication environment. Doorley and Garcia(2007) emphasized, a communication specialist should be conscious of the historical developments, the effects of the changing circumstances, and the process of society's adaptation to these changes, as well as following the new implications consisting of exchanging the communication tools with the publics(p.128). The first reason of that is the importance of having knowledge about the developments regarding the social behavior in order to integrate the corporate communication strategies into the new dynamics of communication environment (Bıçakçı and Genel 2016). Raub and Wessie (1990) highlighted the correlation between the corporate social behavior and the established perception from the aspect of publics (pp.628-629). From this point of view, grasping the extent of corporate reputation and the components constituting the reputation is an important aspect of the professional communication and the first part of this chapter aims to answer the questions and to provide the expected information about the scope of corporate reputation, as well as presenting a wider conceptual framework.

In the second part of chapter, the evolution of the Web technologies and the effects on audience's perception and behavior in social meaning were discussed. The aim of the second part is to understand the relationship between the development of communication technologies and the changes in audience's attitude. In order to carry out the public relations projects on the Web, it is important to understand the cause-and-effect process of the technologies and the reflections on the social, cultural and political areas. The social media playing an important role in the lives of millions is a new "multimedia" platform that the corporate communication departments should absolutely use in an effective way. Especially the communication in social networks must planned in accordance with the company's long-term corporate communication strategy. Before planning, where the company or brand stands in social networks, should carefully examined in order to understand the recall of brand/corporation. Therefore, the companies should cooperate with the communication experts, who can look at the communication from the corporate perspective, and have the knowledge about the corporate communication.

In the final section of this chapter, the research will discuss a Turkish case study in order to reflect the perceived reputation of a Turkish organization and to explain the attitude of Turkish publics through the reflections on the social media regarding the corporate reputation. This chapter is a resource to examine the reflections and effects of social media cluster on corporate communications and implications of corporate reputation.

BACKGROUND

The significant role of reputation determines the company's asset and life cycle both at the market and country level. In academic researches, the importance of reputation was being studied from various aspects (Kanto et al. 2016). According to Chong (2012), the reputation influences the value of the company's equity, ability of attracting and retaining talent, and fundamental license to operate (p.1). Economists think that the reputation is a source of information about company's behavior in specific situations

(Roper and Fill 2012,p.7). A meta-analysis carried out by Orlitzky et al.(2003) on 52 empirical studies revealed a positive association between corporate social performance (CSP) and corporate financial performance (CFP) (as cited in Cassimon et al.,2014 p.2),which means that the social efforts affect the financial performance of the corporation. As a simple explanation, it can be stated that the reputation is the stakeholders' composed perception on the corporate skills of meeting expectations (Çakır 2016, p.23).

It is not only derives from intangible illustrations on the target audience's perception but also turns a significant financial benefit to the company. As Fombrun(1996) stated, the reputation is depicted as the general estimation of the association by its audiences, which can be communicated by the net emotional responses of customers, speculators, work force, and furthermore the public at higher level(p.112). Moreover, the reputation adds value to the actual worth of a company; in other words, the market includes more than just the book value or liquidation value of assets (Doorley and Garcia, 2007 p.4). In fact, the corporate world put the reputation at a central position like a vital element of an organization's sources together with its benefits regarding the financial performance and innovation (Watson and Kitchen 2010 p.2). The other key point to remind is the reputational effect of social performance, which changes to the sector to sector, and within companies various types of social performance (Bramer and Pavelin, 2006). As well as its financial effects, the reputation is also examined as an administrative instrument of company's board. Some researchers discussed the beneficial aspects of the reputation such as its positive effects on credibility and indirectly management(Balmer and Gray,1999).The content of the term is used as corporate reputation from the perspective of corporations (Özbay and Selvi, 2014, p.2). Although the term has been discussed for a long time, it is considered that the components and rules of positioning an active and sustainable reputation are not certainly figured out yet. According to Fombrun's cognitive model, the main reason for the difficulties in the classification of reputation components is the complex communication environment of the company (1996). The consumers' increasing communication consumption and the complexity of communication environment affect the transformation of reputation elements more deeply. Few researchers (Schwaiger 2004; Fombrun and Van Riel 2004) discussed the reputation from the social perspective and the intangible elements of the corporate reputation have been discussed. The studies shown that the intangible elements that implicit the reputation have great impact on perceived reputation. This is because these elements affect to have an emotional bond with the consumers both positively and negatively (Kadıbeşegil, 2015). By raising awareness among the managers about the vital role of the corporation's intangible elements in reputation, the value becomes a primary point regarding the annual strategic plans. The intangible content brings the discussion of the perception of the audiences that is expressed as a complex and temporary process, which includes many different images, and connotations that are created by the experience of audiences.

The diversification of intangible assets arises from the diversified perceptions of different audience groups (Fombrun and Van Riel 1997). As a matter of course, the corporations have relationships with various groups that have origins from various cultures, functions, and regions. Some researchers classified this intangible diversification into two groups based on consumer's experiences. For instance, Schwaiger(2004) put forward two new aspects of the reputation as *competence* and *likeability*. Having a competence reputation depends on the consumer's experience about the corporations. These experiences consist of direct and indirect relations with the corporation. On the other hand, the satisfaction level of these experiences and awareness of corporate affords to maintain likeability (Schwaiger 2004). Although many researchers are trying to classify the components of corporate reputation, these components have constantly been changing because of the differentiation and improvement of the consumer's experiences and perceptions (Fomburn 1996). That is to say, these explanations show the key role of stakeholders in considering the reputation. Despite the corporate communication managers plan the facilities in order to position the corporate reputation, the researches aiming to classify the components of excellent reputation, which show stakeholders' perception and attitude create the most associations with corporate reputation (McGuire et al. 1990; Szwajkowski and Figlewicz, 1999). Because of this reason, many reputation measurements are based on stakeholders' perception and the components identified by stakeholders since the managers have no acknowledge about the projected reputation (Doorley and Garcia 2007).

The reputation measurement model of Fomburn and Foss (2001) showed that there is a close relationship between the perceived perception and evaluation of stakeholders and consisted of reputation (p.p.4-5). If the stakeholders do not have direct participation in the corporation's reputation efforts, then the stakeholder's effect on consisted corporate reputation is very dominant (Matuleviciene and Stravinskiene 2015).Grunig and Hunt (2002) described the stakeholders as a group of people affected by the decisions of an organization or if their decision affects the organization (p.125). Furthermore, the illuminations of the stakeholders' perception have showed the level and quality of communication efforts grounded on the reputation. Thanks to the developing communications technologies, the stakeholders' role on the reputation has increased because of the transformation into the active publics. Grunig and Hunt (2002) stressed that if the stakeholders have active role on corporate decisions or effect on corporate activities they become publics.Thus, the corporations started to have more struggle in order to establish and sustain the high quality communications with both their stakeholders and publics.

Before the new media, the corporations positioned their consumers as their stakeholders in parallel with the "asymmetrical way symmetrical communications" approach. The main reason for this is that the traditional media and publicity channels were not allowed to have active and on-time engagement with consumers into the communication process of the company. The Web 2.0-based Internet platforms, which allows to integration of users to the corporate account lead the corporate managers rethink the rules of having sustainable communication with their stakeholders (Genel 2017). To understand the changing attitudes of stakeholders and the key factors of corporate reputation, every communication professional should grasp the structure and revolution of digital communications technologies as a significant piece of communication component. Doorley and Garcia (2007) mentioned, a public relations specialist should know and be aware of the sociological, economic and cultural conjunctures of the society in both national and international level. The technological developments affect all the fields in a considerable level, should be understood by all the communication professionals. Starting from this point of view, the development process of this newborn communication and its effects on publics, as well as corporate reputation discussed in the following parts.

MAIN FOCUS OF THE CHAPTER

Community Management in Public Relations

The digital revolution brought many opportunities for the public relations specialists in addition to a new challenge: the social networking sites (McLennan and Howell 2010). The consumer-based contents, which can induce both negative and positive effects for corporations, became the most precious issue of the digital corporate communications. Not only the consumers' attitude evolved with the unique communication environment of the social networks, but also the ecosystem forced the change of corporate social behavior towards the publics (Mathews, 2010, p.18). The malpractice of corporate social network communication started to destroy the corporate image by the increasing consumption of social media during the daily lives of people, as well as the word of mouth effect of the cyber interaction (Valck et al. 2009). On the other hand, the social media gets an essence of revolution in corporate communication area. Especially for the public relations domain, it gives an important chance to understand and interact with social publics. As Köksal and Özdemir (2013) stated, the comments written on videos and the published comments about the articles on blogs provide simplicity to understanding the target audiences (p.322).

Nowadays, achieving success in virtual communication became the prerequisite of gaining the trust of society. The community management is a social process that based on the creation of public opinion through the corporate messages (Koçak, 2016 p.223). Many of the previous studies reported that the publics shaped their attention towards the organization in parallel with the messages of masses in social networks (Keskin and Baş 2016). The proactive and effective communication suggested by Grunig and Hunt (2002) years ago is the most appropriate approach to the management of and survival in the cyber domain. In this new media domain having a multidimensional communication environment, it does not seem possible for the organizations to position or maintain their corporate reputation by employing traditional public relations methods (Koçak 2016). Especially the guiding effect of social network companies in economy suggests that, in order to be successful and active in this domain, the organizations must develop successful public relations strategies in terms of content and society management. Because, the technology companies that are capable of dominating the virtual domain are prepared for regulating the appearance rates of the organizations in order to protect their own prestige and usage rates (Perlberg and Seetharaman, 2016).

It is predicted that the production of contents that are attractive and fitting to the social network will be one of the necessities of communication approach in forthcoming period. As highlighted by Fombrun Galdberg and Sever (2000), the social media is one of the leading management domains of today's public relation specialists. This derived from the aspect of emotional bond, which is one of the components of reputation, because the consumers pay more importance to the opinions of sharers in these societies when compared to the importance given to the advertisement-based activities of organization. Understanding the scope of this new attention economy and developing strategies in this parallel are inevitable in order for professional communication specialists to ensure the sustainability of reputation. These debates focus on how the social network public relations should be. According to Weinberg (2009), the social network public relations should be the communication of a large society, rather than the social extensions of the corporate blogs introducing products and services and those of the websites. The content produced by a member constituting a large mass rapidly spread to a large mass, and it even plays guiding role from the aspect of corporate information in digital platforms. Especially the interpersonal communication about corporates/brands between consumers (Lee and Youns 2009), which is conceptualized as word of mouth, plays important role in establishing the corporate content. In fact, the attention and appearance economy, which shapes certain conditions related with the content, acts as a central filter that is in favor of actors having a strong economy (Castels and Cardoso 2005 p.204). In this new economic conjuncture, the organizations that can establish an accurate communication with the target publics achieve an opportunity to develop further advancement and sustainable communication network, whereas the organizations lacking of sharing and content production fall behind.

In Turkey, as in entire world, the social media domain is a corporate communication domain, on which there are wide debates and the actors act in abstentious way. Especially considering from the aspect of reputation, this multi-layered medium consisting of the reputation in the minds of masses plays effective role. The fact that the social media networks play gradually more effective role in users' perceptions towards an organization or a brand necessitates organizations reviewing their communication approaches. The main objective of the present chapter is to reveal how effective the corporate accounts are in establishment of social network users' opinion regarding the organization/brand. From this point of view, in parallel with the results obtained in the chapter, the information that is believed to contribute to communication professionals is provided.

Research Objective

In order to determine the role of social media communication approach in reputation established in the minds of society and organizations, this chapter aims to reveal the effect of collective communication of corporate accounts in social media platforms on brand/corporate reputation from the aspects of both corporate communication and target publics. Another objective of this research is to reveal the effect of corporate social media accounts on the purchasing decisions in establishment of opinion of target publics regarding the organization.

In parallel with this objective, the mobile ethnography method, which is one of the qualitative methods used in researches, and the digital content analysis methods were utilized, and the data obtained from both methods were synthetized. The concept of mobile ethnography refers to the implementation of ethnography method, which is one of the qualitative research methods frequently used in communication studies, in digital platforms. It consists of the combination of *ethno*, which etymologically means people, and *graphy*, which means documentation (Kozinetz 2010). Based on the observation of human behaviors, ethnography is used in brand-related communication studies in order to obtain the data that are important for understanding the rituals and their effects (Baily 1987). For the analysis of digital content influencing the attitude of target publics towards the organization, the corporate social network interaction analyzing method was employed.

Research Method

From the results obtained, all of the contents produced by the organizations and users within the scope of official Twitter account of Vestel brand between 10 July 2017 and 10 September 2017 were analyzed (Table 2). This time period was selected randomly to reflect a process of corporate official account interaction. The main objective in analyzing this content was to reveal the qualification of content, which affected the target publics constituting the sample group. In this analysis, all of the positive, negative, and neutral comments were grouped and discussed by using sentiment analysis technique. Thus, it was aimed to determine the qualification of content affecting the perception in the minds of target publics in journey to the purchasing. Ethnography is both an observation and interviewing technique, what provides to understand the individual behaviour, belief and attitude in a social context (Barbie 2007). For this purpose, ethnography technique were applied to understand visitor perception, experience, expectations during the visits. Additionally, the ethnographies applied as mobile ethnographies, which method is applied via WhatsApp discussions and sharing during the market visiting experience. Ethnographic questions were applied by application during the market visits of participants.

Table 1. The quota of qualitative research sample

Mobil Ethnography	Age	Social Status	Occupation
4	18-25	BC1	Student
4	26-55		White Collars
4	26-55		Blue Collars

Research Sample

Research sample was constructed according two different research methods for sentiment analysis and descriptive analysis. Vestel, one of the strongest actors in the electronics industry, was taken as the corporate representative of study sample in scope of its official twitter account timeline. As a case study the corporation is selected due to being a Turkish company with powerful reputation. The timeline of corporate official twitter account between mentioned dates was followed and all corporate twitter contents have been analyzed as the research sample for examining the reflection of community on real-time audiences. For this sentiment analysis method is used to understand the reflection of users in terms of positive, negative or neutral. After analyzing the corporate twitter account mobile ethnography technique is used as a qualitative method to observe and understand the attitude of consumers who visit electronics markets and how the twitter eco-system affects their attitude during the shopping. From this perspective, in order to find the answers to the questions such as "how has the reputation of Vestel in social media been shaped", "how effective is this digital information distribution in determining the perception of target publics in process of purchasing an electronic product", and "how guiding is the role of organization's social media interaction in this process". The mobile ethnography method was employed with participation of 12 subjects for two weeks in the first step of this research. The sample consists of three main groups representing different age groups, as shown in Table 1.

In this part, purposive sampling technique were applied to select participants. Purposive sampling provides researchers to observe the units that are appropriate for research judgment criteria. Participants represented each socio economic statue (SES) group, as B SES group and C1 SES group based on Turkish Statistical Institute in 2017. In order to understand differentiation perceptions among different social groups. Within the scope of our sample, the study aimed to determine how a role the corporate social media communication has in the perceptions of consumers from different social economic status (SES).These groups were further divided into subgroups named students, white collars, and blue collars, and there were equal number of men and women in each group. This study has certain limitations since it includes only the contents in Twitter among the corporate social media accounts and the sample consisted of only the subjects living in İstanbul.

Research Findings

In the process of mobile ethnography executed within the present study, it was observed that the comments of other users in social media networks play an important role in establishment of participants regarding an organization/brand. While making a decision regarding a brand/organization, the participants were observed to read the comments in corporate social media accounts. The majority of the participants, who visited the social media accounts of brand before going to the point-of-sale, spent less time in electronic product stores of brands, towards which they have negative attitudes, and more time in stores of brands, towards which they have positive attitudes. The participants in this group were asked about which brands have stronger reputation. In their answers, it was observed that the brands, towards which they have positive impressions, came to the forefront in their social media comments, whereas the subjects thought that the reputation of brands, towards which they have negative impressions, was at lower level. Another attention grabbing point is that the participants established their opinions regarding a brand or organization by analyzing the likes and interaction rates of posts sent by the corporate social media accounts of the organizations. A group of participants (26-55 white collars), who did a research before the purchasing process, was observed to be interested less in the products and campaign posts that received less like, whereas they were interested more in the posts with higher numbers of user comments and sharing.

Regarding this group of participants, it is interesting that the participants that were about to buy a TV allocated minimum time to the products of Vestel in the stores, which they visited. Considering the reason for this situation, it was determined that some of the participants (26-55 white collars and blue collars) specified that the comments reporting the complaints about aftersales services, which were posted to corporate accounts, played significant role. On the other hand, the participants, who visited the electronics store without prior research, paid attention to the comments and posts related with the product during their store experience. This group of participants was observed to obtain information about the brand from domains such as Twitter or forums and to make their brand selection in this parallel. Almost half of the participants in this group declared that they paid attention to the products in Vestel TV category because of the campaign opportunities but they avoided from buying them because of the feedbacks in social media. Considering the responses of 12 participants, who were about to buy an electronic product, to the questions about the reputation of brands, it was observed that Vestel brand fell behind in terms of the corporate reputation. Accordingly, majority of the participants criticize Vestel brand from the aspects of aftersales customer services and use of direct message in social media posts, thus Vestel brand loses trust. The majority of participants consider silence or low level of interaction of the company regarding the critics about aftersales complaint comments as a factor, which abuses the trust and destroys the reputation of company.

Most of the participants, who were asked to assess the effect of official twitter account of corporation on the corporate reputation from the aspect of content, declared it as a brand that does not have an assuring reputation in this category. From this perspective, official Twitter account of Vestel consists of the whole of contents prompting negative effect on corporate reputation and image. Considering the results obtained from the mobile ethnography part of research, official Twitter account of corporation, which is out of focus by the target publics in terms of corporate and brand reputation, is discussed in second part.

Given the interaction analysis of corporation official Twitter account during the given period, it can be seen that 40 of total interactions were negative, and that these interactions consists of complaints focusing on the aftersales services and price.12 neutral and 8 positive comments focus on the local brand and nationalism (Figure 1) and do not include the service process. Another point drawing attention in content analysis is that the contents produced and posted in relation with the products and services, in order to announce the activities related with corporate reputation, received very few interactions when compared to the number of followers.

Figure 1. The interaction proportion of the comments

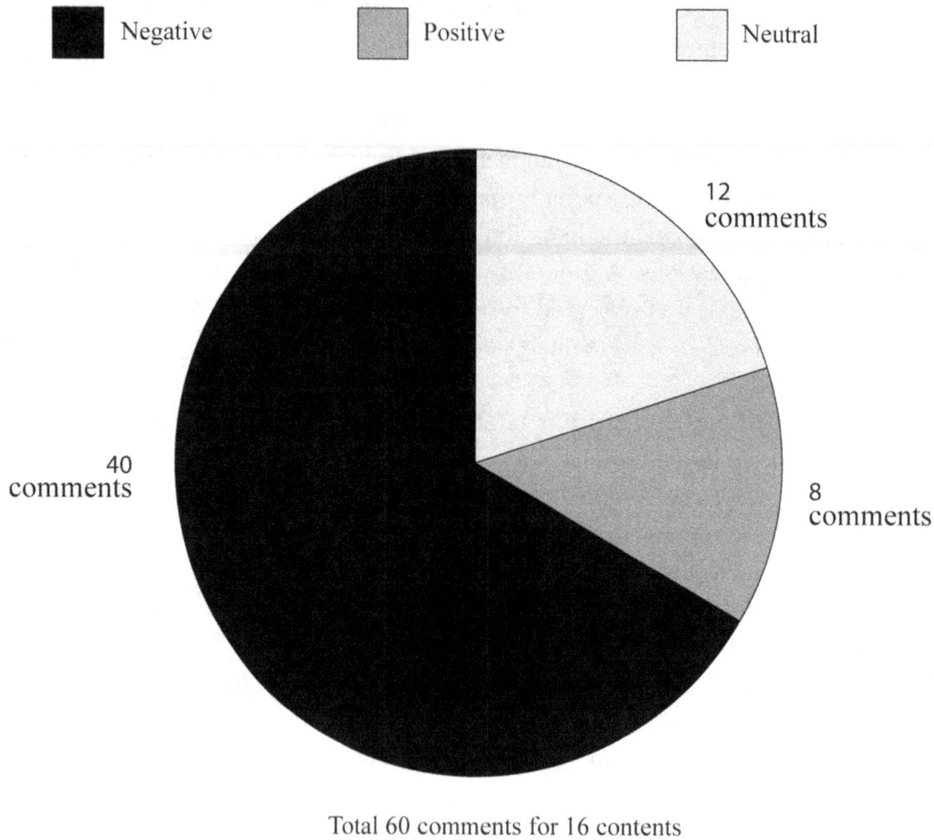

In total, 16 contents were having only 15 interactions in terms of positive response. However official twitter account of organization have 85.9K followers the interactions volume of the contents is very low when compared to the follower volume, which shows that Vestel is one of the corporation that is not able to manage the social media community in an effective way in order to express its contexts and generate interaction in cyber-place.

Figure 2 shows the most of the negative comments of audiences focus on after sales supports and product defects among the 40 negative interactions, what the main issues of reputation are in terms of publics' perception and 7 positive comments on being a domestic brand among the 8 positive comments. Most people complain about the weakness of after sales support services including account executive attitude towards customers during the crisis period, availability, fixing service quality. In parallel with the findings, most of the participants' highlights weaknesses of organizations after sales support services during the mobile ethnographies. The after sales supports connotes the participants incredible corporate characterize when its effects observed during the ethnography. This indicates that social media public relations strategy of company is inefficient and cannot ensure the interaction with target public. Additionally, the results of the research part show that consumers are affected by the social media interactions of brands/corporates' official twitter accounts; even the sample brand is a mal-sample of community management. Hence, the brands/corporations that adapt multilateral symmetrical communications approaches towards the digital publics can sustain the corporate reputation in this digital era.

Figure 2. The classifications of the reactions

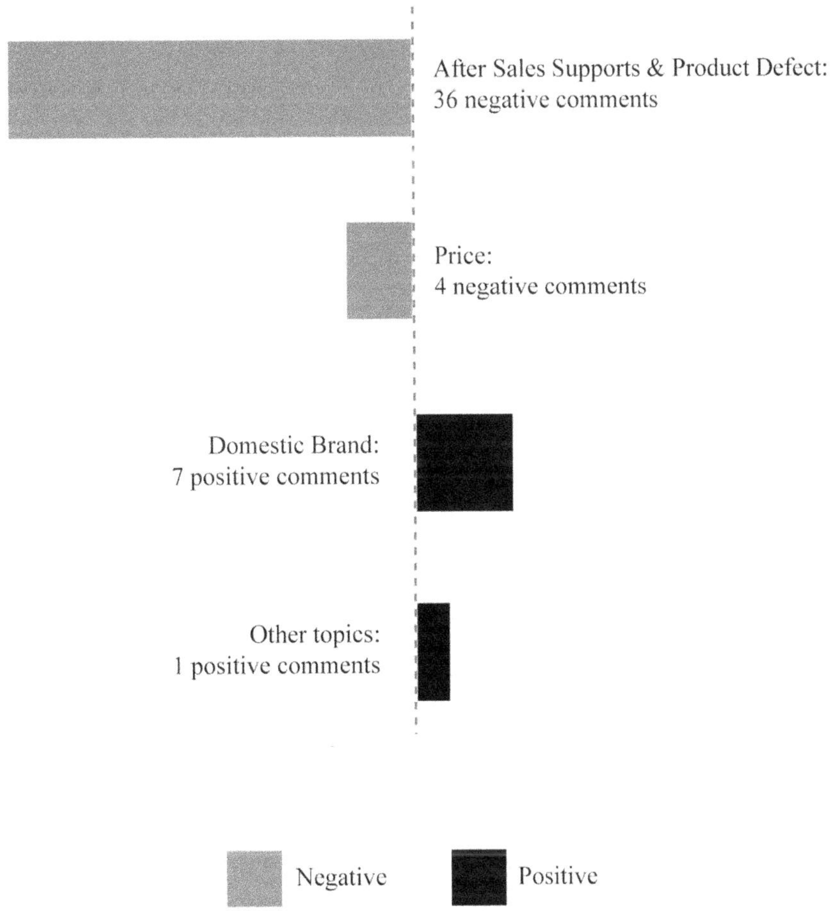

CONCLUSION

The advancing communication technologies bring the individual communication habits into the forefront in terms of corporate communication efforts. The organizations, which were realizing their strategic communication plans by interacting with target publics through traditional media only ten years before, now face with a change. Because of the use of mobile internet and because the consumption of internet in social domain became an environment that re-determines the rules of life, the communication that have been towards the individual has gained a direction from individual to masses, as well as transforming into a multidirectional form. In other words, the instrument replaced the message. Thus, the collective societies defined as the target publics by the organizations and had no exact active role in communication process, changed their roles and they became the publics that actively participate into the communica tion process of organization/brand and even constructing the reflected perception of organization. The active participation of the target publics into the communication process has the communication professionals have difficulties in managing the information flow regarding the organization. This information cluster, which is very hard to manage and distributed very rapidly, becomes one of the determinants of corporate and brand reputation.

From this perspective, the public relations efforts carried out for social media societies, as in examined case, have significant effects on the behavior of target public. Because of its multilayered structure, adopting the communication approaches taking the principle of transparency, as base in managing the corporate data in this new communication environment is very important to ensure the sustainability of corporate reputation. Social media societies come to the forefront as the groups, in which the users maintain interaction because of their sense of belonging. The interaction-based structure of corporate communication executed with this society is the determinant of the quality of corporate information spread over throughout the web. The users having high number of followers play effective role in the distribution of both positive and negative contents. From this aspect, the communication approach that might create brand ambassadors within these societies would feature the target public in production of content and ensure the society with positive motivation. The iconic brands and organizations such as Coca Cola have realized the importance of social media PR and focused on the strategies, in which the old users take part during the content production. However, in Turkey, many organizations and brand have not adopted the interaction-oriented communication approach ensuring the success in social media public relations. Considering the fact that the consumer and influencer group will consist of Z- and Y-generations called digital immigrants very soon, It is anticipated that organizations will not integrate into the dynamics of this new communication environment, will fall behind in terms of corporate reputation in Turkey, as in other countries. At this point, multilayered, symmetrical and interaction-oriented character of communication with this new and multilayered target public will be a strategic unity that might contribute to corporate reputation in perception of publics.

REFERENCES

Albee, A. (2015). *The attention economy: the impact of attention scarcity on modern marketing*. Retrieved from lookbook.com

Bailey, K. D. (1987). *Methods of social research*. New York: The Free Press.

Balmer, J. M. T., & Gray, E. R. (1999). Corporate identity and corporate communications: Creating a competitive advantage. *Corporate Communications*, *4*(4), 171–176. doi:10.1108/EUM0000000007299

Barbie, E. (2007). *The Practice of social research*. Boston: Cengage Learning Publishing.

Bıçakçı, A. B., & Genel, Z. (2016). A theoretical approach for sustainable communication in city branding: multilateral symmetrical communication model. In A. Bayraktar & C. Uslay (Eds.), *Strategic Place Branding Methodologies and Theory for Tourist Attraction* (pp. 41–66). IGI Global.

Çakır, H. (2016). *Corporate reputation management in social media*. İstanbul: Kriter Publishings.

Cassimon, D., Engelen, P. J., & Liederkerke, L. V. (2014). When the firms invest in corporate social responsibility. *Tjalling C.Koopmans Research Institute Discussion Paper, 14*(6), 1715-1728.

Castels, M., & Cardosso, G. (2008). *The network society. From knowledge to policy*. Johns Hopkins Center for Transatlantic Relations Press.

Chong, M. (2012). Importance of corporate reputation. *The Business Times*, *11*(11), 11–15.

Cutlip, S. M., Center, A. H., & Broom, G. M. (2006). *Effective Public Relations*. Upper Saddle River, NJ: Pearson Publishings.

Davenport, T. H., & Beck, J. (2001). *The attention economy*. Boston: Harvard Business School Press. doi:10.1145/375348.376626

Dijkmans, C., Kerkhof, P., & Beukeboom, C. J. (2015). A stage to engage: Social media use and corporate reputation. *Tourism Management Journal*, *47*, 58–67. doi:10.1016/j.tourman.2014.09.005

Donat, J., & Boyd, B. (2004). Public displays of connection. *BT Technology Journal*, *22*(4), 71–82. doi:10.1023/B:BTTJ.0000047585.06264.cc

Doorley, J., & Garcia, H. D. (2007). *Reputation management. The key the successful public relations and corporate communications*. New York: Taylor & Francis Group.

Fombrun, C. J. (1996). Reputation: Realizing value from the corporate image. Harvard Business School Press, 3(2), 101-111.

Fombrun, C. J., Gardberg, N., & Sever, J. (2000). The reputation quotient: A multistakeholder measure of corporate reputation. *Journal of Brand Management*, *7*(4), 241–225. doi:10.1057/bm.2000.10

Fombrun, C. J., & Van Riel, C. (1997). The reputational landscape. *Corporate Reputation Review*, *1*(1), 5–13. doi:10.1057/palgrave.crr.1540008

Fombrun, C. J., & Van Riel, C. (2004). *Fame and fortune: how successful companies build winning reputations*. Upper Saddle River, NJ: Pearson Education, Inc.

Formbrun, C. J., & Foss, C. B. (2005). The reputation quotient. Developing a reputation quotient. *Newsletter of Worldwide Communications Research, 4*(3). Retrieved from www.reputationinstitute.com

Fournier, S., & Lee, L. (2009). Getting brand communities right. *Harvard Business Review*, *87*(4), 105–111. PMID:19736854

Genel, Z. (2017). Sustainable communication as a component of corporate reputation. In A. S. Özdemir (Ed.), *Reputation Management Techniques in Public Relations* (pp. 38–55). IGI Global.

Global Strategic Communications Inc. (n.d.). *Corporate Reputation Review International Journal*. Henry Stewart Publications. Retrieved from www.firesteinco.com/reputation

Grunig, J. E. (2009). Paradigms of global public relations in an age of digitalization. *Prism*, *6*(2), 1–19.

Grunig, J. E., & Hunt, T. (1984). *Managing public relations*. New York: Holt, Rinehart and Winston.

Grunig, J. E., & Hunt, T. (2002). The effect of relationships on reputation and reputation on relationships: a cognitive, behavioral study. *Proceedings of PRSA Educator's Academy 5th Annual International, Interdisciplinary Public Relations Research Conference*.

Henning, T., Malthouse, E. C., Friege, C., Gensler, S., Loschat, L., Rangaswamy, A., & Skiera, B. (2010). The impact of new media on consumer relationships. *Journal of Service Research*, *13*(3), 311–330. doi:10.1177/1094670510375460

Kadıbeşegil, S. (2015). *Reputation management*. İstanbul: Medicat Publishing Ltd.

Kanto, S. D., Run, E. C., & İsa, A. H. (2016). The reputation quotient as a corporate reputation measurement in the Malaysian banking industry: A confirmatory factor analysis. *Social and Behavioral Sciences, 219*(65), 409–415.

Kaplan, A. M., & Haenlein, M. (2009). Users of the world, unite the challenges and opportunities of social media. *Business Horizons, 53*(1), 59–68. doi:10.1016/j.bushor.2009.09.003

Kemp, S. (2017). Digital in 2017. *Global Owerview Houtsuite*. Retrieved from www.wearesocial.com

Keskin, S., & Baş, M. (2016). *The effects of social media on consumers behaviour*. Retrieved from iibfdergisi.gazi.edu.tr/index.php/iibfdergisi/article/view/902

Khang, H., Ki, E., & Ye, L. (2012). Social media research in advertising, communication, marketing, and public relations. *Journalism & Mass Communication Quarterly, 89*(2), 279–298. doi:10.1177/1077699012439853

Kılıç, Ş. O., & Genel, Z. (2018). The impact of social media and technology companies on digital storytelling. In C. S. Csoares & E. Simão (Eds.), Trends, Experiences, and Perspectives on Immersive Multimedia Experiences and Augmented Reality (pp. 147–170). IGI Global Publishing.

Koçak, S. (2015). The role and the importance of public relations in the cities/ countries marketing. *International Multilingual Academic Journal., 2*(1), 82–93.

Köksal, Y., & Özdemir, Ş. (2013). An investigation on place of social media in promotion mix as a communications device. *The Journal of Faculty of Economics Suleyman Demirel University, 18*(1), 323–337.

Kozinetz, V. (2010). *Netnography: doing ethnographic research online*. Sage Publications.

Lee, M. & Youns, J. (2009).*The new community rules marketing on the social web*. O'Reilly Media and Publishing.

Matthews, L. (2010). Social media and the evolution of corporate communications. *The Elon Journal of Undergraduate Research in Communications, 1*(1), 17–23.

Matuleviciene, M., & Stravinskiene, J. (2015). The importance of stakeholders for corporate reputation. *Inzinerine Ekonomika-Engineering Economics, 26*(1), 75–83.

McGuire, J. B., Schneeweis, T., & Branch, B. (1990). Perceptions of firm quality: A cause or result of firm performance. *Journal of Management, 16*(1), 167–180. doi:10.1177/014920639001600112

McLennan, A., & Howell, G. V. J. (2011). Social networks and the challenge for public relations. *Asia Pacific Public Relations Journal, 11*(34), 21–39.

Özbay, D., & Selvi, Y. (2014). The measurement of corporate reputation: A proposal of model. *The Journal of Istanbul University Administration Faculty, 25*(76), 198–212.

Parrish, M., Elliot, N., Riley, N., & Wise, J. (2010). *How to create an effective brand presence on Facebook*. Forrester Research Online Facebook Web Track. Retrieved from go.forrester.com

Perlberg, S., & Seetharaman, D. (2016). Facebook signs deals with media companies, celebrities for facebook live. *The Wall Street Journal*. retrieved from www.wjs.com

Quelch, J. A., & Klein, L. R. (1996). The Internet and ınternational marketing. *Sloan Management Review*, *37*, 60–75.

Raub, W., & Weesie, J. (1990). Reputation and efficiency in social interactions: An example of network effects author. *American Journal of Sociology*, *96*(3), 626–654. doi:10.1086/229574

Roda, C., & Nabeth, T. (2006). Attention management in virtual community environments. *Journée de recherche de l'AIM Innovation et Systèmes d'Information,* 1-12. Retrieved from www.jstor.org

Roper, S., & Fill, C. (2012). *Corporate reputation brand and communication*. London: Harlow Pearson Publishings.

Ryan, D. (2014). *Digital marketing*. İstanbul: Türkiye İş Bankası Publishings.

Schwaiger, M. (2004). Components and parameters of corporate reputation an empirical study. *Schmalenbach Business Review*, *56*(1), 46–71. doi:10.1007/BF03396685

Szwajkowski, E., & Figlewicz, R. E. (1999). Evaluating corporate performance: A comparison of the fortune reputation survey and the Socrates social rating database. *Journal of Managerial*, *11*(2), 137–154.

Toffler, A. (2008). *The third wave*. İstanbul: Koridor Publishings.

Uncles, M. D., Dowling, G. R., & Hammond, K. (2003). Customer loyalty and customer loyalty programs. *Journal of Consumer Marketing*, *20*(4), 294–316. doi:10.1108/07363760310483676

Valck, K., Bruggen, G. H. V., & Wierenga, B. (2009). Virtual communities: A marketing perspective. *Decision Support Systems*, *47*(3), 185–203. doi:10.1016/j.dss.2009.02.008

Van Dijck, J. (2013). *The culture of connectivity: a critical history of social media*. New York: Oxford University Press. doi:10.1093/acprof:oso/9780199970773.001.0001

Vardarlı, K. (2013). *Digital eclipse marketing communications and human*. İstanbul: Mediacat Publishings.

Watson, T., & Kitchen, P. J. (2010). Reputation management: corporate image and communication. *Bournemount University*. retrieved from www. eprints.bournemouth.ac.uk

Weber, L. (2009). *Marketing to the social web: how digital customer communities build your business*. John Wiley & Sons. doi:10.1002/9781118258125

Yalçın, F. G. (2016). *Social Media for small enterprises*. İstanbul: Abaküs Publishings.

KEY TERMS AND DEFINITIONS

Attention Economy: Attention is the most important source of digital economy that determines the quality of corporate communication.

Community Management: In today's world, community management is two-way and symmetrical management of the communication between target audiences and the target audiences themselves in digital platforms.

Digital Communication: The sum of communication practice that the digital platforms that allows the people to connect and interact to each other.

Digital Public Relations: According to the changing communication practices of traditional public relations practices, the applications converted to provide the most accurate communication with the target audience is called digital public relations.

Online Reputation: The collective attitude towards the brand, formed in the perception of target audience from the result of the positive and negative images of the institutions and brands in the digital communication environment.

Public Relations: Public relations is the professional approach of managing the communication circle between an organization and its publics.

Chapter 13
Taxation of Digital Business in Malaysia

Tee Say Kuek
Taylor's University, Malaysia

ABSTRACT

Governments across the world are looking at introducing the "digital tax," which will be imposed on technology companies and digital business players. Digital giants like Google, Amazon, Facebook, Apple, and Microsoft are benefiting from the strong growth of digital business. The Malaysian government has announced in the national 2019 budget that a digital tax will be implemented effective January 1, 2020. The rationale of the tax is that both the international and local businesses in the digital sector must pay their fair share of tax. Malaysia has been taxing income from e-commerce, but it has no guidelines on the taxation of income from digital business. Global digital businesses often avoid paying taxes in Malaysia because they have no physical presence in the country. This chapter looks at how Malaysia is reforming its laws and policies to ensure its tax base fully reflects the scale of transactions and profits generated by the digital economy.

INTRODUCTION

Today, digital business is big business. Digital businesses have become a lucrative segment of the economy. Consumers are spending more money online and the growing digital economy has enabled consumers to be familiar with digital products and services. This new digital age has encouraged the emergence of an enormous variety of new products and services, easily accessed online. The digitization of the global economy creates huge economic opportunities and companies are gearing towards digital sources of revenue and digital channels. Digital giants like Google, Amazon, Facebook, Apple, Microsoft and Alibaba (global companies that transact business in the digital space) are benefitting from the strong growth of digital business. The digital platforms providing search engines, social media, virtual marketplaces and online advertising services have transformed lives for the better. However, it is also a challenge for governments to ensure that the tax systems are fair by also taxing income derives from the digital economy. It is not fair that the lucrative digital platform business can avoid paying tax

DOI: 10.4018/978-1-5225-9697-4.ch013

while conventional business cannot. Therefore, it is important that tax legislations must keep up with the changing business models as a result of advancing technology in business.

TAXING THE DIGITAL BUSINESS

While digital business platforms generate billions of dollars in revenue, many digital enterprises are not liable to pay tax. In fact, tax evasion in the digital economy has become a growing concern to governments worldwide (Bacache-Beauvallet & Bloch 2018). The advent of the digital economy poses great challenges to the international tax arena. Governments worldwide, including Malaysia, are looking at introducing the "digital tax", which will be imposed on technology companies and e-commerce players. Tax authorities across the world are reviewing the ways to collect taxes from digital enterprises under the current international rules. The Organisation for Economic Cooperation and Development's (OECD) view is that the digital economy should be taxed on the same principle that is currently being used to tax traditional businesses. Currently, the international tax law is lagging behind the business models in the digital era.

The reason is international permanent establishment rules are used to determine how much a company should be taxed based on a threshold of its activity in a given country. The concept is mainly based on physical presence such as the existence of offices, factories, warehouses etc. in a country. Based on existing tax rules, these digital companies report their profits in the country where their businesses are based, thereby depriving other countries of potential tax revenue.

The keys to classic business models are of little relevance for Silicon Valley giants like Google, Amazon & others. Today, digital businesses are able to have significant economic or digital presence without necessarily having a substantial physical presence. For instance, in July 2017 the French Government has failed to recover 1.1 billion euros (US$1.3 billion) for years 2005 to 2010 from Google as there was no permanent establishment in France (Reichert 2017). As such, France is pushing for digital tax to be implemented.

There is increasing pressure on governments to ensure that digital business owners pay their fair share of tax. Current taxation concepts for international cases were basically developed for the world in the early 20th century. According to Nellen (2015), tax practitioners are continually facing challenges in both understanding the technology and how tax rules apply. OECD und EU are examining alternative taxation concepts for digital business models. The US government is also keen to find an effective way to tax the new digital economy and is watching EU's plan closely. The Malaysian government has been studying the possibility of collecting taxes (indirect tax and direct tax) from foreign companies that offer digital services in Malaysia. Malaysia has now confirmed that a digital tax will be coming to the country based a similar model and timeline in Singapore. According to the World Bank Group (2018), tax imposition on the digital economy will allow diversification of the Malaysia's revenue sources. Currently there is no common action to tackle the taxing of digital business globally and each country is making its own proposals. There is a need for a global solution to the issue of how, what and where to tax income from the digital economy.

E-COMMERCE IN MALAYSIA

In 2016, the Malaysian Ministry of International Trade and Industry launched a new eCommerce Initiative with the goal of including about 80 percent of small - and medium size enterprises into the world of eCommerce. According to Malaysian Ministry of International Trade and Industry (2016) glossary, e-commerce is defined as, 'Electronic business transactions, commerce or internet trade. May be conducted between companies (B2B) or between companies and customers (B2C) that are wholly or partially conducted over the internet or similar public or private computer networks'.

The Ministry further intends to expand market access for more than 87 million digital customers in the ASEAN region. Some thrust areas of the National eCommerce Strategic Roadmap includes the speeding up the adoption of eCommerce by the sellers, increasing adoption of eProcurement by businesses, lifting non-tariff barriers (such as e-fulfillment, cross-border, e-Payment, and consumer protection), realigning existing economic incentives, making strategic investments in eCommerce players, and promoting national brand to boost cross-border eCommerce.

The high rates of eCommerce usage in Malaysia is due to improved internet and mobile connectivity and government support and encouragement. Malaysia boasts 15.3 million online shoppers (50 percent of the population) and 62 percent of mobile users their devices to shop online (Malaysia Country Commercial Guide, 2017). Online shoppers are attracted by the convenience of online shopping where there is a wide range of products offered with product prices indicated and availability of purchasers' reviews.

TAXATION OF E-COMMERCE TRANSACTIONS IN MALAYSIA

Before the advent of digital business, Malaysia has been taxing income from electronic commerce business. Basically, e-commerce is the buying and selling over the internet. Electronic commerce (e-commerce) is defined as 'any commercial transactions conducted electronically. These include the activity of providing information, promotion and advertising, marketing, supply, order or delivery of goods and services, even though the payment and delivery relating to such transactions may be conducted offline'. Income from e-commerce activities, as with other business and enterprise transactions, are taxable. Individuals and companies involved in e-commerce activities are subject to tax under the Malaysia Income Tax Act (1967).

In 2013, the Inland Revenue Board of Malaysia (IRB) has issued a guideline on the taxation of electronic commerce which explains the income tax treatment in respect of income derived from e-commerce transactions. It must be pointed out that the taxation of e-commerce transactions is not a separate tax from income tax (Veerinder 2013). Among other things, the guidelines explain the scope of charge, the tax liability for business, treatment of server and website and an examination of business models. The guidelines should be read together with the Income Tax Act 1967 (ITA 1967) and other relevant legislations and legal procedures available. There are various laws governing e-commerce such as the Electronic Commerce Act 2006 and the Electronic Government Activities Act 2007, Personal Data Protection Act 2010 and the Digital Signature Act 1997. Basically, the IRB has adopting the principle of neutrality where the same tax treatment is meted out to both e-commerce and conventional business. Therefore, taxpayers should expect the same treatment where the business transactions are the same and carried out in similar context. The OECD has also set out various principles on the right of a country to tax digital transactions.

Malaysia has the right to tax income from e-commerce business if the business is carried on in Malaysia. This is based on the 'business operation' test. The location of the server/website is not a determining factor to decide whether an individual is taxable. This is confirmed by Paragraph 5.1 of the e-commerce guidelines which states that although a server and website facilitate the performance of business activities, it does "not carry any meaning in determining derivation of income."

Paragraph 4 of the IRB's guideline explains the scope of tax liability for a business under the law. The pertinent points are:

Generally, income of a person accruing in or derived from Malaysia is subject to income tax in Malaysia.

Where business operations are carried on in Malaysia, the income attributable to those business operations is deemed to be derived from Malaysia. The scope and extent of business operations in Malaysia is an important factor in considering whether income is derived from Malaysia.

In the context of e-commerce, some determinant business activities that may be taken into account include sourcing of content, procurement of goods, promotions, advertisement, selling, updating and maintaining of website, uploading and downloading of contents, etc.

- In cases where a Double Taxation Agreement (DTA) is applicable, determination of Malaysia's taxing right over the business income is based on the Permanent Establishment (PE) concept.

Paragraph 6 examines various business models of e-commerce with varying assumptions, in each case, stating in conclusion, the IRB's position on whether or not business income is deemed to be derived from Malaysia.

Even though Malaysia has been taxing income from e-commerce, it has no guidelines on the taxation of income from digital business. Tax legislation is generally enacted without the rapid advances in telecommunications technology in mind and its application to the new technological developments tends to be limited to a particular scenario.

This guideline on the taxation of e-commerce is too general and of little use in its application to the digital economy as it applies to business operations carried out in Malaysia or where income is attributable to those business operations deemed to be derived from Malaysia. The digital tax is only for foreign online business, which means businesses that has no establishment in Malaysia and operates from outside the country. In short, digital tax is imposed on foreign companies providing online services or products. These foreign online businesses do not have to pay for GST (now abolished) previously as the GST model only collects tax from online businesses in the country. Digital service providers that are operating outside of Malaysia are not subjected to the same tax obligation. Technological innovation and internet growth have impacted trade relations, production processes and products, and company organization. The digital economy has succeeded in dematerialization of activities and fragmentation of economic functions, assets and risks, thus excluding permanent establishment. Because of these peculiarities, the digital economy poses significant problems for taxation schemes, especially the qualification of the values to be taxed and their territorial location. When it comes to the digital economy and taxation, cross-border transactions pose great challenges for most governments. Taxing digitalized activity was first addressed within the OECD's BEPS project. The issues of base erosions and profit shifting to avoid the payment of income tax have become a major problem for tax jurisdictions all over the world.

INTRODUCTION OF DIGITAL TAX IN MALAYSIA

The 2019 Budget will see the introduction of the digital Tax in Malaysia. During the recent midterm review of the 11th Malaysia Plan, the government has indicated that it plans to introduce a new tax on "online transactions". Malaysia will be the second country in Southeast Asia after Singapore to introduce a tax scheme for the digital business (Chew 2018). The rationale of the tax is to ensure a level playing field between international and local businesses in the digital economy. Global digital businesses normally do not pay taxes in Malaysia as these companies do not have permanent establishments as there is no physical presence in the country. Further, Malaysia cannot tax cross-border transactions in the digital economy as there is no tax rule to provide for it. As these digital businesses declare their profits in their home country, where their headquarters are based, Malaysia is deprived of potential revenue. The Finance Minister has said that if the imposition of digital tax is put aside, the nation will be losing revenue. In addition to this, the digital tax can help to strengthen and widen the government's revenue base. According to the World Bank report, Malaysia's past performance offers substantial optimism about the future of its digital economy and it is important to safeguard future digital tax revenues.

The announcement digital tax was made during a reading of the national budget in the parliament by Malaysian finance minister Lim Guan Eng (Ministry of Finance Malaysia 2018). Lim said in his speech: "For imported online services by consumers, foreign service providers will be required to register and remit related service taxes to the Malaysian customs, effective January 1, 2020." The online services include software, music, video, and any digital advertising. He said that the tax measures will balance competition between retail outlets and online stores, especially those owned by overseas companies. Sales and Service Tax (SST) will be imposed on all imported services and this will enable local service providers in information technology, engineering and graphic designs etc. to compete fairly with foreign firms.

The government did not provide the specifics of the planned taxes at this moment. It is looking at a new mechanism to impose digital tax towards overseas service content providers — foreign entities who provide services in Malaysia, as way to explore new sources of revenue for the country. The Finance Ministry has yet to decide on the tax rate to be imposed on the digital economy players and is still studying on the new mechanism to impose digital tax.

THE IMPACT OF DIGITAL TAX ON MALAYSIAN BUSINESSES AND CONSUMERS

While the reason for imposing digital tax in Malaysia is valid, several professionals and business owners are worried about its possible negative impact on tech companies and e-commerce businesses. The implication of imposing the new tax is that an additional tax has to be paid where there was none in the past. Inevitably, this could lead to the increase in price of online goods and services for all parties (Chew 2018). Sellers and service providers overseas, such as Lazada and Alibaba, will be particularly affected.

According to Laurence and Conor (2018), a new direct digital tax in Malaysia would increase the costs of digital goods and services, which consequentially could increase prices for consumers and businesses. In the short run, the government may collect more revenue from digital tax. However, in the long term the development of the digital economy may be affected especially for new start-ups and small and medium enterprises (SMEs). If digital tax is introduced in Malaysia, other countries will also follow suit and this will hinder Malaysian firms exporting their goods or services to those countries. They reasoned that Malaysia, as an open trading nation, will benefit more from a pro-trade, pro-innovation approach to the digital economy.

Impact on Consumers

Deloitte Malaysia Indirect Tax Partner, Senthuran Elalingam said, "From the consumer's perspective, digital services would be subject to the tax once the law takes effect, and if the service provider decides to pass on the tax by adding it to their existing price, then yes, the price would increase"(The Sun Daily, 2017). If you're an online gamer, or you subscribe to paid online services such as video or audio streaming, the digital tax can affect you as the charges and subscription fees could increase. However, as no guidelines have been determined, both consumers and online service providers will have to wait and see.

Ultimately, as a business practice, sellers and service providers will transfer some of the tax cost to the consumers by increasing the price. Further, if the digital tax rate is high and tax compliance tedious, some foreign sellers may not offer online products and services to Malaysian consumers. Whatever the possible outcomes, an online business promoting a product or service to Malaysian consumer must pay its fair share of tax. The mechanism of collecting and remitting digital tax to the government has not been finalized although discussions are being conducted with credit card companies. Probably, the credit card companies will collect the digital tax when their clients pay with their credit cards and then forward the tax collected to the Customs Department. Details as to the other modes of payment have not been revealed and therefore remain unknown.

Impact on Businesses

There is a fear that the implementation of the digital tax increases the possibility of double taxation to businesses. Currently, the government imposes a 10 percent withholding tax (WHT), which covers some digital transactions. The WHT applies to Malaysian companies' transactions – digital and non-digital – with foreign service providers. The IRB viewed the digital marketing payments to non-resident company as royalty income and hence will be subject to withholding Tax (WHT). WHT approach is an alternative to the collection of digital tax while waiting for future developments by the OECD.

Under the ITA 1967, WHT is applicable to certain payments (interest, royalty, services) made to non-resident companies by Malaysian companies. The Malaysian companies are required to deduct WHT from the gross sum and remit it to the government. With digital tax, is it possible that taxpayers may be subject to double taxation on the same income? There is likelihood that a business might pay both the WHT and SST on some digital transactions. As mentioned before, to lower business costs and avoid double taxation in this context, the government will be introducing a credit system for SST deduction, starting January 1, 2019 (The Borneo Post, 2018). The mechanism for this credit system has yet to be clarified.

At the moment, online services and goods are already subjected to import duties if it is from digital businesses operating outside of Malaysia. Therefore, if the digital tax is implemented, this could mean that consumers will be charged double tax. If they purchase goods online that are imported, they will be charged import duties, and then on top of that will also be charged the digital tax.

On the mechanism of the tax, the Institute for Democracy and Economic Affairs (2018) predicts that there might be two types of taxes that will be introduced. One would be a "direct tax" that targets the profits of foreign digital companies carrying out business in Malaysia. Possibly, the other would be an 'indirect tax' such as SST (a consumption tax) which would be imposed on oversea companies selling digital goods and services to consumers and users in Malaysia.

Amidst the uncertainties, the government has indicated its concerns and is working to introduce a tax scheme that is fair to all the players in the industry (Chew 2018). Malaysian Deputy Finance Minister Datuk Amiruddin Hamzah has said that, "This will definitely be a matter that we will look into deeply. We will come out with a new mechanism, but we are still studying it and we will impose something for them. If we put this matter (digital tax) aside, I think the nation will be losing revenue" (iPrice Group, 2018). The Malaysian Finance Minister Lim Guan Eng has stated that the IRB is expected to collaborate with international bodies to deal with international tax issues relating to the digital and sharing economies.

EU DEVELOPMENT ON DIGITAL TAX

The Malaysian government is observing the current global debate on the taxation of digital business and is assessing its implications on the introduction of digital tax in Malaysia. A global coherent strategy will prevent uncertainty, destabilization of level playing field and new tax abuse through new loopholes. International cooperation and agreement is the best long-term solution. However, discussion among nations is time consuming. The Malaysian Government has indicated that Malaysia would have to wait for the model adopted by EU to be used as a guide to prevent avoidance by digital business. The two standard-setting bodies concurrently studying digital taxation are the European Commission and the OECD.

Most countries in the EU want to tax companies like Apple, Google, Facebook, and Amazon. These companies have been criticized for not paying their fair share of tax in Europe and France is expecting them to pay their fair share (Fortune, 2018).The EU members' corporate tax system (with differing tax rates) most likely contribute to the tax avoidance of the large tech companies. The EU has examined the OECD's interim report on the taxation of the digital economy to the G20 since March 2018. France's proposal has been considered since March 2018, but other European countries have not embraced it. The plan would permit EU countries to tax internet companies' profits earned in their jurisdictions. Currently, digital companies pay an effective tax rate of 9.5% in the EU, whereas traditional businesses pay an effective rate of 23.2%. As can be seen, there is no unanimous agreement on the implementation of digital tax among the countries.

Smaller European countries (e.g. Luxembourg and Ireland), want EU to provide a global reform to digital taxation (Reuters, 2018). However, the discussion has dragged on for years without a solution in sight. The misgiving is that the digital tax may not benefit smaller nations. It may lead to counter measures from the United States where most of its affected companies are based or it may also affect innovation. France and Italy are looking for a quick solution as they have lost millions of euros of tax revenue. The reason is that digital companies are shifting their taxable profits to countries with lower tax rate.

The European Commission has proposed to impose a 3% levy on the revenues of digital businesses with a total annual revenue of over €750mil (RM3.6bil) and a yearly EU taxable revenue of €50mil (RM240mil). Any large tech company will be liable for tax if it makes money from digital advertising in a country or user data, regardless of its physical business presence. If the digital tax is approved by the EU members, it is forecasted that about £4.4bil (RM24bil) will be collected annually in Europe starting from 2019. In the interim, smaller European countries are supportive of the European Commission's proposal for an EU-wide 3 percent tax on digital revenues while waiting for an overhaul of tax rules on digital business.

Meanwhile, Reuters has reported that eleven of the 28 EU states are already considering their own national measures if no common plan is agreed. The disadvantage of this individual action without consensus among the countries in Europe is that it creates disproportionate tax rates across the Europe and undermines one of the aims of the EU.

The EU is not the only the entity looking at digital tax. The UK announced that it would implement a tax by 2020. Therefore, it can be seen that taxation of the digitalized economy will be adopted by more and more countries. Obviously, there would be various approaches to taxing digital businesses.

CONCLUSION

The digital economy plays an increasing role in Malaysia's journey towards becoming a high-income nation. According to the World Bank Group (2018), tax imposition on the digital economy will allow diversification of the Malaysia's revenue sources. The taxation of the digital economy is a multidimensional issue and is often very complicated because it involves cross-border digital transactions (Association of International Certified Professional Accountants, 2018). Effective approach to the taxation of the digitalized economy will be best achieved through multilateral action at the global level instead of different national approaches. According to Grinberg (2018), "One important goal in this difficult environment should be to reestablish some stability to the international tax regime" (p.55). Double taxation treaties, domestic tax incentives and commitments to international trade agreements will have to be reexamined to ensure compatibility and alignment with global proposals and efforts. A global coherent strategy will prevent uncertainty, destabilization of level playing field and new tax abuse through new loopholes.

The Malaysian Government has indicated that Malaysia will consider the model adopted by EU to be used as a guide to prevent avoidance by digital business. Malaysia will probably integrate OECD/EU's appropriate and meaningful solutions in her legislation to tax digital business. However, as discussed earlier, there is no unanimous decision yet on the taxation of digital business among the European countries. This has caused individual country to take unilateral tax measures based on political and revenue considerations. The resulting effect is an uneven tax landscape made up of diverse and different tax policies. Perhaps, in the interim, Malaysia could impose a fixed rate based on the gross income (or a prescribed threshold) of digital business. Meanwhile, digital business owners will have to stay tuned for further updates from the Malaysian government.

REFERENCES

Association of International Certified Professional Accountants. (2018). Taxation of the digitalized economy: A policy paper designed to educate, enlighten and stimulate discussion 2018. Durham, NC: Author.

Bacache-Beauvallet, M., & Bloch, F. (2018). Special issue on taxation in the digital economy. *Journal of Public Economic Theory*, *20*(1), 5–8. doi:10.1111/jpet.12285

Chew, J. (2018, November 5). Malaysia officially the second country in South East Asia to introduce a digital tax. *The Drum*. Retrieved from https://www.thedrum.com/opinion/2018/11/05/malaysia-officially-the-second-country-south-east-asia-introduce-digital-tax

Grinberg, I. (2018). *International Taxation in an Era of Digital Disruption: Analyzing the Current Debate*. Washington, DC: Georgetown Law Faculty Publications and Other Works.

Institute for Democracy and Economic Affairs. (2018). Tax in a Digital Age. Kuala Lumpur: IDEAS Policy Research Berhad. iPrice Group (2018, October17). Malaysia: the 2nd country in SEA with digital Tax. *Focus Malaysia*.

ITA Malaysia. (1967). *Part I to IV, Act 53*. Retrieved from http://www.agc.gov.my/agcportal/uploads/files/Publications/LOM/EN/Pindaan%20Act%2053%20-%2023%2011%202017.pdf

Malaysian Ministry of International Trade and Industry. (2016). *Malaysia's National eCommerce Strategic Roadmap*. Kuala Lumpur: MITI.

Ministry of Finance Malaysia. (2018). *Annual Budget Speech 2019*. Kuala Lumpur: MOF.

Nellen, A. (2015). Taxation and today's digital economy. *Journal of Tax Practice & Procedure*, *17*(2), 17–26.

Reichert, C. (2017, July 13). Google's billion-euro tax bill discharged by French court. *ZDNet*. Retrieved from https://www.zdnet.com/article/googles-billion-euro-tax-bill-discharged-by-french-court/

The Sun Daily. (2017, September 28). Digital tax raises concerns among Malaysian consumers. *The Sun Daily*. Retrieved from https://www.thestar.com.my/business/business-news/2017/09/28/digital-tax-raises-concerns-among-malaysian-consumers/

Veerinder, S. (2013). *Veerinder on Taxation* (3rd ed.). Kuala Lumpur: CCH.

World Bank Group. (2018). *Malaysia's Digital Economy*. Author.

KEY TERMS AND DEFINITIONS

Digital Business: Means the creation of new value chains and business opportunities that are delivered or subscribed over the internet or other electronic network that traditional businesses cannot offer.

Digital Tax: Means the taxation of the revenue of multinational corporations deriving from digital business.

Double Taxation: Means income taxes are paid twice on the same source of earned income or the same income is taxed in two different countries.

Electronic Commerce (E-Commerce): Means as any commercial transactions i.e. the buying and selling of goods or services conducted electronically.

Permanent Establishment: Means the physical presence such as the existence of offices, factories, warehouses, etc. in a country.

Chapter 14
Tools and Techniques Used for Customer Relationship Management:
Review and Case Studies

Geeta Sachdeva
National Institute of Technology Kurukshetra, India

ABSTRACT

Continuing to fulfill the requirements and needs of today's customer is a perplexing job for all the corporations. There have been a number of strategies developed to engage with customers, but few considerations have been paid to string them together in generating well-developed relationships. For of this reason companies are moving towards customer relationship management (CRM) to execute reliable strategies in engaging with customers. CRM emphasizes aiding companies thoroughly to manage the procedures involved in upholding good relationships with customers. This chapter discussed various strategies and examined case studies that adopted different techniques to engage with customers.

INTRODUCTION

In recent times, consumers are not concerned about the amount of profit they are producing for the organization but also have concerns on the quality of relation with the organization. Relationships have become one of the most influential differentiators that organizations should improve personal relationship with their clients, than concerned about the product, which they are offering to them (Yastrow, 2007).

As per Darling and Russ (2000), a relationship is the association amid two or more persons or groups and their contribution with each other, particularly how they act and feel towards each other and interconnect.

In present era, each business works in a linkage of relationships. It is the utmost elementary part of any existing set of objects and so is correct for the organization. It turns as an essential feature for development and pleasure to both those who supply a product or service and those who get it. Relation-

DOI: 10.4018/978-1-5225-9697-4.ch014

ship is a process wherein an organization is required to indulge in making connection with customer even if customer is not eager to be in relationship, this is the duty of organization to place customer on relationship channel and be careful in making relationship (Mathur, A. 2003).

Building relationships with customers is very beneficial for the companies as it gives incessant flow of incomes and returns, that upsurges with the passage of time and even it turns into constructive referrals, novel company prospects and sometimes a challenge to be focused and proficient. Thus, it aids in making robust, positive and equally advantageous connections for a long period. Every company has its restricted possessions and using these limited possessions to optimal level is extremely required. A business's job is to use its assets for making long-term lucrative relations with certain customers who are little in number instead of using its assets for numerous short term, unbalanced relationships or random customer acquisitions. Not all customers might own the similar rapport potential, but it is vital for a company to be attentive in choosing the customers for keeping extended relations with them.

STAGES OF RELATIONSHIPS

DeVito (1993) described that development of relationship is a lengthy procedure it does not occur all of sudden. Behavioral scientist usually uses the six-stage model to define the growth of relationships.

Figure 1. Six-Stage Model of Relationship
Source: DeVito (1993)

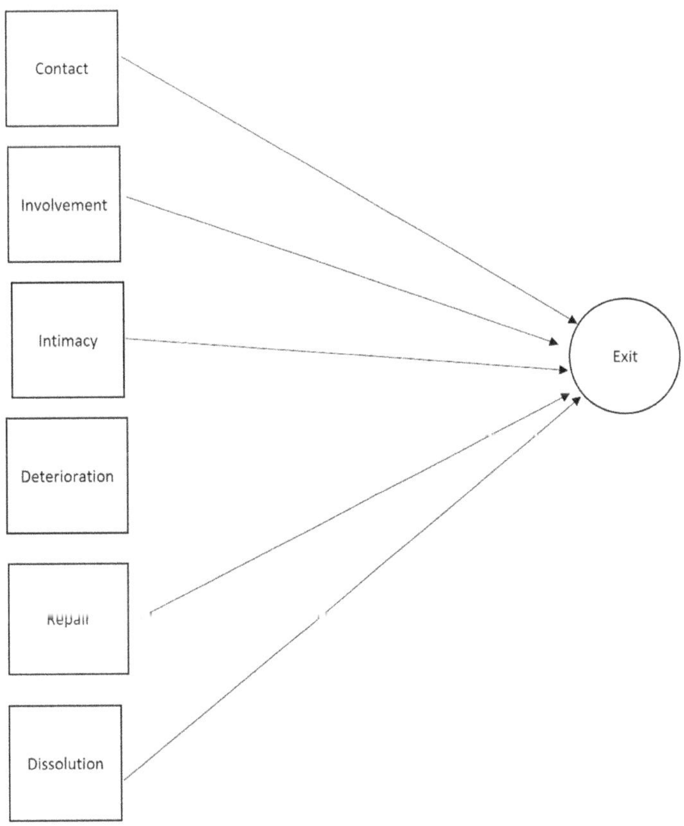

Contact

This is the first stage of relationship. Here persons meet for the first time, the first response is to evaluate other individual and then choose whether to engross or not to engross, and this choice is within very less period and intentional in nature. The difficulty happens when persons do not alter their early impressions, even when there is proof to the contrary. In such a circumstance, engagement finishes there and no relationship grows.

Involvement

This is the stage when persons involve more with one another, creating a light link of friendship, persons try to share information about them and engross in deeper discussions. This stage might result into a test trying to ascertain whether the other individual is ready to go to other level or do not want to move to the next level or might leave things as they are and might not be worried about evolving the relationship further to the next stage.

Intimacy

Relationship becomes deeper and more committed at this stage. At this level, personal commitment takes place, and connection can be felt amongst persons, and the time and exertion that the person is ready to put into this liaison. This might outcome into numerous results such as getting married or individuals publicly stating that they are good friends. Even after this stage, persons might be concerned about or might have apprehension like concern for security, concern for contentment, apprehension for excitement about safeguarding the relationship or fulfillment.

Deterioration

After the intimacy stage, it is possible that encounter and arguments will arise over minor thing. At times unimportant concerns might become reasons for main arguments. In this stage, communication reduces and there is very less expose as persons become offended.

Repair

At this level, relationships can be continued if individual wants and this can happen after the opportunity of repair. Persons might take assistance from a counselor and would work at reestablishing self-disclosure and communication if they were concerned about saving the relationship. A person might make a commitment to alter, but might not trail the same. An uneven relationship further confuses the matter and effective self-disclosure and communication is congested. If interpersonal repair works, then the relationship might become sturdier than it was before.

Dissolution

This is the last stage of relationship. At this stage, sometimes the relationship melts and the persons run the risk of annoyance and might hate each other. The update of the breakdown also becomes publicly which increases to the pressure of the circumstances. The significant communication finishes as the relationship deteriorates.

RELATIONSHIP MARKETING (RM)

Previous, the main emphasis was only on consumption. All human activities were limited only to the accessibility of products for consumption that was available in their scope. Gradually, attention shifted to production. Production done for consumption and then emphasis moved for exchange, with the passage of time actions of production was stretched towards consumption and sales. In sales age, production activities were performed completely for sales and the consideration was only on products. Whatsoever products were produced became marketable due to narrow supply. As the consideration moved to production, selling became a hard job due to enlarged supply. The transactional methodology to marketing was concerned with the key goal to achieve increased sales with the help of efficient management of the marketing mix with beneficial communications amid the customer and the product. The key purpose was to make sales and the factor of achievement in many transactions, income and productivity generally with a comparatively short-term focus. This is the phase when attention was moved from products to customers. This made companies to go in the direction of marketing and associated activities. An understanding and contentment of customers need have become most important for effective existence in the market (Higgins and Smith, 2000). The Relationship Marketing approach has triggered companies shift from the traditional method which concentrated on short-term transactions with a clear opening and ending, to a long-term customer relationship absorbed method.

RELATIONSHIP MARKETING: THE POWER OF CS

Marketing is considered as one eldest activities carried out by man, then again each time it is observed as the utmost topic of the business discipline. Therefore, marketing is observed as one of the utmost lively arenas in the management field. Previous, the focus was on the management of main Ps of the marketing mix such as product, price, promotion, and place and marketers did the same but had little or no consideration on after sales services or grievances of customers (Chadha 2002).

After 1980s onwards, the marketing scene has altered. Expansion in technology have carried radical alteration in accessibility of information to customers' that has led to upsurge in their level of knowledge and diverse variety of products to select from therefore moving towards upsurge in competition. The customer has become the essential point and all choices in the company have started to turn around the profit of the customers. Four Ps of marketing mix are characterized from sellers' point of opinion to stimulus buyer, but from customers' point of view, every marketing tool is vital to be intended to provide customer advantage. There are four such as Consumer, Cost, and Convenience and Communication. In today's atmosphere, the emphasis must be on the customer, not just promotion (Kotler, P. 2003).

Figure 2. Relationship marketing: The Power of Cs
Source: Chadha (2002)

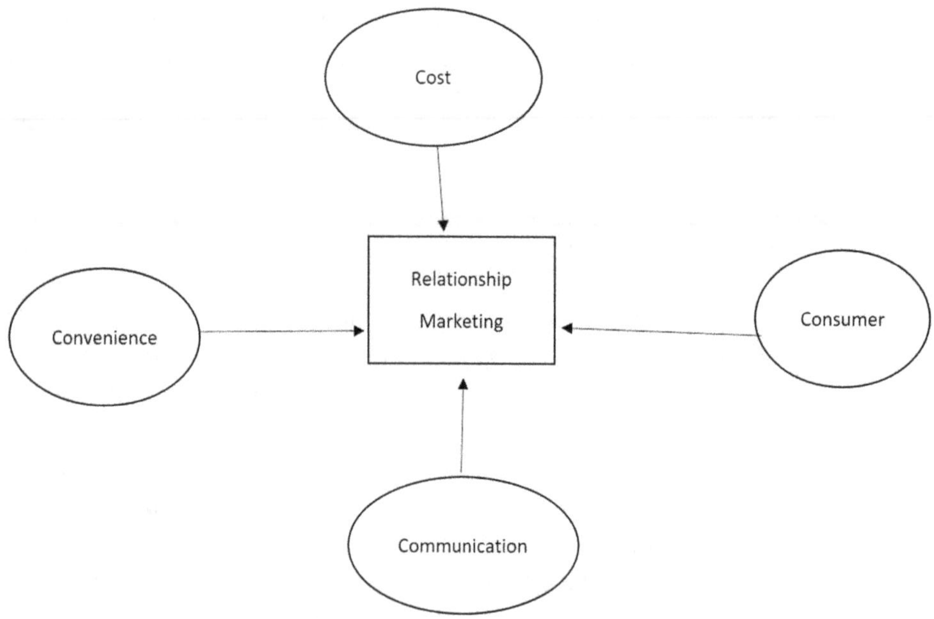

The main goal of relationship marketing is to uphold a healthy relationship with existing clients instead of creating new ones. Moreover, relationship marketing builds and maintains a base of faithful customers who are beneficial for the company (Chadha 2002).Relationship marketing approach recognized that the marketing mix is significant but at the similar time the emphasis to be moved from customer acquirement to customer retaining. Therefore, the fundamentals of RM are disciplined towards all-inclusive approach in recognizing the tastes and likings on single basis to cultivate and improve relationships throughout the customers' life.

RELATIONSHIP MARKETING (RM) AND CRM

Generally, it is observed that relationship marketing (RM) and customer relationship marketing are used interchangeably. Few knowledgeable marketing experts have established that CRM is a development of relationship marketing which increases important notions of customer retention. Relationship marketing is observed as marketing concept whereas customer relationship marketing is observed as a tool to convey out the idea. RM is applied as a strategy and comprises numerous activities. Likewise, maintaining long-term sales, retention, maintaining public relations, marketing and publicity campaigns while CRM includes of the operative errands that contains actions such as congregation of data about the clients, then consolidating and examining it to generate target customers profiles with the key objective of creating and maintaining robust customer relationships. As per Sheth and Parvatiyar (1992), CRM had established since pre industrial times. The source of CRM could be noticed in the eighties of the last century (Kotler et. al 2001). Hakansson (1982) was the first who marked its significance in industry and the word relationship marketing (RM) was primary used by Berry (1983). Mathena et.al

(2009) revealed the development of CRM that began from a single customer to turn as an application framework and contain other business relations.

It is taken as a business strategy that is intended to confirm success, returns and customer gratification (Gartner Group 2002). With this approach companies emphasis to fit themselves as a customer attentive corporation (Garatt, 2000). This approach strives to create, improve and enrich relationship with their targeted customers (Ryals and Payne 2001). In this strategy, companies try to form greater worth for both themselves and for customers (Sheth and Parvatiyar 2001; Rai 2008). It is not limited solitary inside the marketing section rather it should be taken as overall business strategy and should be vigorously include each part of the company (Little and Marandi 2003). This approach should also correctly managed else, it would just be a drain on shareholder worth (Stone and Foss 2001). Overall, it is combined organizational process joined with sales, marketing, services etc. to manage business with customers in a planned manner (Rutenbeck and Blaine 2006). It is developing as the dominant marketing motion for companies working in aggressively competitive environs. As per Gruen (1997), more or less organizations spend six times more to get customers than they do to retain them. Hence, number of companies are now considering their association with current customers to maintain them and upsurge their share of customer is buying. There are many international service firms, which are pioneers in evolving customer-retaining strategies such as, banks have relationship managers for handpicked customers, airlines have recurrent flyer plans to recompense faithful customers, telecom service operators provide customized services to their faithful customers, and tailored services are offered by the hotels for their consistent guests.

EVOLUTION OF CRM

Relationship marketing has not always been the vigorous software that numerous companies trust on today. In the earlier four decades, it has changed out of a variability of other business programs. Through that time, the CRM has experienced huge changes and transformations.

1980 Period

Founded by Robert and Kate Kestnbaum, database marketing collected and analyzed customer information. By adopting statistical tools data was then used to aid to have customize communications with other possible customers. In 1986, an act was introduced to the corporate world to interact with the help of management software. The act permitted the effective storing and organization of customer interaction information. Nearby the close of the decade, the propagation of personal computers and the arrival of server/client architecture made the way for a volatile development in software development.

1990 Period

The opening of the 90s carried the key footstep to the true CRM software. It was towards the sales force automation (SFA) from contact management software. SFA carried numerous of the features of database marketing, automated them, and pooled them with contact management software. It delivered organizations with much more valuable customer information. It also mechanized organizations tasks such as inventory control, customer interaction tracking. By the year1995, sales force automation (SFA) and contact management had grown to look like modern CRM software. However, this developing product still did not have a correct term. Numerous words such as enterprise customer management (ECM) and customer information system (CIS) were in usage. By the end of the year 1995, CRM won out. Some attribute this to the technology research company Gartner, while Tom Siebel is also a possible source. Second half of the decade carried vast changes to the CRM industry. Enterprise resource management (ERP) sellers likewise Oracle and Baan arrived the CRM market, eager to use their size and ERP in-roads to rule the industry. Unlike other software businesses that were transitioning to CRM, SAP arrived the market with the only purpose of exploiting on developing applications. This competition pushed CRM sellers to offer a wider range of services. More services were added to CRM like marketing and sales. The year 1999 was a hectic time for the CRM business. Many noteworthy, high-value acquisitions combined the whole market, whereas emergent e-CRM sellers gave the aggressive competition. By means of intranet, extranet, and internet, e-CRM sellers delivered a level of intra-organizational partnership that had not formerly been obtainable in the CRM market. In the end of year 1990s there was an entrance of the first main Software as a Service (SaaS) vendor. Geared toward smaller industries, Salesforce was overlooked by grander sellers.

2000 Period

In the initial years of the 2000's, Paul Greenberg's book "CRM at the Speed of Light" recommended a further complete CRM system that manages all commercial relationships. By the close of the period, it became the shared thinking across the CRM industry. Through the central of the decade, interoperability with legacy software developed. Software giant such as Microsoft arrived in the CRM market with Dynamics CRM, and Oracle acquired Siebel and many other enterprise application sellers. In the year 2007, Salesforce produced the subsequent large change in the CRM industry. Force.com presented the world to cloud-based CRM. Force.com talked the criticism that cloud-based applications were not Customizable. Social CRM also blasted onto the market with the introduction of Comcast Cares—an application that emphasize more on communication than transaction. Maximum of the big companies rapidly trailed Comcast's example, solidifying the place of social CRM. Through the close of the first decade, and up to the present day, cloud-based and SaaS CRM solutions endure to assimilate extra features such as customer service and social CRM. Cloud-based and SaaS CRM solutions last to attain reputation, mainly because of their initial lesser cost and easy amalgamation with mobile devices.

Thus, CRM is a management tactic that seeks to generate, improve and enrich relationships with prudently targeted customers in order to get maximum customer value, business profitability and therefore stockholders' value. The better use of technology in handling and maximizing value of information has given a new shape to modern CRM. Fundamentally, CRM is a customer attentive corporate strategy that takes together customer lifecycle management, organization process and technology. Embracing a really client concentrated approach can be a resourceful business. Number of administrators have probed how far the investment is worth of it. The response to these types of queries lies in CRM that uses novel technologies that could make over the method of nurturing a trustworthy customer base.

SIGNIFICANCE OF TECHNOLOGY IN CRM

Information Technology enables in selecting the accurate technology. Firstly, it is required to search out initiatives that require improvements through technology and recognizing this initiative is the major task of managers. Victory of CRM is reliant on the selecting the action that includes data management, compound modelling and needs smaller subjectivity and human interference.

Technological Tools

Now days the usage of technology is the utmost thrilling, quickly rising and altering the manner customers attain info regarding products and services. Technology comprises equipment, software and communication links, which companies use to enable or increase their procedures, counting all from simple to complicate. (Stowell, 1997). The utmost extensively used tools are:

Electronic Point of Sale (EPOS): The key advantage of EPOS is the quantity of appropriate and precise info it provides. Advancement in the information technology has meaningfully assisted the possibility for data scrutiny. Apart from the original scanner-related data on sales rate, stock levels, price and margin, venders today have info regarding their demographics, socio-economic and lifestyle features of the customers. Along with this, they can evaluate the influence of an entire host of variables-price, advertising, publicity, position in store, shelf position, number of facings etc. This information aids them to drive their choice of product mix, distribution of shelf space and various publicity strategies. EPOS has surely altered the association amid the buyer and seller (Shipley and Palmer, 1997).

Sales Force Automation: Since 1980, Sales Force Automation (SFA) soft wares offer technical sustenance to sales persons and managers. According to Morgan and Inks (2001) SFA is nowadays perceived as a 'competitive imperative' that provides 'competitive parity' (Engle and Barnes 2000). SFA info could be important to the promotion of customer orientation and the expansion of trustworthy associations between company and customers (Grönroos 2000). Furthermore, 'organizations that use SFA to form superior market sensing and customer-linking capabilities are in a position to inform and guide the internal processes of the firm that are responsible for creating customer value' as noted by (Pullig et al. (2002). It helps in mechanizing and enhancing sales procedures to reduce the sales cycle and upsurge turnover. It aids the organization to track and handle all competent leads, links, and prospects throughout the sales cycle containing customer support. It increases the efficiency of marketing communications programs for producing quality leads as well as better correctness in sales predicting. Organizations can use of internet in providing training to its employees. Detailed product info, specific databases solutions, and sales force support, and a set of inner information on the Internet can increase the output of the organization.

Customer Service Helpdesk: It aids the organization in systematizing the customer support procedures that assist the company to provide supreme quality service to their clients. These types of software aids in logging the info about customers, complaints, and suggestions, etc. It also aids in leading these enquiries to suitable employees inside the organization. It retains data regarding status of customer complaints and stocks all support calls and related communications to concluding resolution, frequently apprising the databank therefore. With an automatic customer service, an organization can decrease the costs of upholding its customer service department while at the similar time cultivating the level and quality of customer service. Customer service using the web delivers more info and tools in the hands of customers that improves customer welfares by letting them to learn more about the product and cultivating their skills in using the product. Companies adopts proper knowledge management system are in better position for creating, evaluating, and using the information (Charband and Jafari Navimipour, 2016 and Zareie and Jafari Navimipour, 2016). In fact, customer knowledge is in the flow of CRM. It is the procedure of recognizing the needs of customers, supplying product and service, and getting feedback from the customers (Lingbo and Kaichao, 2012).

Call Centers: It aids in mechanizing the operations of incoming and outgoing calls created between organization and its customers. These resolutions assimilate the voice switch of automatic telephone systems with agent host software letting for automated call moving to agents, auto display of pertinent customer information, self-service communicating Voice Response systems so on. Nowadays, more inventive network with customers are evolving because of novel technology likewise worldwide telephone based call centers and the Internet. Businesses are now concentrating to propose resolutions that leverage the Internet in building complete CRM systems letting them to manage customer communications in all methods. In any CRM call centers, either inbound or outbound, both the customers and the company could successfully connect through manifold networks likewise call, faxes, live chat and e-mails. This is because a contact center is usually a part of company's overall CRM (Soon, 2007; Sin et al., 2005; Yim et al., 2005). Amongst the inspiring aspects of CRM concept is the tough competitions, which have headed numerous firms into concentrating on how best to maximize connection with customers in order to enhance service quality, customer satisfaction and cost of operation (Nguyen et al, 2007). Because of this fact, call centers are nowadays chosen and most predominant mean via which several firms acquire, obtain and retain long lasting relationship with both their existing and prospective customers (Levin, 2007a).

Therefore, the objectives of this chapter are as follow: (1) To conduct the literature review on CRM, (2) To discuss the various tools and strategies used for CRM, and (3) To discuss the different case studies of CRM practices adopted by different companies.

LITERATURE REVIEW

CRM has developed one of the greatest lively technology subjects of the era. As per Chen and Popovich (2003), CRM is not a notion that is new but somewhat because of latest growth and progresses in information technology, it has presumed practical significance. The concept of CRM has been discovered because customers vary in their likes, preferences and buying habits. As an outcome, it becomes important to recognize customers' tastes, preferences, and companies can offer customized their products and services to gain the utmost benefit (Bose, 2002). Furthermore, CRM is a company-focused effort, which includes all the departments. Moreover, CRM also contains manufacturing, product testing, assembling as well as purchasing, and billing, and human resource, marketing, sales and engineering (Greenberg, 2004). According to (Chou et al, 2002) CRM is an idea regarding how companies can retain their utmost lucrative customers and at the same time cut the cost, upsurge in values of communication which directed towards high profits. Kotler (2000) stated that CRM uses information technology to collect data that can then be used to improve information acquired to generate a more individual collaboration with the customer. Goldenberg (2000) considers that CRM is not only technology applications used for marketing, sales and services but rather when it is effectively executed; it allows companies to have cross functional, customer-driven, technology-integrated business process management approach that maxims relations.

CRM concept was influenced by the philosophies of total quality management and by novel technological models (Zineldin, 2000). However, there is a deficiency of lucidity in the meaning of CRM, though all acknowledged descriptions are sharing roughly the similar fundamental notions likewise customer relationships, customer management, marketing strategy, customer retention, and personalization (Zineldin 2000).

Service quality has been perceived as a vital aspect in the marketing that contribute in the direction of welfares reaped by corporations and this has been emphasized in the literature (Izogo and Ogba, 2015). Service quality is reflected as customer's valuation and gratification regarding the services they take from their companies. Therefore, victory of any service related company is really grounded on the service quality and the gratification of their customers with the services offered to them (Makanyeza, Makanyeza, Chikazhe, and Chikazhe, 2017). Service quality and customer satisfaction are the terms that could be used for each other and service quality guarantees customer gratification or dissatisfaction.

CRM is taken as a central point of organizational strategy that includes internal procedures along with external networks in the direction of providing quality services to the targeted customer segment (Buttle 2004). Payne (2012) also focuses that handling CRM is very difficult and enduring procedure and needs a retort from the companies as the outside environment quickly varies. Thus, it is important that companies view CRM in wider and long-term standpoint. Jham and Khan (2008) also stated that CRM is a comprehensive approach as well as process that emphasis on creating and preserving along with improving the relationship with the customers in order to produce the worth and profit in support of the companies. It is an extensive procedure that helpful for improving the quality with preservation of long lasting connection with customers.

As per Bhattacharya (2011), CRM is the technique to lessen the cost and upsurge the organization performance and quality, which means productivity result through customer loyalty (Rahimi, and Kozak, 2017). It aids the employees to make correct and quick decision while dealing with the customers in diverse parts and touch points. This support in resolving numerous customers' difficulties. Therefore, customer gratification and faithfulness would be attained through an effective CRM application. Thus, companies should find out diverse necessities of the customers and adjust their strategies as per the customer requirement to upsurge the company's effectiveness and quality. Internet and web services enable info and data to transfer and share (Navimipour, 2015; Souri and Navimipour, 2014). The usage of the internet as a medium for trade and information offers an opportunity for organizations to use the Internet as a platform for the delivery of CRM functions on the Web E-CRM (Reid and Catterall, 2015).

TOOLS AND STRATEGIES FOR CRM

Success of CRM is reliant on the selecting the motion that includes data management, complex modelling and needs minor subjectivity/human intervention. Some of the tools and strategies are discussed below:

Process Inside the Company

The first asset of the organizations are human assets who work for generating and keeping relationships with the customers. The key role of employee working in the corporation should be directed towards to satisfy the customers. Employees from top to bottom are required to perform their activities towards customer gratification. This stage includes assembling several activities from recognizing need of probable customer to implementation of need in a rational method for delivering customer satisfaction. This could be performed from customers' point of view to offer satisfactions to them.

Wide Range of Products

Next thing that should be kept in mind that the customers' must unceasingly acquire value addition from the products given by the companies. Customers might presume a lot from the company because of some or the other reason. A pleased customer might be displeased customer in view of the variations that might take place in his or her expectations. Further, corporations should be cognizant about the variations taking place in the technology and effort to offer quality amenities as per tuned with the customers' expectations that changes incessantly.

Studying Paying Capacity of Customers

The pricing is one of the main aspects for customers as well as for the organizations, which should not just be overseen by cost-connected factors. Price fixation should be done after considering the paying ability of the probable customers. There is a prerequisite to control price with the variations in the paying capacity of possible customers. If customers are lost because of price then the companies will have to spend much more in trying to acquire them back. In this procedure, a company might have to give up small shares of the profit at an early phase, but seeing long-term incessant association and future opportunity of earning such price adjustment is worth practicing.

Considering the Changing Need of Customers

Desires of the customers go on changing with the fluctuations in their lives because of their demographic and psychographic aspects. The needs and desires of the customers undergoes a radical change with the variation in stages of life. Corporations must unceasingly match customer desires with the company's requirements in a view of various aspects such as goals, demand, options, values and behavior.

Paying Consideration to Competitors Strategy

Companies must consider the strategy of competitors because the buying pattern of the customers is reliant on the contrast, which customers make between the companies. Performance of the company should always be better than its competitors and it should be confirmed that the customer could observe difference.

Paying Attention to Minimize Dissatisfaction

Firms should be pro-active to all types of condition. Discontented customers might not initiate to complain for their unhappiness, but they can change over to some other firms. To evade displeasure of the customers' the origin source for displeasure has to be recognized and it need to be attended pleasingly.

Keep Watch on Buying Behavior Pattern

It is always advised to have an eye on buying Behavior Pattern of customers. The factors that might affect the buying behavior of customers need to be examined. The outcome of buying decision might be purchase, rejection, postponement, and Search for substitutes.

Provide Differentiated Product and Services

Companies should have diversity of offers with diverse price and brands to encounter the requirement of numerous customers. It is desirable to have four or five brands of diverse class with dissimilar price to meet a specific requirement so that a customer might select one preference contingent on his economic position.

Enhancing Intangible Benefits for Satisfaction

Customer satisfaction can be attained by connecting intangible benefits with the tangible product. An intangible benefit contains aspects likewise: showing courteousness to the customer when he visits, attending prudently to what customer has to say, being efficient in offering service etc. It is vital for companies to have effectual customer friendly communication system, which should be humble and open without any disturbances. In circumstance of any difficulty, customer must feel allowed to contact the company to get resolution of their problem instantaneously. Such efforts would facilitate better relationship with customers.

Reliability Based Pricing Scheme

In this technique, customers are charged on the base of amount of trustworthiness customers' have towards companies. A customer who recurrently buys are charged lesser prices in comparison to the other group of customers. Hotels, Air Travels, Hospitals, etc. mostly use this method of pricing as it inspires customers to unceasingly purchase product or service from the similar company.

Organizations Efforts Towards Customer Friendly Communication

Companies should have effective customer friendly communication system, which should be modest and open devoid of any disturbances. In case of any problem, customer must feel comfortable to communicate with the company at any time and try to get clarification of their problem instantly. For an efficient communication system, special training must be given to the employees who are involved in the communication channel particularly in being available, positive, and friendly to customers.

CASE STUDIES

Apple Inc.

Apple is the most well-known brand in the arena of advanced technology. It provides numerous devices and apparatuses like personal computers, tablets, mobiles, watches, laptops etc. It is focusing on retail and its customers since it came into the market i.e. 2001. CRM is the main attention of the Apple's development strategy and the company itself has become a brand of its own products. In a very short time spa, the company has captured its own market share where in the customers loyalty makes it very tough for other companies to enter and strive. Company has generated a CRM tool, which is completely cloud-based and used by them and by their customers. It is a pyramid effect of businesses benefiting from Apple's CRM data collection, which Apple can also use.

The goal of CRM is to increase the service experience of prevailing and probable customers. Company permits its clients face-to-face communication with its experts for in depth conversation of complications and elucidation through its Apple Genius process of tech support. It has certainly made usage of CRM so comprehensively by handling face-to-face communication and by increasing brand cognizance. Company emphasis on CRM based publicity and targeted emails that has helped them to create a lifetime experience rather than just a buying.

Apple being a successful international company requires a system of CRM so that it could approach each customer on one to one basis. It would also monitor and inspire small businesses for same type of interpersonal CRM. It can be concluded that Apple has made best usage of technology to communicate with the customers by forming cloud based technology.

Amazon

Company has lots of faithful customer base and is the most reliable and preferred E-shopping portal. It has become feasible due to well-managed, effective and properly framed CRM policy. Amazon is well-established company for providing a diversity of decent quality products to the customers all at one place. The finest thing is that company has succeeded to retain its customer relation deprived of any face-to-face interaction with them. The suggestions are displayed to the customer, founded on his earlier purchase aids the customer in selecting the product and makes shopping cool and suitable which is feasible with a click of a button. The smart usage of data make the customer feel appreciated and special is an inventive method of fascinating customers.

Amazon has its own in built software that is tailor-made to their requirements. Its CRM is the reason behind all the useful features offered by them. Its software captures the particulars of every customer connecting to their personal data like location, previous purchases and therefore customize a user's on site experience. The CRM aids the customer to receive the solutions of their questions even before the step of human interference comes. Customers possess to all information linked to the product ordered, delivery time and date, time of delivery, payment choices, return policy etc. It definitely lessens the requirement and cost of having customer service staff.

Amazon customers' needs to make an account that makes easier for them to make forthcoming purchases. Due to these accounts details Amazon get an opportunity for target marketing such as customers can be emailed with offers and promotion grounded upon their previous purchases. Amazon is the innovator for giving recommended product features. When a user is logged in his account, it suggests many products to the customer. This suggestion is grounded on the calculation of the previous purchasing behavior of the customer. Company has also introduced a 'customer who bought this' feature and other features which are very encouraging in increasing sales without pressurizing the customers. Moreover, the return policy of Amazon is very online. In case of any problem with the product, the customer can call the customer service operator who has whole access to the information of the customers buying history etc. It aids and makes the return policy relaxed and all issues are dispensed with efficiency. Smart usage of technology and Data Mining techniques has made the Amazon to gain the customer loyalty and their retention as well.

BMW

BMW is very popular brand in the car-manufacturing segment and is appreciated by the clients for its excellence, design and exclusiveness. BMW is a manufacturer of luxury cars and other vehicles for a limited market segment and attract customer faithfulness for its products. As BMW deals with a specific section of brand conscious customers, relationship management has a vital role. Therefore, it is actual imperative with the organization to uphold customer relations and gather customer information. As BMW has a specific customer section it is imperative to have a CRM software, which would aid in advertising of its products and getting its target audience particularly when there are new releases.

The company has sincerely been working on its direct marketing campaigns and has been making genuine efforts in order to manage its reliability programs more proficiently. Company is trying to improve its position on the internet by using the social media portals. Therefore, BMW has been trying to form up such a CRM policy that would increase and fortify its efforts to be more effective brand in the future. It has applied its idea into a package, which gather and store information regarding their customers and evaluate what exactly their customers' anticipations are from the brand. It is fundamentally using CRM to give information about novel products and services and introduce diverse means in which customers could be made conscious about publicity items. Therefore, BMW has competently used the customer information to search more about what precisely the customers are wanting from the company.

KFC

KFC is an American fast food restaurant chain, which is specialized, in fried chicken. It is the world's second-largest restaurant chain with almost 20,000 locations internationally in 123 countries and territories.

KFC provides free Wi-Fi to all its customers across 548 of its stores in the UK hopeful to lure more clients with the potential of free internet. A logging page requires users to sign up and this data is stored to contact users to sign up, and this information is stored to contact users regarding special deals and promotions.

Apart from the simple data collection, company has introduced a loyalty app to make more use of their CRM system. This app is known as KFC Colonel's Club. It requires customers to download the app and register their details. Customers are provided stamps when they purchase food, and those stamps are added to free rewards. The app trails customer location and aids them find their nearby store and offer particular geographic deals. As the app tracks customer buying habits, KFC is capable to offer targeted deals and marketing. KFC has made best use of technology by making loyalty apps for their frequent customers.

Lufthansa

Lufthansa is the biggest German airline and becomes the largest airline in Europe. It is one of the five founding members of Star Alliance, the world's largest airline alliance, formed in 1997. Lufthansa presently operates more than 500 aircraft. Lufthansa use CRM is to observe its customers and increase return business rates with its Miles and More program. This program permits Lufthansa to target marketing promotions to a particular customer segment founded on their earlier journeys. The program also increases customer service by giving recompenses for faithfulness and allocating every customer a membership level with tiered rewards, grounded upon their frequency of travel with the company. This deal not only make the customer feel prized, it also shows Lufthansa how valued every customer is to their business.

British Airways

British Airways (BA) is the flag carrier and the largest airline in the United Kingdom based on fleet size, or the second largest, behind EasyJet, when measured by passengers carried. British Airways flies over 36 million people to more than 200 destinations. Customer service is the central aspect of British Airways. Companies Teradata CRM solution has allowed them to mechanize numerous continuing movements and customer communications. British Airways' CRM is the energetic force behind their customer loyalty scheme that is the British Airways Executive Club. This scheme is free of cost for everyone and does not include any ongoing charges. It includes all the benefits of normal registration such as special offers, user details are protected for easy booking on forthcoming flights and travel. In this, scheme users get Avios points. It is equates to BA miles that could be used to redeem flights, in booking hotels and pay for taxi hire. Avios could also be used with British Airway's partner group that includes American airlines and Iberia and makes customers easy to use one currency across diverse frequent flyer and connecting programs. This scheme allows users to save their seat and meal choice. Moreover, customers get personalized and targeted communication. Hence, it can be inferred that British Airways has reliability based pricing schemes for their trustworthy and frequent customers which provide them with a lot of personalized schemes.

CONCLUSION

In the competitive global village, it has become necessity for the companies to become customer centric and continue customer centric if they want to succeed and persist. Company must be receptive to the customers and it must deliver customers not only with what they require, worth and wish but also forestall the requirements, desires, and wishes of the customers, and be ready to provide before the customers even identify of their requirements, needs or desires.

Customers are a company's vital source without which the corporation could not perform for all intentions and purposes. The wish to increase customer gratification and retention would continuously drive the requirement to increase CRM systems by the companies. CRM is an incessant learning procedure that objects to upsurge the company's awareness and understanding of its customers. CRM is a multifaceted matter that might cause detailed transformation of customer culture in the business, contingent on what is the initial point and how intensely the business involves in it.

CRM is a tool that aids to track down the altering customer profiles, form in this information to get the essential product design and enhance value to the particular customer. Today's customers are worldwide and have high degree of need for understanding, acknowledgement, approvals and deference. They desire marketers who could offer decent product, provide first class service, repair, resolve complications and advance products. Marketers are endeavoring for a connection with customers, who would be strong and long lasting with the customers.

Nowadays, information technology- aware society has growing craving for the skills of others; therefore, the service industries organizations are rising. Marketers have now comprehended that in the worldwide and highly competitive market place and market space, achievement relies on the organization's capability to attract content and keep its customers.

Shane (2010) stated that information technology helps a lot to increase CRM and communication assures furthest return on investment. The amalgamation of social media and CRM technology assists organizations and help them to create an extraordinary capability to form profound relations with their customers inside a few years and that is why, Social application sellers are progressively tailoring their products in accord to the market. From the above discussions, it is obvious that technology has been used efficiently to improve the usefulness and application of CRM. The requirement is to adjust technology to encounter fresher challenges before CRM. It is vibrant course and correct mind-set of executives is important for the victory. There are some classes of key success factors that are identified in this chapter which can serve as the base to discover the success factors for CRM execution.

These factors are Top management involvement, Wide Range of products, Studying Paying Capacity of Customers, Considering the Changing Need of Customers, Paying Consideration to Competitors Strategy, Paying Attention to Minimize Dissatisfaction, Keep watch on Buying Behavior Pattern, Provide differentiated product and services, Enhancing Intangible Benefits for Satisfaction.

Lastly, if all moves onward, and if the customers perceive satisfaction then competitive advantage could become a reality with the help of improved customer satisfaction, augmented revenue generation, and noteworthy growth in productivity. Therefore, CRM has the optimistic future ahead. In coming times, CRM will be embedded as a strategy for business for most of the organizations. Usage of technology will grow. Radical alterations will be there in coming times, but it is sure that CRM is a voyage, not a journey's end, and customers have their hands on the road map and the steering wheel.

REFERENCES

Berry, L. L. (1983). Relationship marketing in Emerging perspectives on services marketing. American Marketing Association. doi:10.1177/009207039502300402

Bhattacharya, A. (2011). Preeminent Analysis of Customer Relationship Management (CRM). *International Journal of Research in Management and Technology*, *1*(1), 45–51.

Bose, R. (2002). Customer Relationship Management: Key Components for IT success. *Industrial Management & Data Systems*, *102*(2), 89–97. doi:10.1108/02635570210419636

Buttle, F. (2004). *Customer Relationship Management: Concepts and Tools*. Oxford, UK: Butterworth-Heinemann. doi:10.4324/9780080472430

Chadha, K. S. (2002). Indian journal of marketing, Relationship marketing. *Managing Customer Focus, 32*(5), 22–28.

Charband, Y., & Jafari Navimipour, N. (2016). Online knowledge sharing mechanisms: A systematic review of the state of the art literatures and recommendations for future research. *Information Systems Frontiers, 18*(6), 1131–1151. doi:10.100710796-016-9628-z

Chen, I. J., & Popovich, K. (2003). Understanding Customer relationship management (CRM): People, process and technology. *Business Process Management Journal, 9*(5), 672–688. doi:10.1108/14637150310496758

Chou, C. D., Lin, B., Xu, Y., & Yen, C. D. (2002). Adopting Customer relationship management technology. Journal. *Industrial Management & Data Systems, 102*(8), 442–452. doi:10.1108/02635570210445871

Darling and Russ. (2000). Relationship Capital. *Executive Excellence, 17*(5), 14.

DeVito, J. A. (1993). *Messages: Building Interpersonal Communication Skills*. New York: HarperCollins College Publishers.

Engle, R. L., & Barnes, M. L. (2000). Sales force auto-mation usage, effectiveness, and cost–benefit in Germany, England and the United States. *Journal of Business and Industrial Marketing, 15*(4), 216–242. doi:10.1108/08858620010335083

Garett. (2000). *The twelve organizational capabilities: Valuing People at work*. Harper Collins Business.

Gartner. (2002). Retrieved from http://www.gartner.com/technology/home.jsp

Goldenberg, B. (2000). What is CRM? What is an e-customer? Why you need them now. *Proceedings of DCI Customer Relationship Management Conference*, 27-29.

Greenberg, P. (2004). *CRM at the speed of light: essential customer strategies for the 21st century*. Tata McGraw Hill Companies, Inc.

Grönroos, C. (2000). *Service Marketing and Management: a Customer Relationship Management Approach* (2nd ed.). Chichester, UK: John Wiley.

Gruen, T. W. (1997). Relationship Marketing: The Route to Marketing Efficiency and Effectiveness. *Business Horizons, 40*(6), 32–38. doi:10.1016/S0007-6813(97)90065-3

Hakanson. (1982). *International Marketing and Purchasing of Industrial Goods: An Interaction Approach*. New York: John Wiley.

Higgins, M., & Smith, W. (2000). Reconsidering the relationship analogy. *Journal of Marketing Management, 16*(1/3), 81-94. doi:10.1362/026725700785100406

Izogo, E. E., & Ogba, I. E. (2015). Service quality, customer satisfaction and loyalty in automobile repair services sector. *International Journal of Quality and Reliability Management, 32*(3), 250-269. doi:10.1108/IJQRM-05-2013-0075?mobileUi=0

Jafari Navimipour, N., Rahmani, A. M., Habibizad Navin, A., & Hosseinzadeh, M. (2015). Expert Cloud: A Cloud-based framework to share the knowledge and skills of human resources. *Computers in Human Behavior, 46*, 57–74. doi:10.1016/j.chb.2015.01.001

Jham, V., & Khan, K. M. (2008). Customer satisfaction in the Indian banking sector: A study. *IIMB Management Review, 20*(1), 84–93.

Kotler, P. (2000). *Marketing Management*. Upper Saddle River, NJ: Academic Press.

Kotler, P. (2003). *Marketing management*. New Delhi: Pearson Education.

Kotler, P., Clark, E., & Stewart, A. (2001). *Marketing Management*. Pearson Education Australia.

Kotler, P., Keller, K. L., Koshy, A., & Jha, M. (2007). *Marketing Management. A South Asian Perspective*. Pearson Publications.

Levin, G. (2007a). Capture the customer experience by tapping IVR. *Call Center Magazine, 20*(2), 50.

Lingbo, K., & Kaichao, Y. (2012). Research on the knowledge flow in CRM circumstance. *Procedia Engineering, 29*, 3852–3857. doi:10.1016/j.proeng.2012.01.583

Little, E., & Marandi, E. (2003). *Relationship Marketing Management*. Cengage Learning.

Makanyeza, C., Chikazhe, L., & Chikazhe, L. (2017). Mediators of the relationship between service quality and customer loyalty: Evidence from the banking sector in Zimbabwe. *International Journal of Bank Marketing, 35*(3), 540-556. doi:10.1108/IJBM-11-2016-0164?fullSc=1andmbSc=1

Mathena, J., Yetter, A., & Hostetler, H. (2009). *Success with Microsoft Dynamics CRM 4.0*. In *Implementing Customer Relationship Management*. Aprèss.

Mathur, A. (2003). Building Customer Relationships: The Taj Air Caterers Experience, CR emerging concepts tools and applications by Shethparvatiyar and Shainesh. Tata McGraw-Hill Publishing Company Ltd.

Morgan, A., & Inks, S. A. (2001). Technology and the sales force. *Industrial Marketing Management, 30*(5), 463–472. doi:10.1016/S0019-8501(99)00115-7

Nguyen, T. H., Joseph, S. S., & Michael, N. (2007). Strategies for successful CRM implementation. *Journal of Information Management and Computer Security, 15*(2), 102-115. . doi:10.1108/09685220710748001

Parvatiyar, A., & Sheth, J. N. (2001). Customer relationship management: Emerging practice, process, and discipline. *Journal of Economic and Social Research, 3*(2), 1-34. doi:10.1.1.113.2212andrep=rep1andtype=pdf

Payne, A. (2012). *Handbook of CRM: Achieving Excellence in Customer Management*. Oxford, UK: Butterworth-Heinemann. doi:10.4324/9780080476933

Pullig, C., Maxham, J. G. III, & Hair, J. F. Jr. (2002). Sales-force automation systems: An exploratory examination of organizational factors associated with effective implementation and sales-force productivity. *Journal of Business Research, 55*(5), 401–415. doi:10.1016/S0148-2963(00)00159-4

Rahimi, R., and Kozak, M. (2017). Impact of customer relationship management on customer satisfaction: The case of a budget hotel chain. *Journal of Travel and Tourism Marketing, 34*(1), 40-51. doi:. doi:10.1080/10548408.2015.1130108

Rai, K.A. (2008). *Customer Relationship Management: Concepts and Case*. PHI Learning Private limited.

Reid, A., & Catterall, M. (2015). *Hidden data quality problems in CRM implementation marketing, technology and customer commitment in the new economy*. Springer.

Rutenbeck, J., & Blaine, J. (2006). *Tech terms: what every telecommunications and digital media person should know*. Elsevier Inc.

Ryals, L., & Payne, A. (2001). Customer relationship management in financial services: towards information-enabled relationship marketing. *Journal of Strategic Marketing, 9*(1), 3-27. doi:10.1080/713775725

Shane, D. (2010). *Social CRM to soar*. Gartner Information Age.

Sheth, J. N., & Parvatiyar, A. (1992). Towards the theory of Business alliance formation. *Scandinavian International Business Review, 1*(3), 71–87. doi:10.1016/0962-9262(92)90012-U

Shipley, D., & Palmer, R. (1997). Selling to and Managing Key Accounts. In The CIM Handbook of selling and Sales Strategy. Butterworth-Heinemann.

Sin, L. Y., Alan, C. T., & Frederick, H. Y. (2005). CRM: conceptualization and scale Development. *European Journal of Marketing, 39*(11/12), 1264 – 1290. doi:. doi:10.1108/03090560510623253

Soon, H. S. (2007). *An Empirical Analysis on the operational Efficiency of CRM call centers in Korea*. Call Center Industry Research Center.

Souri, A., & Navimipour, N. J. (2014). Behavioral modeling and formal verification of a resource discovery approach in Grid computing. *Expert Systems with Applications, 41*(8), 3831–3849. doi:10.1016/j.eswa.2013.11.042

Stone, N., & Foss, B. (2001, May 3). Where do we go from here. *Marketing Business*.

Stowell, D. M. (1997). *Sales and Marketing, and Continuous Improvement*. San Francisco: Jossey-Bass Publishers.

Yastrow, S. (2007). *We: The ideal customer relationship*. Select Books Inc.

Yim, F. H., Anderson, R. E., & Swaminathan, S. (2005).Customer Relationship Management: Its Dimensions and Effect on Customer Outcomes. *Journal of Personal Selling and Sales Management, 24*(4), 265–280. doi:10.1080/08853134.2004.10749037

Zareie, B., & Jafari, N. (2016). The impact of electronic environmental knowledge on the environmental behaviors of people. *Computers in Human Behavior, 59*, 1–8. doi:10.1016/j.chb.2016.01.025

Zineldin, M. (2000). *Total Relationship Management*. Lund: Studentlitteratur.

Zineldin, M. (2006). The royalty of loyalty: CRM, quality and retention. *The Journal of Consumer Marketing, 23*(7), 430-437. doi:. doi:10.1108/07363760610712975

KEY TERMS AND DEFINITIONS

Buying Behavior Pattern: Factors that might affect the buying behavior of customers need to be examined.

Call Centers: It aids in mechanizing the operations of incoming and outgoing calls created between organization and its customers.

Changing Need of Customers: Corporations' efforts to match customer desires with the company's requirements in a view of various aspects such as goals, demand, options, values, and behavior.

Competitors Strategy: Companies consider the strategy of competitors because the buying pattern of the customers is reliant on the contrast, which customers make between the companies.

Customer Relationship Management: Management tactic that seeks to generate, improve and enrich relationships with prudently targeted customers in order to get maximum customer value, business profitability and therefore stockholders' value.

Customer Service Helpdesk: It aids the organization in systematizing the customer support procedures that assist the company to provide supreme quality service to their clients.

Differentiated Product and Services: Diversity of offers with diverse price and brands are offered to encounter the requirement of numerous customers.

Electronic Point of Sale (EPOS): A technological tool that provides the quantity of appropriate and precise info likewise sales rate, stock levels, price and margin, customers' demographics, socio-economic and lifestyle features of the customers.

Intangible Benefits for Satisfaction: An intangible benefit contains aspects likewise: showing courteousness to the customer when he visits, attending prudently to what customer has to say, being efficient in offering service, etc.

Relationship: Is the association amid two or more persons or groups and their contribution with each other, particularly how they act and feel towards each other and interconnect.

Relationship Marketing: It is to uphold a healthy relationship with existing clients instead of creating new ones. Moreover, relationship marketing builds and maintains a base of faithful customers who are beneficial for the company.

Reliability-Based Pricing Scheme: Customers are charged on the base of amount of trustworthiness customers' have towards companies. A customer who buy recurrently is charged lesser prices in comparison to the other group of customers.

Sales Force Automation: This technological tool as a "competitive imperative" that provides "competitive parity." Useful in mechanizing and enhancing sales procedures to reduce the sales cycle and upsurge turnover.

Chapter 15
Empirical Study of Single Platform E-Payment in South East Asia

P. C. Lai
University of Malaya, Malaysia

Evelyn B. H. Toh
Sunway University, Malaysia

Abdullah Abbas Alkhrabsheh
Albalqa Applied University, Jordan

ABSTRACT

Freedom, choice, and simplicity brought about by the e-commerce and technologies are creating the next internet and mobile wave. The single platform e-payment interactions have emerged in the consumer-centric world. The combination of evolving business drivers, globalization, downsizing, changing customer demands, and the evolution of enabling technology is constructing the customer-centric e-payment solutions. In this chapter, the authors discuss and analyze the e-commerce payment systems with the focus on single platform e-payment. This chapter presents an empirical study of e-payment systems and the implications of the findings on e-payment systems in Southeast Asia. Marketing and management personnel of the e-payment organizations will be able to utilize the study information for developing products and services that encourage the usage of single platform e-payment.

INTRODUCTION

There is an increasing interest in this topic given the problems such as inconvenience, not interesting and unattractiveness of E-payment technology solutions faced by organizations to increase consumers' intention to use E-payment systems (Lai, 2007: 2014; 2016: 2017: 2017; Geron, 2009, Wei, Shuo, Luo, Chen and Ling, 2011; Jovanovic and Organero, 2011; Shuaibi and Muhammad, 2016). Therefore, this paper is addressing the problems faced by organizations through the study of the convenience, design,

DOI: 10.4018/978-1-5225-9697-4.ch015

personality, easy to use, usefulness and intention to use the E-payment. The lack of empirical investigations combining the determinants of the three E-payments (Card, Internet, and Mobile) in one study encourages the study of the single platform E-payment system and this is the research gap in the literature review (Lai: 2014: 2016: 2017: 2018) and the author dominated google search engine with the keyword "Single Platform E-payment".

Previous research and study have covered the design, convenience, perceived usefulness, perceived ease of use and intention to use the single platform E-payment (Lai: 2014; 2016; 2017; 2018; Lai and Zainal, 2015: Lai and Scheele, 2017). This study focuses on consumers-based research orientation such as consumers' intention to use that is measurable with the adoption and extension of Technology Acceptance Model (TAM) (Davis, Bogozzi and Warshaw, 1989) into the stimulus research model (Lai: 2014: 2016: 2017: 2018) to enhance the potential of deploying an integrated single platform E-payment system with personality. Personality is the factor with characteristics that might influence the consumers' intention to use the single platform E-payment and is another gap in the literature. Therefore, this study seeks to investigate the convenience, personality, and design that influence perceived ease of use and perceived usefulness. Furthermore, this study investigates the relationship between perceived ease of use and perceived usefulness with consumers' intention to use one single platform E-payment System.

Another objective of this study is to conduct data splitting. Data splitting is the act of partitioning the available data into two different portions and it is usually for cross-validatory purposes (Picard & Berk, 1990). One portion of the data is used to develop a predictive model while the other to evaluate the model's performance. From this, the researchers hope to point out any discrepancies in the model performance.

THEORETICAL MODEL

Technology Acceptance Model (TAM) was introduced by Fred Davis in 1986. It is specifically tailored for modeling users' acceptance of information systems or technologies or new product acceptance. The goal of Davis (1989) TAM is to explain the general determinants of technology acceptance that lead to explaining users' behavior across a broad range of end-user computing technologies and user populations. In this study will base on Technology Acceptance Model that was formed by Venkatesh and Davis (1996) after the main finding of both perceived usefulness and perceived ease of use were found to have a direct influence on behavior intention, thus eliminating the need for the attitude construct. The two significant beliefs exist in the TAM are the perceived usefulness and perceived ease of use. TAM also postulates that perceived ease of use stimuli perceived usefulness because the easier to use a single platform E-payment system, the more useful users perceive the single platform E-payment system to be. There are empirical studies of the TAM include this correlation and the finding share a significant relationship between these two factors (Moon and Kim, 2001; Van der Heijden, 2003; Shih, 2004).

Factors Influencing the Single Platform E-Payment

Factors influencing the single platform e-payment in this study are personality, design, and convenience. In this study, personality is a new factor. Thus, an in-depth literature review is being discussed here as the rest of the factors are being studied in previous research papers for e-payment. Marketers believe that personality is the factor that wills stimulus the intention to use the single platform e-payment that will help marketers to target this type of personality as customers. Therefore, personality is taken into consideration in this study together with the other factors.

Design

The intention to adopt new technology such as the e-payment platform depends on the technical "design and functionality" of the platform. Basically, users are looking for apps or platform that are attractive as well as user-friendly. Devaraj, Fan, and Kohli (2002) acknowledged that perceived ease of use and usefulness included factors of time-saving and price saving that are major measures of the efficiency for internet retail transactions. Davis (1989) identified the design features that are directly related to perceived ease of use and perceived usefulness. Lin and Hsieh (2006) noted that consumers enjoyed using their phones as electronic payment and valued the benefits of the design that provided ease of use and usefulness. Hence, the following hypothesis can be derived.

H1a: Design has a positive relationship on perceived usefulness.
H1b: Design has a positive relationship on perceived ease of use.

Personality

The term personality refers to the unique set of psychological characteristics that distinguishes a person or group. These characteristics are usually described in terms of traits namely self-confidence, dominance, sociability, autonomy, defensiveness, adaptability, and aggressiveness. In the study of marketing, personality is useful in analyzing consumer behavior and decision making for product or brand choice and in this paper is to study the personality as the stimulus that triggers the motivation to use the single platform E-payment. Schiffman & Kanuk (2010) state that there are three distinct properties of personality – it reflects individual differences, it is consistent and enduring and personality can change. There are many theories that have been put forth in the study of personality.

According to Ajzen (2005), personality traits are defined as a set of characteristics of an individual that exerts a pervasive influence on a broad range of trait-related responses. These trait-related responses are known as attitude towards a belief, object or place. According to Shropshire, Warkentin & Sharma (2015), personality traits have long been used to study a variety of behavioral outcomes. Within the scope of past information research, personality constructs have been used in system use (Klein, Jiang & Tesch, 2005).

According to John & Srivastava (1999), personality traits can be categorized into five broad dimensions or domains. This is known as the five-factor model of personality (FFM). FFM is often referred to as the "Big Five": the domains include Extraversion, Agreeableness, Conscientiousness, Neuroticism (sometimes named by its polar opposite, Emotional Stability), and Openness to Experience (sometimes named Intellect). The Big Five/FFM was developed to represent the variability in individuals' personalities as possible whilst using only a small set of trait dimensions. Many personality psychologists agree that its five domains capture the most important, basic individual differences in personality traits and that many alternative trait models can be conceptualized in terms of the Big Five/FFM structure. Gosling, Rentfrow & Swann (2003) further fine-tuned the Big Five/FFM domains as identified by John & Srivastava (1999) and Barrick & Mount (1991) into the following:-

Extraversion

According to Hogan (1986), as cited by Barrick & Mount (1991), the extraversion dimension consists of two components – ambition (initiative, surgency, ambition, and impetuous) and sociability (sociable, exhibitionist and expressive). In the marketing perspective, this can be associated with risk pervasiveness or avoidance in making purchases (Schiffman & Kanuk, 2010). People who possess this trait are most likely early adopters of technology (Rogers, 2003).

Agreeableness

This dimension is associated with likability. This is likened to social conformity and in the marketing perspective; there are studies on self-congruence and self-image (Sirgy, 1985; Fiske, 1949). Previous researchers have associated this dimension with friendliness (Guildford & Zimmerman, 1949), compliance (Digman & Takemoto-Chock, 1981) and love (Peabody & Goldberg, 1989). As mentioned by Barrick et. al. (1991), other traits for this dimension include, courteous, flexible, trusting, good-natured, cooperative, forgiving, soft-hearted and tolerant.

Conscientiousness

Conscientiousness is the personality trait of a person having an awareness of the impact of their own behavior towards those around them. This personality trait reflects the degree to which a person can be dependable, responsible, perseverant, and achievement driven. Previous studies in the human resources domain have focused on this personality trait for their employee's performance across organizations and cultures (Hassan, Naveed & Yılmaz, 2016). To a certain extent, in marketing studies, this personality trait seems predominant in advertising (Myers, Sen & Alexandrov, 2010).

Neuroticism

Another term for neuroticism is emotional stability. According to Mooradian & Olver (1994), in marketing studies, this personality trait is strongly associated with post-purchase processes. At this stage, some people might experience either a sense of high satisfaction or dissatisfaction in the purchases that they made. In previous studies, Larsen & Ketelaar (1991) have suggested that neurotic consumers tend to focus on negative, punishment signals, whilst extraverts are more inclined to focus on reward signals. Therefore, more effort should be put in by marketers to provide positive signals (e.g., special sales or attractive displays), in order to drown out the unintended negative signals (such as product defects, slipshod service or frequent out-of-stocks) because different personality types attend to each of the signals. Minimizing potential punishment signals is necessary because neurotic consumers may be a disproportionately important source of negative word-of-mouth that "infects" other customers.

Openness to Experience

According to Barrick et. al. (1991), the personality traits that are most commonly associated with this dimension include imaginative, cultured, curious, original, broad-minded, intelligent and artistically sensitive.

The study of personality traits as a role of predictors of beliefs and behavior has been wide spread across a variety of contexts (Mischel, 2004; Pulford & Sohal, 2006). For example, according to (Smits & De Boeck, 2007), the personality trait of agreeableness was linked with inhibition of verbally aggressive behavior, organizational citizenship behavior (Ilies, Scott, & Judge, 2006) as well as consumerism and environmentalism (Hirsh & Dolderman, 2007).

There has also been a growing interest in using personality to explain and understand people's use of information technology (Devito Da Cunha & Greathead, 2007; Oreg & Nov, 2008; and Pratt & Chudoba, 2006). Apart from this, personality traits predispose technology users to behave in certain ways in different situations (Thatcher & Perrewé, 2002). In a study of initial acceptance of ERP (Enterprise Resource Planning), the personality trait of extraversion was shown to be positively related to users' initial acceptance of ERP systems (Pratt & Chudoba, 2006). Other personality traits such as openness to experience were found to moderate the effect of computer-assisted communication on decision-making performance of teams (Colquitt, Hollenbeck, Ilgen, LePine, & Sheppard, 2002). Personality traits such as emotional stability and extraversion were found to moderate the relationships between the paths in a model of monitoring acceptance, therefore, people who scored lower in extraversion and emotional stability were less likely to endorse positive attitudes toward monitoring in the workplace (Zweig & Webster, 2003). Also, Lee, Kozar, & Larsen, (2003) have indicated that there is a need for "a deeper understanding of factors contributing to ease of use and usefulness is needed" and "more efforts to examine the broader environmental factors including personality difference are necessary." Hence, the following hypothesis can be derived.

H2a: Personality has a positive relationship on perceived usefulness.
H2b: Personality has a positive relationship on perceived ease of use.

Convenience

Based on Seiders et al. (2005), this study has applied access and transaction convenience. For example, in a study by Shih & Fang (2004), any new innovation such as the internet is very user friendly with its "point and click" interface therefore, it is likely that potential users may feel that payment systems are less complex to use, and hence are more likely to use them. Dewan & Chen (2005) and Lai (2016) found that consumers preferred convenient and practical E-payment modes that allowed access and transactions anywhere and anytime on their mobile phones that satisfied their daily needs and wants. Lin and Hsieh (2006) illustrated convenience constituted consumers' expectation of service attribute in the specific banking industry. Kim, Mirusmonov, and Lee (2010) and Lai (2016) noted that convenience influenced consumers' intention to use mobile payment through perceived usefulness and perceived ease of use. Hence, the following hypothesis can be derived.

H3a: Convenience has a relationship on perceived usefulness.
H3b: Convenience has a relationship on perceived ease of use.

Perceived Ease of Use (PEU), Perceived Usefulness (PU) and Intention

As mentioned earlier, based on the TAM Model formed by Venkatesh and Davis (1996), both perceived usefulness and perceived ease of use were found to have a direct influence on behavior intention, thus eliminating the need for the attitude construct. In previous studies in the information system settings, the higher the perceived ease of use of any innovation or system, the higher the perceived usefulness (Elkhani, Soltani, & Nazir Ahmad, 2014). Other researchers such as Bhatiasevi & Yoopetch, 2015; Kim, 2014; Lee, Hsieh & Hsu, 2011; Lee, Hsieh, & Ma, 2011; Lee, 2009; Ha & Stoel, 2009; Ramayah & Lo, 2007; Learn & Lin, 2005).

If innovation is considered as relatively easy to use, people or users will be more willing to learn more about its features and finally have the intention to continue using it (Chiu & Wang, 2008). Previous studies on the construct of PU have indicated that there is a relationship between it with continuance intention in the context of e-text (Baker-Eveleth & Stone, 2015; Stone & Baker-Eveleth, 2013), instant messaging (Wang, Ngai, & Wei, 2011), mobile service provider (Abbas & Hamdy, 2015), online travel services (Li & Liu, 2014), e-learning (Lin & Wang, 2012), blog learning (Tang, Tang, & Chiang, 2012) and knowledge creation (Chou, Min, Chang, & Lin, 2009). Hence, the following hypotheses are to be derived.

H4: Perceived ease of use has a relationship on perceived usefulness.
H5: Perceived usefulness has a positive relationship with consumers' intention to use.
H6: Perceived ease of use has a positive relationship with consumers' intention to use.

This study analyzes the relationships between the variables shown in Figure 1 known as the Stimulus research model (Lai: 2014: 2016: 2017: 2018) extension from TAM Model in order to determine their impact on consumers' intention to use the single platform payment system. Further, research in regard to e-payment with different factors was done with the adoption and extension of TAM model into Stimulus research model was done by Lai (2014: 2016: 2017: 2018) with similar research model as shown in Figure 1.

Figure 1. Stimulus Research Model (Lai, 2014: 2016: 2017: 2018)

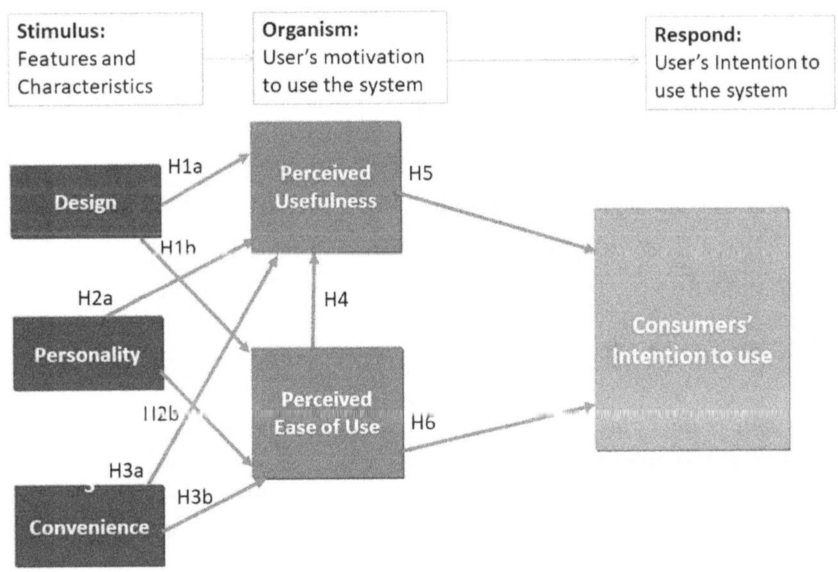

Methodology

This study seeks to conduct an exploratory factor analysis (EFA) as a new variable - personality is added into the equation. As such a total of 270 respondents that fulfil the pre-set requirements were collected and used for this analysis from the online email blast (1 month) of those who used E=Payment from the 874 ASEAN database collected through events. This represents 30% from the database. Based on Sekeran, (2003) using nonprobability sampling, the minimum recommended sample size for this study is 200. The research managed to collect 270 data that was being used here that provided a robust study for this research. In this study, the five-point scale Likert-type of measuring the consumers' intention to use the single platform e-payment system whereby 1 denotes 'strongly disagree' and 5 denotes 'strongly agree'.

When responding to the survey items, participants specify their levels of agreement to the subject given. The five points scale is selected to encourage respondents in order to make both positive or negative choices as prescribed by Cooper, Schindler & Sun (2008) and in order to produce more emphatic information (Oppenheim, 1992). After the data was collected, a rigorous data screening and cleaning were conducted before the EFA was done on SPSS 25. Based on the results of the EFA, a further 322 respondents were collected in order to conduct a confirmatory factor analysis (CFA). The data collected for the CFA was done approximately 1 month after the EFA tests were obtained. The use of Smart PLS 3.2.8 was further used to conduct CFA. The following section explains the EFA tests conducted followed by the results generated by the CFA results from Smart PLS.

Results and Findings

In this study, the analyses were done for each variable separately in order to gather a summary of respondents' demographic profile. This is in order to get the preliminary information as well as the feel of the data (Sekaran, 2003). Table 1 showed the respondents' demographic profiles of the survey.

The highest respondents of 46.8% are in the age range of 26-40 with male respondents of 62.2%. As for the marital status, most of the respondents are single respondents (53.3%). Most of the respondents work at the middle management level (42.2%) and own a combination of all three (3) items mobile phone, internet and card payment (53%).

For this study, the split of the data was necessary to ascertain if the new variable – personality does affect PEU or PEU significantly. The data has undergone rigorous data screening and data cleaning procedures in SPSS 25. This study split the data into two sets because the purpose of this study was to train and test the data set. This is just an attempt to see if the data fits the model in question and see if the predictions are either over fitting or under fitting the model. The subsequent section explains the results obtained from the EFA.

Exploratory Factor Analysis

The first step is to observe the Cronbach α for both the data sets. The Cronbach α for Model 1 is as follows: convenience (0.936), design (0.941), perceived usefulness (0.957), perceived ease of use (0.964) personality (0.918) and consumers' intention to use (0.87). As required reporting, EFA is that the diagonal elements in the Anti-correlation matrix loadings figures are all above the 0.50 cut off point with the communalities being less than 1. As such, there are no items that should be deleted and multicollinearity does not exist.

Table 1. Respondents profile

Variable	Frequency (n= 270)	Percent (Total = 100%)
ASEAN Countries Status		
Developed Countries (Singapore, Brunei)	86	32
Developing Countries (Malaysia, Thailand, Indonesia, Philippines)	146	54
Lesser Developed Countries (Vietnam, Cambodia, Laos, Myanmar)	38	14
Age		
< 25	115	20.6
26 – 40	261	46.8
41 – 55	148	26.5
>55	34	6.1
Gender		
Male	168	62.2
Female	102	37.8
Marital status		
Single	144	53.3
Married	126	46.7
What industry do you work in?		
Education	48	17.8
Banking / Finance	29	10.7
Retail / Hypermarket	29	10.7
Manufacturing / ICT	107	39.6
Other	57	21.1
What is your position level at work?		
Top management	24	8.9
Middle management	114	42.2
Junior management	41	15.2
Professional	33	12.2
Other	58	21.5
Do you own any of the following?		
Mobile / Internet / Card	23	9
Mobile+card / Mobile+internet / card+internet	103	38
Mobile, Internet & card	144	53

Table 2. Factor loadings and reliability results

	Items	Loadings	Communalities	Cronbach's Alpha (α)
Consumer Intention	CI1	.965[a]	0.708	0.887
	CI2	.929	0.767	
	CI3	.892[a]	0.807	
	CI4	.915[a]	0.787	

continued on following page

Table 2. Continued

	Items	Loadings	Communalities	Cronbach's Alpha (α)
Perceived Usefulness	PU1	.975[a]	0.765	0.957
	PU2	.945[a]	0.688	
	PU3	.948[a]	0.742	
	PU4	.959[a]	0.770	
	PU5	.951[a]	0.783	
	PU6	.956[a]	0.757	
	PU7	.966[a]	0.780	
	PU8	.963[a]	0.776	
	PU9	.947[a]	0.769	
	PU10	.966[a]	0.825	
Perceived ease of use	PEU1	.969[a]	0.652	0.964
	PEU2	.967[a]	0.715	
	PEU3	.964[a]	0.787	
	PEU4	.972[a]	0.866	
	PEU5	.975[a]	0.786	
	PEU6	.949[a]	0.872	
	PEU7	.978[a]	0.817	
	PEU8	.970[a]	0.765	
	PEU9	.964[a]	0.834	
	PEU10	.961[a]	0.782	
Personality	P!	.951[a]	0.669	0.918
	P2	.948[a]	0.769	
	P3	.943[a]	0.820	
	P4	.921[a]	0.811	
	P5	.902[a]	0.687	
	P6	.935[a]	0.799	
Convenience	EF1	.953[a]	0.815	0.936
	EF2	.955[a]	0.828	
	EF3	.954[a]	0.790	
	EF4	.959[a]	0.809	
	EF5	.943[a]	0.839	
	EF6	.947[a]	0.849	
Design	D1	.929[a]	0.775	0.941
	D2	.933[a]	0.783	
	D3	.939[a]	0.755	
	D4	.946[a]	0.816	
	D5	.951[a]	0.809	
	D6	.935[a]	0.859	
	D7	.946[a]	0.844	
	D8	.960[a]	0.804	

Table 3. KMO and Bartlett's test

KMO and Bartlett's Test		
Kaiser-Meyer-Olkin Measure of Sampling Adequacy.		0.952
Bartlett's Test of Sphericity	Approx. Chi-Square	13575.081
	Df	946
	Sig.	0.000

As for the communalities in the factor analysis, all the communalities figure is greater than 0.50. This further supports the reason for not deleting any items. The next stage is to do the KMO and Bartlett's test to check on the sampling adequacy (Table 3). This test determines if the responses given from the sample are adequate.

As for the KMO and Bartlett's test, the 0.952 figure exceeds the 0.50 cut off and this denotes the adequacy in sampling. This indicates that the dataset is suitable for EFA. As the dataset has all met the criteria for EFA, the next step is to do the CFA. For this, another set of data is used in order to establish the hypothesis that is proposed. The software that is used to do the CFA is a Variance based SEM called Smart PLS.

Confirmatory Factor Analysis

For the confirmatory factor analysis (CFA) part, a Variance based-SEM (VB-SEM) software called Smart PLS 3.2.8 was utilized. The model that is assessed is reflective and according to Hair, Black, Babin & Anderson (2014), there are certain procedures in analyzing reflective models. Table 4 indicates the systematic evaluation of the PLS-SEM results.

As a prescribed guide to the data analysis, it is important to have threshold values. As such, the following threshold values for assessing the measurement model (outer model) is established (Bagozzi & Yi, 1988; Esposito Vinzi, 2010; Hair et al., 2010; Henseler, Ringle, & Sarstedt, 2015; Henseler et al., 2009) are shown in Table 5.

As seen in Table 6, after running the data set in Smart PLS, the results for the reliability tests are all above 0.70 with the AVE of being above 0.50. According to Hair et. al. (2010), in order for the model to

Table 4. Systematic evaluation of the PLS-SEM Results

Evaluation of the measurement model (Reflective)
? Internal consistency (composite reliability) ? Indicator reliability ? Convergent validity (average variance extracted) ? Discriminant validity
Evaluation of the structural model (Reflective)
? Coefficients of determination (R2) ? Predictive relevance (Q2) ? Size and significance of path coefficients ? f2 effect sizes ? q2 effect sizes

Table 5. Measures and Threshold values for assessment of the measurement model

Assessment Subject	Measures	Threshold values
Indicator Reliability	Factor Loadings	>0.4
Internal Consistency Reliability	Composite Reliability	>0.7
Convergent Validity	Average Variance Extracted (AVE)	>0.5
Discriminant Validity	Fornell-Larcker Criterion	The square root of the AVE of each construct should be higher than its highest correlation with any other construct.
Discriminant Validity	Heterotrait-Monotrait Ratio (HTMT)	Thresholds of 0.85 and 0.9 for HTMT to establish discriminant validity

Table 6. Reliability tests and AVE

	Cronbach's Alpha	rho_A	Composite Reliability	Average Variance Extracted (AVE)
Consumer Intention (CI)	0.872	0.880	0.912	0.721
Convenience	0.921	0.924	0.939	0.720
Design	0.928	0.936	0.941	0.667
PEU	0.958	0.960	0.964	0.728
PU	0.949	0.950	0.956	0.686
Personality	0.921	0.924	0.938	0.717

achieve convergent reliability, there are three types of estimations that have to be established. As mentioned in the previous sections, the Cronbach α generated for the variables in the two data sets indicates that they are reliable. Smart PLS reports a different type of reliability which is known as Composite Reliability. This includes factor loadings, composite reliability (CR), and average variance extracted (AVE) which is used to establish convergent validity. As seen in Table 6, the composite reliability is all above 0.70 and this indicates adequate convergence or internal consistency and the Average Variance Extracted (AVE) is all above 0.50 which is also acceptable.

Table 7. Outer Loading (Indicator reliability)

	Consumer Intention (CI)	Convenience	Design	PEU	PU	Personality
CI1	0.831					
CI2	0.873					
CI3	0.864					
CI4	0.828					
D1			0.714			
D2			0.723			
D3			0.810			
D4			0.829			

continued on following page

Table 7. Continued

	Consumer Intention (CI)	Convenience	Design	PEU	PU	Personality
D5			0.864			
D6			0.849			
D7			0.853			
D8			0.876			
EF1		0.735				
EF2		0.810				
EF3		0.875				
EF4		0.893				
EF5		0.870				
EF6		0.895				
P!						0.780
P2						0.867
P3						0.894
P4						0.874
P5						0.791
P6						0.869
PEU1				0.696		
PEU10				0.884		
PEU2				0.849		
PEU3				0.882		
PEU4				0.890		
PEU5				0.877		
PEU6				0.859		
PEU7				0.885		
PEU8				0.830		
PEU9				0.866		
PU1					0.770	
PU10					0.888	
PU2					0.819	
PU3					0.812	
PU4					0.832	
PU5					0.855	
PU6					0.784	
PU7					0.839	
PU8					0.834	
PU9					0.843	

Table 8. HTMT

Heterotrait-Monotrait Ratio (HTMT)						
	Consumer Intention (CI)	Convenience	Design	PEU	PU	Personality
Consumer Intention (CI)						
Convenience	0.459					
Design	0.525	0.832				
PEU	0.504	0.871	0.802			
PU	0.600	0.830	0.768	0.878		
Personality	0.584	0.605	0.565	0.553	0.598	

As seen in Table 7, the model achieved indicator reliability as the loadings are above 0.7 for all items. Therefore, no items were deleted as they satisfied the criteria of having loadings above 0.70.

As for the discriminant validity shown in Table 8, the HTMT scores are all below the 0.90 threshold. This indicates that the discriminant validity is achieved.

As mentioned above, as a rule of thumb (in Table 8), the outer loadings have to be above 0.7 and the indicator loadings demonstrate that the factor loadings are all 0.01 significance level. This is as highlighted in Table 9. This further illustrates that the model is very robust and the splitting of data does not affect its robustness.

With the reliability and validity of the model and constructs being established in the previous sections, the evaluation of the hypothesized relationships within the inner model should be done. For PLS-SEM, the quality of the model is assessed is based on its ability to predict the endogenous constructs. This can be established by fulfilling the following criteria – Assessing Collinearity issues, assessing the significance and relevance of the structural model relationships, Coefficient of determination (R2) and path coefficients.

Table 9. Factor loadings

	Original Sample (O)	Sample Mean (M)	Standard Deviation (STDEV)	T Statistics (|O/STDEV|)	P Values
CI1 <- Consumer Intention (CI)	0.831	0.832	0.019	43.159	0.000
CI2 <- Consumer Intention (CI)	0.873	0.872	0.018	47.404	0.000
CI3 <- Consumer Intention (CI)	0.864	0.862	0.021	41.420	0.000
CI4 <- Consumer Intention (CI)	0.828	0.826	0.024	33.899	0.000
D1 <- Design	0.714	0.712	0.036	19.939	0.000
D2 <- Design	0.723	0.722	0.032	22.336	0.000
D3 <- Design	0.810	0.810	0.027	30.414	0.000

continued on following page

Table 9. Continued

	Original Sample (O)	Sample Mean (M)	Standard Deviation (STDEV)	T Statistics (|O/STDEV|)	P Values
D4 <- Design	0.829	0.828	0.023	36.785	0.000
D5 <- Design	0.864	0.865	0.030	29.052	0.000
D6 <- Design	0.849	0.850	0.018	46.305	0.000
D7 <- Design	0.853	0.855	0.019	44.398	0.000
D8 <- Design	0.876	0.877	0.015	59.106	0.000
EF1 <- Convenience	0.735	0.734	0.043	17.284	0.000
EF2 <- Convenience	0.810	0.809	0.027	29.785	0.000
EF3 <- Convenience	0.875	0.876	0.019	44.917	0.000
EF4 <- Convenience	0.893	0.893	0.017	51.088	0.000
EF5 <- Convenience	0.870	0.870	0.022	40.358	0.000
EF6 <- Convenience	0.895	0.895	0.018	49.802	0.000
P1 <- Personality	0.780	0.780	0.029	27.185	0.000
P2 <- Personality	0.867	0.867	0.018	48.748	0.000
P3 <- Personality	0.894	0.894	0.014	62.171	0.000
P4 <- Personality	0.874	0.874	0.019	46.603	0.000
P5 <- Personality	0.791	0.790	0.031	25.402	0.000
P6 <- Personality	0.869	0.869	0.019	44.814	0.000
PEU1 <- PEU	0.696	0.699	0.042	16.534	0.000
PEU10 <- PEU	0.884	0.885	0.019	47.221	0.000
PEU2 <- PEU	0.849	0.849	0.031	26.964	0.000
PEU3 <- PEU	0.882	0.882	0.018	50.302	0.000
PEU4 <- PEU	0.890	0.891	0.018	49.857	0.000
PEU5 <- PEU	0.877	0.878	0.019	45.036	0.000
PEU6 <- PEU	0.859	0.860	0.020	42.140	0.000
PEU7 <- PEU	0.885	0.887	0.021	42.911	0.000
PEU8 <- PEU	0.830	0.832	0.029	28.769	0.000
PEU9 <- PEU	0.866	0.867	0.022	40.055	0.000
PU1 <- PU	0.770	0.769	0.033	23.132	0.000
PU10 <- PU	0.888	0.888	0.014	62.305	0.000
PU2 <- PU	0.819	0.820	0.026	31.279	0.000
PU3 <- PU	0.812	0.813	0.025	33.030	0.000
PU4 <- PU	0.832	0.831	0.030	28.012	0.000
PU5 <- PU	0.855	0.856	0.020	43.232	0.000
PU6 <- PU	0.784	0.785	0.045	17.508	0.000
PU7 <- PU	0.839	0.840	0.022	37.773	0.000
PU8 <- PU	0.834	0.833	0.025	33.885	0.000
PU9 <- PU	0.843	0.844	0.020	42.118	0.000

Table 10. Inner VIF values

Inner VIF Values						
	Consumer Intention (CI)	**Convenience**	**Design**	**PEU**	**PU**	**Personality**
Consumer Intention (CI)						
Convenience				**2.692**	3.754	
Design				**2.576**	**2.902**	
PEU	3.345				3.482	
PU	3.345					
Personality				**1.500**	**1.510**	

In order to address any collinearity issues of the model, the inner VIF is studied. The reason for studying the inner VIF is because all the indicators are reflective. Any individual VIF that is greater than 10 should be inspected which usually means that the average VIF is greater than 6. As seen in the results presented in Table 10, all the VIF figures are less than 6 which is acceptable. If the VIF figures are closer to 1, then the model is much stronger, as the factors are not impacted by correlation with other factors.

Table 11. Coefficient of determination (R^2)

	R Square	**R Square Adjusted**
Consumer Intention (CI)	0.308	0.303
PEU	0.713	0.710
PU	0.744	0.741

Table 12. Path Coefficient (direct path)

Mean, STDEV, T-Values, P-Values					
	Original Sample (O) β	**Sample Mean (M)**	**Standard Deviation (STDEV)**	**T Statistics (|O/STDEV|)**	**P Values**
Convenience -> PEU	0.552	0.554	0.059	9.308	**0.000**
Convenience -> PU	0.179	0.171	0.103	1.741	**0.082**
Design -> PEU	0.306	0.304	0.064	4.746	**0.000**
Design -> PU	0.116	0.121	0.055	2.115	**0.035**
PEU -> Consumer Intention (CI)	0.009	0.007	0.083	0.105	**0.916**
PEU -> PU	0.538	0.544	0.084	6.437	**0.000**
PU -> Consumer Intention (CI)	0.547	0.552	0.085	6.416	**0.000**
Personality -> PEU	-0.053	-0.051	0.034	1.548	**0.122**
Personality -> PU	-0.123	-0.121	0.035	3.489	**0.001**

As for the VIF figures for Convenience to PEU and PU is at 2.692 and 3.754 respectively, Design to PEU and PU is at 2.902 and Personality to PEU and PU is at 1.500 and 1.510 respectively. From this, it can be seen that the VIF figures the factors are not impacted by correlation with other factors.

The next step is to conduct the measure of predictive accuracy. According to Hair et. al. (2014), the measure of predictive accuracy is measured with R2 which represents the exogenous variable's combined effect on the endogenous variable(s). The R2 value should range from 0 to 1 with higher levels indicating higher levels of predictive accuracy. As a rule of thumb R2 values of 0.75, 0.50 or even 0.25 for endogenous latent variables are described as substantial, moderate or weak (Hair, Ringle & Sarstedt, 2011). High R2 values also show that the values of the construct can be predicted by the PLS path model (Hair et. al. 2014). As indicated in Table 11, the R2 adjusted values report figures (CI = 0.303, PEU = 0.710 and PU = 0.741). for PEU and PU, the score of R2 is close to the 0.75 indicates that these values provide for substantial predictiveness.

Table 12 denotes the path coefficients (direct) for the model. As seen, the hypotheses Convenience -> PU ($\beta = 0.179$, $p = 0.082$), PEU -> CI ($\beta = 0.009$, $p = 0.916$) and Personality -> PEU ($\beta = -0.053$, $p = 0.122$) are all not significant as p values are all larger than 0.01. All other direct paths indicate that all the other hypotheses are supported.

The summary of the hypotheses results for this study is presented in Table 13. It can be seen that the hypothesis H1 (a and b), H2a, H3b, H4 as well as H5 are supported whereas hypothesis H2b, H3a and H6 are not supported. The summary of hypotheses results of this study has been presented in Table 13.

Figure 2. Path coefficient

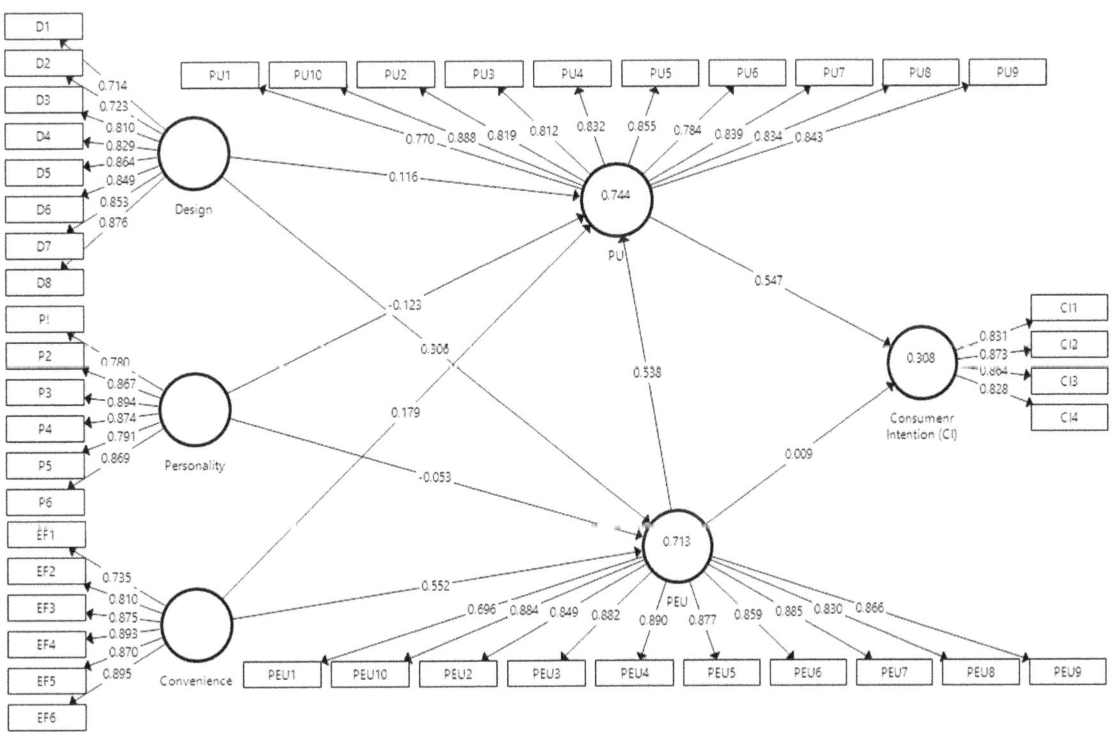

Table 13. Hypotheses summary

Hyp	Hypothesis	Decision
H1a:	Design -> perceived usefulness (PU).	Supported
H1b:	Design -> perceived ease of use (PEU).	Supported
H2a:	Personality -> perceived usefulness (PU).	Supported
H2b:	Personality -> perceived ease of use (PEU).	Not Supported
H3a:	Convenience -> perceived usefulness (PU).	Not Supported
H3b:	Convenience -> perceived ease of use (PEU).	Supported
H4:	Perceived ease of use (PEU) -> perceived usefulness (PU).	Supported
H5:	Perceived usefulness (PU) -> consumers' intention to use (CI).	Supported
H6:	Perceived ease of use (PEU) -> consumers' intention to use (CI)	Not Supported

Theoretical Implication

As mentioned above, the data that was obtained for this study was subjected to data splitting. According to Picard & Berk (1990), data splitting is the act of partitioning available data into two portions, usually for cross-validatory purposes. One portion of the data is used to develop a predictive model and the other to evaluate the model's performance. As seen from the results above, it would seem that the model is stronger when the items are used again to validate the model.

Management Implication

With the emerging of the single platform E-payment system, many companies are facing vital issues in regard to their consumers' technology acceptance. Since consumers play the vital role in organizations bottom line, organizations need to take into consideration of consumers' point of view in regard to their intention to use the single platform E-payment systems for the E-commerce world. This study has many managerial implications for different stakeholders but we will only highlight the top directly impacted parties.

Consumers are concerned with carrying cash that exposes them to theft and loss as well as too many "cards" to carry and manage. Based on consumers' feedback, security (e.g., safe transactions), user-friendly as well as their interest with easy to use on their phone for payment are their priorities. By understanding consumers' preference, technology solution providers will be able to design the solution focused on consumers' needs and want (Lai, 2014: 2016).

As for the telecommunication market, this has reached maturity and on a lookout for a new business like e-payments that can utilize the telco infrastructure for new sources of revenue. Thus, this research provides valuable information for telecommunication companies' strategies for their products and services offering to the intended consumers by understanding consumers' personality, design and convenience factors effect on e-payment. Banks are on the lookout to reduce their high cost of operation (OECD, 2006, Lai, 2010: 2014: 2016). Besides core banking services, banks generate good revenue from transaction payment (e.g., cards payment). Another challenge is to keep the customers satisfied and loyal through innovation (e.g., to have all banking solution in one single platform). Thus, by understanding the additional requirements like personality, design and convenience will help banks to design solution for e-payment consumers.

The study results provide the information needed for the development of new products and services caring for the social-environment by promoting cardless, cashless and contactless (Lai, 2013) that will create new businesses for green jobs in the single platform E-payment environment. Organizations will be able to utilize the study findings for developing products and services that meet the consumers' single platform E-payment system while also fulfilling their objective of corporate social responsibility. Thus, with the single platform e-payment platform, the solutions (e.g: site payment using point of sales, internet payment on mobile) are able to be deployed easily and further examples can be found in the articles of "SMART LIVING for SMART CITIES @ the palm of your hand" and SMART HEALTHCARE @ the palm of our hand" (Lai, 2015; Lai, 2016).

CONCLUSION AND FURTHER RESEARCH

In conclusion, the empirical results from the study suggest that design, personality, convenience, perceived usefulness as well as perceived ease of use can lead to consumers' intention to use a single platform E-payment system. It is noted that the factors of the single platform E-payment system should include users' personality, good design with convenience and supports the ease of use and usefulness of the e-payment solutions. In addition, organizations should look into the single platform E-payment system solutions that are easy to use, user-friendly for e-commerce transactions as well as value for money for the consumers. Having wider strategic alliances for the applications and solutions that are accepted globally can further enhance the potential of the consumers' intention to use a single platform E-payment system.

This book chapter serves as an in-depth of discussion for personality as well as the comparison of the data analysis from the split studies in a study of a single platform E-payment system solutions with the understanding of design, personality, and convenience that can be explored through further studies and research in numerous areas. As seen in the results from the split studies, it seems that the model is strong and robust enough to be used in different settings.

A few areas of interest are, for example, in Information Technology (IT) or Information Communication Technology (ICT). The single platform E-payment system as discussed in this chapter has enabled greater accessibility and availability. At the same time, it also calls for greater security. The E-payment systems technologies for the E-commerce world provide a platform for further research in consumers' buying behaviors and other areas related to marketing. Further, organizations are given a bigger integrated spectrum of management including areas like processes, operations etc. through collaboration and globalization.

REFERENCES

Abbas, H. A., & Hamdy, H. I. (2015). Determinants of continuance intention factor in Kuwait communication market: The Case study of Zain-Kuwait. *Computers in Human Behavior*, *49*(0), 648–657. doi:10.1016/j.chb.2015.03.035

Ajzen, I. (2005). *Attitudes, personality, and behavior* (2nd ed.). Open University Press, Mc-Graw-Hill.

Bagozzi, R. P. (2007). The legacy of the Technology Acceptance Model and a Proposal for a Paradigm Shift. *Journal of the Association for Information Systems*, *8*(4/7), 244–254. doi:10.17705/1jais.00122

Bagozzi, R. P., & Yi, Y. (1988). On the evaluation of structural equation models. *Journal of the Academy of Marketing Science, 16*(1), 74–94. doi:10.1007/BF02723327

Baker-Eveleth, L., & Stone, R. W. (2015). Usability, expectation, confirmation, and continuance intentions to use electronic textbooks. *Behaviour & Information Technology, 34*(10), 992–1004. doi:10.1080/0144929X.2015.1039061

Barrick, M. R., & Mount, M. K. (1991). The Big Five personality dimensions and job performance: A meta-analysis. *Personnel Psychology, 44*(1), 1–26. doi:10.1111/j.1744-6570.1991.tb00688.x

Bhatiasevi, V., & Yoopetch, C. (2015). The determinants of intention to use electronic booking among young users in Thailand. *Journal of Hospitality and Tourism Management, 23*, 1–11. doi:10.1016/j.jhtm.2014.12.004

Chiu, C.-M., & Wang, E. T. G. (2008). Understanding Web-based learning continuance intention: The role of subjective task value. *Information & Management, 45*(3), 194–201. doi:10.1016/j.im.2008.02.003

Chou, S. W., Min, H. T., Chang, Y. C., & Lin, C. T. (2009). Understanding continuance intention of knowledge creation using extended expectation– confirmation theory: An empirical study of Taiwan and China online communities. *Behaviour & Information Technology, 29*(6), 557–57. doi:10.1080/01449290903401986

Colquitt, J., Hollenbeck, J., Ilgen, D., LePine, J., & Sheppard, L. (2002). Computer-assisted communication and team decision-making performance: The moderating effect of openness to experience. *The Journal of Applied Psychology, 87*(2), 402–410. doi:10.1037/0021-9010.87.2.402 PMID:12002966

Cooper, D., & Schindler, P. (2008). *Business research methods* (10th ed.). New York: McGraw-Hill/Irwin.

Davis, F. D. (1989). Perceived usefulness, Perceived ease of use, and User Acceptance of Information Technology. *Management Information Systems Quarterly, 13*(3), 319–340. doi:10.2307/249008

Davis, F. D., Bogozzi, R. P., & Warshaw, P. R. (1989). User acceptance of computer technology: A comparison of two theoretical models. *Management Science, 35*(8), 982–1003. doi:10.1287/mnsc.35.8.982

Devaraj, S., Fan, M., & Kohli, R. (2002). Antecedents of B2C channel satisfaction and preference: Validating e-commerce metrics. *Information Systems Research, 13*(3), 316–333. doi:10.1287/isre.13.3.316.77

Devito Da Cunha, A., & Greathead, D. (2007). Does personality matter? An analysis of code-review ability. *Communications of the ACM, 50*(5), 109–112. doi:10.1145/1230819.1241672

Dewan, S. G., & Chen, L. (2005). Mobile payment adoption in the US: A cross-industry, cross platform solution. *Journal of Information Privacy and Security., 1*(2), 4–25. doi:10.1080/15536548.2005.10855765

Digman, J. M., & Takemoto-Chock, N. K. (1981). Factors in the natural language of personality: Re-analysis, comparison, and interpretation of six major studies. *Multivariate Behavioral Research, 16*(2), 149–170. doi:10.120715327906mbr1602_2 PMID:26825420

Elkhani, N., Soltani, S., & Nazir Ahmad, M. (2014). The effects of transformational leadership and ERP system self-efficacy on ERP system usage. *Journal of Enterprise Information Management, 27*(6), 759–785. doi:10.1108/JEIM-06-2013-0031

Fiske, D. W. (1949). Consistency of the factorial structures of personality ratings from different sources. *Journal of Abnormal and Social Psychology, 44*(3), 329–344. doi:10.1037/h0057198 PMID:18146776

Geron, G. (2009). *Business Aspects of the Internet of Things: Mobile Marketing, Seminar of advanced topics*. Zurich: Florian Michahelles.

Gosling, S. D., Rentfrow, P. J., & Swann, W. B. Jr. (2003). A very brief measure of the Big-Five personality domains. *Journal of Research in Personality, 37*(6), 504–528. doi:10.1016/S0092-6566(03)00046-1

Guildford, J. P. & Zimmerman, W. S. (1949). *The Guildford-Zimmerman Temperament Survey*. Beverly Hills, CA: Sheridan Supply.

Ha, S., & Stoel, L. (2009). Consumer e-shopping acceptance: Antecedents in a technology acceptance model. *Journal of Business Research, 62*(5), 565–571. doi:10.1016/j.jbusres.2008.06.016

Hair, J. F., Black, W. C., Babin, B. J., & Anderson, R. E. (2010). *Multivariate Data Analysis* (7th ed.). Pearson Prentice Hall.

Hair, J. F., Black, W. C., Babin, B. J., & Anderson, R. E. (2014). *Multivariate Data Analysis* (7th ed.). Pearson New.

Harrison, R., & Scheela, W. (2017, September). Beyond institutional voids and the middle income trap? The emerging business angel market in Malaysia. *Asia Pacific Journal of Management*, 1–27.

Hassan, S., Naveed, A., & Yılmaz, A. K. (2016). Impact of the Conscientiousness as Personality Trait on both Job and Organizational Performance. *Journal of Managerial Sciences, 10*(1), 1–14.

Henseler, J., Ringle, C. M., & Sarstedt, M. (2014). A new criterion for assessing discriminant validity in variance-based structural equation modeling. *Journal of the Academy of Marketing Science, 43*(1), 115–135. doi:10.100711747-014-0403-8

Henseler, J., Ringle, C. M., & Sinkovics, R. R. (2009). The use of Partial Least Squares Path Modeling in International Marketing. *Advances in International Marketing, 20*, 277–319. doi:10.1108/S1474-7979(2009)0000020014

Hirsh, J., & Dolderman, D. (2007). Personality predictors of consumerism and environmentalism: A preliminary study. *Personality and Individual Differences, 43*(6), 1583–1593. doi:10.1016/j.paid.2007.04.015

Ilies, R., Scott, B., & Judge, T. (2006). The interactive effects of personal traits and experienced states on intraindividual patterns of citizenship behavior. *Academy of Management Journal, 49*(3), 561–575. doi:10.5465/amj.2006.21794672

John, O. P., & Srivastava, S. (1999), The Big Five-trait taxonomy: History, measurement, and theoretical perspectives. In L.A. Pervin & O.P. John (Eds.), Handbook of Personality: Theory & Research (pp. 120-138). New York: Guildford Press.

Jovanovic, M., & Organero, M. (2011). Analysis of the Latest Trends in Mobile Commerce using the NFC Technology, Multidisciplinary Journals in Science and Technology. *Journal of Selected Areas in Telecommunications, 5*, 1–12.

Kim, C., Mirusmonov, M., & Lee, I. (2010). An empirical examination of factors influencing the intention to use mobile payment. *Computers in Human Behavior, 26*(3), 310–322. doi:10.1016/j.chb.2009.10.013

Kim, S. H. (2014). A Study on Adoption Factors of Korean Smartphone Users : A Focus on TAM (Technology Acceptance Model) and UTAUT (Unified Theory of Acceptance and Use of Technology). *Advanced Science and Technology, 57*, 27–30.

Klein, G., Jiang, J., & Tesch, D. (2002). Wanted: Project teams with a blend of is professional orientations. *Communications of the ACM, 45*(6), 81–87. doi:10.1145/508448.508452

Klein, R. B. (2011). *Principles and practice of structural equation modeling*. New York, NY: Guilford.

Lai, P. C. (2006). The significant of E-business and knowledge-based Customer Relationship in the E-market Place Environment. *INTI Journal, 2*(1), 552–559.

Lai, P. C. (2007). The Chip Technology Management Implication in the Era of Globalization: Malaysian Consumers' Perspective. *Asia Pacific Business Review, 3*(1), 91–96. doi:10.1177/097324700700300107

Lai, P. C. (2010). E-business and E-banking. Japan Society for Software Science and Technology, Itech research group.

Lai, P. C. (2013, May). *WalletSIM™ - Contactless, Cardless, Cashless, Convenience*. Paper presented at Singapore Innovest, Singapore.

Lai, P. C. (2014). *Factors Influencing Consumers' Intention to use a single platform E-payment System* (Thesis). UNITEN.

Lai, P. C. (2015). *Smart living for smart cities @ the palm of your hand*. Research Asia.

Lai, P. C. (2016a). *SMART HEALTHCARE @ the palm of our hand*. ResearchAsia.

Lai, P. C. (2016b). Design and Security impact on consumers' intention to use single platform E-payment, Interdisciplinary. *Information Sciences, 22*(1), 111–122.

Lai, P. C. (2017). The literature review of technology adoption models and theories for the novelty technology. *Journal of Information Systems and Technology Management, 14*(1), 21–38. doi:10.4301/S1807-17752017000100002

Lai, P. C. (2018a). Single platform E-payment Consumers' intention to use. *Journal of Information Technology Management, 29*(2), 22–28.

Lai, P. C. (2018b). Research Methodology for novelty technology. *Journal of Information Systems and Technology Management, 15*, 1–18.

Lai, P. C. (2018c). Security as an extension to TAM Model: Consumers' intention to use a single platform E-payment System. *Asia-Pacific Journal of Management Research and Innovation, 13*(3-4), 110–119. doi:10.1177/2319510X18776405

Lai, P. C. (2018d). Research, Innovation and Development Strategic Planning for Intellectual Property Management. *Economic Alternatives., 12*(3), 303–310.

Lai, P. C., & Ahmad, Z. A. (2015). Perceived Enjoyment of Malaysian consumers' intention to use a single platform E-payment. *SHS Web of Conferences, 18*, 1-9.

Lai, P. C., & Scheela, W. (2018). Convergence of technology in the E-commerce World and Venture Capital Landscape: South East Asia, Global Entrepreneurship and New Venture Creation in the Sharing Economy. IGI-Global.

Larsen, R. J., & Ketelaar, T. (1991). Personality and Susceptibility to Positive and Negative Emotional States. *Journal of Personality and Social Psychology*, *61*(1), 132–140. doi:10.1037/0022-3514.61.1.132 PMID:1890584

Lee, M. C. (2009). Factors influencing the adoption of internet banking: An integration of TAM and TPB with perceived risk and perceived benefit. *Electronic Commerce Research and Applications*, *8*(3), 130–141. doi:10.1016/j.elerap.2008.11.006

Lee, Y., & Kozar, K. (2008). An empirical investigation of anti-spyware software adoption: A multi-theoretical perspective. *Inf. Man*, *45*(2), 109–119.

Lee, Y. H., Hsieh, Y. C., & Hsu, C. N. (2011). Adding Innovation Diffusion Theory to the Technology Acceptance Model : Supporting Employees ' Intentions to use E-Learning Systems E-learning and TAM The Technology Acceptance Model (TAM). *International Forum of Educational Technology & Society*, *14*(4), 124–137.

Lee, Y. H., Hsieh, Y. C., & Ma, C. Y. (2011). A model of organizational employees' e-learning systems acceptance. *Knowledge-Based Systems*, *24*(3), 355–366. doi:10.1016/j.knosys.2010.09.005

Li, H., & Liu, Y. (2014). Understanding post-adoption behaviors of e-service users in the context of online travel services. *Information & Management*, *51*(8), 1043–1052. doi:10.1016/j.im.2014.07.004

Lin, J., & Hsieh, P. (2006). The role of technology readiness in customers' perception and adoption of self-service technologies. *International Journal of Service Industry Management*, *17*(5), 497–517. doi:10.1108/09564230610689795

Lin, W.-S., & Wang, C.-H. (2012). Antecedences to continued intentions of adopting e-learning system in blended learning instruction: A contingency framework based on models of information system success and task-technology fit. *Computers & Education*, *58*(1), 88–99. doi:10.1016/j.compedu.2011.07.008

Luarn, P., & Lin, H. H. (2005). Toward an understanding of the behavioral intention to use mobile banking. *Computers in Human Behavior*, *21*(6), 873–891. doi:10.1016/j.chb.2004.03.003

Mischel, W. (2004). Toward an integrative science of the person. *Annual Review of Psychology*, *55*(1), 1–22. doi:10.1146/annurev.psych.55.042902.130709 PMID:14744208

Moon, J., & Kim, Y. (2001). Extending the TAM for a world wide web context. *Journal of Information & Management Science*, *27*(1), 15–22.

Mooradian, T. A., & Olver, J. M. (1994). Neuroticism, Affect and Postpurchase Processes. In C. T. Allen & D. R. John (Eds.), *NA - Advances in Consumer Research, 21* (pp. 595–600). Provo, UT: Association for Consumer Research.

Moore, G. C., & Benbasat, I. (1991). Development of and instrument to measure the perceptions of adopting and information technology innovation. *Information Systems Research*, *2*(3), 192–222. doi:10.1287/isre.2.3.192

Myers, S. D., Sen, S., & Alexandrov, A. (2010). The Moderating Effect Of Personality Traits on Attitudes toward Advertisements: A Contingency Framework. *Management & Marketing Challenges for Knowledge Society*, *5*(3), 3–20.

Oppenheim, A. N. (1992). *Questionnaire, design, interviewing and attitude measurement*. London: Pinter Pub Ltd.

Oreg, S., & Nov, O. (2008). Exploring motivations for contributing to open source initiatives: The roles of contribution context and personal values. *Computers in Human Behavior*, *24*(5), 2055–2073. doi:10.1016/j.chb.2007.09.007

Peabody, D., & Goldberg, L. R. (1989). Some determinants of factor structures from personality traits descriptors. *Journal of Personality and Social Psychology*, *57*(3), 552–567. doi:10.1037/0022-3514.57.3.552 PMID:2778639

Picard, R. R., & Berk, K. N. (1990). Data Splitting. *The American Statistician*, *2*(44), 140–147.

Pratt, R., & Chudoba, K. (2006). *Is extraversion the next predictor of system adoption? Effects of personality traits on system acceptance*. Paper presented at the Academy of Management Meeting, Atlanta, GA.

Pulford, B., & Sohal, H. (2006). The influence of personality on HE students' confidence in their academic abilities. *Personality and Individual Differences*, *41*(8), 1409–1419. doi:10.1016/j.paid.2006.05.010

Ramayah, T., & Lo, M. C. (2007). Impact of shared beliefs on "perceived usefulness" and "ease of use" in the implementation of an enterprise resource planning system. *Management Research News*, *30*(6), 420–431. doi:10.1108/01409170710751917

Rogers, E. M. (2003). *Diffusion of Innovations* (5th ed.). New York: Free Press.

Schiffman, L., & Kanuk, L. (2010). *Consumer Behaviour* (10th ed.). Prentice Hall.

Seiders, K., Voss, G. B., Grewal, D., & Godfrey, A. L. (2005). Do satisfied customers buy more? Examining moderating influences in a retailing context. *Journal of Marketing*, *69*(4), 26–43. doi:10.1509/jmkg.2005.69.4.26

Sekaran, U. (2003). *Research Methods for Business: A Skill-Building Approach* (4th ed.). John Wiley and Sons, Inc.

Shih, H. P. (2004). Extended technology acceptance model of Internet utilization behavior. *Information & Management*, *41*(6), 719–729. doi:10.1016/j.im.2003.08.009

Shropshire, J., Warkentin, M., & Sharma, S. (2015). Personality, attitudes, and intentions: Predicting initial adoption of information security behavior. *Computers & Security*, *49*, 177–191. doi:10.1016/j.cose.2015.01.002

Shuaibu, K., & Muhammad, A. (2016). Electronic Payment System Challenges in Gombe State: Evidences from the Office of the Accountant General of Gombe State, Nigeria. *Journal of the Humanities and Social Sciences*, *21*(4), 1–7.

Sirgy, M. J. (1985). Using Self-Congruity and Ideal Congruity to predict purchase motivation. *Journal of Business Research*, *13*(3), 195–206. doi:10.1016/0148-2963(85)90026-8

Smits, D., & De Boeck, P. (2007). From anger to verbal aggression: Inhibition at different levels. *Personality and Individual Differences*, *43*(1), 47–57. doi:10.1016/j.paid.2006.11.006

Stone, R. W., & Baker-Eveleth, L. (2013). Students' expectation, confirmation, and continuance intention to use electronic textbooks. *Computers in Human Behavior*, *29*(3), 984–990. doi:10.1016/j.chb.2012.12.007

Tang, J. E., Tang, T. I., & Chiang, C. H. (2012). Blog learning: Effects of users' usefulness and efficiency towards continuance intention. *Behaviour & Information Technology*, *33*(1), 36–50. doi:10.1080/0144929X.2012.687772

Thatcher, J., & Perrewé, P. (2002). An empirical examination of individual traits as antecedents to computer anxiety and computer self-efficacy. *Management Information Systems Quarterly*, *26*(4), 381–399. doi:10.2307/4132314

Van der Heijden, H. (2003). Factors influencing the usage of websites: The case of a generic portal in the Netherlands. *Information & Management*, *40*(6), 541–549. doi:10.1016/S0378-7206(02)00079-4

Venkatesh, V., & Davis, F. (1996). A model of the antecedents of perceived ease of use: Development and test. *Decision Sciences*, *27*(3), 451–481. doi:10.1111/j.1540-5915.1996.tb01822.x

Venkatesh, V., Davis, F., Morris, M., & Michael, G. (2007). Dead of Alive? The development, trajectory, and future of technology adoption research. *Journal of the Association for Information Systems*, *8*(4), 268–286. doi:10.17705/1jais.00120

Vinzi, E., Trinchera, L., & Amato, S. (2010). PLS path modeling: from foundations to recent developments and open issues for model assessment and improvement. Handbook of Partial Least Squares: Concepts, Methods, and Applications in Marketing and Related Fields, 47-82.

Wang, W., Ngai, E. W. T., & Wei, H. (2011). Explaining Instant Messaging Continuance Intention: The Role of Personality. *International Journal of Human-Computer Interaction*, *28*(8), 500–510. doi:10.1080/10447318.2011.622971

Wei, D., Shuo, Z., Luo, G., Chen, Z., & Ling, X. (2011). Analyze on Mobile Payment Based on RFID. *Procedia Environmental Sciences*, *10*, 950–955. doi:10.1016/j.proenv.2011.09.152

Wortley, D. J., & Lai, P. C. (2017). The Impact of Disruptive Enabling Technologies on Creative Education. *3rd International Conference on Creative Education*, 1-3.

Zweig, D., & Webster, J. (2003). Personality as a moderator of monitoring acceptance. *Computers in Human Behavior*, *19*(4), 479–493. doi:10.1016/S0747-5632(02)00075-4

KEY TERMS AND DEFINITIONS

ASEAN: ASEAN is geographically divided into two sub regions, namely Mainland Southeast Asia (or Indochina) and Maritime Southeast Asia. ASEAN consists of countries from Vietnam, Laos, Cambodia, Thailand, Myanmar (Burma), Malaysia, Indonesia, Philippines, Brunei, Singapore, and East Timor.

Card Payment: Card Payment is a plastic card (e.g., credit card or debit card or pre-paid card or electronic-wallet) in order to pay for products and services, but also the one that takes the money directly from our bank account.

Electronic Payment (E-Payment): Electronic payment systems in this chapter will focus on the retail payment systems involving card, internet, and mobile.

Internet Payment: Internet payment system facilitates the acceptance of electronic payment for online transactions that is also known as electronic funds transfer or electronic commerce (e-commerce) through the world wide web.

Mobile Payment: Mobile payment also referred to as mobile commerce, mobile wallet, mobile money and mobile banking are generally referred to payment services operated under financial regulations of each country and performed via a mobile device.

Single Platform E-Payment: A single platform solution technology combining card, internet, and mobile technology for what the users' needs and wants.

APPENDIX 1: "SMART LIVING FOR SMART CITIES @ THE PALM OF YOUR HAND"

A smart city uses information and communication technologies (ICT) to enhance the efficiency, convenience accessibility, performance and interactivity of urban services, to reduce costs and resource consumption and to improve quality of life in the city. Do you know the number of hours' residents of Greater Kuala Lumpur spend stuck in traffic in a single year? 250,000,000 hours (Source: Malaysia Economic Monitor June 2015, World Bank).

Smart city applications are developed with the goal of improving the management of people flows in and out of the cities and allowing for real-time responses to the challenges faced in our daily life. Providing convenient and rapid mobility, connectivity with social cohesion systems to today's urban and suburban consumers can be challenging but possible. Imagine if you can have smart living tools at the palm of your hand using the mobile phone as shown in the diagrams below. Start your day by using the ''iPark™'' (Parking app - The goal is to enhance parking experience by enabling users to view and book parking lots, and use their phones as access cards to parking zones through Near Field Communication. iPark™ saves fuel, time and promotes green environment) to book a parking spot near the public transport terminal (e.g: Kelana Jaya Station) before leaving the house and then able to use the MySIM™ application in the phone already activated with transport pre-paid credit to pay at a touch to ride the Light Rail Transit (LRT) to KL Sentral.

While in the Light Rail Transit (LRT), just use ''Shopbuddy™'' to order and purchase breakfast set at a special price from food outlet (e.g: McDonald) where you can pick up when you arrive and share the promotion on social media with your friends. Just tap/scan to pick up your breakfast. Then, walk to your office and use the MySIM™ application on the phone to open the office door access. While enjoying your breakfast in the office, you can log in to your ''smart home app'' to make sure your child is safe at home and use ''Health app'' to see how many calories you're taking for breakfast this morning as well as how many steps you've walked from home to office.

Lai, P. C. (2015). *Smart living for smart cities @ the palm of your hand.* Research Asia.

APPENDIX 2: "SMART HEALTHCARE INNOVATION @ THE PALM OF OUR HAND"

The Smart HealthCare Innovation solutions allow for a stress-less trip to the hospital for medical links information technology, communications and healthcare to improve the quality and safety of patient care @ the palm of our hand. A long queue of patients and parking space are problems faced at hospitals. Furthermore, visitors and patients have difficulty to reach the exact location in hospitals too especially when they have to visit several different clinics or departments during the visit. Medical prescriptions are also ''alien'' to patients with medical terminology. Therefore, we've come out with solutions on a single platform that can be accessible on a mobile phone by the users.

On the day of appointment with a doctor, the patient can use the mobile phone to get the queue number with estimate time of seeing the doctor using the Queue ticketing system and then reserve a car park space to ensure the parking space is available upon arrival with iPark™ (Your priority Car Park Booking). The hospital is like a maze to visitors and patients. Therefore, the QNavigation™ System is available to assist visitors and patients to direct them to the right location both online and offline (advantage over most existing applications which do not support offline navigation). Upon seeing the doctor and get the prescription, the payment can be made using the MySIM™ e-payment. MySIM™ has the cutting-edge technology that looks like a regular SIM card but with combined Telecommunication SIM, Bankcard SIM and Transport SIM (Touch N Go) plus with an integrated hybrid antenna on the SIM itself which operates at 13.56MHz that can be used for Card, Internet and Mobile Payment works on any phone that uses the SIMCard. MySIM™ can be used to enter the parking space as well as store the owner identity with health information (e.g: allergies, blood type etc) and link to E-payment that can be retrieved by touching at the secured readers in the hospital. The medications information can be transferred to the Medisafe™app (breakthrough technology on imaging with the capability to scan and identify the drug image) on the mobile phone. Basically, Medisafe™ app is to identify the correct medication to be taken at home as an extension to patient safety. The Smart Healthcare Innovation Solution able to provide comfort to patients by reducing their queuing, searching, waiting and parking time. It also lessens stress on staff so that they can focus on their job instead of managing frustrated patients. The use of the e-ticket is eco-friendly and alternative to a paper ticket from queue ticket, parking ticket to the prescription of medications on a mobile phone. This has a positive impact on the well-being of the stakeholders from the perspective of convenience to patients, the productivity of staff to patient safety of the medication.

Lai, P. C. (2016). *SMART HEALTHCARE @ the palm of our hand.* Research Asia.

Chapter 16
A Qualitative Insight Into the Personal Factors Impacting Online Impulse Behavior

Harish Kumar
BML Munjal University, India

Ruchi Garg
BML Munjal University, India

Payal Kumar
BML Munjal University, India

Ritu Chhikara
BML Munjal University, India

ABSTRACT

The purpose of the chapter is to have a deeper understanding of impulse buying and find out the different personal factors that affect the impulse behavior of the consumer in the online context. Phenomenology methodology was used by conducting 12 in-depth interviews with Gen Y as the main respondents. The interview transcripts were analyzed through the method of thematic analysis. This study found that factors such as sudden urge to buy, haptics, risk factors, persuasion, convenience, monotony and boredom, and trust were the dominant personal factors. These factors act as the triggers for consumers to make impulse purchase decisions. This study differentiates the personal and market-oriented factors and broaden the understanding of impulse buying behavior. The findings will enable the marketers to make effective strategies and help the business organizations to increase their revenues.

INTRODUCTION

Impulse buying refers to a buying behavior, which is totally unplanned in nature. The decision is made just before the purchase and doesn't necessarily focus on the actual needs. (Clover, 1950; Stern, 1962; Rook, 1985). Previous studies have shown that share of the impulse buy to total sales has grown signifi-

DOI: 10.4018/978-1-5225-9697-4.ch016

cantly from 40% to 75% from the time the construct was developed till now including brick and mortar stores and online shopping. (Hausman, 2000).

In a study of National Endowment for Financial Education, 2010 report 87% of the adults in America admit that they make an impulse buy. A person on an average spends $110000 for the impulse buy in his/her lifetime. From the past sixty years, researchers have studied different aspects and factors due to which consumers tend to go for impulse buying. However, in the era of internet, rapidly increasing virtual traffic and online market places to buy has led us to focus on different dimension related to impulsive behavior online. Online selling through various online market platforms like amazon.com, flipkart.com etc. with their effective marketing strategies, vast array of products and good discounts to consumers has stimulated impulsive buying.

Social media has also played a very crucial role in changing the mindset of consumers, particularly in impulse buying. Facebook has 2.23 billion users across the world, WhatsApp has 1.5 billion users; YouTube has 1.9 billion users as per Statista (2018). Hence, in this chapter, we look at some personal factors, which are stimulating the consumers to shop impulsively in the online context and also how these factors either market related or personal have an impact on behavioral patterns due to the existence of online markets in comparison to an offline setting.

LITERATURE REVIEW

The phenomena of impulse purchase emerged in 1950 by Clover (1950) when the studies found out that a significant share of the total sales was unplanned and sudden. He described it as an unplanned purchase. Beatty and Ferrell (1998) definition of impulse buy is considered to be the one the most extensive definition "a sudden and immediate purchase with no pre-shopping intentions either to buy the specific product category or to fulfill a specific buying task. The behavior occurs after experiencing an urge to buy and it tends to be spontaneous and without a lot of reflection (i.e., it is 'impulsive')".

Stern (1962) further contributed significantly to the literature he classified impulse behavior in four categories: 1. Pure impulse, 2. Planned impulse, 3. Reminder impulse and 4.Suggestion impulse. This study provided a new land base for further studies. Rook (1985) studied various behavioral component of individual and linked impulse behavior with the hedonic component, materialism, and sensation. Rook further in (1987, 1993, 1995) contributed to the literature, where he referred that impulse behavior is dependent on consumer's mood. Rook and Fisher (1995) defined it as a spontaneous and immediate response. One similarity that exists between online and offline consumer behavior is the perceived usefulness of the consumer that will tell about their repetitive visit to the store with the use of Technology acceptance model, TAM (Koufaris, 2002).

MARKET-ORIENED FACTORS

In a comparative view of significant contribution to the total sales, the offline channel is more dominating over online system. Social media is a very crucial player in the online context, which affects consumer behavior. Facebook is the most influential social platform affecting consumer (Laura and Carlos, 2018).

Impulse buying has also been defined as "a sudden, compelling, hedonically complex purchase behavior in which the rapidity of the impulse purchase decision precludes any thoughtful, deliberate consideration of alternatives or future implications" (Sharma et al, 2010, p. 277).

In the context of online impulse behavior varieties of the product is found to be one of the most critical factor (Brohan, 2000). According to Kuofaris (2002) anonymity is an advantage when you go for shop online as for some type of products consumers don't feel comfortable in the in-store setting. As well as online stores don't have the constructs of store opening timings and a geographical location. Demographic factors are positively connected with impulse behavior. This study also showed that higher income and age group between 25 years to 50 years are more likely to buy impulsively. A study conducted on demographic factors affecting impulse behavior in online and offline setting found that gender and marital status mattered most as compared to others. Incidentally men make more impulse purchase than women. (Kaur, Sharma, 2015).

The online market has a greater variety of product hence it induces more impulse buy. As consumers get lot of option at a single time they get confused about the purchase decision. (Kinney, 2009). Price discounts and offers are found to the great stimulator in common for both online and offline impulse buys (Kim, 2009).

Price sensitivity as a factor is found more in the online context as a consumer can easily compare prices of products in different online markets. (Xu and Huang, 2014; Koski, N. 2004). In addition, online market has more promotional flexibility as compared to physical stores. Promotions can be more customized and easy to target the potential audience.

In the present scenario, people prefer referring online reviews prior to taking a decision, as it provides them reliability when they are going to buy something else. Online reviews also bring positivity for the consumer and it makes their urge to buy stronger and ultimately it induces an impulse purchase. (Kem. Zhang, Haiqin Xu, Zhao, Yu, 2018). Credit card also positively enhances online impulse buying behavior. Apart from this quality of the website is also a positively impacting factor for online impulse buying. (Akram, Umair,2018).

PERSONAL FACTORS

Due to the presence of sensory feelings, offline channels are high on impulsiveness than the online channel (Gupta, 2011). In the in-store shopping, consumer can see and check the product, which is not the case in online shopping. Direct contact between buyer and seller influences the impulse behavior; while in brick and mortar set-up, the consumer has an opportunity to directly interact with the salesperson and gets more satisfaction out of the experience.

A study made by Varma & Agarwal (2014) reveals that most of the purchase made impulsively is offline in nature even though they all are having online access to buy products but they prefer to go out, experience something new from their daily routine and remove monotony.

Lack of time was another factor found that induces men to buy online whereas women prefer buying offline. Consumer prefers to buy products impulsively when they are provided with great convenience value. Easy accessibility of the product is a very dominating factor for both kinds of the impulse buy i.e. online vs offline (Kuofaris, 2002)

Bhatnagar et al. (2000) found that risk factors are more dominating in online purchase with respect to offline purchase. Sometimes there is an issue with the credibility of the website, or defective products delivery, spams, or credit card information stolen. Around 30 percent of online buyers and 25 percent of offline consumers are impulse buyers. It stressed on the hedonic effect in an online setting as well. The study also tells that offline impulse is a more contributory then online impulse purchase. (Aragoncillo, Orus, 2018).

Consumer loyalty is always important for impulsive behavior. Consumer loyalty was found low in online buying in contrast to offline store shopping. Because brick and mortar store provide a sensory feeling, visuals, and tangibility. (Morrisette et al.1999).

The impulsiveness of the consumer depends more on the personal factors than channel factors. Ease of the payment, personal references and a large amount of variety of product availability are one of the most influencing factors in online impulse buy. (Aragoncillo, Orus, 2018)

Consumer sensitive to haptic more preferably goes for in-store shopping as they can feel and touch the physical (Peck and Childers, 2003). In the context of online markets, quality of the website, its attractiveness and free shipping are found to be one of the significant factors for impulse purchase. The retail sector also has a significant revenue share from an impulse purchase. Amazon prime is a great example of how they have been successful in attracting impulse buyers. The key elements for this are instant delivery of the product and its easy access.

Grocery products are the main segment of the total items purchased impulsively. Anger and boredom also contribute positively to impulse behavior. When a person is angry or bored then he is more prone to go for sudden or unplanned shopping. If you are going for a planned shopping chance of impulse buy decrease by 13%.

Sometimes boredom and monotony also trigger impulse buying behavior. Customers are found to shopping just because they were feeling bored and monotonous. (Sundstrom et.al, 2019).

Perceived personalization of the social media advertisements also enhances the tendency of online impulse consumer behavior.

By the study of the literature, it can be seen that researchers have done numerous work on the factor findings which affects online and offline impulse buying behavior. But a major part of them is focused on the factors, which are market-oriented while little work is done on common personal factors of an individual, which impact online and offline impulse behavior simultaneously.

An in-depth study of online impulse behavior is needed for further understanding of impulse behavior. (Aragoncillo, Orus, 2018).

Hence, the complete episode of online impulse buying needs to be explored by phenomenology from their urge to buy till their post-purchase behavior by taking semi-structured in-depth interviews. (Mittal, Sondhi, 2018). It will enable marketers to get more insight into the study of online impulse behavior. It will also enable them to make better marketing strategies and increase their sales as well as add to the existing body of the knowledge to help researchers for further studies.

Most of the factors which contribute to the impulse behavior are market-oriented factors i.e. easy access of the product (Kuofaris, 2002), price discounts and offers Dawson & Kim (2009), Promotion and marketing Koski, N. (2004), Some of the personal factor i.e. Anonymity (Kuofaris, 2002), Hedonic impact, (Rook, 1985), (Sharma et al. 2010) also impacts the impulse behavior. So we propose

P1: Market-related factors are more dominating than personal factors for online impulse behavior.

Weinberg and Gottwald (1982) proposed that both cognitive and affective domain are very crucial in the context of impulse behavior but affective part is more dominating over the cognitive state in terms of the impact on the impulse consumer behavior. (Dawson and Kim, 2009) stated that affective factors are positively related to online impulse behavior whereas the cognitive domain is having a negative impact on online impulse behavior. But there lacks a study on online and offline methods simultaneously for the elaborated. So we further propose

P2: Affective factors are more dominating than cognitive factors.
P3: Affective factors have a positive impact on online impulse buying
P4: Cognitive factors have a negative impact on online impulse behavior.

In the study of impulse behavior online channel is found to be more impulsive than offline channel according to (Verhagen, 2011). But another study made on online and offline channels for impulse behavior reveals that brick and mortar store is high on impulsiveness as compared to shopping online. Kearney (2013), Sharma et.al. (2010). From the above-mentioned results, which seem to be contradictory, there is a need to further explore the impact and validate, which channel is high on impulsiveness. Hence, we propose the following:

P5: Online channel is high on impulsiveness than the offline channel.

Figure 1. The conceptual model

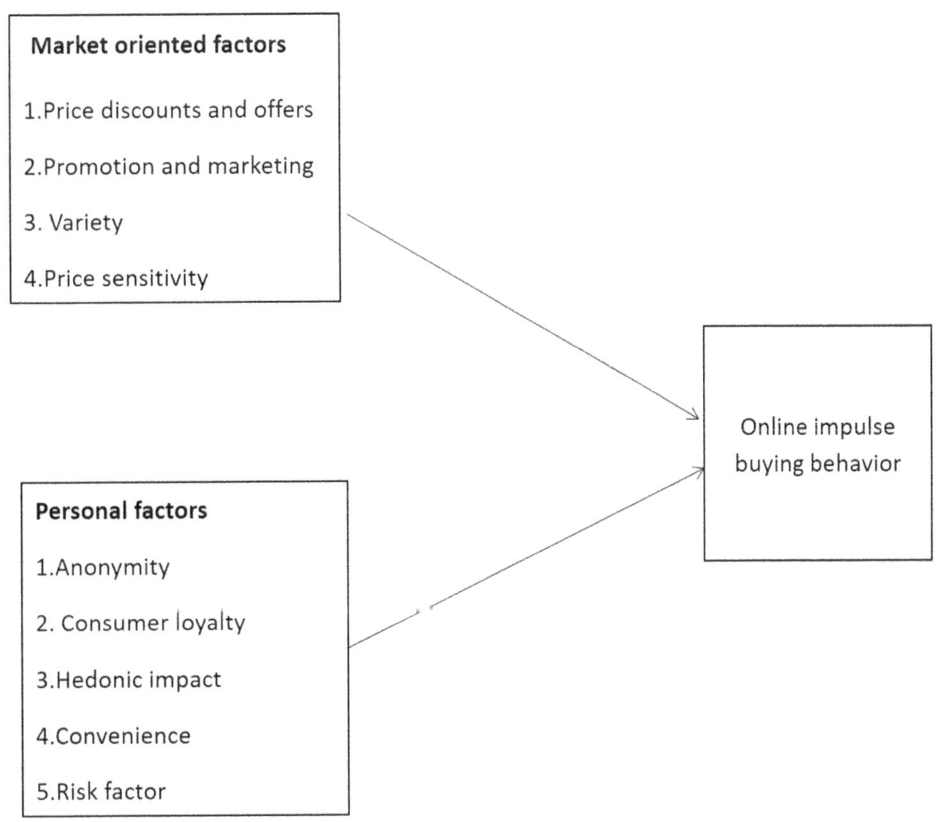

RESEARCH METHOD

A phenomenological study was conducted by taking in-depth semi-structured interviews making for making sure the maximum insight into the phenomena. The interviews were taken at the residence of the respondent so that they feel comfortable without any apprehension of being judged by others.

The questionnaire was prepared after a critical examination of the literature. Various factors and key aspects for the impulse behavior were pointed out and accordingly the questions were prepared. An in-depth semi-structured interview method was used to a deeper understanding of the phenomena. Bastin (2010) and Hausman (2000) has also used this approach. Firstly, respondents were asked about the convenient timing for the interview. On their given time interviews were conducted and their audio recording was done. After that a transcript of was made and then analyzed. The respondents were 18 years and above and living in metro cities. The respondents include both men and women. On-probability convenient sampling was used in the study.

FINDINGS

Monotony and Boredom

When people are sitting idle and they have nothing to do then they go for surfing the internet and instantly see some lucrative product or offer and are hence stimulated to go for an impulse purchase. The same case happens in the offline context as well. During window shopping a consumer is suddenly attracted towards something lucrative buys it.

we go for a Window shopping in an outlet but we ended up buying the small thing from there.

Suddenly it's like if you are online and just getting bored. One day it happened to me as I would just get bored, so I opened a website and I was just scrolling down the products. I bought products for Rupees 2000 but I didn't need them but it was like so attractive that I bought it. So it happens many of the times like when you're getting bored you use your phone and buy a product.

Impulsively, is like it never strikes in my mind like what to buy or not it's just the attractiveness of the website and impulsive behavior it happens normally when you are free.

When I am getting bored so I will scroll through the sites

I always go for Window shopping and I try different clothes but there are few things which I like so I ended up buying them.

Haptics

The inability of the consumer to touch the product or feel the product in the online purchase turns out to be one of the most important factors adversely affecting impulse buying. In case of offline setting, the customer has the privilege to actually see the product, try out and even feel the product so it gives them a better rationale to buy that product thus going for an impulse purchase.

It is basically offline because I don't prefer buying online because I want to get the feel of the product that I am purchasing my size and how I am I looking in that outfit so I need to get that feeling before buying the product

That is the main factor, that I do less online shopping, you when you see a product when you see the clothes stuff and you know the size, most of the times I cannot measure that what I should it be M L Xl, whatever in online it is very difficult to calculate that.

Because I prefer, if I feel the thing and you know I touch the thing, I can I think I can judge it better, the fitting and all mostly about the clothes

Trust

A consumer's trust about the website or online market place is also responsible for his impulse purchase. A consumer having strong confidence in the website/market place tends to be make impulsive purchase. Generally, online market places having low goodwill are not considered good for purchase.

Because these brands are known in India and you are sure that they will deliver. If you are scrolling on Facebook and Instagram in your experience as well you might have seen some random websites giving the same things which you looked at the trusted websites like Amazon. There is a website call soul store that was one risk I took to order a t-shirt, but then again I wasn't sure that they will deliver to my place because they don't even have a COD option. So, when you know how you don't have a COD option you generally don't pay through a debit card and then expect them to deliver. When you don't trust them when you haven't been buying from them, so that is one thing for me that if I don't trust the website and if there is no COD option then I don't go for that website

Because as of now I have a good experience with these two best websites and there is a sense of trust on these websites because I purchase and I feel secure when I purchase that

Risk Factors

The risk is found to be more dominant in online channel. Because of the credit card payment, quality of the product delivered, promised delivery deadline etc. Because of the risk factor, it brings a negative impact on the online impulse consumer behavior as it brings a sense of insecurity in the mindset of the consumer while making an online purchase.

In case of clothes, convenience factor will come, because online I'm hesitant to buy clothes because whenever I buy clothes when they will get delivered so if there is a size issue or some damage so I have to return it back there is no convenience because my product was not delivered as such

Exactly, sometimes I feel so. I was looking for jeans or something else but I didn't feel satisfied from it, when it arrived I was totally dissatisfied

I have purchased two three things from these sites and then I know the quality because basically, the problem with online is that they cannot assure the quality or they cannot assure the product so I have purchased some 2-from these websites and I feel that they give the good quality products.

My preference is when I am back in my University when I'm in a proper City like in Delhi or Chandigarh I will prefer to buy stuff offline, going to store you know is much better and much reliable rather than you know seeing their pictures and then trying and then returning it.

Convenience

In the online channel, consumer has convenience to purchase a product anytime from anywhere with less time consumption hence it triggers impulse buying. Satisfaction level of the consumer is also higher in the online channel.

For sure it is positive that if you are buying it online you are not like, when you reach back home all the way from the traffic and everything then you need to go back and return. So these policies are quite flexible.

I think it's more in online mode because for offline mode we have to plan go for shopping, go to the market and all so I think impulsive shopping is more in online mode.

Actually online marketing, I can use 24/7 from wherever I am. So, I can purchase from wherever I am I am sitting in my hostel room I can purchase a good if I don't like the good I can exchange it. I can get my money back directly to my bank account, if I use the product. If there, is any problem I can refund it. I can return it and get my refund back and so I think online shopping is a very good option for impulsive buying and if I have not been sleeping at night, I go and scroll up, Myntra, Amazon, then I see something I buy it so I think impulsive buying is pretty good for online shopping.

Like as I stay in hostel, so I can't go and buy products every day so online buying helps me to get the product at my doorstep. I just have to go and order it and I will get it the next day like Amazon is providing you Prime, Prime delivery, so you order today you get it next day, so it's basically very easy to get the products. They are providing same day delivery also nowadays so you order it and you get it in the evening you don't have to go anywhere it's at your doorstep.

Sudden Urge to Buy

It is one of the most significant factors responsible for an impulse purchase. Sometimes the customer has a sudden urge to buy a product or avail service and he makes his decision instantly. There is no rationale for the decision, maybe the customer just got attracted towards the product or just made up his mind and bought without any planning.

Actually I am very fond of watches, so in last 3-4 years when these online portals have increased so much, I spontaneously bought a watch and not for myself but for my cousins and everybody, if I see a watch it's good and the amount they are offering is very good, I purchase it.

Once I did, actually not once many times, like when you go on Amazon or something so you find products which you don't need but it's like it's very attractive and I have seen it like once you like a product.

Like, when I went to buy a dress but then I saw boot so I felt the urge to buy that product.

Persuasion/Reference

The customer may get influenced by his peers, friends or others and may go for an unplanned purchase. Earlier the consumer may not be wanting to buy such product randomly but when he saw his peer or friend who bought a particular product then he was instantly motivated to go for it and hence made an impulse purchase.

I felt there was a scene that I saw a girl of my age trying that boots, So…yeah after seeing that so I also felt that I need to also get that product

Peer group can be taken as a good example which happens you know if you see your friend wearing some different dress, some different kind of denim that has come into the market so ya that made me feel that I also want to buy that product so peer group is also a very major factor to influence my Purchase.

Many times, like frequently I tend to do that like if get influenced by someone like this product is very good and all that then some impulse generates

CONCLUSION

A qualitative research undertaking an in-depth interview was carried out. The findings reveal various personal factors are accountable for consumers to go for an impulse purchase apart from different market-oriented factors. Impulse shopping is induced due to stress, anxiety, boredom or even monotony by a consumer i.e. an impulse purchase then makes him feel happy and also refresh his mind. Online channel is not usually a preferred option for impulse purchase as a consumer really wants to have a sense of touch or feel of the product. A brick and mortar set-up provides this feeling and hence a consumer feels much more satisfied about their purchase decision after feeling the product. Online channel lacks this personal aspect and hence consumer usually refrains from making an online purchase.

Consumers trust towards a certain marketplace or website is also very significant. Consumers are found to be more impulsive in case they have a nice past experience with that website or marketplace. Hence, when they go for another purchase they don't think so much about the risk factors of the website or marketplace as they have already experienced it. Hence, there are greater chances of being impulsive in this scenario. Whereas on the other hand if a website does not have a goodwill then consumer will rarely make an impulsive purchase from it.

This study also reveals that consumer finds online shopping riskier as a lot of factors responsible for this. Credit card payments, no quality assurance, timely delivery of the product are some of the major concerns for the consumers, which prohibit them to be impulsive in nature. Consumers feel a strong sense of confidence in the online channel. They do not have time, easy return policy, quick refunds to the accounts are one of the stimulators that induces the sense of impulsiveness in the minds of consumers. A feeling of "must have "the product or unexpectedly getting attracted towards a product, instantly being high intense about the product reveals a sudden urge to buy happens to the impulse consumers and they shop for this without any rationale or pre-planning.

Sometimes, an impulse buyer is also influenced by peers, friends who are using a product and he simultaneously gets a feeling of having the same kind of product. Overall, this chapter provides an enriched glimpse of the different personal factors responsible for the impulse decision in the online context.

THEORETICAL CONTRIBUTION

It will not only help in contrasting the similarities and differences in factors for an impulse buying behavior but also broaden the perspective of impulse buying behavior for others. This study provides a background for further research for scholars as they can get a glimpse of the factors responsible for the consumer behavior in the context of impulse behavior.

PRACTICAL CONTRIBUTION

The findings will enable the marketers to make more effective strategies and help the business organization to increase their revenues. With the help of the identification of the factors the market strategists will be in a better position to get the target customers as well.

LIMITATION AND FUTURE RESEARCH DIRECTION

This study has several limitations. Firstly, the sampling methodology has some constraints because the respondents were asked to recall their most recent impulse purchase. Maybe they would have a different experience in a planned purchase. Secondly, this study neglects situational or demographic factors, which could be impacting the impulse decision as well

Apart from this size of the sample is small and the findings are tentative in nature so generalization becomes difficult. The study has been conducted on the age group of 18-30 years as their needs, income, the behavior is different from the people of age group of 30 years and above so it is interesting to study the consumer behavior of those as well so the better validity of the above mentioned personal factors.

Since this study has taken online channel into consideration, as impulse behavior in brick and mortar stores may be completely different, so researchers should consider exploring this phenomenon in the offline context specifically for the age group 30 years and above.

Table 1 and Table 2 show the different factors impacting impulse buying behavior extracted from the study of the literature.

Table 1. Market oriented factors

Market oriented factors		
Factors	**Findings**	**Author**
1. Price discounts and offers	Various promotions tools in terms of discounts and offers stimulate consumers to go for impulse buying in both kinds of markets.	Dawson & Kim (2009).
2. Promotion and marketing	Promotion of the product to the target audience is more flexible in case of the online market, SEO, SEM, social media and other platform provide more selectivity to online promotion. Even though promotion in an offline setting also encourages impulse behavior.	Koski, (2004); Pessemier, (1982)
3. Variety	Greater variety of products encourages impulse behavior. In online markets, more varieties of products are available in contrast to in store.	Kinney et al.(2009)
4. Price sensitivity	Consumer behavior in online market is more price sensitive due to easier comparison, quick access to different marketplaces	Xu and Huang (2014)

Table 2. Personal factors

Personal factors		
Factors	**Findings**	**Author**
1. Anonymity	Sometime for certain type of products, consumer feels discomfort to buy. In such situation, online channel is more preferred as there is no direct contact with the seller.	Kuoforis (2002)
2. Consumer loyalty	Consumer loyalty in terms of impulse behavior is low in online markets	Morrisette et al. 1999.
3. Hedonic impact	There is a presence of hedonic component in the consumer behavior in both types of channel online as well as offline.	Rook (1985), Sharma et al, (2010), Aragoncillo, Orus (2018).
4. Convenience	Convenience as a factor triggers both kinds of impulse behavior in online and offline. Yet consumer is found to be more satisfied in online shopping as the product is available anytime and can be purchased anywhere.	Kuofaris (2002)
5. Risk factor	Compared to in-store shopping consumers feel more insecure in their behavior when they shop online. Credit card information, product quality, credibility of the website are the main issues. Consumer feels secured while they purchase in-store.	Bhatnagar et al. (2000)

REFERENCES

Akram, U., Hui, P., Kaleem Khan, M., Tanveer, Y., Mehmood, K., & Ahmad, W. (2018). How website quality affects online impulse buying: Moderating effects of sales promotion and credit card use. *Asia Pacific Journal of Marketing and Logistics*, *30*(1), 235–256. doi:10.1108/APJML-04-2017-0073

Aragoncillo, L., & Orus, C. (2018). Impulse buying behaviour: An online-offline comparative and the impact of social media. *Spanish Journal of Marketing-ESIC*, *22*(1), 42–62. doi:10.1108/SJME-03-2018-007

Beatty, S. E., & Ferrell, M. E. (1998). Impulse buying: Modeling its precursors. *Journal of Retailing*, *74*(2), 169–191. doi:10.1016/S0022-4359(99)80092-X

Clover, V. T. (1950). Relative importance of impulse-buying in retail stores. *Journal of Marketing*, *15*(1), 66–70. doi:10.1177/002224295001500110

Dawson, S., & Kim, M. (2009). External and internal trigger cues of impulse buying online. *Direct Marketing: An International Journal*, *3*(1), 20–34. doi:10.1108/17505930910945714

Dodoo, N. A., & Wu, L. (2019). Exploring the anteceding impact of personalised social media advertising on online impulse buying tendency. *International Journal of Internet Marketing and Advertising*, *13*(1), 73–95. doi:10.1504/IJIMA.2019.097905

Gupta, P. (2011). Shopping impulses, online vs off. *The New York Times*. Available at: http://nyti.ms/2le4rY8

Hausman, A. (2000). A multi-method investigation of consumer motivations in impulse buying behavior. *Journal of Consumer Marketing*, *17*(5), 403–426. doi:10.1108/07363760010341045

Kearney, A. T. (2013). *Recasting the retail store in today's ommnichannel world*. Retrieved from http://bit.ly/2kFlQY0

Kollat, D. T., & Willett, R. P. (1969). Is impulse purchasing really a useful concept for marketing decisions? *Journal of Marketing*, *33*(1), 79–83. doi:10.1177/002224296903300113

Koski, N. (2004). Impulse buying on the internet: Encouraging and discouraging factors. *Frontiers of E-business Research*, *4*, 23–35.

Kukar-Kinney, M., Ridgway, N. M., & Monroe, K. B. (2009). The relationship between consumers' tendencies to buy compulsively and their motivations to shop and buy on the Internet. *Journal of Retailing*, *85*(3), 298–307. doi:10.1016/j.jretai.2009.05.002

Kuofaris, M. (2002). Applying the Technology Acceptance Model and Flow Theory to Online Customer Behavior. *Information Systems Research*, *13*(2), 205–253.

LaRose, R. (2001). On the negative effects of e-commerce: A sociocognitive exploration of unregulated on-line buying. *Journal of Computer-Mediated Communication*, *6*(3). doi:10.1111/j.1083-6101.2001.tb00120.x

McAlister, L., & Pessemier, E. (1982). Variety seeking behavior: An interdisciplinary review. *The Journal of Consumer Research*, *9*(3), 311–322. doi:10.1086/208926

Minnesota retailers are reaping rewards from far flung consumers. (2018, November 2). *Star Tribune*.

Mittal, S., Sondhi, N., & Chawla, D. (2017). Process of Impulse Buying: A Qualitative Exploration. *Global Business Review*, *19*(1), 131–146. doi:10.1177/0972150917713368

Peck, J., & Childers, T. L. (2003). To have and to hold: The influence of haptic information on product judgments. *Journal of Marketing*, *67*(2), 35–48. doi:10.1509/jmkg.67.2.35.18612

Rook, D. W. (1987). The buying impulse. *The Journal of Consumer Research*, *14*(2), 189–199. doi:10.1086/209105

Rook, D. W., & Fisher, R. J. (1995). Normative influences on impulsive buying behavior. *The Journal of Consumer Research*, *22*(3), 305–313. doi:10.1086/209452

Rook, D. W., & Hoch, S. J. (1985). Consuming Impulses. In E. C. Hirschman & M. B. Holbrook (Eds.), ACR North American Advances (pp. 23–27). Academic Press.

Sharma, K. C., & Kaur, S. (2015). The Impact of Demographic Factors on Impulse Buying Behaviour of Online and Offline Consumers (A Case Study of Punjab, Haryana, New Delhi and Chandigarh). International Journal of Engineering Technology. *Management and Applied Sciences*, *3*(9), 63–69.

22. Sharma, P., Sivakumaran, B., & Marshall, R. (2010). Impulse buying and variety seeking: A trait-correlates perspective. *Journal of Business Research*, *63*(3), 276–283. doi:10.1016/j.jbusres.2009.03.013

Statista. (n.d.). Retrieved from https://www.statista.com/statistics/272014/global-social-networks-ranked-by-number-of-users/

Stern, H. (1962). The Significance of Impulse Buying Today. *Journal of Marketing*, *26*(2), 59–62. doi:10.1177/002224296202600212

Sundström, M., Hjelm-Lidholm, S., & Radon, A. (2019). Clicking the boredom away–Exploring impulse fashion buying behavior online. *Journal of Retailing and Consumer Services*, *47*, 150–156. doi:10.1016/j.jretconser.2018.11.006

Verhagen, T., & van Dolen, W. (2011). The influence of online store beliefs on consumer online impulse buying: A model and empirical application. *Information & Management*, *48*(8), 320–327. doi:10.1016/j.im.2011.08.001

Zhang, K. Z., Xu, H., Zhao, S., & Yu, Y. (2018). Online reviews and impulse buying behavior: The role of browsing and impulsiveness. *Internet Research*, *28*(3), 522–543. doi:10.1108/IntR-12-2016-0377

KEY TERMS AND DEFINITIONS

Affective Factors: The summative and enduring levels of emotions experienced by a consumer with respect to his/her engagement focus.

Anonymity: A situation where a customer does not want to disclose its identity.

Cognitive Factors: A set of enduring and active mental states that a consumer experiences with respect to the focal object of his/her engagement.

Consumer Socialization: The process undergone by social media users in which they develop the skills, attitude, and knowledge as consumers.

Haptics: The inability of the consumer to touch the product or feel the product.

Impulse Buying: A purchase that is unplanned, the result of exposure to a stimulus, and decided on the spot.

Sudden Urge to Buy: Feeling which incites action on its first instance.

Chapter 17
Ethical Issues With the Use of Social Media in the Connected Business World

Ali Shafiq
Taylor's University, Malaysia

ABSTRACT

With the dawn of social media, the world of communication and interaction changed tremendously. It transformed altogether many other aspects of life – businesses, education, philanthropy, to name a few. However, with a phenomenon of such grand proportions came the associated problems of comparable stature. This chapter deals with some of the most compelling problems which social media brought. It highlights how these problems occur, their consequences, and what should be done to minimize the effects. It is hoped that after reading this chapter the users of social media will exercise caution; the practitioners will play a more responsible role while the theorists will be able to propose novel but practical solutions to these problems.

INTRODUCTION

'Facebook is selling your data', 'Social media is putting people at health risk', 'someone died while taking a perfect selfie'… how many a times we have read such headlines. How many more will come, one wonders! All these headlines start with the incident and end with an explanation, and maybe some conclusions based on what the companies/people should do in this regard. Is that enough? Some time later another similar news will ink the pages, spurring another discussion, availing no fruit at all. Why not nip the problem in the bud – try curtailing it where it all breeds – at the business level. If we can have business realize that they can actually play a pivotal role in addressing the ethical issues, it will actually reduce most of them. This chapter is exactly about it!

Social media is undoubtedly the biggest phenomenon of the 21st century which has affected the lives of, literally, billions of people globally. It is a part of everyday life of people, whether it is in the personal, professional, or business domain. With its myriads of options, there is virtually 'one for everyone'. The prime purpose

DOI: 10.4018/978-1-5225-9697-4.ch017

of any social media is to share contents with one's connections, get and be informed, and be entertained. In all its types and purposes, the process is common: a user creates her profile, makes connections with others, shares her contents and sees what others have shared. But with all the well-intended consequences there are its side-effects too. This chapter deals with some of the most common and perhaps most important ethical problems related to the use of social media in general. It describes how they occur and their effects. These effects are generic enough to include many similar concepts readily available in the literature.

PRIVACY

Privacy is one of the most obvious and often the least bothered about concern when using social media. While any website, mobile app, social media website, or any other online media does ask your permission (before performing an action) but how often we have seriously read whatever is written inside the permission agreement! The users typically agree to everything that is said in it as a result of the blind trust that they put into the service provider (Berreby, 2017). Often this blind agreement is also made because we just don't understand all the terminologies and the language used in the agreement and perhaps don't have the luxury of time to decipher what that alien language means. The result is often a (perceived) 'breach' of privacy where users' personal and usage data is gathered by the service provider and used for various purposes (Berreby, 2017). History has given many examples of such breach of privacy, Facebook-Cambridge Analytica scandal being the worst and most severe of them.

Similar to such privacy issues is the conscious and deliberate divulgence of personal information over these social media which might lead to intrusion and other more severe privacy issues. Sharing on social media is so exciting that it becomes almost impossible to resist sharing personal information on it (Steinberg, 2017). The extent of this sharing, obviously, depends on the users – some are more open to share than others. Though it might sound like innocent fun, yet in many cases such exposure of one's personal life leads to falling that data in wrong hands which might lead to bullying, stalking, and other crimes (Kleinberg, 2015). This risk is increased multiple times if this information is shared in the purview of a meme or hashtag which ultimately becomes a 'trend'.

What It Implies for the Businesses?

Experts and law enforcement authorities of any country have clearly warned against blind sharing of one's personal information on social media and have always cautioned the general public to exercise diligence in sharing personal contents. But is this warning enough to curb the situation? Apparently it is not. What the businesses need to do is to be more transparent in what they say. When an 'agreement' is made, it is important that all the parties fully understands the terms and conditions and then sign. In order for a common person to understand what is written in such agreements, it is necessary that they are written in simple, easy to understand language. This will encourage the consumers to read through the agreement and understand what they are signing up for, and later on not fall into difficult situations.

The companies also have a responsibility towards ethical business practices. Sometimes, in the urge of creating a 'trend', the companies make hashtags which ask people to post their photos or videos using that hashtag. This is a breeding ground for such breach of privacy where naïve consumers can get trapped. The businesses should take a responsibility here and not encourage people to post their personal images for promotional purposes.

NUMBER OF LIKES/COMMENTS

Recently, a short video on China's 'Likes Factory' which makes handsome amount of money just by generating (fake) likes for users on social media. The mechanism is simple – connect thousands of cell phones to internet via a server → use fake Facebook identities to like a page/post → promote the idea/product for a third party → make money!

Word-of-Mouth has always been a great source of information and inspiration to make purchase decisions. People trust it more, and more often than paid promotion because of presupposition that the word-of-mouth comes from an independent third party which has no stake in promoting the product. With the advent of internet and social media, the word-of-mouth has evolved into electronic word-of-mouth (eWoM). In principle it works the same way – many people talking about a product; this 'talk' is used by others as an informational source. However, only the tools have changed for eWoM; now instead of people 'talking' about the product, they post 'comments' in favour or disfavour, press the 'like' icon or any version of it, share it, +1 it, retweet it, or forward it. All these help in generating eWoM which eventually makes a product famous.

This has resulted in companies vehemently promoting their products on social media. Any new product or idea, before actually being launched on mainstream traditional media finds its way onto the social media. This way, long before a product is actually launched the hype is created which translates to product purchase. This equally applies to all types of marketing offers – products services, people, places, ideas, etc. A very helpful aide in this eWoM has been the 'hashtag'.

Now, bad publicity may be better than no publicity as this seems to be the norm on social media. With so much benefits tied with eWoM, why shouldn't they use the social media to become famous. By logic, 'whatever makes us famous should be good for us'. This has resulted in a lot more troubles than the meagre benefits. People have resorted to all sorts of bizarre tactics to come up with something to make them viral. A 13-year old Vietnamese girl accidentally set herself on fire (and luckily survived) in an attempt to put her school on fire, in a trade of 1,000 likes on her Facebook profile (İbrahim, 2016). In another instance, a guy recorded himself taking bath in a bath tub filled with red chilies, actually got himself in excruciating pain. Indeed the saddest of all would be the example of a Pakistani social media celebrity who wanted to follow her dreams and become famous by making online videos and going live, which eventually led to her sad demise.

Talking about celebrities, many deliberately fall into controversies to create a buzz and eWoM. The 'trend' created then raises their popularity which eventually brings them laurels. These stunts are double-edged sword though, for public opinion cannot entirely be controlled. Many celebrities were found drunk and driving, hate speech, or controversial dress-up which resulted in defame and ruining their otherwise shiny careers.

The craze of getting 'likes' and becoming famous is not limited to individuals only. Marketing firms are equally into it for all reasons. Often companies are found creating 'hashtags' for becoming viral. A very recent #10YearChallenge from Facebook became ultra-famous before it got controversial owing to its perceived hidden intentions. #ShareACoke is another famous one which is promoting Coke consumption via a very good message, rejecting the tall verifiable claims about its sugar contents.

What It Implies for the Businesses?

The point in this ethical issue is not to stop sharing good contents, or to stop brands from promoting themselves, or celebrities to stay close to their fandom. All this becomes controversial and raises flags when the users become too obsessed with making something go viral and in their obsession they can go to any length. This in principle disregards the moral duty that they hold towards themselves as well as towards the society at large. Putting oneself in danger to get fame is not a rational choice at all. Or just because the marketers want their products to sell, they let people resort to over consumption or other unhealthy habits. Sadly, there is no one to impose this restriction and it is upon one's own moral compass to draw the line, which means that companies have to ensure that they don't attempt to create harmful hashtags, memes, or viral contents.

FAKE IDENTITIES

Long time ago I once read that if Facebook were to be a country, it would be third largest in the world by population. Fast forward to current time, now Facebook boasts itself of having well-above 2 billion active users which would make it the most populous 'country' of all. This is followed by YouTube and Instagram with 1.9 and 1billion, respectively. Impressive by any means how once small start-ups grew into global giants with a truly global customer base.

However, often little light is shed on the fact that many people have multiple identities on social media, some of which could be fake. It is only logical that one person can only have one real identity on Facebook, and the others have to be the modified version of it. Whom do you trust when such identities become rampant? What are the repercussions? Let's have a look at them:

In real life, you can actually judge one's personality by the looks or behaviors of a person. They need to be consistent in order to be called a personality. They need to be time-tested as well. These personalities let us decide whether to approach, continue with the relationship, or avoid a person. This personality is manifested in the spontaneity, being natural, and consistency of behaviors (Okdie, Duadagno, Bernieri, Geers, & Mclarney-Vesotski, 2011). When any ingredient is missing, we tend to judge a behaviour not in accordance with the known personality; thus suspicion, or disbelief to the least, sets in.

Now, let's see this mechanism in the frame of social media. We typically put our best picture as our profile or display picture at any social media. We want people to see us beautiful, attractive, happy (satisfied), accomplished and successful, and approachable. In natural settings these are not always the characteristics that describe us – so the first trait of 'being fake' is introduced. Atop that if we put 'filters', these traits are enhanced even more. How often have you seen a person with her profile picture when she is sad, or distressed, or crying, or in pain or misery?

Then, when we tend to describe ourselves on social media under our profile, we only have words to help us. How many of us choose negative sounding words? Don't we write passionate, searching for truth, on a quest for knowledge, simple, decent, enjoys nature, etc. rather than chauvinist, racist, liar, personality disorder, tried-but-failed multiple times, etc. We don't, because we don't want to repel people – after all, social media is for connecting people, not dissociating them.

Finally, our posts and the language in it also tell a lot about us and it is us who choose what we post and what we say. Perhaps it loses the spontaneity in it since we have ample time to write/respond. All of this already led people to lower trust levels on social media. It leads to more extreme consequences should these fake identities be trusted and relationships be continued.

Then, there is an altogether different dimension of the same problem; people creating multiple identities. Although sociological studies approve of such happenings and call it 'virtual self', but this approval should be tied with truth. People tend to impersonate themselves as someone else (famous or otherwise) with logically only one intention that I can think of – to deceive people. This deception might be just for fun, or it might have other malicious intentions behind it, but in any case it is deception which, to the least, hurts the other party. Examples of scams, cheating, assaults and rapes, and phishing are aplenty resulting from such fake identities.

What It Implies for the Businesses?

There isn't much which the companies can do about it, except for those who own social media, for it is they who have developed the virtual identities and it is them who can influence people to practice objectivity when using these features. Although it sounds almost utopian, and it is tantamount to killing the (almost) entire charm of social media, yet it is not impossible.

ELIMINATION OF FACE TO FACE CONVERSATIONS

Now this is ironic! Social media was invented to increase and enhance communication. It did (Grieve, Indian, Witteveen, Tolan, & Marrington, 2013), in one way or the other, but perhaps at the expense of real-time face-to-face communication. Many reports have been published and many research articles produced addressing the same issue that social media has actually disconnected people in real-life. One the average, in 2017 people spent around 135 minutes per day on social media which is 2 hours and 15 minutes, a little more than 9% of the whole day. And it is not just a complete turn-on and shut-off phenomenon – the effects of the usage creep through for some time affecting our performance in other activities (Harris, 2017). It has become a very common spectacle to see people texting and not talking in a restaurant, at office, at home, at play. While it is still a form of communication, the benefits of face-to-face far outweigh those obtained online.

I remember listening to the very famous video of Simon Sinek in which he talks about 'what is wrong with the Millennials' where the number 1 reason for their problems is internet and social media powered by immediate gratification. Talking to someone face-to-face requires investment of time and energy; online communication doesn't. Frankly, people feel they can get more tasks done via online communication than face-to-face. The result is a disconnection of ties, loss in warmth of relationships, and no social learning, thereby undermining the very fabric which connects us.

What It Implies for the Businesses?

Why wouldn't people spend most of their time online when (literally) everything is available online! When you have everything, from food delivery to grocery shopping, from ticket purchase to education, from dating to preaching, available online then yes, people will spend all their time online. It is of no help that we go back to the offline mode – it will cause more destruction than the benefit. But can we say the same for social media? Should we make it an inseparable parts of our lives? Should we give it so much importance at the expense of other actual, real-world ties?

IT PROMOTES PROCRASTINATION

In a 2015 psychology blog (Pychyl, 2015), procrastination was defined as the destruction of self-regulation – doing (or not doing) something at the cost of something else. The author of the blog, a PhD in psychology, blamed social media for it; for it is designed to be 'sticky' and the 'stickier' it is, the better it is for the maker. There is a whole mechanism involved in it where the more you stay on a social network, the more chances there are that you will get something of interest, create a favorable (perhaps biased) opinion, and more chances of return. This seems 'perfect, I agree' (just as Collin Farrell tells Tom Cruise in Minority Report) but there is a fundamental flaw tied to this system, i.e., people get stuck to it at the cost of other more important things; and as a result delaying them. This is what is commonly defined as procrastination. There was a time when TV used to do this job. Now, this task is effectively taken over by the social media. Addiction is another name given to it. According to the Independent, an average British checks her cell phone as much as 28 times a day on average (Barr, 2019). Many reports have been written on the amount of time people spend on any given social media and the possible delays caused by this time spent. Most prominent of all is change in eating habits. The 'stickiness' of social media has surely put food on the waiting list whereby people either don't take food on time, or their diets have become irregular (World Economic Forum). This is more common in adolescents than in adults.

EFFECT ON PSYCHOLOGICAL AND PHYSICAL HEALTH

It is no surprise now that social media directly affects one's self-esteem. It can very conveniently raise or lower it in iota of seconds. Feelings of unhappiness, envy, and sadness are commonly reported by many social media related studies (Walker, 2016). These feelings, if prolonged, can lead to relatively permanent change in personality. How does it all happen? one may wonder! Well, it is simple, we always keep our best selves in front of people. With social media such as Facebook, where people only see our 'face' we definitely need to keep a good one, even if we are not feeling like it. Now you may be faking it, but on the other side of the screens are people who don't look into your intentions and take it for real. For them, you are enjoying, happy, accomplished, beautiful, famous, admired, adored, social, and gifted. If they are your sincere friends they may even like it. But a time comes when too much of it becomes offensive leading to sadness, anxiety, and depression. How much can one absorb that another person is having all that he desires while I am not getting anything! Eventually, this comparison leads to unhappiness; unhappiness leads to dissatisfaction; dissatisfaction leads to one exerting more efforts to reach the desired level; or it may make one feel frustrated and eventually depressed.

It is also related to adverse physical health conditions, such as loss of sleep pattern (World Economic Forum) leading to poor sleep quality. A good amount of sleep is vital for psycho-physical health. But when the brain is awake you can't sleep well. Brain is awake either because you have watched too much of social media and developed too many thoughts, or because you have been using it just before your sleep time (World Economic Forum). Similarly, holding a cell phone for extended period of time can lead to cramps; using cell-phone for longer duration staying at one position leads to posture problems and fatigue.

What It Implies for the Businesses?

Take some responsibility and stop it. Understand and confess that it is wrong, and stop promoting it. Rather than creating a treadmill with app-connectivity for 'healthy lifestyle on-the-go', the makers should promote an 'actual' healthy lifestyle without any connectivity. Rather than promoting 'instagrammable food' for posting on social media first, and eating later, a real marketer should promote 'food for eating only'.

The stickiness of the site is a very lucrative business idea, but it should come with a sense of responsibility too. The marketers should put an 'empathy notice' that should stick at the top of every page that they navigate to remind them that their health is more important than being glued to this entertainment website. There should also be a constantly 'sticky' reminder to tell its users that your emotions and others emotions are in your control. It should remind them to use social media emphatically and wisely. Unless businesses take the charge and do something about it, the problems will continue to not only exist, but multiply.

ONLINE SCAMS/FRAUDS

I was shocked to my bones when I read that "Facebook and Google were conned out of $100m in phishing scheme" (Gibbs, 2017). If the technology giants can't handle the sophistication of the scammers, God bless the common user. In Malaysia a total of 8,313 cybercrimes were reported in the year 2018 alone (The Star, 2018). In a similar news much earlier, it is reported that as many as 30 Malaysians fall victim to cybercrimes daily (Cheng, 2015), including identity theft, financial transactions, scams, or even cyberbullying. One journalist puts the lost amount to more than 100 million USD in U.S. alone (Wagner, 2018). While the governments and their agencies all around the world are exerting all possible efforts, it just doesn't seem sufficient, for the scammers are everywhere and ever growing.

I believe part of the culprits represent the consumers too. We cannot simply call them naïve and blame the perpetrators entirely. The consumers have to overcome their urge to get more in less time. The scammers thrive on the same urge. The other, and without a doubt, the major culprit are the actual perpetrators. They have a similar urge – to get more in less time, but with a different style of execution.

What It Implies for the Businesses?

It is upon the governments and the marketers together to educate their citizens and customers. This is as easy and commonly touted solution that seems to be, well, very slowly working. Yet, the scammers are getting sophisticated and they are easily defeating the whole purpose of educating the customers. The other alternative, perhaps the difficult one, is to educate the customers about their needs; to tell them to stop comparing themselves with someone who has more than them, and to always look at those who can only wish for what they already have; to remind them that material possessions can make someone happy, not necessarily satisfied; to make them realize that beauty is more than just a fair complexion, and that it is more than skin-deep. These and many other materialistic motives make customers yearn for more resources, fall into the scams, and lose it all.

CONCLUDING THOUGHTS

This chapter discussed some of the most pressing ethical issues associated with the use of social media, and what can business do to curb, or at least minimize these issues. In my opinion the problems are not a given, but are mediated by users. Hence, I strongly believe the users are in control and many of these issues and many similar can be avoided by simply practicing due diligence. We don't need someone else to instruct us on how to use social media – the will-power should be within us. This will-power comes with awareness. This chapter was written in the hope of making people aware of the problems so that they can reflect on their social media habits and develop mechanisms to counter these. The inertia is great and it is surely hard to resist.

On the flip side, the producers/sellers will want to harness the most out of social media, even at the expense of consumers and they will design all possible means to ensure they achieve it. So the responsibility also lies with the businesses. They have to overcome their profit-maximization desire to ensure that customers' benefits are safeguarded.

This chapter, then invites the policy makers and theorists to come forward and propose ways to regulate such practices. Such regulations will help the consumers in the long run by keeping the social media usage under control.

REFERENCES

Aragon, A., AlDoubi, S., Kaminski, K., Anderson, S. K., & Isaacs, N. (2014). Social Networking: Boundaries and Limits Part 1: Ethics. *TechTrends*, *58*(2), 25–31. doi:10.100711528-014-0734-9

Barr, S. (2019). *Six Ways Social Media Negatively Affects Your Mental Health*. Retrieved 15 February, 2019, from Independent: https://www.independent.co.uk/life-style/health-and-families/social-media-mental-health-negative-effects-depression-anxiety-addiction-memory-a8307196.html

Berreby, D. (2017). *Click to agree with what? No one reads terms of service, studies confirm*. Retrieved 13 February, 2019, from The Guardian: https://www.theguardian.com/technology/2017/mar/03/terms-of-service-online-contracts-fine-print

Calus, V. (2018). Retrieved 26 January 2019, from Planable: https://planable.io/social-media-challenges/

Cheng, N. (2015). *More than 30 Malaysians fall prey to cyber crime daily*. Retrieved from The Star Online: https://www.thestar.com.my/news/nation/2015/10/26/cybercrime-30-msians-daily/#RTz6iSoeOx4XTBeb.99

Gibbs, S. (2017). *Facebook and Google were conned out of $100m in phishing scheme*. Retrieved from The Guardian: https://www.theguardian.com/technology/2017/apr/28/facebook-google-conned-100m-phishing-scheme

Greysen, R. S., Kind, T., & Chretien, K. C. (2010). Online Professionalism and the Mirror of Social Media. *Journal of General Internal Medicine, 25*(11), 1227–1229. doi:10.100711606-010-1447-1

Grieve, R., Indian, M., Witteveen, K., Tolan, G. A., & Marrington, J. (2013, May). Face-to-face or Facebook: Can social connectedness be derived online? *Computers in Human Behavior*, *29*(3), 604–609. doi:10.1016/j.chb.2012.11.017

Harris, S. (2017). *Why keeping your smartphone close is actually making you dumber*. Retrieved 14 February, 2019, from World Economic Forum: https://www.weforum.org/agenda/2017/07/why-keeping-your-smartphone-close-is-actually-making-you-dumber/?fbclid=IwAR0kLUHVAoQjxekvlQCNlyygFHALR5mSiS8-bcjhbQvOqzlAXLja-nH9aL4

İbrahim, A. (Ed.). (2016). *13-year-old girl sets herself on fire in Vietnam in social media dare*. Retrieved 14 February, 2019, from Daily Sabah: https://www.dailysabah.com/asia/2016/10/12/13-year-old-girl-sets-herself-on-fire-in-vietnam-in-social-media-dare

Kleinberg, S. (2015). *Think twice before you share your next photo on social media*. Retrieved 14 February, 2019, from Chicago Tribune: https://www.chicagotribune.com/lifestyles/ct-social-media-safe-posting-20151103-column.html

Okdie, B. M., Duadagno, R. E., Bernieri, F. J., Geers, A. L., & Mclarney-Vesotski, A. R. (2011). Getting to know you: Face-to-face versus online interactions. *Computers in Human Behavior*, *27*(1), 153–159. doi:10.1016/j.chb.2010.07.017

Pychyl, T. A. (2015). *Social Media, the Network Effect and Procrastination: Our self-regulation is being undermined by design*. Retrieved 15 February, 2019, from Psychology Today: https://www.psychologytoday.com/us/blog/dont-delay/201512/social-media-the-network-effect-and-procrastination

Steinberg, S. (2017). *Social Media Etiquette: What's Safe To Share On Social Networks?* Retrieved 13 February, 2019, from Huffington Post: https://www.huffingtonpost.com/scott-steinberg/social-media-etiquette-wh_b_14500916.html

Strober, E. (2016). *5 Problems With Social Media: What the internet is doing to our lives*. Retrieved 26 January, 2019, from the odyssey: https://www.theodysseyonline.com/five-problems-with-social-media

The Star. (2018). *Cybercrime fraud cases stand at 8,313 as at Oct 3*. Retrieved from The Star Online: https://www.thestar.com.my/news/nation/2018/10/09/cybercrime-fraud-cases-stand-at-8313-as-at-oct-3/

Townsend, L., & Wallace, C. (2016). Social Media Research: A Guide to Ethics. The University of Aberdeen.

Wagner, P. (2018). *Internet Scamming is on The Rise*. Retrieved from Internet Usage in the United States: https://www.statista.com/chart/15069/number-of-internet-scams-in-the-us/

Walker, P. (2016). *Facebook Makes You Unhappy And Makes Jealous People Particularly Sad, Study Finds*. Retrieved 16 February, 2019, from Independent: https://www.independent.co.uk/life-style/gadgets-and-tech/facebook-social-media-make-unhappy-jealous-people-particularly-sad-copenhagen-university-study-a7490816.html

World Economic Forum. (n.d.). *Our addiction to screens is damaging more than our health*. Retrieved 15 February, 2019, from https://www.facebook.com/watch/?v=10153727978766479

KEY TERMS AND DEFINITIONS

Appalachia: A geographic and cultural region of the Mideastern United States. The population in media is portrayed as suspicious, backward, and isolated.

Bullying: An intentional action intending to harm, intimidate, or coerce someone who is perceived as weak or vulnerable. Although originating in the physical world, it has creeped into the cyber world too, termed as cyber-bullying.

Hashtag: Denoted by #, it is used immediately before a word or a phrase to identify a specific topic on social media.

Like: Social Media has the option of "liking" or "disliking" a content being shared. This is expressed via a small icon made available with the content and can take many forms (thumbs-up or down, emoji, etc.). The number of likes or dislikes or any other similar emotion denotes how general public has reacted to the contents.

Profile: Just like in our daily lives, our social media also carries our personal details, like our sex, birth date, interests, life goals, etc. This information constitutes our profile. It can be public for others to view or set private. This introduces us to others.

Retweet: Reposting a content on the Twitter. Initially a user Tweets content. If someone shares the same contents it is called retweet.

Stalking: The unwanted and often repeated surveillance of someone by another person or group. This is often a common phenomenon on social media where people scroll through a person's profile/activity log to get more information.

Stickiness: It is the quality of a website or social media which makes the viewers stay longer on it. It has benefit for the website/social media owner as it helps generate revenue.

Trend: A trend is the topic of discussion for many posts on social media, typically for a short period of time. When some topic gets social media attention, people start discussing it and is called the trending topic. It is usually identified with a hashtag (for example, #10YearChallenge, #MeToo, #IceBucketChallenge).

Viral: A piece of information (image, audio/video, message, or any other content) that has been rapidly shared across the internet. Viral content is typically shared among hundreds of thousands of people in a very short amount of time.

Word-of-Mouth: The general discussion about someone or something. This discussion can be in favor, against, or can be mixed, and it gives the listeners/readers a general opinion about the subject of discussion which is majorly based on the polarity of the discussion.

Compilation of References

22. Sharma, P., Sivakumaran, B., & Marshall, R. (2010). Impulse buying and variety seeking: A trait-correlates perspective. *Journal of Business Research*, *63*(3), 276–283. doi:10.1016/j.jbusres.2009.03.013

Abbas, H. A., & Hamdy, H. I. (2015). Determinants of continuance intention factor in Kuwait communication market: The Case study of Zain-Kuwait. *Computers in Human Behavior*, *49*(0), 648–657. doi:10.1016/j.chb.2015.03.035

Abbott, W., Donaghey, J., Hare, J., & Hopkins, P. (2013). An Instagram is worth a thousand words: An industry panel and audience Q&A. *Library Hi Tech News*, *30*(7), 1–6. doi:10.1108/LHTN-08-2013-0047

Abdul-Rahman, M., & Kamarulzaman, Y. (2012). The influence of relationship quality and switching costs on customer Loyalty in the Malaysian Hotel Industry. *Procedia: Social and Behavioral Sciences*, *62*, 1023–1027. doi:10.1016/j.sbspro.2012.09.174

Abzari, M., Ghassemi, R. A., & Vosta, L. N. (2014). Analysing the effect of social media on brand attitude and purchase intention: The case of Iran Khodro Company. *Procedia: Social and Behavioral Sciences*, *143*, 822–826. doi:10.1016/j.sbspro.2014.07.483

Achilleas, K., & Anastasios, S. (2008). Marketing aspects of quality assurance systems: The organic food sector case. *British Food Journal*, *110*(8), 829–839. doi:10.1108/00070700810893359

Ackroyd, A. (2018). *How to Turn Fans Into Brand Champions*. Retrieved from https://www.socialmediaexaminer.com/brand-champions-social-media/

Afolabi, A. O., Ojelabi, R. A., & Oyeyipo, O. (2018). An analysis of social media marketing of indigenous construction firms in Nigeria: A tool for sustainable growth. *International Journal of Construction Supply Chain Management*, *8*, 60–72.

Agarwal, J., & Wu, T. (Eds.). (2018). *Emerging Issues in Global Marketing: A Shifting Paradigm*. New York: Springer. doi:10.1007/978-3-319-74129-1

Agarwal, R., & Prasad, J. (1998). A conceptual and operational definition of personal innovativeness in the domain of Information technology. *Information Systems Research*, *9*(2), 204–215. doi:10.1287/isre.9.2.204

Agnihotri, R., Dingus, R., Hu, M. Y., & Krush, M. T. (2016). Social media: Influencing customer satisfaction in B2B sales. *Industrial Marketing Management*, *53*, 172–180. doi:10.1016/j.indmarman.2015.09.003

Ahmad, A. E. M. K. (2012). Attractiveness factors influencing shoppers' satisfaction, loyalty, and word of mouth: An empirical investigation of Saudi Arabia shopping malls. *International Journal of Business Administration*, *3*(6), 101–112.

Ahmad, S. N., & Juhdi, N. (2010). Organic Food: A Study on Demographic Characteristics and Factors Influencing Purchase Intentions among Consumers in Klang Valley, Malaysia. *International Journal of Business and Management*, *5*(2), 105–118. doi:10.5539/ijbm.v5n2p105

Ahmad, S. Z., Abu Bakar, A. R., & Ahmad, N. (2019). Social media adoption and its impact on firm performance: The case of the UAE. *International Journal of Entrepreneurial Behaviour & Research*, *25*(1), 84–111. doi:10.1108/IJEBR-08-2017-0299

Ahmad, S., & Rosli, J. (2015). The Rise of Online Shopping. *Malaysian Business*, *1*, 20–27.

Ahmed, Z. U., Ghingold, M., & Dahari, Z. (2007). Malaysian shopping mall behavior: An exploratory study. *Asia Pacific Journal of Marketing and Logistics*, *19*(4), 331–348. doi:10.1108/13555850710827841

Ajzen, I. (2005). *Attitudes, personality, and behavior* (2nd ed.). Open University Press, Mc-Graw-Hill.

Akar, E., & Nasir, V. A. (2015). A review of literature on consumers' online purchase intentions. *Journal of Customer Behaviour*, *14*(3), 215–233. doi:10.1362/147539215X14441363630837

Akinci, S., Inan, E. A., & Aksoy, Ş. (2008). Re-assessment of E-S-Qual and E-RecS-Qual in a pure service setting. *Journal of Business Research*, *63*(3), 232–240. doi:10.1016/j.jbusres.2009.02.018

Akpojivi, U., & Bevan-Dye, A. (2014). Mobile advertisements and information privacy perception amongst South African Generation Y students. *Telematics and Informatics*, *32*(1), 1–10. doi:10.1016/j.tele.2014.08.001

Akram, U., Hui, P., Kaleem Khan, M., Tanveer, Y., Mehmood, K., & Ahmad, W. (2018). How website quality affects online impulse buying: Moderating effects of sales promotion and credit card use. *Asia Pacific Journal of Marketing and Logistics*, *30*(1), 235–256. doi:10.1108/APJML-04-2017-0073

Aladwani, A. M., & Palvia, P. C. (2002). Developing and validating an instrument for measuring user-perceived web quality. *Information & Management*, *39*(6), 467–476. doi:10.1016/S0378-7206(01)00113-6

Al-Agaga, A. M., & Nor, K. H. M. (2012). Factors that influence e-loyalty of internet banking users. *International Journal of Electronic Commerce Studies*, *3*(2), 297–304. doi:10.7903/ijecs.1097

Albala, K., & Allen, G. (2007). The Business of Food: Encyclopedia of the Food and Drink Industries. Greenwood.

Albee, A. (2015). *The attention economy: the impact of attention scarcity on modern marketing*. Retrieved from look-book.com

Alexander, J. E., & Tate, M. A. (1999). *Web wisdom: How to evaluate and create information quality on the web*. Mahwah, NJ: Erlbaum.

Al-Gahtani, S., & King, M. (1999). Attitudes. Satisfaction and usage: Factors contributing to each in the acceptance of information technology. *Behaviour and Information Technology Studies: Special Issue on Research Methodology*, *18*(4), 277–297. doi:10.1080/014492999119020

Aliagha, G. U., Qin, Y. G., Ali, K. N., & Abdullah, M. N. (2015). Analysis of shopping mall attractiveness and customer loyalty. *Journal Teknologi*, *74*(2), 15–21.

Alkhouli, S. (2017). The effect of banks website service quality and e-satisfaction on e-loyalty: An empirical study on Swedish banks. *International Journal of Business and Management*, *13*(1), 1–12. doi:10.5539/ijbm.v13n1p1

Allen, J., Browne, M., & Cherrett, T. (2012). Investigating relationships between road freight transport, facility location, logistics management and urban form. *Journal of Transport Geography*, *24*, 45–57. doi:10.1016/j.jtrangeo.2012.06.010

Al-Salamin, H., & Al-Hassan, E. (2016). The Impact of Pricing on Consumer Buying Behavior in Saudi. *European Journal of Business and Management*, *8*(12), 62–73.

Alsamdyai, M. J., Yousif, R. O., & Al-khasawneh, M. H. (2012). The factors influencing consumer satisfaction and continuity to deal with e-banking services in Jordan. *Global Journal of Management and Business Research*, *12*(14), 129–142.

Amato-Mccoy, D. M. (2018, May 30). Study: Social commerce sales are on the rise. *Chain Store age: The business of retail.*

Amer, A., & Chow, J. Y. J. (2017). A downtown on-street parking model with urban truck delivery behavior. *Transportation Research Part A, Policy and Practice*, *102*, 51–67. doi:10.1016/j.tra.2016.08.013

Amin, B. J., & Amin, P. (2013). A conceptual framework to understanding online consumer buying behavior. *International Journal of Online Marketing*, *3*(1), 47–63. doi:10.4018/ijom.2013010104

Ammani, P. (2013). A study of the factors that influence customer preference for shopping malls over local markets. *IUP Journal of Management Research*, *12*(1), 7–21.

Anandarajan, M., Igbaria, M., & Anakwe, U. P. (2000). Technology Acceptance in the Banking Industry: A prospective from a less developed country. *Information Technology & People*, *13*(4), 298–312. doi:10.1108/09593840010359491

Anders, S., & Moeser, A. (2008). Assessing the demand for value-based organic meats in Canada: A combined retail and household scanner-data approach. *International Journal of Consumer Studies*, *32*(5), 457–469. doi:10.1111/j.1470-6431.2008.00707.x

Andreoli, D., Goodchild, A., & Vitasek, K. (2010). The rise of mega distribution centers and the impact on logistical uncertainty. *Transportation Letters*, *2*(2), 75–88. doi:10.3328/TL.2010.02.02.75-88

Anthopoulos, L. G., Siozos, P., & Tsoukalas, L. A. (2007). pplying Participatory Design and Collaboration in Digital Public Services for Discovering and Re-designing E-government Services. *Government Information Quarterly*, *24*(2), 353–376. doi:10.1016/j.giq.2006.07.018

Anuradha, D., & Manohar, H. (2011). Customer shopping experience in malls with entertainment centres in Chennai. *African Journal of Business Management*, *5*(31), 12319–12324. doi:10.5897/AJBM11.902

Anyanwu, G., Nelson, O., & Salawu, A. (2018). Online Advertising Influence for Promoting Preference for E-Shopping in Nigeria: A Study of Jumia. *Academy of Strategic Management Journal*, *17*, 1–9.

Aquilani, B., Serpico, E., Silvestri, C., & Ruggieri, A. (2015). Offline and online customer satisfaction in B2C markets: Towards an overall customer satisfaction framework. In *Handbook of Research on Managing and Influencing Consumer Behavior* (pp. 311–364). IGI Global. doi:10.4018/978-1-4666-6547-7.ch014

Aragon, A., AlDoubi, S., Kaminski, K., Anderson, S. K., & Isaacs, N. (2014). Social Networking: Boundaries and Limits Part 1: Ethics. *TechTrends*, *58*(2), 25–31. doi:10.100711528-014-0734-9

Aragoncillo, L., & Orus, C. (2018). Impulse buying behaviour: An online-offline comparative and the impact of social media. *Spanish Journal of Marketing-ESIC*, *22*(1), 42–62. doi:10.1108/SJME-03-2018-007

Ariff, M. S. M., Leong, O. Y., Norhayati, Z., & Ahmad, J. (2012). Examining dimensions of electronic service quality for internet banking services. *Proceedings of International Congress on Interdisciplinary Business and Social Science 2012*, *65*, 854-859. 10.1016/j.sbspro.2012.11.210

Ariff, M. S. M., Yun, L. O., Zakuan, N., & Ismail, K. (2013). The impacts of service quality and customer satisfaction on customer loyalty in internet banking. *Procedia: Social and Behavioral Sciences*, *81*, 469–473. doi:10.1016/j.sbspro.2013.06.462

Armağan, E., & Çetin, A. (2013). Peer communication and impacts on purchasing decisions: An application on teenagers. *International Journal of Social Sciences and Humanity Studies*, *5*(2), 60–72.

Aryal, K., Chaudhary, P., Pandit, S., & Sharma, G. (2009). Consumers' Willingness To Pay For Organic Products: A Case From Kathamandu Valley. *The Journal of Agriculture and Environment*, *10*, 12–22. doi:10.3126/aej.v10i0.2126

Asgari, N., Ahmadi, M. H., Shamlou, M., Farokhi, A. R., & Farzin, M. (2014). Studying the impact of e-service quality on e-loyalty of customers in the area of e-banking services. *Journal of Management and Sustainability*, *4*(2), 126–133. doi:10.5539/jms.v4n2p126

Ashley, C., & Tuten, T. (2015). Creative strategies in social media marketing: An exploratory study of branded social content and consumer engagement. *Psychology and Marketing*, *32*(1), 15–27. doi:10.1002/mar.20761

Association of International Certified Professional Accountants. (2018). Taxation of the digitalized economy: A policy paper designed to educate, enlighten and stimulate discussion 2018. Durham, NC: Author.

Asubonteng, P., McCleary, K. J., & Swan, J. (1996). Servqual revisited: A critical review of service quality. *Journal of Services Marketing*, *10*(6), 62–81. doi:10.1108/08876049610148602

Athanasopoulou, P. (2009). Relationship quality: A critical literature review and research agenda. *European Journal of Marketing*, *43*(5/6), 583–610. doi:10.1108/03090560910946945

Awan, M. A., Khan, H. U., & Wenqing, Z. (2012). A comparative study on online service quality perception of two major regional economies. *International Journal of e-Education, e-Business, e-Management and e-Learning*, *2*(6), 529-533.

Bacache-Beauvallet, M., & Bloch, F. (2018). Special issue on taxation in the digital economy. *Journal of Public Economic Theory*, *20*(1), 5–8. doi:10.1111/jpet.12285

Badrinarayanan, V., & Becerra, E. P. (2018). Shoppers' attachment with retail stores: Antecedents and impact on patronage intentions. *Journal of Retailing and Consumer Services*. doi:10.1016/j.jretconser.2018.07.012

Bagga, T., & Bhatt, M. (2013). A study of intrinsic factors influencing consumer buying behavior online. *Asia-Pacific Journal of Management Research and Innovation*, *9*(1), 77–90. doi:10.1177/2319510X13483515

Bagozzi, R. P. (2007). The legacy of the Technology Acceptance Model and a Proposal for a Paradigm Shift. *Journal of the Association for Information Systems*, *8*(4/7), 244–254. doi:10.17705/1jais.00122

Bagozzi, R. P., & Dholakia, U. M. (2002). Intentional social action in virtual communities. *Journal of Interactive Marketing*, *16*(2), 2–21. doi:10.1002/dir.10006

Bagozzi, R., & Yi, Y. (1988). On the evaluation of structural equation models. *Journal of the Academy of Marketing Science*, *16*(1), 74–94. doi:10.1007/BF02723327

Bailey, K. D. (1987). *Methods of social research*. New York: The Free Press.

Baker-Eveleth, L., & Stone, R. W. (2015). Usability, expectation, confirmation, and continuance intentions to use electronic textbooks. *Behaviour & Information Technology*, *34*(10), 992–1004. doi:10.1080/0144929X.2015.1039061

Balasubramanian, S., & Mahajan, V. (2001). The Economic Leverage of the Virtual Community. *International Journal of Electronic Commerce*, *5*(3), 103–138. doi:10.1080/10864415.2001.11044212

Balmer, J. M. T., & Gray, E. R. (1999). Corporate identity and corporate communications: Creating a competitive ad vantage. *Corporate Communications*, *4*(4), 171–176. doi:10.1108/EUM0000000007299

Baltes, L. P. (2015). Content marketing-the fundamental tool of digital marketing. *Bulletin of the Transilvania University of Brasov. Economic Sciences. Series V*, *8*, 111.

Banerjee, S., & Dholakia, R. R. (2012). Location-based mobile advertisements and gender targeting. *Journal of Research in Interactive Marketing*, *6*(3), 198–214. doi:10.1108/17505931211274679

Barbie, E. (2007). *The Practice of social research.* Boston: Cengage Learning Publishing.

Barnes, S., & Vidgen, R. (2007). Interactive e-government: Evaluating the web site of the UK Inland Revenue. *Journal of Electronic Government Research*, *3*(1), 19–37. doi:10.4018/jegr.2007010102

Barr, S. (2019). *Six Ways Social Media Negatively Affects Your Mental Health.* Retrieved 15 February, 2019, from Independent: https://www.independent.co.uk/life-style/health-and-families/social-media-mental-health-negative-effects-depression-anxiety-addiction-memory-a8307196.html

Barrick, M. R., & Mount, M. K. (1991). The Big Five personality dimensions and job performance: A meta-analysis. *Personnel Psychology*, *44*(1), 1–26. doi:10.1111/j.1744-6570.1991.tb00688.x

Barrutia, J. M., & Gilsanz, A. (2012). Electronic service quality and value: Do consumer knowledge-related resources matter? *Journal of Service Research*, *16*(2), 231–246. doi:10.1177/1094670512468294

Bartlett-Bragg, A. (2009). Reframing practice: Creating social learning networks. *Development and Learning in Organizations: An International Journal*, *23*(4), 16–20.

Ba, S., & Pavlou, P. A. (2002). Evidence of the effect of trust building technology in electronic markets: Price premiums and buyer behavior. *Management Information Systems Quarterly*, *26*(3), 243–268. doi:10.2307/4132332

Basu, R., & Sondhi, N. (2014). Child socialization practices: Implications for retailers in emerging markets. *Journal of Retailing and Consumer Services*, *21*(5), 797–803. doi:10.1016/j.jretconser.2014.06.008

Bauer, H. H., Falk, T., & Hammerschmidt, M. (2006). eTransQual: A transaction process-based approach for capturing service quality in online shopping. *Journal of Business Research*, *59*(7), 866–875. doi:10.1016/j.jbusres.2006.01.021

Bauer, H. H., Hammerschmidt, M., & Falk, T. (2005). Measuring the quality of e-banking portals. *International Journal of Bank Marketing*, *23*(2), 153–175. doi:10.1108/02652320510584395

Beatty, S. E., & Ferrell, M. E. (1998). Impulse buying: Modeling its precursors. *Journal of Retailing*, *74*(2), 169–191. doi:10.1016/S0022-4359(99)80092-X

Bélanger, F., & Carter, L. (2008). Trust and risk in e-government adoption. *The Journal of Strategic Information Systems*, *17*(2), 165–176. doi:10.1016/j.jsis.2007.12.002

Bell, D. R., Gallino, S., & Moreno, A. (2018). The Store Is Dead—Long Live the Store. *MIT Sloan Management Review*, *59*(3), 59–66. Retrieved from https://faculty.wharton.upenn.edu/wp-content/uploads/2018/03/Long-Live-the-Store.pdf

Bellows, A. C., Onyango, B., Diamond, A., & Hallman, W. K. (2008). Understanding Consumer Interest in Organics: Production Values vs. Purchasing Behaviour. *Journal of Agricultural & Food Industrial Organization*, *6*(2), 12–28.

Bennett, R., & Rundle-Thiele, S. (2002). A comparison of attitudinal loyalty measurement approaches. *Journal of Brand Management*, *9*(3), 193–209. doi:10.1057/palgrave.bm.2540069

Bentler, P. M. (1990). Comparative fit indexes in structural models. *Psychological Bulletin*, *107*(2), 238–246. doi:10.1037/0033-2909.107.2.238 PMID:2320703

Bentler, P., & Bonett, D. (1980). Significance tests and goodness of fit in the analysis of covariance structures. *Psychological Bulletin*, *88*(3), 588–606. doi:10.1037/0033-2909.88.3.588

Bergner, M. (2016). *What Retailers Can Learn from the Showroom Model*. Retrieved January 22, 2019, from https://apparelmag.com/what-retailers-can-learn-showroom-model

Berreby, D. (2017). *Click to agree with what? No one reads terms of service, studies confirm*. Retrieved 13 February, 2019, from The Guardian: https://www.theguardian.com/technology/2017/mar/03/terms-of-service-online-contracts-fine-print

Berry, L. L. (1983). Relationship marketing in Emerging perspectives on services marketing. American Marketing Association. doi:10.1177/009207039502300402

Bhatiasevi, V., & Yoopetch, C. (2015). The determinants of intention to use electronic booking among young users in Thailand. *Journal of Hospitality and Tourism Management*, *23*, 1–11. doi:10.1016/j.jhtm.2014.12.004

Bhattacharya, A. (2011). Preeminent Analysis of Customer Relationship Management (CRM). *International Journal of Research in Management and Technology*, *1*(1), 45–51.

Bıçakçı, A. B., & Genel, Z. (2016). A theoretical approach for sustainable communication in city branding: multilateral symmetrical communication model. In A. Bayraktar & C. Uslay (Eds.), *Strategic Place Branding Methodologies and Theory for Tourist Attraction* (pp. 41–66). IGI Global.

Blight, M. G., Ruppel, E. K., & Schoenbauer, K. V. (2017). Sense of community on Twitter and Instagram: Exploring the roles of motives and parasocial relationships. *Cyberpsychology, Behavior, and Social Networking*, *20*(5), 314–319. doi:10.1089/cyber.2016.0505

Bloch, P. H., & Richins, M. L. (1983). A theoretical model for the study of product importance perceptions. *Journal of Marketing*, *47*(3), 69–81. doi:10.1177/002224298304700308

Bloch, P. H., Ridgway, N. M., & Dawson, S. A. (1994). The shopping mall as consumer habitat. *Journal of Retailing*, *70*(1), 23–42. doi:10.1016/0022-4359(94)90026-4

Bose, R. (2002). Customer Relationship Management: Key Components for IT success. *Industrial Management & Data Systems*, *102*(2), 89–97. doi:10.1108/02635570210419636

Bowden, J. L.-H. (2009). The Process of Customer Engagement: A Conceptual Framework. *Journal of Marketing Theory and Practice*, *17*(1), 63–74. doi:10.2753/MTP1069-6679170105

Bracalente, B., Cossignani, M., & Mulas, A. (2009). *Statistica aziendale*. Milan: McGraw-Hill.

Bremmer, I. (2017). The Mixed Fortunes of the BRICS Countries, in 5 Facts. Time.

Brensinger, R. P., & Lambert, D. M. (1990). *Can the SERVQUAL Scale be Generalized to Business-to-Business Services?* Paper presented at the Knowledge Development in Marketing1990 AMA's Summer Educators' Conference.

Bressolles, G., Durrieu, F., & Senecal, S. (2014). A consumer typology based on e-service quality and e-satisfaction. *Journal of Retailing and Consumer Services*, *21*(6), 889–896. doi:10.1016/j.jretconser.2014.07.004

Britannica. (2016). *Price*. Encyclopedia Britannica.

Brodie, R. J., Ilic, A., Juric, B., & Hollebeek, L. (2013). Consumer engagement in a virtual brand community: An exploratory analysis. *Journal of Business Research*, *66*(1), 105–114. doi:10.1016/j.jbusres.2011.07.029

Brown, C. (2003). Consumers' preferences for locally produced food: A study in southeast MIssouri. *American Journal of Alternative Agriculture*, *18*(4), 213–224. doi:10.1079/AJAA200353

Bughin, J., & Zeisser, M. (2001). The marketing scale effectiveness of virtual communities. *Electronic Markets*, *11*(4), 258–262. doi:10.1080/101967801753405544

Bukhari, A. N., & Kazi, R. (2016). CRM triggers effectiveness through customer selection orientation, business cycle orientation, cross-functional integration and dual value creation: Myth or reality. *Journal of Marketing Management, 4*(1), 163–171.

Buttle, F. (2004). *Customer Relationship Management: Concepts and Tools*. Oxford, UK: Butterworth-Heinemann. doi:10.4324/9780080472430

Cai, S., & Jun, M. (2003). Internet Users Perceptions of On-line Service Quality: A Comparison of On-line Buyers and Information Searchers. *Managing Service Quality, 13*(6), 504–519. doi:10.1108/09604520310506568

Cai, Y., & Shannon, R. (2012). Personal values and mall shopping behaviour: The mediating role of intention among Chinese consumers. *International Journal of Retail & Distribution Management, 40*(4), 290–318. doi:10.1108/09590551211211783

Çakır, H. (2016). *Corporate reputation management in social media*. İstanbul: Kriter Publishings.

Calefato, F., Lanubile, F., & Novielli, N. (2015). The role of social media in affective trust building in customer–supplier relationships. *Electronic Commerce Research, 15*(4), 453–482. doi:10.100710660-015-9194-3

Calus, V. (2018). Retrieved 26 January 2019, from Planable: https://planable.io/social-media-challenges/

Cao, M., Zhang, Q., & Seydel, J. (2005). B2C e-commerce web site quality: An empirical examination. *Industrial Management & Data Systems, 105*(5), 645–661. doi:10.1108/02635570510600000

Carlson, G., & Larco, N. (2017). *Warehousing*. Retrieved from https://cpb-us-e1.wpmucdn.com/blogs.uoregon.edu/dist/f/13615/files/2017/06/Warehousing-Urb-Next-SCI-Carlson-Larco-2017-19ymhh6.pdf

Carter, L., & Bélanger, F. (2005). The utilization of e-government services: Citizen trust, innovation and acceptance factors. *Information Systems Journal, 15*(1), 5–26. doi:10.1111/j.1365-2575.2005.00183.x

Caruana, A. (2002). Service loyalty: The effects of service quality and the mediating role of customer satisfaction. *European Journal of Marketing, 36*(7/8), 811–828. doi:10.1108/03090560210430818

Cassimon, D., Engelen, P. J., & Liederkerke, L. V. (2014). When the firms invest in corporate social responsibility. *Tjalling C.Koopmans Research Institute Discussion Paper, 14*(6), 1715-1728.

Castaldo, S., & Botti, S. (1999). La dimensione emozionale dello shopping. *Economia & Management, 1*, 17–37.

Castels, M., & Cardosso, G. (2008). *The network society. From knowledge to policy*. Johns Hopkins Center for Transatlantic Relations Press.

Čater, T., & Čater, B. (2010). Product and relationship quality influence on customer commitment and loyalty in B2B manufacturing relationships. *Industrial Marketing Management, 39*(8), 1321–1333. doi:10.1016/j.indmarman.2010.02.006

Chadha, K. S. (2002). Indian journal of marketing, Relationship marketing. *Managing Customer Focus, 32*(5), 22–28.

Chaffey, D. (2018). *Global social media research summary 2018*. Retrieved from https://www.smartinsights.com/social-media-marketing/social-media-strategy/new-global-social-media-research/

Chaffey, D. (2010). Applying organisational capability models to assess the maturity of digital-marketing governance. *Journal of Marketing Management, 26*(3-4), 187–196. doi:10.1080/02672571003612192

Chaffey, D., & Ellis-Chadwick, F. (2019). *Digital Marketing*. London: Pearson.

Chai, S., Das, S., & Rao, H. R. (2011). Factors affecting bloggers' knowledge sharing: An investigation across gender. *Journal of Management Information Systems, 28*(3), 309–342. doi:10.2753/MIS0742-1222280309

Chakrabarti, S. (2010). Factors influencing organic food purchase in India – expert survey insights. *British Food Journal*, *112*(8), 902–915. doi:10.1108/00070701011067497

Chang, Y. F. (2013). Exploration of shopping mall customer value propositions in the experience economy. *Актуальні проблеми економіки*, (5), 566-576.

Chang, H. H., & Wang, H.-W. (2011). The moderating effect of customer perceived value on online shopping behaviour. *Online Information Review*, *35*(3), 333–359. doi:10.1108/14684521111151414

Chang, M.-Y., Pang, C., Tarn, J. M., Liu, T.-S., & Yen, D. C. (2015). Exploring user acceptance of an e-hospital service: An empirical study in Taiwan. *Computer Standards & Interfaces*, *38*, 35–43. doi:10.1016/j.csi.2014.08.004

Chang, Y.-T., Yu, H., & Lu, H.-P. (2015). Persuasive messages, popularity cohesion, and message diffusion in social media marketing. *Journal of Business Research*, *68*(4), 777–782. doi:10.1016/j.jbusres.2014.11.027

Charband, Y., & Jafari Navimipour, N. (2016). Online knowledge sharing mechanisms: A systematic review of the state of the art literatures and recommendations for future research. *Information Systems Frontiers*, *18*(6), 1131–1151. doi:10.100710796-016-9628-z

Charters, S., & Pettigrew, S. (2006). Product involvement and the evaluation of wine quality. *Qualitative Market Research*, *9*(2), 181–193. doi:10.1108/13522750610658810

Chau, P. Y. K., & Hu, P. J.-H. (2001). Information Technology Acceptance by Individual Professionals: A Model of Comparison Approach. *Decision Sciences*, *32*(4), 699–719. doi:10.1111/j.1540-5915.2001.tb00978.x

Chebat, J. C., El Hedhli, K., & Sirgy, M. J. (2009). How does shopper-based mall equity generate mall loyalty? A conceptual model and empirical evidence. *Journal of Retailing and Consumer Services*, *16*(1), 50–60. doi:10.1016/j.jretconser.2008.08.003

Chebat, J. C., Michon, R., Haj-Salem, N., & Oliveira, S. (2014). The effects of mall renovation on shopping values, satisfaction and spending behaviour. *Journal of Retailing and Consumer Services*, *21*(4), 610–618. doi:10.1016/j.jretconser.2014.04.010

Chebat, J. C., Sirgy, M. J., & Grzeskowiak, S. (2010). How can shopping mall management best capture mall image? *Journal of Business Research*, *63*(7), 735–740. doi:10.1016/j.jbusres.2009.05.009

Chen, C. (2013). Perceived risk, usage frequency of mobile banking services. *Managing Service Quality: An International Journal*, *23*(5), 410–436. doi:10.1108/MSQ-10-2012-0137

Cheng, N. (2015). *More than 30 Malaysians fall prey to cyber crime daily*. Retrieved from The Star Online: https://www.thestar.com.my/news/nation/2015/10/26/cybercrime-30-msians-daily/#RTz6iSoeOx4XTBeb.99

Cheng, R. (2014). Strategy Research on Development of Green Food and Security Control in Heilongjiang Province. *International Conference on Agricultural and Biosystem Engineering*, *8*, 24-29. 10.1016/j.ieri.2014.09.005

Chen, H. (2018). College-aged young consumers' perceptions of social media marketing: The story of Instagram. *Journal of Current Issues and Research in Advertising*, *39*(1), 22–36. doi:10.1080/10641734.2017.1372321

Chen, I. J., & Popovich, K. (2003). Understanding Customer relationship management (CRM): People, process and technology. *Business Process Management Journal*, *9*(5), 672–688. doi:10.1108/14637150310496758

Chen, M. F. (2007). Consumer Attitude towards organic meats and purchase intentions in relation to organic foods in Taiwan: Moderating effects of food-related personality traits. *Food Quality and Preference*, *18*, 1008–1021. doi:10.1016/j.foodqual.2007.04.004

Chen, S.-C. (2015). Customer value and customer loyalty: Is competition a missing link? *Journal of Retailing and Consumer Services*, *22*, 107–116. doi:10.1016/j.jretconser.2014.10.007

Chen, Y., Fay, S., & Wang, Q. (2011). The role of marketing in social media: How online consumer reviews evolve. *Journal of Interactive Marketing*, *25*(2), 85–94. doi:10.1016/j.intmar.2011.01.003

Cheung, C. M. K., & Lee, M. K. O. (2005). The Asymmetric Effect of Website Attribute Performance on Web Satisfaction: An Empirical Study. *e-Service Journal*, *3*(3), 65–90. doi:10.2979/esj.2004.3.3.65

Chew, J. (2018, November 5). Malaysia officially the second country in South East Asia to introduce a digital tax. *The Drum*. Retrieved from https://www.thedrum.com/opinion/2018/11/05/malaysia-officially-the-second-country-south-east-asia-introduce-digital-tax

Chikandiwa, T., & Sarah, C. (2013). The adoption of social media marketing in South African banks. *European Business Review*, *25*(4), 365–381. doi:10.1108/EBR-02-2013-0013

Chinomona, R., & Sandada, M. (2013). The influence of market related mobile activities on the acceptance of mobile marketing and consumer intention to purchase products promoted by SMS in South Africa. *Journal of Applied Business Research*, *29*(6), 1897–1908. doi:10.19030/jabr.v29i6.8225

Chin, W. W. (1998). Issues and opinions on structural equation modeling. *Management Information Systems Quarterly*, *22*(1), 7–16.

Chiu, C.-M., & Wang, E. T. G. (2008). Understanding Web-based learning continuance intention: The role of subjective task value. *Information & Management*, *45*(3), 194–201. doi:10.1016/j.im.2008.02.003

Chong, A. Y. L. (2013). Understanding mobile commerce continuance intentions: An empirical analysis of Chinese consumers. *Journal of Computer Information Systems*, *53*(4), 22–30. doi:10.1080/08874417.2013.11645647

Chong, M. (2012). Importance of corporate reputation. *The Business Times*, *11*(11), 11–15.

Chopra, S. (2016). How omni-channel can be the future of retailing. *Decision (Washington, D.C.)*, *43*(2), 135–144. doi:10.100740622-015-0118-9

Chou, C. D., Lin, B., Xu, Y., & Yen, C. D. (2002). Adopting Customer relationship management technology. Journal. *Industrial Management & Data Systems*, *102*(8), 442–452. doi:10.1108/02635570210445871

Choudhury, M. M., & Harrigan, P. (2014). CRM to social CRM: The integration of new technologies into customer relationship management. *Journal of Strategic Marketing*, *22*(2), 149–176. doi:10.1080/0965254X.2013.876069

Choudhury, V., & Karahanna, E. (2008). The relative advantage of electronic channels: A multidimensional view. *Management Information Systems Quarterly*, *32*(1), 179–200. doi:10.2307/25148833

Chou, S. W., Min, H. T., Chang, Y. C., & Lin, C. T. (2009). Understanding continuance intention of knowledge creation using extended expectation– confirmation theory: An empirical study of Taiwan and China online communities. *Behaviour & Information Technology*, *29*(6), 557–57. doi:10.1080/01449290903401986

Chretien, K. C., & Kind, T. (2013). Social media and clinical care: Ethical, professional, and social implications. *Circulation*, *127*(13), 1413–1421. doi:10.1161/CIRCULATIONAHA.112.128017 PMID:23547180

Chung, N., & Kwon, S. J. (2009). The effect of customers' mobile experience and technical support on the intention to use mobile banking. *Cyberpsychology & Behavior*, *12*(5), 539–543. doi:10.1089/cpb.2009.0014 PMID:19772441

Chung, N., Song, H. G., & Lee, H. (2017). Consumers' impulsive buying behavior of restaurant products in social commerce. *International Journal of Contemporary Hospitality Management*, *29*(2), 709–731. doi:10.1108/IJCHM-10-2015-0608

Chu, P.-Y., Lee, G.-Y., & Chao, Y. (2012). Service quality, customer satisfaction, customer trust, and loyalty in an e-banking context. *Social Behavior and Personality*, *40*(8), 1271–1283. doi:10.2224bp.2012.40.8.1271

Churchill, G. A. Jr. (1979). A paradigm for developing better measures of marketing constructs. *JMR, Journal of Marketing Research*, *16*(1), 64–73. doi:10.1177/002224377901600110

CIGI-IPSOS. (2018). *Global Survey on Internet Security and Trust*. Retrieved from www.cigionline.org/internet-survey

Clarke, I. (2001). Emerging value propositions for m-commerce. *The Journal of Business Strategy*, *18*(2), 133–149.

Close, A. G., & Kinney, M. K. (2010). Beyond buying: Motivations behind consumer's online shopping cart use. *Journal of Business Research*, *63*(9/10), 986–992. doi:10.1016/j.jbusres.2009.01.022

Clover, V. T. (1950). Relative importance of impulse-buying in retail stores. *Journal of Marketing*, *15*(1), 66–70. doi:10.1177/002224295001500110

Cohen, W. M., & Levinthal, D. A. (1990). Absorptive capacity: A new perspective on learning and innovation. *Administrative Science Quarterly*, *35*(1), 128–152. doi:10.2307/2393553

Colier, J. E., & Bienstock, C. C. (2006). Measuring service quality in e-retailing. *Journal of Service Research*, *8*(3), 260–275. doi:10.1177/1094670505278867

Colliander, J., & Marder, B. (2018). 'Snap happy' brands: Increasing publicity effectiveness through a snapshot aesthetic when marketing a brand on Instagram. *Computers in Human Behavior*, *78*, 34–43. doi:10.1016/j.chb.2017.09.015

Colquitt, J., Hollenbeck, J., Ilgen, D., LePine, J., & Sheppard, L. (2002). Computer-assisted communication and team decision-making performance: The moderating effect of openness to experience. *The Journal of Applied Psychology*, *87*(2), 402–410. doi:10.1037/0021-9010.87.2.402 PMID:12002966

Cook, R. D., & Sanford, W. (1982). *Residuals and influence in regression*. New York: Chapman and Hall.

Cothrel, J. P. (2000). Measuring the success of an online community. *Strategy and Leadership*, *28*(2), 7–21. doi:10.1108/10878570010341609

Cox, J., & Dale, B. G. (2001). Service quality and e-commerce: An exploratory analysis. *Managing Service Quality*, *11*(2), 121–131. doi:10.1108/09604520110387257

Cox, J., & Dale, B. G. (2002). Key quality factors in Web site design and use: An examination. *International Journal of Quality & Reliability Management*, *19*(7), 862–888. doi:10.1108/02656710210434784

Crainic, T. G., Ricciardi, N., & Storchi, G. (2004). Advanced freight transportation systems for congested urban areas. *Transportation Research Part C, Emerging Technologies*, *12*(2), 119–137. doi:10.1016/j.trc.2004.07.002

Crainic, T. G., Ricciardi, N., & Storchi, G. (2009). Models for Evaluating and Planning City Logistics Systems. *Transportation Science*, *43*(4), 432–454. doi:10.1287/trsc.1090.0279

Cristobal, E., Flavian, C., & Guinalıu, M. (2007). Perceived E-Service Quality: Measurement Validation and Effects on Consumer Satisfaction and Website Loyalty. *Managing Service Quality*, *17*(3), 317–340. doi:10.1108/09604520710744326

Crocker, J., & Canevello, A. (2008). Creating and undermining social support in communal relationships: The role of compassionate and self-image goals. *Journal of Personality and Social Psychology*, *95*(3), 555–575. doi:10.1037/0022-3514.95.3.555 PMID:18729694

Cronin, J. J. Jr, & Taylor, S. A. (1992). Measuring Service Quality: A Reexamination and Extension. *Journal of Marketing*, *56*(3), 55–68. doi:10.1177/002224299205600304

Cullen, M., & Kabanda, S. K. (2018). The role of demographic and motivational factors on mobile commerce usage activities in South Africa. *South African Journal of Information Management, 20*(1), 1–8. doi:10.4102ajim.v20i1.817

Culnan, M. J., McHugh, P. J., & Zubillaga, J. I. (2010). How large US companies can use Twitter and other social media to gain business value. *MIS Quarterly Executive, 9*(4), 243–259.

Cummins, S., Peltier, J. W., Schibrowsky, J. A., & Nill, A. (2014). Consumer behavior in the online context. *Journal of Research in Interactive Marketing, 8*(3), 169–202. doi:10.1108/JRIM-04-2013-0019

Cushman & Wakefiled. (2017) *European Shopping Centres The Development Story*. A Cushman & Wakefield Research Publication. Retrieved from http://www.cushmanwakefield.com/en/research-and-insight/2017/european-shopping-centres-the-development-story-nov-17

Cutlip, S. M., Center, A. H., & Broom, G. M. (2006). *Effective Public Relations*. Upper Saddle River, NJ: Pearson Publishings.

Cyr, D., Bonanni, C., Bowes, J., & Ilsever, J. (2005). Beyond trust: Web site design preferences across cultures. *Journal of Global Information Management, 13*(4), 25–54. doi:10.4018/jgim.2005100102

Cyr, D., Hassanein, K., Head, M., & Ivanov, A. (2006). The role of social presence in establishing loyalty in e-service environments. *Interacting with Computers, 19*(1), 43–56. doi:10.1016/j.intcom.2006.07.010

Dabholkar, P. (1996). Consumer evaluations of new technology-based self-service options: An investigation of alternative modes of service quality. *International Journal of Research in Marketing, 13*(1), 29–51. doi:10.1016/0167-8116(95)00027-5

Dablanc, L., & Rakotonarivo, D. (2010). The impacts of logistics sprawl: How does the location of parcel transport terminals affect the energy efficiency of goods' movements in Paris and what can we do about it? *Procedia: Social and Behavioral Sciences, 2*(3), 6087–6096. doi:10.1016/j.sbspro.2010.04.021

Daoud, M., Naqvi, S.K., & Ahmad, A. (2014). Opinion Observer: Recommendation System on ECommerce Website. *International Journal of Computers and Applications, 105*(14), 37–42.

Dardak, R. A., Zainol, A. Z., & Kasim, A. (2009). Consumer's perception, consumption and preference on organic product: Malaysian perspective. *Economic and Technology Management Review, 4*, 95–107.

Darling and Russ. (2000). Relationship Capital. *Executive Excellence, 17*(5), 14.

Daugherty, T., Eastin, M. S., & Bright, L. (2008). Exploring consumer motivations for creating user-generated content. *Journal of Interactive Advertising, 8*(2), 16–25. doi:10.1080/15252019.2008.10722139

Davenport, T. H., & Beck, J. (2001). *The attention economy*. Boston: Harvard Business School Press. doi:10.1145/375348.376626

Davis. (1989). Perceived Usefulness, Perceived Ease of Use, and User Acceptance of Information Technology. *MIS Quarterly, 13*(3), 319-339.

Davis, F. D. (1989). Perceived usefulness, perceived ease of use, and user acceptance of information technology. *Management Information Systems Quarterly, 13*(3), 319–340. doi:10.2307/249008

Davis, F. D., Bagozzi, R. P., & Warshaw, P. R. (1989). User acceptance of computer technology: A comparison of two theoretical models. *Management Science, 35*(8), 982–1003. doi:10.1287/mnsc.35.8.982

Dawson, S., & Kim, M. (2009). External and internal trigger cues of impulse buying online. *Direct Marketing: An International Journal, 3*(1), 20–34. doi:10.1108/17505930910945714

Day, G. S. (1969). A two-dimensional concept of brand loyalty. *Journal of Advertising Research*, *9*(3), 29–35.

De Gregorio, F., & Sung, Y. (2010). Understanding attitudes toward and behaviors in response to product placement. *Journal of Advertising*, *39*(1), 83–96. doi:10.2753/JOA0091-3367390106

de Ruyter, K., Wetzels, M., & Kleijnen, M. (2001). Customer adoption of e-service: An experimental study. *International Journal of Service Industry Management*, *12*(2), 184–207. doi:10.1108/09564230110387542

De Veirman, M., Cauberghe, V., & Hudders, L. (2017). Marketing through Instagram influencers: The impact of number of followers and product divergence on brand attitude. *International Journal of Advertising*, *36*(5), 798–828. doi:10.1080/02650487.2017.1348035

De Vries, L., Gensler, S., & Leeflang, P. S. H. (2012). Popularity of brand posts on brand fan pages: An investigation of the effects of social media marketing. *Journal of Interactive Marketing*, *26*(2), 83–91. doi:10.1016/j.intmar.2012.01.003

De Vries, N. J., & Carlson, J. (2014). Examining the drivers and brand performance implications of customer engagement with brands in the social media environment. *Journal of Brand Management*, *21*(6), 495–515. doi:10.1057/bm.2014.18

Debek, M. (2015). What Drives Shopping Mall Attractiveness? *Polish Journal of Applied Psychology*, *13*(1), 67–118. doi:10.1515/pjap-2015-0026

Del Giudice, M., Campanella, F., & Dezi, L. (2016). The bank of things: An empirical investigation on the profitability of the financial services of the future. *Business Process Management Journal*, *22*(2), 324–340. doi:10.1108/BPMJ-10-2015-0139

Dellarocas, C. (2003). The digitization of word of mouth: Promise and challenges of online feedback mechanisms. *Management Science*, *49*(10), 1407–1424. doi:10.1287/mnsc.49.10.1407.17308

DeLoatch, P. (2018). *Retailers lure shoppers with in-store holiday experiences*. Retrieved January 22, 2019, from https://www.retaildive.com/news/retailers-lure-shoppers-with-in-store-holiday-experiences/541471/

DeLone, W. H., & McLean, E. R. (1992). Information systems success: The quest for the dependent variable. *Information Systems Research*, *3*(1), 60–95. doi:10.1287/isre.3.1.60

DeLone, W. H., & McLean, E. R. (2003). The DeLone and McLean model of information systems success: A ten-year update. *Journal of Management Information Systems*, *19*(4), 9–30. doi:10.1080/07421222.2003.11045748

Dennis, A. R., Pootheri, S. K., & Natarajan, V. L. (1998). Lessons from the early adopters of Web groupware. *Journal of Management Information Systems*, *14*(4), 65–86. doi:10.1080/07421222.1998.11518186

Dennis, C., Merrilees, B., Jayawardhena, C., & Wright, L. T. (2009). E-Consumer behavior. *European Journal of Marketing*, *42*(9), 1121–1139. doi:10.1108/03090560910976393

Dettmann, R. L., & Dimitri, C. (2009). Who's Buying Organic Vegetables? Demographic Characteristics of U.S. Consumers. *Journal of Food Products Marketing*, *16*(1), 79–91. doi:10.1080/10454440903415709

Devaraj, S., Fan, M., & Kohli, R. (2002). Antecedents of B2C channel satisfaction and preference: Validating e-commerce metrics. *Information Systems Research*, *13*(3), 316–333. doi:10.1287/isre.13.3.316.77

Devito Da Cunha, A., & Greathead, D. (2007). Does personality matter? An analysis of code-review ability. *Communications of the ACM*, *50*(5), 109–112. doi:10.1145/1230819.1241672

DeVito, J. A. (1993). *Messages: Building Interpersonal Communication Skills*. New York: HarperCollins College Publishers.

Dewan, S. G., & Chen, L. (2005). Mobile payment adoption in the US: A cross-industry, cross platform solution. *Journal of Information Privacy and Security.*, *1*(2), 4–25. doi:10.1080/15536548.2005.10855765

Dhurup, M., Surujlal, J., & Redda, E. (2014). Customer perceptions of online banking service quality and its relationship with customer satisfaction and loyalty. *Mediterranean Journal of Social Sciences*, *5*, 72–80.

Dick, A. S., & Basu, K. (1994). Customer loyalty: Toward an integrated conceptual framework. *Journal of the Academy of Marketing Science*, *22*(2), 99–113. doi:10.1177/0092070394222001

Dickerson, M. D., & Gentry, J. W. (1983). Characteristics of adopters and non-adopters of home computers. *The Journal of Consumer Research*, *10*(2), 225–235. doi:10.1086/208961

Dickey, I. J., & Lewis, W. F. (2010). Social Media Perceptions and Usage by Generation Y and Relevant Marketing Implications. In *2010 Conference Proceedings of the Society for Marketing Advances*. University of Dayton.

Dickieson, J., & Arkus, V. (2009). *Factors that influence the purchase of organic food: A study of consumer behaviour in the UK*. Cass Business School.

Digman, J. M., & Takemoto-Chock, N. K. (1981). Factors in the natural language of personality: Reanalysis, comparison, and interpretation of six major studies. *Multivariate Behavioral Research*, *16*(2), 149–170. doi:10.120715327906mbr1602_2 PMID:26825420

Dijkmans, C., Kerkhof, P., & Beukeboom, C. J. (2015). A stage to engage: Social media use and corporate reputation. *Tourism Management Journal*, *47*, 58–67. doi:10.1016/j.tourman.2014.09.005

Dilek, S., & Top, S. (2013). Charges on parking in shopping malls: Evidence from Turkey. *Procedia: Social and Behavioral Sciences*, *99*, 382–390. doi:10.1016/j.sbspro.2013.10.506

Dimitri, C., & Dettmann, R. L. (2012). Organic Food Consumers: What Do We Really Know About Them? *British Food Journal*, *114*(8), 1157–1183. doi:10.1108/00070701211252101

Djafarova, E., & Rushworth, C. (2017). Exploring the credibility of online celebrities' Instagram profiles in influencing the purchase decisions of young female users. *Computers in Human Behavior*, *68*, 1–7. doi:10.1016/j.chb.2016.11.009

Dlodlo, N., & Dhurup, M. (2013). Examining social media dimensions among a cohort of Generation Y consumers in South Africa. *Mediterranean Journal of Social Sciences*, *4*, 329.

Dodoo, N. A., & Wu, L. (2019). Exploring the anteceding impact of personalised social media advertising on online impulse buying tendency. *International Journal of Internet Marketing and Advertising*, *13*(1), 73–95. doi:10.1504/IJIMA.2019.097905

Dodson, I. (2016). *The Art of Digital Marketing*. John Wiley & Sons.

Doll, W. J., Xia, W., & Torkzadeh, G. (1994). A confirmatory factor analysis of the end-user computing satisfaction instrument. *Management Information Systems Quarterly*, *18*(4), 453–461. doi:10.2307/249524

Donat, J., & Boyd, B. (2004). Public displays of connection. *BT Technology Journal*, *22*(4), 71–82. doi:10.1023/B:BTTJ.0000047585.06264.cc

Dong, K., Sun, R., Dong, C., Li, H., Zeng, X., & Ni, G. (2018). Environmental Kuznets curve for PM 2.5 emissions in Beijing, China: What role can natural gas consumption play? *Ecological Indicators*, *93*, 591–601. doi:10.1016/j.ecolind.2018.05.045

Doorley, J., & Garcia, H. D. (2007). *Reputation management. The key the successful public relations and corporate communications*. New York: Taylor & Francis Group.

Dubihlela, D., & Dubihlela, J. (2014). Attributes of shopping mall image. customer satisfaction and mall patronage for selected shopping malls in Southern Gauteng. South Africa. *Journal of Economics and Behavioral Studies*, *6*(8), 682.

Duffett, R. G. (2015). Facebook advertising's influence on intention-to-purchase and purchase amongst Millennials. *Internet Research*, *25*(4), 498–526. doi:10.1108/IntR-01-2014-0020

Duffett, R. G. (2017). Influence of social media marketing communications on young consumers' attitudes. *Young Consumers*, *18*(1), 19–39. doi:10.1108/YC-07-2016-00622

Duffett, R. G., & Wakeham, M. (2016). Social media marketing communications effect on attitudes among Millennials in South Africa. *The African Journal of Information Systems*, *8*, 2.

Duggan, M., & Brenner, J. (2012). The demographics of social media users. *Pew Research Center's Internet & American Life Project*. Retrieved from https://www.pewinternet.org/2013/02/14/the-demographics-of-social-media-users-2012/

Dupuy, G., van Schaick, J., & Klaasen, I. T. (2018). *Urban networks: Network urbanism*. Amsterdam: Techne press.

Duverger, P. (2013). Curvilinear effects of user-generated content on hotels' market share: A dynamic panel-data analysis. *Journal of Travel Research*, *52*(4), 465–478. doi:10.1177/0047287513478498

Dwivedi, Y. K., Choudrie, J., & Brinkman, W.-P. (2006). Development of a survey instrument to examine consumer adoption of broadband. *Industrial Management & Data Systems*, *106*(5), 700–718. doi:10.1108/02635570610666458

Easley & Kleinberg. (2010). Networks, Crowds, and Markets: Reasoning about a Highly Connected World. Cambridge University Press.

eCommerceMILO. (2014). Retrieved from https://www.ecinsider.my/2014/12/top-malaysia-ecommerce-stories-2014.html

Edelman, B., Jaffe, S., & Kominers, S. D. (in press). To Groupon or not to Groupon: The profitability of deep discounts. *Marketing Letters*.

Einasto, O. (2014). E-service Quality Criteria in University Library: A Focus Group Study. *Procedia: Social and Behavioral Sciences*, *147*, 561–566. doi:10.1016/j.sbspro.2014.07.163

El Hedhli, K., & Chebat, J. C. (2009). Developing and validating a psychometric shopper-based mall equity measure. *Journal of Business Research*, *62*(6), 581–587. doi:10.1016/j.jbusres.2008.05.016

Elkhani, N., Soltani, S., & Nazir Ahmad, M. (2014). The effects of transformational leadership and ERP system self-efficacy on ERP system usage. *Journal of Enterprise Information Management*, *27*(6), 759–785. doi:10.1108/JEIM-06-2013-0031

Ellison, N. B., Steinfield, C., & Lampe, C. (2007). The benefits of Facebook "friends:" Social capital and college students' use of online social network sites. *Journal of Computer-Mediated Communication*, *12*(4), 1143–1168. doi:10.1111/j.1083-6101.2007.00367.x

Engle, R. L., & Barnes, M. L. (2000). Sales force auto-mation usage, effectiveness, and cost–benefit in Germany, England and the United States. *Journal of Business and Industrial Marketing*, *15*(4), 216–242. doi:10.1108/08858620010335083

Erkip, F. (2005). The rise of the shopping mall in Turkey: The use and appeal of a mall in Ankara. *Cities (London, England)*, *22*(2), 89–108. doi:10.1016/j.cities.2004.10.001

Etezadi-Amoli, J., & Farhoomand, A. (1996). A structural model of end user computing satisfaction and user performance. *Information & Management*, *30*(2), 65–73. doi:10.1016/0378-7206(95)00052-6

Fabrigar, L. R., Wegener, D. T., MacCallum, R. C., & Strahan, E. J. (1999). Evaluating the use of exploratory factor analysis in psychological research. *Psychological Methods*, *4*(3), 272–299. doi:10.1037/1082-989X.4.3.272

Fan, Y., & Li, Y. (2010). Children's buying behaviour in China: A study of their information sources. *Marketing Intelligence & Planning*, *28*(2), 170–187. doi:10.1108/02634501011029673

Faraoni, M., Rialti, R., Zollo, L., & Pellicelli, A. C. (2018). Exploring e-Loyalty Antecedents in B2C e-Commerce: Empirical results from Italian grocery retailers. *British Food Journal*, *121*(2), 574–589. doi:10.1108/BFJ-04-2018-0216

Farrag, D. A., El Sayed, I. M., & Belk, R. W. (2010). Mall shopping motives and activities: A multimethod approach. *Journal of International Consumer Marketing*, *22*(2), 95–115. doi:10.1080/08961530903476113

Fassnacht, M., & Koese, I. (2006). Quality of electronic services: Conceptualizing and testing a hierarchical model. *Journal of Service Research*, *9*(1), 19–31. doi:10.1177/1094670506289531

Federal Department of Town and Country Planning. (2016). *Malaysia National Report for the 3rd UNITED NATIONS Conference on Housing and Sustainable Urban Development (HABITAT III)*. Kuala Lumpur, Malaysia: Author.

Fei, B. (2011). *Study of China's online catering market under the booming of online group purchasing*. UNLV Theses/Dissertations/Professional Papers/Capstones, Paper 648. Retrieved 14 March, from: http://digitalcommons.library.unlv.edu/cgi/viewcontent.cgi?article=1649&context=thesesdissertations

Feinberg, R. A., & Meoli, J. (1991). A brief history of the mall. *ACR North American Advances*, *18*, 426–427.

Felix, R., Rauschnabel, P. A., & Hinsch, C. (2017). Elements of strategic social media marketing: A holistic framework. *Journal of Business Research*, *70*, 118–126. doi:10.1016/j.jbusres.2016.05.001

Fierro, I., Cardona Arbelaez, D. A., & Gavilanez, J. (2017). Digital marketing: A new tool for international education. *Pensamiento & Gestión*, *43*, 220–240.

Figallo, C. (1998). *Hosting Web communities: Building relationships, increasing customer loyalty and maintaining a competitive edge*. New York: John Wiley & Sons, Inc.

Finn, A. (2011). Investigating the non-linear effects of e-service quality dimensions on customer satisfaction. *Journal of Retailing and Consumer Services, 18*, 27-37.

Fischer, E., & Reuber, A. R. (2011). Social interaction via new social media:(How) can interactions on Twitter affect effectual thinking and behavior? *Journal of Business Venturing*, *26*(1), 1–18. doi:10.1016/j.jbusvent.2010.09.002

Fiske, D. W. (1949). Consistency of the factorial structures of personality ratings from different sources. *Journal of Abnormal and Social Psychology*, *44*(3), 329–344. doi:10.1037/h0057198 PMID:18146776

Flanagin, A. J., Metzger, M. J., Pure, R., Markov, A., & Hartsell, E. (2014). Mitigating risk in ecommerce transactions: Perceptions of information credibility and the role of user-generated ratings in product quality and purchase intention. *Electronic Commerce Research*, *14*(1), 1–23. doi:10.100710660-014-9139-2

Flavián, C., Guinalíu, M., & Gurrea, R. (2006). The role played by perceived usability, satisfaction and consumer trust on website loyalty. *Information & Management*, *43*(1), 1–14. doi:10.1016/j.im.2005.01.002

Floh, A., & Treiblmaier, H. (2006). What keeps the e-banking customer loyal? A multigroup analysis of the moderating role of consumer characteristics on e-loyalty in the financial service industry. *Journal of Electronic Commerce Research*, *7*(2), 97–110.

Fogg, B. J., Soohoo, C., Danielson, D. R., Marable, L., Stanford, J., & Tauber, E. R. (2003). *How do Users Evaluate the Credibility of Web Sites? A Study with over 2500 Participants.* Paper presented at the Conference on Designing for User Experiences, San Francisco, CA.

Fombrun, C. J. (1996). Reputation: Realizing value from the corporate image. Harvard Business School Press, 3(2), 101-111.

Fombrun, C. J., Gardberg, N., & Sever, J. (2000). The reputation quotient: A multistakeholder measure of corporate reputation. *Journal of Brand Management*, *7*(4), 241–225. doi:10.1057/bm.2000.10

Fombrun, C. J., & Van Riel, C. (1997). The reputational landscape. *Corporate Reputation Review*, *1*(1), 5–13. doi:10.1057/palgrave.crr.1540008

Fombrun, C. J., & Van Riel, C. (2004). *Fame and fortune: how successful companies build winning reputations*. Upper Saddle River, NJ: Pearson Education, Inc.

Fong, J., & Burton, S. (2006). Electronic Word-of-Mouth: A Comparison of Stated and Revealed Behavior on Electronic Discussion Boards. *Journal of Interactive Advertising*, *6*(2), 7–62. doi:10.1080/15252019.2006.10722119

Formbrun, C. J., & Foss, C. B. (2005). The reputation quotient. Developing a reputation quotient. *Newsletter of Worldwide Communications Research, 4*(3). Retrieved from www.reputationinstitute.com

Fornell, C., & Larcker, D. (1981). Structural equation models with unobservable variables and measurement error: Algebra and statistics. *JMR, Journal of Marketing Research*, *14*(3), 382–388. doi:10.1177/002224378101800313

Fournier, S., & Lee, L. (2009). Getting brand communities right. *Harvard Business Review*, *87*(4), 105–111. PMID:19736854

Franz, R., & Wolkinger, T. (2003). Customer Integration with Virtual Communities. Case study: The online community of the largest regional newspaper in Austria. *Proceedings of the Hawaii International Conference on System Sciences*.

Fuller, R., & Shikaloff, N. (2017). Being Engaged at Work Is Not the Same as Being Productive. *Harvard Business Review*, *16*. Retrieved from https://hbr.org/2017/02/being-engaged-at-work-is-not-the-same-as-being-productive

Ganguli, S., & Roy, S. K. (2011). Generic technology-based service quality dimensions in banking impact on customer satisfaction and loyalty. *International Journal of Bank Marketing*, *29*(2), 168–189. doi:10.1108/02652321111107648

Garett. (2000). *The twelve organizational capabilities: Valuing People at work*. Harper Collins Business.

Gartner. (2002). Retrieved from http://www.gartner.com/technology/home.jsp

Garvin, D. A. (1983). Quality on the Line. *Harvard Business Review*, *61*, 65–73.

Gefen, D. (2002). Customer loyalty in e-commerce. *Journal of the Association for Information Systems*, *3*(1), 27–51. doi:10.17705/1jais.00022

Genel, Z. (2017). Sustainable communication as a component of corporate reputation. In A. S. Özdemir (Ed.), *Reputation Management Techniques in Public Relations* (pp. 38–55). IGI Global.

Gentry, J. W., & Burns, A. C. (1978). How important are evaluative criteria in shopping center patronage. *Journal of Retailing*, *53*(4), 73.

George, T., & Stavros, T. (2013). *The role of psychological commitment and attitudinal loyalty on the relationship between involvement and behavioral loyalty of sports fans*. Available from: http://www.thesportjournal.org

Gerbing, D. W., Anderson, J. C., & Carlo, M. (1993). Evaluation of goodness-of-fit indeces for Stractural Equations Models. *Sociological Methods & Research*, *21*(2), 132–160. doi:10.1177/0049124192021002002

Geron, G. (2009). *Business Aspects of the Internet of Things: Mobile Marketing, Seminar of advanced topics*. Zurich: Florian Michahelles.

Gevaers, R., Van de Voorde, E., & Vanelslander, T. (2014). Cost Modelling and Simulation of Last-mile Characteristics in an Innovative B2C Supply Chain Environment with Implications on Urban Areas and Cities. *Procedia: Social and Behavioral Sciences*, *125*, 398–411. doi:10.1016/j.sbspro.2014.01.1483

Gibbs, S. (2017). *Facebook and Google were conned out of $100m in phishing scheme*. Retrieved from The Guardian: https://www.theguardian.com/technology/2017/apr/28/facebook-google-conned-100m-phishing-scheme

Gibreel, O., AlOtaibi, D. A., & Altmann, J. (2018). Social commerce development in emerging markets. *Electronic Commerce Research and Applications*, *27*, 152–162. doi:10.1016/j.elerap.2017.12.008

Gilmore, A. (1997). Implementing quality in a services marketing context. *Marketing Intelligence & Planning*, *15*(4), 185–189. doi:10.1108/02634509710185306

Global Strategic Communications Inc. (n.d.). *Corporate Reputation Review International Journal*. Henry Stewart Publications. Retrieved from www.firesteinco.com/reputation

Goldenberg, B. (2000). What is CRM? What is an e-customer? Why you need them now. *Proceedings of DCI Customer Relationship Management Conference*, 27-29.

Gomiero, T., Pimentel, D., & Paoletti, M. (2011). Environmental Impact of Different Agricultural Management Practices: Conventional vs. Organic Agriculture. *Critical Reviews in Plant Sciences*, *30*(1), 95–124. doi:10.1080/07352689.2011.554355

Gommans, M., Krishnan, K. S., & Scheffold, K. B. (2001). From brand loyalty to e-loyalty: A conceptual framework. *Journal of Economic and Social Research*, *3*(1), 43–58.

Gorsuch, R. (1983). *Factor Analysis*. Hillsdale, NJ: Erlbaum.

Gosling, S. D., Rentfrow, P. J., & Swann, W. B. Jr. (2003). A very brief measure of the Big-Five personality domains. *Journal of Research in Personality*, *37*(6), 504–528. doi:10.1016/S0092-6566(03)00046-1

Gottlieb, B. H. (1985). Social Networks and Social Support: An Overview of Research, Practice, and Policy Implications. *Health Education Quarterly*, *12*(1), 5–22. doi:10.1177/109019818501200102 PMID:3980240

Gracia, A., & Magistris, T. (2007). Organic Food Product Purchase Behaviour: A Pilot Study. *Spanish Journal of Agricultural Research*, *5*(4), 439–451. doi:10.5424jar/2007054-5356

Greenberg, P. (2004). *CRM at the speed of light: essential customer strategies for the 21st century*. Tata McGraw Hill Companies, Inc.

Greysen, R. S., Kind, T., & Chretien, K. C. (2010). Online Professionalism and the Mirror of Social Media. *Journal of General Internal Medicine, 25*(11), 1227–1229. doi:10.100711606-010-1447-1

Grieve, R., Indian, M., Witteveen, K., Tolan, G. A., & Marrington, J. (2013, May). Face-to-face or Facebook: Can social connectedness be derived online? *Computers in Human Behavior*, *29*(3), 604–609. doi:10.1016/j.chb.2012.11.017

Griffith-Greene, M. (2014). Fake online reviews: 4 ways companies can deceive you. *CBC News*. Retrieved from http://www.cbc.ca/

Grigoroudis, E., Litos, C., Moustakis, V. A., Politis, Y., & Tsironis, L. (2008). The assessment of user-perceived web quality: Application of a satisfaction benchmarking approach. *European Journal of Operational Research*, *187*(3), 1346–1357. doi:10.1016/j.ejor.2006.09.017

Grinberg, I. (2018). *International Taxation in an Era of Digital Disruption: Analyzing the Current Debate*. Washington, DC: Georgetown Law Faculty Publications and Other Works.

Grönroos, C. (2000). *Service Marketing and Management: a Customer Relationship Management Approach* (2nd ed.). Chichester, UK: John Wiley.

Gronroos, C., Heinonen, F., Isoniemi, K., & Lindholm, M. (2000). The NetOffer model: A case example from the virtual marketplace. *management. Decision (Washington, D.C.)*, *38*(4), 243–252.

Gross. (1999, March 22). Building global communities: How business is partnering with sites that draw together like-minded consumers. *BusinessWeek Online*. Retrieved October 17, 2004, from http://businessweek.com/datedtoc/1999/9912.htm

Gruen, T. W. (1997). Relationship Marketing: The Route to Marketing Efficiency and Effectiveness. *Business Horizons*, *40*(6), 32–38. doi:10.1016/S0007-6813(97)90065-3

Grunig, J. E. (2009). Paradigms of global public relations in an age of digitalization. *Prism*, *6*(2), 1–19.

Grunig, J. E., & Hunt, T. (1984). *Managing public relations*. New York: Holt, Rinehart and Winston.

Grunig, J. E., & Hunt, T. (2002). The effect of relationships on reputation and reputation on relationships: a cognitive, behavioral study. *Proceedings of PRSA Educator's Academy 5th Annual International, Interdisciplinary Public Relations Research Conference.*

Gudonaviciene, R., & Alijosiene. S. (2013). Influence of shopping centre image attributes on customer choices. *Economics and Management, 18*(3), 545-552.

Guildford, J. P. & Zimmerman, W. S. (1949). *The Guildford-Zimmerman Temperament Survey*. Beverly Hills, CA: Sheridan Supply.

Gummerus, J., Liljander, V., Pura, M., & Riel, A. V. (2004). Customer loyalty to content-basedWeb sites: The case of an online healthcare service. *Journal of Services Marketing*, *18*(3), 175–186. doi:10.1108/08876040410536486

Gupta, P. (2011). Shopping impulses, online vs off. *The New York Times*. Available at: http://nyti.ms/2le4rY8

Gwebu, K. L., & Wang, J. (2011). Adoption of Open Source Software: The role of social identification. *Decision Support Systems*, *51*(1), 220–229. doi:10.1016/j.dss.2010.12.010

Hagel, J., & Armstrong, A. G. (1997). *Net Gain: Expanding Markets through Virtual Communities*. Harvard Business School Press.

Hair, J. F., Anderson, R. E., Tatham, R. L., & Black, W. C. (1998). Multivariate Data Analysis (5th ed.). Englewood Cliffs, NJ: Prentice Hall.

Hair, J., Anderson, R., Tatham, R., & Black, W. (1995a). Multivariate data analysis. (4th ed.). Prentice-Hall Inc.

Hair, J., Black, W. C., Babin, B. J., Anderson, R. E., & Tatham, R. (2006). *Multivariate Data Analysis*. New York, NY: Pearson Education.

Hajli, N., Sims, J., Zadeh, A. H., & Richard, M.-O. (2017). A social commerce investigation of the role of trust in a social networking site on purchase intentions. *Journal of Business Research*, *71*, 133–141. doi:10.1016/j.jbusres.2016.10.004

Haj-Salem, N., Chebat, J. C., Michon, R., & Oliveira, S. (2016). Why male and female shoppers do not see mall loyalty through the same lens? The mediating role of self-congruity. *Journal of Business Research*, *69*(3), 1219–1227. doi:10.1016/j.jbusres.2015.09.011

Hakanson. (1982). *International Marketing and Purchasing of Industrial Goods: An Interaction Approach*. New York: John Wiley.

Hall, E. T. (1983). *The Dance of Life*. Garden City, NY: Anchor Press.

Hallowell, R. (1996). The relationships of customer satisfaction, customer loyalty, and profitability: An empirical study. *International Journal of Service Industry Management*, *7*(4), 27–42. doi:10.1108/09564239610129931

Hameed, K., Ahsan, K., & Yang, W. (2010). Mobile commerce and applications: An exploratory study and review. *Journal of Computers*, *2*(4), 110–114.

Hanna, R. C., Swain, S. D., & Smith, J. (2015). *Email Marketing in a Digital World: The Basics and Beyond*. New York, NY: Business Expert Press.

Harris, S. (2017). *Why keeping your smartphone close is actually making you dumber*. Retrieved 14 February, 2019, from World Economic Forum: https://www.weforum.org/agenda/2017/07/why-keeping-your-smartphone-close-is-actually-making-you-dumber/?fbclid=IwAR0kLUHVAoQjxekvlQCNlyygFHALR5mSiS8-bcjhbQvOqzlAXLja-nH9aL4

Harris, A., Kelly, S. E., & Wyatt, S. (2014). Autobiologies on YouTube: Narratives of direct-to-consumer genetic testing. *New Genetics & Society*, *33*(1), 60–78. doi:10.1080/14636778.2014.884456 PMID:24772003

Harris, L. C., & Goode, M. M. (2004). The four levels of loyalty and the pivotal role of trust: A study of online service dynamics. *Journal of Retailing*, *80*(2), 139–158. doi:10.1016/j.jretai.2004.04.002

Harrison, R., & Scheela, W. (2017, September). Beyond institutional voids and the middle income trap? The emerging business angel market in Malaysia. *Asia Pacific Journal of Management*, 1–27.

Ha, S., & Stoel, L. (2009). Consumer e-shopping acceptance: Antecedents in a technology acceptance model. *Journal of Business Research*, *62*(5), 565–571. doi:10.1016/j.jbusres.2008.06.016

Hassan, S. H., Loi, W. Y., & Kok, J. R. (2015). Purchasing Intention Towards Organic Food Among Gen Y In Malaysia. *Journal of Agribusiness Marketing*, *7*(2), 16–32.

Hassan, S., Naveed, A., & Yılmaz, A. K. (2016). Impact of the Conscientiousness as Personality Trait on both Job and Organizational Performance. *Journal of Managerial Sciences*, *10*(1), 1–14.

Hausman, A. (2000). A multi-method investigation of consumer motivations in impulse buying behavior. *Journal of Consumer Marketing*, *17*(5), 403–426. doi:10.1108/07363760010341045

Hautz, J., Füller, J., Hutter, K., & Thürridl, C. (2014). Let users generate your video ads? The impact of video source and quality on consumers' perceptions and intended behaviors. *Journal of Interactive Marketing*, *28*(1), 1–15. doi:10.1016/j.intmar.2013.06.003

Ha, Y., & Im, H. (2012). Role of web site design quality in satisfaction and word of mouth generation. *Journal of Service Management*, *23*(1), 79–96. doi:10.1108/09564231211208989

Hennig-Thurau, T., Gwinner, K. P., & Gremler, D. D. (2002). Understanding relationship marketing outcomes. *Journal of Service Research*, *4*(3), 230–247. doi:10.1177/1094670502004003006

Hennig-Thurau, T., Gwinner, K. P., Walsh, G., & Gremler, D. D. (2004). Electronic word-of-mouth via consumer-opinion platforms: What motivates consumers to articulate themselves on the internet? *Journal of Interactive Marketing*, *18*(1), 38–52. doi:10.1002/dir.10073

Henning, T., Malthouse, E. C., Friege, C., Gensler, S., Loschat, L., Rangaswamy, A., & Skiera, B. (2010). The impact of new media on consumer relationships. *Journal of Service Research*, *13*(3), 311–330. doi:10.1177/1094670510375460

Henseler, J., Ringle, C. M., & Sarstedt, M. (2014). A new criterion for assessing discriminant validity in variance-based structural equation modeling. *Journal of the Academy of Marketing Science*, *43*(1), 115–135. doi:10.100711747-014-0403-8

Henseler, J., Ringle, C. M., & Sinkovics, R. R. (2009). The use of Partial Least Squares Path Modeling in International Marketing. *Advances in International Marketing*, *20*, 277–319. doi:10.1108/S1474-7979(2009)0000020014

Herrington, D. J., & Capella, L. M. (1995). Shopper reactions to perceived time pressure. *International Journal of Retail & Distribution Management*, *23*(12), 13 20. doi:10.1108/09590559510103963

Hesse, M. (2004). Land for Logistics: Locational Dynamics, Real Estate Markets and Political Regulation of Regional Distribution Complexes. *Tijdschrift voor Economische en Sociale Geografie*, *95*(2), 162–173. doi:10.1111/j.0040-747X.2004.t01-1-00298.x

He, Z., Xu, S., Shen, W., Long, R., & Chen, H. (2017). Impact of urbanization on energy related CO2 emission at different development levels: Regional difference in China based on panel estimation. *Journal of Cleaner Production*, *140*, 1719–1730. doi:10.1016/j.jclepro.2016.08.155

Higgins, M., & Smith, W. (2000). Reconsidering the relationship analogy. *Journal of Marketing Management*, *16*(1/3), 81-94. doi:10.1362/026725700785100406

Hirsh, J., & Dolderman, D. (2007). Personality predictors of consumerism and environmentalism: A preliminary study. *Personality and Individual Differences*, *43*(6), 1583–1593. doi:10.1016/j.paid.2007.04.015

Ho, C.-I., & Lee, Y.-L. (2007). The development of an e-travel service quality scale. *Tourism Management*, *26*(6), 1434–1449. doi:10.1016/j.tourman.2006.12.002

Hoffman, K. D., & Bateson, J. E. G. (1997). *Essentials of service marketing*. Fort Worth, TX: The Dryden Press.

Hofstede, G. (1984). The cultural relativity of the quality of life concept. *Academy of Management Review*, *9*(3), 389–398. doi:10.5465/amr.1984.4279653

Hofstede, G. (2001). *Culture's consequences: Comparing values, behaviors, institutions, and organizations across nations* (2nd ed.). Thousand Oaks, CA: Sage.

Hofstede, G., Hofstede, G. J., & Minkov, M. (2010). *Cultures and organizations: Software of the mind* (3rd ed.). New York, NY: McGraw-Hill.

Homburg, C., & Giering, A. C. (2001). Personal characteristics as moderators of the relationship between customer satisfaction and loyalty - An empirical analysis. *Psychology and Marketing*, *18*(1), 43–66. doi:10.1002/1520-6793(200101)18:1<43::AID-MAR3>3.0.CO;2-I

Hong, I. B. (2015). Understanding the consumer's online merchant selection process: The roles of product involvement, perceived risk, and trust expectation. *International Journal of Information Management*, *35*(3), 322–336. doi:10.1016/j.ijinfomgt.2015.01.003

Ho, R. C., & Rezaei, S. (2018). Social Media Communication and Consumers Decisions: Analysis of the Antecedents for Intended Apps Purchase. *Journal of Relationship Marketing*, *17*(3), 204–228. doi:10.1080/15332667.2018.1492322

Ho, R., & Vogel, D. (2014). The impact of social networking functionalities on online shopping: An examination of the web's relative advantage. *International Journal of Business Information Systems*, *16*(1), 25–41. doi:10.1504/IJBIS.2014.060834

Horrigan, J. B., Rainie, L., & Fox, S. (2001). *Online communities: networks that nurture long-distance relationships and local ties*. Washington, DC: Pew Internet & American Life Project. Available at: http://www.pewinternet.org

Hossain, M. T., & Lim, P. X. (2016). Consumers' Buying Behavior towards Organic Foods. *Journal of Malaysian Insititute of Management*, *51*(2), 7–25.

House, J. S. (1981). *Work Stress and Social Support*. Reading, MA: Addison- Wesley.

Howell, A. (2018). *Why Kroger's Driverless Grocery Delivery Pilot Is a Harbinger of Disruption*. Retrieved January 10, 2019, from https://urbanismnext.uoregon.edu/2018/09/17/why-krogers-driverless-grocery-delivery-pilot-is-a-harbinger-of-disruption/

Huang, K.-Y., Nambisan, P., & Uzuner, Ö. (2010). *Informational support or emotional support: Preliminary study of an automated approach to analyze online support community contents*. Paper presented at the International Conference on Information Systems (ICIS 2010), St. Louis, MO.

Huang, Z., & Benyoucef, M. (2013). From e-commerce to social commerce: A close look at design features. *Electronic Commerce Research and Applications*, *12*(4), 246–259. doi:10.1016/j.elerap.2012.12.003

Huang, Z., & Benyoucef, M. (2015). User preferences of social features on social commerce websites: An empirical study. *Technological Forecasting and Social Change*, *95*, 57–72. doi:10.1016/j.techfore.2014.03.005

Hudek, R., & Vrcek, N. (2006). *E-service quality evaluation instruments*. Paper presented at the 29th International Convention Proceedings: Microelectronics, Electronics and Electronic Technologies, MEET, Hypermedia and Grid Systems HGS (MIPRO), Croatia.

Hughner, R. S., McDonagh, P., Prothero, A., Shultz, C. J., & Stanton, J. (2007). Who are organic food consumers? A compilation and review of why people purchase orgnic food. *Journal of Consumer Behaviour*, *6*(2-3), 94–110. doi:10.1002/cb.210

Hui, E. C., Zhang, P. H., & Zheng, X. (2013). Facilities management service and customer satisfaction in shopping mall sector. *Facilities*, *31*(5/6), 194–207. doi:10.1108/02632771311307070

Hu, M., Shi, M., & Wu, J. (2013). Simultaneous vs. sequential group-buying mechanisms. *Management Science*, *59*(12), 2805–2822. doi:10.1287/mnsc.2013.1740

Hussain, R., Nasser, A. A., & Hussain, Y. K. (2014). Service quality and customer satisfaction of a UAE-based airline: An empirical investigation. *Journal of Air Transport Management*, 1–9.

Hussien, M. I., & El Aziz, R. A. (2013). Investigating e-banking service quality in one of Egypt's banks: A stakeholder analysis. *The TQM Journal*, *25*(5), 557–576. doi:10.1108/TQM-11-2012-0086

İbrahim, A. (Ed.). (2016). *13-year-old girl sets herself on fire in Vietnam in social media dare*. Retrieved 14 February, 2019, from Daily Sabah: https://www.dailysabah.com/asia/2016/10/12/13-year-old-girl-sets-herself-on-fire-in-vietnam-in-social-media-dare

Ibrahim, E. E., Joseph, M., & Ibeh, K. I. N. (2006). Customers' perception of electronic service delivery in the UK retail banking sector. *International Journal of Bank Marketing*, *24*(7), 475–493. doi:10.1108/02652320610712094

Ilich, K. L., & Hardey, M. (2018). 'It's all about the packaging': Investigation of the motivations, intentions, and marketing implications of sharing photographs of secondary packaging on Instagram. *Information Communication and Society*. doi:10.1080/1369118X.2018.1478983

Ilies, R., Scott, B., & Judge, T. (2006). The interactive effects of personal traits and experienced states on intraindividual patterns of citizenship behavior. *Academy of Management Journal*, *49*(3), 561–575. doi:10.5465/amj.2006.21794672

Insights, H. (2018). *Country Comparison - India*. Retrieved December 1, 2018, from https://www.hofstede-insights.com/country-comparison/india/

Institute for Democracy and Economic Affairs. (2018). Tax in a Digital Age. Kuala Lumpur: IDEAS Policy Research Berhad. iPrice Group (2018, October17). Malaysia: the 2nd country in SEA with digital Tax. *Focus Malaysia.*

International Federation of Organic Agriculture Movements. (2018). *2017 Annual Report of the Organics International.* Retrieved from https://www.ifoam.bio/en/our-library/annual-reports

Internetworldstats.com. (2015). *World Population Stats*. Available at: http://www.internetworldstats.com/stats.htm

Islam, J. U., & Rahman, Z. (2016). The transpiring journey of customer engagement research in marketing. *Management Decision*, *54*(8), 2008–2034. doi:10.1108/MD-01-2016-0028

Ismail El-Adly, M. (2007). Shopping malls attractiveness: A segmentation approach. *International Journal of Retail & Distribution Management*, *35*(11), 936–950. doi:10.1108/09590550710828245

Istat. (2017). *Data*. Retrieved from https://www.istat.it/

ITA Malaysia. (1967). *Part I to IV, Act 53*. Retrieved from http://www.agc.gov.my/agcportal/uploads/files/Publications/LOM/EN/Pindaan%20Act%2053%20-%2023%2011%202017.pdf

Ivory, M. Y., & Hearst, M. A. (2001). The state of the art in automating usability evaluation of user interfaces. *ACM Computing Surveys*, *33*(4), 470–516. doi:10.1145/503112.503114

Izogo, E. E., & Ogba, I. E. (2015). Service quality, customer satisfaction and loyalty in automobile repair services sector. *International Journal of Quality and Reliability Management, 32*(3), 250-269. doi:10.1108/IJQRM-05-2013-0075?mobileUi=0

Izogo, E. E., & Ogba, I.-I. (2015). Service quality, customer satisfaction and loyalty in automobile repair services sector. *International Journal of Quality & Reliability Management*, *32*(3), 250–269. doi:10.1108/IJQRM-05-2013-0075

Jackson, V., Stoel, L., & Brantley, A. (2011). Mall attributes and shopping value: Differences by gender and generational cohort. *Journal of Retailing and Consumer Services*, *18*(1), 1–9. doi:10.1016/j.jretconser.2010.08.002

Jacoby, J. (1971). A model of multi-brand loyalty. *Journal of Advertising Research*, *11*(3), 25–31.

Jafari Navimipour, N., Rahmani, A. M., Habibizad Navin, A., & Hosseinzadeh, M. (2015). Expert Cloud: A Cloud-based framework to share the knowledge and skills of human resources. *Computers in Human Behavior*, *46*, 57–74. doi:10.1016/j.chb.2015.01.001

Jaller, M., Holguín-Veras, J., & Hodge, S. D. (2013). Parking in the City. *Transportation Research Record: Journal of the Transportation Research Board*, *2379*(1), 46–56. doi:10.3141/2379-06

Janda, S., Trocchia, P. J., & Gwinner, K. P. (2002). Consumer perceptions of Internet retail service quality. *International Journal of Service Industry Management*, *13*(5), 412–431. doi:10.1108/09564230210447913

Jawaid, M., & Ahmed, S. J. (2018). Pharmaceutical Digital Marketing and Its Impact on Healthcare Physicians of Pakistan: A National Survey. *Cureus*, *10*(6), e2789. doi:10.7759/cureus.2789 PMID:30112265

Jenifer, L. (2016). Customer orientation in shopping malls of South Chennai - An exploratory study. *International Journal of Applied Research*, *2*(3), 124–128.

Jeong, Y., & Lee, Y. (2010). A study on the customer satisfaction and customer loyalty of furniture purchaser in on-line shop. *Asian Journal on Quality*, *11*(2), 146–156. doi:10.1108/15982681011075952

Jham, V., & Khan, K. M. (2008). Customer satisfaction in the Indian banking sector: A study. *IIMB Management Review*, *20*(1), 84–93.

Jiang, H., & Zhang, Y. (2016). An investigation of service quality, customer satisfaction and loyalty in China's airline market. *Journal of Air Transport Management*, *57*, 80–88. doi:10.1016/j.jairtraman.2016.07.008

Jiang, J. J., Klein, G., & Crampton, S. M. (2000a). A Note on SERVQUAL Reliability and Validity in Information System Service Quality Measurement. *Decision Sciences*, *31*(3), 725–744. doi:10.1111/j.1540-5915.2000.tb00940.x

Jiang, L., Yang, Z., & Jun, M. (2013). Measuring consumer perceptions of online shopping convenience. *Journal of Service Management*, *24*(2), 191–214. doi:10.1108/09564231311323962

Jing, X., & Xie, J. (2011). Group buying: A new mechanism for selling through social interactions. *Management Science*, *57*(8), 1354–1372. doi:10.1287/mnsc.1110.1366

Jo, A., & Mo, A. (2018). Factors influencing customer satisfaction and loyalty to internet banking services among undergraduates of a Nigerian University. *Journal of Internet Banking and Commerce*, *23*(1), 1–20.

John, O. P., & Srivastava, S. (1999), The Big Five-trait taxonomy: History, measurement, and theoretical perspectives. In L.A. Pervin & O.P. John (Eds.), Handbook of Personality: Theory & Research (pp. 120-138). New York: Guildford Press.

Johnson, M. E., & Whang, S. (2002). E-business supply chain management: An overview and framework. *Production and Operations Management*, *11*(4), 413–423. doi:10.1111/j.1937-5956.2002.tb00469.x

Jones, N., Borgman, R., & Ulusoy, E. (2015). Impact of social media on small businesses. *Journal of Small Business and Enterprise Development*, *22*(4), 611–632. doi:10.1108/JSBED-09-2013-0133

Joseph, M., McClure, C., & Joseph, B. (1999). Service quality in the banking sector: The impact of technology in service delivery. *International Journal of Bank Marketing*, *17*(4), 182–191. doi:10.1108/02652329910278879

Jovanovic, M., & Organero, M. (2011). Analysis of the Latest Trends in Mobile Commerce using the NFC Technology, Multidisciplinary Journals in Science and Technology. *Journal of Selected Areas in Telecommunications*, *5*, 1–12.

Jun, M., & Cai, S. (2001). The key determinants of Internet banking service quality: A content analysis. *International Journal of Bank Marketing*, *19*(7), 276–291. doi:10.1108/02652320110409825

Jun, M., & Palacios, S. (2016). Examining the key dimensions of mobile banking service quality: An exploratory study. *International Journal of Bank Marketing*, *34*(3), 307–326. doi:10.1108/IJBM-01-2015-0015

Jun, M., Yang, Z., & Kim, D. (2004). Customers' perceptions of online retailing service quality and their satisfaction. *International Journal of Quality & Reliability Management*, *21*(8), 817–840. doi:10.1108/02656710410551728

Kadıbeşegil, S. (2015). *Reputation management*. İstanbul: Medicat Publishing Ltd.

Kaiser, H. F. (1958). The Varimax criterion for analytic rotation in factor analysis. *Psychometrika*, *23*(3), 187–200. doi:10.1007/BF02289233

Kaiser, H. F. (1974). An index of factor simplicity. *Psychometrika*, *39*(1), 31–36. doi:10.1007/BF02291575

Kamesh, D. B. K., Sasi Bhanu, J., & Sastry, J. K. R. (2018). An architectural approach for assessing quality of web sites. *Journal of Engineering and Applied Sciences (Asian Research Publishing Network)*, *13*(15), 4503–4513.

Kane, K., Robinson-Combre, J., & Berge, J. L. (2010). Tapping into social networking: Collaborating enhances both knowledge management and e-learning. *Vine*, *40*(1), 62–70. doi:10.1108/03055721011024928

Kang, J.-W., & Namkung, Y. (2019). The information quality and source credibility matter in customers' evaluation toward food O2O commerce. *International Journal of Hospitality Management*, *78*, 189–198. doi:10.1016/j.ijhm.2018.10.011

Kang, S. (2018). Warehouse location choice: A case study in Los Angeles, CA. *Journal of Transport Geography*. doi:10.1016/j.jtrangeo.2018.08.007

Kang, Y.-Q., Zhao, T., & Yang, Y.-Y. (2016). Environmental Kuznets curve for CO 2 emissions in China: A spatial panel data approach. *Ecological Indicators*, *63*, 231–239. doi:10.1016/j.ecolind.2015.12.011

Kanto, S. D., Run, E. C., & İsa, A. H. (2016). The reputation quotient as a corporate reputation measurement in the Malaysian banking industry: A confirmatory factor analysis. *Social and Behavioral Sciences*, *219*(65), 409–415.

Kanwar, S. (2018). *Here is why retailers need to invest in social commerce, 21 Feb 2018, Shopping habits are changing*. Retrieved from https://www.digitalcommerce360.com/2018/02/21/retailers-need-invest-social-commerce/

Kaplan, A. M., & Haenlein, M. (2010). Users of the world, unite! The challenges and opportunities of Social Media. *Business Horizons*, *53*(1), 59–68. doi:10.1016/j.bushor.2009.09.003

Kardaras, D., & Karakostas, B. (2006). *E-service adaptation using fuzzy cognitive maps*. Paper presented at the 3rd International IEEE Conference Intelligent Systems.

Katrodia, A., Naude, M. J., & Soni, S. (2018). Determinants of shopping and buying behaviour: A case at Durban shopping malls. *African Journal of Business and Economic Research*, *13*(1), 219–241. doi:10.31920/1750-4562/2018/v13n1a8

Kaur, G., & Quareshi, T. K. (2015). Factors obstructing intentions to trust and purchase products online. *Asia Pacific Journal of Marketing and Logistics*, *27*(5), 758–783. doi:10.1108/APJML-10-2014-0146

Kawira, D. K., Mukulu, E., & Odhiambo, R. (2019). Effect of Digital Marketing on the Performance of MSMES in Kenya. *Journal of Marketing Communications*, *2*, 1–23.

Kaynama, S. A., & Black, C. I. (2000). A proposal to assess the service quality of online travel agencies: An exploratory study. *Journal of Professional Services Marketing*, *21*(1), 63–88. doi:10.1300/J090v21n01_05

Kearney, A. T. (2013). *Recasting the retail store in today's ommnichannel world*. Retrieved from http://bit.ly/2kFlQY0

Keating, B., Rugimbana, R., & Quazi, A. (2003). Differentiating between service quality and relationship quality in cyberspace. *Managing Service Quality: An International Journal*, *13*(3), 217–232. doi:10.1108/09604520310476481

Keegan, B. J., & Rowley, J. (2017). Evaluation and decision making in social media marketing. *Management Decision*, *55*(1), 15–31. doi:10.1108/MD-10-2015-0450

Kemp, S. (2017). Digital in 2017. *Global Owerview Houtsuite*. Retrieved from www.wearesocial.com

Keng, C. J., Huang, T. L., Zheng, L. J., & Hsu, M. K. (2007). Modeling service encounters and customer experiential value in retailing: An empirical investigation of shopping mall customers in Taiwan. *International Journal of Service Industry Management*, *18*(4), 349–367. doi:10.1108/09564230710778137

Keskin, S., & Baş, M. (2016). *The effects of social media on consumers behaviour*. Retrieved from iibfdergisi.gazi.edu.tr/index.php/iibfdergisi/article/view/902

Khang, H., Ki, E., & Ye, L. (2012). Social media research in advertising, communication, marketing, and public relations. *Journalism & Mass Communication Quarterly*, *89*(2), 279–298. doi:10.1177/1077699012439853

Khare, A. (2011). Mall shopping behaviour of Indian small town consumers. *Journal of Retailing and Consumer Services*, *18*(1), 110–118. doi:10.1016/j.jretconser.2010.10.005

Khare, A. (2012). Influence of mall attributes and demographics on Indian consumers' mall involvement behavior: An exploratory study. *Journal of Targeting. Measurement and Analysis for Marketing*, *20*(3-4), 192–202. doi:10.1057/jt.2012.15

Khare, A. (2016). Consumer shopping styles and online shopping: An empirical study of Indian consumers. *Journal of Global Marketing*, *29*(1), 40–53. doi:10.1080/08911762.2015.1122137

Khare, A., Khare, A., & Singh, S. (2012). Attracting shoppers to shop online - Challenges and opportunities for the Indian retail sector. *Journal of Internet Commerce*, *11*(1), 161–185. doi:10.1080/15332861.2012.689570

Khare, A., & Rakesh, S. (2010). Retailers in malls: Retailers' preferences for store space in Indian malls. *Journal of Retail & Leisure Property*, *9*(2), 125–135. doi:10.1057/rlp.2010.1

Kılıç, Ş. O., & Genel, Z. (2018). The impact of social media and technology companies on digital storytelling. In C. S. Csoares & E. Simão (Eds.), Trends, Experiences, and Perspectives on Immersive Multimedia Experiences and Augmented Reality (pp. 147–170). IGI Global Publishing.

Kilsheimer, J. (1997, April 7). Virtual communities; Cyberpals keep in touch online. *The Arizona Republic*, p. E3.

Kim, A. J., & Ko, E. (2012). Do social media marketing activities enhance customer equity? An empirical study of luxury fashion brand. *Journal of Business Research*, *65*(10), 1480–1486. doi:10.1016/j.jbusres.2011.10.014

Kim, C., Mirusmonov, M., & Lee, I. (2010). An empirical examination of factors influencing the intention to use mobile payment. *Computers in Human Behavior*, *26*(3), 310–322. doi:10.1016/j.chb.2009.10.013

Kim, H., Fiore, A. M., Niehm, L. S., & Jeong, M. (2010). Psychographic characteristics affecting behavioral intentions towards pop-up retail. *International Journal of Retail & Distribution Management*, *38*(2), 133–154. doi:10.1108/09590551011020138

Kim, H., & Song, J. (2010). The quality of word-of-mouth in the online shopping mall. *Journal of Research in Interactive Marketing*, *4*(4), 376–390. doi:10.1108/17505931011092844

Kim, M., Kim, J.-H., & Lennon, S. J. (2006). Online service attributes available on apparel retail web sites: An E-S-QUAL approach. *Managing Service Quality*, *16*(1), 51–77. doi:10.1108/09604520610639964

Kim, N., & Kim, W. (2018). Do your social media lead you to make social deal purchases? Consumer-generated social referrals for sales via social commerce. *International Journal of Information Management*, *39*, 38–48. doi:10.1016/j.ijinfomgt.2017.10.006

Kim, S. E., Shaw, T., & Schneider, H. (2003). Web site design benchmarking within industry groups. *Internet Research*, *13*(1), 17–26. doi:10.1108/10662240310458341

Kim, S. H. (2014). A Study on Adoption Factors of Korean Smartphone Users : A Focus on TAM (Technology Acceptance Model) and UTAUT (Unified Theory of Acceptance and Use of Technology). *Advanced Science and Technology*, *57*, 27–30.

Kim, S., Haley, E., & Koo, G.-Y. (2009). Comparison of the paths from consumer involvement types to ad responses between corporate advertising and product advertising. *Journal of Advertising*, *38*(3), 67–80. doi:10.2753/JOA0091-3367380305

Kim, Y., Kang, J., & Kim, M. (2005). Family and Social Interaction, Loneliness, Mall Shopping Motivation, and Mall Spending of Older Consumers. *Psychology and Marketing*, *22*(12), 995–1015. doi:10.1002/mar.20095

Kim, Y., & Peterson, R. A. (2017). A Meta-analysis of Online Trust Relationships in E-commerce. *Journal of Interactive Marketing*, *38*, 44–54. doi:10.1016/j.intmar.2017.01.001

Kin, B., Verlinde, S., & Macharis, C. (2017). Sustainable urban freight transport in megacities in emerging markets. *Sustainable Cities and Society*, *32*, 31–41. doi:10.1016/j.scs.2017.03.011

Kirmani, A., & Rao, A. R. (2000). No pain, no gain: A critical review of the literature on signaling unobservable product quality. *Journal of Marketing*, *64*(2), 66–79. doi:10.1509/jmkg.64.2.66.18000

Kleinberg, S. (2015). *Think twice before you share your next photo on social media*. Retrieved 14 February, 2019, from Chicago Tribune: https://www.chicagotribune.com/lifestyles/ct-social-media-safe-posting-20151103-column.html

Klein, G., Jiang, J., & Tesch, D. (2002). Wanted: Project teams with a blend of is professional orientations. *Communications of the ACM*, *45*(6), 81–87. doi:10.1145/508448.508452

Klein, R. B. (2011). *Principles and practice of structural equation modeling*. New York, NY: Guilford.

Kline, P. (1997). *An Easy Guide to Factor Analysis*. London: Routledge.

Knoll, J. (2016). Advertising in social media: A review of empirical evidence. *International Journal of Advertising*, *35*(2), 266–300. doi:10.1080/02650487.2015.1021898

Koçak, S. (2015). The role and the importance of public relations in the cities/ countries marketing. *International Multilingual Academic Journal.*, *2*(1), 82–93.

Koças, C. (2005). A model of Internet pricing under price-comparison shopping. *International Journal of Electronic Commerce*, *10*(1), 111–134. doi:10.1080/10864415.2005.11043959

Koernig, S. K. (2003). E-scapes: The electronic physical environment and service tangibility. *Psychology and Marketing*, *20*(2), 151–167. doi:10.1002/mar.10065

Ko, H., Roberts, M. S., & Cho, C.-H. (2006). Cross cultural differences in motivations and perceived interactivity: A comparative study of American and Korean internet users. *Journal of Current Issues and Research in Advertising*, *28*(2), 93–104. doi:10.1080/10641734.2006.10505201

Ko, K. H. (1990). Promotion of IT Applications in Singapore: Policy Issues and Strategic Thrusts. In C. M. L. C. Y. Kuo & K. S. Raman (Eds.), *Information Technology and Singapore Society: Trends, Policies and Applications*. Singapore: Singapore University Press.

Köksal, Y., & Özdemir, Ş. (2013). An investigation on place of social media in promotion mix as a communications device. *The Journal of Faculty of Economics Suleyman Demirel University*, *18*(1), 323–337.

Kollat, D. T., & Willett, R. P. (1969). Is impulse purchasing really a useful concept for marketing decisions? *Journal of Marketing*, *33*(1), 79–83. doi:10.1177/002224296903300113

Kortunay, N. (2016). *Measuring internet service quality of e-commerce web sites by using E-S-QUAL in Turkey*. European Scientific Journal.

Koski, N. (2004). Impulse buying on the internet: Encouraging and discouraging factors. *Frontiers of E-business Research*, *4*, 23–35.

Kotler, P. (2000). *Marketing Management*. Upper Saddle River, NJ: Academic Press.

Kotler, P. (2003). *Marketing management*. New Delhi: Pearson Education.

Kotler, P., Keller, K. L., Koshy, A., & Jha, M. (2007). *Marketing Management. A South Asian Perspective*. Pearson Publications.

Kotler, P., Keller, K. L., Koshy, A., & Jha, M. (2009). *Marketing management - A South Asian perspective* (13th ed.). New Delhi, India: Pearson Education.

Koufaris, M. (2002). Applying technology acceptance model and flow theory to online consumer behavior. *Information Systems Research, 13*(2), 205–226. doi:10.1287/isre.13.2.205.83

Kozinetz, V. (2010). *Netnography: doing ethnographic research online*. Sage Publications.

Krejcie, R. V., & Morgan, D. W. (1970). Determining sample size for research activities. *Educational and Psychological Measurement, 30*(3), 607–610. doi:10.1177/001316447003000308

Kukar-Kinney, M., Ridgway, N. M., & Monroe, K. B. (2009). The relationship between consumers' tendencies to buy compulsively and their motivations to shop and buy on the Internet. *Journal of Retailing, 85*(3), 298–307. doi:10.1016/j.jretai.2009.05.002

Kumar, A., & Kashyap, A. K. (2018). Leveraging utilitarian perspective of online shopping to motivate online shoppers. *International Journal of Retail & Distribution Management, 46*(3), 247–263. doi:10.1108/IJRDM-08-2017-0161

Kumar, P., & Verma, A. (2017). Impact of Digital Marketing on Rural Marketing. *Imperial Journal of Interdisciplinary Research, 3*, 705–708.

Kuofaris, M. (2002). Applying the Technology Acceptance Model and Flow Theory to Online Customer Behavior. *Information Systems Research, 13*(2), 205–253.

Kursunluoglu, E. (2011). Customer service effects on customer satisfaction and customer loyalty: A field research in shopping centers in Izmir City-Turkey. *International Journal of Business and Social Science, 2*(17).

Kwon, Y. J., Cui, J., & Kwon, D. (2013). A Study on Comparison Analysis of the System Quality Factors between Korea and China Shopping mall Websites. *Journal of Korea Multimedia Society, 16*(11), 1315–1324. doi:10.9717/kmms.2013.16.11.1315

Ladhari, R. (2009). A review of twenty years of SERVQUAL research. *International Journal of Quality and Service Sciences, 1*(2), 172–198. doi:10.1108/17566690910971445

Ladhari, R. (2010). Developing e-service quality scales: A literature review. *Journal of Retailing and Consumer Services, 17*(6), 464–477. doi:10.1016/j.jretconser.2010.06.003

Lai, P. C. (2010). E-business and E-banking. Japan Society for Software Science and Technology, Itech research group.

Lai, P. C. (2013, May). *WalletSIM™ - Contactless, Cardless, Cashless, Convenience*. Paper presented at Singapore Innovest, Singapore.

Lai, P. C. (2014). *Factors Influencing Consumers' Intention to use a single platform E-payment System* (Thesis). UNITEN.

Lai, P. C., & Ahmad, Z. A. (2015). Perceived Enjoyment of Malaysian consumers' intention to use a single platform E-payment. *SHS Web of Conferences, 18*, 1-9.

Lai, P. C., & Scheela, W. (2018). Convergence of technology in the E-commerce World and Venture Capital Landscape: South East Asia, Global Entrepreneurship and New Venture Creation in the Sharing Economy. IGI-Global.

Lai, I. K. W., & Lai, D. C. F. (2013). User acceptance of mobile commerce: An empirical study in Macau. *International Journal of Systems Science, 45*(6), 1321–1331. doi:10.1080/00207721.2012.761471

Lai, P. C. (2006). The significant of E-business and knowledge-based Customer Relationship in the E-market Place Environment. *INTI Journal, 2*(1), 552–559.

Lai, P. C. (2007). The Chip Technology Management Implication in the Era of Globalization: Malaysian Consumers' Perspective. *Asia Pacific Business Review, 3*(1), 91–96. doi:10.1177/097324700700300107

Lai, P. C. (2015). *Smart living for smart cities @ the palm of your hand.* Research Asia.

Lai, P. C. (2016a). *SMART HEALTHCARE @ the palm of our hand.* ResearchAsia.

Lai, P. C. (2016b). Design and Security impact on consumers' intention to use single platform E-payment, Interdisciplinary. *Information Sciences*, *22*(1), 111–122.

Lai, P. C. (2017). The literature review of technology adoption models and theories for the novelty technology. *Journal of Information Systems and Technology Management*, *14*(1), 21–38. doi:10.4301/S1807-17752017000100002

Lai, P. C. (2018a). Single platform E-payment Consumers' intention to use. *Journal of Information Technology Management*, *29*(2), 22–28.

Lai, P. C. (2018b). Research Methodology for novelty technology. *Journal of Information Systems and Technology Management*, *15*, 1–18.

Lai, P. C. (2018c). Security as an extension to TAM Model: Consumers' intention to use a single platform E-payment System. *Asia-Pacific Journal of Management Research and Innovation*, *13*(3-4), 110–119. doi:10.1177/2319510X18776405

Lai, P. C. (2018d). Research, Innovation and Development Strategic Planning for Intellectual Property Management. *Economic Alternatives.*, *12*(3), 303–310.

Lam, R., & Burton, S. (2006). SME banking loyalty (and disloyalty): A qualitative study in Hong Kong. *International Journal of Bank Marketing*, *24*(1), 37–52. doi:10.1108/02652320610642335

Laroche, M., Teng, L., Michon, R., & Chebat, J. C. (2005). Incorporating service quality into consumer mall shopping decision making: A comparison between English and French Canadian consumers. *Journal of Services Marketing*, *19*(3), 157–163. doi:10.1108/08876040510596830

LaRose, R. (2001). On the negative effects of e-commerce: A sociocognitive exploration of unregulated on-line buying. *Journal of Computer-Mediated Communication*, *6*(3). doi:10.1111/j.1083-6101.2001.tb00120.x

Larsen, R. J., & Ketelaar, T. (1991). Personality and Susceptibility to Positive and Negative Emotional States. *Journal of Personality and Social Psychology*, *61*(1), 132–140. doi:10.1037/0022-3514.61.1.132 PMID:1890584

Latiff, Z. A., & Safiee, N. A. S. (2015). New business set up for branding strategies on social media–Instagram. *Procedia Computer Science*, *72*, 13–23. doi:10.1016/j.procs.2015.12.100

Latour, K. A., & Latour, M. S. (2010). Bridging aficionados' perceptual and conceptual knowledge to enhance how they learn from experience. *The Journal of Consumer Research*, *37*(4), 688–697. doi:10.1086/655014

Laukkanen, T., & Lauronen, J. (2005). Consumer value creation in mobile banking services. *International Journal of Mobile Communications*, *3*(4), 325–338. doi:10.1504/IJMC.2005.007021

Laureti, T., Piccarozzi, M., & Aquilani, B. (2018). The effects of historical satisfaction, provided services characteristics and website dimensions on encounter overall satisfaction: A travel industry case study. *The TQM Journal*, *30*(3), 197–216. doi:10.1108/TQM-07-2017-0080

Lean, O. K., Zailani, S., Ramayah, T., & Fernando, Y. (2009). Factors influencing intention to use e-government services among citizens in Malaysia. *International Journal of Information Management*, *29*(6), 458–475. doi:10.1016/j.ijinfomgt.2009.03.012

Lederer, A. L., Maupin, D. J., Sena, M. P., & Zhuang, Y. (2000). The technology acceptance model and the World Wide Web. *Decision Support Systems*, *29*(3), 269–282. doi:10.1016/S0167-9236(00)00076-2

Lee, M. & Youns, J. (2009).*The new community rules marketing on the social web.* O'Reilly Media and Publishing.

Lee, Y. H., Hsieh, Y. C., & Hsu, C. N. (2011). Adding Innovation Diffusion Theory to the Technology Acceptance Model : Supporting Employees ' Intentions to use E-Learning Systems E-learning and TAM The Technology Acceptance Model (TAM). *International Forum of Educational Technology & Society, 14*(4), 124–137.

Leech, N., Barrett, K., & Morgan, G. A. (2005). *SPSS for intermediate statistics: Use and interpretation* (2nd ed.). London: Lawrence Erlbaum Associates.

Leeflang, P. S., Verhoef, P. C., Dahlström, P., & Freundt, T. (2014). Challenges and solutions for marketing in a digital era. *European Management Journal, 32*(1), 1–12. doi:10.1016/j.emj.2013.12.001

Lee, G.-G., & Lin, H.-F. (2005). Customer perceptions of e-service quality in online shopping. *International Journal of Retail & Distribution Management, 33*(2), 161–176. doi:10.1108/09590550510581485

Lee, J. E., & Watkins, B. (2016). YouTube vloggers' influence on consumer luxury brand perceptions and intentions. *Journal of Business Research, 69*(12), 5753–5760. doi:10.1016/j.jbusres.2016.04.171

Lee, J., Lee, J., & Feick, L. (2001). The impact of switching costs on the customer satisfaction-loyalty link: Mobile phone service in France. *Journal of Services Marketing, 15*(1), 35–48. doi:10.1108/08876040110381463

Lee, J., Park, D.-H., & Han, I. (2008). The effect of negative online consumer reviews on product attitude: An information processing view. *Electronic Commerce Research and Applications, 7*(3), 341–352. doi:10.1016/j.elerap.2007.05.004

Lee, L. F., Hutton, A. P., & Shu, S. (2015). The role of social media in the capital market: Evidence from consumer product recalls. *Journal of Accounting Research, 53*(2), 367–404. doi:10.1111/1475-679X.12074

Lee, M. C. (2009). Factors influencing the adoption of internet banking: An integration of TAM and TPB with perceived risk and perceived benefit. *Electronic Commerce Research and Applications, 8*(3), 130–141. doi:10.1016/j.elerap.2008.11.006

Lee, Y. H., Hsieh, Y. C., & Ma, C. Y. (2011). A model of organizational employees' e-learning systems acceptance. *Knowledge-Based Systems, 24*(3), 355–366. doi:10.1016/j.knosys.2010.09.005

Lee, Y., & Kozar, K. (2008). An empirical investigation of anti-spyware software adoption: A multi-theoretical perspective. *Inf. Man, 45*(2), 109–119.

Leigh, N. G., & Hoelzel, N. Z. (2012). Smart Growth's Blind Side. *Journal of the American Planning Association, 78*(1), 87–103. doi:10.1080/01944363.2011.645274

Leonardi, P. M. (2017). The social media revolution: Sharing and learning in the age of leaky knowledge. *Information and Organization, 27*(1), 47–59. doi:10.1016/j.infoandorg.2017.01.004

Leong, Y. L. (1997). ECH Programme Hits Its Stride. *Computerworld, 3*(13).

Lester, G., & Saftner, R. A. (2011). Organically versus Conventionally Grown Produce: Common Production Inputs, Nutritional Quality, and Nitrogen Delivery between the Two Systems. *Journal of Agricultural and Food Chemistry, 59*(19), 10401–10406. doi:10.1021/jf202385x PMID:21910454

Levin, G. (2007a). Capture the customer experience by tapping IVR. *Call Center Magazine, 20*(2), 50.

Liang, T. P., Ho, Y. T., Li, Y. W., & Turban, E. (2012). What Drives Social Commerce: The Role of Social Support and Relationship Quality. *International Journal of Electronic Commerce, 16*(2), 69–90. doi:10.2753/JEC1086-4415160204

Liang, T.-P., & Turban, E. (2011). Introduction to the special issue social commerce: A research framework for social commerce. *International Journal of Electronic Commerce, 16*(2), 5–14. doi:10.2753/JEC1086-4415160201

Liang, T., & Wei, C. P. (2004). Introduction to the special issue: Mobile commerce applications. *International Journal of Electronic Commerce*, *8*(3), 7–17. doi:10.1080/10864415.2004.11044303

Liao, C., Liu, C.-C., Liu, Y.-P., To, P.-L., & Lin, H.-N. (2011). Applying the expectancy disconfirmation and regret theories to online consumer behavior. *Cyberpsychology, Behavior, and Social Networking*, *14*(4), 241–246. doi:10.1089/cyber.2009.0236 PMID:21067306

Liberati, A., Altman, D. G., Tetzlaff, J., Mulrow, C., Gøtzsche, P. C., Loannidis, J. P., ... Moher, D. (2009). The PRISMA statement for reporting systematic reviews and meta-analyses of studies that evaluate health care interventions: Explanation and elaboration. *Italian Journal of Public Health*, *6*, 354–391. PMID:19621070

Li, C.-Y. (2017). How social commerce constructs influence customers' social shopping intention? An empirical study of a social commerce website. *Technological Forecasting and Social Change*, *144*, 283–294. doi:10.1016/j.techfore.2017.11.026

Li, C.-Y., & Ku, Y.-C. (2018). The power of a thumbs-up: Will e-commerce switch to social commerce? *Information & Management*, *55*(3), 340–357. doi:10.1016/j.im.2017.09.001

Li, H., & Liu, Y. (2014). Understanding post-adoption behaviors of e-service users in the context of online travel services. *Information & Management*, *51*(8), 1043–1052. doi:10.1016/j.im.2014.07.004

Li, H., Liu, Y., & Suomi, R. (2009). Measurement of e-service quality: An empirical study in online travel service. *Proceedings of 17th European Conference on Information Systems*, 1127-1139.

Likert, R. (1932). A technique for the measurement of attitudes. *Archives de Psychologie*, *22*, 5–55.

Lin, F.-J., Huarng, K., Chen, Y.-M., & Lin, S.-M. (2004). *Quality Evaluation of Web Services.* Paper presented at the IEEE International Conference on E-Commerce Technology for Dynamic E-Business, Beijing, China.

Lin, C.-Y., & Shih, K.-H. (2013). Service quality of mobile banking systems. In *Proceedings of Confernence on Active Citizenship by Management Knowledge Management and Innovation* (pp. 515–521). Zadar, Croatia: Knowledge and Learning.

Lingbo, K., & Kaichao, Y. (2012). Research on the knowledge flow in CRM circumstance. *Procedia Engineering*, *29*, 3852–3857. doi:10.1016/j.proeng.2012.01.583

Lin, J. C. C., & Lu, H. (2000). Towards an understanding of the behavioural intention to use a web site. *International Journal of Information Management*, *20*(3), 197–208. doi:10.1016/S0268-4012(00)00005-0

Lin, J., & Hsieh, P. (2006). The role of technology readiness in customers' perception and adoption of self-service technologies. *International Journal of Service Industry Management*, *17*(5), 497–517. doi:10.1108/09564230610689795

Lin, L.-Y., & Chen, C.-S. (2006). The influence of the country-of-origin image, product knowledge and product involvement on consumer purchase decisions: An empirical study of insurance and catering services in Taiwan. *Journal of Consumer Marketing*, *23*(5), 248–265. doi:10.1108/07363760610681655

Lin, W.-S., & Wang, C.-H. (2012). Antecedences to continued intentions of adopting e-learning system in blended learning instruction: A contingency framework based on models of information system success and task-technology fit. *Computers & Education*, *58*(1), 88–99. doi:10.1016/j.compedu.2011.07.008

Lin, Y. (2018). E-urbanism: E-commerce, migration, and the transformation of Taobao villages in urban China. *Cities (London, England)*. doi:10.1016/j.cities.2018.11.020

Little, E., & Marandi, E. (2003). *Relationship Marketing Management.* Cengage Learning.

Liu, C., & Arnett, K. P. (2000). Exploring the factors associated with Web site success in the context of electronic commerce. *Information & Management, 38*(1), 23–33. doi:10.1016/S0378-7206(00)00049-5

Liu, C., & Forsythe, S. (2010). Post-adoption online shopping continuance. *International Journal of Retail & Distribution Management, 38*(2), 97–114. doi:10.1108/09590551011020110

Liu, S.-H., Chou, C.-H., & Liao, H.-L. (2015). An exploratory study of product placement in social media. *Internet Research, 25*(2), 300–316. doi:10.1108/IntR-12-2013-0267

Li, X., Hess, T. J., & Valacich, J. S. (2006). Using Attitude and Social Influence to Develop an Extended Trust Model for Information Systems. *The Data Base for Advances in Information Systems, 37*(2 & 3), 108–124. doi:10.1145/1161345.1161359

Li, Y. (2009). Measuring e-commerce dimensions. *Journal of Computer Information Systems*, 2–12.

Li, Y., Tan, K., & Xie, M. (2002). Measuring web-based service quality. *Total Quality Management, 13*(5), 685–700. doi:10.1080/0954412022000002072

Li, Y.-W., Yang, S.-M., & Liang, T.-P. (2015). Website interactivity and promotional framing on consumer attitudes toward online advertising: Functional versus symbolic brands. *Pacific Asia Journal of the Association for Information Systems, 7*(2), 41–58. doi:10.17705/1pais.07203

Lloyd, A. Y. K., Chan, R. S. C., Yip, L., & Chan, A. (2014). Time buying and time saving: Effects on service convenience and the shopping experience at the mall. *Journal of Services Marketing, 28*(1), 36–49. doi:10.1108/JSM-03-2012-0065

Loiacono, E. T., Watson, R. T., & Goodhue, D. L. (2007). WebQual: An Instrument for Consumer Evaluation of Web Sites. *International Journal of Electronic Commerce, 11*(3), 51–87. doi:10.2753/JEC1086-4415110302

Loiacono, E. T., Watson, R. T., & Hoodhue, D. L. (2002). WEBQUAL: measure of web site quality. *Marketing Educators Conference: Marketing Theory and Applications, 13*, 432-437.

Loonam, M., & O'Loughlin, D. (2008). Exploring e-service quality: A study of Irish online banking. *Marketing Intelligence & Planning, 26*(7), 759–780. doi:10.1108/02634500810916708

Lovelock, C. (2001). *Services Marketing: People, Technology and Strategy*. Upper Saddle River, NJ: Prentice Hall.

Luarn, P., & Lin, H. (2003). A customer loyalty model for e-serve context. *Journal of Electronic Commerce Research, 4*(4), 156–167.

Luarn, P., & Lin, H. H. (2005). Toward an understanding of the behavioral intention to use mobile banking. *Computers in Human Behavior, 21*(6), 873–891. doi:10.1016/j.chb.2004.03.003

Lu, B., Fan, W., & Zhou, M. (2016). Social presence, trust, and social commerce purchase intention: An empirical research. *Computers in Human Behavior, 56*, 225–237. doi:10.1016/j.chb.2015.11.057

Luczak, C., & Younkin, N. (2012). Net generation: A conceptual framework of the consumer socialization process. *Academy of Marketing Studies Journal, 16*(2), 47.

Lu, J. (2001). Measuring cost/benefits of e-business applications and customer satisfaction. *Proceedings of the 2nd International Web Conference.*

Lu, J., Yu, C. S., Liu, C., & Yao, J. E. (2003). Technology acceptance model for wireless Internet. *Internet Research, 13*(3), 206–222. doi:10.1108/10662240310478222

Luo, M. M., Chea, S., & Chen, J.-S. (2011). Web-based information service adoption: A comparison of the motivational model and the uses and gratifications theory. *Decision Support Systems, 51*(1), 21–30. doi:10.1016/j.dss.2010.11.015

Luo, M. M.-l., Remus, W., & Chea, S. (2006). Technology Acceptance of Internet-based Information Services: An Integrated Model of TAM and U&G Theory. *Proceedings of the Twelfth Americas Conference on Information Systems.*

Lu, Q., He, Z. L., & Stoffella, P. J. (2012). Land Application of Biosolids in the USA: A Review. *Applied and Environmental Soil Science, 11*, 1–3. doi:10.1155/2012/201462

Luque-Ayala, A., & Marvin, S. (2015). Developing a critical understanding of smart urbanism? *Urban Studies (Edinburgh, Scotland), 52*(12), 2105–2116. doi:10.1177/0042098015577319

Lu, Y., Zhao, L., & Wang, B. (2010). From virtual community members to C2C e-commerce buyers: Trust in virtual communities and its effect on consumers' purchase intention. *Electronic Commerce Research and Applications, 9*(4), 346–360. doi:10.1016/j.elerap.2009.07.003

Madell, D. E., & Muncer, S. J. (2007). Control over social interactions: An important reason for young people's use of the internet and mobile phones for communication? *Cyberpsychology & Behavior, 10*(1), 137–140. doi:10.1089/cpb.2006.9980

Madjar, N. (2008). Emotional and informational support from different sources and employee creativity. *Journal of Occupational and Organizational Psychology, 81*(1), 83–100. doi:10.1348/096317907X202464

Madu, C. N., & Madu, A. A. (2002). Dimensions of e-quality. *International Journal of Quality & Reliability Management, 19*(3), 246–259. doi:10.1108/02656710210415668

Maduku, D. K., Mpinganjira, M., & Duh, H. (2016). Understanding mobile marketing adoption intention by South African SMEs: A multi-perspective framework. *International Journal of Information Management, 36*(5), 711–723. doi:10.1016/j.ijinfomgt.2016.04.018

MagazineM. (2014). Retrieved from https://marketingmagazine.com.my/magazines/

Magutu, P. O., Mwangi, M., Nyaoga, R. B., Ondimu, G. M., Kagu, M., Mutai, K., ... Nthenya, P. (2011). E-commerce products and services in the banking industry: The adoption and usage in commercial banks in Kenya. *Journal of Electronic Banking Systems, 2011*, 1–19.

Mahinda, E., & Whitworth, B. (2006). *Using The WOSP Model To Improve End-User Productivity Of Information Systems.* Paper presented at the International Conference on Business IT (BIZIT 2006): Collaborating with ICT Innovations for Business Survival, Kuala Lumpur, Malaysia.

Maidenberg, M. (2017, October 24). As Amazon Moves In, Demand for Warehouse Space Climbs. *The New York Times.* Retrieved from www.nytimes.com/2017/10/24/business/amazon-ecommerce-warehouse-demand.html?smprod=nytcore-iphone&smid=nytcore-iphone-share&_r=0

Makanyeza, C., Chikazhe, L., & Chikazhe, L. (2017). Mediators of the relationship between service quality and customer loyalty: Evidence from the banking sector in Zimbabwe. *International Journal of Bank Marketing, 35*(3), 540-556. doi:10.1108/IJBM-11-2016-0164?fullSc=1andmbSc=1

Makena, K. (2018). *Waymo partners with Walmart to test grocery pickup service in Arizona.* Retrieved from www.theverge.com/2018/7/25/17611760/waymo-walmart-self-driving-vehicles-groceries-discounts

Makgopa, S. S. (2016). Online social media usage of car dealerships in Gauteng Province, South Africa. *Problems and Perspectives in Management, 14*, 601–607. doi:10.21511/ppm.14(3-3).2016.02

Malaysian Ministry of International Trade and Industry. (2016). *Malaysia's National eCommerce Strategic Roadmap.* Kuala Lumpur: MITI.

Malhotra, N. K., & McCort, J. D. (2001). A cross-cultural comparison of behavior intention models: Theoretical consideration and an empirical investigation. *International Marketing Review, 18*(3), 235–268. doi:10.1108/02651330110396505

Malik, R. (2017). An Empirical Study of Digital Marketing and its Elements. *IJSRST, 3*, 715–718.

Malviya, S. (2015). Exploring mobile banking service quality dimensions for public and private sector banks in Indore district of Madhya Pradesh. *International Journal of Advance Research in Computer Science and Management Studies, 3*(1), 243–252.

Manasra, E. A. A., Zaid, M. K. S. A., & TaherQutaishat, F. (2013). Investigating the Impact of Website Quality on Consumers' Satisfaction in Jordanian Telecommunication Sector. *Arab Economic and Business Journal, 8*, 31-37.

Mangold, W., & Smith, K. T. (2012). Selling to Millennials with online reviews. *Business Horizons, 55*(2), 141–153. doi:10.1016/j.bushor.2011.11.001

Mao, E., & Palvia, P. (2006). Testing an Extended Model of IT Acceptance in the Chinese Cultural Context. *The Data Base for Advances in Information Systems, 37*(2 & 3), 20–32. doi:10.1145/1161345.1161351

Massicotte, M. C., Michon, R., Chebat, J. C., Sirgy, M. J., & Borges, A. (2011). Effects of mall atmosphere on mall evaluation: Teenage versus adult shoppers. *Journal of Retailing and Consumer Services, 18*(1), 74–80. doi:10.1016/j.jretconser.2010.10.001

Mathena, J., Yetter, A., & Hostetler, H. (2009). *Success with Microsoft Dynamics CRM 4.0.* In *Implementing Customer Relationship Management.* Aprèss.

Mathur, A. (2003). Building Customer Relationships: The Taj Air Caterers Experience, CR emerging concepts tools and applications by Shethparvatiyar and Shainesh. Tata McGraw-Hill Publishing Company Ltd.

Matthews, L. (2010). Social media and the evolution of corporate communications. *The Elon Journal of Undergraduate Research in Communications, 1*(1), 17–23.

Matuleviciene, M., & Stravinskiene, J. (2015). The importance of stakeholders for corporate reputation. *Inzinerine Ekonomika-Engineering Economics, 26*(1), 75–83.

Max, R. (2018). *Mall Analytics.* Retrieved from https://behavioranalyticsretail.com/mall-analytics/

Mazaheri, E., Richard, M. O., & Laroche, M. (2011). Online consumer behavior: Comparing Canadian and Chinese website visitors. *Journal of Business Research, 64*(1), 958–965. doi:10.1016/j.jbusres.2010.11.018

Mazaheri, E., Richard, M. O., Laroche, M., & Ueltschy, L. C. (2014). The influence of culture, emotions, intangibility, and atmospheric cues on online behavior. *Journal of Business Research, 67*(1), 253–259. doi:10.1016/j.jbusres.2013.05.011

McAlister, L., & Pessemier, E. (1982). Variety seeking behavior: An interdisciplinary review. *The Journal of Consumer Research, 9*(3), 311–322. doi:10.1086/208926

McCain, S. L. C., Jang, S., & Hu, C. (2005). Service quality gap analysis toward customer loyalty: Practical guidelines for casino hotels. *International Journal of Hospitality Management, 24*(3), 465–472. doi:10.1016/j.ijhm.2004.09.005

McCay-Peet, L., & Quan-Haase, A. (2016). A model of social media engagement: User profiles, gratifications, and experiences. In H. O'Brien & M. Lalmas (Eds.), *Why engagement matters: Cross-disciplinary perspectives and innovations on user engagement with digital media.* Heidelberg, Germany: Springer Verlag. doi:10.1007/978-3-319-27446-1_9

McGuire, J. B., Schneeweis, T., & Branch, B. (1990). Perceptions of firm quality: A cause or result of firm performance. *Journal of Management, 16*(1), 167–180. doi:10.1177/014920639001600112

McKinnon, A. C. (1983). The development of warehousing in England. *Geoforum*, *14*(4), 389–399. doi:10.1016/0016-7185(83)90036-2

McKinsey Global Institute. (2016). *Urban World: The Global Consumers to Watch*. Retrieved from https://www.mckinsey.com/global-themes/urbanization/urban-world-the-global-consumers-to-watch/~/media/57c6ad7f7f1b44a6bd2e24f0777b4cd6.ashx

McKinsey. (2017). *Meeting millennials where they shop: Shaping the future of shopping malls*. Retrieved from www.mckinsey.com/industries/capital-projects-and-infrastructure/our-insights/meeting-millennials-where-they-shop-shaping-the-future-of-shopping-malls

McKnight, D. H., Choudhury, V., & Kacmar, C. (2002b). Developing and Validating Trust Measures for e-Commerce: An Integrative Typology. *Information Systems Research*, *13*(3), 334–359. doi:10.1287/isre.13.3.334.81

McLennan, A., & Howell, G. V. J. (2011). Social networks and the challenge for public relations. *Asia Pacific Public Relations Journal*, *11*(34), 21–39.

McWilliam, G. (2002). Building stronger brands through online communities. *Sloan Management Review*, *41*(3), 43–54.

Michaelidou, N., & Hassan, L. M. (2008). The role of health consciousness, food safety concern and ethical identity on attitudes and intentions towards organic food. *International Journal of Consumer Studies*, *32*(2), 163–170. doi:10.1111/j.1470-6431.2007.00619.x

Michon, R., Chebat, J. C., & Turley, L. W. (2005). Mall atmospherics: The interaction effects of the mall environment on shopping behavior. *Journal of Business Research*, *58*(5), 576–583. doi:10.1016/j.jbusres.2003.07.004

Miller, J. L., Craighead, C. W., & Karwan, K. R. (2000). Service recovery: A framework and empirical investigation. *Journal of Operations Management*, *18*(4), 387–400. doi:10.1016/S0272-6963(00)00032-2

Ministry of Finance Malaysia. (2018). *Annual Budget Speech 2019*. Kuala Lumpur: MOF.

Minnesota retailers are reaping rewards from far flung consumers. (2018, November 2). *Star Tribune*.

Mirabi, V., Akbariyeh, H., & Tahmasebifard, H. (2015). A Study of Factors Affecting on Customers Purchase Intention. *Journal of Multidisciplinary Engineering Science and Technology*, *2*(1), 267–273.

Mischel, W. (2004). Toward an integrative science of the person. *Annual Review of Psychology*, *55*(1), 1–22. doi:10.1146/annurev.psych.55.042902.130709 PMID:14744208

MITI, MDEC, & AT Kearney. (2016). *National eCommerce Strategic Roadmap Overview*. Retrieved from http://www.miti.gov.my/miti/resources/Gallery_Walk.pdf

Mittal, A., & Jhamb, D. (2016). Determinants of shopping mall attractiveness: The Indian context. *Procedia Economics and Finance*, *37*, 386–390. doi:10.1016/S2212-5671(16)30141-1

Mittal, S., Sondhi, N., & Chawla, D. (2017). Process of Impulse Buying: A Qualitative Exploration. *Global Business Review*, *19*(1), 131–146. doi:10.1177/0972150917713368

Mittal, V., & Tsiros, M. (2007). Customer Loyalty in Electronically Mediated Environments. *Journal of Value Chain Management*, *1*(1/2), 80–109.

Mobarek, A. (2007). E-banking practices and customer satisfaction - a case study in Botswana. *Proceedings of 20th Australasian Finance & Banking Conference 2007 Paper*. Retrieved from http://ssrn.com/abstract=1011112

Mohd, F., & Osman, S. (2005). Towards the future of mobile commerce (m-commerce) in Malaysia. *Proceedings of IADIS International Conference Web Based Communities 2005*, 276-280.

Molesworth, M., & Suortti, J.-P. (2002). Buying cars online: The adoption of the web for high-involvement, high-cost purchases. *Journal of Consumer Behaviour: An International Research Review*, *2*(2), 155–168. doi:10.1002/cb.97

Moliner, M. A., Sánchez, J., Rodríguez, R. M., & Callarisa, L. (2007). Relationship quality with a travel agency: The influence of the postpurchase perceived value of a tourism package. *Tourism and Hospitality Research*, *7*(3-4), 194–211. doi:10.1057/palgrave.thr.6050052

Mollen, A., & Wilson, H. (2010). Engagement, telepresence and interactivity in online consumer experience: Reconciling scholastic and managerial perspectives. *Journal of Business Research*, *63*(9-10), 919–925. doi:10.1016/j.jbusres.2009.05.014

Moon, J., & Kim, Y. (2001). Extending the TAM for a world wide web context. *Journal of Information & Management Science*, *27*(1), 15–22.

Mooradian, T. A., & Olver, J. M. (1994). Neuroticism, Affect and Postpurchase Processes. In C. T. Allen & D. R. John (Eds.), *NA - Advances in Consumer Research, 21* (pp. 595–600). Provo, UT: Association for Consumer Research.

Moore, G. C., & Benbasat, I. (1991). Development of and instrument to measure the perceptions of adopting and information technology innovation. *Information Systems Research*, *2*(3), 192–222. doi:10.1287/isre.2.3.192

Moore, N. (2006). *How to do research: a practical guide to designing and managing research projects* (3rd ed.). London: Facet Publishing.

Morgan, A., & Inks, S. A. (2001). Technology and the sales force. *Industrial Marketing Management*, *30*(5), 463–472. doi:10.1016/S0019-8501(99)00115-7

Morgan, R. M., & Hunt, S. D. (1994). The commitment-trust theory of relationship marketing. *Journal of Marketing*, *58*, 20–38. doi:10.1177/002224299405800302

Mosbeh, R., & Soliman, K. S. (2008). An exploratory analysis of factors affecting users' adoption of corporate intranet; A Tunisian study. *Management Research News*, *31*(5), 375–385. doi:10.1108/01409170810865172

Moustakis, V., Litos, C., Dalivigas, A., & Tsironis, L. (2004). *Website Quality Assessment Criteria. IQ*, *5*, 59–73.

Murthy, D., Gross, A., & McGarry, M. (2016). Visual Social Media and Big Data. Interpreting Instagram Images Posted on Twitter. *Digital Culture & Society*, *2*(2), 113–134. doi:10.14361/dcs-2016-0208

Myers, S. D., Sen, S., & Alexandrov, A. (2010). The Moderating Effect Of Personality Traits on Attitudes toward Advertisements: A Contingency Framework. *Management & Marketing Challenges for Knowledge Society*, *5*(3), 3–20.

Namukasa, J. (2013). The influence of airline service quality on passenger satisfaction and loyalty: The case of Uganda airline industry. *The TQM Journal*, *25*(5), 520–532. doi:10.1108/TQM-11-2012-0092

Narahari, A. C., & Kuvad, D. (2017). Customer Behaviour towards Shopping Malls – A Study in Bhavnagar (Gujarat State, India). *IJARIIE*, *3*(2), 211–224.

Negi, R. (2009). User perceived service quality of mobile communications: Experience from Ethiopia. *International Journal of Quality & Reliability Management*, *26*(7), 699–711. doi:10.1108/02656710910975769

Negoita, O. D., Purcarea, A. A., Popescu, M., Niculescu, A., & Coman, C. N. (2018). Digital Marketing Tools Used by Companies. *FAIMA Business & Management Journal*, *6*, 66–76.

Nellen, A. (2015). Taxation and today's digital economy. *Journal of Tax Practice & Procedure*, *17*(2), 17–26.

Nguyen, T. H., Joseph, S. S., & Michael, N. (2007). Strategies for successful CRM implementation. *Journal of Information Management and Computer Security, 15*(2), 102-115. . doi:10.1108/09685220710748001

Nittala, R. (2015). Factors influencing online shopping behavior of urban consumers in India. *International Journal of Online Marketing, 5*(1), 38–50. doi:10.4018/IJOM.2015010103

Niu, H.-J. (2013). Cyber peers' influence for adolescent consumer in decision-making styles and online purchasing behavior. *Journal of Applied Social Psychology, 43*(6), 1228–1237. doi:10.1111/jasp.12085

Nusair, K., & Kandampully, J. (2008). The antecedents of customer satisfaction with online travel services: A conceptual model. *European Business Review, 20*(1), 4–19. doi:10.1108/09555340810843663

Nyadzayo, M. W., & Khajehzadeh, S. (2016). The antecedents of customer loyalty: A moderated mediation model of customer relationship management quality and brand image. *Journal of Retailing and Consumer Services, 30*, 262–270. doi:10.1016/j.jretconser.2016.02.002

Nysveen, H., Pedersen, P. E., & Skard, S. E. R. (2015). *A review of mobile services research: Research gaps and suggestions for future research on mobile apps.* SNF Working Paper No 01/15.

O'Brien, H. (2011). Exploring user engagement in online news interactions. *Proc. Am. Soc. Information Science Technology, 48*(1), 1–10.

Ok, S.-J., & Shon, J.-H. (2006, December). *The Determinant of Internet Banking Usage Behavior in Korea: A Comparison of Two Theoretical Models.* Paper presented at the CollECTeR '06, Adelaide, Australia.

Okdie, B. M., Duadagno, R. E., Bernieri, F. J., Geers, A. L., & Mclarney-Vesotski, A. R. (2011). Getting to know you: Face-to-face versus online interactions. *Computers in Human Behavior, 27*(1), 153–159. doi:10.1016/j.chb.2010.07.017

Oliver Richard, L. (1997). *Satisfaction: A behavioral perspective on the consumer.* New York, NY: Irwin-McGraw-Hill.

Oliveria, P., Roth, A. V., & Gilland, W. (2002). Achieving competitive capabilities in e-services. *Technological Forecasting and Social Change, 69*(7), 721–739. doi:10.1016/S0040-1625(01)00188-3

Oliver, R. L. (1999). Whence customer loyalty. *Journal of Marketing, 63*(4), 33–44. doi:10.1177/00222429990634s105

Oni, O. A., Shumba, P. M., & Matiza, T. (2014). The Impact of Social Media-Based Marketing on the Turnover of Retailers Based in Polokwane, South Africa. *Mediterranean Journal of Social Sciences, 5*, 307–316.

Oppenheim, A. N. (1992). *Questionnaire, design, interviewing and attitude measurement.* London: Pinter Pub Ltd.

Oreg, S., & Nov, O. (2008). Exploring motivations for contributing to open source initiatives: The roles of contribution context and personal values. *Computers in Human Behavior, 24*(5), 2055–2073. doi:10.1016/j.chb.2007.09.007

Osborne, J., & Waters, E. (2002). Four assumptions of multiple regression that researchers should always test. *Practical Assessment, Research & Evaluation, 8*(2). Retrieved from http://PAREonline.net/getvn.asp?v=8&n=2

Othmani, L., & Bouslama, P. N. (2015). Highlighting the Influence of Virtual Communities on the online shoppers trust. *Journal of Internet Social Networking & Virtual Communities, 6*, 1–8.

Özbay, D., & Selvi, Y. (2014). The measurement of corporate reputation: A proposal of model. *The Journal of Istanbul University Administration Faculty, 25*(76), 198–212.

Ozer, A., Argan, M. T., & Argan, M. (2013). The effect of mobile service quality dimensions on customer satisfaction. *Social and Behavioral Sciences, 11*(99), 428–438.

Padel, S., & Foster, C. (2005). Exploring the gap between attitudes and behaviour: Understanding why consumers buy or do not buy organic food. *British Food Journal, 107*(8), 606–625. doi:10.1108/00070700510611002

Palmer, J. W. (2000). Electronic commerce in retailing: Convenience, search costs, delivery and price across retail formats. *Information Technology Management, 1*(1-2), 25–43. doi:10.1023/A:1019152403937

Palmer, J. W. (2002). Web Site Usability, Design and Performance Metrics. *Information Systems Research, 13*(2), 151–167. doi:10.1287/isre.13.2.151.88

Pandolph, S. (2018). *The Social Commerce Report: How Facebook, YouTube, Pinterest, and other popular apps are upending the e-commerce space*. Business Insider. Retrieved from https://www.businessinsider.my/social-commerce-report-2018-1/?r=US&IR=T

Parasuraman, A., & Berry, L. L. (1985). A conceptual model of service quality and its implications for future research. *Journal of Marketing Science, 49*, 41–50.

Parasuraman, A., Berry, L. L., & Zeithaml, V. A. (1991). Understanding customer expectations of service. *Sloan Management Review, 32*(3), 39–48.

Parasuraman, A., Berry, L. L., & Zeithaml, V. A. (1991a). Refinement and Reassessment of the SERVQUAL Scale. *Journal of Retailing, 67*(4), 420–450.

Parasuraman, A., Zeithaml, V. A., & Berry, L. L. (1985). A conceptual model of service quality and its implications for future research. *Journal of Marketing, 49*(4), 41–50. doi:10.1177/002224298504900403

Parasuraman, A., Zeithaml, V. A., & Berry, L. L. (1988). Servqual. *Journal of Retailing, 64*(1), 12–37.

Parasuraman, A., Zeithaml, V. A., & Berry, L. L. (1988). SERVQUAL: A multi-item scale for measuring consumer perceptions of service quality. *Journal of Retailing, 64*, 2–40.

Parasuraman, A., Zeithaml, V. A., & Berry, L. L. (1988). Servqual: A multiple-item scale for measuring consumer perc. *Journal of Retailing, 64*(1), 12.

Parasuraman, A., Zeithaml, V. A., & Malhotra, A. (2005). E-S-QUAL a multiple-item scale for assessing electronic service quality. *Journal of Service Research, 7*(3), 1–21. doi:10.1177/1094670504271156

Park, C., & Jun, J.-K. (2003). A cross-cultural comparison of Internet buying behavior: Effects of Internet usage, perceived risks, and innovativeness. *International Marketing Review, 20*(5), 534–553. doi:10.1108/02651330310498771

Park, Y. A., & Gretzel, U. (2007). Success factors for destination marketing web sites: A qualitative meta-analysis. *Journal of Travel Research, 46*(1), 46–63. doi:10.1177/0047287507302381

Parrish, M., Elliot, N., Riley, N., & Wise, J. (2010). *How to create an effective brand presence on Facebook*. Forrester Research Online Facebook Web Track. Retrieved from go.forrester.com

Parsons, A. G. (2003). Assessing the effectiveness of shopping mall promotions: Customer analysis. *International Journal of Retail & Distribution Management, 31*(2), 74–79. doi:10.1108/09590550310461976

Parvatiyar, A., & Sheth, J. N. (2001). Customer relationship management: Emerging practice, process, and discipline. *Journal of Economic and Social Research, 3*(2), 1-34. doi:10.1.1.113.2212andrep=rep1andtype=pdf

Pate, S. S., & Adams, M. (2013). The influence of social networking sites on buying behaviors of millennials. *Atlantic Marketing Journal, 2*, 92–109.

Pavlou, P. (2003). Consumer acceptance of electronic commerce: Integrating trust and risk with the technology acceptance model. *International Journal of Electronic Commerce*, *7*, 69–103.

Payne, A. (2012). *Handbook of CRM: Achieving Excellence in Customer Management*. Oxford, UK: Butterworth-Heinemann. doi:10.4324/9780080476933

Peabody, D., & Goldberg, L. R. (1989). Some determinants of factor structures from personality traits descriptors. *Journal of Personality and Social Psychology*, *57*(3), 552–567. doi:10.1037/0022-3514.57.3.552 PMID:2778639

Pearson, S. (1996). Building brands directly: Creating business value from customer relationships. *Macmillan Business*, *20*(6), 68–82.

Peck, J., & Childers, T. L. (2003). To have and to hold: The influence of haptic information on product judgments. *Journal of Marketing*, *67*(2), 35–48. doi:10.1509/jmkg.67.2.35.18612

Pedersen, P. E. (2005). Adoption of mobile Internet services: An exploratory study of mobile commerce early adopters. *Journal of Organizational Computing and Electronic Commerce*, *15*(2), 203–222. doi:10.120715327744joce1503_2

Peng, L., Zhang, W., Wang, X., & Liang, S. (2019). Moderating effects of time pressure on the relationship between perceived value and purchase intention in social E-commerce sales promotion: Considering the impact of product involvement. *Information & Management*, *56*(2), 317–328. doi:10.1016/j.im.2018.11.007

Pentina, I., Prybutok, V. R., & Zhang, X. (2008). The Role of Virtual Communities as Shopping Reference Groups. *Journal of Electronic Commerce Research*, *9*(2), 114–136.

Pepitone, J. (2011). Groupon anxiety: The online-coupon firm will have to move fast to retain its impressive lead. *Economist*, *17*, 70–71.

Perlberg, S., & Seetharaman, D. (2016). Facebook signs deals with media companies, celebrities for facebook live. *The Wall Street Journal*. retrieved from www.wjs.com

Perrin, Andrew. (2015). Social media usage. *Pew Research Center*.

Petersen, A. (1999, January 6). Some places to go when you want to feel right at home: Communities focus on people who need people. *The Wall Street Journal*, p. B6.

Peters, K., Chen, Y., Kaplan, A. M., Ognibeni, B., & Pauwels, K. (2013). Social media metrics—A framework and guidelines for managing social media. *Journal of Interactive Marketing*, *27*(4), 281–298. doi:10.1016/j.intmar.2013.09.007

Peterson, E. R., Sillman, A., & McCaffrey, C. R. (2018). *Where Are the Global Millennials?* Retrieved January 24, 2019, from https://www.atkearney.com/web/global-business-policy-council/article?/a/where-are-the-global-millennials-

Pett, M. A., Lackey, N. R., & Sullivan, J. J. (2003). *Making Sense of Factor Analysis: The use of factor analysis for instrument development in health care research*. Sage Publications Inc. doi:10.4135/9781412984898

Peyper, L. (2015). *Trends and tastes in e-commerce*. Finweek.

Phua, J., Jin, S. V., & Kim, J. J. (2017). Gratifications of using Facebook, Twitter, Instagram, or Snapchat to follow brands: The moderating effect of social comparison, trust, tie strength, and network homophily on brand identification, brand engagement, brand commitment, and membership intention. *Telematics and Informatics*, *34*(1), 412–424. doi:10.1016/j.tele.2016.06.004

Picard, R. R., & Berk, K. N. (1990). Data Splitting. *The American Statistician*, *2*(44), 140–147.

Pitney Bowes. (2017). *Pitney Bowes Parcel Shipping Index Reveals 48 Percent Growth in Parcel Volume since 2014.* Retrieved from http://news.pb.com/article_display.cfm?article_%0Aid=5784

Pomsanam, P., Napompech, K., & Suwanmaneepong, S. (2014). Factors Driving Thai Consumers' Intention to Purchase Organic Foods. *Asian Journal of Scientific Research*, *7*(4), 434–446. doi:10.3923/ajsr.2014.434.446

Porter, C. E. (2004). A Typology of Virtual Communities: A Multi-Disciplinary Foundation for Future Research. *Journal of Computer-Mediated Communication*, *10*(1), 101–121. Retrieved from https://academic.oup.com/jcmc/article/10/1/JCMC1011/4614445

Prashar, S., Singh, H., Parsad, C., & Vijay, T. S. (2017). Predicting Indian Shoppers' Malls Loyalty Behaviour. *Vikalpa*, *42*(4), 234–250.

Pratt, R., & Chudoba, K. (2006). *Is extraversion the next predictor of system adoption? Effects of personality traits on system acceptance.* Paper presented at the Academy of Management Meeting, Atlanta, GA.

Preece, J. (2001). Sociability and usability in online communities: Determining and measuring success. *Behaviour & Information Technology*, *20*(5), 347–356. doi:10.1080/01449290110084683

Premkumar, G., & Bhattacherjee, A. (2008). Explaining information technology usage:Atest of competing models. *Omega*, *36*(1), 64–75. doi:10.1016/j.omega.2005.12.002

PRISMA. (2015). *Welcome to the Preferred Reporting Items for Systematic Reviews and Meta-Analyses (PRISMA) website!* Retrieved from http://www.prisma-statement.org/

Prologis Research. (2016). *Global E-Commerce Impact on Logistics Real Estate.* Retrieved January 21, 2019, from www.prologis.com/logistics-industry-research/global-e-commerce-impact-logistics-real-estate

Pulford, B., & Sohal, H. (2006). The influence of personality on HE students' confidence in their academic abilities. *Personality and Individual Differences*, *41*(8), 1409–1419. doi:10.1016/j.paid.2006.05.010

Pullig, C., Maxham, J. G. III, & Hair, J. F. Jr. (2002). Sales-force automation systems: An exploratory examination of organizational factors associated with effective implementation and sales-force productivity. *Journal of Business Research*, *55*(5), 401–415. doi:10.1016/S0148-2963(00)00159-4

Puriwat, W., & Tripopsakul, S. (2017). The impact of e-service quality on customer satisfaction and loyalty in mobile banking usage: Case study of Thailand. *Polish Journal of Management Studies*, *15*(2), 183–193. doi:10.17512/pjms.2017.15.2.17

Pychyl, T. A. (2015). *Social Media, the Network Effect and Procrastination: Our self-regulation is being undermined by design.* Retrieved 15 February, 2019, from Psychology Today: https://www.psychologytoday.com/us/blog/dont-delay/201512/social-media-the-network-effect-and-procrastination

Quach, T. N., Thaichon, P., & Jebarajakirthy, C. (2016). Internet service providers' service quality and its effect on customer loyalty of different usage patterns. *Journal of Retailing and Consumer Services*, *29*, 104–113. doi:10.1016/j.jretconser.2015.11.012

Quelch, J. A., & Klein, L. R. (1996). The Internet and international marketing. *Sloan Management Review*, *37*, 60–75.

Quintal, V., Phau, I., Sims, D., & Cheah, I. (2016). Factors influencing generation Y's purchase intentions of prototypical versus me-too brands. *Journal of Retailing and Consumer Services*, *30*, 175–183. doi:10.1016/j.jretconser.2016.01.019

Qu, W. G., Pinsonneault, A., Tomiuk, D., Wang, S., & Liu, Y. (2015). The impacts of social trust on open and closed B2B e-commerce: A Europe-based study. *Information & Management*, *52*(2), 151–159. doi:10.1016/j.im.2014.07.002

Rabbanee, F. K., Ramaseshan, B., Wu, C., & Vinden, A. (2012). Effects of store loyalty on shopping mall loyalty. *Journal of Retailing and Consumer Services*, *19*(3), 271–278. doi:10.1016/j.jretconser.2012.02.001

Radder, L., Pietersen, J., Wang, H., & Han, X. (2010). Antecedents of South African high school pupils' acceptance of universities' SMS advertising. *International Business & Economics Research Journal*, *9*, 29–39.

Rahimi, R., and Kozak, M. (2017). Impact of customer relationship management on customer satisfaction: The case of a budget hotel chain. *Journal of Travel and Tourism Marketing*, *34*(1), 40-51. doi:. doi:10.1080/10548408.2015.1130108

Rahman, M. A., & Ramli, M. F. (2016). The influence of relationship quality on customer loyalty in the dual-banking system in the northern states of peninsular Malaysia. *Procedia: Social and Behavioral Sciences*, *219*, 606–613. doi:10.1016/j.sbspro.2016.05.040

Rai, K.A. (2008). *Customer Relationship Management: Concepts and Case*. PHI Learning Private limited.

Rajagopal, D. (2008). *Growing Shopping Malls and Behavior of Urban Shoppers*. EGADE Working Paper No. 2008-05-MKT. Available at SSRN: https://ssrn.com/abstract=1299024

Rajapopal, P. (2011). Determinants of shopping behavior of urban consumers. *Journal of International Consumer Marketing*, *23*(2), 83–104. doi:10.1080/08961530.2011.543051

Rajput, N., & Khanna, A. (2014). Dynamics of young indian consumers' buying behvior towards branded apparels: Gender perspective. *Archives of Business Research*, *2*(5), 84–106. doi:10.14738/abr.25.596

Ramayah, T., & Lo, M. C. (2007). Impact of shared beliefs on "perceived usefulness" and "ease of use" in the implementation of an enterprise resource planning system. *Management Research News*, *30*(6), 420–431. doi:10.1108/01409170710751917

Rambe, P. (2017). Social media marketing and business competitiveness: Evidence from South African tourism SMMEs. *Problems and Perspectives in Management*, *15*(2), 411–423. doi:10.21511/ppm.15(2-2).2017.10

Rapp, A., Beitelspacher, L., Grewal, D., & Hughes, D. (2013). Understanding social media effects across seller, retailer, and consumer interactions. *Journal of the Academy of Marketing Science*, *41*(5), 547–566. doi:10.100711747-013-0326-9

Rasheed, F., & Abadi, M. F. (2014). Impact of Service Quality. Trust and Perceived Value on Customer Loyalty in Malaysia Services Industries. *Procedia: Social and Behavioral Sciences*, *164*(August), 298–304. doi:10.1016/j.sbspro.2014.11.080

Raub, W., & Weesie, J. (1990). Reputation and efficiency in social interactions: An example of network effects author. *American Journal of Sociology*, *96*(3), 626–654. doi:10.1086/229574

Rauyruen, P., & Miller, K. E. (2006). Relationship quality as a predictor of B2B customer loyalty. *Journal of Business Research*, *60*(1), 21–31. doi:10.1016/j.jbusres.2005.11.006

Razak, N. S. A., Ahmad, A. H., & Marimuthu, M. (2016). The Effect of Website Quality on Repurchase Intention in Travel Agency's Website in Malaysia. *First International Conference on Advance Business and Social Sciences*, 21-29.

Rechinhheld, F., & Sasser, W. (1990). Zero defections: Quality comes to service. *Harvard Business Review*, *68*(5), 105–111.

Reichert, C. (2017, July 13). Google's billion-euro tax bill discharged by French court. *ZDNet*. Retrieved from https://www.zdnet.com/article/googles-billion-euro-tax-bill-discharged-by-french-court/

Reichheld, F. F., & Schefter, P. (2000). E-loyalty: Your secret weapon on the web. *Harvard Business Review*, *78*, 105–113.

Reid, A., & Catterall, M. (2015). *Hidden data quality problems in CRM implementation marketing, technology and customer commitment in the new economy*. Springer.

Reimers, V., & Clulow, V. (2009). Retail centres: It's time to make them convenient. *International Journal of Retail & Distribution Management*, *37*(7), 541–562. doi:10.1108/09590550910964594

Resnick, M. L. (2015). The Shopping Mall Of The Customer Experience Future. *Proceedings of the Human Factors and Ergonomics Society Annual Meeting*, *59*(1), 1127–1131. doi:10.1177/1541931215591164

Riel, A. C. R. v., Semeijn, J., & Pauwels, P. (2003). Online Travel Service Quality: The Importance of Pre-transaction Services. METEOR, Maastricht research school of Economics of Technology and Organizations.

Rishika, R., Kumar, A., Janakiraman, R., & Bezawada, R. (2013). The effect of customers' social media participation on customer visit frequency and profitability: An empirical investigation. *Information Systems Research*, *24*(1), 108–127. doi:10.1287/isre.1120.0460

Ritholtz, B. (2018). *Don't Blame Amazon for the Retail Apocalypse*. Retrieved from https://www.bloomberg.com/opinion/articles/2018-04-09/trump-is-wrong-that-amazon-caused-the-u-s-retail-apocalypse

Robbins, T. L., & Miller, J. L. (2004). Considering customer loyalty in developing service recovery strategies. *The Journal of Business Strategy*, *21*(2), 95–109.

Robinson, J. (2009). *Triandis theory of interpersonal behaviour in understanding software privace behaviour in the South African context (Masters degree)*. Johannesburg: University of the Witwatersrand.

Roda, C., & Nabeth, T. (2006). Attention management in virtual community environments. *Journée de recherche de l'AIM Innovation et Systèmes d'Information,* 1-12. Retrieved from www.jstor.org

Rogers, E. M. (1962). *Diffusions of Innovations. The Free Press.*

Rogers, E. M. (2003). *Diffusion of Innovations* (5th ed.). New York: Free Press.

Romadhoni, B., & Hadiwidjojo, D., Noermijati, & Aisjah, S. (2015). Relationship between e-service quality, e-satisfaction, e-trust, e-commitment in building customer e-loyalty: A literature review. *International Journal of Business and Management Invention*, *4*(2), 1–9.

Rook, D. W., & Hoch, S. J. (1985). Consuming Impulses. In E. C. Hirschman & M. B. Holbrook (Eds.), ACR North American Advances (pp. 23–27). Academic Press.

Rook, D. W. (1987). The buying impulse. *The Journal of Consumer Research*, *14*(2), 189–199. doi:10.1086/209105

Rook, D. W., & Fisher, R. J. (1995). Normative influences on impulsive buying behavior. *The Journal of Consumer Research*, *22*(3), 305–313. doi:10.1086/209452

Roper, S., & Fill, C. (2012). *Corporate reputation brand and communication*. London: Harlow Pearson Publishings.

Rose, S., Clark, M., Samouel, P., & Hair, N. (2012). Online customer experience in e-retailing: An empirical model of antecedents and outcomes. *Journal of Retailing*, *88*(2), 308–322. doi:10.1016/j.jretai.2012.03.001

Rose, S., Hair, N., & Clark, M. (2011). Online customer experience: A review of the business to consumer online purchase context. *International Journal of Management Reviews*, *13*(1), 24–39. doi:10.1111/j.1468-2370.2010.00280.x

Rotchanakitumnuai, S. (2008). Measuring e-government service value with the EGOVSQUAL-RISK model. *Business Process Management Journal*, *14*(5), 724–737. doi:10.1108/14637150810903075

Rousseau, G. G., & Venter, D. J. (2014). Mall shopping preferences and patronage of mature shoppers. *SA Journal of Industrial Psychology, 40*(1), 1-12.

Rowley, J. (2006). An analysis of the e-service literature: Towards a research agenda. *Internet Research*, *16*(3), 339–359. doi:10.1108/10662240610673736

Rupp, M. A., Odette, K. L., Kozachuk, J., Michaelis, J. R., Smither, J. A., & McConnell, D. S. (2019). Investigating learning outcomes and subjective experiences in 360-degree videos. *Computers & Education*, *128*, 256–268. doi:10.1016/j.compedu.2018.09.015

Rust, R. T. (2001). The rise of e-service. *Journal of Service Research*, *3*(4), 283–284. doi:10.1177/109467050134001

Rust, R. T., & Lemon, K. N. (2001). E-service and the consumer. *International Journal of Electronic Commerce*, *5*(3), 85–101. doi:10.1080/10864415.2001.11044216

Rutenbeck, J., & Blaine, J. (2006). *Tech terms: what every telecommunications and digital media person should know*. Elsevier Inc.

Ryals, L., & Payne, A. (2001). Customer relationship management in financial services: towards information-enabled relationship marketing. *Journal of Strategic Marketing*, *9*(1), 3-27. doi:10.1080/713775725

Ryan, D. (2014). *Digital marketing*. İstanbul: Türkiye İş Bankası Publishings.

Saarijärvi, H., Joensuu, J., Rintamaki, T., & Yrjölä, M. (2018). One person's trash is another person's treasure: Profiling consumer-to-consumer e-commerce in Facebook. *International Journal of Retail & Distribution Management*, *46*(11/12), 1092–1107. doi:10.1108/IJRDM-04-2017-0091

Sabate, F., Berbegal-Mirabent, J., Cañabate, A., & Lebherz, P. R. (2014). Factors influencing popularity of branded content in Facebook fan pages. *European Management Journal*, *32*(6), 1001–1011. doi:10.1016/j.emj.2014.05.001

Safeena, R., Hundewale, N., & Kamani, A. (2011). Customer's adoption of mobile-commerce a study on emerging economy. *International Journal of e-Education, e-Business, e-. Management Learning*, *1*(3), 228–233.

Saha, P., Nath, A., & Salehi-Sangari, E. (2010). Success of Government E-Service Delivery: Does Satisfaction Matter? In EGOV 2010 LNCS (Vol. 6228, pp. 204-215). IFIP International Federation for Information Processing.

Said, I., Gambo, N., & Ismail, R. (2016). An evaluation into the architectural factors attracting customers to Malaysian shopping malls. *Journal of Business and Retail Management Research*, *11*(1), 138–153.

Saji, K. B. (2013). Role of content strategy in social media brand communities: A case of higher education institutes in India. *Journal of Product and Brand Management*, *22*(1), 40–51. doi:10.1108/10610421311298687

Saleki, Z. S., Seyedsaleki, S. M., & Rahimi, M. R. (2012). Organic Food Purchasing Behaviour in Iran. *International Journal of Business and Social Science*, *3*(13), 278–285.

Salisbury, W. D., Pearson, R. A., Pearson, A. W., & Miller, D. W. (2001). Perceived security and World Wide Web purchase intention. *Industrial Management & Data Systems*, *101*(4), 165–176. doi:10.1108/02635570110390071

Salomon, D. (2013). Moving on from Facebook: Using Instagram to connect with undergraduates and engage in teaching and learning. *College & Research Libraries News*, *74*(8), 408–412. doi:10.5860/crln.74.8.8991

Santos, J. (2003). E-service quality: A model of virtual service quality dimensions. *Managing Service Quality*, *13*(3), 233–246. doi:10.1108/09604520310476490

Santouridis, I., & Trivellas, P. (2010). Investigating the impact of service quality and customer satisfaction on customer loyalty in mobile telephony in Greece. *The TQM Journal*, *22*(3), 330–343. doi:10.1108/17542731011035550

Santouridis, I., Trivellas, P., & Tsimonis, G. (2012). Using ES-QUAL to measure internet service quality of e-commerce web sites in Greece. *International Journal of Quality and Service Sciences*, *4*(1), 86–98. doi:10.1108/17566691211219751

Sashi, C. M. (2012). Customer engagement, buyer-seller relationships, and social media. *Management Decision*, *50*(2), 253–272. doi:10.1108/00251741211203551

Saxe, R., & Weitx, B. A. (1982). The SOCO Scale: A Measure of the Customer Orientation of Sales people. *Journal of Marketing*, *19*, 343–351. doi:10.1177/002224378201900307

Schaefer, C., Coyne, J. C., & Lazarus, R. S. (1981). The health-related functions of social support. *Journal of Behavioral Medicine*, *4*(4), 381–406. doi:10.1007/BF00846149 PMID:7338894

Schaupp, L. C., & Bélanger, F. (2005). A Conjoint Analysis of Online Consumer Satisfaction. *Journal of Electronic Commerce Research*, *6*(2), 95–111.

Schiffman, L., & Kanuk, L. (2010). *Consumer Behaviour* (10th ed.). Prentice Hall.

Schindler, R. M. (2001). Internet Forums as Influential Sources of Consumer Information. *Journal of Interactive Marketing*, *15*(3), 31–40. doi:10.1002/dir.1014

Schuler, D. (1996). *New Community Networks – Wired for Change*. New York: Addison-Wesley.

Schwaiger, M. (2004). Components and parameters of corporate reputation an empirical study. *Schmalenbach Business Review*, *56*(1), 46–71. doi:10.1007/BF03396685

Seattle Traffic. (2019). *UPS pilot kicks off with a public/private partnership of a new urban delivery system*. Retrieved January 10, 2019, from https://www.seattletraffic.org/a-special-delivery-ups-pilot-kicks-off-with-a-public-private-partnership-creating-a-new-urban-delivery-system/

See-To, E. W. K., & Ho, K. K. W. (2014). Value co-creation and purchase intention in social network sites: The role of electronic Word-of-Mouth and trust–A theoretical analysis. *Computers in Human Behavior*, *31*, 182–189. doi:10.1016/j.chb.2013.10.013

Seiders, K., Voss, G. B., Grewal, D., & Godfrey, A. L. (2005). Do satisfied customers buy more? Examining moderating influences in a retailing context. *Journal of Marketing*, *69*(4), 26–43. doi:10.1509/jmkg.2005.69.4.26

Sekaran, U. (2003). *Research Methods for Business: A Skill-Building Approach* (4th ed.). John Wiley and Sons, Inc.

Semeijn, J., Riel, A. C. R., Birgelen, M. J. H., & Streukens, S. (2005). E-services and offline fulfilment: How e-loyalty is created. *Managing Service Quality*, *15*(2), 182–194. doi:10.1108/09604520510585361

Seneler, C. O., Basoglu, N., & Daim, T. U. (2010). An empirical analysis of the antecedents of adoption of online services; A prototype-based framework. *Journal of Enterprise Information Management*, *23*(4), 417–438. doi:10.1108/17410391011061753

Severin, V., Louviere, J. J., & Finn, A. (2001). The stability of retail shopping choices over time and across countries. *Journal of Retailing*, *77*(2), 185–202. doi:10.1016/S0022-4359(01)00043-4

Shachaf, P., & Oltmann, S. M. (2007). E-quality and e-service equality. *Proceedings of the 40th Hawaii International Conference on System Sciences*.

Shah, M. (2017). *Traditional Media vs New Media: Which is Beneficial?* Retrieved from https://www.techfunnel.com/martech/traditional-media-vs-new-media-beneficial/

Shaikh, A. A., & Karjaluoto, H. (2015). Mobile banking adoption: A literature review. *Telematics and Informatics*, *32*(1), 129–142. doi:10.1016/j.tele.2014.05.003

Shane, D. (2010). *Social CRM to soar*. Gartner Information Age.

Shareef, M. A., Kumar, U., Kumar, V., & Dwivedi, Y. K. (2009). Identifying critical factors for adoption of e-government. *Electronic Government: An International Journal*, *6*(1), 70–96. doi:10.1504/EG.2009.022594

Sharma, K. C., & Kaur, S. (2015). The Impact of Demographic Factors on Impulse Buying Behaviour of Online and Offline Consumers (A Case Study of Punjab, Haryana, New Delhi and Chandigarh). International Journal of Engineering Technology. *Management and Applied Sciences*, *3*(9), 63–69.

Sheikhshoaei, F., & Oloumi, T. (2011). Applying the technology acceptance model to Iranian engineering faculty libraries. *The Electronic Library*, *29*(3), 367–378. doi:10.1108/02640471111141106

Sheng, T., & Liu, C. (2010). An empirical study on the effect of e-service quality on online customer satisfaction and loyalty. *Nankai Business Review International*, *1*(3), 273–283. doi:10.1108/20408741011069205

Sheth, J. N., & Parvatiyar, A. (1992). Towards the theory of Business alliance formation. *Scandinavian International Business Review*, *1*(3), 71–87. doi:10.1016/0962-9262(92)90012-U

Shih, H. P. (2004). Extended technology acceptance model of Internet utilization behavior. *Information & Management*, *41*(6), 719–729. doi:10.1016/j.im.2003.08.009

Shim, S., Eastlick, M., Lotz, S. L., & Warrington, P. (2001). An online pre-purchase intentions model: The role of intention to search. *Journal of Retailing*, *77*(3), 397–416. doi:10.1016/S0022-4359(01)00051-3

Shin, D.-H. (2010). The effects of trust, security and privacy in social networking: A security-based approach to understand the pattern of adoption. *Interacting with Computers*, *22*(5), 428–438. doi:10.1016/j.intcom.2010.05.001

Shipley, D., & Palmer, R. (1997). Selling to and Managing Key Accounts. In The CIM Handbook of selling and Sales Strategy. Butterworth-Heinemann.

Shropshire, J., Warkentin, M., & Sharma, S. (2015). Personality, attitudes, and intentions: Predicting initial adoption of information security behavior. *Computers & Security*, *49*, 177–191. doi:10.1016/j.cose.2015.01.002

Shuaibu, K., & Muhammad, A. (2016). Electronic Payment System Challenges in Gombe State: Evidences from the Office of the Accountant General of Gombe State, Nigeria. *Journal of the Humanities and Social Sciences*, *21*(4), 1–7.

Siamagka, N.-T., Christodoulides, G., Michaelidou, N., & Valvi, A. (2015). Determinants of social media adoption by B2B organizations. *Industrial Marketing Management*, *51*, 89–99. doi:10.1016/j.indmarman.2015.05.005

Signore, O. (2005, September). A comprehensive model for web sites quality. In *Web Site Evolution, 2005, (WSE 2005). Seventh IEEE International Symposium on* (pp. 30-36). IEEE. 10.1109/WSE.2005.1

Sikundla, T., Mushunje, A., & Akinyemi, B. E. (2018). Socioeconomic drivers of mobile phone adoption for marketing among smallholder irrigation farmers in South Africa. *Cogent Social Sciences*, *4*(1), 1–12. doi:10.1080/23311886.2018.1505415 PMID:30310826

Sin, L. Y., Alan, C. T., & Frederick, H. Y. (2005). CRM: conceptualization and scale Development. *European Journal of Marketing, 39*(11/12), 1264 – 1290. doi:. doi:10.1108/03090560510623253

Singh, H., & Prashar, S. (2014). Anatomy of shopping experience for malls in Mumbai: A confirmatory factor analysis approach. *Journal of Retailing and Consumer Services*, *21*(2), 220–228. doi:10.1016/j.jretconser.2013.08.002

Singh, H., & Sahay, V. (2012). Determinants of shopping experience: Exploring the mall shoppers of national capital region (NCR) of India. *International Journal of Retail & Distribution Management, 40*(3), 235–248. doi:10.1108/09590551211207184

Singh, J., Srivastava, S., Sharma, S., Nath, S., & Karmakar, A. (2016). Customer perception of e-service quality in online travel companies in India. *International Journal of Applied Business and Economic Research., 14*(7), 5245–5254.

Singh, J., & Wilkes, R. (1996). When consumers complain: A path analysis of the key antecedents of consumer complaint response estimates. *Journal of the Academy of Marketing Science, 24*(4), 350–365. doi:10.1177/0092070396244006

Singh, N., & Matsuo, H. (2004). Measuring cultural adaptation on the web: A content analytic study of US and Japanese Web sites. *Journal of Business Research, 57*(8), 864–872. doi:10.1016/S0148-2963(02)00482-4

Sirakaya-Turk, E., Ekinci, Y., & Martin, D. (2015). The efficacy of shopping value in predicting destination loyalty. *Journal of Business Research, 68*(9), 1878–1885. doi:10.1016/j.jbusres.2015.01.016

Sirgy, M. J. (1985). Using Self-Congruity and Ideal Congruity to predict purchase motivation. *Journal of Business Research, 13*(3), 195–206. doi:10.1016/0148-2963(85)90026-8

Sit, J., Merrilees, B., & Birch, D. (2003). Entertainment-seeking shopping centre patrons: The missing segments. *International Journal of Retail & Distribution Management, 31*(2), 80–94. doi:10.1108/09590550310461985

Sjöblom, M., Törhönen, M., Hamari, J., & Macey, J. (2019). The ingredients of Twitch streaming: Affordances of game streams. *Computers in Human Behavior, 92*, 20–28. doi:10.1016/j.chb.2018.10.012

Smed, A. S., Kærgård, L. M., & Daugbjerg, C. (2013). A Matter of Trust: How Trust Influence Organic Consumption. *The Journal of Agricultural Science, 5*(7), 91–106.

Smith, A. G. (2001). Applying evaluation criteria to New Zealand government Web sites. *International Journal of Information Management, 21*(2), 137–149. doi:10.1016/S0268-4012(01)00006-8

Smith, D., Menon, K. S., & Sivakumar, K. (2005). Online Peer and Editorial Recommendations, Trust, and Choice in Virtual Markets. *Journal of Interactive Marketing, 19*(3), 15–37. doi:10.1002/dir.20041

Smits, D., & De Boeck, P. (2007). From anger to verbal aggression: Inhibition at different levels. *Personality and Individual Differences, 43*(1), 47–57. doi:10.1016/j.paid.2006.11.006

Snyman, L., & Visser, J. H. (2014). The adoption of social media and social media marketing by dentists in South Africa. *South African Dental Journal, 69*, 258–264. PMID:26548200

Social Media Marketing. (2019). *The No 1 Social Media Agency in Malaysia Discusses the Trends*. Retrieved from https://www.dmhubtraining.com

Social Media. (n.d.). *Merriam-Webster online*. Retrieved from http://www.merriam-webster.com/dictionary/socialmedia

Sohn, C., & Tadisina, S. K. (2008). Development of e-service quality measure for internet-based financial institutions. *Total Quality Management & Business Excellence, 19*(9), 903–918. doi:10.1080/14783360802224412

Somasundram, C., Razali, Z., & Santhirasegaram, V. (2016). A Review on Organic Food Production in Malaysia. *Horticulturae, 2*(3), 4–12. doi:10.3390/horticulturae2030012

Sønderskov, K. M., & Daugbjerg, C. (2011). The state and consumer confidence in eco-labeling: Organic labeling in Denmark, Sweden, The United Kingdom and The United States. *Agriculture and Human Values, 28*(4), 507–517. doi:10.100710460-010-9295-5

Song, J. H., & Zinkhan, G. M. (2003, March). Features of web site design, perceptions of web site quality, and patronage behavior. In ACME 2003 proceedings (pp. 106-114). ACME.

Soon, H. S. (2007). *An Empirical Analysis on the operational Efficiency of CRM call centers in Korea*. Call Center Industry Research Center.

Sotiriadis, M. D., & Van Zyl, C. (2013). Electronic word-of-mouth and online reviews in tourism services: The use of twitter by tourists. *Electronic Commerce Research*, *13*(1), 103–124. doi:10.100710660-013-9108-1

Souri, A., & Navimipour, N. J. (2014). Behavioral modeling and formal verification of a resource discovery approach in Grid computing. *Expert Systems with Applications*, *41*(8), 3831–3849. doi:10.1016/j.eswa.2013.11.042

Sparks, B. A., & Bradley, G. L. (2017). A "Triple A" typology of responding to negative consumer-generated online reviews. *Journal of Hospitality & Tourism Research (Washington, D.C.)*, *41*(6), 719–745. doi:10.1177/1096348014538052

Spisak, K. (2019). *2019 Social Media Trends & Statistics*. Retrieved from http://Business2community.com

Spiteri, L. F. (2000). Access to electronic commerce sites on the World Wide Web: An analysis of the effectiveness of six Internet search engines. *Journal of Information Science*, *26*(3), 173–183. doi:10.1177/016555150002600307

Srivastava, M., & Kaul, D. (2014). Social interaction, convenience and customer satisfaction: The mediating effect of customer experience. *Journal of Retailing and Consumer Services*, *21*(6), 1028–1037. doi:10.1016/j.jretconser.2014.04.007

Stamenkov, G., & Dika, Z. (2016). Bank employees' internal and external perspectives on e-service quality, satisfaction and loyalty. *Electronic Markets*, *26*(3), 291–309. doi:10.100712525-016-0221-6

Stanoevska-Slabeva, K. (2002). Toward a community-oriented design of Internet platforms. *International Journal of Electronic Commerce*, *6*(3), 71–95. doi:10.1080/10864415.2002.11044244

Statista. (n.d.). Retrieved from https://www.statista.com/statistics/272014/global-social-networks-ranked-by-number-of-users/

Stefanou, C. J., Sarmaniotis, C., & Stafyla, A. (2003). CRM and customer-centric knowledge management: An empirical research. *Business Process Management Journal*, *9*(5), 617–634. doi:10.1108/14637150310496721

Steinberg, S. (2017). *Social Media Etiquette: What's Safe To Share On Social Networks?* Retrieved 13 February, 2019, from Huffington Post: https://www.huffingtonpost.com/scott-steinberg/social-media-etiquette-wh_b_14500916.html

Stephanie, A. J., Abdul Nasir, Z., & Nur Fadziana, F. M. (2008). *A Study on the Acceptance of E-Ticketing in Universiti Utara Malaysia Bus Service*. Paper presented at the Knowledge Management International Conference, Langkawi, Malaysia.

Stern, H. (1962). The Significance of Impulse Buying Today. *Journal of Marketing*, *26*(2), 59–62. doi:10.1177/002224296202600212

Stevens, J. (2001). Applied multivariate statistics for the social sciences (3rd ed.). Mahwah, NJ: Lawrence Erlbaum.

Stiglingh, M. (2014). A measuring instrument to evaluate e-service quality in arevenue authority setting. *Public Relations Review*, *40*(2), 216–225. doi:10.1016/j.pubrev.2013.12.001

Stone, N., & Foss, B. (2001, May 3). Where do we go from here. *Marketing Business*.

Stone, R. W., & Baker-Eveleth, L. (2013). Students' expectation, confirmation, and continuance intention to use electronic textbooks. *Computers in Human Behavior*, *29*(3), 984–990. doi:10.1016/j.chb.2012.12.007

Stowell, D. M. (1997). *Sales and Marketing, and Continuous Improvement*. San Francisco: Jossey-Bass Publishers.

Strang, K. D. (2011). Multicultural face of organizations. In M. A. Sarlak (Ed.), *The new faces of organizations in the 21st century* (Vol. 5, pp. 1–21). Duluth, MN: North American Institute of Science and Information Technology.

Strang, K. D., & Vajjhala, N. R. (2015). Impact of socialized uncertainty on group decision making: An experiment with emerging executives. *International Journal of Risk and Contingency Management*, *4*(2), 45–58. doi:10.4018/IJRCM.2015040104

Strang, K. D., & Vajjhala, N. R. (2017). Student resistance to a mandatory learning management system in online supply chain courses. *Journal of Organizational and End User Computing*, *29*(3), 49–67. doi:10.4018/JOEUC.2017070103

Straub, D., Boudreau, M.-C., & Gefen, D. (2004). Validation guidelines for IS positivist research. *Communications of the Association for Information Systems*, *13*, 380–427. doi:10.17705/1CAIS.01324

Strober, E. (2016). *5 Problems With Social Media: What the internet is doing to our lives.* Retrieved 26 January, 2019, from the odyssey: https://www.theodysseyonline.com/five-problems-with-social-media

Suh, B. W., Eves, A., & Lumbers, M. (2012). Consumers' Attitude and Understanding of Organic Food: The Case of South Korea. *Journal of Foodservice Business Research*, *12*(1), 49–63. doi:10.1080/15378020.2012.650524

Suki, N. M. (2014). Passenger satisfaction with airline service quality in Malaysia: A structural equation modeling approach. *Research in Transportation Business & Management*, *10*, 26–32. doi:10.1016/j.rtbm.2014.04.001

Sun, H., & Zhang, P. (2003). *A new perspective to analyze user technology acceptance.* Working Paper, Syracuse University.

Sundström, M., Hjelm-Lidholm, S., & Radon, A. (2019). Clicking the boredom away–Exploring impulse fashion buying behavior online. *Journal of Retailing and Consumer Services*, *47*, 150–156. doi:10.1016/j.jretconser.2018.11.006

Sundström, M., & Radon, A. (2015). Utilizing the concept of convenience as a business opportunity in emerging markets. *Organizations and Markets in Emerging Economies*, *6*(2), 7–21.

Surjadaja, H., Ghosh, S., & Antony, F. (2003). Determining and assessing the determinants of e-service operations. *Managing Service Quality*, *13*(1), 39–44. doi:10.1108/09604520310456708

Swaid, S. I. (2009). Measuring the quality of e-service: Scale development and initial validation. *Journal of Electronic Commerce Research*, *10*(1), 13–28.

Swanson, S. R., & Kelley, S. W. (2001). Attributions and outcomes of the service recovery process. *Journal of Marketing Theory and Practice*, *9*(4), 50–65. doi:10.1080/10696679.2001.11501903

Sweeney, J. C., & Lapp, W. (2004). Critical Service Quality Encounters on the Web: An Exploratory Study. *Journal of Services Marketing*, *18*(4), 276–289. doi:10.1108/08876040410542272

Sylvie, R., & Ina, F. (2010). A new measure of e-service quality in France. *International Journal of Retail & Distribution Management*, *38*(7), 497–517. doi:10.1108/09590551011052106

Szwajkowski, E., & Figlewicz, R. E. (1999). Evaluating corporate performance: A comparison of the fortune reputation survey and the Socrates social rating database. *Journal of Managerial*, *11*(2), 137–154.

Szwarc, P. (2005). *Researching customer satisfaction and loyalty: how to find out what people really think.* London, UK: Kogan Page.

Taherdoost, H., Sahibuddin, S., Ibrahim, S., Kalantari, A., Jalaliyoon, N., & Ameri, S. (2012). *Examination of Electronic Service Definitions* Paper presented at the International Conference on Advanced Computer Science Applications and Technologies (ACSAT), Kuala Lumpur, Malaysia. 10.1109/ACSAT.2012.51

Taherdoost, H. (2016a). How to Design and Create an Effective Survey/Questionnaire; A Step by Step Guide. *International Journal of Academic Research in Management*, *5*(4), 37–41.

Taherdoost, H. (2016b). Validity and Reliability of the Research Instrument; How to Test the Validation of a Questionnaire/Survey in a Research. *International Journal of Academic Research in Management*, *5*(3), 28–36.

Taherdoost, H. (2017a). Determining Sample Size; How to Calculate Survey Sample Size. *International Journal of Economics and Management Systems*, *2*, 237–239.

Taherdoost, H. (2017b). Understanding of E-service Security Dimensions and its effect on Quality and Intention to Use. *Information and Computer Security*, *25*(5), 535–559. doi:10.1108/ICS-09-2016-0074

Taherdoost, H. (2018). Development of an adoption model to assess user acceptance of e-service technology: E-Service Technology Acceptance Model. *Behaviour & Information Technology*, *37*(2), 173–197. doi:10.1080/0144929X.2018.1427793

Taherdoost, H. (2018b). A review of technology acceptance and adoption models and theories. *Journal of Procedia Manufacturing*, *22*, 960–967. doi:10.1016/j.promfg.2018.03.137

Taherdoost, H., Sahibuddin, S., & Jalaliyoon, N. (2013). E-Services Usage Evaluation; Applications' level of Co-Creation and Digitalization. *International Journal of Academic Research in Management*, *2*(1), 10–18.

Tan, A., & Huey, Q. S. (2009). Consumer Purchase Decisions of Organic Food Products: An Ethnic Analysis. *Journal of International Consumer Marketing*, *22*(1), 47–58. doi:10.1080/08961530902844949

Tandon, A., Gupta, A., & Tripathi, V. (2016). Managing shopping experience through mall attractiveness dimensions: An experience of Indian metro cities. *Asia Pacific Journal of Marketing and Logistics*, *28*(4), 634–649. doi:10.1108/APJML-08-2015-0127

Tang, J. E., Tang, T. I., & Chiang, C. H. (2012). Blog learning: Effects of users' usefulness and efficiency towards continuance intention. *Behaviour & Information Technology*, *33*(1), 36–50. doi:10.1080/0144929X.2012.687772

Tan, K. C., Xie, M., & Li, Y. N. (2003). A service quality framework for Web-based information systems. *The TQM Magazine*, *15*(3), 164–172. doi:10.1108/09544780310469262

Taylor, D. G., Lewin, J. E., & Strutton, D. (2011). Friends, fans, and followers: Do ads work on social networks? *Journal of Advertising Research*, *51*(1), 258–275. doi:10.2501/JAR-51-1-258-275

Taylor, S., & Todd, P. (1995a). Understanding information technology usage: A Test of Competing Models. *Information Systems Research*, *6*(2), 144–176. doi:10.1287/isre.6.2.144

Tee, M. T. (2017). *She Bet RM60k On Women Wanting A Better Way To Deal With "That" Monthly Flow*. Retrieved from https://vulcanpost.com/621319/malaysia-cotton mermaid reusable-cloth-pad/

Teixeira, N., Pereira, H. G., & Dionísio, P. (2018). Online consumer generated content it's for real! the rise of social influence marketing. *The Business & Management Review*, *9*(3), 358–366.

Teo, J. S. E., Taniguchi, E., & Qureshi, A. G. (2012). Evaluating City Logistics Measure in E-Commerce with Multiagent Systems. *Procedia: Social and Behavioral Sciences*, *39*, 349–359. doi:10.1016/j.sbspro.2012.03.113

Thaichon, P., Lobo, A., & Mitsis, A. (2014). An empirical model of home internet services quality in Thailand. *Asia Pacific Journal of Marketing and Logistics*, *26*(2), 190–210. doi:10.1108/APJML-05-2013-0059

Thaichon, P., Lobo, A., Prentice, C., & Quach, T. N. (2014). The development of service quality dimensions for internet service providers: Retaining customers of different usage patterns. *Journal of Retailing and Consumer Services*, *21*(6), 1047–1058. doi:10.1016/j.jretconser.2014.06.006

Thatcher, J., & Perrewé, P. (2002). An empirical examination of individual traits as antecedents to computer anxiety and computer self-efficacy. *Management Information Systems Quarterly*, *26*(4), 381–399. doi:10.2307/4132314

The Star. (2018). *Cybercrime fraud cases stand at 8,313 as at Oct 3*. Retrieved from The Star Online: https://www.thestar.com.my/news/nation/2018/10/09/cybercrime-fraud-cases-stand-at-8313-as-at-oct-3/

The Sun Daily. (2017, September 28). Digital tax raises concerns among Malaysian consumers. *The Sun Daily*. Retrieved from https://www.thestar.com.my/business/business-news/2017/09/28/digital-tax-raises-concerns-among-malaysian-consumers/

Thompson, B. (2004). *Exploratory and confirmatory factor analysis: understanding concepts and applications*. Washington, DC: American Psychological Association. doi:10.1037/10694-000

Thong, J.YL, Hong, S.-J., & Tam, K.Y. (2006). The effects of post-adoption beliefs on the expectation-confirmation model for information technology continuance. *International Journal of Human-Computer Studies, 64*(9), 799-810.

Thuy, P. N., & Hau, L. N. (2010). Service personal values and customer loyalty: A study of banking services in a transitional economy. *International Journal of Bank Marketing*, *28*(6), 465–478. doi:10.1108/02652321011077706

Ting, H., Ming, W. W. P., de Run, E. C., & Choo, S. L. Y. (2015). Beliefs about the use of Instagram: An exploratory study. *International Journal of business and innovation, 2*(2), 15-31.

Todd, P. R., & Melancon, J. (2018). Gender and live-streaming: Source credibility and motivation. *Journal of Research in Interactive Marketing*, *12*(1), 79–93. doi:10.1108/JRIM-05-2017-0035

Toffler, A. (2008). *The third wave*. İstanbul: Koridor Publishings.

Torkzadeh, G., & Dhillon, G. (2002). Measuring factors that influence the success of Internet commerce. *Information Systems Research*, *13*(2), 187–204. doi:10.1287/isre.13.2.187.87

Townsend, L., & Wallace, C. (2016). Social Media Research: A Guide to Ethics. The University of Aberdeen.

Trompenaars, F., & Hampden-Turner, C. (1997). *Riding the waves of culture: Understanding cultural diversity in business* (2nd ed.). Boston, MA: Nicholas Brealey.

Tsai, H.-T., Huang, H.-C., Jaw, Y.-L., & Chen, W.-K. (2006). Why on-line customers remain with a particular e-retailer: An integrative model and empirical evidence. *Psychology and Marketing*, *23*(5), 447–464. doi:10.1002/mar.20121

Tsai, S. P. (2010). Shopping mall management and entertainment experience: A cross-regional investigation. *Service Industries Journal*, *30*(3), 321–337. doi:10.1080/02642060802123376

Tsekouropoulos, G., Andreopoulou, Z., Koliouska, C., Koutroumanidis, T., Batzios, C., & Lefakis, P. (2012). Marketing policies through the internet: The case of skiing centers in Greece. *Scientific Bulletin-Economic Sciences*, *11*(1), 66–78.

Tshuma, P., Makhathini, S., Siketile, P. N., & Taruvinga, A. (2010). Consumer perceptions on organic products in the Eastern Cape; the case of East London: South Africa. *Journal of Environmental. Agricultural and Food Chemistry*, *9*(3), 458–467.

Turban, E., King, D., McKay, J., Marshall, P., Lee, J., & Viehland, D. (2008). *Electronic Commerce 2008: A Managerial Perspective*. Pearson.

Turban, E., Lee, J. K., King, D., Liang, T. P., & Turban, D. (2010). *Electronic Commerce 2010: A Managerial Perspective*. Prentice Hall.

Udo, G. J., Bagchi, K. K., & Kirs, P. J. (2010). An assessment of customers' e-service quality perception, satisfaction and intention. *International Journal of Information Management, 30*(6), 481–492. doi:10.1016/j.ijinfomgt.2010.03.005

UN Habitat. (2013). *Explore data*. Retrieved January 10, 2019, from http://urbandata.unhabitat.org/explore-data/?indicators=urban_agglomeration_population_density

Uncles, M. D., Dowling, G. R., & Hammond, K. (2003). Customer loyalty and customer loyalty programs. *Journal of Consumer Marketing, 20*(4), 294–316. doi:10.1108/07363760310483676

UNDESA. (2014). World Urbanization Prospects. *Undesa, 32*. doi:10.4054/DemRes.2005.12.9

Unglesbee, B. (2018). *Walmart has big plans to cash in on Toys R Us' demise*. Retrieved January 24, 2019, from https://www.retaildive.com/news/walmart-has-big-plans-to-cash-in-on-toys-r-us-demise/531413/

United Nations Department of Economic and Social Affairs Population Division. (2016). *The World's Cities in 2016 – Data Booklet* (ST/ESA/ SER.A/392). Retrieved from http://www.un.org/en/development/desa/population/publications/pdf/urbanization/the_worlds_cities_in_2016_data_booklet.pdf

Valck, K., Bruggen, G. H. V., & Wierenga, B. (2009). Virtual communities: A marketing perspective. *Decision Support Systems, 47*(3), 185–203. doi:10.1016/j.dss.2009.02.008

Van der Heijden. (2000). *Using the technology acceptance model to predict website usage: Extensions and Empirical Test*. Serie Research Memoranda.

Van der Heijden, H. (2003). Factors influencing the usage of websites: The case of a generic portal in the Netherlands. *Information & Management, 40*(6), 541–549. doi:10.1016/S0378-7206(02)00079-4

Van der Waldt, D. R., Rebello, T. M., & Brown, W. J. (2009). Attitudes of young consumers towards SMS advertising. *African Journal of Business Management, 3*, 444–452.

Van Dijck, J. (2013). *The culture of connectivity: a critical history of social media*. New York: Oxford University Press. doi:10.1093/acprof:oso/9780199970773.001.0001

Van Doorn, J., Lemon, K. N., Mittal, V., Nass, S., Pick, D., Pirner, P., & Verhoef, P. C. (2010). Customer engagement behavior: Theoretical foundations and research directions. *Journal of Service Research, 13*(3), 253–266. doi:10.1177/1094670510375599

Van Iwaarden, J., Van der Wiele, T., Ball, L., & Millen, R. (2003). Applying SERVQUAL to web sites: An exploratory study. *International Journal of Quality & Reliability Management, 20*(8), 919–935. doi:10.1108/02656710310493634

van Riel, A. C. R., Liljander, V., & Jurriens, P. (2001). Exploring consumer evaluations of e-services: A portal site. *International Journal of Service Industry Management, 12*(4), 359–377. doi:10.1108/09564230110405280

Van Riel, A. C. R., Semeijn, C., & Janssen, W. (2003). E-service quality expectations: A case study. *Total Quality Management, 14*(4), 437–450. doi:10.1080/1478336032000047255

Van Riel, C. R. A., Semeijn, J., & Pauwels, P. (2004). Online travel service quality: The importance of pre-transaction services. *Total Quality Management & Business Excellence, 15*(4), 475–493. doi:10.1080/1478336042000183578

VanMeter, R., Syrdal, H. A., Powell-Mantel, S., Grisaffe, D. B., & Nesson, E. T. (2018). Don't Just "Like" Me, Promote Me: How Attachment and Attitude Influence Brand Related Behaviors on Social Media. *Journal of Interactive Marketing, 43*, 83–97. doi:10.1016/j.intmar.2018.03.003

Vardarlı, K. (2013). *Digital eclipse marketing communications and human*. İstanbul: Mediacat Publishings.

Vatanasombut, B., Stylianou, A., & Igbaria, M. (2004). How to retain online customers. *Communications of the ACM*, *47*(6), 65–69. doi:10.1145/990680.990682

Vazifehdoust, H., Taleghani, M., Esmaeilpour, F., Nazari, K., & Khadang, M. (2013). Factors influence consumers' green purchasing behavior. *Management Science Letters*, *2*(9), 2489–2500. doi:10.5267/j.msl.2013.08.013

Veerinder, S. (2013). *Veerinder on Taxation* (3rd ed.). Kuala Lumpur: CCH.

Venaik, S., & Brewer, P. (2013). Critical issues in the Hofstede and GLOBE national culture models. *International Marketing Review*, *30*(5), 469–482. doi:10.1108/IMR-03-2013-0058

Venkatesh, V., & Bala, H. (2008). Technology acceptance model 3 and a research agenda on interventions. *Decision Sciences*, *39*(2), 273–315. doi:10.1111/j.1540-5915.2008.00192.x

Venkatesh, V., & Davis, F. (1996). A model of the antecedents of perceived ease of use: Development and test. *Decision Sciences*, *27*(3), 451–481. doi:10.1111/j.1540-5915.1996.tb01822.x

Venkatesh, V., & Davis, F. D. (2000). A theoretical extension of the technology acceptance model: Four longitudinal field studies. *Management Science*, *46*(2), 186–204. doi:10.1287/mnsc.46.2.186.11926

Venkatesh, V., Davis, F., Morris, M., & Michael, G. (2007). Dead of Alive? The development, trajectory, and future of technology adoption research. *Journal of the Association for Information Systems*, *8*(4), 268–286. doi:10.17705/1jais.00120

Venkatesh, V., Morris, M. G., Davis, G. B., & Davis, F. D. (2003). User acceptance of information technology: Toward a unified view. *Management Information Systems Quarterly*, *27*(3), 425–478. doi:10.2307/30036540

Venkatesh, V., Thong, J. Y. L., & Xu, X. (2012). Consumer acceptance and use of information technology: Extending the unified theory of acceptance and use of technology. *Management Information Systems Quarterly*, *36*(1), 157–178. doi:10.2307/41410412

Verhagen, T., & van Dolen, W. (2011). The influence of online store beliefs on consumer online impulse buying: A model and empirical application. *Information & Management*, *48*(8), 320–327. doi:10.1016/j.im.2011.08.001

Verhoef, P. C., & Langerak, F. (2001). Possible determinants of consumers' adoption of electronic grocery shopping in the Netherland. *Journal of Retailing and Consumer Services*, *8*(5), 275–285. doi:10.1016/S0969-6989(00)00033-3

Vijayasarathy, L. R. (2004). Predicting consumer intentions to use on-line shopping: The case for an augmented technology acceptance model. *Information & Management*, *41*(6), 747–762. doi:10.1016/j.im.2003.08.011

Vinzi, E., Trinchera, L., & Amato, S. (2010). PLS path modeling: from foundations to recent developments and open issues for model assessment and improvement. Handbook of Partial Least Squares: Concepts, Methods, and Applications in Marketing and Related Fields, 47-82.

Virnoche, M. E., & Marx, G. T. (1997). Only connect-E. M. Forster in an age of electronic communication: Computer-mediated association and community networks. *Sociological Inquiry*, *67*(1), 85–100. doi:10.1111/j.1475-682X.1997.tb00431.x

Virtanen, H., Björk, P., & Sjöström, E. (2017). Follow for follow: Marketing of a start-up company on Instagram. *Journal of Small Business and Enterprise Development*, *24*(3), 468–484. doi:10.1108/JSBED-12-2016-0202

Voon, J. P., Ngui, K. S., & Agrawal, A. (2011). Determinants of Willingness to Purchase Organic Food: An Exploratory Study Using Structural Equation Modeling. *The International Food and Agribusiness Management Review*, *14*(2), 103–120.

Wagner, P. (2018). *Internet Scamming is on The Rise*. Retrieved from Internet Usage in the United States: https://www.statista.com/chart/15069/number-of-internet-scams-in-the-us/

Wakefield, K. L., & Baker, J. (1998). Excitement at the mall: Determinants and effects on shopping response. *Journal of Retailing, 74*(4), 515–539. doi:10.1016/S0022-4359(99)80106-7

Walker, P. (2016). *Facebook Makes You Unhappy And Makes Jealous People Particularly Sad, Study Finds*. Retrieved 16 February, 2019, from Independent: https://www.independent.co.uk/life-style/gadgets-and-tech/facebook-social-media-make-unhappy-jealous-people-particularly-sad-copenhagen-university-study-a7490816.html

Wallace, D. W., Giese, J. L., & Johnson, J. L. (2004). Customer retailer loyalty in the context of multiple channel strategies. *Journal of Retailing, 80*(4), 249–263. doi:10.1016/j.jretai.2004.10.002

Wang, J. (2009). *Study of online group purchasing*. Retrieved from from: http://d.g.wanfangdata.com.cn/Periodical_scxdh200928025.aspx

Wang, R. Y., & Strong, D. M. (1996). Beyond accuracy: What data quality means to data consumers. *Journal of Management Information Systems, 12*(4), 5-33.

Wang, W., Ngai, E. W. T., & Wei, H. (2011). Explaining Instant Messaging Continuance Intention: The Role of Personality. *International Journal of Human-Computer Interaction, 28*(8), 500–510. doi:10.1080/10447318.2011.622971

Wang, X., Yu, C., & Wei, Y. (2012). Social media peer communication and impacts on purchase intentions: A consumer socialization framework. *Journal of Interactive Marketing, 26*(4), 198–208. doi:10.1016/j.intmar.2011.11.004

Wang, X., Yuen, K. F., Wong, Y. D., & Teo, C. C. (2018). An innovation diffusion perspective of e-consumers' initial adoption of self-collection service via automated parcel station. *International Journal of Logistics Management, 29*(1), 237–260. doi:10.1108/IJLM-12-2016-0302

Wang, Y., Zhang, X., Kubota, J., Zhu, X., & Lu, G. (2015). A semi-parametric panel data analysis on the urbanization-carbon emissions nexus for OECD countries. *Renewable & Sustainable Energy Reviews, 48*, 704–709. doi:10.1016/j.rser.2015.04.046

Watson, T., & Kitchen, P. J. (2010). Reputation management: corporate image and communication. *Bournemount University.* retrieved from www. eprints.bournemouth.ac.uk

Weber, L. (2009). *Marketing to the social web: how digital customer communities build your business*. John Wiley & Sons. doi:10.1002/9781118258125

Wei, D., Shuo, Z., Luo, G., Chen, Z., & Ling, X. (2011). Analyze on Mobile Payment Based on RFID. *Procedia Environmental Sciences, 10*, 950–955. doi:10.1016/j.proenv.2011.09.152

White, R. (2008). The Role of Entertainment in Shopping Centers & Malls. *Leisure eNewsletter, 8*(5), 1-15.

Whiting, A., & Williams, D. (2013). Why people use social media: A uses and gratifications approach. *Qualitative Market Research, 16*(4), 362–369. doi:10.1108/QMR-06-2013-0041

Widiatmika, G. N., & Subawa, N. S. (2017). Effect of e-service quality and recovery service quality mobile banking services to e-trust, e-satisfaction and e-loyalty mobile banking users of local bank customer in Bali, Indonesia. *Imperial Journal of Interdisciplinary Research, 3*(3), 1252–1260.

Wills, B. (2009). The business case for environmental sustainability (Green): Achieving rapid returns from the practical integration of lean & green. *Business Case for Environmental Sustainability*, 1-15.

Wilson, V., & Makau, C. (2018). Online marketing use: Small and medium enterprises (SMEs) experience from Kenya. *ORSEA Journal*, *7*, 63–77.

Wingfield, N., & Hanrahan, T. (1999). Web firm salon buys 'the Well,' an online pioneer. *The Wall Street Journal*, p. B9.

Wixom, B. H., & Todd, P. A. (2005). A theoretical integration of user satisfaction and technology acceptance. *Information Systems Research*, *16*(1), 85–102. doi:10.1287/isre.1050.0042

Wolfinbarger, M., & Gilly, M. C. (2003). Etailq: Dimensionalizing, Measuring and Predicting Etail Quality. *Journal of Retailing*, *79*(3), 183–198. doi:10.1016/S0022-4359(03)00034-4

Wood, S. L., & Jr, L. (2002). Prior knowledge and complacency in new product learning. *The Journal of Consumer Research*, *29*(3), 416–426. doi:10.1086/344425

World Bank Group. (2018). *Malaysia's Digital Economy*. Author.

World Economic Forum. (n.d.). *Our addiction to screens is damaging more than our health*. Retrieved 15 February, 2019, from https://www.facebook.com/watch/?v=10153727978766479

Wortley, D. J., & Lai, P. C. (2017). The Impact of Disruptive Enabling Technologies on Creative Education. *3rd International Conference on Creative Education*, 1-3.

Wu, Shi, & Hu. (2015). Threshold Effects in Online Group Buying. *Management Science*, *61*(9), 2025–2040.

Wu, J., & Wang, S. (2005). What drives mobile commerce? An empirical evaluation of the revised technology acceptance model. *Information & Management*, *42*(5), 719–729. doi:10.1016/j.im.2004.07.001

Wu, K. W. (2011). Customer loyalty explained by electronic recovery service quality: Implications of the customer relationship re-establishment for consumer electronics e-tailers. *Contemporary Management Research*, *7*(1), 21–44. doi:10.7903/cmr.1101

Wu, Y.-L., Tao, Y.-H., & Yang, P.-C. (2008). The use of unified theory of acceptance and use of technology to confer the behavioral model of 3G mobile telecommunication users. *Journal of Statistics & Management Systems*, *11*(5), 919–949. doi:10.1080/09720510.2008.10701351

Xie, T. (2004). Strategic alliances: Incorporating the impact of e-business technological innovations. *Journal of Business and Industrial Marketing*, *19*(3), 208–222. doi:10.1108/08858620410531342

Xiong, L., & Hu, C. (2011). *Hotel Viral Marketing via Social Networks: A Strategic Pricing Lesson from Group Buying*. Retrieved from http://scholarworks.umass.edu/cgi/viewcontent.cgi?article=1312&context=gradconf_hospitality

Xiong, L., & Hu, C. (2010). Harness the power of viral marketing in hotel industry: A network discount strategy. *Journal of Hospitality and Tourism Technology*, *1*(3), 234–244. doi:10.1108/17579881011078368

Yalçın, F. G. (2016). *Social Media for small enterprises*. İstanbul: Abaküs Publishings.

Yang, H., & Tsai, F.-S. (2007). General E-S-QUAL scales applied to websites satisfaction and loyalty model. *Communications of the IIMA*, *7*(2), 115–126.

Yang, Z. (2001). Consumer perceptions of service quality in internet-based electronic commerce. *Proceedings of EMAC Conference*.

Yang, Z., Cai, S., Zhou, Z., & Zhou, N. (2005). Development and validation of an instrument to measure user perceived service quality of information presenting Web portals. *Information & Management*, *42*(4), 575–589. doi:10.1016/S0378-7206(04)00073-4

Yang, Z., & Jun, M. (2002). Consumer perception of e-service quality: From Internet purchaser and non-purchaser perspectives. *Journal of Business Strategies Huntsville*, *19*(1), 19–41.

Yang, Z., Peterson, R. T., & Cai, S. (2003). Services quality dimension of Internet retailing: An exploratory analysis. *Journal of Services Marketing Science*, *17*(7), 685–690. doi:10.1108/08876040310501241

Yang, Z., Peterson, R. T., & Huang, L. (2001). Taking the pulse of internet pharmacies. *Marketing Health Services*, *21*(2), 5–10. PMID:11406905

Yap, B. W., Ramayah, T., & Shahidan, W. N. W. (2012). Satisfaction and trust on customer loyalty: A PLS approach. *Business Strategy Series*, *13*(4), 154–167. doi:10.1108/17515631211246221

Yastrow, S. (2007). *We: The ideal customer relationship*. Select Books Inc.

Yaya, L. H. P., Marimon, F., & Casadesus, M. (2011). Customer's loyalty and perception of ISO 9001 in online banking. *Industrial Management and Data Systems, 111*(8), 1194-1213. doi:10.1108/02635571111170767

Ye, B. H., Barreda, A. A., Okumus, F., & Nusair, K. (2019). Website interactivity and brand development of online travel agencies in China: The moderating role of age. *Journal of Business Research*, *99*, 382–389. doi:10.1016/j.jbusres.2017.09.046

Yenisey, M. M., Ozok, A. A., & Salvendy, G. (2005). Perceived security determinants in ecommerce among Turkish University students. *Behaviour & Information Technology*, *24*(4), 259–274. doi:10.1080/0144929042000320992

Ye, Q., Law, R., Gu, B., & Chen, W. (2011). The influence of user-generated content on traveler behavior: An empirical investigation on the effects of e-word-of-mouth to hotel online bookings. *Computers in Human Behavior*, *27*(2), 634–639. doi:10.1016/j.chb.2010.04.014

Yim Yiu, C., & Xu, S. Y. (2012). A tenant-mix model for shopping malls. *European Journal of Marketing*, *46*(3/4), 524–541. doi:10.1108/03090561211202594

Yim, F. H., Anderson, R. E., & Swaminathan, S. (2005).Customer Relationship Management: Its Dimensions and Effect on Customer Outcomes. *Journal of Personal Selling and Sales Management, 24*(4), 265–280. doi:10.1080/08853134.2004.10749037

Yin, S., Wu, L., Du, L., & Chen, M. (2010). Consumers' Purchase Intention of Organic Food in China. *Journal of the Science of Food and Agriculture*, *90*(8), 1361–1367. doi:10.1002/jsfa.3936 PMID:20474056

Yiridoe, E. K., Bonti-Ankomah, S., & Martin, R. C. (2005). Comparison of consumer perceptions and preference toward organic versus conventionally produced foods: A review and update of the literature. *Renewable Agriculture and Food Systems*, *20*(4), 193–205. doi:10.1079/RAF2005113

Yiu, C. Y., & Yau, Y. (2006). An ecological framework for the strategic positioning of a shopping mall. *Journal of Retail & Leisure Property*, *5*(4), 270–280. doi:10.1057/palgrave.rlp.5100037

Yoo, B., & Donthu, N. (2001). Developing a scale to measure perceived quality of an Internet shopping site (SITEQUAL). *Quarterly Journal of Electronic Commerce*, *2*(1), 31–46.

Yoon, C. (2009). The effects of national culture values on consumer acceptance of e-commerce: Online shoppers in China. *Information & Management*, *46*(1), 294–301. doi:10.1016/j.im.2009.06.001

Yoon, C.-H., & Lim, D.-S. (2018). The Effect of the Big Five and the MBTI on Impulsive and Compulsive Buying Behaviors: An Integrated Analysis in Online Shopping. *Journal of International Trade & Commerce*, *14*(3), 101–117.

Young, A. L., & Quan-Haase, A. (2013). Privacy Protection Strategies on Facebook. *Information Communication and Society*, *16*(4), 479–500. doi:10.1080/1369118X.2013.777757

Yu, E., Jung, C., Kim, H., & Jung, J. (2018). Impact of viewer engagement on gift-giving in live video streaming. *Telematics and Informatics*, *35*(5), 1450–1460. doi:10.1016/j.tele.2018.03.014

Yuen, M. K. (2018). *Animal doctors needed*, 6 May 2018. Retrieved from https://www.thestar.com.my/news/nation/2018/05/06/animal-doctors-needed/

Yu, J., Ha, I., Choi, M., & Rho, J. (2005). Extending the TAM for a t-commerce. *Information & Management*, *42*(7), 965–976. doi:10.1016/j.im.2004.11.001

Yu, M., Lee, Y.-S., & Lee, J.-E. (2017). A study on the constituent factors and customer characteristics of Chinese internet shopping malls (centering around purchase satisfaction, customer loyalty and repurchase intention of Chinese female college students). *Journal of Engineering and Applied Sciences (Asian Research Publishing Network)*, *12*(2), 6344–6349.

Yun, G. W., Park, S.-Y., & Ha, L. (2008). Influence of cultural dimensions on online interactive review feature implementations: A comparison of Korean and US retail web sites. *Journal of Interactive Marketing*, *22*(3), 40–50. doi:10.1002/dir.20116

Yusta, A. I., & Newell, S. J. (2011). Consumer beliefs and motivations that influence repeat online purchases. *International Journal of Electronic Marketing and Retailing*, *4*(4), 270–292. doi:10.1504/IJEMR.2011.045611

Yusuf, A. S., Hussin, C., Razak, A., & Busalim, A. H. (2018). Influence of e-WOM engagement on consumer purchase intention in social commerce. *Journal of Services Marketing*, *32*(4), 493–504. doi:10.1108/JSM-01-2017-0031

Zagata, L. (2012). Consumers' beliefs and behavioural intentions towards organic food. Evidence from the Czech Republic. *Appetite*, *59*(1), 81–89. doi:10.1016/j.appet.2012.03.023 PMID:22504401

Zahra, S. A., & George, G. (2002). Absorptive capacity: A review, reconceptualization, and extension. *Academy of Management Review*, *27*(2), 185–203. doi:10.5465/amr.2002.6587995

Zareie, B., & Jafari, N. (2016). The impact of electronic environmental knowledge on the environmental behaviors of people. *Computers in Human Behavior*, *59*, 1–8. doi:10.1016/j.chb.2016.01.025

Zeist, R. H. J., & Hendriks, P. R. H. (1996). Specifying software quality with the extended ISO model. *Software Quality Journal*, *5*(4), 273–284. doi:10.1007/BF00209185

Zeithaml, V. A., Parasuraman, A., & Malhotra, A. (2000). *A conceptual framework for understanding e-service quality: Implications for future research and managerial practice.* MSI Working Paper Series, Report No. 00-115, Cambridge.

Zeithaml, V. A., Parasuraman, A., & Malhotra, A. (2000). *Conceptual framework for understanding e-service quality: Implications for future research and managerial practice.* Retrieved from http://www.msi.org/reports/a-conceptual-framework-for-understanding-e-service-quality-implications-for/

Zeithaml, V. A. (2002). Service excellence in electronic channels. *Managing Service Quality*, *12*(3), 135–138. doi:10.1108/09604520210429187

Zeithaml, V. A., Berry, L. L., & Parasuraman, A. (1996). The behavioral consequences of service quality. *Journal of Marketing*, *60*(2), 31–46. doi:10.2307/1251929

Zeithaml, V. A., Berry, L., & Parasuraman, A. (1996). The behavioral consequences of service quality. *JMR, Journal of Marketing Research*, *60*(2), 31–46.

Zeithaml, V. A., Parasuraman, A., & Malhotra, A. (2002). Service quality delivery through web sites: A critical review of extant knowledge. *Journal of the Academy of Marketing Science*, *30*(4), 362–375. doi:10.1177/009207002236911

Zhang, J., & Daugherty, T. (2009). Third-person effect and social networking: Implications for online marketing and word-of-mouth communication. *American Journal of Business*, *24*(2), 53–64. doi:10.1108/19355181200900011

Zhang, K. Z., Xu, H., Zhao, S., & Yu, Y. (2018). Online reviews and impulse buying behavior: The role of browsing and impulsiveness. *Internet Research*, *28*(3), 522–543. doi:10.1108/IntR-12-2016-0377

Zhang, L., Zhu, J., & Liu, Q. (2012). A meta-analysis of mobile commerce adoption and the moderating effect of culture. *Computers in Human Behavior*, *28*(5), 1902–1911. doi:10.1016/j.chb.2012.05.008

Zhang, M., Guo, L., Hu, M., & Liu, W. (2017). Influence of customer engagement with company social networks on stickiness: Mediating effect of customer value creation. *International Journal of Information Management*, *37*(3), 229–240. doi:10.1016/j.ijinfomgt.2016.04.010

Zhang, X., Gao, Y., Yan, X., de Pablos, P. O., Sun, Y., & Cao, X. (2015). From e-learning to social-learning: Mapping development of studies on social media-supported knowledge management. *Computers in Human Behavior*, *51*, 803–811. doi:10.1016/j.chb.2014.11.084

Zhang, X., & Prybutok, V. (2005). A consumer perspective of e-service quality. *IEEE Transactions on Engineering Management*, *52*(4), 461–477. doi:10.1109/TEM.2005.856568

Zheng, X., Cheung, C. M. K., Lee, M. K. O., & Liang, L. (2015). Building brand loyalty through user engagement in online brand communities in social networking sites. *Information Technology & People*, *28*(1), 90–106. doi:10.1108/ITP-08-2013-0144

Zhen, J., & Mansori, S. (2012). Young Female Motivations for Purchase of Organic Food in Malaysia. *International Journal of Contemporary Business Studies*, *3*(5), 61–72.

Zhong, J., & Nieminen, M. (2015). Resource-based co-innovation through platform ecosystem: Experiences of mobile payment innovation in China. *Journal of Strategy and Management*, *8*(3), 283–298. doi:10.1108/JSMA-03-2015-0026

Zhou, L., Dai, L., & Zhang, D. (2007). Online shopping acceptance model - A critical survey of consumer factors in online shopping. *Journal of Electronic Commerce Research*, *8*(1), 41–62.

Zikmund, W. G., Babin, B. J., Carr, J. C., & Griffin, M. (2013). *Business research methods*. Mason, OH: Cengage Learning.

Zineldin, M. (2000). *Total Relationship Management*. Lund: Studentlitteratur.

Zineldin, M. (2006). The royalty of loyalty: CRM, quality and retention. *The Journal of Consumer Marketing, 23*(7), 430-437. doi:. doi:10.1108/07363760610712975

Zweig, D., & Webster, J. (2003). Personality as a moderator of monitoring acceptance. *Computers in Human Behavior*, *19*(4), 479–493. doi:10.1016/S0747-5632(02)00075-4

About the Contributors

Ree C. Ho is senior lecturer at Taylor's University, Malaysia. Dr. Ho has vast academic and administrative experiences in higher education institutes. His academic portfolio includes dean, principal lecturer, stream coordinator, program leader and etc. Prior to his academic career, he worked in the capacity of business analyst, project manager, and regional manager in the development of business enterprise systems. He has published in a number of indexed journals and his current research interests include e-commerce, social commerce, digital marketing, mobile business apps, and business analytics.

* * *

Abdullah Abbas Alkhrabsheh received his PhD in Business Administration from UNITEN Malaysia and currently working as a lecture with Al-balqa Applied University in management faculty. He teaches organisational behaviour, crisis management, human resource management and strategic management. His research interest include organisation behaviour, consumer behaviour and management related areas.

Vijayabanu C is currently an Associate Professor at School of Management, SASTRA Deemed University in India. She obtained her Ph.D in Commerce-Human Resource Management in 2000 at Bharathidasan University, India. Her current research interests focus on the areas behavioral studies –Personality, Perception: attitudes & values. She handles courses such as, Human Resource Management, organizational behaviour and specialization courses such as Change Management, Training & Development, etc. She brings to her classes enriched knowledge of 5 years of Research & 16 years of academic experience. She has produced 3 doctoral scholars successfully and currently Guiding 4 Ph.D scholars .She is an Associate Member in NIPM (National Institute of Personnel Management). She has presented papers in international and national level conferences and seminars. She has published a number of research articles and case studies in referred Scopus indexed journals. She has served on the Editorial Review Boards of several academic journals, including Business theory and practice, Journal of Management Social Science and Humanities and Journal of Business Economics and Management.

Ritu Chhikara is an Assistant Professor at School of Management, BML Munjal University. She holds a PhD in Retail Management from Faculty of Management Studies, University of Delhi. Prior to PhD she worked with Microsoft India, in Sales and Marketing domain. She was involved in their public sector education business. Dr Ritu has a Master's in Business Administration with specialization in Marketing from FMS, Delhi.

Shopee Dube is currently employed by University of Johannesburg (UJ), Department of Applied Information Systems in South Africa, as an IT Senior lecturer and deputy Head of Department since 2007. She obtained a PhD in Informatics from UJ, Master of Computer Science (Cum Laude) from National University of Science and Technology (NUST) and Bachelor of Computer Science (Cum Laude) from Andrews University, Michigan in USA. She strives to integrate her professional experience gained over the years in teaching and learning to impact knowledge to her students. The lecturer position has enhanced her experience in postgraduate supervision at Honours, Masters and Doctoral levels. Dr Dube, currently serves as an external moderator and/or examiner for Information Systems modules for local universities. She is also a reviewer for some journals and has served as a Program Committee Co-Chair for The 2nd and 4th International Conference On the Internet, Cyber Security and Information Systems in 2017 and 2019. Dr Dube, generated accredited research outputs by publishing in international journals and several conferences proceedings. Her research areas of specialization are digital marketing, IT project management in virtual teams and Fourth Industrial Revolution.

Ruchi Garg is an assistant professor at BML Munjal University, Gurgaon. She completed her fellowship in management from Management development Institute, Gurugram. Her research interests are Brand Love, Consumer brand relationship, sustainability communication and consumer behavior.

Zeynep Genel completed her undergraduate degree at İstanbul University in 1998 on Public Relations She took her first MA degree in 2004 at Marmara University on Public Relations and Advertising, and second MA degree in 2008 at Marmara University on Journalism. Dr. Genel took her doctoral degree in 2015 at Yeditepe University, on Media Studies. She has lectured at Okan University's New Media department since 2016. Her research and publications focus corporate reputation, marketing communications, city branding, influencer marketing and sustainability.

Ali Hassan is a PhD student of Economics at Malaya University, Malaysia. His thesis is concerning the economic evaluation of Spinal Cord Injuries in Malaysia. Currently, he is a member of Research and Development Department (Research Club) of Hamta Group. His research interests are Policy Modeling, Macroeconomics, Econometrics, Technology, Innovation and Development.

Refiloe Gladys Khoase is a Post Doctoral Researcher at the University of KwaZulu-Natal, Pietermaritzburg Campus. She obtained her PhD in Management from the same university (UKZN) in 2015. Prior to that, she obtained Master of Commerce in Management (2011), Bachelor of Commerce Honours in Management (2007), and Bachelor or Business Administration in Business Management (2006) all from the same Institution (UKZN).

Harish Kumar is JRF (Junior Research Fellowship) awardee with 7th rank in management subject having 99.9 percentile pursuing Ph.D. in marketing. He has done MBA M.com. His research interest are consumer behavior and artificial intelligence. He has also qualified national eligibility test (NET) 5 times as well.

Payal Kumar is Professor and Chair (OB/HR), and Head of Research and International Relations at BML Munjal University. She has published widely including as a series editor of a 5 volume series on Leadership and Followership for Palgrave Macmillan. She is on several editorial boards and is senior reviewer for the Journal of Organizational Behaviour.

Patrick Ndayizigamiye obtained his PhD (Information Systems and Technology), Master of Commerce (Information Systems and Technology), and Bachelor of Social Sciences Honours (Information Systems and Technology) degrees from the University of KwaZulu-Natal in South Africa. For the past two years (2017 and 2018) Patrick was employed as a Postdoctoral researcher funded by the South Africa's National Research Foundation (NRF). Patrick is currently employed as a Senior Lecturer in the Department of Applied Information Systems at the University of Johannesburg in South Africa. He has 8 years of experience in teaching information systems modules and has published in international journals and conference proceedings. He has also presented his research outputs at many local and international conferences. His current research interest is in the design and deployment of mobile health interventions to provide healthcare services in Resource-Limited Settings. He is also an external advisor/supervisor of Masters and PhD students in the discipline of Information Systems and Technology.

Vera Nsahlai is a Masters student at the University of KwaZulu-Natal. She graduated with a Post-Graduate Diploma in Marketing and Supply Chain Management in 2019. Prior to that, she graduated in 2018 with a Bachelor of Social Science with majors in Marketing and Media Studies.

Michela Piccarozzi is an assistant professor at the Department of Enterprise and Engineering, Society and Management (DEIM) - University of 'Tuscia' of Viterbo. Interests: innovation; University Spin-off (USOs); strategic planning, business plan and firms creation's process; innovative start-ups.

Kanesh Gopal Rajadurai has 8 years' experience in the field of Education and Engineering. Trained as an engineer, he later pursued his passion in education and marketing, while gaining professional qualifications in Management and Marketing. While an avid educator, he started his career in the engineering industry and progressed to the education world after completing his postgraduate studies. He has a degree in Engineering, a Masters in Management Science and a PhD in Management. Dr. Kanesh's Areas of Research interest amongst others are Services Marketing, Organizational Behavior, Marketing Educational Psychology, Adolescent Behavior, Consumer Behavior and Social issues pertaining to teenagers and young adults.

Eleonora Rapiti is enrolled for the second year of the PhD in "Economics, management and quantitative methods" at the University of Tuscia, Viterbo (Italy). She graduated in 2014 from the University of Tuscia with a Bachelor's Degree in Business Economics with a thesis titled "Stochastic approach to modeling the balance sheet requirement premium risk in optic Solvency II", with the final degree mark 110 (out of 110) cum laude. In 2016 she obtained her Master's Degree in Administration, Finance and Control from the University of Tuscia with a thesis titled "The impact of terrorism on the financial markets", with the final degree mark 110 (out of 110) cum laude. Her research interests include: circular economy, quality management, online marketing and communications.

Geeta Sachdeva works in the Department of Humanities & Social Sciences in the Institute of National Importance NIT i.e. National Institute of Technology, Kurukshetra (India). She Has has total 11 years of teaching experience. She has done MBA in field of Human Resource Management and Marketing. She has published several Papers in various National and International Journals.

Karthikeyan Shanmugam, B.Sc, MBA, is currently pursuing PhD (Full Time) at School of Management, SASTRA Deemed University, India in the area of behavioral finance which remains as the area of his own interest. He received his master's degree in business administration at SASTRA Deemed University, Tamilnadu in India. He has 5 years of Industry & 8 years of academic experience. He has rich experience in handling specialized business courses in Finance and HR to both Under-Graduate and Post-Graduate students. He has presented and published a number of research articles in national and international conferences.

Cecilia Silvestri is Researcher of Commodity Science at the Department of Enterprise and Engineering, Society and Management(DEIM) at the University of Tuscia, Viterbo (Italy) where she held the course Quality and Customer Relationships. She had her PhD in 2011 in "Economics and local development" at the University of Tuscia. Consistent with carried out studies, her research has developed along the following guidelines: (1) Quality of goods, products and services. Studies and research on the quality according to the approaches of "Total Quality Management" and standards "ISO 9000", (2) The relationship between quality and consumers, with particular reference to satisfaction and loyalty, (3) Quality and innovation in the agro-food, (4) Innovation and technology transfer, with particular attention to the role of technological innovation for territorial development.

Kenneth David Strang has over 270 publications and 36 years of experience in business, project management and teaching. Ken has a Doctorate in Project Management (Operations Research), MBA in Strategic Management, BSBA in Marketing, AS (IT) all with summa cum laude honors. He is a licensed Project Management Professional (PMI, USA) a Fellow Life Management Institute with distinction (LOMA, USA), a Certified Research Professional (IIPMR, USA), a Certified Network Administrator(Novell), and a Certified Procurement Professional (IIPMR, USA). He won a Behaviour Energy Climate Change Fellowship from the American Council for an Energy-Efficient Economy, an Emerald Literati award and a Duke of Edinborough community service medal. He is a full professor and he worked for reputable organizations including IBM, Blue Cross as well as University of Technology.

Teck Choon Teo received the M.A. and Masters of Management degrees from Macquarie University, M.Ed. from Monash University and D.B.A. from University of South Australia. During his academic career 2001-19, he was the chair of academic Board in various private educational institutions in Singapore. Since 2018, he has been with RVi Institute Mandalay, Myanmar, where he is currently serving as an Associate Dean and Vice Principal (Strategic Planning). His research interests are in the fields of creative leadership, organisational change and educational technology. He is a co-author of Strategic Thinking and Insights (2018) with Prof Patrick Low. He is also an active board member of Chinese American Scholar Association (CASA) and Fellow of Chartered College of Teaching (UK).

Narasimha Rao Vajjhala is an Assistant Professor at the School of IT and Computing at the American University of Nigeria. He is a senior member of ACM and IEEE He has over 13 years of experience in teaching mainly programming and database-related courses at both graduate and undergraduate level in Europe and Africa. He has edited a peer-reviewed book, published 2 monographs, 9 peer-reviewed book chapters, 14 refereed international conference proceedings, 14 peer-reviewed journal articles, and one review article. He has also worked as a consultant in technology firms in Europe and has experience participating in an EU-funded project. He has supervised several undergraduate senior design projects and graduate theses. He has completed a Doctorate in Information Systems and Technology (United States); holds a Master of Science in Computer Science and Applications (India), and a Master of Business Administration with specialization in Information Systems (Switzerland), and an undergraduate degree in Computer Science (India).

Savdeep Vasudeva is working as an Assistant Professor in the Department of Business Management of DAV Institute of Engineering & Technology, Jalandhar (Punjab) India. He has completed his PhD in Management from I.K Gujral Punjab Technical University in the year 2017 and has contributed different research papers in International Journals. Before that, he has done MBA with specialization in Information Technology from Punjab Technical University in the year 2000. He also holds a B.Sc. degree (with Economics and Computer Science) which he has completed in the year 1998 from Guru Nanak Dev University. In addition to this, he also possesses a Certificate in Computing from IGNOU, New Delhi. He has a total work experience of 18+ years. It is comprised of 12+ years of teaching and 6 years of industrial experience. During his stay in industry, he has worked in different techno-managerial capacities and is into teaching from last 12+ years.

Index

Q

R

S

T

U

V

W

www.ingramcontent.com/pod-product-compliance
Lightning Source LLC
LaVergne TN
LVHW060410300926
849162LV00006B/1388